W9-CFS-757

REAL-TIME SOFTWARE FOR CONTROL: PROGRAM EXAMPLES IN C

REAL-TIME SOFTWARE FOR CONTROL: PROGRAM EXAMPLES IN C

David M. Auslander
University of California, Berkeley

Cheng H. Tham
Sherpa Corporation

Prentice Hall
Englewood Cliffs, New Jersey 07632

Library of Congress Cataloging-in-Publication Data

Auslander, David M.
Real time software for control : program examples in C / David M. Auslander, Cheng H. Tham.
p. cm.
Includes bibliographical references.
ISBN 0-13-762824-2
1. Real-time control--Computer programs. 2. C (Computer program language) I. Tham, Cheng H. (Cheng Haam) II. Title.
TJ217.7.A87 1989
629.8'955133--dc20 89-36478
CIP

Editorial/production supervision
and interior design: *Jacqueline A. Jeglinski*
Cover design: *Ben Santora*
Manufacturing buyer: *Denise Duggan/Mary Ann Gloriande*

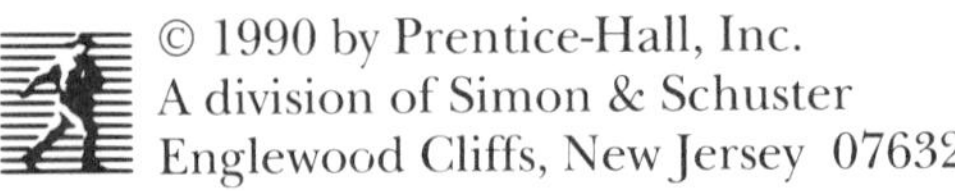

The publisher offers discounts on this book when ordered in bulk quantities. For more information, write:

Special Sales/College Marketing
Prentice-Hall, Inc.
College Technical and Reference Division
Englewood Cliffs, NJ 07632

Printed in the United States of America
10 9 8 7 6 5 4 3 2 1

ISBN 0-13-762824-2

Prentice-Hall International (UK) Limited, *London*
Prentice-Hall of Australia Pty. Limited, *Sydney*
Prentice-Hall Canada Inc., *Toronto*
Prentice-Hall Hispanoamericana, S.A., *Mexico*
Prentice-Hall of India Private Limited, *New Delhi*
Prentice-Hall of Japan, Inc., *Tokyo*
Simon & Schuster Asia Pte. Ltd., *Singapore*
Editora Prentice-Hall do Brasil, Ltda., *Rio de Janeiro*

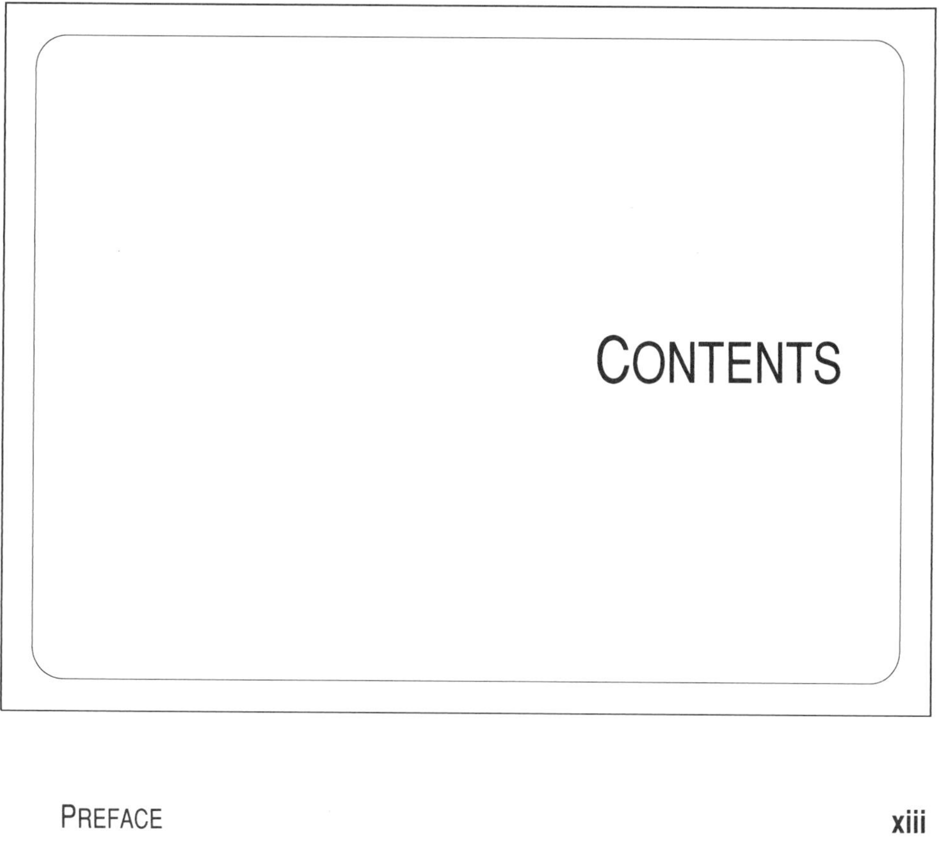
CONTENTS

PREFACE

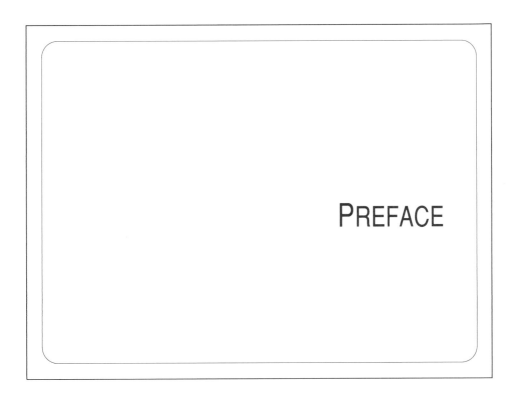

Engineers from all disciplines must be able to conceptualize, design, and prototype systems that depend on computers as operational components. The software in these computers is *real-time,* in the sense that its operation must be synchronized with events occurring in the physical system and with time.

Performance, reliability, and cost are products of the integral design of a machine and its control intelligence. Part count reductions, self-diagnostic ability, adaptation to changing environments, faster operation—these are all benefits of appropriate replacement of hardware with software. Our hypothesis is that *all* engineers need to know the fundamentals of intergrated real-time software, whether they are designing, supervising design, purchasing, or using sophisticated engineering systems.

Real-time software functions in an environment in which the various system components operate asynchronously. The events associated with changes in software state, changes in state of the physical system, and time, do not repeat in a predictable way. This environment puts a premium on good design practice, since system "bugs" cannot be reproduced at will for diagnosis as they usually can in purely numerical programs. Furthermore, the asynchronous nature of the system increases the likelihood that a system will contain very low probability bugs, bugs that don't show up in laboratory testing, but could appear in production versions of the system long after its initial release.

Our approach to real-time software emphasizes design practices that result in fewer bugs in the first place: modular programs, data hiding, mutual exclusion, task isolation, simulation. The text uses a graduated approach, starting with strictly synchronous software (although the complete system remains asynchronous), adding interrupts, simple scheduling, and then event-driven scheduling.

All of the text material is illustrated with extensive examples, with complete code in C included. The text presents solutions in a language-independent form, with C-specific discussion of the examples following the text material in each chapter.

Motor-driven systems are used as the physical example throughout the text. Motors are ubiquitous in the engineering world, and they also can be small, inexpensive, and safe—ideal properties for use in a teaching laboratory.

The material in this text is the subject of a one-semester graduate course in the Mechanical Engineering Department, University of California at Berkeley. It is supplemented with a C-language tutorial. The course has no formal prerequisites, and is successfully completed by students from Mechanical Engineering as well as other engineering departments. In particular, students are not expected to have any prior C or real-time experience.

The course is heavily laboratory-based. In the early part of the course, example programs from the text are used as the basis for lab exercises. The students are asked to test, modify, or enhance these programs. This provides a functioning starting point for students, and helps to minimize the frustration commonly associated with development of real-time software from scratch. It also helps teach an incremental style of design—test, enhance the design, retest, etc.—which we feel allows students to build confidence in their ability to get a job done.

The text can be used even in situations in which an actual lab is not available, since the use of simulations is encouraged throughout. Simulations are carried all the way to real-time operation, with the physical system existing as a simulation in a separate task module.

The book is also intended for use as a professional self-study text. In that case, some prior study in C would be useful. Because the example code includes simulation-based programs, completion of the text does not require an extensive laboratory.

Real-time Software for Control: Program Examples in C

CHAPTER 1

SYNCHRONOUS PROGRAMMING

Real-time computer systems must interact with the outside world on terms that are dictated by events taking place there. The computations that are done in response to those events must not only produce the correct results, but they must also produce those results at the right time. Unlike a real-time system, the success of a scientific or engineering computation is rarely related to when the result appears, although the user's patience and total computing expenses are related to the computation time. A further distinction in real-time computing is that the total computing environment consists of many semi-independent tasks that must be synchronized properly.

Many varieties of computers and systems qualify as "real-time." In this text, our concerns will focus on engineering systems in which there are interactions between a computer and some form of physical system. There are also often interactions with an operator. The physical system usually contains several measuring devices, which the computer must interrogate to get information, and several actuators, which receive signals from the computer to control their actions. Some systems have only one or the other of sensors or actuators, while most have both (Fig. 1.1). The computer (or computers) used can range from thumbnail size to room size (microprocessors to superminis), but the basic techniques for designing effective real-time systems are the same: careful conceptual design, systematic implementation, exhaustive validation, and thoughtful choice of software and hardware development tools. A major focus here will be on the use of high-level computing languages for implementation of real-time systems.

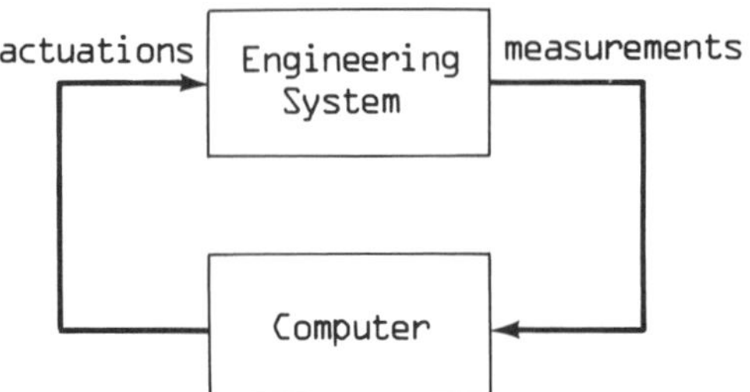

Figure 1.1

1.1 MOTOR SPEED CONTROL

We have chosen the control of electric motors as our theme. Motors are widely used and appear in so many different kinds of engineering systems that they cross virtually all disciplinary boundaries. When different methods of actuation and speed and position measurement are considered, motors also offer examples of situations that are typical of almost any real-time system. Motor systems are also easy and inexpensive to build in a laboratory, and so offer an excellent learning environment. On the other hand, the programs developed in the course of exploring the theme of motor control are generic to other control problems, and could be applied to many of them with little or no change.

A simple motor control system is shown schematically in Fig. 1.2. From the point of view of real-time system design, the simplicity of the job, even for this very simple-looking physical system, will depend on how much we demand of the computer. If the analog-to-digital (A/D) and digital-to-analog (D/A) converters can operate with little or no intervention from the computer, if the only interaction with the operator takes place at the beginning and end of an experiment, and if the algorithm chosen for computing the output signal to the power amplifier as a function of the measured motor speed depends only on the most recent measurement, then the real-time system will also be quite simple. With these restrictions, we can embark on our first example.

1.2 THE CONTROL ALGORITHM

At the heart of most real-time computation systems there are usually some key calculations. This could be a trend analysis of incoming data, spectral analysis for recognizing changes in system characteristics, generation of waveforms for system excitation, or, in this case, computation of the actuation signal on the basis of the measured motor velocity. Although these calculations are absolutely critical to proper system operation, the actual amount of program code devoted to them is usually embarrassingly small!

Control of motor speed is accomplished by increasing the voltage to the power amplifier if the speed is too low, and decreasing it if the speed is too high. A simple rule for doing this is to make the change in actuation voltage proportional to the velocity error, the difference between the actual velocity and the

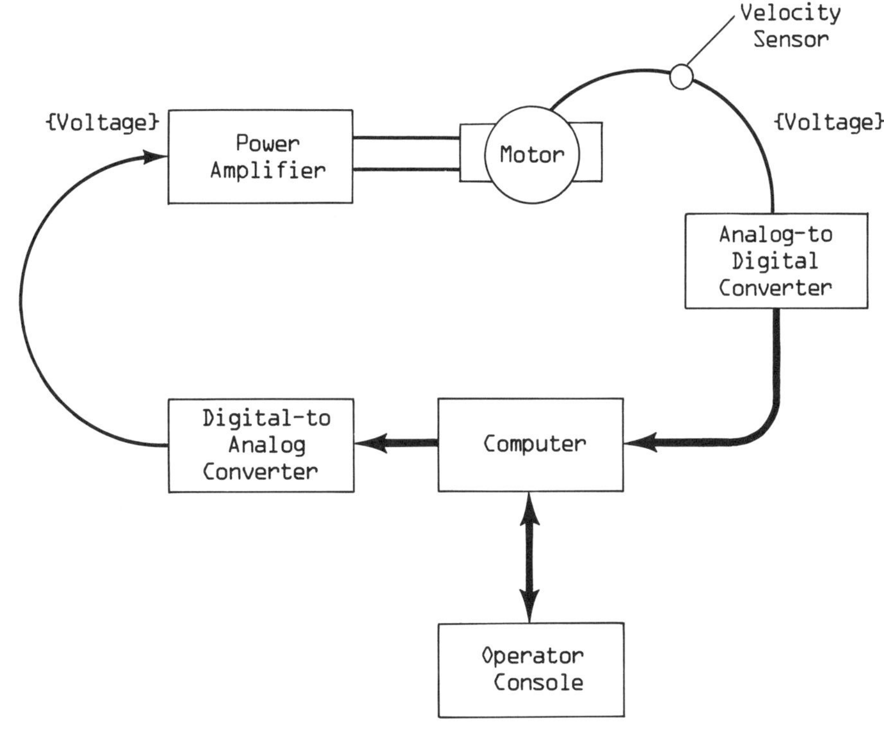

Figure 1.2

desired value

$$m = k_p \varepsilon + c \tag{1.1}$$

where m is the controller output, k_p is the proportionality constant ("gain"), ε is the error

$$\varepsilon = r - v_m \tag{1.2}$$

and c is a constant bias that is applied to the output voltage, often to compensate for steady loads such as gravity or friction. r is the desired ("reference") voltage, and v_m is the motor speed (scaled to the same units as r).

1.3 PROGRAM STRUCTURE

The equations expressing the control algorithm, when coded for computer implementation, must be embedded in a program that will interact properly with the system (motor) being controlled. If, in this case, the external environment is limited to a single motor, a relatively simple program structure emerges. Because the calculation of the controller output, m, does not depend either implicitly or explicitly on time, the strategy for the real-time portion of the program is to run the control calculation as often as possible. The basic real-time constraint in this case is whether the length of time required to complete one controller calculation cycle is short enough to maintain effective control. If it isn't, the only solution is to find some way to make it run faster, a more expensive processor, a better compiler, use of assembly language in key places, and so on.

Real-time programs consist of sets of semi-independent modules, often called *tasks*. Each of these tasks is a sequence of program instructions written in a standard programming language. To illustrate the structure of the tasks, we will use a form of "pseudocode," that is, free-form statements about actions to be taken, but organized to look very much like a program in one of the structured languages (C, Pascal, etc.). The convention we will use is to identify program blocks by indentation, with no further beginning or end of block marker. No formal syntax will be used for loops or conditionals; whatever form suits the need will be used. Blocks that consist of functionally grouped statements but do not require any formal blocking will be set off with blank lines. No GO-TO's will be used within tasks.

The motor control outlined above makes a good first example because its simple structure has only one task. That task has three parts: the beginning, in which the user interaction and initialization activity takes place, the middle part, which contains the real-time portion, and the final section, where performance reports are made (the final section can be omitted). The full program could be diagrammed as shown in Fig. 1.3, with each of the three sections represented as a program block. (The details of how these program structures are implemented with specific computers and compilers are given in the appendices in the form of fully commented programs, with additional explanatory material if necessary. These programs show the implementation for the final program structure selected for each of the problems.)

```
Get user input (gains, setpoint, number of iterations, ...)

Initialize I/O ports, internal control variables

For specified number of iterations:
        Read the velocity
        Compute the controller output
        Send output to the motor

Report results
```

Figure 1.3

This structure is simple and will work, but leaves no control to the operator once the parameters are set. Particularly in laboratory environments, it is very common to want to "play" with a system as a means of understanding its behavior and finding the best control parameters ("tuning" the gains). In that situation, the user likes to make one change at a time, see its effect, then make another change. An alternate structure to accommodate such repetitive activity would be to make all actions depend on a user command. These actions would include changing parameters, initializing, and initiating the actual control. This leads to the following, more complex, but more useful structure (Fig. 1.4).

```
Main:
        Repeat continuously:
                Get user command (single letter commands)
                Interpret and execute the command

Command Interpreter:
        Execute block that matches the single letter command:
                e       exit from program
                k       set controller gain
                s       set the setpoint (desired velocity)
                g       control for specified number of iterations
                i       initialize the system
                other   print an error message
```

Figure 1.4

The control module, initializing module, and results reporting module (which isn't included in the menu) now become subsidiary to the command interpreter. Otherwise, they look very much like the version in Fig. 1.3.

Further protocol is required to establish the way in which information can be passed to the various modules that are called by the command interpreter. Each module can do its own prompting and ask for the data from the user, but that usually leads to a lack of uniformity in the user interface, particularly if all the modules were not written by the same person or if they were written at different times. A simple solution to this is to put the information to be passed to the lower level program on the same line as the command itself. When the command interpreter calls a function, it also passes the remainder of the line to it as an argument. To specify the number of iterations for control, for example, the "g" command, the user would type:

```
g 50
```

As long as the protocol is similar for each of the commands, i.e., one or more numbers following the command letter, the user interface remains consistent. Likewise, the programming necessary to decode the additional numbers is not too difficult because almost all high-level computer languages provide for a format decoding that works on an internal buffer of characters.

1.4 DEBUGGING: SIMULATING REAL-TIME

Debugging of real-time programs is a difficult problem because the computer and the real world to which it is relating are operating asynchronously. This means that it is often not possible to duplicate the situations that are causing problems. This is in distinct contrast to debugging a computational program. In the latter case, all the action takes place in the computer, which is a strictly sequential machine, and, unique among engineering systems, will always duplicate its actions *exactly*. Although debugging is still a major problem, the ability to debug by repeatedly reproducing the same error is a boon!

We would like to take advantage of this property of computers as long as possible in debugging real-time problems. Extensive planning and program design remain the main bulwarks against excessive debugging time, but some amount of debugging always seems to be necessary. Before entering the real-time phase of operation, it would be nice to be reasonably sure that the computational part of the program is correct. This can be done by operating the program with another program (or program section) that simulates the real-time part of the system. The extra work involved in producing the simulation will pay off handsomely in overall productivity. It might also add some additional insight into the nature of the problem leading to improved solution methods.

At this stage, an advantage of using a high-level language is that with proper choice of the language and compiler, it becomes possible to do the simulation studies on one computer and then transport the program to a different computer for real-time operation when the simulation studies are complete. This could not be done efficiently with assembly language programs because the languages differ from one computer to another.

The structure of the real-time control module and the simulator are shown in Fig.1.5. The simulator has two functions. It has to increment "time," and it has to compute the change in the controlled system that would take place during that time. The interesting property of the simulated real-time environment is that it makes the control computer appear to have an infinitely fast computing speed. For example, in this system, the control program must first read the value of the velocity from the analog-to-digital converter, then compute the voltage to be sent to the digital-to-analog converter for transmission to the motor's power amplifier. All of that computation takes a finite amount of time. There is some delay between the time that the velocity measurement process is started and the time that the new voltage command signal gets to the amplifier. This introduces a certain amount of delay into the system, and that delay can affect the quality of control. In the simulated system, however, "time," that is, simulated time, is suspended while the computation takes place. By breaking the process into finer divisions, some of these effects can be simulated also; however, simulated time will always stand still while the control computation is taking place.

```
Control:
        For specified number of iterations
                Read velocity instrument
                Compute controller output
                Send value to power amplifier
                Simulate one increment in time

Simulation:
        Compute motor velocity change for this time step
        Increment time
```

Figure 1.5

In most cases, since it is the computational validity that is being tested rather than whether the particular control algorithm will successfully control the motor, it is usually satisfactory at this stage to substitute a very simple model of the system under control. For the motor, the simplest useful model is of a pure rotational inertia with no friction, no compliance in the drive train, and no lag in the power amplifier. This can be expressed in differential equation form as:

$$\frac{dv}{dt} = \frac{T}{m} \tag{1.3}$$

where T is the torque applied to the motor and m is its mass (rotational inertia). A simple approximation of this equation for computer solution is:

$$v(t+\Delta t) = v(t) + \left(\frac{T}{m}\right)\Delta t \tag{1.4}$$

If the control sample time is long, it may be necessary to use a Δt that is a fraction of the sample time and solve Eq. (1.4) several times to advance the solution one full sample time. Fig. 1.6 shows the program structure for solving the differential equation.

For n iterations (where $n = T/\Delta t$)
    $v = v + (T * \Delta t \neq m)$

Figure 1.6

The emphasis in this model of real-time is on producing an environment in which the numerical validity of the program can be tested. Errors due to timing conflicts must be debugged in actual real-time operation. To accomplish that, the model of the control object (i.e., the motor) does not require a great deal of fidelity with the real thing. If the simulation were to be used to tune the control gains, for example, a more accurate model would have to be used. In most circumstances, it would be better to use a simulation language for that purpose.

1.5 INTEGER AND FLOATING POINT: REAL-TIME CONSIDERATIONS

In the discussion thus far, we have not made any reference to the way in which numbers are represented internally in the computer's memory, or to the way in which the basic arithmetical operations are carried out. These details are of critical importance to real-time programs.

There are two common ways that numbers can be dealt with in computers: as integers, or as floating point quantities. For computational purposes, the integer representation includes positive and negative values (with zero usually counted as positive), that is, signed integers. Floating point numbers, more properly called scientific notation, are represented in two parts, a mantissa and an exponent, both signed. The value of the number is the mantissa times the base of the number system raised to the power given by the exponent:

$$value = mantissa \; * \; base^{exponent} \tag{1.5}$$

For ordinary numbers, the base is 10. In internal computer representations, the base can be either 2 or 10, with 2 being more common in engineering applications. A normalized floating point number is one for which the magnitude of the mantissa is always within a range given by:

$$(base^{r-1}) \le mantissa < base^{r} \tag{1.6}$$

For decimal numbers, for example, a normalized mantissa might be constrained to the range $0.1 \le mantissa < 1$.

Both of these are finite precision representations. For the integers, the precision is expressed by the range of integer values that can be represented. Some integer examples are: a 3-bit signed integer can represent numbers from −4 to +3; an 8-bit integer can represent numbers from −128 to +127; a 16-bit integer can represent numbers from −32,768 to +32,767; a 32-bit signed integer can represent −2,147,483,648. For integers, the precision is expressed as maximum positive and maximum (absolute value) negative numbers. For floating point numbers, the precision limitations are expressed as a number of significant digits for the mantissa, and a maximum positive and negative integer value for the exponent.

By contrast, neither precision nor range is normally considered when expressing an engineering quantity. The normal assumption is that whatever computing instrument is used, it will have sufficient precision and range to deal with the numbers involved. As a result, quantities in engineering units can have vastly different ranges in order to use common units. The floating point number representation falls closest to common usage. Using this representation, as long as the quantity does not fall into the extreme edge of the range of exponents available, the overall computing precision will be independent of the value. In most cases, there will be some round-off error associated with every calculation.

Integer calculations, on the other hand, pose much greater computing difficulty. The precision associated with an integer value depends on its magnitude. Small (absolute value) numbers have very low precision, measuring precision in an intuitive way as percentage change required to move from the current value to the next allowable value. For an integer of value 1, for example, it takes a 100% change to get to its nearest neighbors. All quantities used must therefore be scaled if integer representations are to be used. The internal value will be related to the actual value (in engineering units) by an arbitrary scale factor. The scaling process must compromise between two problems: (1) to maintain sufficient precision; and (2) to avoid exceeding the allowable range, even in intermediate results of calculations. For example, the controller output equation requires that the error be multiplied by the proportional gain and then added to the bias to get the controller output value. If all quantities are scaled for integer arithmetic, they will all have approximately the same range of allowable values. For many control applications, that will mean that the control gain will be a number near unity. That is precisely the range, however, where integer arithmetic has its least precision, and so will not allow for fine tuning the controller's gain. To avoid that, the gain can be represented as a ratio of numbers, so the calculation becomes:

$$output = (k_{num} * error) \;/\; k_{den} + bias \tag{1.7}$$

The position of the parentheses in this calculation is not arbitrary; the parentheses control the computing order. The multiplication must be done before the division so that the round-off error will be minimized. If, for example, k_{num}, *error*, and k_{den} are all about the same magnitude, if the division were done first, the result would be near unity and all precision would be lost. On the other hand, the scaling of the problem must be done in such a way that the product, $k_{num} * error$, does not ever exceed the integer range. If it does, in most cases the result will have a very large error and, often, will have the opposite sign of the true product.

Floating point is clearly much easier to work with. Except for extreme cases, engineering units can be used directly with no problems of precision or range. The catch is that floating point is much slower in computing time than integer, as much as 100 times slower, or, alternatively, to get computing times for floating point even close to integer times (but usually still slower) requires the use of additional computing hardware that is quite expensive.

The suggested procedure for approaching the integer/floating point decision is to start in the simulated real-time mode using floating point. Because scaling is almost never required for programs using floating point numeric representation, the validation and debugging can proceed without the need to worry about scaling. Because time is being simulated, the computing time is not a factor either. When this step is complete, a set of time trials can be made to find out the execution time for the key modules in the program (some compilers provide links to "profilers" that make it very easy to get these statistics). If the performance is within the system specifications, it may be possible to leave the floating point in place and proceed with the system development. If the performance is close to specification, it might be possible to identify one or two key modules and recode them for integer calculation, leaving the rest of the program intact. If, however, it appears that integer calculation will be necessary throughout the program, the simulated real-time system can be used to great advantage in doing the conversion.

The first step in the conversion is to decide what class of integer to use. All processors have a "most natural" word size, that is, the number of bits that can be processed in parallel. This determines the natural integer precision for that processor. For microprocessor systems, the most common are 8-bit and 16-bit word sizes. Eight-bit precision means that the integer number range is –128 to +127 (for a given word size, there are a total of 2^n possible numbers, where n is the word size). This range is inadequate for most control-type problems. Sixteen-bit precision implies a range of –32,768 to 32,767. This range is adequate for many control problems, but scaling must be done very carefully to preserve precision and avoid overflows. The next most common integer size is 32-bit, providing a range of approximately $\pm 2.15 \times 10^9$. This range is large enough to make the problem of scaling for specified precision while avoiding overflow relatively simple for most control tasks.

The use of a high-level language insulates the programmer from the details of how the arithmetic is implemented on a specific processor. Any processor can implement arithmetic operations with any desired precision level, at the cost of increased computational time. In making the choices, therefore, it is important to know the characteristics of the computer to know what precision level is likely to work well. Most processors implement some arithmetic operations at one level above their most natural level. Eight-bit processors have some 16-bit operations and 16-bit processors have some 32-bit operations. Most compilers allow at least limited 8-bit operations, and full 16- or 32-bit integer arithmetic.

Using a combination of the overall desired precision level and the characteristics of the processor in use (or the target processor if the simulation is being run on a computer different than the one that will actually be used for control), a first choice can be made for the integer arithmetic precision level. If possible, the choice should be the most natural and therefore most efficient integer mode of the target computer. Using a high-level language, changes can easily be made to other modes, but using a larger word size than the natural size will cause a significant computing time penalty. Before changing all of the program variable declarations, however, the original, floating point version of the program should be "instrumented" with print statements to give the values of internal variables and intermediate computation results throughout the program. This might require breaking program statements into several parts in order to get at the intermediate results.

At this point, the simulated real-time program will be turned into a simulated integer arithmetic program. This is done by scaling all of the variables as if they were integers, but leaving them in floating point form. The program should then be run over as wide a range of operating conditions as possible, recording all of the data from the "print" statements that have been introduced. This data is used primarily to check that no overflows occur anywhere in the program, for any of its operating ranges. The overall results can be compared with the original floating point simulation program to make sure that overall precision requirements are being met.

The final step in the integer conversion is the actual substitution of new declarations for all the appropriate variables. With the integer mode simulation already done, there should be few further conversion problems. The "instrumented" version of the program can be run to verify the intermediate and final results.

1.6 RUNNING IN REAL-TIME

The final version of the program, either integer or floating point, is now ready for real-time operation. For this motor control problem, the changes that must be made are: (1) Remove the simulated motor module; (2) Insert a function to read the analog-to-digital converter; and (3) Insert a function to send results to the digital-to-analog converter.

A/D converters typically are available with conversion word widths of 8 to 16 bits, with 8, 10, and 12 bits being the most common. The output of the converter is an integer, so the same scaling conditions discussed above in connection with integer variables apply to it. The conversion precision is usually chosen on the basis of problem requirements since the measurement input will be a primary precision-limiting step. The narrower the conversion word, the cheaper and faster the converter will be. Once a conversion precision has been chosen, the voltage range at the input to the converter must be set so that the full range of the converter is used. This is done by setting gains in the analog circuit at the input to the converter or in the converter itself. The A/D converter function used in the simulated real time studies should have had the same conversion factor (motor speed -> voltage -> converter output) as the real converter, so the program ranges and scaling factors should not be affected by the change to a real A/D converter.

Operating the converter requires consideration of multiplexing and speed of conversion. In order to save cost, A/D converters are often multiplexed, that is, an electronic switch is placed ahead of the converter so that it can be attached to any of a number of different signals. The conversion speed is a factor because the program must wait, or do something else, while the conversion is taking place. Many converters can complete a conversion in less than 100 microseconds, so it is usually not worth trying to do anything else in that time. The logic for getting a value from a specified multiplexor channel is shown in Fig. 1.7.

```
Get A/D value:
        Set multiplexor channel
        Start the conversion
        Wait for conversion to finish
        Read the result
```

Figure 1.7

Digital-to-analog converters (D/As) are much easier to use than A/Ds. No multiplexor is involved and the conversion is done very quickly. The programming required is just sending a value to the D/A's output port. The A/D and D/A modules should be coded and tested separately. With these modules installed in place of the real-time simulation functions, the program is ready to control an actual motor. The sample time that the controller will achieve depends entirely on the speed with which the computer can make a full cycle through the program. This is most easily checked by using an oscilloscope to measure the width of the "staircase" on the D/A output.

Functional testing can now begin to check that the control algorithm is working properly and then to tune the controller gains.

INTRODUCTION TO EXAMPLE PROGRAMS

1.7 ABOUT EXAMPLE PROGRAMS

The programs in this section are designed to provide examples of how one might implement the concepts discussed in the various chapters. The programs are designed to run on the ubiquitous IBM-PC, and almost all are written in the **C** programming language. There are a few modules written in 808x assembly language, but one cannot write real-time programs to control devices without having to resort to assembly language once in a while. Not all readers are familiar with the C programming language, and some of you may be just learning the language. Because of this, the descriptive text for the example programs in the earlier chapters will devote more space to descriptions of language features. In addition to describing the function and organization of the program modules, we also try to point out why certain language features are used and why certain functions are implemented the way they are. Although execution speed is always important, we believe that good programming practices such as structured design, input checking, data hiding, and encapsulation can be equally important, especially in a large application. Such practices need not adversely affect performance, but we do recognize that real-time process control programs operate under different conditions from, say, a spreadsheet, and sometimes rules may have to be bent to meet performance requirements.

Almost all real-time control programs have to deal with hardware; it may be an analog-to-digital converter, a parallel port, or a motor. It is impossible to write stand-alone example programs that can accommodate all the possible interface devices that a reader may need. It is also not realistic to expect readers to obtain the hardware setup required by the example programs. In view of these difficulties, some of the example programs include a module that simulates the external hardware environment. Simulation is a very useful tool for debugging program logic and developing new applications where it may be difficult if not impossible to run tests on the actual hardware.

We hope that readers who are implementing computer-based real-time control projects will find these example programs useful as starting points or as modules that can be incorporated into their applications.

1.8 THE C LANGUAGE STANDARD

At this time, the C programming language is undergoing a transition from the informal de facto standard established by the book *The C Programming Language* by Kernighan and Ritchie (commonly referred to as K&R), and the ANSI draft standard proposed by the X3J11 committee. There are several new language features in the draft standard, and many C compiler vendors have already implemented them. Some of the features have been stable for quite some time now and are very unlikely to change in the future.

The example programs makes use of some ANSI C features such as the *void* type and function prototyping. The *void* type is used to declare functions that do not return a value,[1] and as a generic pointer type, an absence that is sorely felt in the old K&R standard. Function prototyping is a feature that allows a function's return type and the type of its arguments to be declared before the function is used or outside of the file where the function resides. This allows the compiler to check if the correct number of arguments are passed to the function and if the arguments are of the correct type.

1.9 COMPILERS

The example programs were compiled with Microsoft C, version 5.0, and linked using the Microsoft linker, version 3.61. The code and compilation commands suggested here are totally compatible with the version 4.00 compiler and the version 3.51 linker. It is unlikely that you will have to modify the code in order to compile the programs since we have tried to avoid compiler dependent features. The few assembly language modules were assembled using the version 4.00 Microsoft MASM assembler.

1.10 PROGRAMMING PRACTICES

Program organization and certain programming practices common to all the programs are described in this section.

1.10.1 FILE MODULES

The module concept organizes a program into groups of related functions. For example, a device driver module for an analog-to-digital converter contains functions that initialize and otherwise control the ADC, and maintains data required by all the routines[2] in the module. The module provides a set of interface routines that allows other routines outside of the module to set the channel and perform

[1]This is known as a *procedure* in Pascal.

[2]We use the term *routine* to refer to both functions that return a value and those that do not. In C, the term *function* is commonly used to denote both types of functions; a function in C is assumed to return an integer unless declared otherwise.

analog-to-digital conversion. Routines outside of the module cannot call on routines or access data not specifically made *visible* outside of the module.[3] Thus, a module is a sort of black box with a defined interface.

The module concept encourages one to conceptualize the program as a collection of functional blocks that communicate with other blocks through well defined-interface routines. As long as the module interface is unchanged, its contents can be replaced without affecting the rest of the program. Although this may not seem important in small programs, large programs are very difficult to manage and maintain unless some form of modular organization is used. This will become obvious in the later chapters as the example programs increase in size and complexity.

The module concept is central to the **Modula-2** language, and a variant of it is implemented in **Ada** as *packages*. Unfortunately, C does not directly support modules, though many of the concepts can be implemented in C by treating a file as a module. In C, a routine that is declared to be *static* can only be called by name by other routines within the same file; it is not visible outside of the file. Such routines can be thought of as being "private" to the module.

A data variable defined outside of any routine is visible to all routines. However, as with routines, the variable can be made to be visible only within a file in which it is defined by declaring it to be static. Routines and variables outside of the module can have the same name without fear of accidental name conflicts (a particularly insidious type of bug).

How do we make the interface routines (and perhaps data) known to other functions outside the module? The simplest way is by means of a header file declaring the names, return type, and arguments of the interface routines. Visible routines and data are declared to be *extern*, which means that the code and data are probably not in the current file, i.e., external to the current file. Thus, each module has its own header file, and we have adopted the convention that the header file has the same name as the module file, but with the .h extension instead of the .c extension. Other program modules wishing to use the services of a particular module merely have to include the appropriate header file.

C automatically assumes that a routine returns an integer unless declared otherwise. Thus, all functions that do not return integers should be declared before they are called, preferably with a function prototype. Declaring a function before it is used or defined is also known as a *forward declaration*. In the module file, there is a section near the beginning of the file for forward declarations of functions private to the module. Strictly speaking, forward declarations for private routines should use the static keyword, but some compilers may not accept the use

---

[3]The term *visible* in this context means that the item can be referenced directly by name; a function is visible if it can be called by name, a data variable is visible if it can be read and assigned-to by name.

of the static keyword in a forward declaration.[4] Because of this, we have avoided the static keyword in forward declarations for private routines.

Function prototyping is a more advanced form of forward declaration that not only declares the return type, but also the type and order of the function arguments. This allows compilers to check that the correct types are being passed to functions. Since not all compilers have implemented this feature yet, function prototyping is only enabled if the symbol ANSI is defined. The file modules in the example programs are organized into sections:

header files and imported declarations
global data visible outside of the module
forward declarations
private data
interface or entry functions
private functions
initialization functions

Grouping related items together makes it easier to locate specific items for modification, and there are fewer chances of introducing bugs due to multiple and possibly different declarations for the same item.

Each routine in the module is preceded by a short comment block describing the routine. The type of routine is indicated by the words PROCEDURE or FUNCTION, used in the Pascal sense. This is followed by the name of the routine in capital letters; this makes it easier to search for the place where the routine is defined using a program or text editor. The return type and arguments are described next. There is an optional REMARK section that describes any special features or algorithm used in the routine.

1.10.2 THE ENVIRONMENT FILE—ENVIR.H

Many of the example program modules include a header file named *envir.h*. This header file specifies the environment under which the program is compiled and executed. This is useful if the program is to run on different computers or has to be compiled by different compilers. This is not uncommon, especially in "embedded systems," as real-time control programs are often developed and debugged on large computers or workstations and later transferred to the microcomputer that actually controls the hardware. Code that depends on certain features of the environment, such as the computer, operating system, or compiler can be isolated and conditionally compiled using the information in the *envir.h* file.

---

[4] We know of a compiler that quietly accepts static forward declarations, but generates incorrect code!

1.10.3 INPUT AND OUTPUT PORTS—INOUT.H

Computers based on Intel CPUs, such as the IBM-PC family, have special instructions to access i/o ports, and most compiler vendors supply functions to read from and write to i/o ports. Unfortunately, there is no consensus on the names of these functions. To simplify matters, we have chosen to use the function names *in()* and *out()* for routines that read a byte from a port and write a byte to a port, respectively. These names are mapped to the appropriate compiler library names by macros defined in *inout.h*; here is an excerpt:

```
#if CIC86           /* Computer Innovations C86 */
#define in(port)                inportb((unsigned)(port))
#define out(port, value)    outportb((unsigned)(port), value)
#endif

#if MICROSOFT       /* Microsoft C Version 4.00 & 5.00 */
#define in(port)                inp((unsigned)(port))
#define out(port, value)    outp((unsigned)(port), value)
#endif
```

1.10.4 FLOATS AND DOUBLES

C has two floating point types: *float* for single precision and *double* for double precision floating point types. For historical reasons, the C language specifies that floats are always expanded into doubles in expressions and when passed to a function.[5] The example program uses doubles rather than floats for floating point variables, as we feel that in most cases, the reduction in conversion overhead more than compensates for the slight increase in storage requirement and data transfer time. There is also another reason relating to the use of function prototypes in the proposed ANSI standard. The proposed standard in its current form allows single precision calculations for greater speed without automatic expansion into double precision. Function prototypes that declare arguments as floats may have problems with functions that expect float type parameters to be expanded into doubles. Using doubles for all floating point variables avoids this problem during the transition from K&R C to ANSI C.

---

[5]The historical reason for this convention of automatically converting floats to doubles is that C was developed on early PDP-11 computers. Programs running on early PDP-11s cannot determine whether the floating point unit is in single or double precision mode; this presents an obvious problem for multi-tasking systems since the precision mode of the floating point unit could have been changed by another program. The solution the creators of C came up with was to always use double precision.

SYNCHRONOUS PROGRAMMING EXAMPLES

1.11 INTRODUCTION

The first example program is an implementation of proportional speed control for a d.c. motor. The computer controls the motor speed by means of a digital-to-analog converter (D/A) connected to a linear power amplifier which drives the motor. Motor speed is obtained from an analog tachometer, the output of which is read by an analog-to-digital converter (A/D). There are two versions of the program. The first version assumes that all the hardware (i.e., motor, power amplifier, and so on) is present. The analog interface is designed for the Metrabyte DASH-8 and DAC-02 data acquisition and control boards. Readers with different data acquisition boards will have to modify the A/D and D/A drivers, which should not be too difficult since the drivers are well encapsulated. The second version of the program does not require any external hardware; the motor plant and analog interfaces are simulated in software in a manner that is transparent to the control program.

The following files are required:

envir.h The environment specification file.

inout.h Maps the *in()* and *out()* port access functions to the equivalent functions in the compiler vendor's library.

main0.c Main program module of the example program.

cntrl0.h Declarations for cntrl0.c.

cntrl0.c Implements the control algorithm.

rtsim0.c Simulates the motor, power amplifier, 12-bit ADC and DAC interfaces.

dash8.h Declarations for dash8.c.

dash8.c Driver module for Metrabyte DASH-8 analog-to-digital data acquisition board.

dac2.h Declarations for dac2.c.

dac2.c Driver module for Metrabyte DAC-02 digital-to-analog control board.

To compile the "real hardware" version of the program, type:

```
cl main0.c cntrl0.c dash8.c dac2.c
```

To compile the simulation version, type:

```
cl /DSIMRT main0.c cntrl0.c rtsim0.c
```

The /DSIMRT is a Microsoft C compiler option that is equivalent to putting a #define SIMRT statement at the beginning of the program files. This statement "defines" the symbol SIMRT, which tells the compiler to include code that is placed between the directives:

```
#ifdef SIMRT
 ...
#endif
```

This is intended for code that is only needed in the simulation version.

1.12 MAIN MODULE—MAIN0.C

The main program module implements a simple interface that allows users to enter speed setpoints and other control parameters. Each parameter is associated with a single character; the user enters the parameter by typing the character followed by the parameter value and a carriage return. For example, to specify a speed setpoint of 100 units, the user types s 100 followed by a carriage return.

Let us look at how user input is processed. When the program is first invoked, it calls *menu()* to print a list of all the valid commands, the letter associated with each command, and the arguments that are expected by each command. We believe that programs should endeavor to make life easier for their users; the user should never have to keep scraps of paper around to remind them of the commands. The reminder should be printed after each command, or there should be a command to print it. All user interactions take place inside an endless loop formed by the *for(;;)* statement. The only way out is via an exit command that allows the program to perform any "cleaning up" that is required (such as stopping the motor) before calling *exit()* to terminate the program.

The first statement in the loop is to print a prompt to let the user know that an entry is expected. The prompt string is defined by:

```
#define PROMPT "-"
```

which directs the C macro preprocessor[6] to substitute all occurrences of the symbol PROMPT with the string "-". By defining the prompt this way, it can be changed later by merely changing the #define statement; one does not have to

[6]The macro preprocessor makes a pass through the code before the actual compiler, expanding #define's and other preprocessor directives. The preprocessor is not really part of the compiler proper, but the trend shown in the ANSI draft standard for C is to make it part of the standard C environment.

search through the entire file for all the places where the prompt string is used. The prompt is printed using the standard C library function *fputs()* instead of the more common *printf()* because on some computer systems (mainly large UNIX systems), *printf()* will not print anything until a newline ('\n'), carriage-return ('\r'), or end-of-file (EOF) character is sent to the output stream. The standard definition for *fputs()* states that the specified string will be printed immediately, and almost all compiler implementations conform to this definitiion. User input is obtained by *fgets()*, which copies the input characters into the supplied buffer, *cbuf*. The input characters are then passed to *cmdint()* for interpretation.

The command "interpreter," *cmdint()*, expects the input to conform to a format where the first character must be the letter associated with a command. Parameter values may start at the second character and must be separated by blank (spaces or tabs) if there is more than one parameter value. This is not ideal as far as "idiot-proofing" is concerned, but it is very simple to implement. Large, sophisticated user interfaces are outside the scope of this section. However, programs intended to be used by people other than the original author or programs that deal with critical data should incorporate much better error checking and recovery.

Each command is handled by an individual routine. A *switch* statement is used to implement a multi-way branch to the appropriate routine based on the first character of the input line. The *switch* statement is generally more efficient than a long series of *if...else* statements when there is a large number of possible execution paths, the choice of which depends on the value of some variable or expression. A pointer[7] to the input string, starting at the second character, is passed to the command routine, which is responsible for extracting any parameters it requires from the rest of the input string.[8] Since the input string is declared as a character array

```
char cline[];
```

a pointer to the second character can be written as the address of the second element in the array, i.e., *&cline[1]* where '*&*' is the address-of operator. The command routines are located in the file *cntrl0.c*.

[7]A pointer is equivalent to an address or memory location. A variable can be referenced either directly by its name, or indirectly through its memory location by means of a pointer.

[8]A note about terminology: the C language does not support a special string type; strings are implemented as NUL (ASCII value of 0) terminated character arrays. Since arrays are often referenced through pointers, we often use the term string to refer to arrays of characters or pointers that point into such arrays.

1.13 CONTROL MODULE—CNTRL0.C

The routines in this module are organized into three groups: the command processing routines, the main control routine, and the device interface routines. The command routines are passed through a pointer to the input string starting at the second character. In this simple example, the parameters are extracted by passing this string to *sscanf()*, which works much like *scanf()* except that it takes its input from a string instead of the standard input. Error checking is left as an exercise.

Readers may notice that an initialization command is required to initialize the system. With real hardware, this will initialize the A/D and D/A; under simulation, this will initialize the simulation model. The question of whether to require an explicit initialization command or to have the initialization done automatically when the program starts up depends on the requirements of the application. In this example, the program is designed as an experimental tool, and the initialization command allows the experiment (or simulation) to be restarted.

1.13.1 The Control Loop

The program uses a very simple P control algorithm and runs the control loop as fast as possible. The control output, *m*, is calculated from the formula

$$m = kp*(vref - v) + vcon;$$

where *kp* is the proportional gain, *vref* is the speed, set-point, *v* is the actual speed, and *vcon* is the constant term. A very wide dynamic range is ensured by using floating point variables throughout. However, the operating range of real devices is much more limited, and the theoretical output value must be modified to take the limitations of the DAC into consideration.

1.13.2 Programming Notes

Note that the D/A output limits are not hard-coded into the control code, but are obtained by calling *da_limits()*, a routine supplied by the digital-to-analog (DAC) driver module. The control program thus does not need to know output limits until run time, and the output interface module can change the limits to accommodate different hardware or simulation conditions without affecting the main control program.

It can be very disconcerting if a program does not offer any feedback to the user as to what it is doing. The example program has an option to print the current motor velocity and the actuator output at every cycle of the control loop. However, in time critical programs (and almost all real-time programs are time critical), one must weigh the performance cost of displaying status information in real-time against the desire for such information. It may not matter in simulation, but real-time status display can consume a significant amount of time, especially when controlling systems with short time constants and quick response from the controller is required. However, such status displays may be the only way a user or machine operator can know what is going on in the process. The system designer must therefore consider what needs to be displayed and how often to display it.

Within the control routine, motor velocity is obtained from *getv()*, and control output is sent to the motor by *mact()*. These two functions hide from the control routine the details of how velocity is obtained and control is effected. In fact, the motor velocity interface need not even be an ADC; it could instead be a quadrature encoder. Similarly, the output actuator could be a PWM (Pulse Width Modulation) amplifier. The two input/output functions can also take care of converting between device units and the units used by the control program.

For example, a more sophisticated version of the program may use radians-per-second or revolutions-per-minute as speed units; *getv()* will have to convert the raw device readings into the appropriate units and cast[9] the result into a floating point value before returning it to the control program.

In the *control()* routine, there is a statement of the form:

```
#ifdef SIMRT
    tstep();
#endif
```

This tells the C macro preprocessor to include the call to *tstep()* in the program for subsequent compilation if the symbol SIMRT is defined. The routine *tstep()* causes the simulation equation to step forward in time by one time increment (defined by the *i* user command). The use of this "conditional compilation" feature allows the same C source file to generate both the real hardware version and the simulation version of the program.

1.14 SIMULATION MODULE—RTSIM0.C

This module consists of 3 main sections: the ADC simulation, the DAC simulation, and the motor plant simulation. All the interface functions of the dash8.c and dac2.c driver modules are simulated.

The motor plant is described by a simple difference equation that uses the Euler method to solve for the speed given the torque, inertia, and time step. This is intended only to demonstrate the use of simulation; interested readers may wish to substitute a more sophisticated simulation using the Runge-Kutta method and perhaps incorporate friction in the model. The simulation can be as sophisticated as you want to make it.

---

[9] A cast in C is where a value of one type is converted into another type. For example, in mact(), the argument *value* is casted from a **double** into an **int** by preceding it with **(int)**, i.e., the desired type enclosed in brackets.

The torque term is obtained from the D/A simulation, which converts the D/A output value to a torque value using an arbitrary conversion factor. If you are simulating a real setup, the conversion factor will depend on the characteristics of the motor, power amplifier, and the D/A. The *da_write()* routine simulates a 12-bit bipolar[10] D/A of the sort used in the Metrabyte DAC-02 control board. Only the least significant 12 bits are used. For positive arguments, a bitwise *AND* operation is performed on the argument with a mask consisting of all 1's in the least significant 12 bits and 0's in the most significant bits. For example:

```
value &= 0xfff;
```

where *0xfff* is the mask value in hexadecimal[11] notation. This statement is equivalent to

```
value = value & 0xfff;
```

If the argument is negative, we still want only the least significant 12 bits, but the most significant bits have to be set to 1's instead of 0's to preserve its sign (in 2's complement notation) when calculating the torque value. This is done by performing a bitwise *OR* with a mask consisting of 0's in the least significant 12 bits and 1's in the most significant bits. For example:

```
value |= ~0xfff;
```

The '~' bitwise complement operator changes all 1 bits to 0 and all 0 bits to 1. The result (in this example, 0xf000) is then bitwise or'ed with the variable *value* and the result assigned back to *value*.

Why use such a roundabout method instead of just using 0xf000 directly? The reason is portability. Integers are implemented as 16-bit quantities by most of the C compilers that run on the IBM-PC. However, this is not true for all C compilers[12] for the IBM-PC, and most definitely cannot be assumed for compilers intended for computers based on the Motorola 68000 family or even the Intel 80386. In the example, or'ing with 0xf000 will be incorrect with a compiler that uses 32-bit integers. Problems of this sort are particularly difficult to find, especially if the code is buried deep in a large program. Since we want to turn on all the bits above the 12th bit, but leave the lower 12 bits alone, the best solution is to use the complement of 0xfff; this way, the compiler takes care of expanding the result into the correct number of bits.

---

[10]Bipolar in this context means that the D/A can put out both positive and negative voltages.

[11]Base 16 numbering system: 0 1 2 3 4 5 6 7 8 9 A B C D E F

[12]The C standard, such as it is, does not specify how many bits an *int* or any other type should have, only that some types may not have fewer bits than others. For example, a *long* type must be represented by the same or greater number of bits than an *int* type.

There is a related problem known as the byte ordering problem where bytes in a multi-byte word are ordered differently by different CPUs. This problem may affect you if you are porting code that performs bit manipulation (such as device drivers) between, say, Intel processors and Motorola processors.

Low-level "bit fiddling" is common in programs that control hardware. Fortunately, C is a language designed for implementing operating systems and as such, provides operators for performing low-level bitwise operations. Judicious use of these operators can often result in more efficient code since they may have a direct machine instruction analogue. However, they can be rather obscure for the uninitiated.

A word about assignments of the form

```
t += dt;
```

This may seem somewhat obscure, but it can allow the compiler to generate more efficient code. This is worth noting because, after all, execution time is always a concern in real-time programs. The compiler can generate more efficient code since t need only be evaluated once, and its address can be kept in a register for faster access. It probably makes very little difference with a simple variable like t, but consider the case where we have a complicated expression like

$$a[b+c[d*e[f][g]+h]] = a[b+c[d*e[f][g]+h]] + x;$$

1.15 METRABYTE DASH-8 A/D DRIVER—DASH8.C

The file module, *dash8.c*, implements a driver for the analog-to-digital converter on the Metrabyte DASH-8 board. This module also serves as an example of how one might implement simple device drivers. Such programs are very hardware dependent, but as long as the function call interface is well designed and consistent, other modules need not be concerned with the details of the implementation. We have chosen the Metrabyte DASH-8 simply because we have it; your particular ADC board may be entirely different, but the same design principles apply.

1.15.1 PRINCIPLES OF OPERATION

The A/D on the DASH-8 has 8 multiplexed channels. It presents 4 i/o ports to the system:

1. the control port
2. the status port
3. the low byte of the converted value
4. the high byte of the converted value

The channel is first specified by writing the channel value (0 to 7) to the control port. A conversion will be initiated by writing any value to the high-byte port address. While a conversion is in progress, the busy bit in the status port will be set; hence, the program must wait until the busy bit is cleared before reading the low-byte and high-byte ports for the result.

1.15.2 INITIALIZATION

The A/D input ports should be read once when the system is first powered up since they may contain stray and invalid data. This is done by the *ad_init()* routine. In general, device drivers should have an initialization routine to put the device into a known state and initialize variables used by the module.

1.15.3 MORE BIT FIDDLING

The 12-bit result is split between two bytes: the least significant nibble[13] is presented at the most significant nibble of the low-byte port, and the two most significant nibbles are presented at the high-byte port. The resulting 12-bit word is assembled into a 16-bit integer using the >> and << bitwise shift operators and bit-masking operations. In the example,

```
in(ADLO) >> 4
```

means to shift to the right by 4 bits the value obtained from port ADLO (the low-byte port). This shifts the least significant nibble of the 12-bit result into the correct position. To ensure that no extraneous bits are included, we mask out all but the low-order nibble:

```
(in(ADLO) >> 4) & 0x000F
```

The binary '**&**' operator performs the bitwise AND operation on the operand bitfields. For example:

```
  01101011
& 00001111
  --------
  00001011
```

The result bit position is 1 if and only if the corresponding bits in both operands are 1s. Thus, to extract the low-order 4 bits in a byte, we apply a mask consisting of 1 bit in the low-order nibble and 0 bits in the high-order nibble. Depending on the machine/compiler combination, it may be a good idea to mask the result of a

---

[13]A nibble is 4 bits.

rightward shift because on some systems, if the most significant bit of word is 1, a 1 bit may be shifted in from the left[14] instead of 0's.

Thus, to obtain the 12-bit value:

```
rval  = (in(ADLO) >> 4) & 0x000F;
rval |= (in(ADHI) << 4) & 0x0FF0;
```

The least significant nibble is first shifted into position. Next, the most significant byte is shifted into position and or'ed with the least significant nibble. Multiplication and division can be used to accomplish the same result, but the computation overhead may be unacceptable, especially when the operation has to be performed frequently in a time critical control loop.

1.16 METRABYTE DAC-02 D/A DRIVER—DAC2.C

The DAC-02 has two 12-bit digital-to-analog converter channels. Each channel consists of two output ports; one for the low byte and one for the high byte. The output bits are partitioned between the two ports in a manner similar to the DASH-8 partitioning. The most significant byte of the 12-bit output value is sent to the high-byte port, and the remaining nibble is sent to the upper 4 bits of the low-byte port.

The DAC-02 can be configured for bipolar operation. This means that it can put out both positive and negative voltages. It uses an "offset binary" encoding scheme where sending a value of 0 to the output ports results in −10 volts and a value of 0xFFF (4095 in decimal) results in +10 volts. The *da_write()* routine hides this inconvenience from the application by accepting values in the −2048 to 2047 range and applying an offset to it before sending it out to the DAC.

---

[14]This is known as an arithmetic right shift.

```
/***********************************************************************

FILE
    envir.h  -  defines program environment

LAST UPDATE
    16 August 1987
        remove unnecessary clutter

    Copyright(c) 1985,1986,1987  D.M. Auslander and C.H. Tham

***********************************************************************/

/***********************   Operating System   ***********************/

#define UNIX    0       /* 4.2 BSD, implies UNIX C compiler */
#define PCDOS   1       /* includes generic MSDOS family */
#define CPM     0       /* the CP/M family, including MP/M */


/*******************   Hardware or Machine Type   *******************/

#define IBMPC       1       /* standard PC, PC/XT, PC/AT */
#define COMPUPRO    0       /* Compupro 8086 or Dual Processor */
#define INTEL310    0       /* Intel 310 development system */


/***************************   Compilers   ***************************/

#define CIC86       0       /* Computer Innovations C86 ver. 2.20M */
#define DESMET      0       /* Desmet C */
#define LATTICE     0       /* Lattice C ver. 2.15 */
#define MICROSOFT   1       /* Microsft C ver. 4.00 */

#if MICROSOF
#define ANSI                /* use proposed ANSI C features */
#endif

/***********************************************************************

FILE
    inout.h  -  maps compiler's 8-bit i/o function names

REMARKS
    Different compilers call their 8-bit port i/o routines by different
    names.  This file contains macros to map these names to the generic
    in() and out().  This makes programs much more portable across
    different compilers

    Note: compiler #define's must be placed before this file.

***********************************************************************/


#if CIC86           /* Computer Innovations C86 */

#define in(port)            inportb((unsigned)(port))
#define out(port, value)    outportb((unsigned)(port), value)

#endif

#if DESMET          /* Desmet C  */

#define in(port)            _inb(port)
#define out(port, value)    _outb(port, value)

#endif

#if LATTICE         /* Lattice C (Version 2.15) */

#define in(port)            inp(port)
#define out(port, value)    outp(port, value)

#endif

#if MICROSOFT       /* Microsoft C Version 4.00 and 5.00 */

#define in(port)            inp(port)
#define out(port, value)    outp((port), value)

#endif

/***********************************************************************

FILE
    dash8.h  -  interface declarations for dash8.c

LAST UPDATE
    18 November 1987

***********************************************************************/


#ifdef ANSI

extern void ad_init(void);
extern void ad_start(int);
extern int  ad_read(int);
extern int  ad_wread(int);
```

```
#else

extern void ad_init();
extern void ad_start();
extern void ad_read();
extern void ad_wread();

#endif

/************************************************************************

FILE
    dac2.h  -  interface declarations for dac2.c

LAST UPDATE
    18 November 1987

************************************************************************/

#ifdef ANSI

extern void da_init();
extern void da_limits(int *, int *);
extern int  da_write(int, int);

#else

extern void da_init();
extern void da_limits();
extern int  da_write();

#endif

/************************************************************************

FILE
    main0.c  -  d.c. motor speed control example, main program module

ROUTINES
    main    -  main program
    cmdint  -  command processor

REMARKS
    This program module, together with cntrl0.c and rtsim0.c implements
    simple control of the speed of a d.c. motor.  This is the main
    program module and it implements a command processor.  The other
    two module implements the P control algorithm (cntrl0.c) and a
    simulation of the motor set-up (rtsim0.c).

    To generate the simulation program under Microsoft C version 4.00
    and above, type: cl main0.c cntrl0.c rtsim0.c

LAST UPDATE
    18 March 1985
        recast in module form
    1 December 1987
        restructure and modify for MSC 4.00 and 5.00

    Copyright(C) 1984-1987  D.M. Auslander and C.H. Tham

************************************************************************/

/************************************************************************
                          I M P O R T S

    This section contains ALL the declarations from other modules
    required in this program.  Such "imports" are gathered here
    instead of scattered all over this file to make them easier
    to find and reduces the chance of introducing bugs through
    inconsistent multiple declarations of the same item.

************************************************************************/

#include <stdio.h>      /* standard C header file */

#include "envir.h"      /* program environment declarations */
#include "cntrl0.h"     /* extern declarations for cntrl0.c */


/************************************************************************
    P R I V A T E    D A T A    A N D    D E C L A R A T I O N S

    These variables and declarations are visible to all routines in
    this file.  Variables declared as "static" are not visible
    outside of this file.  In computer jargon, their "name space" is
    restricted to this file.  This enhances data security by preventing
    routines outside this file from inadvertently modifying these
    values though accidental use of an external variable with the
    same name.

************************************************************************/

#define PROMPT "-"      /* defines the command processor prompt */


/************************************************************************
          F O R W A R D    D E C L A R A T I O N S

    In C, functions are assumed to return an integer unless declared
    otherwise.  Here, the return type of all functions which do not
    return integers (or anything at all) are declared.  The symbol
    string "ANSI" is used by the C macro processor's conditional
    compilation feature to enable "function prototyping" for
```

```
    compilers that support this proposed ANSI C feature.

    The statement below declares cmdint() and menu() to be functions
    which do not return a value.  If the symbol "ANSI" is defined
    anywhere prior to the #ifdef statement, function prototyping
    is used as an added consistency check.

*********************************************************************/

#ifdef ANSI

void cmdint(char *);
void menu(void);

#else

void cmdint();
void menu();

#endif


/*********************************************************************
                  E N T R Y    R O U T I N E S

    Entry routines are those that can be called directly by functions
    outside this module or file.  Here, we have only one entry
    routine, the main() function.

*********************************************************************/

main()
{
    char cbuf[100];     /* space for the user-typed command line */


    menu();             /* print menu of commands */

    for (;;)            /* an endless loop */
    {
        fputs(PROMPT, stdout);      /* print a prompt */

        fgets(cbuf, 100, stdin);    /* get command line from user */

        cmdint(cbuf);               /* interpret and execute commands */
    }
}


/*********************************************************************
```

```
                    P R I V A T E    R O U T I N E S

    The following routines are declared "static".  These routines
    can be directly accessed only by routines inside this file; they
    are not "visible" to routines outside this file.  Hence they are
    private to this file.  Private routines help avoid name conflicts
    in large programming projects.

*********************************************************************/

/*-------------------------------------------------------------------
PROCEDURE
    CMDINT  -  command interpreter

SYNOPSIS
    static void cmdint(cline)
    char cline[];

PARAMETER
    cline  -  command line in the form of an array of characters

REMARKS
    The first character of the command string, cline[0], specifies the
    command.  The rest of the command line is passed to the specific
    "command function" as &cline[1], which is the address of the rest
    of the line.

    Recognized commands are:

        k  -  controller gains
        s  -  set point
        i  -  initialize the system
        g  -  start (i.e. go)
        ?  -  help

LAST UPDATE
    18 March 1985
-------------------------------------------------------------------*/

static void cmdint(cline)
char cline[];          /* command string is terminated by NULL char */
{


    switch (cline[0])
    {
        case 'k':                /* set controller gains; remainder */
                                 /*  of the command line is passed  */
            gain(&cline[1]);     /*  to the function gain() for     */
            break;               /*  decoding.                      */
```

```
        case 's':               /* set the setpoint */

            setv(&cline[1]);
            break;

        case 'i':               /* initialize the system */

            init(&cline[1]);
            break;

        case 'g':               /* "go," i.e., start control. */

            control(&cline[1]);
            break;

        case 'e':               /* return to operating system. */

            exit(0);

        case '?':               /* print list of commands */
        case 'h':

            menu();
            break;

        default:                /* unrecognized commands */

            printf("command not found: %s", cline);
    }

}


/*----------------------------------------------------------------------
PROCEDURE
    MENU  -  print a reminder of commands

SYNOPSIS
    static void menu()

LAST UPDATE
    17 November 1987
----------------------------------------------------------------------*/

static void menu()
{

    printf("k <P gain> <constant term>    -  control gains\n");
    printf("s <speed reference>           -  speed reference\n");
    printf("i <delta t>                   -  sampling time\n");
    printf("g <# of iterations> <print each iteration>  -  start\n");
    printf("h                                    -  print menu of commands\n");
    printf("e                                    -  exit program\n");

}


/***********************************************************************

FILE
    cntrl0.c  -  d.c. servo speed control example, control code

ROUTINES
    control  -  execute control algorithm
    gain     -  interpret command line for P gain
    setv     -  interpret command line for setpoint
    getv     -  get velocity reading
    mact     -  send controller output to actuator

REMARKS
    implements simple P control of d.c. motor speed.

LAST UPDATE
    18 March 1985  by  Haam
        recast in module form
    1 December 1987
        restructure and modify for MSC 4.00 and 5.00

    Copyright(C) 1984-1987, D.M.Auslander and C.H. Tham

***********************************************************************/

/***********************************************************************
                            I M P O R T S

    This section contains ALL the declarations from other modules
    required in this program.  Such "imports" are gathered here
    instead of scattered all over this file to make them easier
    to find and reduces the chance of introducing bugs through
    inconsistent multiple declarations of the same item.

***********************************************************************/

#include <stdio.h>

#include "envir.h"      /* environment definitions */
#include "dash8.h"      /* declarations for dash8.c */
#include "dac2.h"       /* declarations for dac2.c */
#include "cntrl0.h"     /* exported declarations for this module */
```

```
/*************************************************************************
           F O R W A R D    D E C L A R A T I O N S

    In C, functions are assumed to return an integer unless declared
    otherwise.  Here, the return type of all functions which do not
    return integers (or anything at all) are declared.  The symbol
    string "ANSI" is used by the C macro processor's conditional
    compilation feature to enable "function prototyping" for
    compilers that support this proposed ANSI C feature.

    This section only declares functions that are local to this
    module; functions visible outside this module are already
    declared in the header file cntrl0.h #include'd above.

*************************************************************************/

#ifdef ANSI

double getv(void);
void   mact(double);

#else

double getv();
void   mact();

#endif


/*************************************************************************
         P R I V A T E    D A T A    V A R I A B L E S

    These variables and declarations are visible to all routines in
    this file.  Variables declared as "static" are not visible
    outside of this file.  In computer jargon, their "name space" is
    restricted to this file.  This enhances data security by preventing
    routines outside this file from inadvertently modifying these
    values though accidental use of an external variable with the
    same name.

*************************************************************************/

#define ADCHANNEL    0            /* A/D channel that we will use */
#define DACHANNEL    0            /* D/A channel used by this module */

static double vref = 1000.0;      /* velocity setpoint  */
static double kp = 1.0;           /* proportional gain */
static double vcon = 0.0;         /* constant term in the controller */
static double mmin;               /* lower limit for controller output */
static double mmax;               /* upper limit for controller output */
```

```
/*************************************************************************
                 E N T R Y    R O U T I N E S

    Entry routines are those that can be called directly by functions
    outside this module or file.

*************************************************************************/

/*-----------------------------------------------------------------------
PROCEDURE
    CONTROL  -  implements P control algorithm

SYNOPSIS
    void control(cline)
    char *cline;

PARAMETERS
    cline  -  pointer to user's argument string

LAST UPDATE
    15 October 1984
-----------------------------------------------------------------------*/

void control(cline)
char *cline;
{
    long nitr;              /* number of iterations */
    long i;                 /* iteration counter */
    double v;               /* the motor velocity */
    double m;               /* controller output */
    int damin, damax;       /* output argument range of D/A */
    int prnt;               /* 1 = print control output, 0 = no print */

    /*-----------------------------------------------------------------
       Get number of iterations and print flag from the command
       line, cline.  Sscanf() is just like scanf() except that the
       input is a string instead of the standard input (keyboard).
    -----------------------------------------------------------------*/

    sscanf(cline, "%ld %d", &nitr, &prnt);

    printf("number of iterations = %ld\n", nitr);    /* verify */

    da_limits(&damin, &damax);       /* find D/A output limits */

    mmin = (double)damin;
    mmax = (double)damax;

    for (i = 1; i <= nitr; i++)      /* main iteration loop */
    {
        v = getv();                  /* get motor velocity */
```

```
        m = kp * (vref - v) + vcon; /* the control equation */

        if (m > mmax)               /* limit value of m to allowable */
            m = mmax;               /*   d/a and actuator range.     */
        else if (m < mmin)
            m = mmin;

        if (prnt)
            printf("v = %f, m = %f\n", v, m);

        mact(m);        /* send controller output to the actuator. */

#ifdef SIMRT
        tstep();        /* time simulation: step ahead one step in time */
#endif

    }   /* end of main iteration loop. */

}



/*---------------------------------------------------------------------
PROCEDURE
    GAIN  -  interpret the input line specifying controller gain(s)

SYNOPSIS
    void gain(cline)
    char *cline;

PARAMETERS
    cline  -  input line

LAST UPDATE
    15 October 1984
---------------------------------------------------------------------*/

void gain(cline)
char *cline;
{

    sscanf(cline, "%lf %lf", &kp, &vcon);       /* decode input line */

#if DEBUG
    printf("<gain> kp = %lf, vcon = %lf\n", kp, vcon);
#endif

}
```

```
/*---------------------------------------------------------------------
PROCEDURE
    SETV  -  get velocity setpoint from the command line

SYNOPSIS
    void setv(cline)
    char *cline;

PARAMETERS
    cline  -  user's command line

LAST UPDATE
    15 October 1984  by  Haam
---------------------------------------------------------------------*/

void setv(cline)
char *cline;
{

    sscanf(cline,"%lf", &vref);

#if DEBUG
    printf("<setv> vref = %lf\n", vref);
#endif

}



/**********************************************************************

    The following section contains routines which interface between
    high level control code and functions which perform the hardware
    dependent functions of operating the A/D and D/A.  As such, they
    are necessarily dependent on the device driver interface.

**********************************************************************/

/*---------------------------------------------------------------------
PROCEDURE
    INIT  -  system initialization

SYNOPSIS
    void init()

REMARKS
    Performs any initializations required.

LAST UPDATE
    1 December 1987
---------------------------------------------------------------------*/
```

```
void init(cline)
char *cline;
{

    ad_init();              /* initialize A/D */
    da_init();              /* initialize D/A */

#ifdef SIMRT
    sim_init(cline);        /* initialize simulation module */
#endif

}



/*------------------------------------------------------------------------
FUNCTION
    GETV  -  returns motor velocity

SYNOPSIS
    static double getv()

RETURNS
    current motor velocity (units unspecified)

REMARKS
    Reads channel 0 of the A/D converter, convert the value to a
    double type and return this converted value.

LAST UPDATE
    15 October 1984
------------------------------------------------------------------------*/

static double getv()
{

    return((double)ad_wread(ADCHANNEL));
}



/*------------------------------------------------------------------------
PROCEDURE
    MACT  -  send controller output to actuator

SYNOPSIS
    static void mact(value)
    double value;

PARAMETER
    value  -  controller output

REMARKS
    Convert output to integer and send it to D/A converter

LAST UPDATE
    15 October 1984
------------------------------------------------------------------------*/

static void mact(value)
double value;
{

    da_write(DACHANNEL, (int)value);
}


/************************************************************************

FILE
    rtsim0.c  -  d.c. speed control, simulation module

ENTRY ROUTINES
    tstep      -  advance one time step

    ad_init    -  simulates A/D initialization
    ad_start   -  simulates starting an A/D read
    ad_read    -  simulates reading A/D value
    ad_wread   -  simulates read from A/D

    da_init    -  simulates D/A initialization
    da_limits  -  returns simulation D/A output limits
    da_write   -  simulates write to D/A

PRIVATE ROUTINE
    simul   -  motor plant simulation

INITIALIZATION ROUTINE
    sim_init   -  initialize simulation

REMARKS
    This module simulates the interface and motor hardware and the
    passage of "real" time.  This module must thus provide the same
    interface functions as the modules controlling the hardware.

    A simulation allows algorithms to be debugged and fine-tuned
    without the need for an actual hardware setup.

LAST UPDATE
    1 December 1987
        restructure and modify for MSC 4.00 and 5.00

    Copyright(C) 1984-1987  D.M. Auslander and C.H. Tham
```

```
**********************************************************************/

/**********************************************************************
                          I M P O R T S
**********************************************************************/

#include "envir.h"          /* environment specifications */


/**********************************************************************
             F O R W A R D   D E C L A R A T I O N S
**********************************************************************/

#ifdef ANSI

void simul(void);

#else

void simul();

#endif


/**********************************************************************
                 P R I V A T E   D A T A
**********************************************************************/

#define ADSCALE       512.0     /* scale speed to A/D units */
#define ADMAX        2047       /* max A/D input value */
#define ADMIN       -2048       /* min A/D input value */

#define DASCALE      2047.0     /* scale D/A value to torque */
#define DAMIN       -2048       /* min. output value accepted */
#define DAMAX        2047       /* max. output value accepted */

static double inertia = 1.0;        /* motor system inertia */
static double speed;                /* simulated motor velocity */
static double t;                    /* time */
static double dt;                   /* step size in time */
static double torque = 0.0;         /* motor torque */


/**********************************************************************
  E N T R Y   R O U T I N E S   -   T I M E   S I M U L A T I O N
**********************************************************************/

/*----------------------------------------------------------------------
PROCEDURE
    TSTEP  -  advance time forward one step

SYNOPSIS
    tstep()

LAST UPDATE
    10 October 1984
----------------------------------------------------------------------*/

tstep()
{

    simul();        /* compute one time step in the differential */
                    /*   equation for the motor system.          */

    t += dt;        /* increment time by dt */

}



/**********************************************************************
  E N T R Y   R O U T I N E S   -   A / D   S I M U L A T I O N

    These routines dummies the routines in dash8.c which drives the
    Metrabyte DASH8 A/D board.  The channel parameter is ignored.

**********************************************************************/

void ad_init()
{

    speed = 0.0;

}


void ad_start(channel)
int channel;
{
    /* nothing */
}


int ad_read(channel)
int channel;
{
    int rval;                       /* return value */


    rval = ADSCALE * speed;         /* scale and convert to int type */

    if (rval > ADMAX)               /* apply converter limits */
```

```
        rval = ADMAX;
    else if (rval < ADMIN)
        rval = ADMIN;

    return(rval);
}


int ad_wread(channel)
int channel;
{

    return(ad_read(channel));
}



/**********************************************************************
   E N T R Y    R O U T I N E S   -   D / A    S I M U L A T I O N

    These routines dummies the routines in dac2.c which drives the
    Metrabyte DAC02 D/A board.  The channel parameter is ignored.

    The DAC2 is a 12-bit digital-to-analog converter configured for
    bipolar output.  Thus, the output parameter values range from
    -2048 to 2047.  Only lower 12 bits will be used, treating those
    12 bits as a 2's complement signed number.  Thus if the output
    value is negative, the lower 12 bits will be preserved and all
    higher order bits will be converted to 1's.

    Note the use of ~0xfff instead of 0xf000, this makes the program
    more portable across machines with different integer sizes.

**********************************************************************/

void da_init()
{

    torque = 0.0;

}


void da_limits(lo, hi)
int *lo, *hi;
{

    *lo = DAMIN;
    *hi = DAMAX;

}
```

```
void da_write(channel, value)
int channel, value;
{

    if (value < 0)            /* OR with a binary number having 0's for */
        value |= ~0xfff;      /*   the lower 12 bits and 1's elsewhere  */
    else
        value &= 0xfff;       /* for positive values, just save the     */
                              /*   lower 12 bits.                        */

    torque = value / DASCALE;   /* rescale for motor drive torque. */

}



/**********************************************************************
                  P R I V A T E    R O U T I N E S

    The following routines are declared "static".  These routines
    can be directly accessed only by routines inside this file; they
    are not "visible" to routines outside this file.  Hence they are
    private to this file.  Private routines enhances data security
    and helps avoid unexpected name conflicts in large programming
    projects.

**********************************************************************/

/*--------------------------------------------------------------------
PROCEDURE
    SIMUL  -  simulates motor plant

SYNOPSIS
    static void simul()

REMARKS
    Solve the motor system differential equation.  This version uses
    the Euler method for integration; it isn't very efficient, but its
    easy to program!

LAST UPDATE
    10 October 1984
--------------------------------------------------------------------*/

static void simul()
{

    speed += torque * dt / inertia;     /* pure inertial load */

}
```

```
/*********************************************************************
          I N I T I A L I Z A T I O N    R O U T I N E
*********************************************************************/

/*-------------------------------------------------------------------
PROCEDURE
    INIT  -  system initialization

SYNOPSIS
    sim_init(cline)
    char *cline;

PARAMETER
    cline  -  user's input command line

REMARKS
    In a "real" real-time program, this function would be used to set
    up interrupts, set clock modes, etc.  In this simulation version,
    it sets time to zero and sets the motor simulation initial conditions.

LAST UPDATE
    18 October 1984
-------------------------------------------------------------------*/

sim_init(cline)
char *cline;
{

    sscanf(cline, "%lf", &dt);  /* get the step size. */

#if DEBUG
    printf("<init> dt = %lf\n", dt);
#endif

    t = 0.0;                    /* reset time */

    speed = 0.0;                /* motor is initially at rest */
    torque = 0.0;

}


/*********************************************************************

FILE
    dash8.c  -  driver for Metrabyte DASH-8 analog to digital i/o board

ROUTINES
    ad_init     -  initialize A/D
    ad_start    -  start an A/D conversion
    ad_read     -  read A/D channel
    ad_wread    -  start conversion and wait for result

REMARKS
    The DASH-8 is a 8-channel 12-bit ADC with a typical conversion time
    of 25 microseconds (35 microseconds max.).  Analog range is +/- 5V.
    Although the DASH-8 has options for faster 8-bit conversions, on-
    board 8253 timer/counter, digital i/o lines and interrupt operation,
    we shall not use them in the interest of simplicity.

LAST UPDATE
    1 May 1985

    Copyright (c) 1985  D.M. Auslander and C.H. Tham

*********************************************************************/

/*********************************************************************
                        I M P O R T S
*********************************************************************/

#include <stdio.h>

#include "envir.h"          /* environment declarations */
#include "inout.h"          /* i/o mapping macros */
#include "dash8.h"          /* exported declarations for this module */


/*********************************************************************
                    P R I V A T E    D A T A
*********************************************************************/

#define MINCHAN     0           /* lowest valid channel number */
#define MAXCHAN     7           /* highest valid channel number */

#define ADMAX   0x0FFF          /* max value of A/D */
#define ADMIN   0               /* min value returned by A/D */

#define ADBASE  0x340           /* base address of A/D */

#define ADLO    ADBASE          /* low byte of A/D */
#define ADHI    ADBASE+1        /* high byte of A/D */
#define ADSTAT  ADBASE+2        /* A/D status port */
#define ADCTL   ADBASE+2        /* A/D control port */

#define ADBUSY  0x80            /* A/D not-finished bit */

static char adctl = 0;          /* A/D control word */


/*********************************************************************
                  E N T R Y    R O U T I N E S
```

```
***********************************************************************/

/*----------------------------------------------------------------------
PROCEDURE
    AD_START  -  initiate A/D conversion

SYNOPSIS
    void ad_start(channel)
    int channel;

LAST UPDATE
    18 November 1987
----------------------------------------------------------------------*/

void ad_start(channel)
int channel;
{

    if ((channel >= MINCHAN) && (channel <= MAXCHAN))
    {
        adctl &= ~0x7;              /* clear channel select bits */
        adctl |= channel;           /* set channel select bits */

        out(ADCTL, adctl);          /* select channel */
        out(ADHI, 0);               /* start 12-bit conversion */
    }
    else
    {
        printf("ad_start: channel out of range\n");
    }

}



/*----------------------------------------------------------------------
PROCEDURE
    AD_READ  -  read A/D channel

SYNOPSIS
    int ad_read(channel)
    int channel;

RETURNS
    signed 12-bit value

REMARKS
    The data format is:

        DASH-8 value    voltage     return value
        0x0             -5.0000 V      0xF800
        0x800                 0 V           0
        0xFFF           +4.9976 V      0x07FF

    The return value is transformed to a signed integer between -2048
    to +2047 corresponding to -5V and +5V since there is an intuitive
    correspondence between signed values and signed voltages.

    If the channel argument is out of range, ad_read() returns 0.

LAST UPDATE
    18 November 1987
----------------------------------------------------------------------*/

int ad_read(channel)
int channel;
{
    int rval;        /* return value */


    if ((channel >= MINCHAN) && (channel <= MAXCHAN))
    {
        while (in(ADSTAT) & ADBUSY)          /* wait for A/D to finish */
            ;

        rval = (in(ADLO) >> 4) & 0x000F;     /* get 12-bit value */
        rval |= (in(ADHI) << 4) & 0x0FF0;    /* in normal format */

        rval -= 0x800;                /* convert to signed value */
    }
    else
    {
        printf("ad_read: channel out of range\n");

        rval = 0;
    }

    return(rval);
}



/*----------------------------------------------------------------------
FUNCTION
    AD_WREAD  -  initiate A/D and wait for result

SYNOPSIS
    int ad_wread(channel)
    int channel;

PARAMETER
```

```
    channel  -  channel number (0..7)

RETURNS
    signed 12 bit value

REMARKS
    A convenient combination of ad_start() and ad_read().

LAST UPDATE  :
    18 November 1987
----------------------------------------------------------------------*/

int ad_wread(channel)
int channel;
{

    if ((channel >= MINCHAN) && (channel <= MAXCHAN))
    {
        ad_start(channel);
        return(ad_read(channel));
    }
    else
    {
        printf("ad_wread: channel out of range\n");
        return(0);
    }

}



/***********************************************************************
          I N I T I A L I Z A T I O N    R O U T I N E
***********************************************************************/

/*---------------------------------------------------------------------
PROCEDURE
    AD_INIT  -  initialize A/D

SYNOPSIS
    void ad_init()

REMARKS
    Initialize to power-up state: interrupts disabled, digital outputs
    zero and channel select at zero.

LAST UPDATE
    1 May 1985
----------------------------------------------------------------------*/

void ad_init()
{

    adctl = 0;                  /* reset control word map variable */
    out(ADCTL, 0);              /* reset A/D itself */
}

/***********************************************************************

FILE
    dac2.c  -  driver for Metrabyte DAC-02 digital to analog i/o board

ROUTINES
    da_init    -  initialize D/A
    da_limits  -  return output limits of D/A
    da_write   -  D/A output

REMARKS
    The DAC-02 is a 2-channel 12-bit DAC using 8 consecutive i/o
    addresses.  Data has to be "left-justified" and sent out in 2 bytes,
    least significant byte first.  One can also use the 16-bit i/o
    instructions, but we will not do so here.

LAST UPDATE
    1 May 1985

    Copyright (c) 1985  D.M. Auslander and C.H. Tham

***********************************************************************/

/***********************************************************************
                          I M P O R T S
***********************************************************************/

#include <stdio.h>

#include "envir.h"          /* environment declarations */
#include "inout.h"          /* i/o mapping macros */
#include "dac2.h"           /* exported declarations for this module */


/***********************************************************************
                     P R I V A T E    D A T A
***********************************************************************/

#define DABASE  0x330           /* base address of D/A */

#define DAMIN   -2048           /* min. output value accepted */
#define DAMAX    2047           /* max. output value accepted */

#define DALO0   DABASE          /* D/A 0 low byte */
#define DAHI0   DABASE+1        /* D/A 0 high byte */
```

```
#define DALO1   DABASE+2        /* D/A 1 low byte */
#define DAHI1   DABASE+3        /* D/A 1 high byte */


/************************************************************************
                 E N T R Y    R O U T I N E S
************************************************************************/

/*-----------------------------------------------------------------------
PROCEDURE
    DA_LIMITS  -  returns D/A output limits.

SYNOPSIS
    void da_limits(lo, hi)
    int *lo, *hi;

PARAMETERS
    lo  -  pointer to low limit
    hi  -  pointer to high limit

REMARKS
    The limits are returned by means of side effects.  This routine
    enables other routines to perform limit checks in a more device
    independent manner.

LAST UPDATE
    1 May 1985
-----------------------------------------------------------------------*/

void da_limits(lo, hi)
int *lo, *hi;
{

    *lo = DAMIN;
    *hi = DAMAX;

}


/*-----------------------------------------------------------------------
FUNCTION
    DA_WRITE  -  write output to D/A

SYNOPSIS
    int da_write(chan, value)
    int chan, value;

PARAMETERS
    chan  -  channel number (0 or 1)
    value -  output value

RETURNS
    0  if all is well,  -1 if error

REMARKS
    The channel number is checked, but no range checking is performed on
    the output value in the interest of speed.  The calling routine is
    responsible for such checks - that's what da_limits() is for.

    The DAC uses an offset binary format where 0 will put out -10 volts
    and 4095 will put out +10 volts.

    The output value is scaled such that:

          -2048     --->     -10V
              0     --->       0V
          +2047     --->     +10V

LAST UPDATE
    1 May 1985
-----------------------------------------------------------------------*/

int da_write(chan, value)
int chan, value;
{
    int rval;        /* error indication return value */


    value = 0x800 + value;          /* convert to offset binary */

    switch (chan)
    {
        case 0:      /* channel 0 */

            out(DALO0, value << 4);          /* send low byte */
            out(DAHI0, value >> 4);          /* send high byte */

            rval = 0;                        /* indicate all O.K. */

            break;

        case 1:      /* channel 1 */

            out(DALO1, value << 4);
            out(DAHI1, value >> 4);

            rval = 0;

            break;

        default:     /* bad channel number */
```

```
            rval = -1;
            break;
    }

    return(rval);
}


/**********************************************************************
          I N I T I A L I Z A T I O N     R O U T I N E
**********************************************************************/

/*--------------------------------------------------------------------
PROCEDURE
    DA_INIT  -  initialize D/A

SYNOPSIS
    void da_init()

REMARKS
    Initialize both output channels to 0 volts.

LAST UPDATE
    1 May 1985
--------------------------------------------------------------------*/

void da_init()
{

    out(DALO0, 0x00);                /* zero channel 0 */
    out(DAHI0, 0x80);

    out(DALO1, 0x00);                /* zero channel 1 */
    out(DAHI1, 0x80);

}
```

CHAPTER 2

TIME

The mathematical function used for the control algorithm in the previous chapter made no reference to time, so the program could be run as often as the processor was able to. This is very simple and convenient for programming, but unusual. Most real-time programs require some synchronization with "real" time. In this chapter, we shall consider an algorithm that makes use of data sampled at known instants of time. It is still the only task present, so synchronous programming can still be used, but some mechanism must be added to determine time.

2.1 PROPORTIONAL PLUS INTEGRAL (PI) CONTROL

The proportional control algorithm has the disadvantage in that, when the error is zero, its output is fixed by the constant bias term. In general, there will only be a single setpoint for which the preset bias is correct. For all other setpoints, the inability of the controller to provide different biases for different setpoints will mean that after all of the transient behavior has died away, the output will not be at its desired value but will have some steady-state error. Whether or not this happens depends on the nature of the behavior of the system under control. If we imagine a frictionless motor, once it has reached its desired speed it will coast at that speed forever if no energy is removed from the system. If a controller is built in such a way that the control output represents torque applied to the motor, then maintenance of setpoint speed will not require any torque, and an offset bias of zero will work for all setpoint values.

Even without violating the assumption of no friction, whether the system will work satisfactorily with zero for an offset bias depends on the type of power amplifier that is used. A power amplifier that controls voltage across the motor will allow current to flow when its voltage is zero, thus dissipating energy and causing the motor to slow down. A non-zero bias voltage is needed to maintain speed, so, with only proportional (P) control, there will be a steady-state error in speed. A power amplifier that controls the current flow to the motor will act very much like a torque source, so will come closer to having no steady-state error. All real systems have some dissipation, however, so even a current-controlled system will have some steady-state offset.

Rather than use a constant bias voltage in the controller, the control algorithm can be designed to automatically adjust its bias voltage to whatever level is necessary to ensure that there is no steady-state error. This is done by substituting a term that acts on accumulated error for the constant bias. This can be expressed as an integral

$$m = k_p \varepsilon + k_i \int \varepsilon \, dt \tag{2.1}$$

As long as the error is not zero, the integral will continue to increase. When the error finally reaches zero, the value of the integral will remain, providing the needed bias to hold the error at zero. For computer control systems, the integral is approximated as a summation

$$m = k_p \varepsilon + k_i \sum \varepsilon \tag{2.2}$$

From an implementation point of view, it is simpler to separate the accumulation process from the control output computation. This can be done with the general form shown in Fig. 2.1.

```
error = setpoint - velocity
accumulation = accumulation + error
m = kp * error + ki * accumulation
```

Figure 2.1

The rate at which the accumulation term builds up depends on how often the process is sampled. It is thus necessary to control the timing of the sampling process, so that the sampling is done uniformly, and at a specified interval. A further point that must be considered is that the addition of the integral term (to give a PI control) reduces the system stability margin. If the integral gain, k_i is too high, it is possible to produce unstable behavior. k_i is therefore usually kept as small as possible consistent with reducing the error to zero in a reasonable amount of time.

2.2 CLOCKS

To a computer, a clock is a device that generates a sequence of pulses with a constant time interval between the pulses. To "keep time," it is necessary to count each of the pulses and keep track of the count. Within this context, there are several ways of recording the passage of time. The clock/calendar model is to maintain a record of "absolute" time. Absolute time, however, implies that the count can go on forever, which, in a finite precision machine such as a computer, can lead to difficulties in defining the means of storing the number. In ordinary timekeeping, we switch from the clock to the calendar for long time periods, but rarely maintain a precision of better that one second. For real-time problems, the precision level of interest is usually somewhere between a microsecond (10^{-6} sec) and a millisecond (10^{-3} sec). Cumulatively keeping track of microseconds means 3.6×10^9 counts per hour! Since real-time computers can run continuously for days, weeks, or even years, the bookkeeping problem is substantial. Furthermore, use of such a large format number to keep track of time can use up significant amounts of computing time if the time has to be updated frequently.

Fortunately, many real-time tasks only need to know relative time rather than absolute time, so the model of an interval timer can be used instead of the clock/calendar model. In these cases, the nature of the task is such that at the time it is run, the interval to the next time it must run again is already known. The interval timer is then set for that time, and when it runs out, the task is run again.

A third view of time is the stopwatch model. In this case, an event will happen at some indeterminate time in the future, but, when that event happens, something must be done (perhaps only record the time of the event). The interval timer and stopwatch models do not have as severe a precision problem as the absolute timekeeper, but there can still be problems with precision and word size. A 16-bit (unsigned) integer can keep track of 65535 counts. Even at a millisecond precision level, that is only about one minute. 32-bit integers can keep track of about 4 billion counts (4×10^9) which is adequate for most problems, but dealing with 32-bit integers can be slow for many computers.

2.3 CLOCK IMPLEMENTATION

The original source for the pulse train that is the fundamental timekeeper must be a physical device, usually a crystal oscillator, but, if the accuracy and stability of a crystal is not needed, it could be a tuned circuit. The rest of the clock can be implemented in either hardware or software, depending on the precision and duration requirements. When implemented in hardware, the basic pulse interval is usually from around one microsecond to around one millisecond. Devices called *programmable clocks* usually have several operating modes so that they can be used in either interval timing mode or stopwatch (event detection) mode.

Programmable timers usually also allow for variable count rate by dividing the basic pulse rate by a user-specified amount (every other pulse, every third, etc.). Because they are hardware devices, the duration is limited by the word size of the counter; 16-bits is common, but others are available.

Clock/calendar hardware clocks are also available, mainly for maintaining time and date information for operating systems. They usually have much cruder precision and are not as useful for real-time applications as programmable clocks.

At the other end of the spectrum, if the pulse interval is in the range of a millisecond or more, it is possible to implement the rest of the clock entirely in software. Hardware solutions are necessary for faster pulse trains to avoid using a large fraction of the computing time for the clock software. As pulse intervals get down toward a microsecond, it becomes impossible for a computer to keep up at all. Software solutions are much more flexible than hardware clocks because changes in precision, word size, and so on, can all be taken care of with programming changes. Mode changes and special needs for event detection can also be accommodated more easily.

The program structure for an interval timer implemented in software is shown in Fig. 2.2. The clock-set module is executed to start the interval timer by presetting a counter to the desired number of "ticks." Each pulse represents one tick of the clock. The clock module is executed whenever a pulse from the clock is detected. The clock module must also contain some means of communicating with the other parts of the program that use the time information. This can be done by providing a function that returns the current value of the counter. Another function normally supplied returns a clock-done *flag,* a logic variable that indicates whether the clock has run out yet. Its advantage is that its form is the same regardless of the means of implementing the clock, so programs using that information do not have to "know" the form of the internal counter used in the clock program.

```
clock-set(interval):
        counter = interval * scaling-factor
        clock-done = FALSE
        turn on the pulse generator and
                enable the detection circuitry
        return

clock:              (This module is called whenever a clock
                pulse is detected)
        counter = counter - 1
        if(counter <= 0)
                clock-done = TRUE
        return
```

Figure 2.2

It would also be possible to make the counter and clock-done flag available directly to programs as global variables. This method is less attractive, even though it requires slightly less computing time, because it compromises the isolation of the clock service module. Imagine, for example, a programming error resulting in a statement that changed the value of the clock counter in a module that was only supposed to use the clock, not change it. All other parts of the program that use the clock would then operate improperly, implying that the error is somewhere in the clock service functions when it is not. Careful modularization and "protection" of variables that are local to a module can go a long way toward more reliable and easy-to-debug programs.

The programming logic for using a hardware programmable timer is very similar. The clock-set program must transmit the interval information to the timer hardware and start it running. The maintenance of the count is done by the hardware timer, so the only further software requirement is a function that can tell if time has run out.

2.4 USING TIME IN CONTROL—PARALLEL PROCESSES

The primary interaction between the control program and the timekeeper is the flag variable, clock-done, which is available by a function call. For the purpose of designing the control program, it is useful to assume that time is being kept by a process that is completely independent of the control program, and running parallel with it. The parallel process assumption implies that nothing going on in the control program will interfere with the timekeeping function, and no constraints on execution time have to be applied to the control program other than the requirement that it be able to complete its work by the time of the next sample. With this structure in mind, the control program shown in Fig. 2.3 will behave the same as the control program developed for proportional control, except that sampling and control will only take place at specified times.

```
clock-set(sample-interval)

For number of iterations specified
        Do control
        Wait until clock-done = TRUE
        clock-set(sample-interval)
                                        (Reset the clock for the next
                                        sample)
```

Figure 2.3

One feature of this program is noted in the comment at the top of Fig. 2.3, that is, the time interval must be entered in units of ticks. Although a seemingly minor detail, this requirement makes the use of the high-level program dependent on the details of the low-level implementation. To run the program, the user must be aware of clock implementation information. Most users have no need for such information, so a better implementation might be to call the clock-set function with the sample time in units of seconds (or, perhaps, milliseconds) and convert to ticks in clock-set. The decisions on how to best insulate the user from unnecessary detail must be made early in the program design cycle. Once they become embedded, changes might have to be made throughout the program to alter the level at which information can be accessed.

Such decisions, however, have a variety of consequences. In this case, the conversion of sample interval from seconds to ticks normally would only have to be done once, during the setup phase of the program. By moving that conversion to a lower level (in clock-set), the user is indeed insulated from that detail, but the conversion must now be performed for every sample interval. Thus, convenience and portability may affect efficiency. A further difficulty is in deciding what "convenience" really is. Users of packaged programs are constantly frustrated on the one hand by features that are buried too deeply in the program for them to change and, on the other hand, by an overwhelming choice of features and parameters, which often interact with each other.

2.5 ACHIEVING PARALLELISM

If the clock is implemented with a hardware timer, the parallel operation assumed above is achieved naturally. Suitable circuitry must be provided so that the clock can be set and interrogated. In all other respects, though, the clock and the computer are independent devices. When the counting part of the clock is implemented in software, both the clock software and the control software must be run in the same computer. Since the computer is a strictly sequential device, true parallel operation cannot be achieved. If the computer is fast enough, however, both tasks can be carried out with an appearance of concurrent operation even though they run in sequence. If this is to be done in a manner that is "invisible" to the control program, a facility must be available that can suspend the execution of the control program whenever a pulse is detected, run the clock counting function, and then resume execution of the suspended program. This is called an *interrupt* mechanism and is present on most microprocessors.

The interrupt provides for pseudo-parallel operation as long as the computation that takes place during the interrupt does not significantly interfere with the *background* calculation. In most cases, this is accomplished by making the interrupt routine (the *foreground*) short enough and infrequent enough so that the appearance to the user is that the background calculation is just running on a slightly slower processor.

The mechanism of the interrupt is that the hardware device causing the interrupt (the input port where the pulse train signal is connected in our case) sends a signal to the processor requesting an interrupt. If the processor's operating mode is such that the signal can be recognized, it initiates the interrupt by suspending the execution of its current program and saving whatever internal processor information is necessary to restart that task when the interrupt has been completed. The processor then starts the execution of the foreground task, the "clock" module described above. When the foreground task has completed its work, the process is reversed. A signal is sent to the device that caused the interrupt indicating that interrupt processing is complete, the saved information is used to restore the processor state to where it was when the interrupt first occurred, and the background process is resumed. This sequence of events is illustrated in Fig. 2.4.

1. Hardware device requests an interrupt
2. Processor recognizes request
3. Execution of existing task is continued to the end
   of the current machine instruction
4. Internal processor status information is saved
5. Foreground task is started
6. Foreground task finishes
7. Background task's status information is restored
8. Background resumes

Figure 2.4

2.6 INTERRUPT HARDWARE

There are three main functions that must be accomplished by the interrupt control hardware:

1. Maintain *masking* information to decide whether or not an interrupt request should be honored,
2. Establish the *priority* of the current interrupt relative to already active interrupts, and
3. Determine the identity of the interrupt (what device caused the interrupt) and communicate the location (in memory) of the interrupt service function to the processor (*vectoring*).

The hardware that is used to perform these functions is often separate from the CPU, so it is possible to use different interrupt control schemes with the same CPU hardware.

The communication between the interrupt control hardware and the CPU to set the various modes, parameters, etc., is done through input and output ports. Most interrupt controllers allow for several modes of operation; they can be complex, and the operating instructions must be studied carefully!

The 3 functions described above, while always present in some form, are not always implemented to the same degree of sophistication. Masking, for example, implies the ability to selectively *enable* or *disable* individual interrupts. In simple interrupt processors, there may only be a global enable/disable present while others may allow for control of groups of devices.

The priority function can also have several levels of implementation. The simplest level disables all interrupts as soon as an interrupt request has been honored. This method gives all interrupts equal priority. Once the interrupt service function starts, the decision can be made in software whether (or when) to re-enable interrupts so that other interrupts can be allowed before processing of the current interrupt is complete. At the other end of the spectrum, a fully prioritized interrupt control maintains a separate priority for each interrupt. When an interrupt service routine starts running, it sets a CPU register to indicate its operating priority level. If another interrupt device requests service, the priority of that interrupt is compared to the priority level. If the requesting interrupt has a higher priority, its request is honored. Otherwise, it is held in abeyance.

A middle, and fairly common, priority control establishes priorities with groups of devices and stores the priority level information about the currently operating interrupt. The operating priority may not be accessible from the CPU, so remains fixed at the level set by the device. In order for the priority control to work, there must be appropriate mechanisms to signal to the interrupt controller that a particular interrupt service function has completed its work so that that priority level can be cleared.

The simplest possible vectoring method is for all interrupts to cause execution of the same interrupt service routine. This leaves to the software the task of determining the source of the interrupt and then executing the associated service function. This method requires a minimum of hardware, but is costly in computation time. It is not used frequently anymore, because interrupts are normally used for servicing time-critical tasks. Dedicated interrupt request lines between the interrupt controller and devices can be used to establish a time efficient compromise. There can be as many unique devices as there are wires provided for the interconnection. Beyond that, each wire must be shared. Because of the unique connection, however, the interrupt controller can determine the identity of the interrupting device very quickly and communicate the associated vector (i.e., memory address) to the CPU.

When a system has many devices, however, a more flexible method—a fully vectored interrupt—is necessary. To achieve full vectorization, each individual interrupt must be able to specify a unique vector. An interchange between the interrupt controller and the device is often used for this purpose. When the interrupt controller recognizes an interrupt, it sends a signal to the device asking for its interrupt vector. The device then sends the vector address to the interrupt controller, which passes it on to the CPU. The interchange between the interrupt controller and the device interface takes some time, but very much less time than would be needed to do the same interchange in software.

2.7 XIGNAL: A SOFTWARE INTERRUPT CONTROLLER

Interrupt hardware is usually complex. Many details must be attended to in order to set up and use the interrupt controller. The "xignal" facility is a software package that, for almost all real-time problems, allows that setup to be done once, then used for many programs in a way that makes the interrupts very simple to implement.

"Xignal" looks to the user like a fully vectored interrupt, except that communication with it only requires knowledge of some code names for the available interrupts. The name "xignal" is used to avoid conflicts with programs named "signal" that are part of several operating systems and compiler packages. Figure 2.5 shows a sample of using "signal" to set up an interrupt using a clock (the syntax is patterned after the "signal" facility of the UNIX operating system). The first call shown will cause the function timer-service to be called whenever the clock interrupts. The second call resets the interrupt hardware back to its original state after the real-time portion of the program is over.

```
xignal(SIGTMR, timer-service)
        .
        .
        .
xignal(SIGTMR, signal-default)
```

Figure 2.5

A general purpose package such as "signal" ("xignal") is never quite as time efficient as a module written for a specific purpose, but it should be fast enough for most needs.

THE TIME ELEMENT

2.8 INTRODUCTION

In this section, we will implement a proportional plus integral control algorithm that has to sample at known time intervals. In addition, we will show how to use interrupts from the built-in timer/counter of the IBM-PC to obtain real time information. Using interrupts normally requires an intimate knowledge of the hardware and assembly language programming. Fortunately, we have developed a set of routines, collected together in the xignal.lib library that allows one to set up interrupt-driven programs for the IBM-PC without having to delve into the hardware and assembly language programming. However, we have also included an example of how to "roll your own" interrupt driven timer functions using a mix of C and assembly language. Readers should know that real-time programming often requires the use of assembly language to meet performance goals and to manipulate hardware.

The programs in this section are:

envir.h	The environment specification file.
inout.h	Maps the *in* () and *out* () port access function names to the compiler's name for the equivalent functions.
main1.c	Main program module of the example program which implements the user interface.
cntrl1.h	Declarations for cntrl1.c.
cntrl1.c	Implements the PI control algorithm.
rtsim1.c	Simulation module.
dash8.h	Declarations for the DASH-8 ADC interface.
dac2.h	Declarations for the DAC-02 DAC interface.
time0.h	Declarations for the time0.c timer module.
time0.c	Simple timer implementation using ftime() calls.
main2.c	Another implementation of main1.c with a better command processor.
sigtime.c	A simple program to count 10 seconds using the xignal package.
xignal.h	Declarations for the xignal package.
xignal.lib	The xignal package library.
timeintc.c	Simple program to count 10 seconds using stand-alone timer interrupts.
time1.h	Declarations for the time1.c module.

time1.c Implements timer using timer interrupts.

alarm.h Declarations for the alarm.c module.

alarm.c Manipulates the PC's timer hardware.

8259.h Declarations of port addresses, vectors, and other miscellaneous information on the 8259 Programmable Interrupt Controller in the IBM-PC.

timeinta.asm Assembly language interface with the interrupt system.

2.9 SIMPLE PI CONTROL

The program consists of 3 modules: main1.c, cntrl1.c, and rtsim1.c, which are based on similar modules in Chapter 1. The main difference is that the time element is built into the control algorithm in cntrl1.c, which has to sample the speed and send out the control output at fixed time intervals (the sampling period). Time synchronization is provided by the following functions: *settimer()* sets the count-down timer for a given interval in milliseconds, and *timeout()* returns a value of 1 if the previously set interval has elapsed, and returns a value of 0 otherwise.

In the beginning of the control loop, *settimer()* is called to set time interval to the sample period. Since *settimer()* requires its argument to be in milliseconds and of type **long**, the sample period variable is converted to milliseconds and cast to the appropriate type before being passed to *settimer()*. Near the end of the control loop, the program tests if the timer has already timed out; if so, this means that the control loop cannot complete within the sample interval. The sampling interval is too short or the computer is too slow; either way, we cannot carry on since the controller cannot perform at the proper sampling interval. In real-time control applications, it is important to know if the system can perform at the specified level since the controlled system can become unstable if the controller cannot keep up with it. If the timer has not timed out prematurely, the program waits until it is time to run the loop again.

Note that the implementation of the timer functions are hidden from the control algorithm. Simulated or real-time can be used without affecting the control algorithm.

2.9.1 TIMER SIMULATION

Rtsim1.c contains a simple simulation of a count-down timer in addition to the ADC and DAC simulations. The count-down interval is stored in the form of a tick count. This is set by *settimer()*, which converts the desired interval from milliseconds to a tick count based on some assumed clock tick frequency in ticks per second defined by the variable *freq*. During each step of the control plant simulation, the number of ticks corresponding to the simulation step size (*dt*) is decremented from the timer tick count. If the tick count becomes zero or negative, a flag is set to indicate that "time is up"; this flag is used by the *timeout()* routine.

To create a program using simulated time:

```
cl /DSIMRT main1.c cntrl1.c rtsim1.c
```

2.10 REAL-TIME

There are several ways to obtain real-time information.

2.10.1 USING *ftime()*

Perhaps the simplest is to use the *ftime()* function supplied by the compiler vendor. This function originated on UNIX systems and is spreading to microcomputer implementations of C compiler libraries. Most of the recent high-end C compiler libraries have a variant of this function. *ftime()* gets the current system time and stores it in the structure pointed to by its argument. The resolution is that of the system clock, approximately 55 milliseconds for the IBM-PC family. Thus, time intervals can be determined by making calls to *ftime()* and obtaining the difference between the returned time information. This method of telling real-time is implemented in *time0.c*.

To generate a program using *ftime()* to tell time:

```
cl /DSIMRT /FTIME main1.c cntrl1.c rtsim1.c time0.c
```

2.10.2 USING THE XIGNAL PACKAGE

Another way involves the use of timer interrupts. A simple way to make use of timer interrupts without having to know the hardware details and assembly language programming is provided by the xignal package. This package is modelled on the UNIX signal family of functions; we named it xignal to avoid possible confusion with some compilers' library functions. The package comes in two parts: a declaration header file, *xignal.h*, and a library file, *xignal.lib*. A demonstration program, *sigtime.c*, shows how to use xignal to install a timer interrupt service routine. This is done by calling xignal with the name of the service routine as its second argument. This routine, named *tmr_isr()* in the example, runs whenever a timer interrupt occurs. On the IBM-PC, this would be about every 55 milliseconds. The interrupt service routine counts off 18 interrupt ticks and sets a flag. The background routine checks this flag; if it is set, it means that 1 second has elasped. The flag is immediately cleared and a count of seconds printed. When 10 seconds are up, the background loop exits and restores the system's time functions to their original state by calling xignal with *XIG_DFL* as its second argument.

Interested readers can try implementing a version of time0.c using the xignal package. Further documentation of the xignal package will be provided in later sections.

2.10.3 USING TIMER INTERRUPTS DIRECTLY

This is where we get down to the nitty-gritty of using timer interrupts. The description of the interrupt handling process will necessarily involve aspects of the 8088/8086 architecture and the Intel 8259 Programmable Interrupt Controller, which some readers may find heavy going. Explanations of the detailed operations of these two devices are clearly beyond the scope of this book. There are several excellent books on the 8088 to which the reader can refer; these are listed in the bibliography. The gory details of the 8259 are described in the *Intel Microcontroller Peripherals Handbook.* What we shall attempt to do here is to give a general overview of the interrupt handling process in the IBM-PC so that readers will have a sufficient conceptual understanding of the whole process to be able to follow the sample programs.

There is an example program, similar to *sigtime.c*, that uses timer interrupts. To create the program, do the following:

```
masm timeinta /ml;
cl /Gs timeintc.c time1.c alarm.c timeinta
```

The 8088 microprocessor uses vectored interrupts. Whenever a device interrupts the processor, it is responsible for telling the CPU which interrupt service routine should be executed. In other words, the external device provides a "vector" that points out its own service routine. An interrupt vector table is maintained by the CPU; there are 256 entries in the table, and each vector entry contains the address of an interrupt service routine.

If a program wishes to catch interrupts, it must first choose an interrupt vector and put the address of an interrupt service routine in the corresponding entry of the vector table. On the IBM-PC, external device vectors range from 8 to 15 (the timer uses vector number 8). An address consists of two parts: the segment plus an offset from the beginning of the segment. The maximum size of a segment is 64k bytes. Most real-time control programs that you are going to write will use the "small memory model"; all progam code must fit within a single segment and all data in another segment. Since the interrupt service routine consists of program instructions, it resides within the code segment.

The module *timeinta.asm* provides a function, *setivec(),* to install a routine as an interrupt service routine. This function takes 2 arguments; the first is the vector number, and the second is a pointer to the routine. In C, using a routine name without the brackets at the end indicates that we want the address of the routine. Thus, to install the routine *tick()* as the timer service routine, we call *setivec(TMRVEC, tick);* where *TMRVEC* is the timer vector number defined in *8259.h*.

It is very important point to note that the CPU must be prevented from responding to externally generated interrupts when a new vector entry is being installed. You do not want a timer interrupt to occur just as the program is changing the timer interrupt vector entry! The CPU interrupt response can be inhibited by using the *disable()* function (defined in *timeinta.asm*). When the new vector entry is installed, the CPU's interrupt response is re-enabled with the *enable()* function.

Note also that the original contents of the vector entry table must be saved so that we can restore the system when the program exits. If this is not done, the computer will surely crash after the program exits. An example of how this is done is found in the *init_tmr()* routine in the *time1.c* module. The segment and offset components of the vector are read using the *peekw()* function (defined in *timeinta.asm*) which allows one to read any memory location. The original vector is restored in *rstr_tmr()* by "poking" the original vector contents back. Note that such manipulations of the vector table must take place with interrupts disabled.

Next, let us consider what happens when an external device such as the timer makes an interrupt request. All external interrupt requests (except the 8087's) are first processed by the 8259A Programmable Interrupt Controller. The interrupt controller is designed to provide a powerful but simple interface between devices and the CPU. Each 8259 can handle 8 interrupt request inputs, and each request is associated with a priority and a vector number. These and other parameters are normally set up by the operating system.

An external device (e.g., the timer) requests an interrupt by signalling one of the 8259's interrupt request input lines. The 8259 looks at all current interrupt requests and selects the one with the highest priority. It then compares the priority of the request with the priority of any interrupt routines that are currently in service. If there are no interrupt routines currently in service, or if the priority of the request is higher than that of the routine currently in service, the 8259 will pass the interrupt request on to the CPU. The CPU can respond to the interrupt request or ignore it. Let us suppose that the CPU is set up to respond to external interrupts, i.e., interrupts are "enabled." On receipt of an interrupt request, the CPU stops execution after the current instruction and enters the "Interrupt Acknowledge Sequence." During this phase, the 8259 sends the vector number to the CPU and marks the request as "currently in service." The CPU saves the current state of the flag register and its current place in the code segment. It then uses the vector number to index into the interrupt vector table and obtain the address of the interrupt service routine, which is then executed.

The interrupt service routine should save all the registers that it will use so that the program can resume where it left off when the interrupt occurred. If there are calls to interrupt handlers written in C, all the registers must be saved since we do not know which registers will be used by the C functions (there are ways to find out, but it is usually not worth the extra work).

Here, we encounter one of the disadvantages of the segmented memory architecture used by the 8088. The interrupt may occur at any time; it may occur when the program is calling DOS to print characters to the screen or to perform disk i/o. Typically, DOS service routines operate with different segments from the program; so unless the program's data segment is restored by the interrupt service routine, data reads and writes will wreak havoc with the system. Under Microsoft

C, the program's data segment is referenced by DGROUP; we can thus use it to set up the data segment register in the interrupt service routine.

Another point to note is that the 8259 must be informed that the service routine has finished; otherwise, it will not allow another interrupt request from the same source to be passed on to the CPU. Worse, all lower priority requests will also be blocked. The completion of the current service routine is signaled by sending an "end-of-interrupt" (EOI) control byte to the 8259. This is done just before the service routine exits.

2.11 IN CONCLUSION

The sample program modules, *timeintc.c*, *time1.c*, and *timeinta.asm*, are designed to illustrate the setup and handling of timer interrupts using a combination of C and assembly language. The reason that assembly language is used is that very low level operations such as saving and restoring the registers, setting up the program data segment, and executing an "iret" instruction cannot be done in C. Version 5.00 of the Microsoft compiler has a special *interrupt* keyword that is supposed to do the appropriate setup and termination clean-up, but it is not a standard C feature and is not sufficiently stable at this time for us to recommend using it unless you are knowledgeable in both C and assembly language.

We have also provided a module, *alarm.c*, which manipulates the IBM-PC's 8253 timer/counter chip. This is used by the *time1.c* module. We think readers will find it useful for their real-time programming projects on the IBM-PC.

```
/************************************************************************

FILE
    envir.h  -  defines program environment

LAST UPDATE
    16 August 1987
        remove unnecessary clutter

    Copyright(c) 1985,1986,1987  D.M. Auslander and C.H. Tham

************************************************************************/

/***********************   Operating System   ***********************/

#define UNIX    0       /* 4.2 BSD, implies UNIX C compiler */
#define PCDOS   1       /* includes generic MSDOS family */
#define CPM     0       /* the CP/M family, including MP/M */


/******************   Hardware or Machine Type   ******************/

#define IBMPC       1       /* standard PC, PC/XT, PC/AT */
#define COMPUPRO    0       /* Compupro 8086 or Dual Processor */
#define INTEL310    0       /* Intel 310 development system */


/**************************   Compilers   ************************/

#define CIC86       0       /* Computer Innovations C86 ver. 2.20M */
#define DESMET      0       /* Desmet C */
#define LATTICE     0       /* Lattice C ver. 2.15 */
#define MICROSOFT   1       /* Microsft C ver. 4.00 */

#if MICROSOFT
#define ANSI                /* use proposed ANSI C features */
#endif

/************************************************************************

FILE
    inout.h  -  maps compiler's 8-bit i/o function names

REMARKS
    Different compilers call their 8-bit port i/o routines by different
    names.  This file contains macros to map these names to the generic
    in() and out().  This makes programs much more portable across
    different compilers

    Note: compiler #define's must be placed before this file.

************************************************************************/

#if CIC86           /* Computer Innovations C86 */

#define in(port)            inportb((unsigned)(port))
#define out(port, value)    outportb((unsigned)(port), value)

#endif

#if DESMET          /* Desmet C  */

#define in(port)            _inb(port)
#define out(port, value)    _outb(port, value)

#endif

#if LATTICE         /* Lattice C (Version 2.15) */

#define in(port)            inp(port)
#define out(port, value)    outp(port, value)

#endif

#if MICROSOFT       /* Microsoft C Version 4.00 and above */

extern int inp(unsigned);
extern int outp(unsigned, int);

#define in(port)            inp(port)
#define out(port, value)    outp((port), value)

#endif

/************************************************************************

FILE
    main1.c  -  d.c. motor speed control example, main program module 1

ROUTINES
    main    -  main program
    cmdint  -  command processor

REMARKS
    This program module, together with cntrl0.c and rtsim0.c implements
    simple control of the speed of a d.c. motor.  This is the main
    program module and it implements a command processor.

    The other two module implements the P control algorithm (cntrl1.c)
    and a simulation of the motor set-up (rtsim1.c).
```

```
    To generate the simulation program under Microsoft C version 4.00
    and above, type: cl /DSIMRT main1.c cntrl1.c rtsim1.c

    This version differs from main0.c in that its command processor
    includes commands to set the clock and sample interval.

LAST UPDATE
    18 January 1988
        minor maintenance

    Copyright (c) 1984-1988  D.M. Auslander and C.H. Tham

***********************************************************************/

/***********************************************************************
                            I M P O R T S
***********************************************************************/

#include <stdio.h>

#include "envir.h"          /* program environment declarations */
#include "cntrl1.h"         /* extern declarations for cntrl1.c */


/***********************************************************************
            F O R W A R D   D E C L A R A T I O N S
***********************************************************************/

#ifdef ANSI

void cmdint(char *);
void menu(void);

#else

void cmdint();
void menu();

#endif


/***********************************************************************
    P R I V A T E   D A T A   A N D   D E C L A R A T I O N S
***********************************************************************/

#define PROMPT  "READY "    /* defines the command processor prompt */
#define BUFSIZE 100         /* command input buffer size */


/***********************************************************************
                E N T R Y   R O U T I N E S
***********************************************************************/

main()
{
    char cbuf[BUFSIZE];     /* space for the user-typed command line */


    menu();                 /* print menu of commands */

    for (;;)                /* an endless loop. */
    {
        fputs(PROMPT, stdout);          /* print a prompt */

        fgets(cbuf, BUFSIZE, stdin);    /* get command line from user */

        cmdint(cbuf);                   /* interpret and execute commands */
    }
}


/***********************************************************************
            P R I V A T E   R O U T I N E S
***********************************************************************/

/*----------------------------------------------------------------------
PROCEDURE
    cmdint  -  command interpreter

SYNOPSIS
    static void cmdint(cline)
    char cline[];

PARAMETERS
    cline  -  user's command line (a null terminated character array)

DESCRIPTION
    Since single-letter commands are used, the first character of the
    command line denotes the command.  A switch statement is used to
    decide which command is specified.  The rest of the command line
    is then passed to appropriate routines which extract the arguments
    (if any) to the command.

LAST UPDATE
    18 March 1985
----------------------------------------------------------------------*/

static void cmdint(cline)
char cline[];
{
```

```
switch(cline[0])          /* Execute different sections of code  */
{                         /*   depending on 1st char of cline[]  */
    case 'k':
                              /* set controller gain, the remainder */
        gain(&cline[1]);      /*   of the string is sent to the     */
                              /*   function gain() for decoding     */
        break;

    case 's':

        setv(&cline[1]);      /* set the setpoint */
        break;

    case 'g':

        control(&cline[1]); /* "go," i.e., start control. */
        break;

    case 'i':

        init(&cline[1]);      /* initialize the system */
        break;

    case 't':

        smpset(&cline[1]);  /* set sample interval. */
        break;

    case '?':
    case 'h':                 /* "help," print the command list */

        menu();               /* print menu of commands */
        break;

    case 'e':

        exit(0);              /* Return to operating system. */
        break;

    default:                  /* no match found */

        printf("command not found: %s\n", cline);
  }

}


/*-----------------------------------------------------------------------
PROCEDURE
    MENU  -  print a reminder of commands

SYNOPSIS
    static void menu()

LAST UPDATE
    17 November 1987
------------------------------------------------------------------------*/

static void menu()
{

    printf("\nCommand List Usage: command [argument(s)]\n");

    printf("command  arguments         remarks\n");
    printf("-------  ---------         -------\n");
    printf(" h                         : print this menu\n");
    printf(" i       delta_t           : initialize\n");
    printf(" k       kp ki const       : set controller gains\n");
    printf(" s       setpoint          : specify setpoint\n");
    printf(" t       sample_interval   : set sample interval\n");
    printf(" g       iterations prnt   : start\n");
    printf(" e                         : exit\n");

    printf("\n");

}
/**************************************************************************

FILE
    cntrl1.h  -  exported declarations for cntrl1.c

LAST UPDATE
    1 December 1987

**************************************************************************/

#ifdef ANSI

extern void control(char *);
extern void gain(char *);
extern void setv(char *);
extern void smpset(char *);
extern void init(char *);

#else

extern void control();
extern void gain();
extern void setv();
extern void smpset();
extern void init();
```

```
#endif
/*************************************************************************

FILE
    cntrl1.c  -  control code

ROUTINES
    control   -  execute control algorithm
    gain      -  interpret command line for P gain
    setv      -  interpret command line for setpoint
    getv      -  get velocity reading
    mact      -  send controller output to actuator

REMARKS
    Implements PI control and uses a timer to determine sample
    intervals.

LAST UPDATE
    1 December 1987
        restructure and modify for MSC 4.00 and 5.00

    Copyright(C) 1984-1987, D.M.Auslander and C.H. Tham

*************************************************************************/

/*************************************************************************
                            I M P O R T S
*************************************************************************/

#include <stdio.h>

#include "envir.h"       /* environment definitions */
#include "dash8.h"       /* declarations for dash8.c */
#include "dac2.h"        /* declarations for dac2.c */
#include "time0.h"       /* declarations for time0.c */
#include "cntrl1.h"      /* exported declarations for this module */


/*************************************************************************
            F O R W A R D   D E C L A R A T I O N S
*************************************************************************/

#ifdef ANSI

double getv(void);
void   mact(double);

#else

double getv();
void   mact();

#endif


/*************************************************************************
            P R I V A T E   D A T A   V A R I A B L E S
*************************************************************************/

#define ADCHANNEL   0            /* A/D channel that we will use */
#define DACHANNEL   0            /* D/A channel used by this module */

static double vref = 1000.0;     /* velocity setpoint  */
static double kp = 1.0;          /* proportional gain */
static double ki = 0.2;          /* integral gain. */
static double vcon = 0.0;        /* constant term in the controller */
static double mmin;              /* lower limit for controller output */
static double mmax;              /* upper limit for controller output */
static double tsamp = 0.5;       /* controller sample interval (sec). */
static double isum;              /* integrator accumulated value. */


/*************************************************************************
                    E N T R Y   R O U T I N E S
/*************************************************************************

/*-----------------------------------------------------------------------
PROCEDURE
    control  -  this function does the control

SYNOPSIS
    void control(cline)
    char *cline;

PARAMETER
    cline  -  user's input line

REMARKS
    Implements PI control.

    The control output is calculated in two parts - first with only
    P action and add I action.  The output is limited to what the
    actuator can put out, with provisions against reset windup.

    Note that the timer is set in milliseconds.

LAST UPDATE
    1 December 1987
-----------------------------------------------------------------------*/

void control(cline)
char *cline;
{
```

```
    long nitr;           /* number of iterations */
    long i;              /* iteration counter */
    double v;            /* the motor velocity */
    double m1;           /* intermediate result in control calculation. */
    double m;            /* controller output */
    int damin, damax;    /* output argument range of D/A */
    int prnt;            /* 1 = print control output, 0 = no print */


    /*-----------------------------------------------------------------
        Get number of iterations and print flag from the command
        line, cline.  Sscanf() is just like scanf() except that the
        input is a string instead of the standard input (keyboard).
    -------------------------------------------------------------------*/

    sscanf(cline, "%ld %d", &nitr, &prnt);

    printf("number of iterations = %ld\n", nitr);   /* verify */

    da_limits(&damin, &damax);      /* find D/A output limits */

    mmin = (double)damin;
    mmax = (double)damax;

    isum = 0.0;             /* initialize integrator. */


    for (i = 0; i < nitr; i++)
    {
        SetTimer((long)(tsamp * 1000L));    /* set countdown timer in ms */

        v = getv();                 /* get motor velocity */

        isum += vref - v;           /* integrate error term */

        /*-----------------------------------------------------------
            First calculate control output without integral term.
        -------------------------------------------------------------*/

        m1 = kp * (vref - v)  +  vcon;

        /*-----------------------------------------------------------
            Check for actuator limits and apply "reset windup".
            Limit value of m to allowable D/A and actuator range
            and set integral term to zero if system is outside
            linear zone.
        -------------------------------------------------------------*/

        if (m1 > mmax)          /* output exceeds actuator limit */
        {
            m1 = mmax;          /* set output to actuator maximum */
            isum = 0.0;         /* set integral term to zero */
        }
        else if (m1 < mmin)
        {
            m1 = mmin;
            isum = 0.0;
        }

        m = m1 + ki * isum;     /* now add in integral term. */

        mact(m);                /* send control output to actuator */

        if (prnt)
            printf("v = %lf, m = %lf\n", v, m);

        if (TimeUp())           /* timer has run out */
        {
            printf("sample time too short\n");
            exit(1);
        }

        while (!TimeUp())
        {
#if SIMRT
            tstep();    /* advance time */
#endif
        }
    }   /* end of control loop */

}



/*-----------------------------------------------------------------------
PROCEDURE
    GAIN  -  interpret the input line specifying controller gain(s)

SYNOPSIS
    void gain(cline)
    char *cline;

PARAMETERS
    cline  -  input line

LAST UPDATE
    15 October 1984
-------------------------------------------------------------------------*/

void gain(cline)
char *cline;
{
```

```
    sscanf(cline, "%lf %lf %lf", &kp, &ki, &vcon);  /* decode input line */

#if DEBUG
    printf("<gain> kp = %lf, ki = %lf, vcon = %lf\n", kp, kp, vcon);
#endif

}



/*-----------------------------------------------------------------------
PROCEDURE
    SETV  -  get velocity setpoint from the command line

SYNOPSIS
    void setv(cline)
    char *cline;

PARAMETERS
    cline  -  user's command line

LAST UPDATE
    15 October 1984
-----------------------------------------------------------------------*/

void setv(cline)
char *cline;
{

    sscanf(cline,"%lf", &vref);

#if DEBUG
    printf("<setv> vref = %lf\n", vref);
#endif

}



/*-----------------------------------------------------------------------
PROCEDURE
    SMPSET  -  set sample time

SYNOPSIS
    smpset(cline)
    char *cline;

PARAMETER
    cline  -  user's command line

DESCRIPTION
    Extract sample time from user's command line and use it to set the
    sample time on the timer.

LAST UPDATE
    1 December 1987
-----------------------------------------------------------------------*/

void smpset(cline)
char *cline;
{

    sscanf(cline, "%lf", &tsamp);

#if DEBUG
    printf("<smpset> tsamp = %lf\n", tsamp);
#endif

}



/***********************************************************************

    The following section contains routines which interface between
    high level control code and functions which perform the hardware
    dependent functions of operating the A/D and D/A.  As such, they
    are necessarily dependent on the device driver interface.

***********************************************************************/

/*-----------------------------------------------------------------------
PROCEDURE
    INIT  -  system initialization

SYNOPSIS
    void init()

REMARKS
    Performs any initializations required.

LAST UPDATE
    1 December 1987
-----------------------------------------------------------------------*/

void init(cline)
char *cline;
{

    ad_init();                /* initialize A/D */
    da_init();                /* initialize D/A */
```

```
#ifdef SIMRT
    sim_init(cline);        /* initialize simulation module */
#endif

}


/*----------------------------------------------------------------------
FUNCTION
    GETV  -  returns motor velocity

SYNOPSIS
    static double getv()

RETURNS
    current motor velocity (units unspecified)

REMARKS
    Reads channel 0 of the A/D converter, convert the value to a
    double type and return this converted value.

LAST UPDATE
    1 December 1987
----------------------------------------------------------------------*/

static double getv()
{

    return((double)ad_wread(ADCHANNEL));
}



/*----------------------------------------------------------------------
PROCEDURE
    MACT  -  send controller output to actuator

SYNOPSIS
    static void mact(value)
    double value;

PARAMETER
    value  -  controller output

REMARKS
    Convert output to integer and send it to D/A converter

LAST UPDATE
    1 December 1987
----------------------------------------------------------------------*/

static void mact(value)
double value;
{

    da_write(DACHANNEL, (int)value);
}


/***********************************************************************

FILE
    rtsim1.c  -  d.c. speed control, simulation module 1

ENTRY ROUTINES
    tstep      -  advance one time step
    SetTimer   -  set count-down timer
    TimeUp     -  has count down completed?

    ad_init    -  simulates A/D initialization
    ad_start   -  simulates starting an A/D read
    ad_read    -  simulates reading A/D value
    ad_wread   -  simulates read from A/D

    da_init    -  simulates D/A initialization
    da_limits  -  returns simulation D/A output limits
    da_write   -  simulates write to D/A

PRIVATE ROUTINE
    simul   -  motor plant simulation

INITIALIZATION ROUTINE
    sim_init   -  initialize simulation

REMARKS
    This module simulates the interface and motor hardware and the
    passage of "real" time.  This module must thus provide the same
    interface functions as the modules controlling the hardware.

    To use "real" time, compile this module with the /DFTIME switch;
    this will cause tstep() to use ftime() calls to tell time.


LAST UPDATE
    1 December 1987
        restructure and modify for MSC 4.00 and 5.00

    Copyright(C) 1984-1987  D.M. Auslander and C.H. Tham

***********************************************************************/

/***********************************************************************
```

```
                              I M P O R T S
*********************************************************************/

#include <stdio.h>

#include "envir.h"          /* environment specifications */

#ifdef FTIME                /* include stuff to run simulation in */
                            /*   real time using ftime() calls.    */

#include <sys\types.h>
#include <sys\timeb.h>

#endif


/*********************************************************************
              F O R W A R D   D E C L A R A T I O N S
*********************************************************************/

#ifdef ANSI

void simul(void);

#ifndef FTIME
void runtimer(void);
#endif

#else

void simul();

#ifndef FTIME
void runtimer();
#endif

#endif


/*********************************************************************
                    P R I V A T E   D A T A
*********************************************************************/

#define ADSCALE       512.0     /* scale speed to A/D units */
#define ADMAX        2047       /* max A/D input value */
#define ADMIN       -2048       /* min A/D input value */

#define DASCALE      2047.0     /* scale D/A value to torque */
#define DAMIN       -2048       /* min. output value accepted */
#define DAMAX        2047       /* max. output value accepted */

static double inertia = 1.0;         /* motor system inertia */
static double speed;                 /* simulated motor velocity */
static double t;                     /* time */
static double dt;                    /* step size in time */
static double torque = 0.0;          /* motor torque */

#ifndef FTIME

static long freq = 1000L;         /* timer frequency (ticks/sec) */
static long ticks;                /* how many ticks to timeout */
static int tflag;                 /* set to 1 if timer runs out */

#endif

static long millidt;              /* step size dt in milliseconds */


/*********************************************************************
                    T I M E   S I M U L A T I O N
*********************************************************************/

#ifndef FTIME                    /* simulate timer hardware */

/*-------------------------------------------------------------------
PROCEDURE
    TSTEP  -  advance time forward one step

SYNOPSIS
    void tstep()

LAST UPDATE
    10 October 1984
-------------------------------------------------------------------*/

void tstep()
{

    simul();          /* compute one time step in the differential */
                      /*   equation for the motor system.         */

    t += dt;          /* increment time by dt */

    runtimer();       /* simulate timer run */
}


/*-------------------------------------------------------------------
PROCEDURE
    SETTIMER  -  set countdown timer

SYNOPSIS
```

```
    void SetTimer(ms)
    long ms;

PARAMETER
    period -  count down period in milliseconds

LAST UPDATE
    15 January 1988
-----------------------------------------------------------------------*/

void SetTimer(ms)
long ms;
{

    ticks = ((ms * freq) + 500L) / 1000L;    /* 500 is for rounding */

    tflag = 0;                               /* timeout flag to false */

}


/*-----------------------------------------------------------------------
FUNCTION
    TIMEUP  -  has timer timed out?

SYNOPSIS
    int TimeUp()

RETURNS
    1 if timer runs out, 0 otherwise

LAST UPDATE
    1 March 1985
-----------------------------------------------------------------------*/

int TimeUp()
{

    return(tflag);
}


/*-----------------------------------------------------------------------
PROCEDURE
    RUNTIMER  -  simulates timer run

SYNOPSIS
    static void runtimer()

LAST UPDATE
    19 March 1985
-----------------------------------------------------------------------*/

static void runtimer()
{

    if (!tflag)               /* if timeout, just return, otherwise... */
    {
        /* decrement tick count by # of ticks corresponding to dt sec */

        ticks -= (long)(dt * freq + 0.5);    /* 0.5 is for rounding */

        if (ticks <= 0L)      /* time has run out */
            tflag = 1;
    }

}


#else   /* else use "real" time */


/*-----------------------------------------------------------------------
PROCEDURE
    TSTEP  -  advance time forward one step

SYNOPSIS
    void tstep(void)

REMARKS
    This routine runs the simulation and then waits dt seconds (millidt
    is dt converted to milliseconds) using ftime() library calls.

    Thus, dt determines how often the simulation is run and is more or
    less independent of the sampling time.

LAST UPDATE
    18 January 1988
-----------------------------------------------------------------------*/

void tstep()
{
    struct timeb start;          /* starting time */
    struct timeb now;            /* current time */


    simul();

    ftime(&start);
```

```
    do
    {
        ftime(&now);
    }
    while (((now.time - start.time) * 1000)
        + now.millitm - start.millitm < millidt);

}


#endif  /* else ifndef FTIME */


/**********************************************************************
                     A / D   S I M U L A T I O N

    These routines dummies the routines in dash8.c which drives the
    Metrabyte DASH8 A/D board.  The channel parameter is ignored.

**********************************************************************/

void ad_init()
{

    speed = 0.0;

}


void ad_start(channel)
int channel;
{
    /* nothing */
}


int ad_read(channel)
int channel;
{
    int rval;                   /* return value */


    rval = ADSCALE * speed;     /* scale and convert to int type */

    if (rval > ADMAX)           /* apply converter limits */
        rval = ADMAX;
    else if (rval < ADMIN)
        rval = ADMIN;

    return(rval);
}
```

```
int ad_wread(channel)
int channel;
{

    return(ad_read(channel));
}


/**********************************************************************
                     D / A   S I M U L A T I O N

    These routines dummies the routines in dac2.c which drives the
    Metrabyte DAC02 D/A board.  The channel parameter is ignored.

    The DAC2 is a 12-bit digital-to-analog converter configured for
    bipolar output.  Thus, the output parameter values range from
    -2048 to 2047.  Only lower 12 bits will be used, treating those
    12 bits as a 2's complement signed number.  Thus if the output
    value is negative, the lower 12 bits will be preserved and all
    higher order bits will be converted to 1's.

    Note the use of ~0xfff instead of 0xf000, this makes the program
    more portable across machines with different integer sizes.

**********************************************************************/

void da_init()
{

    torque = 0.0;

}


void da_limits(lo, hi)
int *lo, *hi;
{

    *lo = DAMIN;
    *hi = DAMAX;

}


void da_write(channel, value)
int channel, value;
{

    if (value < 0)           /* OR with a binary number having 0's for */
        value |= ~0xfff;     /*   the lower 12 bits and 1's elsewhere  */
```

```
    else
        value &= 0xfff;      /* for positive values, just save the      */
                             /*    lower 12 bits.                       */

    torque = value / DASCALE;   /* rescale for motor drive torque. */

}


/*********************************************************************
                 P R I V A T E    R O U T I N E S

    The following routines are declared "static".  These routines
    can be directly accessed only by routines inside this file; they
    are not "visible" to routines outside this file.  Hence they are
    private to this file.  Private routines enhances data security
    and helps avoid unexpected name conflicts in large programming
    projects.

*********************************************************************/

/*-------------------------------------------------------------------
PROCEDURE
    SIMUL  -  simulates motor plant

SYNOPSIS
    static void simul()

REMARKS
    Solve the motor system differential equation.  This version uses
    the Euler method for integration; it isn't very efficient, but its
    easy to program!

LAST UPDATE
    12 January 1988
        add friction term to make it more interesting
-------------------------------------------------------------------*/

static void simul()
{
    double friction;


    friction = speed / 10.0;    /* this is quite arbitrary */

    speed += (torque - friction) * dt / inertia;

}


/*********************************************************************
         I N I T I A L I Z A T I O N    R O U T I N E
*********************************************************************/

/*-------------------------------------------------------------------
PROCEDURE
    INIT  -  system initialization

SYNOPSIS
    sim_init(cline)
    char *cline;

PARAMETER
    cline  -  user's input command line

REMARKS
    In a "real" real-time program, this function would be used to set
    up interrupts, set clock modes, etc.  In this simulation version,
    it sets time to zero and sets the motor simulation initial conditions.

LAST UPDATE
    18 October 1984
-------------------------------------------------------------------*/

sim_init(cline)
char *cline;
{

    sscanf(cline, "%lf", &dt);  /* get the step size. */

#if DEBUG
    printf("<init> dt = %lf\n", dt);
#endif

    t = 0.0;                        /* reset time */
    millidt = (long)(dt * 1000  +  0.5);

    speed = 0.0;                    /* motor is initially at rest */
    torque = 0.0;

}


/*********************************************************************

FILE
    dash8.h  -  interface declarations for dash8.c

LAST UPDATE
    18 November 1987
```

```
**********************************************************************/

#ifdef ANSI

extern void ad_init(void);
extern void ad_start(int);
extern int  ad_read(int);
extern int  ad_wread(int);

#else

extern void ad_init();
extern void ad_start();
extern void ad_read();
extern void ad_wread();

#endif

/**********************************************************************

FILE
    dac2.h  -  interface declarations for dac2.c

LAST UPDATE
    18 November 1987

**********************************************************************/

#ifdef ANSI

extern void da_init(void);
extern void da_limits(int *, int *);
extern int  da_write(int, int);

#else

extern void da_init();
extern void da_limits();
extern int  da_write();

#endif

/**********************************************************************

FILE
    time0.h  declarations for time0.c

LAST UPDATE
    15 January 1988

**********************************************************************/

#ifdef ANSI

extern void SetTimer(long);
extern int  TimeUp(void);

#else

extern void SetTimer();
extern int  TimeUp();

#endif
/**********************************************************************

FILE
    time0.c  -  simple timer routine using ftime() calls

ROUTINES
    SetTimer   -  set timer for specified interval
    TimeUp     -  is time up?

REMARKS
    These functions use the Microsoft C compiler library's ftime()
    calls to tell time.  They will run under DOS and not interfere
    with DOS's date/time keeping.

    Time resolution is same as system clock - approx. 55 milliseconds.

LAST UPDATE
    12 January 1988
        creation

    Copyright(C) 1988, D.M.Auslander and C.H. Tham

**********************************************************************/

/**********************************************************************
                           I M P O R T S
**********************************************************************/

#include <stdio.h>
#include <sys\types.h>
#include <sys\timeb.h>

#include "time0.h"

/**********************************************************************
           P R I V A T E    D A T A    V A R I A B L E S
**********************************************************************/

static struct timeb start;       /* record starting time */
static long period;              /* countdown period in milliseconds */
```

```
/************************************************************************
                    E N T R Y    R O U T I N E S
/************************************************************************

/*-----------------------------------------------------------------------
PROCEDURE
    SETTIMER  -  set countdown timer

SYNOPSIS
    void SetTimer(ms)
    long ms;

PARAMETER
    ms -  count down period in milliseconds

LAST UPDATE
    18 January 1988
-----------------------------------------------------------------------*/

void SetTimer(ms)
long ms;
{

    ftime(&start);      /* record starting time */

    period = ms;

}



/*-----------------------------------------------------------------------
FUNCTION
    TIMEUP  -  has timer timed out?

SYNOPSIS
    int TimeUp()

RETURNS
    1 if timer runs out, 0 otherwise

LAST UPDATE
    18 January 1988
-----------------------------------------------------------------------*/

int TimeUp()
{
    struct timeb now;           /* current time */


    ftime(&now);
    if (((now.time - start.time) * 1000)
            + now.millitm - start.millitm < period)
        return(0);
    else
        return(1);

}


/************************************************************************

FILE
    main2.c  -  d.c. motor speed control example, main program module 2

ROUTINES
    main    -  main program
    cmdint  -  command processor
    fstr    -  extract command word
    help    -  print list of commands

REMARKS
    This module is similar to main1.c but implements a better command
    interpreter.

    To generate the simulation program under Microsoft C version 4.00
    and above, type: cl /DSIMRT main2.c cntrl1.c rtsim1.c

LAST UPDATE
    18 January 1988
        minor tidying-up

    Copyright (c) 1984-1988  D.M. Auslander and C.H. Tham

************************************************************************/

/************************************************************************
                            I M P O R T S
************************************************************************/

#include <stdio.h>

extern void exit();         /* this is needed for the command table */

#include "envir.h"          /* program environment declarations */
#include "cntrl1.h"         /* extern declarations for cntrl1.c */


/************************************************************************
            F O R W A R D    D E C L A R A T I O N S
************************************************************************/
```

```
#ifdef ANSI

void cmdint(char *);
char *getcmd(char *, char *);
void menu(void);

#else

void cmdint();
char getcmd();
void menu();

#endif


/************************************************************************
   P R I V A T E   D A T A   A N D   D E C L A R A T I O N S
************************************************************************/

#define PROMPT  "READY "    /* defines the command processor prompt */
#define BUFSIZE 100         /* command input buffer size */

/*-----------------------------------------------------------------
   The following declares a data structure for associating a
   command string with the routine that acts on the contents
   of that command string.  This is done using a C construct
   known as a "struct" (record to you Pascal enthusiasts).

   The structure has 2 fields:

       1) the command name in the form of a NUL terminated string
       2) a pointer to the associated function
----------------------------------------------------------------*/

#define CMDLEN  12      /* max length of command name */

struct command {

    char cmd[CMDLEN+1]; /* command string (+1 for NUL terminator) */

    void (*cmdfunc)();  /* pointer to command function.  Note the  */
                        /*   parentheses in the declaration - they */
                        /*   are very important and must be placed */
                        /*   exactly right! (See K & R, page 209). */
};


/*-----------------------------------------------------------------------
   This is the command interpreter table, an array of commands and
   their associated function pointers.  Note that commands have a
   long and a short form.

   The interpreter table is an array of structures.  Each structure
   in the array is initialized with a command name and an associated
   function pointer (function name used without brackets).

   The function pointers must be declared ahead so that the compiler
   knows that the names refer to functions and not data variables,
   and assigns the proper function addresses (entry points).
-----------------------------------------------------------------------*/

static struct command cmdtable[] = {

    {"gains",       gain},        /* specify controller gains */
    {"k",           gain},

    {"setpoint",    setv},        /* specify setpoint */
    {"s",           setv},

    {"initialize",  init},        /* initialize */
    {"i",           init},

    {"sample-time", smpset},      /* specify sample time */
    {"t",           smpset},

    {"help",        menu},        /* print help menu */
    {"h",           menu},

    {"go",          control},     /* start controller */
    {"g",           control},

    {"exit",        exit},        /* program exit */
    {"e",           exit},
};


static int ncmds;       /* number of entries in command table */


/************************************************************************
                    M A I N   P R O G R A M
************************************************************************/

main()
{
    char cbuf[BUFSIZE];     /* space for the user-typed command line */


    ncmds = sizeof(cmdtable) / sizeof(struct command);

    menu();                 /* print command list to start. */

    for(;;)                 /* an endless loop. */
```

```
    {
        fputs(PROMPT, stdout);  /* print a prompt so that user will */
                                /*   know that the program expects  */
                                /*   an input.                      */

        fgets(cbuf, BUFSIZE, stdin);    /* read a NULL terminated string */
                                        /*   from the "standard input"   */
                                        /*   (normally the user console) */

        cmdint(cbuf);           /* call the routine that interprets  */
                                /*   the command line.               */
    }
}


/**********************************************************************
                    P R I V A T E     R O U T I N E S
**********************************************************************/

/*---------------------------------------------------------------------
PROCEDURE
    CMDINT  -  command interpreter

SYNOPSIS
    static void cmdint(cline)
    char cline[];

PARAMETERS
    cline  -  command line

DESCRIPTION
    The command word is isolated and matched against the list of valid
    commands in the command table.  If a match is found, the routine
    associated with that command is executed.

LAST UPDATE
    1 December 1987
---------------------------------------------------------------------*/

static void cmdint(cline)
char cline[];
{
    char cword[CMDLEN+1];   /* storage to hold the command word. */
    char *prest;            /* ptr to rest of line after command word */
    struct command *pcom;   /* ptr to the command structure list. */
    int i;                  /* iteration counter */


    prest = getcmd(cline, cword);       /* isolate the command word */

    /*----------------------------------------------------------------
        Search the command list for a match on the command word.
    ----------------------------------------------------------------*/

    pcom = cmdtable;    /* initialize the pointer to the command list */

    for (i = 0; i < ncmds; i++)
    {
        /*  note: strcmp() returns zero if strings match  */

        if (strcmp(pcom->cmd, cword) == 0)
        {
            /*------------------------------------------------------
                Command word matches a name entry in the command
                interpreter table.  The associated function is
                executed  --  again, watch the parentheses!
            ------------------------------------------------------*/

            (*pcom->cmdfunc)(prest);    /* execute associated func */

            break;                      /* break out of "for" loop */
        }

        pcom++;                         /* not found, next item. */
    }

    if (i >= ncmds)     /* did not match any of the valid commands */
    {
        printf("command not found : %s\n", cline);
    }
}


/*---------------------------------------------------------------------
FUNCTION
    GETCMD  -  isolate command word from input string

SYNOPSIS
    static char *getcmd(line, word)
    char line[], word[];

PARAMETERS
    line  -  command line
    word  -  where to put the command word

RETURNS
    pointer to rest of line (after the command word)

DESCRIPTION
```

```
    Command words are assumed to be delimited by blanks.  Thus this
    routine finds the first blank-terminated word in the command line
    and copies it into the 'word' argument.

    The command line is a NUL terminated character array which is
    passed to this routine in the form of a NUL terminated character
    array.  Note that the command line CANNOT begin with a blank.

    getcmd() returns NULL if the input command line begins with a blank
    or carriage-return.

LAST UPDATE
    18 October 1984
----------------------------------------------------------------------*/

static char *getcmd(line, word)
char line[], word[];
{
    int i;      /* loop index */


    for (i = 0; i < CMDLEN; i++)
    {
        if ((line[i] == ' ') || (line[i] == '\n') || (line[i] == '\0'))
            break;      /* end of word found, get out of loop */

        word[i] = line[i];      /* Copy the character to w. */
    }

    word[i] = 0;        /* terminate output word with NUL character */

    return(&line[i]);   /* return a pointer to the remainder of line. */

}



/*----------------------------------------------------------------------
PROCEDURE
    MENU  -  print a list of commands

SYNOPSIS
    static void menu()

LAST UPDATE
    22 September 1984
----------------------------------------------------------------------*/

static void menu()
{
    fputs("\n                COMMAND LIST\n\n", stdout);
    fputs("full command (or single-letter equivalent) arguments\n\n", stdout);

    fputs("initialize    (i)   delta_t\n", stdout);
    fputs("sample-time   (t)   tsamp\n", stdout);
    fputs("gains         (k)   kp ki const\n", stdout);
    fputs("setpoint      (s)   setpoint_value\n", stdout);
    fputs("go            (g)   number_of_iterations print(0/1)\n", stdout);
    fputs("exit          (e) \n", stdout);
    fputs("help          (h) \n\n", stdout);

}


/***********************************************************************

FILE
    sigtime.c  -  timer test using xignal package

SYNOPSIS
    #include "xignal.h"

    cl /Gs sigtime.c /link xignal

REMARKS
    Prints the seconds for 10 seconds.  DOS's time keeping function is
    temporarily suspended, but will be restored at the end of the test.

    This program uses the PC's system clock, ticking at approx. 18.2
    interrupts per second.

    Note that the program must be compiled with the /Gs flag to disable
    stack checking; otherwise a run time error may result because the
    interrupt service routine, tmr_isr() may run on a different stack.

LAST UPDATE
    12 September 1987
        name change from signal to xignal

    Copyright(c) 1987-1988  D.M. Auslander and C.H. Tham

***********************************************************************/

/***********************************************************************
                             I M P O R T S
***********************************************************************/

#include <stdio.h>

#include "envir.h"
#include "xignal.h"
```

```
/***********************************************************************
                       P R I V A T E   D A T A
***********************************************************************/

static int tick = 0;            /* count of interrupts */
static int time = 0;            /* time in seconds */
static int flag = 0;            /* flag each 1 second period */


/***********************************************************************
                           R O U T I N E S
/***********************************************************************

/*----------------------------------------------------------------------
PROCEDURE
    TMR_ISR  -  timer service routine

SYNOPSIS
    static void tmr_isr()

REMARKS
    This routine is called by xignal's low level timer interrupt handler
    at every timer interrupt (approx. every 55 milliseconds).  It counts
    off 18 ticks and sets a flag to indicate 1 second has elasped.

LAST UPDATE
    12 September 1987
----------------------------------------------------------------------*/

static void tmr_isr()
{

    if (++tick >= 18)           /* approx. 18 interrupts per second */
    {
        tick = 0;               /* reset */
        flag = 1;               /* indicate 1 sec is up */
    }
}



/*----------------------------------------------------------------------
PROCEDURE
    MAIN  -  main program

REMARKS
    Calls xignal() to install tmr_isr() as the "high-level" timer
    interrupt service routine.  Variable 'flag' is set whenever 1
    second has elasped.  The original timer vector is restored before
    the program exits by a call to xignal() using the XIG_DFL argument.

LAST UPDATE
    17 September 1987
----------------------------------------------------------------------*/

main()
{

    xignal(XIGTMR, tmr_isr);        /* set up tmr_isr */

    while (time < 10)               /* not 10 seconds yet */
    {
        if (flag)
        {
            flag = 0;                   /* reset flag */
            printf("%2d\n", ++time);    /* print seconds */
        }
    }

    xignal(XIGTMR, XIG_DFL);        /* restore timer interrupts */

}


/***********************************************************************

FILE
    xignal.h    (IBM-PC version)

SYNOPSIS
    #include "xignal.h"

LAST UPDATE
    22 May 1985  by  Haam
        downgrade requirement for envir.h
    02 October 1985  by  Haam
        add stuff for Compupro
    10 September 1987  by  Haam
        name change to xignal

AUTHOR
    Haam  Tham  18 February 1985

***********************************************************************/

/*********************  locals - for IBM-PC  *********************/

#if IBMPC

#define XIGALL      0               /* vectors 0 to 15 */

#define XIGTMR      1
```

```
#define XIGKB       2
#define XIGCGA      3
#define XIGCOM2     4
#define XIGCOM1     5
#define XIGLPT2     6
#define XIGFDSK     7
#define XIGPRN      8

#define XIGFPE      9

#define XIGAUX      XIGCOM1
#define XIGLPT1     XIGPRN


#define NXIG        10


#define XIGTMR0     XIGTMR      /* compatibility with Compupro version */
#define XIGKEYB     XIGKB

#endif  /* if IBMPC */


/*********************  locals - for Compupro  *********************/

#if COMPUPRO

#define XIGALL      0

#define XIGPIO4     1
#define XIGSRX4     3
#define XIGSTX4     4
#define XIGSRX2     5
#define XIGSTX2     6

#define XIGTMR0     12
#define XIGTMR1     13
#define XIGTMR2     14
#define XIGSCRN     17
#define XIGKEYB     18

#define XIGFPE      20


#define NXIG        21


#define XIGTMR      XIGTMR0     /* compatibility with IBM version */
#define XIGKB       XIGKEYB

#endif  /* if COMPUPRO */
```

```
/**************  Some Standard Xignal Definitions  **************/

extern XIG_IGN();           /* actual functions are used instead of */
extern XIG_DFL();           /*  casting (*int())() since some       */
extern BADXIG();            /*  compilers cannot perform the cast.  */

extern  int (*xignal(int, int (*)()))();


/******  Floating Point Stuff, modelled on UNIX definitions  ******/

#define     FPE_INTOVF  0x1         /* integer overflow */
#define     FPE_INTDIV  0x2         /* integer divide by zero */
#define     FPE_FLTOVF  0x3         /* floating overflow */
#define     FPE_FLTDIV  0x4         /* floating divide by zero */
#define     FPE_FLTUND  0x5         /* floating underflow */


#define XIGALRM     XIGTMR  /* Unix to Local xignal number mapping */


/*******************************************************************

FILE
    timeintc.c  -  timer demo program using time1.c

REMARKS
    Prints the seconds for 10 seconds.  DOS's time keeping function is
    temporarily suspended, but will be restored at the end of the test.

    This program must be linked with the timeinta.asm module.  The
    low level timer interrupt service routine in timeinta.asm, tmrisr(),
    will save the registers and call tick(), which is defined in this
    module.  Here is how to generate an executable program:

        masm timeinta /ml;
        cl /Gs timeintc.c timeinta

    This module must be compiled using the /Gs flag because it contains
    a routine that will be called inside an interrupt service routine.

    This program uses the PC's system clock frequency of approx. 18.2
    timer interrupts per second.  If you want to use a different
    tick frequency, refer to alarm.c for functions to change it.

LAST UPDATE
    18 January 1988

    Copyright(c) 1987-1988  D.M. Auslander and C.H. Tham

*******************************************************************/
```

```
/**********************************************************************
                              I M P O R T S
**********************************************************************/

#include "envir.h"

#ifdef ANSI

extern void     tmrisr(void);
extern void     setivec(int, unsigned, long);
extern long     getivec(int);

#else

extern void     tmrisr();
extern void     setivec();
extern long     getivec();

#endif

/**********************************************************************
                          P R I V A T E   D A T A
**********************************************************************/

#define VECTOR  8                  /* timer interrupt vector number */

static int tock = 0;               /* count of interrupts */
static int flag = 0;               /* flag each 1 second period */

/**********************************************************************
                              R O U T I N E S
**********************************************************************/

/*---------------------------------------------------------------------
PROCEDURE
    TICK  -  high level timer interrupt service routine

SYNOPSIS
    void tick(void)  -  called by low level interrupt handler tmrisr()

REMARKS
    Count 18 timer interrupts (equivalent to 1 second) and set flag

LAST UPDATE
    26 January 1988
---------------------------------------------------------------------*/

void tick()
{
    if (++tock >= 18)
    {
        tock = 0;
        flag = 1;
    }
}


/*---------------------------------------------------------------------
PROCEDURE
    MAIN  -  the main program

LAST UPDATE
    26 January 1988
        take advantage of new setivec() and getivec()
---------------------------------------------------------------------*/

main()
{
    long orig_isr;         /* place to save original timer vector */
    int seconds = 0;       /* elasped time in seconds, initialized to 0 */


    orig_isr = getivec(VECTOR);      /* save original vector contents */

    setivec(VECTOR, sizeof(tmrisr), (long)tmrisr);  /* install tmrisr() */

    while (seconds < 10)             /* not 10 seconds yet */
    {
        while (!flag)                /* wait for 1 second indication */
            ;

        flag = 0;                    /* reset flag */

        printf("%d\n", ++seconds);   /* print elasped time in seconds */
    }

    setivec(VECTOR, sizeof(orig_isr), orig_isr);

}


/**********************************************************************

FILE
    time1.h  declarations for time1.c

LAST UPDATE
    15 January 1988

**********************************************************************/
```

```
#ifdef ANSI

extern void SetTimer(long);
extern int  TimeUp(void);
extern void ResetTimer(void);
extern void InitTimer(long);

#else

extern void SetTimer();
extern int  TimeUp();
extern void ResetTimer();
extern void InitTimer();

#endif
/**********************************************************************

FILE
    time1.c  -  simple timer routine that uses real-time

ENTRY ROUTINES
    SetTimer    -  set timer interval
    TimeUp      -  has timer run out?
    ResetTimer  -  restore timer to default state

    tick        -  timer interrupt service routine

INITIALIZATION ROUTINE
    InitTimer  -  initialize time module

REMARKS
    Need to be linked with alarm.c and timeinta.asm

LAST UPDATE
    23 January 1986
        fix minor LINT complaints
    26 January 1988
        revise to used getivec() and new version of setivec()

    Copyright(c) 1986-1988  D.M. Auslander and C.H. Tham

**********************************************************************/

/**********************************************************************
                              I M P O R T S
**********************************************************************/

#include "envir.h"
#include "8259.h"
#include "inout.h"
#include "alarm.h"

/*
 *  The following routines are to be found in timeinta.asm
 */

#ifdef ANSI

extern void     tmrisr(void);
extern void     setivec(int, unsigned, long);
extern long     getivec(int);
extern int      enable(void);
extern int      disable(void);

#else

extern void     tmrisr();
extern void     setivec();
extern long     getivec();
extern int      enable();
extern int      disable();

#endif


/**********************************************************************
                        P R I V A T E   D A T A
**********************************************************************/

static long mstick;             /* milliseconds per tick */
static long dtime;              /* count down in ticks */
static long orig_isr;           /* pointer to original timer isr */


/**********************************************************************
                        E N T R Y   R O U T I N E S
**********************************************************************/

/*----------------------------------------------------------------------
PROCEDURE
    TICK  -  timer interrupt service routine

SYNOPSIS
    called by timer interrupt

REMARKS
    Interrupts are enabled when tick is called.  However, we know
    that the low level isr, tmrisr() will not send an EOI to the
    8259 until this routine is done, interrupts are effectively
    disabled since the timer interrupt has the highest priority.

LAST UPDATE
    6 June 1985
```

```
-----------------------------------------------------------------------*/

void tick()
{

    if (dtime > 0L)
        --dtime;
}


/*-----------------------------------------------------------------------
PROCEDURE
    SETTIMER  -  set timer

SYNOPSIS
    void SetTimer(ms)
    long ms;

PARAMETER
    ms  -  time interval in milliseconds

REMARKS
    (mstick >> 1) is equivalent to mstick/2, thus the formula
    is equivalent to: dtime = (ms / mstick)  +  0.5

LAST UPDATE
    5 June 1985
-----------------------------------------------------------------------*/

void SetTimer(ms)
long ms;
{

    dtime = (ms + (mstick >> 1)) / mstick;

}



/*-----------------------------------------------------------------------
FUNCTION
    TIMEUP  -  has timer run out?

SYNOPSIS
    int TimeUp()

RETURNS
    1  if timeup, 0 otherwise or error

LAST UPDATE
    23 January 1986
-----------------------------------------------------------------------*/

int TimeUp()
{

    return(dtime <= 0L ? 1 : 0);
}


/*-----------------------------------------------------------------------
PROCEDURE
    RESETTIMER  -  restore timer to original state

SYNOPSIS
    void ResetTimer()

REMARKS
    Restoring the vector contents must be atomic; hence we disable
    interrupts to prevent the CPU from responding should a timer
    interrupt occur during the process.

LAST UPDATE
    26 January 1988
        revised for new setivec() and getivec()
-----------------------------------------------------------------------*/

void ResetTimer()
{
    int istat;      /* interrupt status */


    istat = disable();

    setivec(TMRVEC, sizeof(orig_isr), orig_isr);    /* restore vector */

    setalarm(-1.0);         /* restore DOS timer interrupt frequency */

    if (istat)
        enable();

}


/***********************************************************************
            I N I T I A L I Z A T I O N   R O U T I N E S
***********************************************************************/


/*-----------------------------------------------------------------------
PROCEDURE
```

```
    INITTIMER  -  initialize this module

SYNOPSIS
    InitTimer(ms)
    long ms;

PARAMETER
    ms  -  milliseconds per tick

REMARKS
    Interrupt vector contents are obtained and set using setivec()
    and getivec(), defined in timeinta.asm.  This initialization
    routine writes directly to the 8259 interrupt controller to ensure
    that time interrupt requests are not disabled by a previos program.

LAST UPDATE
    26 January 1988
        revised for new setivec() and getivec()
----------------------------------------------------------------------*/

void InitTimer(ms)
long ms;
{
    int istat;       /* interrupt status */


    if (ms > MAX_MS)                /* range check - cannot exceed */
        ms = MAX_MS;                /*  hardware constraints.      */

    mstick = ms;

    orig_isr = getivec(TMRVEC);     /* save original vector contents */

    istat = disable();              /* disable interrupts */

    setivec(TMRVEC, sizeof(tmrisr), (long)tmrisr);

    out(MASKPORT, in(MASKPORT) & ~TMRMASK);      /* unmask timer IRQ */
    out(EOIPORT, TMREOI);                        /* send EOI just in case */

    setalarm((double)ms);        /* set timer tick interrupt rate */

    if (istat)                   /* if interrupts were enabled before  */
        enable();                /*  disable() was called, enable them */

}

/***********************************************************************

FILE
    alarm.h  -  all the declarations needed for alarm.c
```



```
LAST UPDATE
    25 August 1985

***********************************************************************/

#define CLOCKFREQ    1193180L        /* clock frequency */

#define DOS_COUNT    0xFFFF          /* DOS timer count */
#define MAX_MS       55L             /* max interval in milliseconds */

#define TIMER_CTL    0x43            /* 8253 timer control port */
#define TIMER        0x40            /* timer 0 port */

#ifdef ANSI

extern int       setalarm(double);
extern int       rsetalarm(long);
extern long      alarm_count(void);
extern double    alarm_time(void);

#else

extern int       setalarm();
extern int       rsetalarm();
extern long      alarm_count();
extern double    alarm_time();

#endif
/***********************************************************************

FILE
    alarm.c -  set hardware timer (8253 timer 0) - IBM-PC version

ROUTINES
    setalarm     -  set hardware timer alarm in milliseconds (double).
    rsetalarm    -  a "raw" form of setalarm(), using ticks
    alarm_count  -  returns the current count (long).
    alarm_time   -  returns the current time in millisec (double).

REMARKS
    These procedures are obviously hardware dependent. The 8253 timer 0
    is set to mode 3, 16-bit binary count.  The maximum period on the
    IBM PC is limited to about 54.9 milliseconds, which is the default
    tick frequency used by DOS.

    To reduce overheads for very time critical applications, rsetalarm()
    allows the period to be specified in clock ticks to eliminate the
    millisecond to tick conversion overhead.

    If the interval argument is zero or negative, the timer is reset to
    the DOS default state.
```

```
LAST UPDATE
    3 May 1985
        add rsetalarm().
    12 January 1988
        change all floats to doubles

    Copyright (c) 1985-1988  D.M. Auslander and C.H. Tham

*************************************************************************/

/*************************************************************************
                            I M P O R T S
*************************************************************************/

#include <stdio.h>

#include "envir.h"      /* environment declarations */
#include "inout.h"      /* in() and out() function mapping macros */
#include "alarm.h"      /* address and other declarations */


/*************************************************************************
                    P R I V A T E    D A T A
*************************************************************************/

static long count = 0xFFFFL;    /* current count, init to DOS default */


/*************************************************************************
                    E N T R Y    R O U T I N E S
*************************************************************************/

/*-----------------------------------------------------------------------
PROCEDURE
    SETALARM  -  set timer interrupt period in milliseconds

SYNOPSIS
    int setalarm(ms)
    double ms;

PARAMETERS
    ms  -  interval in milliseconds

RETURNS
    0  normal return
    1  error return

REMARKS
    Since the max. interval for the IBM PC corresponds to a maximum
    count of 65535, the maximum value of ms is limited to 54.9 ms.

    If ms is zero or negative, timer will be reset to DOS default.

LAST UPDATE
    23 August 1985 by D. M. Auslander
        change to float input format
    12 January 1988  by  Haam
        change floats to doubles
-----------------------------------------------------------------------*/

int setalarm(ms)
double ms;
{

    if ((ms > 0.0) && (ms <= MAX_MS))   /* argument is valid */
    {
        count = (CLOCKFREQ * ms) / 1000.0 + 0.5;

        out(TIMER_CTL, 0x36);        /* mode 3, 16-bit binary count */

        out(TIMER, count & 0xFF);    /* send least sig. byte first */
        out(TIMER, (count >> 8) & 0xFF);
    }
    else if (ms <= 0.0)              /* reset to DOS clock rate */
    {
        out(TIMER_CTL, 0x36);

        out(TIMER, DOS_COUNT & 0xFF);
        out(TIMER, (DOS_COUNT >> 8) & 0xFF);

        count = DOS_COUNT;
    }
    else    /* bad input - do nothing */
    {
        return(1);      /* error return */
    }

    return(0);          /* normal return */
}


/*-----------------------------------------------------------------------
PROCEDURE
    RSETALARM  -  raw form of setalarm using clock ticks instead of ms.

SYNOPSIS
    rsetalarm(ticks)
    long ticks;

PARAMETERS
    ticks  -  interval in clock ticks (1,193,180 Hz raw clock)
```

```
RETURNS
    0  normal return
    1  error return

REMARKS
    This raw form is intended for time critical programs that
    cannot afford the overhead of converting milliseconds to ticks.
    For even more time critical applications, the range check
    can be omitted.

    The clock frequency is defined in alarm.h as CLOCKFREQ.

LAST UPDATE
    3 May 1985
----------------------------------------------------------------------*/

int rsetalarm(ticks)
long ticks;
{

    if ((ticks > 0L) && (ticks < 65536L))
    {
        out(TIMER_CTL, 0x36);

        out(TIMER, ticks & 0xFF);   /* send least sig. byte first */
        out(TIMER, (ticks >> 8) & 0xFF);

        count = ticks;
    }
    else if (ticks <= 0L)           /* reset to DOS default */
    {
        out(TIMER_CTL, 0x36);

        out(TIMER, DOS_COUNT & 0xFF);
        out(TIMER, (DOS_COUNT >> 8) & 0xFF);

        count = DOS_COUNT;
    }
    else
        return(1);  /* error return */

    return(0);      /* normal return */
}


/*----------------------------------------------------------------------
PROCEDURE
    ALARM_COUNT  -  get the current count value

SYNOPSIS
    long alarm_count()

RETURNS
    the current count used by the timer

LAST UPDATE
    21-Aug-85 by D. M. Auslander
----------------------------------------------------------------------*/

long alarm_count()
{

    return(count);
}


/*----------------------------------------------------------------------
PROCEDURE
    ALARM_TIME  -  get the current timer interval in millisec

SYNOPSIS
    double alarm_time()

RETURNS
    count * 1000 / CLOCKFREQ

LAST UPDATE
    23-Aug-85 by D. M. Auslander
----------------------------------------------------------------------*/

double alarm_time()
{

    return((double)count * 1000.0 / CLOCKFREQ);
}

/***********************************************************************

FILE
    8259.h  -  8259A definitions, IBM-PC version

SYNOPSIS
    #include "8259.h"

DESCRIPTION
    This file contains useful definitions for default operation of the
    Intel 8259A Programmable Interrupt Controller in the IBM-PC.

LAST UPDATE
    30 April 1985
```

```
   Copyright(c) 1985,1986  D.M. Auslander and C.H. Tham

************************************************************************/


#define BASE8259     0x20              /* base address */

#define EOIPORT      (BASE8259+0)      /* where to send EOI */
#define MASKPORT     (BASE8259+1)      /* 8259 mask port */

#define BASEVEC      8                 /* base vector */

#define TMRVEC       BASEVEC           /* timer vector */
#define KBVEC        (BASEVEC+1)       /* keyboard vector */
#define COM2VEC      (BASEVEC+3)       /* COM2 device vector */
#define COM1VEC      (BASEVEC+4)       /* COM1 or (AUX) vector */
#define PRNVEC       (BASEVEC+7)       /* parallel printer vector */

#define AUXVEC       COM1VEC           /* an alternative definition */

#define TMRMASK      0x01              /* disable timer mask */
#define KBMASK       0x02              /* disable keyboard mask */
#define COM2MASK     0x08              /* disable COM2 mask */
#define COM1MASK     0x10              /* disable COM1 mask */
#define PRNMASK      0x80              /* disable printer port mask */

#define AUXMASK      COM1MASK

#define TMREOI       0x60              /* timer specific EOI */
#define KBEOI        0x61              /* keyboard specific EOI */
#define COM2EOI      0x63              /* COM2 specific EOI */
#define COM1EOI      0x64              /* COM1 specific EOI */
#define PRNEOI       0x67              /* printer specific EOI */

#define NSEOI        0x20              /* non specific EOI */

;***********************************************************************
;
; FILE
;       timeinta.asm  -  timer interrupt demo, assembly portion
;
; REMARKS
;       This module implements some of the very basic functions needed
;       to set up a timer interrupt service routine.
;
;       The C language service routine MUST be named tick() and the
;       low level interrupt handler is named here as tmrisr().
;
;       Note that this module is designed to be used with Microsoft C
;       version 4.00 and above; it will probably work with version 3.00
;       also.  All global names are preceeded by an underscore and you
;       must assemble using the /ml flag to preserve case sensitivity:
;
;               masm timeinta /ml;
;
; LAST UPDATE
;       15 January 1988  by  Haam
;               special version to demo how to roll your own timer isr
;
;       Copyright(c) 1986-1988  D.M. Auslander and C.H. Tham
;
;***********************************************************************

        EOIPORT         EQU             20h             ; where to send the EOI byte
        SEOI            EQU             60h             ; specific EOI byte for the timer

        INCLUDE model.h                                 ; memory model definitions

IF LCODE
        EXTRN   _tick:FAR                       ; tick is in different code segment
ENDIF

        INCLUDE prologue.h                      ; setup stuff

IFE LCODE
        EXTRN   _tick:NEAR                      ; tick is in same code segment
ENDIF


        PUBLIC  _tmrisr                         ; this means tmrisr() is visible

        PUBLIC  _setivec, _getivec
        PUBLIC  _enable, _disable



;----------------------------------------------------------------------
; PROCEDURE
;       TMRISR  -  timer interrupt service routine
;
; SYNOPSIS
;       void tmrisr(void), vectored to by timer interrupt
;
; REMARKS
;       Saves the registers and switch to the program's data segment which
;       is defined by DGROUP in all memory models.  The CPU's interrupt
;       response is enabled with a sti instruction almost immediately to
;       allow higher priority interrupts to interrupt this interrupt, not
;       that it makes much difference in the IBM-PC since the timer is the
;       highest priority interrupt.
;
;       A specific EOI (end-of-interrupt) byte is sent to the 8259 Interrupt
```

```
;       Controller at the end of the service function, tick().  This tells
;       the 8259 that we are done servicing the timer interrupt.  Without
;       an EOI notification, the 8259 will not allow another timer interrupt
;       (plus all lower priority interrupts) to be passed to the CPU.
;
;       There are ways around this, for example, by using the special mask
;       mode, but that is beyond the scope of this exercise.
;
; LAST UPDATE
;       10 January 1988
;----------------------------------------------------------------------

IF LCODE
_tmrisr         PROC    FAR
ELSE
_tmrisr         PROC    NEAR
ENDIF

        sti                             ; enable CPU's interrupt response

        push    ax                      ; save registers in pusha order
        push    cx
        push    dx
        push    bx
        push    bp
        push    si
        push    di

        push    ds                      ; save data and extra segments
        push    es

        mov     ax, SEG DGROUP          ; switch to program's data segment
        mov     ds, ax

        call    _tick

        mov     al, SEOI                ; send specific EOI
        out     EOIPORT, al

        pop     es                      ; restores data and extra segments
        pop     ds

        pop     di                      ; restores registers in popa order
        pop     si
        pop     bp
        pop     bx
        pop     dx
        pop     cx
        pop     ax

        iret

_tmrisr         ENDP


;----------------------------------------------------------------------
; PROCEDURE
;       SETIVEC  -    install a function as interrupt service routine
;
; SYNOPSIS
;       void setivec(vecno, sizeof(isr), isr)
;       int vecno;
;       void (*isr)();
;
; PARAMETERS
;       vecno         -  vector number (0..255)
;       sizeof(isr)   -  sizeof the function pointer
;       isr           -  routine to be vectored to
;
; REGISTERS
;       AX, BX, CX, DX
;
; REMARKS
;       Installs isr as an interrupt service routine.  If isr is a
;       32-bit pointer in segment:offset form, then the specified segment
;       is used.  If isr contains just the 16-bit offset as indicated by
;       the sizeof(isr) argument, the current code segment will be assumed
;       for the segment portion.
;
;       Note how interrupts are disabled and restored when writing to the
;       vector entry by using the flag register.
;
; LAST UPDATE
;       12 February 1988
;               add sizeof(isr) argument for greater flexibility
;----------------------------------------------------------------------

IF LCODE
_setivec                PROC    FAR
ELSE
_setivec                PROC    NEAR
ENDIF

        push    bp
        mov     bp, sp                  ; set up stack frame

        push    ds                      ; save DS

        mov     bx, [bp+AP]             ; get vector number
        shl     bx, 1                   ; multiply by 4 to get byte offset
        shl     bx, 1                   ;  into interrupt vector table
```

```
        mov     ax, [bp+AP+4];          ; get offset portion of isr

        cmp     WORD PTR [bp+AP+2], 2 ; isr contains 16-bit offset only?
        je      siv_1                   ; yes, goto siv_1

        mov     dx, [bp+AP+6]           ; isr is 4 bytes, get segment portion
        jmp     siv_2                   ; skip over stuff for 2-byte pointers

siv_1:                                  ; ptr is short, use CS for segment

        push    cs
        pop     dx                      ; copy CS into DX

siv_2:                                  ; prepare to set vector...

        xor     cx, cx                  ; zero CX to access vector table

        pushf                           ; save flags, hence also interrupt status
        cli                             ; disable interrupts - critical section

        mov     ds, cx                  ; data segment now points to vector table

        mov     [bx], ax                ; set isr's offset component
        mov     [bx+2], dx              ; set isr's segment component

        popf                            ; restore previous interrupt status

        pop     ds                      ; restore DS

        pop     bp
        ret

_setivec        ENDP


;-------------------------------------------------------------------------
; FUNCTION
;       GETIVEC  -  return 32-bit pointer to interrupt service routine
;
; SYNOPSIS
;       long getivec(vecno)
;       int vecno;
;
;       void far *getivec(vecno)
;       int vecno;
;
; PARAMETER
;       vecno  -  vector number (0..255)
;
; RETURNS
;       segment in DX and offset in AX
;
; REGISTERS
;       AX, BX, DX
;
; REMARKS
;       Two alternative declarations for the return value are possible:
;       one can declare it as a 32-bit long or a far pointer, depending
;       on whether your compiler supports Microsoft's far pointer type.
;
;       Personally, I prefer a 32-bit long return type since the "far"
;       keyword is definitely non standard.
;
;       It is assumed that the vector entry will not be asynchronously
;       changed while we are reading it, hence we do not disable interrupts.
;
; LAST UPDATE
;       12 February 1988
;-------------------------------------------------------------------------

IF LCODE
_getivec                PROC    FAR
ELSE
_getivec                PROC    NEAR
ENDIF

        push    bp
        mov     bp, sp                  ; establish stack frame

        push    es                      ; save ES

        mov     bx, [bp+AP]             ; get vector number
        shl     bx, 1                   ; multiply by 4 to get byte offset
        shl     bx, 1                   ;  into interrupt vector table

        xor     ax, ax                  ; zero AX
        mov     es, ax                  ; ES now points into vector table

        mov     ax, es:[bx]             ; get offset component
        mov     dx, es:[bx+2]           ; get segment component

        pop     es

        pop     bp
        ret

_getivec        ENDP


;-------------------------------------------------------------------------
```

```
; FUNCTION
;       ENABLE  -  enable 8086 external interrupt response
;
; SYNOPSIS
;       int enable()
;
; RETURNS
;       1  if interrupts was previously enabled, 0 otherwise
;
; LAST UPDATE
;       9 January 1986
;----------------------------------------------------------------------

IF LCODE
_enable         PROC    FAR
ELSE
_enable         PROC    NEAR
ENDIF

        pushf
        pop             ax              ; get flags for interrupt status

        mov             al, ah          ; I flag bit was in AH, now moved to AL
        shr             al, 1           ; shift I flag bit to the bit-0 position
        and             ax, 1           ; mask out all other flag bits

        sti                             ; enable CPU interrupt response

        ret

_enable         ENDP


;----------------------------------------------------------------------
; FUNCTION
;       DISABLE  -  disable 8086 external interrupt response
;
; SYNOPSIS
;       int disable()
;
; RETURNS
;       1  if interrupts was previously enabled, 0 otherwise
;
; LAST UPDATE
;       9 January 1986
;----------------------------------------------------------------------

IF LCODE
_disable                PROC    FAR
ELSE
_disable                PROC    NEAR
ENDIF

        pushf                           ; get flags and hence interrupt flag bit

        cli                             ; disable CPU interrupt response

        pop             ax              ; pop flags into AX

        mov             al, ah          ; I flag bit was in AH, now moved to AL
        shr             al, 1           ; shift I flag bit to the bit-0 position
        and             ax, 1           ; mask out all other flag bits

        ret

_disable                ENDP


        INCLUDE epilogue.h

        END
```

CHAPTER 3

ASYNCHRONOUS SIGNAL PROCESSING

The problem solved in the last chapter involved one task in the background—controlling the motor—and one task in the foreground—keeping time. The A/D and D/A conversions were assumed to be fast enough to be run as part of the backgound program and required no attention except when a conversion was needed. Not all measurement or actuation systems are that simple. In this chapter, the same motor control problem is presented, but the speed measurement is made with a pulse generating device and the motor actuation is done using pulse-width modulation (PWM). Both measurement and actuation, if implemented in software, require constant attention from the computer. That attention is normally required much more often than the control sampling interval and is not synchronous with the control sampling.

3.1 PULSE-WIDTH MODULATION

It is often useful to control the voltage across a motor in such a way that only two values are used, usually zero and some other value. The usefulness derives from two sources: (1) The easiest signal to produce with a computer is a binary (i.e., two-valued) signal; and (2) the most efficient way to modulate power flow is with amplifiers that can only operate at full-on or full-off. One way to achieve the appearance of continuous speed control in this environment is with pulse-width modulation.

A pulse-width modulated signal is a constant frequency, two-valued signal in which the proportion of the period for which the signal is "on" and the proportion for which it is "off" can be varied. The percentage of on-time is called the *duty cycle*; 25% and 50% duty cycle signals are shown in Fig. 3.1. The actual voltage value associated with "on" and "off" will depend on the application.

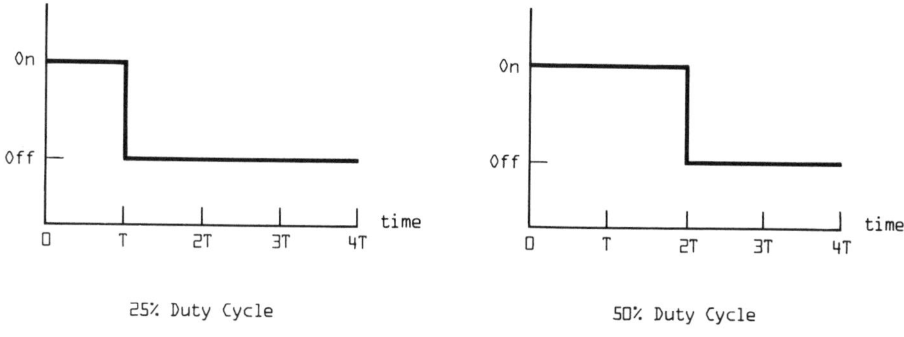

Figure 3.1

For pulse-width modulation to be effective, the chosen frequency of the PWM signal must be high enough so that the motor will not have time to respond to the rapid on/off changes, but, instead, the speed of the motor will reflect the average power level over many cycles. This average power level is controlled by the duty cycle. This will serve to control the speed of a motor that is only intended to rotate in one direction. If bidirectional rotation is required, it will be necessary to add an additional output value so that there will be three states, On-Forward, Off, and On-Reverse. To preserve the binary nature of the solution, both in terms of the computer output signals and the power amplifying elements, this is most easily handled by providing two signals, one for on/off as in the uni-directional case, and the other for direction.

3.2 PROGRAMMING FOR PULSE-WIDTH MODULATION

From the perspective of the background control program, the type of actuation used should be of no consequence. Thus, the function that sends a command value for actuation is unchanged. The actual generation of the pulse-width modulated signal is accomplished by a foreground program that makes use of an interval timer. The simplest way to program this is to fix the duty cycle at the beginning of each period. Any changes in duty cycle that are received will take effect from the next period. This can introduce a short delay into the control, but if the frequency of the PWM signal is substantially higher than the sampling frequency for control, which is normally the case, the delay will be short.

Every time the background updates the pulse-width information, there is the possibility of an interrupt in the middle of the update process. An interrupt at that time carries with it the potential for a subtle but important error. The interrupt mechanism on most computers will actually cause the interrupt to occur at the end of the current instruction that the CPU is executing. If the information being transferred requires more than one instruction to complete the update, an interrupt could conceivably leave the pulse-width information half changed. The value used by the foreground PWM generation function would be corrupted, resulting in an incorrect duty cycle being used. The error would occur infrequently, but could have serious consequences. Such errors are very hard to debug because they have probabilities of one part in many thousands, and do not occur at any regular interval.

There are two major methods of preventing such errors from occurring. The first is through *mutual exclusion.* During the data transfer time, an "interrupt disable" can be used to prevent any foreground processes from running. The other method is to provide a data transfer area that is separate from the variable actually used by the foreground PWM function. This data transfer area includes space for the new value of the variable, and a flag indicating when a data transfer is in progress. Normally, the PWM function would use the value from the data transfer area to set the duty cycle. If, however, the flag indicated that a transfer was in progress, the previous value would be used to avoid the possiblility of using incorrect information.

The output function that is called from the background is straightforward; it takes the command value, scales that to a duty cycle, and stores it for the next cycle. Two further levels of scaling are needed. The first level is the conversion from duty cycle to an on-time and an off-time based on the pulse actuation frequency, and the second is the conversion from time to ticks for use with the actual clock. Depending on the same convenience vs. efficiency trade-off made in the last chapter, the conversion can be done in this function or at a lower level.

The foreground function runs whenever its interval timer generates an interrupt. Note the assumption that this foreground function, and by implication all others, has access to its own private timer. The design of the foreground function will proceed under that assumption. In some cases there will be sufficient hardware timers to meet all these needs for independent timers. If there aren't enough timers, software will have to be used in such a way that each function thinks that it has an independent timer. In that way, the design of the PWM software can proceed without having to make any assumptions about how many or what kind of timers are available. The design of software for emulating multiple timers will be discussed shortly.

The PWM foreground function is shown in Fig. 3.2 (Timer #1 is used to time the sampling period). When the timer interrupt occurs, the PWM function must decide whether this is the end of the off-time, and thus the end of one cycle and the beginning of the next, or the end of the on-time and thus in the middle of a cycle. If it is the beginning of a new cycle, the timer is set for the on-time of the next cycle, then the output signal is set to "on." If it is the middle of the cycle, the timer is set for the off-time and the output signal is set to "off."

```
Timer #2 Interrupt:

    If (state is Beginning-of-cycle)
        Compute on-time and off-time for current duty cycle
        Set Timer #2 for on-time
        Set output port for Motor-On
        Set state for next entry to Middle-of-cycle
        Return from interrupt

    Else
        Set Timer #2 for off-time
        Set output port for Motor-Off
        Set state for next entry to Beginning-of-cycle
        Return from interrupt
```

Figure 3.2

In order to run properly, several pieces of information must be remembered between foreground executions. The state information, which is used to decide which path to take on entry into the interrupt function, and the on-time and off-time information, must be remembered from the last time the background program called the function to set a new duty cycle. Because they must be remembered even after the function is no longer running, these variables must be stored in fixed memory locations, thus rendering this function non-re-entrant. Not being re-entrant is not serious for this kind of interrupt routine because it is not used as a general purpose function. The only way that it could be called while still running would be if there were insufficient computing time to finish its work between clock interrupts. If that were the case, it would be impossible to run the system; a longer period for the PWM signal would have to be used.

A second interesting problem involves the accuracy of timing. When the (hardware) timer runs out, some time elapses until the function that services the interrupt runs, and further time until the function in Fig. 3.2 starts running. Therefore, the time from the end of a timing cycle to resetting the timer is "lost," resulting in inaccurate control of the frequency of the PWM signal. For relatively low frequencies, the inaccuracy due to interrupt *latency* is not serious, but it becomes more significant as the signal gets faster. The best way to minimize or eliminate the latency errors is to use a timer that automatically resets itself when the interval it is timing runs out. This can work directly in a clock that is being used to time a fixed period, since the period does not change from cycle to cycle. The PWM signal, however, uses different on-/and off-times, and these times can change from one cycle to the next. If two timers were used, however, one of them could be used for timing the PWM period, which doesn't change, so that the clock could use automatic reset. If the automatic reset is achieved within one "tick" of the clock, there is no latency error at all. There would still be some latency error in the on-time, which would use the second clock. A correction based on the average latency time would reduce that error.

Hardware clock/timers are available that allow for two interrupts within a single operating cycle. Programming such a timer to interrupt at the end of the on-time and then again at the end of the PWM period makes direct implementation of pulse-width modulation quite simple.

A more elaborate, and more accurate, scheme is to use a clock that *always* resets itself when it finishes timing. If there is no preset interval to set (as there is when the timer is used in automatic reset mode), the timer will restart in stopwatch mode (counting up from zero). When a command for a new interval arrives, the interval that is set is adjusted for whatever time has elapsed since the last interrupt (unless the clock has been turned off by an explicit command).

3.3 PULSE-FREQUENCY MODULATION (PFM)

The velocity measurement is derived from a device that generates a fixed number of pulses per revolution. The pulse-generating mechanism is often optical, but can be magnetic, electrical, or mechanical. We will initially assume a system with unidirectional motion, which only requires a single pulse train. Two 90-degree out-of-phase pulse trains (*quadrature*) are needed to deduce the direction of motion. We will be discussing use of quadrature signals later in this chapter in the context of position control where bidirectional motion is essential. We will consider the unidirectional velocity measurement first.

Measuring velocity from pulses has several interesting conceptual problems that must be resolved before design of the software can proceed. Unless the motor velocity will only be measured in a narrow range, the timing and precision problems at low velocities and high velocities must be handled differently. The choice in processing is whether to measure frequency or period. The frequency (pulses/time) is proportional to velocity and will require minimum further processing for control tasks that require a velocity measurement. The period (time/pulse) is proportional to the inverse of frequency.

At high velocities, pulses arrive very frequently. Counting the number of pulses received in a fixed time interval provides an accurate and easily programmed measurement of frequency. At the upper limit, the frequency is limited by both the hardware's and software's ability to respond without missing pulses. Direct pulse-to-pulse period measurement is impractical at high speed because the pulses are so close together that the measurement of the time between pulses becomes very imprecise. A recently developed velocity measurement technique is to record the period of a specified number of pulses to give a result that is proportional to period but with a lower requirement on clock speed.

At low motor velocities, the problems are reversed. Measurement of frequency is impractical because the number of pulses in any reasonable amount of time is too small for adequate precision in the result. Use of a very high speed clock is also impractical because the number of counts that could accumulate between pulses would require extended precision numbers which are often not available with hardware timers. The most practical measurement to make at low velocities is thus the direct period measurement between successive pulses. As the velocity approaches zero, however, as it does for all positioning systems, this period measuring scheme has the problem that the "next" pulse *never* arrives! A *timeout* must be defined to specify the time period for a velocity that is low enough to be considered zero.

The method of velocity measurement also has an effect on the control algorithm. It is desirable to compute the controller error based on the most recent information possible. "Velocity" is a quantity that has instantaneous meaning for the motor itself, so it would be desirable for the controller to be able to use the current value of velocity in its calculations. For normal velocities, an analog tachometer (with an A/D) gives a measure of the instantaneous velocity. A pulse-generating system, on the other hand, always has some delay in producing the information because the pulse rate is finite. The needs for precision must therefore be balanced against the needs of the controller for current information. Very precise measurements can only be made by waiting for large numbers of pulses to be counted, or by using very fast clocks and very closely spaced pulses. These requirements run counter to the needs at low velocities, and, ultimately, must be balanced with cost and computing load considerations. As the velocity decreases, the interaction with the controller gets worse, because the pulse rate may become slower than the controller's sampling rate. In this case, the information needed is simply not available, so the controller will be forced to use a slower sampling rate.

This is not to say that the pulse generating measurement methods do not have some advantages. The most important advantage is in very precise, wide-range measurement of position where they are far better than most analog systems. One common solution is to use both methods—analog for velocity measurement, and pulse-generating for position measurement. This increases the system cost, so there is strong motivation to make do with only one kind of transducer.

3.4 UNIDIRECTIONAL VELOCITY MEASUREMENT

Like the PWM function, the velocity measurement runs in the foreground as an independent task. The most recent value measured is always accessible to the control program through a function call that returns that information. The method of measurement used is to record the period for a group of pulses. The function that is used to communicate with the background returns the measurement in the form of three values: the period measured, the number of pulses associated with that period, and a flag that can be used by the background program to decide if a zero velocity should be presumed. The flag is set to "one" every time a new period is recorded by the foreground program, and is set to zero every time the background program reads the value. If, upon reading a velocity value, the flag is zero, the background program knows that no pulses have arrived since the last measurement. The number of pulses to be grouped can be changed by a function call from the background, or by adding foreground code to make that number adaptive to the most recent measurements.

The function to realize the velocity measurement, shown in Fig. 3.3 makes use of a stopwatch (event) type of timer and an interrupt that is caused by the arrival of a pulse. When the interrupt arrives, the pulse count is incremented and checked against the goal. If the specified number of interrupts has been received, the current time is read from the timer, and the timer is reset for the next cycle. An initialization function, shown in Fig. 3.4, is used to arm the interrupt, initialize the pulse count, and start the timer.

```
Pulse Interrupt:
        Increment Pulse_Count
        If (Pulse_Count >= N_Group)
                Read time and store it
                Reset event timer
                Store new N_Group
                Pulse_Count = 0
                Flag = 1

        Return from interrupt
```

Figure 3.3

```
Initialize Pulse Detector:
        Pulse_Count = 0
        Flag = 0
        Start Event Timer
        Enable pulse input interrupt
```

Figure 3.4

3.5 SOFTWARE IMPLEMENTATION OF MULTIPLE TIMERS

If enough hardware timers were available to satisfy all of the foreground modules, the preceding solution would be complete. In many cases, however, the number of "logical" timers needed is greater than the number actually available. Then software must be used to provide an emulation of multiple timers. The usual hardware/software trade-off applies, that is, the software solution requires fewer components and therefore has less expensive hardware, but, for similar processors, will run more slowly. In the case of timing, running more slowly implies a slower base frequency for the clock and thus less precision in time measurements.

The design we will use makes use of the simplest kind of clock possible, one that can cause interrupts at a fixed frequency, and assumes that only one such clock is available. For software implementation, a clock rate of no faster than about 1 millisecond would be usual for this kind of implementation.

Both interval timers and event timers will be implemented. The event timers will follow the model used in the velocity measurement above, in that the actual start and stop signals to the timer will come from another software module rather than from a physical interrupt. The event timers are the easiest to handle (see Fig. 3.5). An array is established with the number of elements equal to the number of event timers being emulated. At each tick of the clock, all of the elements in the array are incremented by one. Reading and resetting the event timer are accomplished by getting the appropriate value from the array, or setting that value to zero to start a new count.

```
Clock Interrupt:
        For i = 1 to Number_of_event_timers
                event_time(i) = event_time(i) + 1
        Return from interrupt

Read i-th event timer's time:      (These two operations should be done with
        Return event_time(i)       interrupts disabled so they cannot be
                                   interrupted)
Reset i-th event timer:
        event_time(i) = 0
```

Figure 3.5

A similar structure is used for the interval timers, with an array of elements, one for each timer (see Fig. 3.6). These timers are used as down counters, so they are initialized to the desired interval, and an action is taken when the count reaches zero. The action to be taken is to run the interrupt (foreground) modules that are outlined above, so the initialization procedure for the timer involves sending the name of the function to be executed to the timer module as well as the interval to be timed. An additional array will be required to store the names (or addresses) of these functions. For the background control part of the program, the associated foreground module sets the timer-done flag so that the control program will run. Only the new interval time is sent on a reset, on the assumption that the function to be executed will not change.

```
Initialize i-th interval timer(interval, function):
        interval_time(i) = interval
        foreground_function(i) = function
        re_entry_flag(i) = 0
        active_flag(i) = 1

        Return

Clock interrupt:
        For i = 0 to Number_of_interval_timers
                if(active_flag(i) = 1)
                        Decrement interval_time(i)
                        if(interval_time(i) <= 0)
                                if(re_entry_flag(i) = 1)
                                        error
                                re_entry_flag(i) = 1
                                active_flag(i) = 0
                                Execute foreground_function(i)
                                re_entry_flag = 0
        Return from interrupt

Reset i-th interval timer(interval):
        interval_time(i) = interval
        active_flag(i) = 1
        Return
```

Figure 3.6

Two flag variables are required for proper control of the interval timers. The first is an active/inactive flag. Decrementing and testing are only done on active timers. A timer becomes inactive when its time runs out, and becomes active again when it is reset. The second flag, an in-service flag, prevents re-entry into the foreground function being executed if another interrupt should occur before it is done. Whether or not such an interrupt is allowed depends on the specific hardware used. However, it makes sense to allow such interrupts so that clock pulses can be counted while a foreground function is being executed.

If the foreground functions must be complete before any further clock interrupts are allowed to occur, the basic clock frequency might be limited to an undesirably low value. Two possible conflicts can arise from re-entry interrupts that occur while a foreground function is still executing. The first is that a different foreground routine will be scheduled for execution as a result of the interrupt. Using the form of scheduling that is in this design, the newly scheduled function will execute and complete before the currently running function is allowed to complete. This could cause some timing problems, but would generally not be a problem. The second problem is more serious and we will use a flag variable to guard against its occurrence. That is when the new clock interrupt causes the *same* foreground function to be scheduled for execution as is already running. As was noted above, in general, the foreground modules are not re-entrant so this cannot be allowed. A reasonable interpretation of this condition is that it represents a user scheduling error that should be flagged and cause an error condition in the program.

The flag variable used to detect this condition is set to 1 (for busy) when the function is started, and is set to zero (not busy) when the function is done. Before calling the function, the flag is checked. If it is already "one," an error message is printed.

The precision and range of these timing functions depend on the integer precision used for the variables. For a 1 millisecond clock, 16-bit signed integers will give a range of about 32 seconds, and 16-bit unsigned integers will give a range of about 65 seconds. For 32-bit integers, the ranges are about 2 million seconds and 4 million seconds, respectively. On many computers, however, there will be a computing time penalty for using 32-bit integers.

3.6 POSITION CONTROL

With velocity control based on a pulse-generating tachometer, all of these fundamental tools can also be used for position control if a quadrature signal is used in place of the single pulse train. The most straightforward control structure to use leaves the velocity control in place and adds an additional control loop for position (see Fig. 3.7). For this *cascade* control configuration, the output of the position loop is the setpoint for the velocity loop.

The mathematical form of the position controller is exactly the same as that of the velocity controller. A P (proportional) or PI (proportional plus integral) control can be used. A derivative (D) term could be added to make a PID control. The derivative term, which is proportional to the rate-of-change of error, helps in stabilizing the system behavior but is not always necessary. A "D" term could be used if desired for the velocity control as well. In computer control, where the PID is approximated with difference equations, the derivative is usually approximated with a term proportional to the difference between the current error and the previous error.

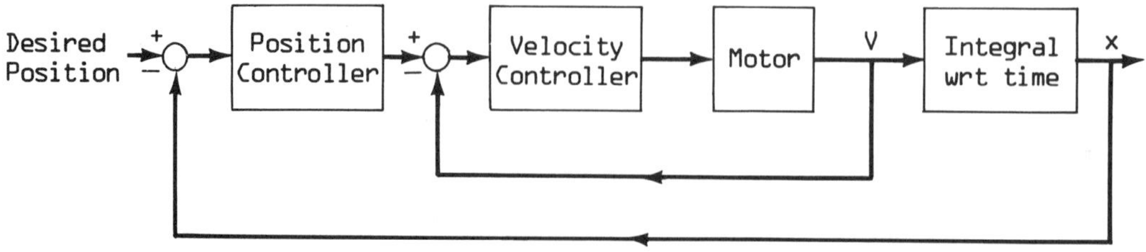

Figure 3.7

As a variant to the control algorithm, the controller output can be expressed in difference form rather than absolute form. For a PID control, this takes the form;

$$\Delta\, m = k_p(\varepsilon - \varepsilon_{-1}) + k_i\varepsilon + k_d(\varepsilon_{-2}\varepsilon_{-1} + \varepsilon_{-2}) \tag{3.1}$$

and

$$m = m_{-1} + \Delta\, m$$

where the "-1" subscript indicates the previous value and the "-2" subscript refers to the value delayed by two time units. This form of the PID control algorithm has two main advantages. The first is that it is easier to apply limits to the controller output. In the absolute form, separate limits must be imposed for the integrated value and for the controller output, whereas in this form a single limit applied to m is sufficient since the integrated value is never explicit. The second advantage to this form is that the P and/or the D term can be written in terms of the output variable instead of the error. Since they are both difference terms, this is equivalent to assuming that the setpoint is always constant. This avoids the very large change in controller output that accompanies a change in setpoint and makes the control action much smoother, although somewhat slower. Where wear and tear on actuators is an important design factor, or when uncontrolled resonances could be excited, this feature can be very useful. If this option is exercised, the integral term must be retained with $k_i \neq 0$ because it is the only term that contains the setpoint.

Another anomaly in the incremental form of the PID algorithm occurs if only the P term is implemented. In that case, whenever the output saturates, an offset value will appear. If an I term is present, the offset will be absorbed into the integral action and will not usually cause any problems. This problem is not very common because one of the reasons for implementing control with the incremental form is that it handles the integral action better. For pure P control, the incremental form does not have any advantages.

The implementation of a cascade position/velocity control is shown in Fig. 3.8. It is assumed that the velocity and the position loops have the same sampling interval, so they can be written as a single combined background task. The timing control is identical to the method described in Fig. 2.3, so it will not be repeated here. The addition of the derivative (difference) term and the incremental form of the controller equations make the timing control even more critical than in the PI case.

```
Controller:
        old2_position_error = old1_position_error
        old1_position_error = position_error
        position_error = position_setpoint - position

        delta_mp = kpp * (position_error - old1_position_error)
                + kpi * position_error
                + kpd * (position_error - 2 * old1_position_error
                                + old2_position_error)
        mp = mp + delta_mp

        old2_velocity_error = old1_velocity_error
        old1_velocity_error = velocity_error
        velocity_error = mp - velocity

        delta_mv = kvp * (velocity_error - old1_velocity_error)
                + kvi * velocity_error
                + kvd * (velocity_error - 2 * old1_velocity_error
                                + old2_velocity_error)
        mv = mv + delta_mv
        Return
```

Figure 3.8

3.7 MEASURING POSITION

The basic quadrature measurement consists of a pair of 90 degree out-of-phase square waves, as shown in Fig. 3.9

Using 1 = *On* and 0 = *Off*, forward motion will trace out the AB sequence 10 11 01 00 10 ..., while reverse motion will trace out 10 00 01 11 10 ... . The direction of motion is uniquely determined by the sequence followed. For example, if the previous AB value were 01 and the current value is 00, then a forward step has been taken. Likewise, for the transition 01 to 11, a reverse step has been taken. The program to keep track of position by incrementing a position counter when a

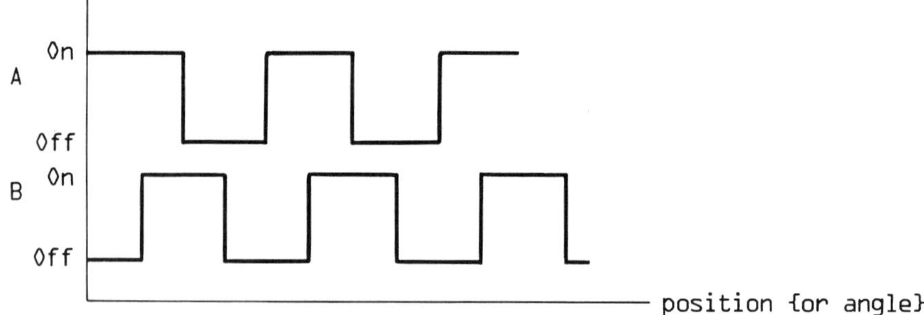

Figure 3.9

forward step is taken and decrementing it when a backward step is taken can be written in the form of a finite-state machine (see Fig. 3.10). That is, if the previous "state," i.e., the AB value for the previous step, is known, there are two possible valid transitions and two invalid transitions. The two valid transitions are for a forward or backward step, and the two invalid ones mean that there was either a data error or a complete transition was missed, due to a pulse rate that was too high for the computer, for example. The interrupts are set up so that an interrupt occurs whenever there is a transition (high-to-low or low-to-high) on either the A or the B inputs.

```
Quadrature interrupt:
    old_state = AB
    Read input port and set AB
    Execute the code block corresponding to old_state:
                    (00, 01, etc are the binary values)

        00:  if (AB = 10) increment position
             else if (AB = 01) decrement position
             else ERROR

        01:  if (AB = 00) increment position
             else if (AB = 11) decrement position
             else ERROR

        11:  if (AB = 01) increment position
             else if (AB = 10) decrement position
             else ERROR

        10:  if (AB = 11) increment position
             else if (AB = 00) decrement position
             else ERROR
    Return
```

Figure 3.10

The measurement of velocity only has to be slightly modified from the scheme already outlined because of the possibility of velocity reversals. These can be accommodated by the addition of a "forward/reverse" flag in the "increment" and "decrement" modules accessed above. The velocity timing is done as normal as long as there are no velocity reversals. Velocity reversals can be checked by comparing the previous value of the forward/reverse flag to the current value. If it has changed, there has been a velocity reversal. Whenever such a reversal occurs, the best current estimate of velocity is zero. Regardless of the number of pulses that are being collected, whenever a reversal occurs the output velocity should be updated. However, the current output is a period (i.e., number of pulses and associated time) that cannot be used to express a velocity of zero! Some sort of signal must be used for this case. An easy one is to use the "number of pulses" variable; set to zero it can be used to indicate zero velocity since a period cannot be measured for no pulses.

ASYNCHRONOUS PROGRAMMING EXAMPLES

3.8 INTRODUCTION

Many real-time applications have to deal with asynchronous events, such as detecting and timing external signals or generating signals at intervals determined by external circumstances. The asynchronous nature of the events and the often tight response-time constraints require special considerations in software design. Real time applications can often benefit from the use of more than one clock or timer. Unfortunately, many small control computers have only one hardware-based timer. Hence, this section will lead off by presenting a simple implementation of two timers in software that are synchronized with the single hardware timer of the IBM-PC. Next, we will present modules for pulse-width modulation, pulse-frequency demodulation, and quadrature decoding. Asynchronous events are detected via interrupts, and these modules have routines that need to be installed as interrupt service routines. Fortunately, the *xignal* package is available to take most of the work out of setting up interrupt service routines. This package will be discussed in detail in the example program section of a later chapter. If interrupt latency and performance constraints preclude the use of the *xignal* package, you can "roll your own" interrupt front-end routines using the *timeintc.* and *timeinta.asm* examples of Chapter 2 as a guide. The final example is a general implementation of multiple count-down and count-up timers in software. This module, *time.c,* is part of the *clotho* kernel, which is designed to support real-time control applications. We shall return to *time.c* in the example programs for Chapter 5, where it is used to implement multiple independent real-time control tasks.

The sample program modules are:

panic.c This supplies a function to terminate program execution and restore the CPU state.

time2.h Declarations for time2.c.

time2.c Implements two count-down timers in software; the soft timers are clocked off the IBM-PC's single hardware timer.

pwm.h Declarations for pwm.c.

pwm.c Implements pulse-width modulation using the IBM-PC's parallel printer port.

quad0.h Declarations for quad0.c.

quad0.c Position information using single-ended 2-channel quadrature input on the IBM-PC's parallel port.

quad1.h	Declarations for quad1.c.
quad1.c	Similar to quad0.c but includes velocity information based on a fixed velocity sampling time.
pfm.h	Declarations for both pfm0.c and pfm1.c.
pfm0.c	Infers velocity from input pulses generated by a pulse-frequency modulation "tachometer."
pfm1.c	Similar to pfm0.c but uses adaptive pulse group sizing to accomodate a wider velocity range.
time.h	Declarations for time.c.
time.c	A general implementation of multiple timers in software.
cascade0.c	Demonstrate cascaded position and velocity control loops for PID control.

The modules in this section also require several files described in the example program section of Chapter 2: envir.h, inout.h, 8259.h, alarm.h, alarm.c, xignal.h, and xignal.lib.

3.9 PROGRAM TERMINATION

The module *panic.c* is designed to restore the PC's timer settings and interrupt status just prior to emergency program termination. Programs that modify interrupt vectors and timer frequency should restore the computer to some semblance of its original state when they exit, otherwise the computer will most likely "crash" when it vectors to nonexistent interrupt code after the program exits. Putting all the clean-up chores into one routine seems like a good idea. This simple example also illustrates some of the issues that must be considered when programming for asynchronous environments, even in something as simple as printing an error message.

This module has just one routine, *panic(),* which prints a parting message and restores the IBM-PC's hardware timer interrupt frequency and any vectors that have been changed through *xignal().* This, of couse, assumes that interrupt handlers were installed through *xignal().* The PC's timer interrupt frequency is reset to the DOS default value using *setalarm()* from the *alarm.c* module.

Note that *panic()* first disables all interrupts (except the NMI—nonmaskable interrupt) by calling *xignal()* with the XIGALL (specifying all xignal handlers) and XIG_IGN (tells xignal to ignore signals) parameters. This is to prevent the error message from being interrupted since the IBM-PC takes about a millisecond to print each character and interrupts may occur during this time which cannot be handled due to the error condition. After printing the error message, *panic()* restores all the xignal handlers to their default state (XIG_DFL), resets the PC's clock, and exits.

Why not just disable interrupts with *disable()* when printing the message? The reason is that *printf()* and related library functions call on DOS, and through

DOS the BIOS, to perform the actual output. BIOS functions always enable interrupts by executing a *sti* instruction. An alternative is to mask the 8259 interrupt controller, but since the 8259 mask port is write-only, a program cannot tell which interrupts were masked and which were not masked.

3.10 TWO SOFTWARE TIMERS

Since there is only one hardware timer available on the IBM-PC, software is used to simulate multiple timers that work much like hardware timers and are synchronized to the PC's single hardware timer through the timer interrupt. In addition to providing time telling functions, *time2.c* allows routines to be asynchronously executed when a soft timer times out. This implementation may be regarded as a precursor to the general multiple timer implementation; it is much simpler and provides only two nonprioritized count-down timers.

There are three reasons for this. First, most of the example programs here require at most two timers and a minimal implementation incurs much less overheads. Tests on an IBM-PC have shown that the response time with *time2.c* and *xignal* is about 670 microseconds from when the hardware timer interrupts to when the timeout service routine starts executing. This is about four times faster than the general implementation (*time.c*) using six soft timers. The extra performance may be critical to applications with severe performance constraints. Second, this minimal version is much easier to understand than the more general version; it can serve as an introduction to the more complicated general implementation. Third, it uses less code and data space, a not unimportant consideration if you need to squeeze your control program into a small EPROM.

In *time2.c*, there are two count-down variables, *time0* and *time1*, which track the number of timer interrupts left before the soft timer runs out. A timeout service routine may be associated with each timer; if a soft timer times out and there is a routine attached to it, that routine is executed. The timeout routine is installed by passing the function name of the routine to *SetTsr()* (a mnemonic for Set Timeout Service Routine). This timeout routine is referenced as a pointer to a function that does not return anything.[1] In the case of soft timer 0, this pointer is declared as

```
static void (*isr0)().
```

This declares *isr0* to be a pointer to a function that does not return a value; the *static* keyword means that this pointer variable cannot be referenced by routines outside of *time2.c*.

---

[1]The name of a function (without the brackets) is interpreted as a pointer to the function itself. Thus, to pass a pointer to a function as an argument, just use the function name.

The timeout service routines may optionally accept arguments; these are specified in the form of pointers that point to a memory location containing the actual arguments. If no arguments are required, the pointers are set to NULL. These argument pointers for the two timers are declared as

```
static void *argp0, *argp1;
```

The optional argument pointers allow the same timeout service routine to be installed for both timers, but the routine may act on different data sets for different timers. For example, say we are controlling two motors using a PID control algorithm, but each motor requires different control gains. The routine that implements the PID control loop can be installed as the timeout service routine for both timers, but the argument pointers point at different areas containing the control gains and i/o port addresses for each motor. To further illustrate, assume that the parameters are in the form of an array, one for each motor:

```
double paramset0[3], paramset1[3];

void control(param)
double *param;
{
  ...
}

init()
{
  ...
  SetTsr(0, control, (void *)paramset0);
  SetTsr(1, control, (void *)paramset1);
  ...
}
```

In the above example, the address of the parameter array is passed to *SetTsr()* as the argument pointer. Note that the *type* of the parameter address is cast into a void pointer before being passed to *SetTsr()* .

The generalized *void* pointer type is a fairly recent innovation in C. Prior to their introduction in the draft ANSI C standard, the concept of a general purpose pointer was not explicitly supported by the C language. One has to make do with *char* pointers, since they tend to have the least restrictive alignment requirements.[2] Now, almost all C compilers support the void type, and it is a stable feature of the ANSI draft standard.

---

[2]For example, C compilers designed for PDP-11s require that integers be aligned on even memory addresses while characters can be stored at odd or even addresses. Floats, doubles ,and structures may have even more restrictive alignment requirements. It depends largely on the compiler.

3.10.1 INITIALIZATION

The initialization routine, *InitTime()*, is passed a *long* argument specifying the timer interrupt frequency in milliseconds. The PC's timer is set to the desired "tick" frequency using *setalarm()*. The IBM-PC family uses a default tick frequency of about 55 milliseconds. Many real-time control applications (such as PWM) require much finer timing resolution, especially if the CPU is fast enough to handle it. The initialization routine must therefore allow the timer tick frequency to be changed to suit the needs of the application. The timer interrupt service routine, *chronos()*, is installed using *xignal()*. Bear in mind that by taking over the timer interrupt, DOS's timekeeping functions are bypassed.

3.10.2 TIMER INTERRUPT SERVICE ROUTINE

The *chronos()* routine is invoked at every timer interrupt. Its basic functions are to synchronize the software timers to the PC's hardware timer, decrement the count-down timers, and invoke the timeout service routine if a soft timer has timed out and such a routine is installed.

If the soft timer has not timed out yet, the tick count is decremented. A *Specific End-Of-Interrupt [seoi()]* byte is sent to the 8259 interrupt controller;[3] this fools the interrupt controller into thinking that *chronos()* has finished, thus allowing another timer interrupt request to be passed to the CPU. This also allows lower priority interrupt requests to be passed through. The timer interrupt on the PC has the highest priority; if the timer interrupt service routine did not issue an EOI notification, all other interrupt requests will be held back by the 8259. A consequence of sending a "premature" EOI is that another timer interrupt can occur in the middle of a timeout service routine. While timeout service routines should be re-entrant, they should not be invoked re-entrantly unless there are special reasons (such as task scheduling/dispatching) for doing so. That a timeout routine has to be called again even before it is finished indicates that it is taking far too long to execute. Allowing the same timeout routine to be called in this situation will pile calls upon calls until the stack overflows, causing a system crash. To guard against this, flag variables *isf0* and *isf1* (short for In-Service Flag) are used to indicate if a timeout routine is currently executing and should not be invoked re-entrantly.

However, this should not prevent the other timeout service routine from being executed. The execution of timeout service routines can thus overlap, allowing one routine to interrupt the other. Using *time2.c*, one can set up a simple control system with two "concurrent" control loops installed as timeout service routines, with the proviso that the sampling interval of each loop be much longer than its execution time.

---

[3]The *seoi()* function is part of the xignal package.

What if both timers timeout at the same time? In that case, *timer0*'s timeout routine will be executed first, and *timer1*'s timeout routine will be executed at the next timer interrupt. Consequently, there is a one "tick" uncertainty in the execution instance of the second timeout service routine. In this scheme, a small preference is given to the first timer, but the timeout routines are not mutually exclusive, i.e., the execution of one routine does not prevent the other routine from being executed, albeit with a delay of 1 timer tick. The issues of explicit priority and exclusion control are addressed by the more general multiple software timer implementation, *time.c*, which will be discussed later.

Note that each timeout routine is only allowed to be executed once per timeout. The timer has to be reset before the timeout service routine can be activated again at the next timeout. This prevents the timeout routine from being called over and over again should the control routine fail to reset the timer. An auto-reload feature can be easily implemented if desired.

Note that although the timeout service routines are not called re-entrantly, *chronos()* itself is invoked re-entrantly. This introduces the possibility that *chronos()* may be interrupted while in the process of reading or updating flags (or other data) and the new instance of *chronos()* may read or modify the same data. Therefore, access to such data must be carefully controlled to prevent the two instances of *chronos()* from simultaneously writing to the same variable, or for one instance to be reading and the other to be writing to the same variable at the same time. A simple expedient is to simply disable interrupts during data access. This creates a *critical section* where no other process (in this case, *chronos()* itself) can access the same data at the same time. This is also known as *mutual exclusion*.

Note the placement of *enable()* and *disable()* function calls in *chronos()*. Interrupts are disabled when determining if a timer has timed out and if there is a timeout routine to execute. If there is, flags are set and interrupts enabled before executing the timeout routine. Interrupts are again disabled to clear the *isf0* or *isf1* flags, and then re-enabled before *chronos()* exits.

There are other methods of implementing critical sections, such as atomic test-and-set instructions and semaphores, some of which can be used in multiprocessor systems communicating with shared memory. Disabling interrupts has the advantage that it is simple, easy to understand, and easy to implement; the disadvantages are that it works only on single processor systems and effectively creates a single, program-wide critical section for all data access. The other methods allow different critical sections to be implemented for different groups of data; entering a critical section for one group does not exclude other tasks from accessing their data.

3.11 THE PARALLEL PRINTER PORT

Since the following set of program modules uses the IBM-PC's parallel printer port for output (Pulse-Width Modulation) and input (Pulse-Frequency Modulation and

Quadrature), a little background information on the parallel printer port seems to be indicated. Readers are advised to refer to the appropriate IBM-PC Technical Reference Manual for more information. As its name suggests, the IBM-PC's parallel *printer* port is just that: a parallel port designed to interface to printers using the parallel *Centronics* printer control protocol. It has 12 latched TTL output points and 5 TTL level input points. There are actually two variants of the device: the standalone Parallel Printer Adapter with port addresses[4] from 0x378 to 0x37A, and the much more common combination Monochrome Display and Printer Adapter with port addresses from 0x3BC to 0x3BE. The example programs assume the latter device. Port 0x3BC is a normal 8-bit digital output port; reading this port will return the last byte written to it unless the external device is driving them (which it should not do), in which case the data will be or'ed with the value last written to the port. The pin numbers[5] corresponding to the output bits are:

Bit 7	Bit 6	Bit 5	Bit 4	Bit 3	Bit 2	Bit 1	Bit 0
Pin 9	Pin 8	Pin 7	Pin 6	Pin 5	Pin 4	Pin 3	Pin 2

The example programs use the port at 0x3BE as an input port although it is normally an output port. The port is somewhat strange compared to a normal parallel input port. Only the least significant 5 bits are available (bits 0 to 4), and of these, bits 0, 1, and 3 are inverted (i.e., a digital high input will read as a 0). Input data at bit 3 is or'ed with the bit 3 value last written to the port. In addition to all of this, if a 1 value is written to bit 4, an interrupt will be generated whenever the input voltage on pin 10 goes from high to low. The pin numbers corresponding to the input bits are:

Bit 3	Bit 2	Bit 1	Bit 0
Pin 17	Pin 16	Pin 14	Pin 1

There are also 5 input bits available at 0x3BD, but they are not used in the example programs and we will not delve into them in this book.

The PC's parallel printer port has several shortcomings when used as a parallel port for digital control applications. It has relatively few input points and there is only one interrupt trigger that cannot be set up to generate an interrupt on any condition other than a falling edge. For certain pulse detection applications, such as detecting pulse frequency modulated signals, extra circuitry may be required to invert the pulse before feeding it to pin 10 if we want to trigger on the rising edge of the pulse. These caveats aside, the capabilities of the parallel printer port are quite adequate for generating PWM signals, detecting quadrature pulses, and pulse frequency-modulated signals.

---

[4]All addresses are hexadecimal and are expressed using the C language's hexadecimal notation.

[5]These are pin numbers for the PC's printer port DB25 connector.

3.12 PULSE WIDTH MODULATION

This program module, *pwm.c*, provides pulse-width modulation services to control programs. Pulses are sent out through the parallel printer port using an on-off bit and a direction bit. The *time2.c* module is used for timing, and it is assumed that the time module has been initialized when *pwm_init()* is called. Two basic services are provided to calling programs: *setpfreq()* sets the pulse frequency, and *setdcycle()* sets the duty cycle. The sign of the duty cycle argument determines the direction.

3.12.1 INITIALIZATION

The initialization routine, *pwm_init()*, accepts a timer number argument which specifies which timer has been allocated to it. Turning the output on and off is performed by the *pulse()* routine, which is installed as a timeout service routine. Since *pulse()* need not be accessed directly outside of this module, it is declared as static, i.e., private to this module only. As a safety precaution, the duty cycle is set to zero and the pulse output bit is turned off.

3.12.2 PULSE-WIDTH MODULATION

Pulse-width control is achieved using the algorithm described in Chapter 3, Fig. 3.2. The period defined by the pulse frequency is divided into an on-time and an off-time based on the desired duty cycle. For example, a pulse frequency of 10 Hz and a duty cycle of 70% will result in an on-time of 70 milliseconds and an off-time of 30 milliseconds. Note that *pulse()* is only invoked when the timer times out at the end of a pulse-on period or pulse-off period. For example, if *pulse()* is invoked at the end of a pulse-off period (as determined by the variable state*), it sets the timer to the pulse-on interval. Pulse()* will not be called again until the timer times out at the end of the time-on period. Direction is handled by *or*'ing the output byte with the direction bit-mask before sending it to the parallel port.

3.12.3 PULSE FREQUENCY

The maximum pulse actuation frequency is constrained mainly by the maximum timer interrupt frequency that the system can reliably handle; this in turn depends on the CPU speed and interrupt latency.[6] These performance issues require detailed knowledge of the underlying hardware, and are best handled outside of this module. Consequently, *setpfreq()* cannot check if the desired pulse frequency is possible without knowing the timer interrupt frequency; it must assume that this detail has been taken care of by the rest of the program.

---

[6]The interrupt latency is the delay between the time when a device (such as the timer) generates an interrupt request and the time when the interrupt service routine starts to execute.

The *ontime* and *offtime* variables are accessed asynchronously by *pulse()*, hence they must be updated inside a critical section, which in this example is implemented by disabling interrupts. To minimize the time spent inside the critical section, the calculations are performed outside of the critical section, and results are stored in temporary local variables for later assignment to *ontime* and *offtime* inside the critical section. The functions *enable()* and *disable()* return the interrupt state prior to the function call. This information is used to restore the proper interrupt state when leaving a critical section. As a rule, background routines should not arbitrarily enable interrupts since they can be called by routines that need interrupts to be disabled because they are in their own critical section. This is an important point to keep in mind if you implement critical sections by disabling interrupts.

3.12.4 DUTY CYCLE

Duty cycle is set by calling *setdcycle()* with the duty cycle as a value between -1.0 (100% in the reverse direction) and 1.0 (100% in the forward direction). As before, the on and off time intervals are calculated outside a critical section and then assigned to *ontime* and *offtime* inside a critical section. The direction bit-mask is also set here.

3.13 PULSE-FREQUENCY MODULATION

A cheap and simple method of measuring motor speed is to attach to the motor a device that generates pulses as the motor rotates. This can be as simple as a slotted disk that interrupts a beam of light. The motor speed can be inferred from the frequency of the pulses thus generated.

To detect the pulses using an IBM-PC, the pulses (suitably buffered and electrically isolated) are fed into the parallel printer port (pins 10 and 1) which is set up to generate an interrupt whenever a high-to-low transition occurs on pin 10.

The sample program module, *pfm0.c,* implements the basic algorithm described in Chapter 3, which determines the velocity from the time it takes to detect a specified number[7] of consecutive pulses. This method's usefulness is limited to a fairly narrow pulse frequency range. The second sample program module, *pfm1.c,* extends the pulse frequency range it can work with by using an adaptive pulse group sizing technique. These two modules have a lot of code in common; we shall first describe *pfm0.c* and then point out where *pfm1.c* differs from it. These two modules require the *xignal* package and the *time.c* software timer module.

---

[7]This number is termed the pulse group size.

3.13.1 INITIALIZATION

In order to make this module more flexible, the displacement-per-pulse scaling factor is passed to *pfm_init()*. This pulse scaling factor is then multiplied by 1000 because the soft timer returns time in milliseconds, and premultiplying by 1000 allows faster conversion of the pulse interval to velocity. The function *NewITimer()* returns a number specifying an interval timer that is now allocated for use by this module.

Note that the interval timer must be initialized before the parallel port interrupts are enabled; otherwise, the initial timer readings will be invalid and the calculated velocity will consequently be incorrect until there are sufficient incoming pulses to make up a group and cause the interval timer to be reset. This is especially important for systems with low pulse rates and initial acceleration times much greater than the controller's velocity sampling rate.

3.13.2 PULSE INPUT

The parallel port interrupt service routine, *pulse()*, assumes that the hardware is set up such that bit 0 (as defined by INMASK) will read high whenever a pulse triggers the interrupt. It checks if a pulse is actually present at bit 0 as a condition for processing it. This serves as insurance against false triggering, which is an important design consideration when using edge-triggered interrupts in the electrically noisy environment of an electric motor. If it has collected enough pulses to make up a group, the time interval to collect the group is recorded in the variable *period* and the interval is reset to zero. The pulse count is also reset and *pflag* is set to indicate that a complete pulse group has been collected and timed.

3.13.3 CALCULATING VELOCITY

With a complete pulse group, the velocity is easily calculated from the displacement represented by the number of pulses in a group and the time over which the pulses were collected. If there are insufficient pulses to make up a group, the velocity is determined from the current pulse count and the interval so far.

Note that *pflag*, the current pulse count, *pcount*, and the time, *period*, must be accessed within a critical section. The reason is quite obvious: these variables are used to calculate the speed and we do not want them to be changed in the middle of the calculations. To minimize the period over which interrupts are disabled, these variables are copied to temporary local variables and the calculations are done with the copies outside of the critical section.

The algorithm implemented by *pfm0.c* is simple and works well if the velocity (and pulse frequency) do not vary much from the operating point. The choice of the group size must take into account the pulse frequency and the resolution of the interval timer. At high pulse frequencies, it takes less time to form a group, and the accuracy of the velocity reading is determined by the resolution of the timer. At low pulse frequencies, accuracy is determined by the interval between pulses compared to the frequency that *pfm_getv()* is called. The velocity algorithm, by using the current pulse count and interval, is able to adapt more effectively to low pulse frequencies than high pulse frequencies. However, there will be a noticeable variation in the velocity readings at low pulse frequencies.

3.13.4 Adaptive Group Size

Given the importance of a good match between the group size and pulse frequency, we can have the main control algorithm associate an "ideal" group size with different velocity ranges and call on *pfm_group()* to set the group size. The advantage of this method is that the control program has access to more information such as the sampling rate and the timer resolution. This demands a closer coupling between the control algorithm and the actual velocity interface, trading better performance against reduced flexibility in how the interface is implemented. Another solution, demonstrated in *pfm1.c*, is to have the PFM module change the group size in response to changes in pulse frequency. This is carried out in *pfm_getv()*, which is where *pfm1.c* differs from *pfm0.c*.

At high pulse rates, velocity accuracy is limited by timer resolution. Therefore, if the time it takes to collect enough pulses to form a group is less than a certain value, then pulses are deemed to be arriving too quickly. The response is to double the group size. This is done by left shifting the *group* variable by 1 bit:

```
group <<= 1;
```

This is followed by an overflow check that works like this: if a non-zero bit pattern representing a positive integer is left-shifted far enough, the most significant bit in the integer will be set, causing the integer to be interpreted as a negative number. An overflow is indicated if this happens.

The time criteria for increasing the group size should ideally be based on the desired velocity accuracy and timer resolution. For example, given a velocity accuracy of 10% and a timer resolution of 5 milliseconds, the group interval must not be less than 50 milliseconds.[8] This minimum group interval is defined by MINPERIOD.

At low pulse rates, the group size is halved until the group interval is less than some limit defined by MAXPERIOD or the group size becomes one, whichever is reached first. This MAXPERIOD is determined by the velocity sampling rate since, ideally, there should be enough new pulses to form a group within the velocity sampling period. At very low pulse rates when the group size becomes unity, velocity is determined using the interval between individual pulses.

[8] This only tells us the accuracy of the average velocity over the period when the pulses forming the group are counted.

Readers may wonder why the group size is halved or doubled instead of being adjusted proportionately. The reason is simple: it is much faster to perform a shift than a multiplication and/or division operation. Since the group size is adjusted within a global critical section that prevents *pulse()* from running, speed is important. Readers may also find that this method works just as well, if not better, than using a proportional size adjustment algorithm.

3.14 QUADRATURE DECODING

In many motion control applications, quadrature signals are decoded by special circuits to give position information. However, there will be cost-sensitive applications where performance requirements allows quadrature decoding to be performed in software. TTL level quadrature signals can be fed into the IBM-PC's parallel printer port, which is set up to generate an interrupt on a high-to-low transition at pin 10. A simple circuit for doing so is shown in Fig. 3.11.

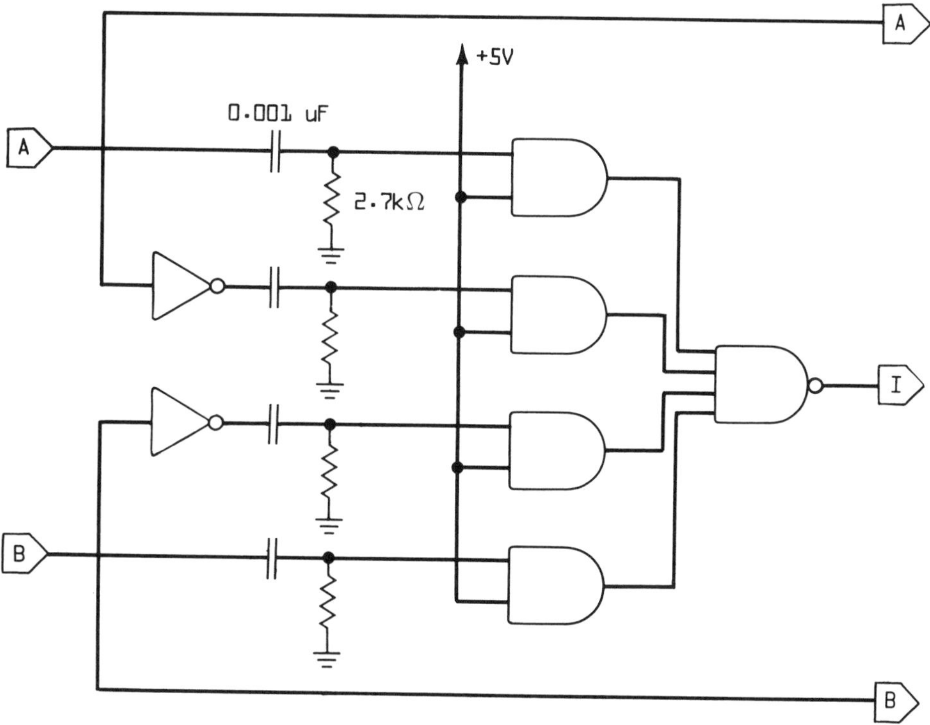

Figure 3.11

The sample program module *quad0.c* implements the state transition diagram (see Fig. 3.10) in the routine named *pulse()*, which is installed as the parallel port interrupt service routine. Position information is calculated in *quad_getp()*, by multiplying the pulse count with a scaling factor. In *quad1.c*, velocity is obtained from the difference in pulse count and the sampling interval, with modifications for direction reversal. Let us examine *quad0.c* first.

3.14.1 INITIALIZATION

The initialization routine, *quad_init()*, requires the pulse-to-displacement scaling factor as an argument. The current state of the parallel port input points corresponding to the two quadrature channels are recorded. The four possible input states are represented in two state variables, *curstate* and *oldstate*, using the parallel port input bit pattern after masking out all bits other than the two quadrature channel bits.

C Programming Note: An assignment statement has a value, the assigned value, associated with it. In C, one can assign the result of an assignment statement to another variable, keeping in mind that the order of evaluation is from right to left. This is demonstrated in *quad_init()* by the statement:

```
curstate = oldstate = in(INPORT) & PHASEMASK;
```

which assigns to *curstate* the same value that is assigned to *oldstate*.

3.14.2 POSITION DECODING

Position decoding is done in the interrupt service routine using a state table. When *pulse()* is invoked, the previous state is saved in *oldstate* and the current state is read from the port into *curstate*. Using the quadrature bits to represent state obviates the need to further translate the input into a state value. There are only two "legal" transitions from each state; any illegal transition is flagged as an error and duly reported the next time a position reading is requested through the *quad_getp()* routine. The two legal transitions correspond to forward and reverse motion, and the pulse count is incremented or decremented accordingly.

There are many ways to implement a state table. In this example, a *switch* statement is used because it clearly illustrates the structure of this simple state table. Some compilers can generate very efficient code for *switch* statements by using an indexing scheme instead of sequential comparisons. Sometimes, knowing a little more about the language implementation helps to code an algorithm in a way that allows the compiler to optimize for speed.

Position information in the desired units is returned by *quad_getp()*. Note that a copy of *pcount* is used in the unit conversion calculations rather than *pcount* itself since *pcount* may be changed in the middle of the calculations by the interrupt service routine. Although we cannot recommend it, it is possible to dispense with forming a critical section in this case when making a copy of *pcount* because *pcount* is a 16-bit integer, and a *mov* operation on a 16-bit entity is not interruptible on the Intel 808x family of processors. In general, this is not a safe assumption to make,[9] and one should always follow good asynchronous programming practice and access such variables inside a critical section.

3.14.3 CALCULATING VELOCITY

Getting velocity information in addition to position is complicated by direction reversals. In *quad1.c*, the parallel port interrupt service routine calls the functions *incp()* and *decp()* to increment and decrement the pulse count and to update the various flags and indicators. Let us look at *incp()*. It first increments the pulse count, *pcount*. Since we have defined an increasing pulse count as moving in the forward direction, if the *direction* flag indicates that we were previously moving in the reverse direction, we can infer that a direction reversal has occurred. The *direction* flag is updated to reflect the current direction, and the *revflag* is set to indicate a direction reversal. The current pulse count is saved in *rcount* to be used later in determing the velocity.

The velocity function, *quad_getv()*, assumes that it is called at a constant time interval corresponding to the velocity sampling rate, *tsamp*. This simplifying assumption obviates the need for an interval timer and reduces the execution time overhead. However, a soft interval timer can easily be added (see *pfm0.c*) should your application require it. Note that variables that may be asynchronously changed are copied into temporary variables; calculations are always performed with variables that remain unchanged until the calculation completes.

If a direction change has not occurred, the velocity is calculated from the difference between the current pulse count, the pulse count when *quad_getv()* was last called, and the velocity sampling interval:

$$velocity = (cur\_count - last\_count) * pscale / tsamp.$$

If the direction has changed, as indicated by *revflag*, the velocity is calculated thus:

$$velocity = (cur\_count - rev\_count) * pscale / tsamp;$$

where *rev_count* is a copy of the pulse count at the moment of direction change. Although the velocity calculated using this formula will be less than the actual velocity, it will give the correct sign (hence direction). We cannot use *last_count* if there has been a change in direction because *cur_count* may not have passed *last_count* yet, especially if the acceleration in the new direction is low.

---

[9] It assumes that *pcount* will remain an integer, that the compiler-generated code acts on 16-bit entities, that an integer is 16-bits, that the program will never be ported to a different CPU, and that the CPU documentation is correct.

3.15 MULTIPLE TIMERS IN SOFTWARE

Time.c is a general implementation of multiple count-down and interval timers in software. Readers are advised that *time.c* will be easier to understand after first reading through the code and description for the similar, but much simpler *time2.c*. This module is used in the *clotho* real-time kernel to synchronize task dispatching and scheduling; that is why it includes a *config.h* configuration file. The number of count-down timers is specified by MAXDTIMERS, and the number of interval count-up timers is specified by MAXITIMERS. Other declarations in *config.h* may be ignored for now.

Time.c differs from the earlier minimal implementation, *time2.c*, in several ways:

1. It supports interval timers, which are count-up timers, and a *clock* variable, which keeps track of the number of hardware timer interrupts since the timer interrupt is first enabled.
2. Any number of timers can be specified at compile time through MAXDTIMERS and MAXITIMERS in the *config.h* file. The maximum number of timers is constrained only by performance.
3. The count-down timers are prioritized. If two or more timers time out at the same time, only the timeout service routine with the highest priority timer will be executed; the rest will have to wait until until the current timeout service routine completes. This differs from *time2.c*, where the second timeout service routine can interrupt the execution of the first timeout service routine.
4. The flag arrays, *tm_used[]* and *tm_lock[]*, are designed to support timer management and task scheduling. A count-down timer value is only decremented if the timer is "in use" and not "locked." The lock feature is designed to allow a task scheduler to freeze time for background tasks when high-priority foreground tasks are executing. In a multi-tasking environment, timers are resources that can be allocated and deallocated, and the *tm_used* flag indicates if the timer is currently allocated to a task.
5. Timers must be allocated before they can be used.

3.15.1 INITIALIZATION

The initialization routine, *InitTime()*, accepts an argument telling the module the number of milliseconds per timer interrupt. This version differs from *time2.c* in that the timer interrupt service routine, *chronos()*, is not installed by the initialization routine. The reason lies in the fact that *time.c* is designed as part of a multitasking real-time kernel where a timer interrupt may cause the current task to be suspended and another task to be dispatched. This requires special "housekeeping" at each timer interrupt that can only be performed by the kernel. Hence, installation of *chronos()* as the timer interrupt service routine must be performed by the kernel outside of the timer module. In applications that do not require the *clotho* kernel, the timer interrupt service routine will have to be installed during the program initialization phase, perhaps using *xignal*.

3.15.2 TIMER ALLOCATION

A timer must be allocated before it can be used. This service is performed by *NewDTimer()* for count-down timers and by *NewITimer()* for interval timers. Both functions return a timer number that must be used to specify which timer is being accessed. *NewDTimer()* expects to be passed a pointer to the timeout service routine, a pointer to the arguments (if any), and a timer priority. The base type of both pointers is *void*, which is interpreted as a generic pointer type for the arguments and a pointer to a function-that-does-not-return-a-value[10] for the timeout service routine. The convention for priority is that the higher the priority, the larger the priority number.

If there is no timeout service routine to be associated with the timer, NULL pointers of the appropriate type can be specified; for example:

```
NewDTimer((void (*)())NULL, (void *)NULL, priority);
```

Note the use of casts to associate a *type* with the NULL symbol: *(void(*)())* casts to a pointer to a function that does not return a value, and *(void*)* casts to a generic pointer. Although casts are not absolutely necessary in this case, it is still good practice to use it since it tells someone reading the code that the first argument is a function pointer and the second argument is a generic pointer. It also allows the compiler to perform a more rigorous syntax check and help prevent subtle errors due to data size mismatches, especially when changing memory models on the 808x family of processors.

Why do timers have to be allocated? When developing large programs, it is often difficult to keep track of resource usage, such as which timers are allocated to which modules. This problem is alleviated by requiring a function call that returns the number of a free timer that is now allocated to the calling module, greatly reducing the possibility of two modules using the same timer for different purposes at the same time.

3.15.3 CHRONOS

Timer interrupts are normally intercepted by a low-level interrupt service routine that saves the CPU registers and performs other housekeeping functions before calling *chronos()*. Since interrupts may have been enabled by the low-level interrupt service routine, *chronos()* must first disable interrupts before it can safely manipulate its own data. This is especially important since *chronos()* can be

[10]This is termed a *procedure* in Pascal, or a *subroutine* in Fortran.

invoked in a re-entrant manner. The *clock* variable and all interval timers, *tm_itime[]*, are incremented regardless of whether or not they are allocated; given the small number of interval timers, it is faster to do so than to incur the overhead of first checking if the timer is allocated. In contrast, count-down timers, *tm_dtime[]*, are only decremented if they are allocated (indicated by *tm_used[]*) and if the timer count is not locked (indicated by *tm_lock[]*). This will minimize the number of timers that have to be checked later for installed timeout service routines. Note that the timer arrays are incremented or decremented indirectly by means of a pointer, *p* . For example, *++(*p)* increments the value of the variable pointed to by *p* . With most compilers, this method is faster than using an explicit array reference such as *tm_dtime[i]* since a pointer can simply be incremented to point at the next timer (an addition operation) while the address of an array element has to be calculated each time (a multiplication plus an addition). Some of the more advanced optimizing compilers will actually convert array references inside a loop into the equivalent pointer operations. However, one cannot depend on that.

The next part of *chronos()* is only active if the symbol FOREGROUND is defined as a non-zero value when the module was compiled. This enables simple applications that do not require the foreground processing capabilities of timeout service routines to recover the code space for foreground processing and reduce the execution time overhead to service the timer interrupt. Before a timeout service routine can be executed, it must satisfy several conditions. First, the timer must have timed out (obviously!). Second, if two or more timers have timed out, only the timeout routine with the highest priority will be considered. Third, the timeout routine must have an equal or higher priority than any timeout service routine currently in service. Fourth, a timeout service routine can only be invoked once per timeout. This is to prevent a high priority timed out routine from being executed at each timer interrupt and starving the other timeout routines of CPU time.

A timeout condition is indicated if the timer's count in *tm_dtime[]* is zero or negative. The routines currently in service are identified by the *tm_isf[]* flag array, and *maxpri* is set to the highest priority of all the in-service routines. The next step is to identify a timeout service routine of a newly timed out timer that satisfies the conditions. The code may look as if it will require a significant amount of computation, but in reality, the overhead is minimal since in C, boolean expressions are evaluated from left to right, and the first "untrue" condition will terminate further evaluation of *&&* expressions. The *index* variable is set to the timer index for the new service routine (if such a routine is found).

Before the timeout service routine executes, the in-service flag may be set to indicate that the routine is currently in-service. Also, interrupts may be enabled and a Specific End-Of-Interrupt (EOI) sent to the 8259 interrupt controller. These are options selected at compile time by defining the symbols ISF and AUTO_EOI to non-zero. Normally, both options will be turned on. These features are implemented as options to allow for flexibility in special applications where the timeout service routine may directly manipulate the 8259 interrupt controller, and/or where the timeout service routines are re-entrant. Since *chronos()* is re-entrant, it may be used in programs where the timeout service routine never returns. An example of this is a foreground task scheduler/dispatcher of a multi-tasking system. The scheduler will want to control exactly when it gives up control to dispatch a task; thus, we should not send EOIs or enable interrupts in *chronos()*, but leave that to the scheduler/dispatcher to do so, perhaps via *CisDTimer()*.

In the current design, waiting timeout routines can only be executed when a hardware timer interrupt occurs; thus, if the current timeout routine completes, the next timeout routine must wait until the next timer interrupt before it can run. It is relatively easy to modify *chronos()* such that waiting timeout routines are executed as soon as the current one finishes. This is left as an exercise, but please keep in mind that any such modifications must be re-entrant.

3.15.4 Multi-tasking Using Only Chronos

The *time.c* module, by providing for asynchronous prioritized timeout service routines, allows a simple time-based multi-tasking control system to be constructed. Each independent control loop can be implemented as a timeout service routine attached to a timer set to the proper sampling rate. The only caveat is that the overhead exacted by priority resolution and other features may be a significant portion of the control loop sampling time. On a 4.77 MHz IBM-PC using *xignal* for low-level interrupt processing, the effective timer interrupt latency (the time between a hardware timeout and the execution of a soft timer timeout service routine) is just under 3 milliseconds with 4 count-down timers and 2 interval timers. This figure will vary depending on the number of software timers and how many of them have timed out at the same time.

3.16 CASCADE CONTROL

Cascade0.c is an implementation of Fig. 3.7 and 3.8. There are two control loops, an inner velocity loop and an outer position loop; position is controlled by controlling velocity. The setpoint of the inner velocity loop is the control output of the outer position loop. This module is similar in arrangement to *cntrl1.c* described in the example program section of Chapter 2. This example is also interesting in that it uses the quadrature module, *quad1.c*, for position and velocity feedback, and the PWM module, *pwm.c*, to generate control output. The duty cycle is the output value expressed as a fraction of the maximum output in the appropriate direction. Notice how the functions *getv()* and *getp()* hide the details of position and velocity measurements from the main control loop.

```
/************************************************************************

FILE
    panic.c  -  abort execution

ROUTINES
    panic  -  print error message and die

REMARKS
    When using interrupts on the IBM PC, one should restore interrupts
    to their default states before performing an error exit.

    This module assumes that the xignal package was used for interrupts
    and uses a xignal() call to restore all affected interrupts before
    terminating.

LAST UPDATE
    25 January 1988
        calls setalarm() also

    Copyright(c) 1985-1988  D.M. Auslander and C.H. Tham

************************************************************************/

#include "envir.h"
#include "xignal.h"
#include "alarm.h"


void panic(mesg)
char *mesg;
{

    xignal(XIGALL, XIG_IGN);                /* ignore all signals */

    printf("\nABORT - %s\n\n\07", mesg);          /* print error message */

    xignal(XIGALL, XIG_DFL);                /* restore defaults */

    setalarm(-1.0);                         /* restore clock */

}

/************************************************************************

FILE
    time2.h  declarations for time2.c

LAST UPDATE
    25 January 1988

************************************************************************/

#ifdef ANSI

void    chronos(void);
void    SetTsr(int, void(*)(), void *);
void    SetDTimer(int, long);
long    ReadDTimer(int);
int     TimeUp(int);
void    InitTime(long);

#else

void    chronos();
void    SetTsr();
void    SetDTimer();
long    ReadDTimer();
int     TimeUp();
void    InitTime();

#endif
/************************************************************************

FILE
    time2.c  -  implements 2 timers clocked off IBM PC's single timer

ROUTINES
    chronos     -  timer interrupt service routine
    SetDTimer   -  set countdown timer
    ReadDTimer  -  read countdown timer
    TimeUp      -  time up yet?
    InitTime    -  initialize this module

REMARKS
    This is a simple implementation of two software timers which works
    much like hardware timers.  This module is needed since the IBM PC
    has only one timer and we need two timers to implement PI control
    with pulse width modulation.

    The xignal package and alarm.c are used to setup the timer interrupt.

    This module is a precursor to the full-blown general implementation
    of multiple timers in software.  If you want to use the general
    multiple software timer implementation, you should examine this
    module first as it is much easier to understand than the general
    implementation.

    Each timer is associated with an "interrupt" service routine which
    is executed whenever the associated timer/counter times out.

    Because of the speed limitations of the IBM PC, timer resolution
```

```
    is set at 1 millisecond.  Hence, SetDTimer() time argument is in
    milliseconds.  However, there is no reason why real clock ticks
    cannot be used instead of milliseconds.

    Since this is a special implementation to satisfy the requirements
    of pulse width modulation, each soft-timer is implemented with a
    count variable instead of using an array of counters as in the
    general implementation.  However, the implementation is such that
    the module is independent of any specific applications - you can use
    this module for any applications on the IBM PC that requires just
    two timers.  This also incurs less overheads than the general
    implementation.

    Because this program replaces interrupt vectors used by DOS/BIOS,
    we cannot simply exit when an error is encountered, but must restore
    the DOS/BIOS interrupts to their default state first.  This is done
    in the panic() function (in file error.c).

    You will need to link this module with alarm.obj and xignal.lib

LAST UPDATE
    25 January 1988
        use void types and modify chronos()

    Copyright(c) 1985-1988  D.M. Auslander and C.H. Tham

*************************************************************************/

/************************************************************************
                            I M P O R T S
*************************************************************************/

#include <stdio.h>

#include "envir.h"          /* environment definitions */
#include "8259.h"           /* 8259 programming declarations */
#include "xignal.h"         /* declarations for xignal package */
#include "alarm.h"          /* declarations for alarm.c */


/************************************************************************
                    P R I V A T E    D A T A
*************************************************************************/

static long mstick;                     /* milliseconds per 'tick' */
static long halftick;                   /* half of mstick */

static long time0, time1;               /* time values for both timers */
static void (*isr0)(), (*isr1)();       /* pointers to timeout routines */
static void *argp0, *argp1;             /* routine argument pointers */
static int isf0, isf1;                  /* routine in-service flags */
static int flag0, flag1;                /* flags to indicate timeout */


/************************************************************************
                    E N T R Y    R O U T I N E S
*************************************************************************/

/*-----------------------------------------------------------------------
PROCEDURE
    chronos  -  timer interrupt service routine

SYNOPSIS
    void chronos() - called when hardware timer interrupt

REMARKS
    The software timer counters are decremented.  If any of the counts
    are zero or less, the associated "interrupt" service routine is
    executed provided the other conditions (timer has been set, there
    is an interrupt service routine declared and that routine is not
    currently in service) are satisfied.

    Note that no priority scheme is implemented.

    The user is responsible for ensuring that the timeout routines do
    not take too long to execute.  If another interrupt arrives and a
    timeout routine is still not finished, the other timeout routine
    (if installed) will be executed instead (if it is not similarly
    occupied, of course).  This means that the first timeout routine
    will miss the interrupt.

    The latest modification (Jan 88) only allows the timeout routine
    to execute once; a SetDTimer() call has to be made again before
    it will respond to another timer interrupt.  This is to prevent
    the routine from being called at every timer interrupt if the
    associated timer has timed out.  In a way, this is rather like
    edge-triggered interrupts that are reset by calling SetDTimer().

LAST UPDATE
    25 January 1988
        execute isr only once, must reset timer to execute again.
-----------------------------------------------------------------------*/

static void chronos()
{

    if (time0 > 0L)
        --time0;

    if (time1 > 0L)
        --time1;
```

```
    disable();              /* disables CPU's interrupt response */

    seoi(TMRVEC);           /* send Specific EOI to 8259 */

    /*----------------------------------------------------------------------
        If the timer has timed out, and there is a timeout routine
        associated with the timer and if the timeout routine is not
        currently executing, invoke the timeout routine, passing to
        it a pointer to possible arguments.
    ----------------------------------------------------------------------*/

    if ((time0 <= 0L) && (isr0 != (void(*)())NULL) && (isf0 == 0) && !flag0)
    {
        flag0 = 1;          /* timer has timed out */

        isf0 = 1;           /* routine in service */

        enable();           /* enable interrupts */

        (*isr0)(argp0);     /* execute service routine */

        disable();          /* disable interrupts */

        isf0 = 0;           /* routine done */
    }

    if ((time1 <= 0L) && (isr1 != (void(*)())NULL) && (isf1 == 0) && !flag1)
    {
        flag1 = 1;          /* timer has timed out */

        isf1 = 1;           /* routine in service */

        enable();           /* enable interrupts */

        (*isr1)(argp1);     /* execute service routine */

        disable();          /* disable interrupts */

        isf1 = 0;           /* routine done */
    }

    enable();               /* enable interrupts before exit */

}



    /*----------------------------------------------------------------------
PROCEDURE
    SetTsr  -  set timeout service routine and argument pointer

SYNOPSIS
    void SetTsr(timer, isf, argp)
    int timer
    void (*isf)(), *argp;

PARAMETERS
    timer  -  timer number (0 or 1)
    isf    -  pointer to timeout service routine
    argp   -  pointer to argument storage

LAST UPDATE
    25 January 1988
        clear flag0 and flag1
------------------------------------------------------------------------*/

void SetTsr(timer, isf, argp)
int timer;
void (*isf)(), *argp;
{
    int istat;      /* interrupt status */


    if (timer == 0)
    {
        istat = disable();

        isr0 = isf;
        isf0 = 0;
        argp0 = argp;
        flag0 = 0;

        if (istat)
            enable();
    }
    else if (timer == 1)
    {
        istat = disable();

        isr1 = isf;
        isf1 = 0;
        argp1 = argp;
        flag1 = 0;

        if (istat)
            enable();
    }
    else
    {
        fputs("bad timer number in SetTsr", stderr);
    }
```

```
}


/*-----------------------------------------------------------------------
PROCEDURE
    SETDTIMER  -  set count down timer

SYNOPSIS
    void SetDTimer(timer, ms)
    int timer;
    long ms;

PARAMETERS
    timer  -  timer number (0 or 1)
    ms     -  time in milliseconds

REMARKS
    The halftick addition is used for rounding to the nearest tick.

    Because time0 and time1 are of type long (4 bytes on most 8088 C
    compilers), assignment will not be atomic; hence it has to be done
    inside a critical section.  Calculations are done outside the
    critical section to minimize the time interrupts have to be
    disabled.

    The timeout service routine disable flag is only cleared if the
    new setting is greater than 0.

LAST UPDATE
    25 January 1988
        assignment inside critical section
-----------------------------------------------------------------------*/

void SetDTimer(timer, ms)
int timer;
long ms;
{
    int istat;      /* interrupt status */
    long tmp;       /* temporary for tick count */
    int flag;       /* flag status */


    tmp = (ms + halftick) / mstick;
    flag = (ms > 0L) ? 0 : 1;

    switch (timer)
    {
        case 0:

            istat = disable();

            time0 = tmp;
            flag0 = flag;

            if (istat)
                enable();

            break;

        case 1:

            istat = disable();

            time1 = tmp;
            flag1 = flag;

            if (istat)
                enable();

            break;

        default:

            fputs("bad timer number in SetDTimer", stderr);
    }

}


/*-----------------------------------------------------------------------
FUNCTION
    READDTIMER  -  read time remaining

SYNOPSIS
    long ReadDTimer(timer)
    int timer;

PARAMETER
    timer  -  timer select (0 or 1)

RETURNS
    time remaining in milliseconds, resolution is mstick.

LAST UPDATE
    25 January 1988
        assignment to variable t inside critical section
-----------------------------------------------------------------------*/

long ReadDTimer(timer)
int timer;
{
```

```
    int istat;          /* interrupt status */
    long t;             /* timer value */


    switch(timer)
    {
        case 0:

            istat = disable();

            t = time0;

            if (istat)
                enable();

            break;

        case 1:

            istat = disable();

            t = time0;

            if (istat)
                enable();

            break;

        default:
            fputs("bad timer number in ReadDTimer", stderr);
    }

    return(t * mstick);
}



/*----------------------------------------------------------------------
FUNCTION
    TIMEUP  -  has timer run out?

SYNOPSIS
    int TimeUp(timer)
    int timer;

PARAMETER
    timer  -  timer select (0 or 1)

RETURNS
    1 if true, 0 otherwise

LAST UPDATE
    22 April 1985
----------------------------------------------------------------------*/

int TimeUp(timer)
{
    int flag;           /* TimeUp flag */


    switch (timer)
    {
        case 0:
            flag = flag0;
            break;
        case 1:
            flag = flag1;
            break;
        default:
            flag = 1;
            fputs("bad timer number in TimeUp", stderr);
    }

    return(flag);
}


/***********************************************************************
            I N I T I A L I Z A T I O N   R O U T I N E S
***********************************************************************/

/*----------------------------------------------------------------------
PROCEDURE
    INITTIME  -  initialize this module

SYNOPSIS
    InitTime(ms)
    long ms;

PARAMETER
    ms  -  milliseconds per tick of driving hardware timer

LAST UPDATE
    25 January 1988
        also setup timer hardware and interrupts
----------------------------------------------------------------------*/

void InitTime(ms)
long ms;
{
```

```
    mstick = ms;
    halftick = mstick / 2L;      /* for rounding purposes */

    time0 = time1 = 0;
    isf0  = isf1  = 0;
    isr0  = isr1  = (void (*)())NULL;
    argp0 = argp1 = (void *)NULL;
    flag0 = flag1 = 1;

    xignal(XIGTMR, chronos);     /* install chronos() as timer isr */

}
/*********************************************************************

FILE
    pwm.h  -  declarations for pwm.c module

LAST UPDATE
    25 January 1988

*********************************************************************/


#ifdef ANSI

void    setpfreq(double);
void    setdcycle(double);
void    pwm_init(int);

#else

void    setpfreq();
void    setdcycle();
void    pwm_init();

#endif
/*********************************************************************

FILE
    pwm.c  -  Pulse Width Modulation using timer and parallel port

ENTRY ROUTINES
    pulse      -  interrupt service routine
    setpfreq   -  set pulse frequency
    setdcycle  -  set duty cycle

INITIALIZATION ROUTINE
    pwm_init   -  initialize for pwm

REMARKS
    This module uses the IBM-PC's parallel printer port to send out
    pulse width modulated motor control pulses.  One timer is needed
    to time the pulses.  Since the overall control program probably
    needs a timer also, it must tell the initialization routine
    which timer this module can use.  The time2.c module is assumed.

    The maximum pulse frequency is limited by the timer resolution
    and execution speed.

LAST UPDATE
    26 January 1988

    Copyright(c) 1984-1988, D.M.Auslander and C.H. Tham

*********************************************************************/

/*********************************************************************
                             I M P O R T S
*********************************************************************/

#include <stdio.h>

#include "envir.h"           /* environment definitions */
#include "inout.h"           /* in() and out() mapping */
#include "time2.h"           /* time2.c module declarations */

#include "pwm.h"             /* exported declarations */

#ifdef ANSI
extern int enable(void);
extern int disable(void);
#else
extern int enable();
extern int disable();
#endif


/*********************************************************************
          P R I V A T E   D A T A   V A R I A B L E S
*********************************************************************/

#define OUTPORT     0x3BC   /* parallel port address */
#define PULSEON     0x01    /* pulse on output byte */
#define PULSEOFF    0x00    /* pulse off output byte */
#define FORWARD     0x10    /* direction bit OR mask for forward */
#define REVERSE     0x00    /* direction bit OR mask for reverse */

static int ptimer;          /* timer number to use with this module */
static long period;         /* cycle period in milliseconds */
static long ontime;         /* on period in milliseconds */
static long offtime;        /* off period in milliseconds */
static int state;           /* current output state, 0 - off, 1 - on */
```

```
static int direction;       /* direction, FORWARD or REVERSE */
static double dcycle;       /* PWM duty cycle */


/***********************************************************************
                    E N T R Y    R O U T I N E S
 ***********************************************************************/

/*-----------------------------------------------------------------------
PROCEDURE
    SETPFREQ  -  set pulse frequency in hertz

SYNOPSIS
    void setpfreq(f)
    double f;

PARAMETER
    f  -  pulse frequency

REMARKS
    Adjust ontime and offtime to new cycle period.  Since they are
    accessed asynchronously by pulse(), they must be modifed with
    interrupts disabled.  To minimize the interval with interrupts
    disabled, the calculations are stored in temporary variables,
    only assignment is performed with interrupts disabled.

LAST UPDATE
    25 January 1988
-----------------------------------------------------------------------*/

void setpfreq(f)
double f;
{
    int istat;              /* interrupt status */
    long on, off;           /* temporary for ontime and offtime */


    period = (long)(1000.0 / f  +  0.5);       /* cycle time in ms */

    on = (long)(dcycle * period  +  0.5);
    off = period - ontime;

    istat = disable();      /* begin critical section */

    ontime = on;
    offtime = off;

    if (istat)              /* end critical section */
        enable();

}
```

```
/*-----------------------------------------------------------------------
PROCEDURE
    SETDCYCLE  -  set duty cycle

SYNOPSIS
    void setdcycle(dc)
    double dc;

PARAMETER
    dc  -  duty cycle, between 0.0 and 1.0

REMARKS
    Adjust ontime and offtime to new duty cycle.  Since they are
    accessed asynchronously by pulse(), they must be modifed with
    interrupts disabled.

    To minimize the time where interrupts are disabled, the new on
    and off times are calculated and stored in temporary variables;
    only the assignment to ontime and offtime takes place in the
    critical section.

LAST UPDATE
    25 January 1988
-----------------------------------------------------------------------*/

void setdcycle(dc)
double dc;
{
    long on, off;       /* temporary copies of ontime and offtime */
    int istat;          /* interrupt status */


    if ((dc >= -1.0) && (dc <= 1.0))    /* range check */
    {
        if (dc < 0.0)
        {
            direction = REVERSE;        /* set direction mask */
            dcycle = -dc;               /* record absolute duty cycle */
        }
        else
        {
            direction = FORWARD;
            dcycle = dc;
        }

        on = (long)(dcycle * period  +  0.5);
        off = period - on;

        istat = disable();

        ontime = on;
```

```
        offtime = off;

        if (istat)
            enable();
    }
    else
        fprintf(stderr, "setdcycle: invalid duty cycle %lf\n", dc);

}


/*********************************************************************
                P R I V A T E   R O U T I N E
*********************************************************************/

/*-----------------------------------------------------------------------
PROCEDURE
    PULSE  -  pulse control timeout routine

SYNOPSIS
    static void pulse(), called by timer service routine when timeout.

REMARKS
    The timer is reset as soon as possible to reduce timing offsets.

LAST UPDATE
    25 January 1988
-----------------------------------------------------------------------*/

static void pulse()
{

    if (state == PULSEOFF)                   /* is in pulse off state */
    {
        SetDTimer(ptimer, ontime);           /* set timer for on interval */

        out(OUTPORT, PULSEON | direction);   /* pulse on */

        state = PULSEON;                     /* record current state */
    }
    else
    {
        SetDTimer(ptimer, offtime);

        out(OUTPORT, PULSEOFF | direction);

        state = PULSEOFF;
    }

}
```

```
/*********************************************************************
           I N I T I A L I Z A T I O N   R O U T I N E
*********************************************************************/

/*-----------------------------------------------------------------------
PROCEDURE
    PWM_INIT  -  initialize and start PWM pulses

SYNOPSIS
    void pwm_init(timer)
    int timer;

PARAMETER
    timer  -  which timer to use

REMARKS
    Assumes timing is done using time2.c and install pulse() as the
    timeout routine for the specified timer.  Defaults initial duty
    cycle to 0.5 and pulse frequency to quarter MAXFREQ.

LAST UPDATE
    25 January 1988
-----------------------------------------------------------------------*/

void pwm_init(timer)
int timer;
{

    ptimer = timer;                /* record timer number */

    period = 1000L;                /* default 1 second */

    setdcycle(0.0);                /* direction is set in setdcycle() */

    out(OUTPORT, PULSEOFF);        /* make sure outputs are off */
    state = PULSEOFF;

    SetTsr(timer, pulse, (void *)NULL);

}
/*********************************************************************

FILE
    quad0.h  -  declarations for quad0.c

LAST UPDATE
    26 January 1988

*********************************************************************/

#ifdef ANSI
```

```
double quad_getp(void);

#else

double quad_getp();

#endif

/**********************************************************************

FILE
    quad0.c  -  quadrature position measurement routines

ENTRY ROUTINE
    quad_getp  -  get position

PRIVATE ROUTINE
    pulse  -  parallel port interrupt service routine

INITIALIZATION ROUTINE
    quad_init  -  initialize this module

REMARKS
    This module uses bits 0 and 1 of the IBM-PC parallel port for the
    2 quadrature channels.  The parallel port interrupt service routine
    is set up using the xignal package; hence you need to link with
    xignal.lib

LAST UPDATE
    26 January 1988

    Copyright(c) 1985-1988  D.M. Auslander and C.H. Tham

**********************************************************************/

/**********************************************************************
                              I M P O R T S
**********************************************************************/

#include "envir.h"

#include "inout.h"
#include "xignal.h"


/**********************************************************************
                         P R I V A T E    D A T A
**********************************************************************/

static int oldstate;          /* previous state of quadrature input */
static int curstate;          /* current quadrature state */
static int pcount;            /* position indicator */
static int error;             /* error flag, initialized to false */
static double pscale;         /* count to displacement scaling factor */

#define PHASEMASK    0x03     /* mask for bits 0 and 1 on parallel port */

#define STATE00      0x00     /* quadrature states */
#define STATE01      0x01
#define STATE10      0x02
#define STATE11      0x03

#define INPORT       0x3BE    /* parallel input port address */


/**********************************************************************
                         E N T R Y    R O U T I N E S
**********************************************************************/

/*-----------------------------------------------------------------------
FUNCTION
    QUAD_GETP  -  read position value

SYNOPSIS
    double quad_getp()

RETURNS
    incremental position in inches

LAST UPDATE
    26 January 1988
        change to double return type
-----------------------------------------------------------------------*/

double quad_getp()
{
    int istat;        /* interrupt status */
    int count;        /* copy of pcount */


    if (error)
    {
        printf("quadrature state transistion error\n");

        error = 0;                    /* reset error flag */
    }

    istat = disable();                /* begin critical section */

    count = pcount;

    if (istat)                        /* exit critical section */
```

```
        enable();

    return(count * pscale);
}


/*********************************************************************
                P R I V A T E   R O U T I N E
*********************************************************************/

/*--------------------------------------------------------------------
PROCEDURE
    PULSE  -  quadrature pulse input interrupt service routine

SYNOPSIS
    called by parallel port interrupt service routine

REMARKS
    implements figure 3.10 in main text

LAST UPDATE
    18 April 1985
--------------------------------------------------------------------*/

static void pulse()
{

    oldstate = curstate;                /* update state variables */

    curstate = in(INPORT) & PHASEMASK;  /* read quadrature signal */

    switch (oldstate)
    {
        case STATE00:

            if (curstate == STATE01)
                --pcount;
            else if (curstate == STATE10)
                ++pcount;
            else
                error = 1;

            break;

        case STATE01:

            if (curstate == STATE11)
                --pcount;
            else if (curstate == STATE00)
                ++pcount;
            else
                error = 1;

            break;

        case STATE11:

            if (curstate == STATE10)
                --pcount;
            else if (curstate == STATE01)
                ++pcount;
            else
                error = 1;

            break;

        case STATE10:

            if (curstate == STATE00)
                --pcount;
            else if (curstate == STATE11)
                ++pcount;
            else
                error = 1;
    }

}


/*********************************************************************
          I N I T I A L I Z A T I O N   R O U T I N E S
*********************************************************************/

/*--------------------------------------------------------------------
PROCEDURE
    QUAD_INIT  -  initialize

SYNOPSIS
    void quad_init(scale)
    double scale;

PARAMETERS
    scale  -  displacement per quadrature count

LAST UPDATE
    26 January 1988
        calling routine specifies scaling factor
--------------------------------------------------------------------*/

void quad_init(scale)
double scale;
```

```
{

    pscale = scale;

    pcount = 0;
    error = 0;

    curstate = oldstate = in(INPORT) & PHASEMASK;

    xignal(XIGPRN, pulse);  /* install pulse() as service routine */

}
/***********************************************************************

FILE
    quad1.h  -  declarations for quad1.c

LAST UPDATE
    26 January 1988

***********************************************************************/

#ifdef ANSI

double  quad_getp(void);
double  quad_getv(void);
void    quad_init(double, double);

#else

double  quad_getp();
double  quad_getv();
void    quad_init();

#endif

/***********************************************************************

FILE
    quad1.c  -  quadrature position and velocity measurement routines

ENTRY ROUTINE
    quad_getp  -  get position

PRIVATE ROUTINE
    pulse  -  parallel port interrupt service routine

INITIALIZATION ROUTINE
    quad_init  -  initialize this module

REMARKS
    This module extends quad0.c by measuring velocity as well as
    position using quadrature signals.

    For simplicity, this module assumes that quad_getv() will be
    called at fixed intervals corresponding to the sampling period.
    The velocity is then calculated by counting pulses over a sample
    interval.  Unless the velocity is very slow, calculating velocity
    at every quadrature state transistion may incur too much overhead.

    Note also that the pulse count variables are integers instead of
    long integers.  On an IBM-PC, ints are faster and access can be
    assumed to be atomic with most compilers.  However, there is a
    greater chance of overflow.  Whether to use ints or longs depends
    on the requirements of your application (and how paranoid you
    are about overflows).

    You may want to use an interval timer instead of assuming a
    fixed sampling interval.  See pfm0.c and time.c for an example
    of how a software interval timer in time.c may be used.

    This module requires the xignal package to set up the parallel
    port interrupt handler.

LAST UPDATE
    27 January 1988

    Copyright(c) 1985-1988  D.M. Auslander and C.H. Tham

***********************************************************************/

/***********************************************************************
                        I M P O R T S
***********************************************************************/

#include "envir.h"

#include "inout.h"
#include "xignal.h"


/***********************************************************************
            F O R W A R D    D E C L A R A T I O N S
***********************************************************************/

#ifdef ANSI

void incp(void);
void decp(void);

#else
```

```
void incp();
void decp();

#endif

/**********************************************************************
                     P R I V A T E     D A T A
**********************************************************************/

#define PHASEMASK   0x03    /* mask for bits 0 and 1 on parallel port */

#define STATE00     0x00    /* quadrature states */
#define STATE01     0x01
#define STATE10     0x02
#define STATE11     0x03

#define INPORT      0x3BE   /* parallel input port address */

#define FORWARD     1       /* forward direction flag value */
#define REVERSE     0       /* reverse direction flag value */

static int oldstate;     /* previous state of quadrature input */
static int curstate;     /* current quadrature state */
static int pcount;       /* current pulse count */
static int rcount;       /* reference count, for computing velocity */
static int error;        /* error flag, initialized to false */
static int revflag;      /* direction reversal flag */
static int direction;    /* direction flag */
static double pscale;    /* displacement per count */
static double tsamp;     /* sampling period */

/**********************************************************************
                   E N T R Y     R O U T I N E S
**********************************************************************/

/*-------------------------------------------------------------------------
FUNCTION
    QUAD_GETP  -  read position value (same as in quad0.c)

SYNOPSIS
    double quad_getp()

RETURNS
    incremental position in inches

LAST UPDATE
    26 January 1988
        change to double return type
-------------------------------------------------------------------------*/

double quad_getp()
{
    int istat;        /* interrupt status */
    int count;        /* copy of pcount */


    if (error)
    {
        printf("quadrature state transistion error0);

        error = 0;                      /* reset error flag */
    }

    istat = disable();                  /* begin critical section */

    count = pcount;

    if (istat)                          /* exit critical section */
        enable();

    return(count * pscale);
}


/*-------------------------------------------------------------------------
FUNCTION
    QUAD_GETV  -  derive velocity from quadrature pulses

SYNOPSIS
    double quad_getv()

RETURNS
    velocity in rev/sec

REMARKS
    For simplicity, we assume getv() is called at intervals of tsamp
    seconds.  However, you may wish to use an interval timer instead
    of making this assumption.

    The velocity is derived from the diffrence between the current
    pulse count and the pulse count when this routine is last called
    in the previous sampling instance.  If there is a change in
    direction between the current and last call (as indicated by the
    revflag), velocity is derived using the pulse count when the direction
    reversal takes place (rcount) instead of the count when this routine
    is last called (lcount).  This gives a reasonable estimate of the
    actual velocity.

    If you are using an interval timer instead of assuming fixed
    sampling time, substitute calls to read and reset the interval
```

```
    timer instead of using tsamp.

LAST UPDATE
    27 January 1988
        use rcount when direction changes.
----------------------------------------------------------------------*/

double quad_getv()
{
    static int last_count = 0;      /* pcount at last call */
    int cur_count;                  /* current value of pcount */
    int rev_count;                  /* copy of rcount */
    int istat;                      /* interrupt status */
    double velocity;                /* computed velocity */


    if (error)
    {
        printf("quadrature state transistion error\n");

        error = 0;              /* reset error flag */
    }

    /*----------------------------------------------------------------
        Copies of pcount and rcount are made with interrupts
        disabled to prevent their being asynchronously changed by
        pulse() during velocity computation.  This precaution
        may be omitted to reduce overheads if the resultant error
        in velocity is not significant.  Real time programming
        is full of such trade-offs.
    ----------------------------------------------------------------*/

    istat = disable();

    cur_count = pcount;
    rev_count = rcount;

    if (revflag)    /* a direction reversal has taken place */
    {
        revflag = 0;

        if (istat)      /* interrupts enabled after clearing revflag */
            enable();

        velocity = (cur_count - rev_count) * pscale / tsamp;
    }
    else
    {
        if (istat)
            enable();

        velocity = (cur_count - last_count) * pscale / tsamp;
    }

    last_count = cur_count;

    return(velocity);
}



/**********************************************************************
                P R I V A T E     R O U T I N E S
**********************************************************************/

/*--------------------------------------------------------------------
PROCEDURE
    PULSE  -  quadrature pulse input interrupt service routine

SYNOPSIS
    static void pulse(), called by parallel port interrupt service routine

REMARKS
    Basically the same as that in quad0.c, except that it calls
    procedures decp() and incp() to update the pulse count and
    set revflag if there is a change in direction.

LAST UPDATE
    26 January 1988
        use new void type
----------------------------------------------------------------------*/

static void pulse()
{

    oldstate = curstate;                /* update state variables */

    curstate = in(INPORT) & PHASEMASK;  /* read quadrature signal */

    switch (oldstate)
    {
        case STATE00:

            if (curstate == STATE01)
                decp();
            else if (curstate == STATE10)
                incp();
            else
                error = 1;

            break;
```

```
        case STATE01:

            if (curstate == STATE11)
                decp();
            else if (curstate == STATE00)
                incp();
            else
                error = 1;

            break;

        case STATE11:

            if (curstate == STATE10)
                decp();
            else if (curstate == STATE01)
                incp();
            else
                error = 1;

            break;

        case STATE10:

            if (curstate == STATE00)
                decp();
            else if (curstate == STATE11)
                incp();
            else
                error = 1;
    }

}


/*-------------------------------------------------------------------------
PROCEDURE
    INCP  -  increment pulse count

SYNOPSIS
    static void incp()

REMARKS
    Updates direction indicator and mark current pulse count

LAST UPDATE
    27 January 1988
        mark current pcount instead of using flag
-------------------------------------------------------------------------*/

static void incp()
{

    ++pcount;               /* increment pulse count */

    if (direction == REVERSE)   /* direction reversal is indicated */
    {
        direction = FORWARD;
        rcount = pcount;
        revflag = 1;
    }

}


/*-------------------------------------------------------------------------
PROCEDURE
    DECP  -  decrement pulse count

SYNOPSIS
    static void decp()

REMARKS
    Updates direction indicator and mark current pulse count

LAST UPDATE
    27 January 1988
        mark current pcount instead of using flag
-------------------------------------------------------------------------*/

static void decp()
{

    --pcount;               /* decrement pulse count */

    if (direction == FORWARD)   /* direction reversal is indicated */
    {
        direction = REVERSE;
        rcount = pcount;
        revflag = 1;
    }

}


/*************************************************************************
          I N I T I A L I Z A T I O N    R O U T I N E S
*************************************************************************/

/*-------------------------------------------------------------------------
```

```
PROCEDURE
    QUAD_INIT  -  initialize

SYNOPSIS
    void quad_init(scale, period)
    double scale, period;

PARAMETERS
    scale  -  displacement per quadrature count
    period -  sampling period

LAST UPDATE
    26 January 1988
        calling routine specifies scaling factor
-----------------------------------------------------------------------*/

void quad_init(scale, period)
double scale, period;
{

    pscale = scale;
    tsamp = period;

    pcount = 0;
    rcount = 0;
    error = 0;
    revflag = 0;
    direction = FORWARD;        /* arbitrary choice */

    curstate = oldstate = in(INPORT) & PHASEMASK;

    xignal(XIGPRN, pulse);  /* install pulse() as service routine */

}

/************************************************************************

FILE
    pfm0.h  -  declarations for pfm0.c and pfm1.c

LAST UPDATE
    26 January 1988

************************************************************************/

#ifdef ANSI

double  pfm_getv(void);
void    pfm_group(int);
void    pfm_init(int, double);

#else

double  pfm_getv();
void    pfm_group();
void    pfm_init();

#endif
/************************************************************************

FILE
    pfm0.c  -  simple unidirectional velocity measurement using
               Pulse Frequency Modulation

ENTRY ROUTINES
    pfm_getv   -  read velocity value
    pfm_group  -  set pulse group size

PRIVATE ROUTINE
    pulse      -  pulse interrupt service routine

INITIALIZATION ROUTINE
    pfm_init  -  initialize this module

REMARKS
    Velocity is calculated from the time interval it takes for a certain
    number of pulses to be detected.  If the pulse rate is such that not
    enough pulses have arrived to form a group when a velocity reading is
    desired, then the velocity is calculated from the current pulse count
    instead of the group count.

    This module requires the use of an interval timer to time the group
    interval.  Interval timers are implemented in software in the time.c
    module and are clocked off the single countdown timer available in the
    IBM PC.  The function ReadITimer() returns the interval value in
    milliseconds and the procedure SetITimer() resets the interval to 0.

    This module uses the xignal package and time.c to set up parallel
    port interrupts and pulse timing.  Thus, it must be linked with
    time.obj and xignal.lib

LAST UPDATE
    26 January 1988
        change names and eliminate getgroup()

    Copyright(c) 1985-1988  D.M. Auslander and C.H. Tham

************************************************************************/

/************************************************************************
                              I M P O R T S
************************************************************************/
```

```
#include "envir.h"          /* environment */

#include "inout.h"          /* in() and out() mapping */
#include "time.h"           /* timer module declarations */
#include "xignal.h"         /* xignal package declarations */


/**********************************************************************
                     P R I V A T E   D A T A
**********************************************************************/

#define INPORT  0x3BE       /* parallel input port address */
#define INMASK  0x01        /* mask for pulse bit */

static double pscale;           /* pulses per unit displacement */
static int itimer;              /* interval timer number */
static int pflag = 0;           /* a group has arrived */
static long period = 0L;        /* time period for last group */
static int pcount = 0;          /* pulse count */
static int group = 1;           /* number of pulses per group */


/**********************************************************************
                  E N T R Y   R O U T I N E S
**********************************************************************/

/*---------------------------------------------------------------------
FUNCTION
    PFM_GETV  -  return velocity reading

SYNOPSIS
    double pfm_getv()

RETURNS
    displacement per second

REMARKS
    If there are insufficient pulses to make up a group, the velocity
    is based on the current pulse count instead of the group number.

    Note that pflag (and pcount) is accessed with interrupts disabled.

    pscale is a conversion factor to give velocity in revs/sec or
    whatever unit is convenient.

LAST UPDATE
    26 January 1988
---------------------------------------------------------------------*/

double pfm_getv()
{
    double v;               /* temporary velocity value */
    long time;              /* time period - copy of global period */
    int count;              /* copy of pcount */
    int istat;              /* interrupt status */


    istat = disable();                      /* begin critical section */

    if (pflag)                              /* whole group collected */
    {
        pflag = 0;                          /* reset immediately */
        time = period;

        if (istat)                          /* exit critical section */
            enable();

        v = (group * pscale) / time;        /* calculate velocity */
    }
    else    /* not enough pulses for a group since last pfm_getv() */
    {
        count = pcount;
        time = ReadITimer(itimer);

        if (istat)                          /* exit critical section */
            enable();

        /* base velocity on current pulse count instead of group */

        v = (count * pscale) / time;
    }

    return(v);
}



/*---------------------------------------------------------------------
ROUTINES
    PFM_GROUP  -  set pulse group size

SYNOPSIS
    void pfm_group(size)
    int size;

PARAMETER
    size  -  number of pulses in a group

LAST UPDATE
    26 January 1988
        name change
---------------------------------------------------------------------*/
```

```
void pfm_group(size)
int size;
{
    int istat;       /* interrupt status */


    istat = disable();

    group = size;

    if (istat)
        enable();
}



/**********************************************************************
                  P R I V A T E   R O U T I N E
**********************************************************************/

/*-----------------------------------------------------------------------
PROCEDURE
    PULSE  -  pulse interrupt service routine

SYNOPSIS
    static void pulse()  -  called by lower level interrupt service routine

REMARKS
    If pulse count enough for a group, reset interval timer and record
    the time interval for the group.

LAST UPDATE
    8 April 1985
-----------------------------------------------------------------------*/

static void pulse()
{

    if (in(INPORT) & INMASK)    /* a pulse is detected */
    {
        ++pcount;

        if (pcount >= group)                /* enough for a group */
        {
            period = ReadITimer(itimer);    /* record group period */

            SetITimer(itimer);              /* reset interval timer */
            pcount = 0;                     /* reset pulse count */
            pflag = 1;                      /* indicate data available */
        }
    }
}


/**********************************************************************
          I N I T I A L I Z A T I O N   R O U T I N E S
**********************************************************************/

/*-----------------------------------------------------------------------
PROCEDURE
    PFM_INIT  -  initialize

SYNOPSIS
    void pfm_init(scale)
    double scale;

PARAMETERS
    scale  -  pulse scaling factor: displacement per pulse

REMARKS
    The scale is multiplied by 1000 because the interval timer
    readings are in milliseconds.

LAST UPDATE
    28 January 1988
        allocate interval timer here instead of externally
-----------------------------------------------------------------------*/

void pfm_init(scale)
double scale;
{

    pscale = scale * 1000.0;

    itimer = NewITimer();    /* allocate an interval timer */

    group = 100;             /* default to 100 pulses in a group */

    SetITimer(itimer);       /* initialize interval timer */

    xignal(XIGPRN, pulse);   /* set pulse() as parallel port isr */

    out(INPORT, 0x14);       /* enable parallel port interrupts */
}

/**********************************************************************

FILE
    pfm1.c  -  unidirectional velocity measurement using
               Pulse Frequency Modulation with adaptive pulse group size.

ENTRY ROUTINES
```

```
    pfm_getv    -  read velocity value
    pfm_group   -  set pulse group size

PRIVATE ROUTINE
    pulse       -  pulse interrupt service routine

INITIALIZATION ROUTINE
    pfm_init  -  initialize this module

REMARKS
    This differs from pfm0.c in that the group size used in velocity
    calculation adapts to the arrival rate of the pulses.

    If the pulses arrive too slowly, as determined by MAXPERIOD and
    the sampling time, the group size is halved since we do not want
    the group interval to exceed the sampling time.  If the problem
    persists, the group size is reduced again until the lower limit
    of one, in which case velocity is based on the interval between
    consecutive pulses.

    However, if the pulses are arriving too rapidly, then the group
    size should be increased as the interval timer cannot accurately
    measure small intervals.  The minimum period, MINPERIOD criteria
    to determine if we should increase the group size is based on the
    resolution of the interval timer.  In this case, the interval timer
    has a poor resolution and MINPERIOD reflects this.

LAST UPDATE
    26 January 1988
        change names and eliminate getgroup()

    Copyright(c) 1985-1988  D.M. Auslander and C.H. Tham

*************************************************************************/

/************************************************************************
                            I M P O R T S
*************************************************************************/

#include "envir.h"          /* environmemnt */

#include "inout.h"          /* in() and out() mapping */
#include "time.h"           /* timer module declarations */
#include "xignal.h"         /* xignal package declarations */


/************************************************************************
                        P R I V A T E   D A T A
*************************************************************************/

#define MINPERIOD   50L     /* minimum group period, timer limit */

#define MAXPERIOD   200L    /* max group period, sampling time limit */

#define INPORT  0x3BE       /* parallel input port address */
#define INMASK  0x01        /* mask for pulse bit */

#define MAXINT  0x7FFF      /* max value for 16-bit integer */

static double pscale;       /* pulses per unit displacement */
static int itimer;          /* interval timer number */
static int pflag = 0;       /* a group has arrived */
static long period = 0L;    /* time period for last group */
static int pcount = 0;      /* pulse count */
static int group = 1;       /* number of pulses per group */


/************************************************************************
                    E N T R Y   R O U T I N E S
*************************************************************************/

/*-----------------------------------------------------------------------
FUNCTION
    PFM_GETV  -  get velocity reading, adaptive version

SYNOPSIS
    double pfm_getv()

RETURNS
    displacement per second

REMARKS
    This version differs from that in pfm0.c in that the group size
    is adjusted to keep the period (i.e. the time interval needed to
    collect the number of pulses forming a group) between MINPERIOD
    and MAXPERIOD.

    If the group period is less than MINPERIOD, pulses are arriving
    too fast for the resolution of the timer.  The group size is
    doubled.

    If the group period is greater than MAXPERIOD, pulses are
    arriving too slowly to form a group when a velocity reading is
    required.  The group size is halved (with a floor of 1).

LAST UPDATE
    26 January 1988
        name change and other minor modifications
-----------------------------------------------------------------------*/

double pfm_getv()
{
    long time;          /* time period - copy of global period */
```

```
int count;          /* copy of pcount */
int istat;          /* interrupt status */


istat = disable();                  /* begin critical section */

if (pflag)                          /* data available */
{
    pflag = 0;                      /* reset immediately */
    time = period;
    count = group;

    /*-----------------------------------------------------------------
        If the period is less than some predefined minimum,
        pulses are arriving too fast.  Double the group size.
    -----------------------------------------------------------------*/

    if (period <= MINPERIOD)        /* pulses arriving too fast, */
        group <<= 1;                /*  double the group size.   */

    if (group < 0)                  /* group variable overflow! */
        group = MAXINT;             /* set to max integer value */
}
else    /* not enough pulses for a group since last pfm_getv() */
{
    /*-----------------------------------------------------------------
        Base velocity on the current pulse count instead of the
        group count.  This is more accurate than returning the
        previous velocity value.  If the current pulse count is
        zero, then the velocity is too low for the resolution
        of this routine; it is effectively zero.
    -----------------------------------------------------------------*/

    time = ReadITimer(itimer);
    count = pcount;

    /*-----------------------------------------------------------------
        If the elasped time since the start of the current group
        exceeds MAXPERIOD, either the pulses are arriving too
        slowly or the group size is too big, or both.  The group
        size is halved.
    -----------------------------------------------------------------*/

    if (time > MAXPERIOD)       /* pulses are arriving too slowly */
        if (group > 1)
            group >>= 1;        /* halve group size, floor of 1 */
}

if (istat)                      /* exit critical section */
    enable();

    return(count * pscale / time);
}


/*--------------------------------------------------------------------------
ROUTINES
    PFM_GROUP  -  set pulse group size

SYNOPSIS
    void pfm_group(size)
    int size;

PARAMETER
    size  -  number of pulses in a group

LAST UPDATE
    26 January 1988
        name change
--------------------------------------------------------------------------*/

void pfm_group(size)
int size;
{
    int istat;      /* interrupt status */


    istat = disable();

    group = size;

    if (istat)
        enable();

}


/**************************************************************************
                  P R I V A T E     R O U T I N E
**************************************************************************/

/*--------------------------------------------------------------------------
PROCEDURE
    PULSE  -  pulse interrupt service routine

SYNOPSIS
    static void pulse()  -  called by lower level interrupt service routine

REMARKS
    If pulse count enough for a group, reset interval timer and record
    the time interval for the group.
```

```
LAST UPDATE
    8 April 1985
----------------------------------------------------------------------*/

static void pulse()
{

    if (in(INPORT) & INMASK)        /* verify pulse */
    {
        ++pcount;

        if (pcount >= group)                /* enough for a group */
        {
            period = ReadITimer(itimer);    /* record group period */

            SetITimer(itimer);              /* reset interval timer */
            pcount = 0;                     /* reset pulse count */
            pflag = 1;                      /* indicate data available */
        }
    }

}


/**********************************************************************
            I N I T I A L I Z A T I O N     R O U T I N E S
**********************************************************************/

/*----------------------------------------------------------------------
PROCEDURE
    PFM_INIT  -  initialize

SYNOPSIS
    void pfm_init(scale)
    double scale;

PARAMETERS
    scale  -  pulse scaling factor: displacement per pulse

REMARKS
    The scale is multiplied by 1000 because the interval timer
    readings are in milliseconds.

LAST UPDATE
    28 January 1988
        allocate interval timer here instead of externally
----------------------------------------------------------------------*/

void pfm_init(scale)
double scale;
{

    pscale = scale * 1000.0;

    itimer = NewITimer();   /* allocate an interval timer */

    group = 100;            /* default to 100 pulses in a group */

    SetITimer(itimer);      /* initialize interval timer */

    xignal(XIGPRN, pulse);  /* set pulse() as parallel port isr */

    out(INPORT, 0x14);      /* enable parallel port interrupts */
}


/**********************************************************************

FILE
    time.h  -  timer module definitions

LAST UPDATE
    26 January 1988
        add ANSI function prototypes

**********************************************************************/

/************************   Timer Type Codes   ***********************/

#define DTIMER      0x01        /* count-down timer type */
#define ITIMER      0x02        /* interval timer type */


/****************************   Exports   ***************************/

#ifdef ANSI

extern void chronos(void);
extern int  NewDTimer(void(*)(), void *, int);
extern void FreeDTimer(int);
extern void SetDTimer(int, long);
extern long ReadDTimer(int);
extern void StopDTimer(int);
extern void StartDTimer(int);
extern void CisDTimer(int);
extern void SetTsr(int, void(*)(), void *, int);
extern int  NewITimer(void);
extern void FreeITimer(int);
extern void SetITimer(int);
extern long ReadITimer(int);
extern long ReadClock(void);
```

```
extern void InitTime(long);

#else

extern void chronos();
extern int  NewDTimer();
extern void FreeDTimer();
extern void SetDTimer();
extern long ReadDTimer();
extern void StopDTimer();
extern void StartDTimer();
extern void CisDTimer();
extern void SetTsr();
extern int  NewITimer();
extern void FreeITimer();
extern void SetITimer();
extern long ReadITimer();
extern long ReadClock();
extern void InitTime();

#endif
/************************************************************************

FILE
    time.c  -  timing routines

ENTRY ROUTINES
    chronos       -  timer interrupt service routine

    NewDTimer     -  allocate new countdown timer
    FreeDTimer    -  deallocate countdown timer
    SetDTimer     -  set countdown timer
    ReadDTimer    -  read countdown timer
    StopDTimer    -  freeze timer
    StartDTimer   -  unfreeze timer

    CisDTimer     -  set tm_isf field to 0

    NewITimer     -  allocate new interval timer
    FreeITimer    -  deallocate interval timer
    SetITimer     -  set interval timer
    ReadITimer    -  read interval timer

    ReadClock     -  time telling

PRIVATE ROUTINES
    reset_dtimer  -  reset countdown timer
    reset_itimer  -  reset interval timer

INITIALIZATION ROUTINES
    InitTime      -  initialize timer module
    InitSysTime   -  system initialization for task scheduling

DESCRIPTION
    These routines implement multiple timers in software, using a
    single hardware clock as the real-time base.  Actual and
    simulation routines are included.

    Note the implementation of multiple prioritized timer interrupts
    in chronos().  Only countdown timers are associated with interrupt
    service routines.

    The first two timers are reserved by the kernel for time telling
    and task scheduling.

LAST UPDATE
    03 May 1985
        restructure allocation routines
    04 February 1986
        put enable() & disable() in #if BACKGROUND
    1 December 1987
        implement tm_flag[]
    26 January 1988
        use the new void types and add ANSI features

    Copyright (c) 1985-1988  D.M. Auslander  and  C.H. Tham

***********************************************************************/

/***********************************************************************
                            I M P O R T S
***********************************************************************/

#include <stdio.h>

#include "envir.h"          /* environment definitions */

#include "config.h"         /* system configuration header */
#include "8259.h"           /* hardware dependent declarations */
#include "time.h"           /* time module declarations */

#ifdef ANSI
extern int  enable(void);   /* enable CPU interrupt response */
extern int  disable(void);  /* disable CPU interrupt response */
extern void seoi(int);      /* send specific EOI to 8259 */
extern void panic(char *);  /* abort execution */
#else
extern int  enable();       /* enable CPU interrupt response */
extern int  disable();      /* disable CPU interrupt response */
extern void seoi();         /* send specific EOI to 8259 */
extern void panic();        /* abort execution */
#endif
```

```
/*********************************************************************
            F O R W A R D   D E C L A R A T I O N S
*********************************************************************/

#ifdef ANSI

void    reset_dtimer(int);
void    reset_itimer(int);

#else

void    reset_dtimer();
void    reset_itimer();

#endif

/*********************************************************************
                    P R I V A T E   D A T A
*********************************************************************/

#define MAXINT  0x7FFF                  /* max. integer value */
#define MAXLONG 0x7FFFFFFL              /* max. long integer value */

static long tm_dtime[MAXDTIMERS];       /* count down timers */

static int tm_used[MAXDTIMERS];         /* timer in use flag */
static int tm_lock[MAXDTIMERS];         /* used for virtual time */
static int tm_flag[MAXDTIMERS];         /* timeout flags */
static int tm_pri[MAXDTIMERS];          /* priority (countdown only) */

static int tm_isf[MAXDTIMERS];          /* interrupt in service flag */
static void (*tm_tsr[MAXDTIMERS])();       /* timeout service routines */
static void *tm_argp[MAXDTIMERS];       /* ptr to arguments */

static long tm_itime[MAXITIMERS];       /* interval timers */
static int tm_iused[MAXITIMERS];        /* interval timer in use flag */

static long clock;                      /* countdown since system started */
static long mstick;                     /* milliseconds per tick */


#define ISF         1                   /* whether to use tm_isf field */
#define AUTO_EOI    0                   /* enable and send EOI to 8259 */

#define UNUSED      0                   /* timer unused */
#define USED        1                   /* timer in use */
#define UNLOCK      0                   /* timer unlocked */
#define LOCK        1                   /* timer locked */

/*********************************************************************
                   E N T R Y   R O U T I N E S
*********************************************************************/

/*--------------------------------------------------------------------
PROCEDURE
    CHRONOS  -  Timer Interrupt Service Routine

DESCRIPTION
    First decrements count down timers.  Count down timers are only
    decremented if they are in use (ie. allocated to a task) and
    if the timer is not locked.  Interval timers are the exception
    and are all incremented regardless since its probably faster to
    do so than check if they are in use.

    Next, the countdown timer array, tm_dtime[], is scanned for zero
    or negative times.  If time is zero or negative, see if user has
    specified an interrupt service routine (tm_tsr not NULL).  If so,
    set the In Service Flag (tm_isf) and execute the routine, clearing
    tm_isf on completion.

    If two or more service routines are due for service, the one with
    the highest priority will be executed first.  Only service routines
    with equal or higher priority can interrupt a currently in service
    routine.  Priority is set by the user when the timer is allocated.
    The larger the number, the higher the priority.

    Service routines are passed a pointer which may point to a scalar
    argument or an aggregate argument block (eg. structures).  This
    pointer is cast to a char type pointer.

    If this routine is run in a simulation environment, there may be
    simulation routines that have to be executed at every time step,
    regardless of whether a service routine is executed or not.  This
    is provided for by the external routine simintr() which is executed
    at every "tick".

    Chronos() may be used in programs where the "interrupt" routine
    never returns;  the "interrupt" service routine may be a task
    dispatcher or scheduler.  In such cases, two courses of action are
    possible depending on whether the dispatcher/scheduler
    is foregroung or background.  In the case of a background scheduler,
    we normally want to disable the in service flag and also
    reset the hardware interrupt controller.  This is to allow
    another timer interrupt to be generated and passed to
    chronos() without the intervention of the dispatcher/scheduler.
    For a foreground dispatcher/scheduler that uses the timer, it will
    want to control exactly when it gives up control, so we do not want
    to send EOI's or enable interrupts here, but allow the foreground
    dispatcher/scheduler to do so with CisDTimer().

    The in-service-flag may be ignored by means of the ISF conditional
```

```
    compilation switch.  The service routine has the task of reseting
    the hardware interrupt controller.  CisDTimer() performs both actions.

    Chronos() functions like a level triggered interrupt controller.
    As long as other conditions are satisfied, a zero or negative
    count will result in execution of the associated service routine.

    Note the use of register pointers for speed.

    New:    A timeout service routine is only invoked once when the
            count-down timer times out.  The timer must be reset by
            SetDTimer() before the timeout handler can be invoked again.

LAST UPDATE
    28 February 1985
        add ISF test
    04 February 1986
        use enable() and disable() only if BACKGROUND
    1 December 1987
        lock timer when isr active, release on reset
    26 January 1988
        use the new void pointer types
-----------------------------------------------------------------------*/

void chronos()
{
    int maxpri;                 /* max. pri. of in-service routine */
    int index;                  /* index into timer array */
    int istat;                  /* interrupt status on entry */
    int i;                      /* iteration counter */
    register long *p;           /* fast pointer to timer times */


    istat = disable();          /* critical section, disable interrupts */


    ++clock;                    /* update clock */

    /*-----------------------------------------------------------------
        Upon system clock interrupt, increment all interval timers.
        May be faster than checking if they are used b4 incrementing.
    -----------------------------------------------------------------*/

    for (p = tm_itime, i = 0; i < MAXITIMERS; i++, p++)
        ++(*p);

    /*-----------------------------------------------------------------
        If a countdown timer is active and it is not locked, its
        time value is decremented.  Does not check if timer has
        timed out since this is taken care of by tm_flag[] and to
        do so here will increase the overheads.  The tm_lock[]
        check is needed because we may need to stop certain timers.
        Have to check if timer is in use because a timeout service
        routine may be attached to a timer.
    -----------------------------------------------------------------*/

    for (p = tm_dtime, i = 0; i < MAXDTIMERS; i++, p++)
        if ((tm_used[i] == USED) && (tm_lock[i] == UNLOCK))
            --(*p);

#if FOREGROUND      /* use timeout service routines */

    /*-----------------------------------------------------------------
        Find the highest priority of all timer interrupt routines
        currently in service and set maxpri to that priority.
    -----------------------------------------------------------------*/

    maxpri = -MAXINT;

    for (i = 0; i < MAXDTIMERS; i++)
        if ((tm_isf[i] > 0) && (tm_pri[i] > maxpri))
            maxpri = tm_pri[i];

    /*-----------------------------------------------------------------
        Find any pending service routine with greater or equal
        priority.  If index >= 0, such a routine exists and index
        is its offset in tm_tsr[].
    -----------------------------------------------------------------*/

    index = -1;

    for (i = 0; i < MAXDTIMERS; i++)
    {
        if ((tm_dtime[i] <= 0L) && (tm_pri[i] >= maxpri)
            && (tm_isf[i] == 0) && (tm_tsr[i] != (void(*)())NULL)
            && (tm_lock[i] == UNLOCK) && (tm_flag[i] == 0))
        {
            index = i;
            maxpri = tm_pri[i];
        }
    }

    if (index >= 0)
    {
#if ISF
        tm_isf[index] += 1; /* indicate routine in service */
#endif
#if AUTO_EOI
        enable();

        seoi(TMRVEC);           /* specific EOI to intrp. controller */
#endif
```

```
        tm_flag[index] = 1;     /* prevent further use until reset */

        (*(tm_tsr[index]))(tm_argp[index]);

#if AUTO_EOI
        disable();
#endif
#if ISF
        tm_isf[index] -= 1; /* indicate routine done */
#endif
    }

#endif  /* if FOREGROUND */

    if (istat)
        enable();               /* release mutual exclusion */

}


/*-----------------------------------------------------------------------
FUNCTION
    NewDTimer  -  allocate countdown timer

SYNOPSIS
    int NewDTimer(func, argp, pri)
    void (*func)(), *argp;
    int pri;

PARAMETERS
    func  -  pointer to service routine
    argp  -  pointer to argument(s)
    pri   -  priority

RETURNS
    timer index if successful, -1 if not.

LAST UPDATE
    26 January 1988
        change func type to void
-----------------------------------------------------------------------*/

int NewDTimer(func, argp, pri)
void (*func)(), *argp;
int pri;
{
    int i;                      /* iteration variable */
    int istat;                  /* interrupt status */

    istat = disable();      /* disable interrupts, critical section */

    for (i = 0; i < MAXDTIMERS; i++)
        if (tm_used[i] != USED)
            break;

    if (i < MAXDTIMERS)
    {
        tm_pri[i] = pri;
        tm_tsr[i] = func;
        tm_argp[i] = argp;
        tm_lock[i] = UNLOCK;
        tm_flag[i] = 0;
        tm_used[i] = USED;
    }
    else
        i = -1;

    if (istat)              /* exit critical section, re-enable intrp */
        enable();

    return(i);
}


/*-----------------------------------------------------------------------
PROCEDURE
    FreeDTimer  -  free allocated timer

SYNOPSIS
    void FreeITimer(timer)
    int timer;

PARAMTERS
    timer  -  timer index number

DESCRIPTION
    Set associated used field to 0, indicating timer is free.  Note that
    you MUST ensure that the timer you are returning is obtained with
    NewDTimer.  Otherwise, you will screw-up the system for sure.

LAST UPDATE
    3 May 1985
-----------------------------------------------------------------------*/

void FreeDTimer(timer)
int timer;
{

    if ((timer < 0) || (timer >= MAXDTIMERS))
```

```
    {
        panic("FreeDTimer: nonexistent countdown timer");
    }
    else if (tm_used[timer] == USED)
    {
        reset_dtimer(timer);
    }
    else
        panic("FreeDTimer: countdown timer not allocated");

}


/*-------------------------------------------------------------------------
PROCEDURE
    SETDTIMER  -  set countdown timer

SYNOPSIS
    void SetDTimer(n, ms)
    int n;
    long ms;

PARAMETERS
    n   -  timer id
    ms  -  time in milliseconds

DESCRIPTION
    Set countdown timer 'n' for ms milliseconds.  If ms is less than
    the resolution of the time-base, tm_dtime is set to zero.
    A negative value of ms deallocates the timer.

LAST UPDATE
    1 December 1987
        reset tm_flag
-------------------------------------------------------------------------*/

void SetDTimer(n, ms)
int n;
long ms;
{
    int istat;        /* interrupt status */
    long tmp;         /* temporary to hold tick calculations */
    int flag;         /* temporary to hold flag state */


    if ((n < 0) || (n >= MAXDTIMERS))
        panic("SetDTimer: nonexistent timer");
    else if (tm_used[n] == UNUSED)
        panic("SetDTimer: timer not allocated");

    tmp = ms / mstick;
    flag = (ms > 0L) ? 0 : 1;

    istat = disable();       /* guarantee mutual exclusion */

    if (ms >= 0L)
    {
        tm_dtime[n] = tmp;
        tm_flag[n] = flag;
    }
    else        /* release timer */
    {
        tm_used[n] = UNUSED;
        tm_tsr[n] = (void(*)())NULL;
    }

    if (istat)
        enable();            /* release mutual exclusion */

}


/*-------------------------------------------------------------------------
FUNCTION
    ReadDTimer  -  read countdown timer

SYNOPSIS
    long ReadDTimer(n)
    int n;

PARAMETER
    n  -  timer number

RETURNS
    time in milliseconds

REMARKS
    The time left is only accurate to the precision allowed by the
    system clock rate.  If quantization is 10 ms, then ReadDTimer()
    will report 10 ms even if actual time left is 1 ms.

LAST UPDATE
    12 February 1985  by  author
-------------------------------------------------------------------------*/

long ReadDTimer(n)
int n;
{

    if ((n < 0) || (n >= MAXDTIMERS))
```

```
        panic("ReadDTimer: nonexistent timer");

    return(tm_dtime[n] * mstick);
}



/*----------------------------------------------------------------------
PROCEDURE
    STOPDTIMER  -  stop timer from counting down

SYNOPSIS
    void StopDTimer(n)
    int n;

PARAMETER
    n  -  timer number

DESCRIPTION
    This routine should only be used by the system to freeze timers
    used by background process for virtual timing, ie. time proceeds
    only when that process is running.  An important use is for
    background scheduling.

    As this is an internal system routine, error checking is lax.

SEE ALSO
    StartDTimer() to restart stopped timers

LAST UPDATE
    12 February 1985
----------------------------------------------------------------------*/

void StopDTimer(n)
int n;
{
    int istat;              /* interrupt status */


    if ((n < 0) || (n >= MAXDTIMERS))
        panic("StopDTimer: nonexistent timer");

    istat = disable();

    tm_lock[n] = LOCK;

    if (istat)
        enable();
}
```



```
/*----------------------------------------------------------------------
PROCEDURE
    STARTDTIMER  -  stop timer from counting down

SYNOPSIS
    void StartDTimer(n)
    int n;

PARAMETER
    n  -  timer number

REMARKS
    This routine should only be used by the system to restart timers
    frozen by a StopDTimer call.

SEE ALSO
    StopDTimer() to stop timers

LAST UPDATE
    12 February 1985  by  author
----------------------------------------------------------------------*/

void StartDTimer(n)
int n;
{
    int istat;          /* interrupt status */


    if ((n < 0) || (n >= MAXDTIMERS))
        panic("StartDTimer: nonexistent timer");

    istat = disable();

    tm_lock[n] = UNLOCK;

    if (istat)
        enable();

}



/*----------------------------------------------------------------------
PROCEDURE
    CISDTIMER  -  clear in service flags (software and hardware)

SYNOPSIS
    void CisDTimer(n)
    int n;

PARAMTER
```

```
    n  -  countdown timer number

REMARKS
    The purpose is to allow another invocation of the timeout service
    routine at the next timer interrupt.

LAST UPDATE
    1 December 1987
        clear tm_flag
------------------------------------------------------------------------*/

void CisDTimer(n)
int n;
{
    int istat;          /* interrupt status */


    if ((n < 0) || (n >= MAXDTIMERS))
        panic("CisDTimer: nonexistent timer");

    istat = disable();

    tm_isf[n] = 0;
    tm_flag[n] = 0;

    seoi(TMRVEC);    /* send specific EOI to interrupt controller */

    if (istat)
        enable();

}



/*-----------------------------------------------------------------------
PROCEDURE
    SETTSR  -  install timeout service routine

SYNOPSIS
    void SetTsr(n, func, argp, pri)
    void (*func)(), *argp;
    int n, pri;

PARAMETERS
    n     -  timer id
    func  -  pointer to service routine
    argp  -  pointer to argument structure
    pri   -  priority

REMARKS
    There had better be no mistakes when specifying timer.

LAST UPDATE
    26 January 1988
        use the new void types
------------------------------------------------------------------------*/

void SetTsr(n, func, argp, pri)
void (*func)(), *argp;
int n, pri;
{
    int istat;              /* interrupt status */


    if ((n < 0) || (n >= MAXDTIMERS))
        panic("SetTsr:  nonexistent timer");

    istat = disable();

    tm_pri[n] = pri;
    tm_tsr[n] = func;
    tm_argp[n] = argp;
    tm_lock[n] = UNLOCK;
    tm_flag[n] = 0;
    tm_used[n] = USED;

    if (istat)
        enable();

}



/*-----------------------------------------------------------------------
FUNCTION
    TIMEUP  -  has timer run out?

SYNOPSIS
    int TimeUp(n)
    int n;

PARAMETER
    n  -  timer number

RETURNS
    0  if timer has not timed out
    1  if it has timed out

LAST UPDATE
    29 January 1988
        created as this makes more sense than reading the timer
------------------------------------------------------------------------*/
```

```
int TimeUp(n)
int n;
{

    if ((n < 0) || (n >= MAXDTIMERS))
        panic("TimeUp:  nonexistent timer");

    return(tm_dtime[n] <= 0L ? 1 : 0);
}



/*-----------------------------------------------------------------------
FUNCTION
    NewITimer  -  allocate interval timer

SYNOPSIS
    int NewITimer()

RETURNS
    timer index if successful, -1 if not.

LAST UPDATE
    3 May 1985
-----------------------------------------------------------------------*/

int NewITimer()
{
    int istat;                  /* interrupt status */
    int i;                      /* iteration variable */


    istat = disable();  /* disable interrupts, critical section */

    for (i = 0; i < MAXITIMERS; i++)
        if (tm_iused[i] != USED)
            break;

    if (i < MAXITIMERS)
    {
        reset_itimer(i);

        tm_iused[i] = USED;
    }
    else
        i = -1;

    if (istat)          /* exit critical section, re-enable intrp */
        enable();

    return(i);
}



/*-----------------------------------------------------------------------
PROCEDURE
    FreeITimer  -  free allocated interval timer

SYNOPSIS
    void FreeITimer(timer)
    int timer;

PARAMTERS
    timer  -  timer index number

DESCRIPTION
    Set associated used field to 0, indicating timer is free.  Note that
    you MUST ensure that the timer you are returning is obtained with
    NewITimer.  Otherwise, you will screw-up the system for sure.

LAST UPDATE
    3 May 1985  by  author
-----------------------------------------------------------------------*/

void FreeITimer(timer)
int timer;
{

    if ((timer < 0) || (timer >= MAXITIMERS))
    {
        panic("FreeITimer: nonexistent interval timer");
    }
    else if (tm_iused[timer] == USED)
    {
        reset_itimer(timer);
    }
    else
        panic("FreeITimer: interval timer not allocated");

}



/*-----------------------------------------------------------------------
PROCEDURE
    SetITimer  -  set interval timer

SYNOPSIS
    void SetITimer(n);
    int n;
```

```
PARAMETERS
    n   -  timer id

REMARKS
    Set interval time value to 0.

LAST UPDATE
    13 October 1984
-----------------------------------------------------------------------*/

void SetITimer(n)
int n;
{

    if ((n < 0) || (n >= MAXITIMERS))
        panic("SetITimer: nonexistent timer");

    tm_itime[n] = 0;

}



/*-----------------------------------------------------------------------
FUNCTION
    ReadITimer  -  read interval timer

SYNOPSIS
    long ReadITimer(n);
    int n;

PARAMETERS
    n   -  timer id

RETURNS
    interval value in milliseconds

LAST UPDATE
    13 October 1984
-----------------------------------------------------------------------*/

long ReadITimer(n)
int n;
{

    if ((n < 0) || (n >= MAXITIMERS))
        panic("ReadITimer: nonexistent timer");

    return(tm_itime[n] * mstick);
}
```

```
/*-----------------------------------------------------------------------
FUNCTION
    ReadClock  -  read system time

SYNOPSIS
    long ReadClock()

RETURNS
    time elasped in milliseconds since system is born

LAST UPDATE
    12 February 1985
-----------------------------------------------------------------------*/

long ReadClock()
{

    return(clock * mstick);
}



/**********************************************************************
                    P R I V A T E    R O U T I N E S
**********************************************************************/

/*-----------------------------------------------------------------------
PROCEDURE
    reset_dtimer  -  reset countdown timer

SYNOPSIS
    static reset_dtimer(n)
    int n;

PARAMETER
    n  -  timer id

LAST UPDATE
    1 December 1987
        clear tm_flag
-----------------------------------------------------------------------*/

static void reset_dtimer(n)
int n;
{

    tm_dtime[n] = MAXLONG;
    tm_used[n] = UNUSED;
    tm_lock[n] = UNLOCK;
    tm_flag[n] = 0;
    tm_pri[n] = PZERO - 1;
```

```
    tm_isf[n] = 0;
    tm_tsr[n] = (void(*)())NULL;
    tm_argp[n] = (void *)NULL;

}


/*----------------------------------------------------------------------
PROCEDURE
    reset_itimer  -  reset interval timer

SYNOPSIS
    static void reset_itimer(n)
    int n;

PARAMETER
    n  -  timer id

LAST UPDATE
    12 February 1985
----------------------------------------------------------------------*/

static void reset_itimer(n)
int n;
{

    tm_itime[n] = 0L;
    tm_iused[n] = UNUSED;

}


/***********************************************************************
           I N I T I A L I Z A T I O N    R O U T I N E S
***********************************************************************/

/*----------------------------------------------------------------------
PROCEDURE
    INITTIME  -  initialize this module

SYNOPSIS
    void InitTime(ms)
    long ms;

PARAMETER
    ms  -  milliseconds per tick

LAST UPDATE
    12 February 1985
        separate countdown and interval timers.
----------------------------------------------------------------------*/

void InitTime(ms)
long ms;
{
    int i;                    /* iteration variable */


    mstick = ms;
    clock = 0L;


    for (i = 0; i < MAXDTIMERS; i++)
    {
        reset_dtimer(i);
    }

    for (i = 0; i < MAXITIMERS; i++)
    {
        reset_itimer(i);
    }

}


#ifdef CLOTHO       /* used by clotho kernel only */

/*----------------------------------------------------------------------
PROCEDURE
    INITSYSTIME  -  allocate and initialize timers for system

SYNOPSIS
    void InitSysTime(dispatcher)
    void (*dispatcher)();

PARAMETER
    dispatcher  -  pointer to clotho's scheduler/dispatcher

REMARKS
    timer 0  -  reserved for normal dispatcher
    timer 1  -  reserved for control-task dispatcher/scheduler

LAST UPDATE
    12 February 1985
----------------------------------------------------------------------*/

void InitSysTime(dispatcher)
void (*dispatcher)();
{

    if ((SLC_TIMER >= MAXDTIMERS) || (STL_TIMER >= MAXDTIMERS))
```

```
        panic("InitSysTime: check SLC_TIMER & STL_TIMER < MAXDTIMERS");

    tm_used[SLC_TIMER] = USED;
    tm_lock[SLC_TIMER] = UNLOCK;
    tm_flag[SLC_TIMER] = 0;

    tm_used[STL_TIMER] = USED;
    tm_lock[STL_TIMER] = UNLOCK;
    tm_flag[STL_TIMER] = 0;

#if FOREGROUND

    /*****  set up timer for time-slice priority dispatcher  *****/

    tm_tsr[SLC_TIMER] = dispatcher;
    tm_argp[SLC_TIMER] = (void *)SLC_TIMER;
    tm_pri[SLC_TIMER] = PZERO + 1;  /* has low priority */
    tm_dtime[SLC_TIMER] = 0;        /* start background next */


    /*****  set up timer for control-task STL dispatcher  *****/

    tm_tsr[STL_TIMER] = dispatcher;
    tm_argp[STL_TIMER] = (void *)STL_TIMER;
    tm_pri[STL_TIMER] = MAXINT;     /* has very high priority */
    tm_dtime[STL_TIMER] = MAXLONG;

#endif

}

#endif  /* ifdef CLOTHO */
/***********************************************************************

FILE
    cascade0.c  -  cascade PID position and velocity control

ROUTINES
    control  -  the cascade controller
    pgain    -  get position gains
    vgain    -  get velocity gains
    smpset   -  set sampling interval
    getv     -  get velocity
    getp     -  get position

REMARKS
    This implements the cascade control configuration of figure 3.7
    in the book.  There are two control loops, an inner velocity
    loop and an outer position loop.  The input to the velocity loop
    is the output of the position loop.

    This example demonstrates the use of time2.c, quad1.c and a
    modified pwm.c for timing and i/o interface.  You need to modify
    pwm.c in order to use it with quad1.c (refer to remarks for
    the mact() routine).

    This file contains only the control implementation.  You have
    to implement the user interface and perhaps the simulation
    module.  For examples of user interface and simulation modules,
    you can refer to cntrl1.c and rtsim1.c.

LAST UPDATE
    27 January 1988
        use quad1.c and pwm.c

***********************************************************************/

/***********************************************************************
                            I M P O R T S
***********************************************************************/

#include <stdio.h>

#include "envir.h"          /* environment definitions */

#include "time2.h"
#include "quad1.h"
#include "pwm.h"


/***********************************************************************
                F O R W A R D   D E C L A R A T I O N S
***********************************************************************/

#ifdef ANSI

double  getv(void);
double  getp(void);
void    mact(double);

#else

double  getv();
double  getp();
void    mact();

#endif

/***********************************************************************
                      P R I V A T E   D A T A
***********************************************************************/
```

```
#define SCALE   1000.0      /* quadrature states per unit displacement */
#define PWMFREQ 50.0        /* pwm frequency */
#define TMRFREQ 50L         /* timer "tick" frequency in milliseconds */

#define LOOPTIMER   0       /* timer number for control loop */
#define PWMTIMER    1       /* timer number for pwm pulse timing */

static double mvmax =  2047.0;  /* max velocity actuator output */
static double mvmin = -2048.0;  /* min velocity actuator output */

static double tsamp = 0.5;      /* sampling interval */

static double Kpp, Kpi, Kpd;    /* position P, I and D gains */
static double Kvp, Kvi, Kvd;    /* velocity P, I and D gains */
static double pref;             /* position set point */
static double perr0;            /* position error at current time k */
static double perr1;            /* position error at time (k - 1) */
static double perr2;            /* position error at time (k - 2) */
static double verr0;            /* velocity error at current time k */
static double verr1;            /* velocity error at time (k - 1) */
static double verr2;            /* velocity error at time (k - 2) */


/*********************************************************************
                    E N T R Y    R O U T I N E S
*********************************************************************/

/*-----------------------------------------------------------------------
PROCEDURE
    CONTROL  -  implements cascade position-velocity control

SYNOPSIS
    void control(cline)
    char *cline;

PARAMETER
    cline  -  pointer to input line.

REMARKS
    The error terms are initialized to zero.  When this routine starts,
    it is equivalent to applying a step position reference input.
    Note also that mp and mv, the position and velocity outputs, must
    be initialized too.

LAST UPDATE
    1 April 1985
---------------------------------------------------------------------*/

void control(cline)
char *cline;
{
    double p;               /* position */
    double v;               /* velocity */
    double mp;              /* postion controller output */
    double delta_mp;        /* change in mp */
    double mv;              /* velocity controller output */
    double delta_mv;        /* change in mv */
    long i;                 /* iteration counter */
    long nitr;              /* # of iterations */
    int prnt;               /* 1 - print control output, 0 - do not print */


    /*  get user specified iteration limit and print switch  */

    sscanf(cline, "%ld %d", &nitr, &prnt);

#ifdef DEBUG
    printf("number of iterations = %ld\n", nitr);
#endif

    /* initialize position and velocity error variables */

    perr0 = perr1 = perr2 = 0.0;
    verr0 = verr1 = verr2 = 0.0;
    mp = 0.0;
    mv = 0.0;


    for (i = 0L; i < nitr; i++)
    {
        SetDTimer(LOOPTIMER, (long)(tsamp * 1000));

        /* calculate position control parameters */

        perr2 = perr1;          /* update position errors */
        perr1 = perr0;

        p = getp();             /* read position */

        perr0 = pref - p;       /* calculate new position error */

        delta_mp = Kpp * (perr0 - perr1)  +  Kpi * perr0
                        +  Kpd * (perr0  -  2.0 * perr1  +  perr2);

        mp += delta_mp;


        /* calculate velocity control parameters */

        verr2 = verr1;          /* update velocity errors */
        verr1 = verr0;
```

```
        v = getv();             /* read velocity */

        verr0 = mp - v;         /* calculate new velocity error */

        delta_mv = Kvp * (verr0 - verr1)  +  Kvi * verr0
                       +  Kvd * (verr0  -  2.0 * verr1  +  verr2);

        mv += delta_mv;

    /*  Check for actuator limits and apply "reset windup" control.  */
    /*  Limit value of m to allowable D/A and actuator range and     */
    /*  set integral term to zero if system is outside linear zone.  */

        if (mv > mvmax)         /* output exceeds actuator limit */
            mv = mvmax;         /* set output to actuator maximum */
        else if (mv < mvmin)
            mv = mvmin;

        mact(mv);       /* send controller output to the actuator. */

        if (prnt)
            printf("p = %f, v = %f, mp = %f,  mv = %f\n", p, v, mp, mv);

        if (TimeUp(LOOPTIMER))
        {
            printf("sample time too short\n");
            exit(1);
        }

        while (!TimeUp(LOOPTIMER))
        {
#ifdef SIMRT
            tstep();    /* advance time */
#endif
        }
    }   /* end of iteration loop. */

}



/*----------------------------------------------------------------------
PROCEDURES
    PGAIN  -  interpret the input line specifying position gains
    VGAIN  -  interpret the input line specifying velocity gains

SYNOPSIS
    void pgain(cline)
    char *cline;

    void vgain(cline)
    char *cline;

PARAMETERS
    cline  -  input command line

LAST UPDATE
    26 January 1988
        change to void return
----------------------------------------------------------------------*/

void pgain(cline)
char *cline;
{

    sscanf(cline, "%lf %lf %lf", &Kpp, &Kpi, &Kpd);

#ifdef DEBUG
    printf("<pgain> Kpp = %lf, Kpi = %lf, Kpd = %lf\n", Kpp, Kpi, Kpd);
#endif

}


void vgain(cline)
char *cline;
{

    sscanf(cline, "%lf %lf %lf", &Kvp, &Kvi, &Kvd);

#ifdef DEBUG
    printf("<vgain> Kvp = %lf, Kvi = %lf, Kvd = %lf\n", Kvp, Kvi, Kvd);
#endif

}



/*----------------------------------------------------------------------
PROCEDURE
    SETP  -  get position setpoint from the command line

SYNOPSIS
    void setp(cline)
    char *cline;

PARAMETERS
    cline  -  user's command line

LAST UPDATE
    26 January 1988
        change to void return type
```

```
---------------------------------------------------------------------------*/

void setp(cline)
char *cline;
{

    sscanf(cline,"%lf", &pref);

#ifdef DEBUG
    printf("<setv> pref = %lf\n", pref);
#endif

}



/*---------------------------------------------------------------------------
PROCEDURE
    SMPSET  -  set sample time

SYNOPSIS
    void smpset(cline)
    char *cline;

PARAMETER
    cline  -  user's command line

REMARKS
    Extract sample time from user's command line and use it to set the
    sample time on the timer.

LAST UPDATE
    26 January 1988
        change to void return type
---------------------------------------------------------------------------*/

void smpset(cline)
char *cline;
{

    sscanf(cline,"%lf", &tsamp);

#ifdef DEBUG
    printf("<smpset> tsamp = %lf\n", tsamp);
#endif

}

/***************************************************************************
                P R I V A T E   R O U T I N E S
***************************************************************************/

/*---------------------------------------------------------------------------
FUNCTIONS
    GETV  -  returns motor velocity
    GETP  -  returns motor position

SYNOPSIS
    static double getv()
    static double getv()

RETURNS
    current motor velocity and position (units unspecified)

REMARKS
    This example shows how easy it is to use quadl.c (or any other
    method) for position and velocity.  You can plug in other methods
    just as easily.

LAST UPDATE
    27 January 1988
        show use of quadl.c instead of ADC and DAC.
---------------------------------------------------------------------------*/

static double getv()
{

    return(quad_getv());
}


static double getp()
{

    return(quad_getp());
}



/*---------------------------------------------------------------------------
PROCEDURE
    MACT  -  send out controller output

SYNOPSIS
    static void mact(output)
    double output;

PARAMETERS
    output  -  controller output

REMARKS
```

```
    This example shows the use of PWM output using pwm.c

    Note that the control algorithm has already limited the output to
    between mvmax and mvmin and that mvmin is negative.

LAST UPDATE
    26 January 1988
        substitute pwm for DAC
-----------------------------------------------------------------------*/

static void mact(output)
double output;
{
    double dutycycle;


    if (output >= 0.0)
    {
        dutycycle = output / mvmax;
    }
    else
    {
        dutycycle = -(output / mvmin);
    }

    setdcycle(dutycycle);

}



/*-----------------------------------------------------------------------
PROCEDURE
    INIT  -  system initialization

SYNOPSIS
    void init()

REMARKS
    Initialize the time2.c, quad1.c and the yet to be written pwm1.c.

LAST UPDATE
    27 January 1988
        initialize quad1 and a modified pwm.
-----------------------------------------------------------------------*/

void init(cline)
char *cline;
{

    InitTime(TMRFREQ);          /* init time.c module */

    quad_init(SCALE, tsamp);

    pwm_init(PWMTIMER);
    setpfreq(PWMFREQ);

}
```

CHAPTER 4

DATA STRUCTURES

Motivated by the need to develop a user command language that allows for more flexibility and readability than the single character commands introduced earlier, this chapter will provide a brief exploration of the use of structured data in real-time programs. Methods of organizing data are useful features of computing languages for real-time systems. To maximize portability and ease of use, these methods of "structuring" data allow for the collection of data of various types and references to that data in ways that are not dependent on the internal details of the computer's memory organization.

4.1 DATA ORGANIZATION

Data structures are used to group together all data relevant to a specific entity. When data is grouped this way, the individual data items often represent a variety of data types. For example, the description of a motor might include floating point data for items such as its torque constant, windage loss, etc., integer data for number of poles, character for manufacturer's name, and so on. Older computing languages allowed only a single kind of data structure within the language syntax—arrays. Arrays allowed grouping of information but only if all the information could be expressed in the same form (all integer, all float, etc.) and then only into multidimensional Cartesian spaces. More general data groupings are required for real-time problems because the information to be grouped is rarely all of the same form.

Data groupings are called structures in some languages and *records* in others. In either case, the term refers to a data grouping that acts very much like a simple data type in that variables can be assigned to that type. Unlike a simple data type declaration such as integer, that refers to a single variable, a "structure" declaration refers to the whole aggregate. Reference to an element within the grouping is done by attaching a *field* reference to the variable name. We will denote the attachment with a dot, "."

First, let's define a data structure for a control loop. Assume that a program must control several objects, each of which is described by a set of attributes. The definition is shown in Fig. 4.1, starting with a name for the loop, data input channel number, data output channel number, etc.

```
structure control_loop:
        character_string        loop_name
        integer                 input_channel
        integer                 output_channel
        float                   process_output_value
        float                   setpoint
        float                   proportional_gain
        float                   integral_gain
        float                   derivative_gain
        float                   output_low_limit
        float                   output_high_limit
        float                   controller_output_value
        float                   sample_interval
```

Figure 4.1

The definition called "control_loop" is a *template* that describes the data items needed to define a control loop. It does not define a variable or reserve space for it. It only declares a data type.

A single-loop control problem would only require one such definition, for example, a variable called "cl" (see Fig. 4.2). That variable could be used in a control calculation as shown in the figure. Its storage would have to be in fixed memory since the information would have to be remembered from one sample period to the next.

The combination "variable.field" is used in exactly the same way as a simple variable. In fact, for the single-loop case there is no particular advantage to using the structure at all; the variables "setpoint," "process_output_value," etc., would do just as well. The notational advantage begins to appear for the multi-loop case. Rather than declaring arrays of all of the individual variables, setpoint[i], etc., an array of structures can be declared (square brackets, [], will be used to indicate

Control function:

```
old2_error = old1_error
old1_error = error
error = cl.setpoint - cl.process_output_value
delta_m = cl.proportional_gain * (error - old1_error)
            + ...
            ...
```

Figure 4.2

array subscripts to avoid confusion with function calls). The notation

```
cl[i].setpoint
```

will then access one of the members of the structure for the i-th loop. The major advantage to this notation is the statement within the language syntax that the quantity referenced is part of the control_loop structure. The data for each array element will be stored together, so that data referring to a given control loop will always be grouped in memory. The grouping of data in memory is important when memory is allocated and used dynamically, but is less important when fixed, predefined arrays are used.

4.2 POINTER VARIABLES

Variables that can "point" to other variables are an important tool in manipulating structured data. All variables are stored and referenced within memory by an *address* representing the physical location in the memory at which the variable can be found. A variable thus has two attributes: (1) its address, and (2) the contents at that address representing the "value" of the variable. A pointer variable is one whose value (contents) is the address of some other variable. In order to operate with pointer variables, we need some additional notation. We will use the prefix operator "&" to indicate "address-of" when it appears as a prefix operator. Thus, "&*x*" would be read as, "the address of the variable *x*." The address-of operator is necessary for giving values to pointer variables, since the value of a pointer is the address of something else. If a variable *x* is declared to be an integer, and *px* is declared to be a pointer to an integer, the statement

```
px = &x
```

indicates that the *value* of *px* is being set to the *address* of *x*. (It should be noted that there is considerable variation among languages as to the operations that are permitted with pointer variables. The notation used here is closest to the C language.)

Making use of a pointer variable requires that we be able to access the contents of the address it is pointing to. This is accomplished with the prefix operator "*". With the definitions above for *x* and *px*, the notation **px* would refer to the contents of the memory location pointed at by *px*. Because the value of *px* had been set to the address of *x*, **px* would then give the value of *x*. The "*" and the "&" operators are thus complementary. The notation **(&x)* produces the same result as *x* by itself. A variety of notations are used for these concepts in different languages.

A pointer can point at a structure. For example, the pointer variable *pc* can be declared to be a pointer to the data type defined by the "cl" structure defined above. Its value could be set by a statement of the form

```
pc = &cl[i]
```

To use *pc*, we would have to access a particular element of "cl", say the setpoint. Since **pc* accesses the "thing pointed to," we would have to add the field reference to get

```
(*pc).setpoint
```

for a reference to the setpoint field of control_loop. Because precedence of execution of these operators is not as intuitively clear as it is with the arithmetic operators, we will use parentheses whenever there is any possibility of ambiguity.

The *(*x).y* expression is very commonly used, so we will use an arrow operator, "->" as a shorthand

```
pc->setpoint
```

to save some typing and make a graphic statement about the meaning of the expression.

4.3 POINTER ARITHMETIC

Because pointer variables are references to places in a sequential address space, arithmetic with pointers is used to move within that space or to find out how far apart elements in that space are. To keep programs written with pointer variables portable, the arithmetic should be defined in such a way that it does not depend on the way that a particular computer's memory is built or accessed. If, for example, a pointer variable is incremented by one, *pc*+1, the new reference should be to the next object *of the type pc is pointing to.* In the case of *pc*, that would be the next control loop. The change in value of *pc* in the sense of absolute memory address would depend on the computer and could be different in different computers, or even different compilers on the same computer. Within that context for pointer arithmetic, addition of integers to pointers makes sense, as does subtraction of integers from pointers and subtraction of pointers from each other. Because pointers represent absolute references to memory addresses, however, addition of one pointer to another does not make sense, nor does multiplication or division of pointers or pointers and integers.

There is thus an anomaly in pointer variables that is explained by the definition that arithmetic is defined in terms of sizes of the items pointed at. If the value of a pointer variable is printed, it must give the absolute memory address of the object being pointed at. If the values of two pointer variables are printed, the difference between them will be different than the printed value of the difference of the two variables, that is:

$$value(pc1) - value(pc2) \neq value(pc1 - pc2)$$

The first difference will be dependent on the computer being used; the second will not.

4.4 LINKED LISTS

Groups of items that each have the same internal data structure can be related in many ways. Putting them together by declaring a variable to be an array of elements of the same structured data type provides one connection, the array index. Adjacency is determined by incrementing and decrementing the index. There could be other relationships, however. For example, in the control loop case, there might be groupings of the control loops according to the place where the loop is located (all loops located in one part of the plant), the types of processes being controlled (all pressure loops, all temperature loops, etc.), and so on. These relationships can be built into the data structure by including *lnk* in the definition of the data structure so that elements of the array can be linked in as many ways as desired. Links are implemented with pointer variables. By including link pointers in the structure, the actual links can be built when the structures are defined or changed dynamically. Because the link variables point directly at specific data blocks, the relationships can be established regardless of the order in which the data blocks were originally defined, and can even be used if groups of data blocks are separated in memory.

As an example, we might want to organize the information in a system consisting of many control loops so that related loops can be found quickly. To do that, we could augment the "control_loop" definition with two links: one for the process that particular control loop is imbedded in (a distillation column, for example), and the other for the type of control (temperature, flow, pressure). The new definition for the structure of type "control_loop" (see Fig. 4.3), includes the two links defined as pointers to variables of type "structure control_loop."

```
structure control_loop:

        character_string                    loop_name
                .
                .
                .
        pointer_to structure control_loop   process_type_link
        pointer_to structure control_loop   variable_type_link
```

Figure 4.3

To use this "linked list," we must also define pointers to the first item in each category. Then, if we should want to find the process variable values for all of the control loops associated with, for example, distillation column number 4, the procedure would be to first find the pointer to the first control loop associated with that distillation column. Then, follow the trail of pointers, from block to block. Each block would have its process_type_link pointing to the next block that is part of the same distillation column. The last data block in the chain would have a null pointer.

Linkages of this sort can be used to scan through a data structure accessing only items of specified class. The same result could be obtained by scanning all entries in the list and discarding those not in the class, but computing time can be reduced substantially by using links.

The links can be set up by using the address-of operator in statements of the form

```
cl[i].process_type_link = &cl[j]
```

Once the links are set up, a function to list all of the control loops belonging to a particular class could be written, for example, as shown in Fig. 4.4. There would have to be a separate pointer for each class pointing to the first data item in that class, and there would also have to be a convention for ending the list. A common convention is to use a "null" pointer, with the value of the constant "null" set to an illegal or unused address for data structures (often zero or -1). There is no need to specify what value null will have since that should be made specific to compiler/computer combinations. On some computers, attempting to access the address associated with a null pointer will cause a hardware trap.

Using a single link gives a forward reference in the list, that is, connections can be traced from the beginning of the list to the end. It is sometimes useful to be able to move in either direction. To do that, a doubly linked list must be constructed by including pointers to both the next item and to the previous item.

```
List loops in class(pointer_to_first)

        pointer_to structure loop p      (declaration for pointer
                                          variable local to this function)

        p = pointer_to_first

        Repeat code block while p != null
                Print p->loop_name
                p = p->process_type_link
```

Figure 4.4

Doubly linked lists are extremely useful, for example, when items must be inserted or deleted from the middle of the list. With pointers in both directions available, it is an easy matter to change the pointers on both sides of the item being added or deleted to reflect the new structure.

4.5 A SIMPLE INTERPRETER FOR SETPOINT CALCULATION

The cascade control structure used for position control in the previous chapter gets its setpoint from the output of another control loop. The structure defined here to describe a loop, "control_loop," has an entry for setpoint, but nothing to indicate where the setpoint comes from. With that structure, the only way to make the connection between the output of the position loop and the input to the velocity loop would be by writing it into the control algorithm program. That would make the program very specific, however, and would mean that different functions would have to be used for every loop that used any form of setpoint interconnection. A major portion of the design of real-time software comes in drawing the boundary between program code and data in such a way that the program remains as general as possible, with this sort of interconnection information built into the data structure.

One way to build a more general structure is to include a general calculation module for the setpoint that is represented entirely in the data structure. It can thus be customized for any setpoint model, and can be changed at any time, even when the real time control is running. The simplest possible form would be to leave the current setpoint entry in the data structure and add an additional entry that is a pointer to another control loop. When the control is executed for the loop, before computing the error the referenced loop's controller output value would be copied into the current loop's setpoint value. A loop that has its setpoint determined externally could use a "null" entry to indicate that its setpoint is not to be touched. The data structure definition and code to access the dependent setpoint are shown in Fig. 4.5. An alternate to the -> notation in the figure would be to write, for example, "(*loop_pointer).setpoint" in place of "loop_pointer ->setpoint".

```
structure loop:
        .
        .
        .
        float                          setpoint
        pointer_to structure loop      setpoint_source
        .
        .

control function(loop_pointer)         (The argument points to the data
                                       item for the loop to be controlled)
        if(loop_pointer->setpoint_source != null)
                loop_pointer->setpoint =
                (loop_pointer->setpoint_source)->controller_output_value

                ...
```

Figure 4.5

This would work for the cascade control, but would not be adequate for other common schemes, such as ratio control, in which the ratio of two setpoints is kept at a constant value. A more general "calculator" scheme must then be used. A simple calculator algorithm can be built by using reverse Polish notation (RPN, as used on Hewlett-Packard calculators, also called "postfix" notation). RPN uses a list of items and a data stack. As the list is scanned, each item is checked to see whether it represents a data item or a function (or operator). If it is a data item, its value is put on the stack. If it is a function, the function is executed. When a function is executed, it takes its data from the stack, and returns its result to the stack. The final result is left on the stack, and is copied to the current setpoint value.

Each of the items that can be encountered must have a two-part definition. The first part tells what kind of item it is, and the second part is the item itself. For this control problem, there would have to be at least three kinds of items: pointers to other control_loops (as in the simpler example, above), function references, and constants. The function references would be executed, and the other two would put data to the stack. The functions would perform simple arithmetic, addition, subtraction, etc. A fourth item type would be a "null" item, terminating the list.

The calculation list can itself be described by a data structure, which we will call "rpn." It has an interesting structure, however. Each element of the list has two entries, but the second entry has several alternative forms. Since the alternatives can never be present at the same time, it makes no sense to reserve separate space for each of them. Instead, a form of structure is used in which the alternative items occupy overlapping space, so we will call it an "overlapping structure" (also called "unions" in C and "variant records" in Pascal and Ada). The rpn data structure can then be described as in Fig. 4.6, where the overlapping structure name "alt_item" is embedded in the rpn structure.

```
overlapping_structure alt_item
          pointer_to function                rpn_operation
          pointer_to structure loop          rpn_loop
          float                              rpn_constant

structure rpn
          integer                            item_type
          overlapping_structure alt_item     item_entry
```

Figure 4.6

The access to the overlapping structure is exactly the same as the access to a normal structure except that only one of the defined fields can be present at any given time.

The function to evaluate one of these lists is given in Fig. 4.7. The choice of paths includes the four choices described above with one additional choice in the case of the pointer to another loop block that allows for access to either the setpoint or the controller output from that block.

4.6 DYNAMIC MEMORY ALLOCATION

Allocation of memory through fixed, predefined arrays is satisfactory for systems in which the sizes of various lists and tables is known in advance, but does not work well when programs are written for general purpose use. Typical programs have a number of such lists and tables. When fixed memory allocations are used, the program will "crash" when the first size limit is reached, even if there is substantial space left in other areas. This forces the program to be over-allocated, resulting in large load modules for the program even though only a few users will come near to using the full capacity.

The solution to this dilemma is to define the data structures needed for each of the lists, but to allocate memory space for them as needed. There are two forms

```
Evaluate an RPN list(pointer_to_list)

        type = pointer_to_list->item_type

        Repeat code block while type != null
                Execute block corresponding to value of type:

                        1: (type 1 is for execution of a function)
                          Execute pointer_to_list->item_entry.rpn_operation

                        2: (type 2 uses the controller output from another loop)
                          Put value on stack --
                          pointer_to_list->item_entry.rpn_loop->
                                controller_output_value

                        3: (type 3 uses the setpoint from another loop)
                          Put value on stack --
                          pointer_to_list->item_entry.rpn_loop->setpoint

                        4: (type 4 is a constant)
                          Put value on stack --
                          pointer_to_list->item_entry.rpn_constant

                Increment pointer_to_list
                type = pointer_to_list->item_type

        Return top-of-stack value
```

Figure 4.7

of dynamic memory allocation space available. We have already referred to the first type in the discussion of the re-entrant properties of functions. Space that is used for variables that are local to a function is recovered when the function completes execution. The space for these variables, often called *automatics* because they come in to existence "automatically" upon entry to the function, is made available in a section of memory organized as a *stack* It is called a stack because space is allocated in much the same way that a pile of objects is "stacked." The most important property of a stack is that objects must be removed in the reverse of the order in which they were placed on the stack. This organization fits the needs of automatic variables storage very well. When a function is called, it is allocated space at the "top" of the stack. When the function returns, the space is freed for re-use.

The stack order of allocation/deallocation also works properly when function calls are nested, i.e., A calls B calls C, etc. Each function in turn gets space at the top of the stack. Since they must return in reverse order, the space is freed correctly, uncovering the space allocated to the function resuming execution after the "return." Recursive calls, when a function calls itself either directly or indirectly, are handled the same as other calls; new working space is allocated at the top of the stack. Each recursive call thus has its own private working space. The depth of nesting, recursively or non-recursively, is limited only by the total amount of memory reserved for the stack.

The well-ordered dynamic memory allocation of the stack, however, cannot meet all memory allocation needs. One need it could meet, but that is not implemented in most compilers, is the allocation of memory for automatic array variables whose dimensions are not known until the function is called. Memory allocation and deallocation that happen unpredictably, though, cannot use the stack. Such unpredictable memory requests are allocated from an area of memory called the *heap* to distinguish it from the more orderly stack.

This second form of memory allocation requires explicit requests for space, unlike the automatic allocation of space that is done each time a function is entered. The format for a request is to call a function, giving the size of the object and how many objects space is to be reserved for (some languages are more restrictive in how the space allocator may be used). To allocate space for ten "loop" structures, the call would look like

```
pointer_to_new_space = allocate_memory(10,size_of(structure loop))
```

where the function returns a pointer to the space that has been allocated. Space can be freed in the same manner if it is no longer needed, by the call:

```
free_memory(pointer_to_old_space)
```

Instead of using fixed array space for lists, allocated space can be used in small amounts, as needed. This will leave the list scattered all over memory, however, so explicit links will have to be used for all connections between blocks, or special blocks must be reserved for connecting one area of allocated space to another. A program that sets up its tables and lists in this manner, however, will only run out of space when the allocatable space is used up, regardless of the order in which the tables are filled.

4.7 STORAGE MANAGEMENT

Because the space used from the heap usually belongs to lists that must remain in existence independent of the functions that are executing, there is no way to predict the order in which the space will be allocated and freed. Whenever space is freed, the memory allocation function will make an attempt to consolidate the adjoining, unused space into as large blocks as possible. However, it is still possible to go through many allocation/deallocation cycles in such a way that the heap ends up very fragmented, possibly to the point that although there may be sufficient total space in the heap, it is broken into such small groups that is is unusable.

The act of recovering space from the heap for re-use is often called *garbage collection.* Simply freeing and coalescing free space under program control is the first step in garbage collection, but it is sometimes necessary to do more. In those cases when memory becomes very fragmented, it is necessary to copy the sections of the heap that are used, one by one, into one end of the heap space so that the free space can be collected into a large block. If this is to be done, the design of the data structure must include sufficient linkage so that when each block is copied, all necessary references to it can be changed.

Use of memory allocators of the type described above, that provide arbitrary-sized amounts of memory, can sometimes lead to unpredictable behavior. The unpredictability can come from unavailability of space due to fragmentation, or, if more sophisticated garbage collection is used, from computational delays while the garbage collector works. To avoid these problems, and to assure more predictable real-time behavior, some real-time systems allocate and deallocate memory only in fixed block sizes. This removes some flexibility from the program, and can lead to less efficient usage of memory, but guarantees that fragmentation can never occur.

4.8 CONTROL COMMAND LANGUAGE

There are two goals in the improvement of the command control language that are used to interact with the motor control program. The first is to relax the requirement that all commands be single letter, so that more mnemonic command names can be used. The second is to change the program so that the command structure becomes part of the program data structure, rather than part of the code as it has been. The method used for passing information to different program functions will be retained, that is, after the command has been decoded, the remainder of the line will be sent to the function for decoding there. Fig. 4.8 shows the data structure for this command protocol. It has two parts: the first is the text of the command, and the second is a pointer to the function to be executed if that command is matched.

A function can now be written that interprets a command list consisting of entries of this form. The command list is assumed to be in an array of structures of type "commands," command_list. The function shown in Fig. 4.9 will scan the list for a match with the command word portion of the line it is passed as an argument. The function first_word separates the command word from the rest of the line; the loop continues for N_Commands, the number of currently defined commands.

```
structure commands

        character_string        command_name
        pointer_to_function     command_function
```

Figure 4.8

```
Command_interpreter(line)              (line is the string of characters
                                        that the user entered)
        pointer_to_commands = &command_list[0]
                                       (Initialize a pointer to the beginning
                                        of the list)
        Use first_word to separate "line" into command_word and
                rest_of_line
        found = FALSE                  (found is a variable that is used to
                                        check to see if a match was found for
                                        command_word)

        Repeat the code block for i = 1 to N_Commands

                if(command_word = pointer_to_commands->command_name)
                        Execute pointer_to_commands->command_function
                        found = TRUE
                        Break out of the loop

        if(found = FALSE)Print "command not found" message
```

Figure 4.9

When upgrading the user interaction in a system, it is a good idea, if possible, to retain the old commands. In this case, that represents no problem since single-letter commands can be represented in the new structure as well as in the old one. Users can then make a graceful transition to the new protocol.

DATA STRUCTURE EXAMPLES

4.9 INTRODUCTION

As applications become larger and more complex, there is a greater need to structure the program into more manageable units. A simple single-loop process control application has a relatively small number of variables which are easily managed by the engineer/programmer. A large system with many control loops and scheduling requirements will result in an unmanageable proliferation of simple data variables unless the data (and program) are properly organized and structured. In this section, we will explore ways of organizing data using the data structuring facilities of the **C** programming language. The subject will be approached in the context of real-time control applications, using cascade control as the base example.

The following are the example programs in this section:

envir.h	Environment declarations.
dash8.h	Declarations for A/D interface (simulated in this example).
dac2.h	Declarations for D/A interface (simulated in this example).
pidloop.h	Simple PID control data structure.
main2.c	Main program module and command processor for cascade control example.
cascade1.h	Declarations of interface routines in cascade1.c.
cascade1.r	PID cascade control using data structure defined in pidloop.c.
rtsim2.c	Simulation module for cascade control example.

4.10 REVIEW OF DATA STRUCTURES AND TYPES IN C

Data structures are related to the concept of *types* since the way data are represented gives rise to structural properties. C is a typed language[1] in that a *type* is associated with all data variables. A variable's type tells us what kind of variable it is and what sort of operations are allowed on the variable. A simple data type is one that cannot be decomposed into simpler elements. For example, *int* and *double* are simple data types, whereas *char[]* is not since it is an array of multiple *char* units. A complex data type is derived from simpler data types; an array is an example of a data type derived from elements of the same type. A structure, or *struct*, is

[1]Albeit not a strongly typed one like Pascal.

an aggregate data type in that it can comprise data elements of different types.[2] The members of a structure may be simple data types or they may be other complex data types.

A *struct* declaration has the following form:

```
struct tag {
        type variable_name;
        ......
};
```

The *struct* keyword declares a structure; an optional name (the *tag*) may be associated with the structure. This name, if declared, follows immediately after the *struct* keyword. The members of a structure are enclosed by curly braces and are declared just like ordinary variables. However, they do not share the same *name space* as ordinary variables, that is, a structure member named *var1* is not the same as an ordinary variable named *var1*. If members of two different structures have the same name, are the two members the same? For example:

```
struct a {
        int var1;
        int var2;
};

struct b {
        int var1;
        int var3;
};
```

Does *var1* of *struct a* bear any relation to *var1* of *struct b*? According to the ANSI C draft standard, different structures have different name spaces, i.e., members of different structure types are distinct from each other even though they may have the same name. Thus, *var1* of *struct a* is not the same as *var1* of *struct b*. This applies for members of *union*s as well as *struct*s.

A *union* is similar to a *struct* and is declared in the same manner, for example:

```
union c {
        char cvar;
        int avar[16];
        double dvar;
};
```

A *union* differs from a *struct* in that its members all share the same storage space.[3]

---

[2]This is analogous to the *record* in Pascal.

[3]This is equivalent to the *variant record* in Pascal.

In the above example, a variable of type *union c* may contain a *char*, an array of *int*, or a *double* at any one time, but not all at the same time. Only enough storage for the largest member (in this case, the *avar* array) is allocated; the program has to keep track of what is being stored.

The *typedef* feature is commonly used with structure declarations to associate alternative names with a type. For example:

```
typedef struct _pidloop PLOOP;
```

declares that *PLOOP* is a name that can be used in place of *struct _pidloop*. The benefits of the *typedef* facility are that it allows meaningful names to be used instead of complicated structure declarations, which helps to make the program easier to understand and hence reduces the chance of errors.

4.11 CASCADE CONTROL REVISITED

This is a re-implementation of the cascade position and velocity control example of Chapter 3, this time using data structures to encapsulate the parameters for the position and velocity control loops. The parameter data structure is defined in the file *pidloop.h*, and the cascade control algorithm is implemented in *cascade1.c*. The main module, *main2.c*, contains a command interpreter—the commands and the associated routines are implemented by an array of structures. There is also a simulation module, *rtsim2.c*, adapted from Chapter 2. To create the program, type:

```
cl /DSIMRT main2.c cascade1.c rtsim2.c
```

Let us now look at the data structure declarations in *pidloop.h*.

4.11.1 CONTROL LOOP DESCRIPTORS

The PID control loop is described by a data structure:

```
#define NAMESIZE            12    /* max characters for loop name */

struct _pidloop {
      char cl_name[NAMESIZE+1]; /* loop name,*/
                                /*+1 for NUL terminator */
      int cl_inchan;            /* input channel number */
      int cl_outchan;           /* output channel number */
      double cl_setpoint;       /* controller setpoint */
      double cl_feedback;       /* controller feedback value */
      double cl_kp;             /* proportional gain */
      double cl_ki;             /* integral gain */
      double cl_kd;             /* derivative gain */
      double cl_err0;           /* error at (k)-th instant */
```

```
        double cl_err1;              /* error at (k-1)-th instant */
        double cl_err2;              /* error at (k-2)-th instant */
        double cl_output;            /* controller output */
        double cl_outmin;            /* lower limit of output value */
        double cl_outmax;            /* upper limit of output value */
        double cl_tsamp;             /* sampling interval */
};

typedef struct _pidloop PIDLOOP;
```

This data structure is designed to encapsulate the parameters and variables needed for a PID control loop. In addition to the proportional, integral, and differential gains, there are fields for the error terms, setpoint, feedback, and even sampling rate. All the data needed to implement a PID control loop are described by this data structure. The use of such descriptors helps separate the data from the code, allowing the same code to be applied to different control loops. In the cascade control example, the position and velocity loops are described by two such descriptors. The outputs of the position and velocity loops are calculated by the same routine using information contained in the respective loop descriptors.

There is an implicit assumption here that input and output go through an A/D and D/A, respectively; hence the *cl_inchan* and *cl_outchan* fields for specifying the channel numbers. Readers may wonder why the field names have a "cl_" prefix. This is a practice left over from the dark ages before the ANSI C standard where, depending on which compiler you are using, *struct* and *union* members may all share the same name space with the result that the same field name cannot be used in a different structure type. It was (and maybe still is) common practice to prefix field names with a unique mnemonic related to the structure type.

While *struct _pidloop* describes a PID loop very nicely, it is restricted to PID control. A more general control parameter descriptor can be created by using an array for the parameters. The parameters in the array can be specific to the control algorithm used and the same data structure can thus be used by different control loops with different control algorithms. Here is an example of a control loop expressed in this manner:

```
#define NAMESIZE 12          /* max # of characters for name */
#define NPARAM 16            /* max # of parameters in cl_param[] */
#define NIOCHAN 4            /* max # of i/o channels */

struct _cloop {
        char cl_name[NAMESIZE+1];      /* loop name, */
                                       /* +1 for NUL terminator */
        int cl_channel[NIOCHAN];       /* i/o channel numbers */
        double cl_param[NPARAM];       /* control parameters */
        double cl_tsamp;               /* sampling interval */
};

typedef struct _cloop CLOOP;
```

To customize it for PID control, we define array indices for the different parameters:

```
#define IN_CHAN             0
#define OUT_CHAN      1

#define SETPOINT      0
#define FEEDBACK      1
#define KI                  2
#define KP                  3
#define KD                  4
#define ERR0                5
#define ERR1                6
#define ERR2                7
#define OUTPUT              8
#define OUT_MIN             9
#define OUT_MAX             10
```

These declarations would normally be put into a separate file that will be included to customize *struct _cbcp* for PID control.

4.11.2 INITIALIZATION

Let us return to the cascade control example. There are three interrelated initialization routines, all of which reside in *cascade1.c*. The first is *init()*, which is called whenever the user issues the *initialize* command. This initializes the input/output devices and calls *init_cascade()* to initialize the control module. If the program is compiled for simulation, the argument string *cline* containing the simulation time-step is passed to *sim_init()* to initialize the simulation module. The simulation module must be initialized for the program to execute properly.

The *init_cascade()* routine allocates storage for the position and velocity PID loop descriptors and calls *init_pid()* to initialize them. It is more convenient to have a routine like *init_pid()* assign values to the various parameter fields in the PIDLOOP descriptor than to code the assignments in-line.

In this example, storage for the two descriptors is allocated dynamically using the general memory allocation function *calloc()*, which returns a pointer to an allocated block of memory. The amount of memory is specified by the number of items (the first argument), and the size of each item (the second argument). The size of the PIDLOOP descriptor is obtained via the *sizeof* operator[4] which evaluates the size of its operand in bytes.[5] Since *calloc()* returns a *void* pointer (it may be a

[4]Note that *sizeof* is not a function, but an operator that is evaluated at compile time, i.e., when the program module is compiled.

[5]The size unit is dependent on the compiler and the memory architecture of the underlying computer. Generally, the unit is the same size as the *char* type, which may not be 8-bits on some systems.

char pointer in some implementations), it should be cast to the proper pointer type, which in this case is *PIDLOOP **. There is another memory allocation function called *malloc()* which accepts a single argument specifying the size of the desired block. When allocating memory for structures, *calloc()* is preferred since the allocated memory is cleared to zero and is guaranteed to satisfy all alignment requirements. It is always a good idea to test if the allocation is successful (i.e., a non-NULL pointer is returned); writing into an unallocated memory block is almost guaranteed to crash the program.

Dynamic memory allocation is not really necessary in this simple example since the number of parameter descriptors is known in advance. However, this seems like a good place to introduce it. An example in later chapters will involve control of multiple motors where the number of motors is not known until run time. In that case, the parameter structures must be allocated dynamically.

Since the position and velocity parameter structures are allocated dynamically and *init_cascade()* can be called by several routines to initialize or reset the parameters, there must be a mechanism to prevent the loop descriptors from being allocated again and again. Also, since the user can specify the parameters in any order, the loop descriptors must be allocated before the specified parameters can be assigned. A flag variable, *initflag,* is used to indicate if memory for the data structures has been allocated. This allows the specification command routines to know if they need to call *init_cascade()* to allocate the position and velocity descriptors. The flag also allows *init_cascade()* to know when to bypass the allocation and not overwrite user-specified parameters.

4.11.3 CONTROL

The main control loop in *control()* first sets a timer for the sample period. The position and velocity are obtained via *getp()* and *getv()* and are assigned to the *cl_feedback* fields of the position and velocity loop descriptors. Ideally, one wants the position and velocity at the same instance, but this is not usually possible. To better approximate simultaneity, the feedback functions *getp()* and *getv()* should be called as close together in time as possible. Since both the position and velocity loops use the PID algorithm, the control outputs can be determined by passing a pointer to the appropriate descriptor to the *pid()* calculation routine. In this cascade control example, the output of the position loop becomes the setpoint for the velocity loop. The output of the velocity loop is sent to the actuator through the *vmact()* routine.

Comparing this example with the earlier example *cascade0.c* from Chapter 3, we can see that the control loop is greatly simplified since most of the calculations are moved into the *pid()* routine. We have also introduced position, velocity, and actuation scaling factors in the input and output routines. The factors are defined as 1.0 in this example using #define macros, so they do not really make any difference, but it is very easy to change them to suit your application.

Although both the position and velocity loops use PID control, it is not necessary to use the same control algorithm for both loops. Different control algorithms can be integrated with a more general data structure (discussed in the Control Loop Descriptors section) and different calculation routines for each scheme.

4.12 LINKED LISTS IN CASCADE CONTROL

Cascade control need not be restricted to a two-level cascade. One can implement a general multi-level cascade with a different control algorithm for each loop by adding fields to the parameter structure. Expanding on the *struct _cloop* example, we can have:

```
struct _loop {
        char name[NAMESIZE+1];      /* loop name, */
                                    /* +1 for NUL terminator */

        int channel[NIOCHAN];       /* i/o channel numbers */
        double param[NPARAM];       /* control parameters */
        double tsamp;               /* sampling interval */
        int timer;                  /* timer number */

        void (*reference)();        /* get reference or setpoint */
        void (*control)();          /* control calculation routine */
        void (*feedback)();         /* feedback i/o routine */
        void (*actuate)();          /* output i/o routine */

        struct _loop *setpoint;     /* to loop that determines */
                                    /*  setpoint */
        struct _loop *group;        /* to others in the same group */
        struct _loop *process;      /* to similar processes */
                                    /* (eg. pressure) */
 };
```

The control descriptor is even more general now since the control algorithm and input/output routines are encapsulated in the descriptor itself in the form of function pointers. The execution control routine need not know anything about the details of the control loop other than the sampling period. For example, the execution control routine might look something like this:

```
struct _loop aloop;
  ...
void execloop(loop)
struct _loop *lptr;
{
     while (1)
     {
          SetDTimer(lptr->timer, (long)(lptr->tsamp * 1000L));
```

```
        (*lptr->reference)(lptr);          /* get setpoint */
        (*lptr->feedback)(lptr);           /* get feedback */
        (*lptr->control)(lptr);            /* calculate control */
        (*lptr->actuate)(lptr);            /* output */

        WaitDTimer(lptr->timer);           /* wait for timeout */
    }
}
```

A pointer to the loop descriptor is passed to each of the four routines, allowing the same routines to be used for different loops. If there is no action associated with a function (for example, position loop output actuation in the cascade control program), the function pointer should be set to point to a do-nothing routine such as:

```
void empty(ignored)
struct _loop *ignored;
{
        return;
}
```

To handle cases where the setpoint is the output of another loop, there is a field, *struct _loop *setpoint*, that points to the loop from which the setpoint is obtained. If this pointer is not NULL, the setpoint can be obtained from the output element of the parameter array in the structure pointed to.

As an organizational aid, links are provided to other descriptors in the system. The *group* pointer points at the next control descriptor in the same group. For example, a distillation column will need to control flow rates, temperature, pressure, and a host of other process parameters, each with their own control loops. All the control descriptors associated with a particular distillation column can be chained together via the *group* pointer field, and the entire chain can be referenced with a single pointer pointing to the head of the chain. For example:

```
struct _loop *column1;
struct _loop *loop;
 ...
for (loop = column1, loop != NULL; loop = loop->group)
        function(loop);
```

This simplified example shows how all the control processes for the entire distillation column can be referenced. A common application is to scan the process descriptor list for status information to update a display on the operator station.

It is often useful to be able to reference all process loops controlling the same type of process parameters, wherever they are in the system. For example, one may wish to know how a valve failure is affecting all the temperature control loops. The *process* pointer is designed to facilitate such references.

The data structures we have described work well for cascade control and other schemes where the setpoint of a control loop is a function of the output of another loop. It is not adequate for control schemes where the setpoint is a function of two or more loops (ratio control) or where the output of a loop must be applied to several other loops. One solution is to extend the data structure with additional fields or to use an array of descriptor pointers and leave the interpretation of the fields to a function, like we did with the parameters. Another solution is to use a more general calculation scheme such as the rpn calculator and a stack, as described in the text. The design must consider how the various calculation and data structuring schemes fit in with the overall control architecture and other requirements.

As an exercise, consider the control architecture for an electric wheelchair where each wheel is independently powered. The speed and position of each wheel must be controlled and coordinated with each other and with the desired speed, position, and orientation of the wheelchair.

4.13 COMMAND INTERPRETATION USING TABLES

In previous command interpreters, the command letter and the function associated with the command are encoded in the program code itself. In *main2.c*, the command input string and the associated function are described by an array of structures known as the command table. Commands can be added, deleted, or modified by editing the command table; the code to interpret the command is not affected at all. Each command is described by a data structure of the form:

```
#define CMDLEN  12

struct command {
        char cmd[CMDLEN+1]; /* command string */
                            /* (+1 for NUL terminator) */
        void (*cmdfunc)();  /* pointer to command function. */
};
```

The *cmd* field is a *char* array holding the command string; the *cmdfunc* field points to the routine that acts on that command. The command table is an array of such structures; here is an excerpt:

```
static struct command cmdtable[] = {

    { "posgains",     pgain },   /* specify position control gains */
    { "pk",           pgain },
```

```
    { "velgains",     vgain },  /* specify velocity control gains */
    { "vk",           vgain },

           ....
};
```

The line: *static struct command cmdtable[]* declares that *cmdtable[]* is an array of structures of type *struct command*, and that *cmdtable* is private to the module in which it is defined. Each array member is initialized by placing the data for the structure fields within curly braces[6] in the same order as the order in which the fields are declared.

In this example, the first field is a NUL terminated string constant, and the second is a pointer to the routine associated with the command.[7] It is important that *pgain* and *vgain* are declared as routines before they are used as initializers:

```
extern void pgain(char *);
extern void vgain(char *);
```

The declarations (which are actually function prototypes in this example) are placed in the *cascade1.h* header file which is included in the "import" section of the module. The advantage of organizing programs into modules and using a consistent module naming convention becomes evident here—since the declarations are found in *cascade1.h*, the actual routines probably reside in *cascade1.c*. Because the same header file is also included in *cascade1.c*, any inconsistencies between the declarations and the routine definition will be caught by the compiler when *cascade1.c* is compiled.

The reader will notice that it is very easy to have different commands refer to the same routine. It is merely a matter of adding an entry into the command table. In the example, each command has a long form and a short form—the user can type *posgains* or *pk* followed by the gain values to set the position control gains.

4.13.1 INTERPRETATION

The interpretation process takes place in two phases. The first step is to extract the command and parameter strings from the line typed in by the user. Once this is done, the interpreter searches the command table for an entry matching the command string and then invokes the associated routine, passing to it the parameter string.

---

[6]Unlike *struct, union* cannot be initialized at compile time.

[7]A function name used without the braces is taken to mean the address of the function.

Isolating the command and parameter string is done by the *getcmd()* routine. *Getcmd()* is passed two arguments: the user input string and a pointer to a character array to hold the command string. Entries are assumed to be separated by blanks, and the first entry is the command string. The first entry is copied to the array intended for the command string together with an ASCII NUL terminator.[8] A pointer to the rest of the input line is returned to be passed to the command action routine.

The standard *strcmp()* routine is used to compare the command string extracted by *getcmd()* against the *cmd* field of each table entry. Note how the command table entries are referenced and how the code steps through the table. A *struct command* pointer, *pcom*, is set to the start of the table. To point at the next entry, it is only necessary to increment *pcom*—the compiler knows the size and alignment of *struct command* and will add the correct value to *pcom* to point it at the next entry in the table.

This is an important difference between integer and pointer arithmetic. The only arithmetic operations allowed on pointers are addition and subtraction, and the base unit depends on the size and alignment of the data structure pointed to. To illustrate, say *p* and *q* are pointers defined and initialized thus:

```
struct example {
     char c;
     int i;
} *p, *q, array[10];

 ...

p = &array[0];
q = &array[5];
```

The result of *p +2* is the address of *array[2]*. What is the result of *q-p* ?[9] A word of warning: pointer arithmetic is only meaningful if the operand pointers or the result point into the same array.

Instead of using pointers, the command table entries can be referenced directly as array elements:

```
for (i = 0; i < ncmds; i++)
{
     if (strcmp(cmdtable[i].cmd, cword) == 0)
     ...
}
```

It does not make a great deal of difference whether the command table is referenced as an array or via pointers. In general, pointers may be faster since to

---

[8]Remember that in C, the ends of strings are marked with a NUL character.

[9]The answer is 5.

compute the address of *cmdtable[i]*, the compiler may generate code to multiply *i* with the size of each element, taking alignment into account, and add the result to the address of the start of the table. Contrast this with *pcom*++, where the compiler only needs to generate code to add the aligned structure size to the current value of *pcom*. The speed difference can be important in certain time critical applications. An example that comes to mind is the *chronos()* routine in *time.c*, which is described in the sample program section of Chapter 2.

4.13.2 END OF TABLE

Because interpreter sequentially searches the command table entries for a match, it needs to know when it has reached the end of the table. One solution is to know how many entries there are in the table. Note how the number of entries in the command table is calculated in *main()*:

```
ncmds = sizeof(cmdtable) / sizeof(struct command);
```

The *sizeof* operator can be applied to variables as well as types. This ability to calculate the number of entries is very important since it allows the command table to be edited without having to manually count the number of entries. The command table is small enough that one can just count the number of entries, but manual counting is an error-prone process and is not feasible for very large tables.

Another solution is to mark the end of the table with a NULL entry–NULL command string and NULL routine pointer.

4.14 SIMPLE INPUT CHECKING

To make the program less prone to manifestations of Murphy's Law, the command routines check if the command line contains the correct number of parameters and if the parameters are of the correct type. This is accomplished simply by checking the value returned by *sscanf()*. This value corresponds to the number of items in the input string that match the format specification. For example, the gain commands, *pgain()* and *vgain()* in *cascade1.c*, expect three floating point parameters corresponding to the proportional, integral, and differential gains. Thus:

```
sscanf(cline, "%lf %lf %lf", &kp, &ki, &kd)
```

must return a value of 3 for a valid input string *cline*. Checking the number of entries is but the first step. A well-designed user interface should also check if the input values are reasonable and will not cause any damage to the system. This is complicated by nonorthogonal parameters. For example, in a high-speed data acquisition application, the sampling rate and duration of the sampling run are both affected by the number of samples that can be stored in memory. The maximum sampling rate that can be specified thus depends on what sampling duration has been specified, and vice versa.

The reader may wonder why input checking is so important in real-time applications, especially since it results in bigger programs and does not contribute to execution speed. The answer is that a great deal of real-time software is employed in controlling machinery or processes. A software malfunction in such applications can have very costly consequences. Many malfunctions (euphemistically referred to as bugs) are caused by input conditions that are not anticipated by the designer. In the real world, human operators will make mistakes and sensors can malfunction.

```
/************************************************************************

FILE
    envir.h  -  defines program environment

LAST UPDATE
    16 August 1987
        remove unnecessary clutter

    Copyright(c) 1985,1986,1987  D.M. Auslander and C.H. Tham

************************************************************************/

/**********************   Operating System   **********************/

#define UNIX     0      /* 4.2 BSD, implies UNIX C compiler */
#define PCDOS    1      /* includes generic MSDOS family */
#define CPM      0      /* the CP/M family, including MP/M */


/******************   Hardware or Machine Type   ******************/

#define IBMPC        1       /* standard PC, PC/XT, PC/AT */
#define COMPUPRO     0       /* Compupro 8086 or Dual Processor */
#define INTEL310     0       /* Intel 310 development system */


/**************************   Compilers   ************************/

#define CIC86        0       /* Computer Innovations C86 ver. 2.20M */
#define DESMET       0       /* Desmet C */
#define LATTICE      0       /* Lattice C ver. 2.15 */
#define MICROSOFT    1       /* Microsft C ver. 4.00 */

#if MICROSOFT
#define ANSI                 /* use proposed ANSI C features */
#endif

/************************************************************************

FILE
    dash8.h  -  interface declarations for dash8.c

LAST UPDATE
    18 November 1987

************************************************************************/

#ifdef ANSI

extern void ad_init(void);
extern void ad_start(int);
extern int  ad_read(int);
extern int  ad_wread(int);

#else

extern void ad_init();
extern void ad_start();
extern int ad_read();
extern int ad_wread();

#endif

/************************************************************************

FILE
    dac2.h  -  interface declarations for dac2.c

LAST UPDATE
    18 November 1987

************************************************************************/

#ifdef ANSI

extern void da_init(void);
extern void da_limits(int *, int *);
extern int  da_write(int, int);

#else

extern void da_init();
extern void da_limits();
extern int  da_write();

#endif


/************************************************************************

FILE
    pidloop.h   -  simple control loop data structure definition

LAST UPDATE
    10 March 1988
        name changes

    Copyright (c) 1985-1988  D.M. Auslander and C.H. Tham

************************************************************************/
```

```
#define NAMESIZE        12      /* max characters for loop name */

struct _pidloop {
    char cl_name[NAMESIZE];     /* pointer to cntrol loop name string */

    int cl_inchan;              /* input channel number */
    int cl_outchan;             /* output channel number */

    double cl_setpoint;         /* controller setpoint */
    double cl_feedback;         /* controller feedback value */

    double cl_kp;               /* proportional gain */
    double cl_ki;               /* integral gain */
    double cl_kd;               /* derivative gain */

    double cl_err0;             /* error at (k)-th instant */
    double cl_err1;             /* error at (k-1)-th instant */
    double cl_err2;             /* error at (k-2)-th instant */

    double cl_output;           /* controller output */

    double cl_outmin;           /* lower limit of output value */
    double cl_outmax;           /* upper limit of output value */

    double cl_tsamp;            /* sampling interval */

};


typedef struct _pidloop PIDLOOP;

/*************************************************************************

FILE
    main2.c  -  d.c. motor speed control example, main program module 2

ROUTINES
    main    -  main program
    cmdint  -  command processor
    fstr    -  extract command word
    help    -  print list of commands

REMARKS
    This module is similar to main1.c but has a slightly better
    command interpreter.  This particular example is designed for the
    cascade1.c control module of chapter 4 example programs.

    To generate the simulation version of the example program:
        cl /DSIMRT main2.c cascade1.c rtsim2.c

LAST UPDATE
    18 January 1988
        minor tidying-up

    Copyright (c) 1984-1988  D.M. Auslander and C.H. Tham

*************************************************************************/

/*************************************************************************
                              I M P O R T S
*************************************************************************/


#include <stdio.h>
#include <stdlib.h>         /* standard ANSI library function declarations */
#include <string.h>         /* standard string function declarations */

#include "envir.h"          /* program environment declarations */
#include "cascade1.h"       /* cascade control definitions */

/*************************************************************************
              F O R W A R D   D E C L A R A T I O N S
*************************************************************************/


#ifdef ANSI

static void     cmdint(char *);
static char *   getcmd(char *, char *);
static void     menu(void);

#else

void    cmdint();
char    getcmd();
void    menu();

#endif

/*************************************************************************
    P R I V A T E   D A T A   A N D   D E C L A R A T I O N S
*************************************************************************/


#define PROMPT  "READY "        /* defines the command processor prompt */
#define BUFSIZE 100             /* command input buffer size */

/*-----------------------------------------------------------------------
    The following declares a data structure for associating a
    command string with the routine that acts on the contents
    of that command string.  This is done using a C construct
    known as a "struct" (record to you Pascal enthusiasts).

    The structure has 2 fields:
```

```
        1) the command name in the form of a NUL terminated string
        2) a pointer to the associated function
-----------------------------------------------------------------*/

#define CMDLEN  12      /* max length of command name */

struct command {

    char cmd[CMDLEN+1]; /* command string (+1 for NUL terminator) */

    void (*cmdfunc)();  /* pointer to command function.  Note the  */
                        /*   parentheses in the declaration - they */
                        /*   are very important and must be placed */
                        /*   exactly right! (See K & R, page 209). */
};


/*-----------------------------------------------------------------
    This is the command interpreter table, an array of commands and
    their associated function pointers.  Note that commands have a
    long and a short form.

    The interpreter table is an array of structures.  Each structure
    in the array is initialized with a command name and an associated
    function pointer (function name used without brackets).

    The function pointers must be declared ahead so that the compiler
    knows that the names refer to functions and not data variables,
    and assigns the proper function addresses (entry points).
-----------------------------------------------------------------*/

static struct command cmdtable[] = {

    { "posgains",   pgain },,       /* specify position control gains */
    { "pk",         pgain },

    { "velgains",   vgain },        /* specify velocity control gains */
    { "vk",         vgain },

    { "setpoint",   setpos },       /* specify position setpoint */
    { "s",          setpos },

    { "sampletime", setsmp },       /* specify sample time */
    { "t",          setsmp },

    { "go",         control },      /* start controller */
    { "g",          control },

    { "initialize", init },         /* initialize */
    { "i",          init },

    { "help",       menu },         /* print help menu */
    { "h",          menu },

    { "exit",       exit },         /* program exit */
    { "e",          exit }
};

static int ncmds;       /* number of entries in command table */

/*********************************************************************
                    M A I N     P R O G R A M
*********************************************************************/

/*-----------------------------------------------------------------
PROCEDURE
    MAIN  -  this is the main program

REMARKS
    Note how the number of entries in the command table is determined
    through the use of the sizeof() operator.

LAST UPDATE
    18 January 1988
        minor tidy up
-----------------------------------------------------------------*/

main()
{
    char cbuf[BUFSIZE];     /* space for the user-typed command line */


    ncmds = sizeof(cmdtable) / sizeof(struct command);

    menu();                 /* print command list to start. */

    for(;;)                 /* an endless loop. */
    {
        fputs(PROMPT, stdout); /* print a prompt so that user will */
                               /*   know that the program expects  */
                               /*   an input.                      */

        fgets(cbuf, BUFSIZE, stdin);   /* read a NULL terminated string */
                                       /*   from the "standard input"   */
                                       /*   (normally the user console) */

        cmdint(cbuf);          /* call the routine that interprets  */
                               /*   the command line.               */
    }

}
```

```
/**********************************************************************
                    P R I V A T E   R O U T I N E S
**********************************************************************/

/*-----------------------------------------------------------------
PROCEDURE
    CMDINT  -  command interpreter

SYNOPSIS
    static void cmdint(cline)
    char cline[];

PARAMETERS
    cline  -  command line

DESCRIPTION
    The command word is isolated and matched against the list of valid
    commands in the command table.  If a match is found, the routine
    associated with that command is executed.

LAST UPDATE
    1 December 1987
-----------------------------------------------------------------*/

static void cmdint(cline)
char cline[];
{
    char cword[CMDLEN+1];    /* storage to hold the command word. */
    char *prest;             /* ptr to rest of line after command word */
    struct command *pcom;    /* ptr to the command structure list. */
    int i;                   /* iteration counter */


    prest = getcmd(cline, cword);        /* isolate the command word */

    /*------------------------------------------------------------
        Search the command list for a match on the command word.
    ------------------------------------------------------------*/

    pcom = cmdtable;    /* initialize the pointer to the command list */

    for (i = 0; i < ncmds; i++)
    {
        /*  note: strcmp() returns zero if strings match  */

        if (strcmp(pcom->cmd, cword) == 0)
        {
            /*-------------------------------------------------------
                Command word matches a name entry in the command
                interpreter table.  The associated function is
                executed  --  again, watch the parentheses!
            -------------------------------------------------------*/

            (*pcom->cmdfunc)(prest);     /* execute associated func */

            break;                       /* break out of "for" loop */
        }

        pcom++;                          /* not found, next entry */
    }

    if (i >= ncmds)      /* did not match any of the valid commands */
    {
        printf("command not found : %s\n", cline);
    }

}



/*-----------------------------------------------------------------
FUNCTION
    GETCMD  -  isolate command word from input string

SYNOPSIS
    static char *getcmd(line, word)
    char line[], word[];

PARAMETERS
    line  -  command line
    word  -  where to put the command word

RETURNS
    pointer to rest of line (after the command word)

DESCRIPTION
    Command words are assumed to be delimited by blanks.  Thus this
    routine finds the first blank-terminated word in the command line
    and copies it into the 'word' argument.

    The command line is a NUL terminated character array which is
    passed to this routine in the form of a NUL terminated character
    array.  Note that the command line CANNOT begin with a blank.

    getcmd() returns NULL if the input command line begins with a blank
    or carriage-return.

LAST UPDATE
    20 March 1988
        dump leading blanks
-----------------------------------------------------------------*/
```

```
static char *getcmd(line, word)
char line[], word[];
{
    int i;      /* index into line[] */
    int j;      /* index into word[] */


    for (i = 0; (line[i] == ' ') || (line[i] == ''); i++)
        ;               /* skip leading spaces and tabs */

    for (j = 0; j < CMDLEN; j++, i++)
    {
        if ((line[i] == ' ') || (line[i] == '\n') || (line[i] == '\0'))
            break;      /* end of word found, get out of loop */

        word[j] = line[i];      /* copy the character to word[] */
    }

    word[j] = '\0';     /* terminate command word with NUL character */

    return(&line[i]);   /* return a pointer to the remainder of line */

}


/*--------------------------------------------------------------------
PROCEDURE
    MENU  -  print a list of commands

SYNOPSIS
    static void menu()

LAST UPDATE
    22 September 1984
--------------------------------------------------------------------*/

static void menu()
{

    fputs("                 COMMAND LIST\n\n", stdout);
    fputs("full command (or single-letter equivalent) arguments\n\n", stdout);

    fputs("initialize    (i)    delta_t\n", stdout);
    fputs("sampletime    (t)    tsamp\n", stdout);
    fputs("posgains      (pk)   kp ki kd\n", stdout);
    fputs("velgains      (vk)   kp ki kd\n", stdout);
    fputs("setpoint      (s)    position setpoint\n", stdout);
    fputs("go            (g)    number_of_iterations print(0/1)\n", stdout);
    fputs("exit          (e)    \n", stdout);
   uts("help          (h)    \n\n", stdout);
```

```
}

extern void    control(char *);
extern void    pgain(char *);
extern void    vgain(char *);
extern void    setpos(char *);
extern void    setsmp(char *);
extern void    init(char *);
/**********************************************************************

FILE
    cascade1.c  -  position and velocity control using cascaded PID

ENTRY ROUTINES
    control   -  the cascade controller

    pgain     -  get position gains
    vgain     -  get velocity gains
    smpset    -  set sampling interval

    getv      -  get velocity
    getp      -  get position

PRIVATE ROUTINES
    initpid  -  initialize cloop fields
    pid      -  perform PID control

INITIALIZATION ROUTINE
    init_cascade  -  allocate and initialize data structures

REMARKS
    This module implements the PID cascade control configuration of
    figure 3.7 in the book.  This implementation differs from the
    previous cascade0.c in that the velocity and position control
    loops are described by a special data structure of type PIDLOOP.

    Representing each control loop by a structure variable of type
    PIDLOOP leads to a more elegant and flexible control system.  It
    allows one to easily implement complex and deeply nested cascade
    control systems by merely connecting the various control loops
    through the main control program.

    In this demonstration program, the two loops are connected by
    control() such that the input to the innner velocity loop is the
    output of the outer position loop.

    This file contains only the control implementation.  You have
    to implement the user interface and perhaps the simulation
    module.  Please refer to cntrl1.c and rtsim1.c for examples of
    user interface and simulation modules.
```

```
LAST UPDATE
    20 March 1988
        check number of fields converted by sscanf()

**********************************************************************/

/*********************************************************************
                          I M P O R T S
**********************************************************************/

#include <stdio.h>
#include <stdlib.h>      /* standard library function declarations */
#include <string.h>      /* standard string function declarations */

#include "envir.h"       /* environment definitions */
#include "dash8.h"       /* declarations for dash8.c */
#include "dac2.h"        /* declarations for dac2.c */
#include "time0.h"       /* declarations for time0.c */
#include "pidloop.h"     /* PIDLOOP data strcuture declarations */
#include "cascade1.h"    /* export declarations for this module */

/*********************************************************************
              F O R W A R D    D E C L A R A T I O N S
**********************************************************************/

#ifdef ANSI

static double getv(void);           /* get velocity */
static double getp(void);           /* get position */
static void   vmact(void);          /* send velocity control output to actuator */
static void   pid(PIDLOOP *);       /* basic PID control */
static void   init_cascade(void); /* initialize this module */
static void   init_pid(PIDLOOP *, char *, int, int, double, double, double,
                double, double, double, double, double, double);

#else   /* no function prototypes */

double getv();
double getp();
void   vmact();

void   pid();

void   init_cascade();
void   init_pid();

#endif

/*********************************************************************
                     P R I V A T E    D A T A
**********************************************************************/

static int initflag = 0;          /* has system been initialized? */

static PIDLOOP *vloop;            /* pointer to velocity control loop */
static PIDLOOP *ploop;            /* pointer to position control loop */

static double tsamp = 1.0;        /* sampling interval in seconds */

#define VINCHAN     0             /* velocity input ADC channel */
#define VOUTCHAN    0             /* velocity output DAC channel */
#define PINCHAN     1             /* position input ADC channel */
#define POUTCHAN    -1            /* dummy position DAC channel */

#define ADCTOP      1.0           /* ADC units to position units */
#define ADCTOV      1.0           /* ADC units to velocity units */
#define MTODAC      1.0           /* output units to DAC units */

#define MPMIN   -1.0e+6           /* min position actuator output */
#define MPMAX    1.0e+6           /* max position actuator output */

/*********  default PID gains and other control parameters  **********/

#define VKP     5.0               /* velocity PID gains */
#define VKI     0.1
#define VKD     0.0

#define VREF    0.0               /* default velocity setpoint */

#define VERR0   0.0               /* velocity errors at k, k-1 and k-2 */
#define VERR1   0.0
#define VERR2   0.0

#define PREF    0.0               /* default position setpoint */

#define PKP     2.0               /* position PID gains */
#define PKI     0.1
#define PKD     0.0

#define PERR0   0.0               /* position errors at k, k-1 and k-2 */
#define PERR1   0.0
#define PERR2   0.0

/*********************************************************************
                     E N T R Y    R O U T I N E S
**********************************************************************/

/*-------------------------------------------------------------------
PROCEDURE
    CONTROL  -  implements cascade position-velocity control

SYNOPSIS
    void control(cline)
```

```
    char *cline;

PARAMETER
    cline  -  pointer to input line.

REMARKS
    The error terms are initialized to zero.  When this routine starts,
    it is equivalent to applying a step position reference input.

LAST UPDATE
    10 March 1988
        fixup for ANSI features
    20 March 1988
        check number of fields converted by sscanf()
----------------------------------------------------------------*/

void control(cline)
char *cline;
{
    int nitr;           /* # of iterations */
    int prnt;           /* 1 - print control output, 0 - do not print */
    int i;              /* iteration counter */


    if (!initflag)                  /* if system not initialized, do so */
        init_cascade();

    /*  get user specified iteration limit and print switch  */

    if (sscanf(cline, "%d %d", &nitr, &prnt) != 2)
    {
        printf("invalid or insufficient parameters\n");
        return;
    }

    for (i = 0; i < nitr; i++)
    {
        /*--------------------------------------------------------
            Set countdown timer to sampling period in milliseconds.
        ------------------------------------------------------*/

        SetTimer((long)(tsamp * 1000L));

        /*--------------------------------------------------------
            Obtain the current position and call pid() to calculate
            the position loop's control output value.
        ------------------------------------------------------*/

        ploop->cl_feedback = getp();    /* get current position */
        vloop->cl_feedback = getv();    /* get current velocity */

        pid(ploop);                     /* calc. position control o/p */

        /*------------------------------------------------------
            The output of the position loop is the setpoint for the
            velocity loop.  Here we copy the position output to the
            velocity setpoint, get the current velocity and pass the
            parameters to pid() to calculate the control output for
            the velocity loop.
        -----------------------------------------------------*/

        vloop->cl_setpoint = ploop->cl_output;

        pid(vloop);     /* calculate velocity loop output */

        vmact();        /* send control output to velocity actuator */

        if (prnt)
            printf("%d: p = %.31f, v = %.31f, mp = %.21f, mv = %.21f\n",
                i, ploop->cl_feedback, vloop->cl_feedback,
                ploop->cl_output, vloop->cl_output);

        if (TimeUp())                   /* premature time-out */
        {
            printf("sample time too short\n");
            exit(1);
        }

        while (!TimeUp())
        {
#if SIMRT
            tstep();    /* advance simulation time step */
#endif
        }
    }

}


/*-------------------------------------------------------------------
PROCEDURES
    PGAIN  -  interpret the input line specifying position gains
    VGAIN  -  interpret the input line specifying velocity gains

SYNOPSIS
    void pgain(cline)
    char *cline;

    void vgain(cline)
    char *cline;

PARAMETERS
```

```
    cline  -  input line

REMARKS
    Checks the initflag to ensure that the vloop and ploop data
    structures are allocated and if not, to allocate and initialize
    them through init_cascade().

LAST UPDATE
    1 December 1987
        declare return type as void
    20 March 1988
        check number of fields converted by sscanf()
----------------------------------------------------------------*/

void pgain(cline)
char *cline;
{
    double kp, ki, kd;      /* P, I and D gains */


    if (sscanf(cline, "%lf %lf %lf", &kp, &ki, &kd) == 3)
    {
#ifdef DEBUG
        printf("<pgain> kp = %.3lf, ki = %.3lf, kd = %.3lf\n", kp, ki, kd);
#endif

        if (!initflag)
            init_cascade();

        ploop->cl_kp = kp;
        ploop->cl_ki = ki;
        ploop->cl_kd = kd;
    }
    else
        printf("invalid or insufficient position gains\n");

}


void vgain(cline)
char *cline;
{
    double kp, ki, kd;      /* P, I and D gains */


    if (sscanf(cline, "%lf %lf %lf", &kp, &ki, &kd) == 3)
    {
#ifdef DEBUG
        printf("<vgain> kp = %.3lf, ki = %.3lf, kd = %.3lf\n", kp, ki, kd);
#endif
        if (!initflag)
            init_cascade();

        vloop->cl_kp = kp;
        vloop->cl_ki = ki;
        vloop->cl_kd = kd;
    }
    else
        printf("invalid or insufficient velocity gains\n");

}


/*----------------------------------------------------------------
PROCEDURE
    SETPOS  -  get position setpoint from command line

SYNOPSIS
    void setpos(cline)
    char *cline;

PARAMETERS
    cline  -  user's command line

REMARKS
    Note how this differs from pgain() and vgain() in that the value
    is sscanf'ed directly into the cl_setpoint field instead of going
    through temporary variables.

LAST UPDATE
    1 December 1987
        declare return type as void
    20 March 1988
        check number of fields converted by sscanf()
----------------------------------------------------------------*/

void setpos(cline)
char *cline;
{

    if (!initflag)
        init_cascade();         /* initialize controller */

    if (sscanf(cline,"%lf", &(ploop->cl_setpoint)) == 1)
    {
#ifdef DEBUG
        printf("<setpos> position setpoint = %.3lf\n", ploop->cl_setpoint);
#endif
    }
    else
        printf("invalid position setpoint\n");
```

```
}


/*-----------------------------------------------------------------
PROCEDURE
    SETSMP  -  set sample time

SYNOPSIS
    void setsmp(cline)
    char *cline;

PARAMETER
    cline  -  user's command line

DESCRIPTION
    Extract sample time from user's command line and use it to set the
    sample time on the timer.

LAST UPDATE
    20 March 1988
        check number of fields converted by sscanf()
-----------------------------------------------------------------*/

void setsmp(cline)
char *cline;
{

    if (sscanf(cline, "%lf", &tsamp) == 1)
    {
        if (!initflag)
        {
            init_cascade();          /* initialize controller */
        }
        else    /* set both position and velocity tsamps to be the same */
        {
            ploop->cl_tsamp = tsamp;
            vloop->cl_tsamp = tsamp;
        }

#ifdef DEBUG
        printf("<setsmp> tsamp = %lf\n", tsamp);
#endif
    }
    else
        printf("invalid sampling period\n");

}


/*-----------------------------------------------------------------
PROCEDURE
    INIT  -  process system initialization command

SYNOPSIS
    void init()

REMARKS
    This routine must be called before control() is called.

LAST UPDATE
    10 March 1988
        add call to init_cascade() to reset parameters
-----------------------------------------------------------------*/

void init(cline)
char *cline;
{

    ad_init();                  /* initialize A/D */
    da_init();                  /* initialize D/A */

    init_cascade();             /* initialize or reset parameters */

#ifdef SIMRT
    sim_init(cline);            /* initialize simulation module */
#endif

}

/************************************************************************

    The following section contains routines which interface between
    high level control code and functions which perform the hardware
    dependent functions of operating the A/D and D/A.  As such, they
    are necessarily dependent on the device driver interface.

************************************************************************/

/*-----------------------------------------------------------------
FUNCTIONS
    GETV  -  returns motor velocity
    GETP  -  returns motor position

SYNOPSIS
    static double getv()
    static double getp()

RETURNS
    current motor velocity (units unspecified)
    current motor position (units unspecified)
```

```
REMARKS
    Reads the ADC channel specified by the cl_inchan field.

    Note that the source for the channel number is assumed here, but
    that's O.K. because this is a static function that services this
    module only.

    The alternative is to pass the channel number as an argument, but
    that means that the control() function must know how velocity and
    position is obtained, which is less desirable as it spreads the
    application specific parameters into three places: the PIDLOOP data
    structure, the control() routine and these two routines, instead
    of just the data structure and these two routines.

    Note that the conversion of raw ADC units to velocity and position
    units uses parameterized ADCTOV and ADCTOP conversion factors.

LAST UPDATE
    1 March 1988
----------------------------------------------------------------*/

static double getv()
{

    return((double)ad_wread(vloop->cl_inchan) * ADCTOV);
}


static double getp()
{

    return((double)ad_wread(ploop->cl_inchan) * ADCTOP);
}



/*-----------------------------------------------------------------
PROCEDURE
    VMACT  -  send velocity control output to actuator

SYNOPSIS
    static void vmact()

REMARKS
    Output is converted from logical to physical units required by the
    DAC (using MTODAC) and rounded to the nearest integer.

    Note that the DAC channel is specified in the cl_outchan field.

LAST UPDATE
    1 March 1988
----------------------------------------------------------------*/

static void vmact()
{
    int channel;
    int value;


    channel = vloop->cl_outchan;
    value = (int)((vloop->cl_output * MTODAC) + 0.5);

    da_write(channel, value);

}


/*********************************************************************
               P R I V A T E   R O U T I N E S
/*********************************************************************

/*-----------------------------------------------------------------
PROCEDURE
    PID  -  apply PID control for 1 iteration

SYNOPSIS
    static void pid(param)
    PIDLOOP *param;

PARAMETERS
    param  -  pointer to control loop data structure

REMARKS
    Using data in control loop, calculate controller output and store
    it in the cl_output field.

LAST UPDATE
    11 May 1985
----------------------------------------------------------------*/

static void pid(param)
PIDLOOP *param;
{
    double delta_m;          /* change in controller output */


    param->cl_err2 = param->cl_err1;     /* update error terms */
    param->cl_err1 = param->cl_err0;
    param->cl_err0 = param->cl_setpoint - param->cl_feedback;

    delta_m = param->cl_kp * (param->cl_err0 - param->cl_err1)
              +  param->cl_ki * param->cl_err0
```

```
            + param->cl_kd * (param->cl_err0 - (2.0 *  param->cl_err1)
                               + param->cl_err2);

    param->cl_output += delta_m;                 /* update output value */

    if (param->cl_output > param->cl_outmax)     /* apply output limits */
    {
        param->cl_output = param->cl_outmax;
    }
    else if (param->cl_output < param->cl_outmin)
    {
        param->cl_output = param->cl_outmin;
    }

}


/*********************************************************************
          I N I T I A L I Z A T I O N    R O U T I N E S
*********************************************************************/

/*-------------------------------------------------------------------
PROCEDURE
    INIT_CASCADE  -  allocate and initialize data structures

SYNOPSIS
    void init_cascade()

REMARKS
    Sets init flag to true to indicate system initialized.

    The vloop and ploop structures are only allocated the first
    time this routine is called.  The PID gains and setpoints are
    preserved on subsequent calls.  This is to allow init() to call
    this routine when the user wants to reset/restart the program.

LAST UPDATE
    10 March 1988
        modify to preserve gains on subsequent calls.
-------------------------------------------------------------------*/

static void init_cascade()
{
    int damin, damax;         /* min and max DAC output values */
    double mvmin, mvmax;      /* min and max of velocity control values */
    double kp, ki, kd;        /* copies of P, I and D gains */


    if (!initflag)       /* allocate velocity loop control structure */
    {
        if ((vloop = (PIDLOOP *)calloc(1, sizeof(PIDLOOP))) == (PIDLOOP *)NULL)
        {
            printf("cannot allocate velocity parameter structure\n");
            exit(1);
        }
        else    /* initialize PID gains to defaults */
        {
            kp = VKP;
            ki = VKI;
            kd = VKD;
        }
    }
    else        /* preserve current PID gains */
    {
        kp = vloop->cl_kp;
        ki = vloop->cl_ki;
        kd = vloop->cl_kd;
    }

    /*-------------------------------------------------------------
        Initialize velocity PID loop control parameters.
    -------------------------------------------------------------*/

    da_limits(&damin, &damax);      /* find D/A output limits */

    mvmin = (double)damin / MTODAC;
    mvmax = (double)damax / MTODAC;

    init_pid(vloop, "vloop", VINCHAN, VOUTCHAN, kp, ki, kd,
              VERR0, VERR1, VERR2, mvmin, mvmax, tsamp);

    if (!initflag)       /* allocate position PID control structure */
    {
        if ((ploop = (PIDLOOP *)calloc(1, sizeof(PIDLOOP))) == (PIDLOOP *)NULL)
        {
            printf("cannot allocate position parameter structure\n");
            exit(1);
        }
        else
        {
            kp = PKP;
            ki = PKI;
            kd = PKD;
        }
    }
    else
    {
        kp = ploop->cl_kp;
        ki = ploop->cl_ki;
        kd = ploop->cl_kd;
    }
```

```
    /*---------------------------------------------------------------
        Since the output of the position loop does not directly
        drive an actuator, we used pre-defined output limits
        MPMIN and MPMAX which are set for a very wide range.
    ---------------------------------------------------------------*/

    init_pid(ploop, "ploop", PINCHAN, POUTCHAN, kp, ki, kd,
             PERR0, PERR1, PERR2, MPMIN, MPMAX, tsamp);

    initflag = 1;       /* system initialized */

}

/*--------------------------------------------------------------------
PROCEDURE
    INIT_PID  -  initialize data structure parameters for PID control

SYNOPSIS
    static void init_pid(param, name, ichan, ochan, kp, ki, kd,
                         e0, e1, e2, omin, omax, tsamp)

    PIDLOOP *param;
    char *name;
    int ichan, ochan;
    double kp, ki, kd, e0, e1, e2, omin, omax, tsamp;

PARAMETERS
    param          -  pointer to control loop parameter structure
    name           -  pointer to name or id string
    ichan, ochan   -  input and output i/o channel numbers
    kp, ki, kd     -  P, I and D gains
    e0, e1, e2     -  error terms at k, k-1 and k-2
    omin, omax     -  lower and upper output limits
    tsamp          -  sampling interval

REMARKS
    The basic function of this routine is to copy the initialization
    argument parameters into the appropriate fields of the control
    loop data structure.

    The name field is not used at present, but is maintained for
    possible future use as a means to find or reference particular
    control loops in an application with a large number of control
    loops.

    The error terms can be initialized to different values for
    different starting or initial conditions.

LAST UPDATE
    10 March 1988
        explicitly NUL terminate name string
--------------------------------------------------------------------*/

static void init_pid(param,name,ichan,ochan,kp,ki,kd,e0,e1,e2,omin,omax,tsamp)
PIDLOOP *param;
char *name;
int ichan, ochan;
double kp, ki, kd, e0, e1, e2, omin, omax, tsamp;
{

    /*-------------------------------------------------------------
        strncpy() may not add a NUL terminator if name length
        exceeds NAMESIZE, so to make sure, we NUL terminate it.
    -------------------------------------------------------------*/

    strncpy(param->cl_name, name, NAMESIZE);
    param->cl_name[NAMESIZE] = '\0';     /* NUL terminate name */

    param->cl_inchan = ichan;
    param->cl_outchan = ochan;
    param->cl_kp = kp;
    param->cl_ki = ki;
    param->cl_kd = kd;
    param->cl_err0 = e0;
    param->cl_err1 = e1;
    param->cl_err2 = e2;
    param->cl_outmin = omin;
    param->cl_outmax = omax;
    param->cl_tsamp = tsamp;

    param->cl_feedback = 0.0;
    param->cl_output = 0.0;

}

/*********************************************************************

FILE
    rtsim1.c  -  d.c. speed control, simulation module 1

ENTRY ROUTINES
    tstep       -  advance one time step
    SetTimer    -  set count-down timer
    TimeUp      -  has count down completed?

    ad_init     -  simulates A/D initialization
    ad_start    -  simulates starting an A/D read
    ad_read     -  simulates reading A/D value
    ad_wread    -  simulates read from A/D

    da_init     -  simulates D/A initialization
    da_limits   -  returns simulation D/A output limits
```

```
    da_write   -  simulates write to D/A

PRIVATE ROUTINE
    simul   -  motor plant simulation

INITIALIZATION ROUTINE
    sim_init   -  initialize simulation

REMARKS
    This module simulates the interface and motor hardware and the
    passage of "real" time.  This module must thus provide the same
    interface functions as the modules controlling the hardware.

    To use "real" time, compile this module with the /DFTIME switch;
    this will cause tstep() to use ftime() calls to tell time.

LAST UPDATE
    1 December 1987
        restructure and modify for MSC 4.00 and 5.00
    12 March 1988
        modify for cascade1.c & include declarations to satify /W3

    Copyright(C) 1984-1987  D.M. Auslander and C.H. Tham

**********************************************************************/

/*********************************************************************
                            I M P O R T S
**********************************************************************/

#include <stdio.h>

#include "envir.h"      /* environment specifications */
#include "dash8.h"      /* declarations for dash8.c */
#include "dac2.h"       /* declarations for dac2.c */
#include "time0.h"      /* declarations for time0.c */

/*********************************************************************
            F O R W A R D   D E C L A R A T I O N S
**********************************************************************/

#ifdef ANSI

extern void tstep(void);          /* these are referened outside of */
extern void sim_init(char *);     /*   this simulation module.      */

static void simul(void);          /* these are not referenced outside */
                                  /*   of this simulation module.     */
static void runtimer(void);

#else

extern void tstep();
extern void sim_init();

void simul();
void runtimer();

#endif

/*********************************************************************
                    P R I V A T E   D A T A
**********************************************************************/

#define VEL_SCALE       512.0   /* scale speed to A/D units */
#define POS_SCALE       512.0   /* scale position to A/D units */

#define ADMAX        2047       /* max A/D input value */
#define ADMIN       -2048       /* min A/D input value */

#define DASCALE      2047.0     /* scale D/A value to torque */
#define DAMIN       -2048       /* min. output value accepted */
#define DAMAX        2047       /* max. output value accepted */

static double inertia = 1.0;        /* motor system inertia */
static double speed;                /* simulated motor velocity */
static double position;             /* simulated motor position */
static double t;                    /* time */
static double dt;                   /* simulation step size in seconds */
static double torque = 0.0;         /* motor torque */

static long freq;               /* timer frequency (ticks/sec) */
static long ticks;              /* how many ticks to timeout */
static int tflag;               /* set to 1 if timer runs out */

static int initflag = 0;        /* indicates if module initialized */

/*********************************************************************
                    T I M E   S I M U L A T I O N
**********************************************************************/

/*------------------------------------------------------------------
PROCEDURE
    TSTEP  -  advance time forward one step

SYNOPSIS
    void tstep()

LAST UPDATE
    10 March 1988
        check if simulation is initialized
------------------------------------------------------------------*/
```

```
void tstep()
{

    if (initflag)
    {
        simul();        /* compute one time step in the differential */
                        /*   equation for the motor system.          */

        t += dt;        /* increment time by dt */

        runtimer();     /* simulate timer run */
    }
    else
    {
        printf("simulation module not initialized\n");

        tflag = 1;
    }

}


/*-----------------------------------------------------------------
PROCEDURE
    SETTIMER  -  set countdown timer

SYNOPSIS
    void SetTimer(ms)
    long ms;

PARAMETER
    period -  count down period in milliseconds

LAST UPDATE
    15 January 1988
-----------------------------------------------------------------*/

void SetTimer(ms)
long ms;
{

    tflag = 0;                                  /* timeout flag to false */

    ticks = ((ms * freq) + 500L) / 1000L;      /* 500 is for rounding */

    if (ticks <= 0L)
        printf("simulation time step too coarse\n");

}


/*-----------------------------------------------------------------
FUNCTION
    TIMEUP  -  has timer timed out?

SYNOPSIS
    int TimeUp()

RETURNS
    1 if timer runs out, 0 otherwise

LAST UPDATE
    1 March 1985
-----------------------------------------------------------------*/

int TimeUp()
{

    return(tflag);
}


/*-----------------------------------------------------------------
PROCEDURE
    RUNTIMER  -  simulates timer run

SYNOPSIS
    static void runtimer()

LAST UPDATE
    20 March 1988
        one tick per simulation time step
-----------------------------------------------------------------*/

static void runtimer()
{

    if (!tflag)             /* if timeout, just return, otherwise... */
    {
        --ticks;

        if (ticks <= 0L)    /* time has run out */
            tflag = 1;
    }

}


/***********************************************************************
                    A / D   S I M U L A T I O N

    These routines dummy the routines in dash8.c which drive the
```

```
    Metrabyte DASH8 A/D board.

    Channel 0 reads speed and channel 1 reads position for cascade1.c

*********************************************************************/

void ad_init()
{

    speed = 0.0;
    position = 0.0;

}


void ad_start(channel)
int channel;
{
    /* nothing */
}


int ad_read(channel)
int channel;
{
    int rval;                     /* return value */


    if (channel == 0)
    {
        rval = (int)(VEL_SCALE * speed);    /* scale and convert to int type */
    }
    else if (channel == 1)
    {
        rval = (int)(POS_SCALE * position);
    }
    else
        rval = 0;

    if (rval > ADMAX)                 /* apply converter limits */
        rval = ADMAX;
    else if (rval < ADMIN)
        rval = ADMIN;

    return(rval);
}


int ad_wread(channel)
int channel;
{
    return(ad_read(channel));
}


/*********************************************************************
                    D / A   S I M U L A T I O N

    These routines dummy the routines in dac2.c which drive the
    Metrabyte DAC02 D/A board.  The channel parameter is ignored.

    The DAC2 is a 12-bit digital-to-analog converter configured for
    bipolar output.  Thus, the output parameter values range from
    -2048 to 2047.  Only lower 12 bits will be used, treating those
    12 bits as a 2's complement signed number.  Thus if the output
    value is negative, the lower 12 bits will be preserved and all
    higher order bits will be converted to 1's.

    Note the use of ~0xfff instead of 0xf000, this makes the program
    more portable across machines with different integer sizes.

*********************************************************************/

void da_init()
{

    torque = 0.0;

}


void da_limits(lo, hi)
int *lo, *hi;
{

    *lo = DAMIN;
    *hi = DAMAX;

}


int da_write(channel, value)
int channel, value;
{

    if (value < 0)          /* OR with a binary number having 0's for */
        value |= ~0xfff;    /*   the lower 12 bits and 1's elsewhere  */
    else
        value &= 0xfff;     /* for positive values, just save the     */
                            /*   lower 12 bits.                       */

    torque = value / DASCALE;   /* rescale for motor drive torque. */
```

```
    return(0);              /* indicate all is well */
}

/*************************************************************************
                 P R I V A T E   R O U T I N E S

    The following routines are declared "static".  These routines
    can be directly accessed only by routines inside this file; they
    are not "visible" to routines outside this file.  Hence they are
    private to this file.  Private routines enhance data security
    and help avoid unexpected name conflicts in large programming
    projects.

*************************************************************************/

/*-----------------------------------------------------------------------
PROCEDURE
    SIMUL  -  simulates motor plant

SYNOPSIS
    static void simul()

REMARKS
    Solve the motor system differential equation.  This version uses
    the Euler method for integration; it isn't very efficient, but its
    easy to program!

LAST UPDATE
    12 January 1988
        add friction term to make it more interesting
    12 March 1988
        add position using trapeziod integration
-----------------------------------------------------------------------*/

static void simul()
{
    double friction;        /* friction term */
    double pspeed;          /* previous speed */


    pspeed = speed;

    friction = speed * 0.1;     /* this is quite arbitrary */

    speed += (torque - friction) * dt / inertia;

    position += 0.5 * (pspeed + speed) * dt;

}

/*************************************************************************
         I N I T I A L I Z A T I O N   R O U T I N E
*************************************************************************/

/*-----------------------------------------------------------------------
PROCEDURE
    SIM_INIT  -  system initialization

SYNOPSIS
    void sim_init(cline)
    char *cline;

PARAMETER
    cline  -  user's input command line

REMARKS
    In a "real" real-time program, this function would be used to set
    up interrupts, set clock modes, etc.  In this simulation version,
    it sets time to zero and sets the motor simulation initial conditions.

LAST UPDATE
    20 March 1988
        adapt timer resolution to simulation time step
-----------------------------------------------------------------------*/

void sim_init(cline)
char *cline;
{

    sscanf(cline, "%lf", &dt);  /* get the step size. */

#ifdef DEBUG
    printf("<init> dt = %lf\n", dt);
#endif

    t = 0.0;                    /* reset time */

    freq = (long)(1.0 / dt  +  0.5);    /* adapt timer frequency */

    speed = 0.0;                /* motor is initially at rest */
    position = 0.0;
    torque = 0.0;

    initflag = 1;               /* simulation module is now initialized */

}
```

CHAPTER 5

MULTIPLE INDEPENDENT PROCESSES

Thus far, we have explored program structures that can provide for a single background task, control of a motor in the examples, and as many foreground interrupt-driven tasks as are necessary to service the needs of the backgound. It is often desirable to extend this structure to include several independent or semi-independent background tasks as well, either to make better use of the available computational resource or to concentrate all of the control activities for a group of processes in a single processor so that they can be coordinated more easily. In the motor case, for example, if the motors are part of a machine tool or a robot, the coordinated control could be used to provide path or contouring control for machining, welding, or other such activities.

The simplest implementation for multiple background tasks occurs when all of the tasks are of similar nature and complexity. We will examine that situation first by extending the previous programs to the control of an arbitrary number of motors; each motor will use the same control algorithm but will have independent sets of controller gains and sample intervals.

5.1 DATA STRUCTURE FOR MULTIPLE MOTOR CONTROL

Because the control algorithms are the same for all of the motors being controlled, the differentiation between motors can be done in the programs's data structure rather than by using multiple copies of the code portion of the program.

The existing program code will have to be modified to operate on information stored in the data structure rather than on simple variables, but otherwise will require very little change. An additional section of program code will have to be added to handle scheduling so that the proper timing will be used in activating the control loops. The PID control loop structure is extremely general. Although the examples refer to control of motors, the actual control objects could be almost any kind of system that is subject to feedback control. If general setpoint calculations were desired, the interpreter described in Chapter 4 could be added to the data structure used here.

The data structure shown in Fig. 5.1 is very similar to the sample data structure used for a control loop in the previous chapter. It includes all of the information needed to schedule and run each control loop. The control is set up for a PID algorithm using the direct calculation method. The accumulated error must be stored separately along with its minimum and maximum values, and the previous error must also be stored so the derivative term can be calculated.

Structure motors:

integer	in_channel	(input channel number)
integer	out_channel	(output channel number)
float	velocity	(current velocity)
float	setpoint	
float	kp	(proportional gain)
float	ki	(integral gain)
float	kd	(derivative gain)
float	integral	(accumulated error)
float	int_minimum	(minimum allowed integrator value)
float	int_maximum	(maximum allowed integrator value)
float	previous_error	
float	bias	(constant in controller equation)
float	m	(controller output)
float	m_minimum	
float	m_maximum	
float	t_sample	(sampling interval)

Figure 5.1

5.2 ALGORITHM IMPLEMENTATION: PRECISION

This data structure is written with all of the control quantities expressed as floating point numbers which, for a relatively slow process or a very fast processor, might give adequate response speed in motor control. In many cases, however, the floats will have to be changed to integers in order to improve the performance and allow for a suitable short sampling interval. If the floating point representation can be maintained, there are no appreciable precision problems associated with round-off errors in most cases. When the change is made to integer representation, however, the form in which the alogrithm is implemented has a significant effect on precision.

There are two major implementations of the PID algorithm that have already been presented—the incremental form and the absolute form. The advantage of the incremental form is that output limits can be applied more cleanly than in the absolute form, where output limits have to be applied separately to the integral section and to the overall controller output. To review, the need for output limits comes from two sources. The controller output must be limited to the range used by the output interface (a D/A converter, for example), or to the range allowed by the actuator input, whichever is lower. In the absolute form of the PID algorithm, the integral is computed by maintaining a summation of the past errors and then inserting that summation into the controller output equation with the integral gain. If a very large change in setpoint is called for, the controller output will go into saturation (i.e., the limit will become active) until the process output gets close to the setpoint, when linear behavior should be resumed. If the integral summation is not limited, it will continue its summation all the time that the system is in saturation. Because the error is large for that whole time, the summation term will become very large. As the process output approaches the setpoint, the controller output should start to drop so that an equilibrium at the setpoint can be approached. However, if the integrator has a very large value at that point, the controller will be held at saturation. In fact, the integrator will not even start decreasing until after the setpoint has been crossed and the error changes sign. The result of this is a response behavior that exhibits a very large overshoot and oscillatory approach to the setpoint, or even instability.

As an illustration, we will simulate the behavior of a simple motor system model. The response of the motor to a step input in voltage is shown in Fig. 5.2. This is the uncontrolled (open-loop) response of the motor and shows that a steady-state velocity is reached for a constant input voltage. This form of step response indicates that integral control action will be required if the controlled system is to have no steady-state error, as shown in Fig. 5.3, so the effect of different forms of integral limiting can be demonstrated. Fig. 5.4 shows the response of the system with PI control (k_d is set to zero to simplify the controller design) using the incremental (difference) form of the algorithm and a setpoint change large enough to cause controller output saturation. Fig. 5.5 shows the response for the same setpoint change with the absolute form of the PI algorithm having output limiting, but no integrator limiting and Fig. 5.6 shows the response with integrator limiting added also.

These results indicate the superiority of the incremental form of controller algorithm, but, in a manner that is typical of many real time problems, when the floating point algorithms used in the above examples are converted to integer

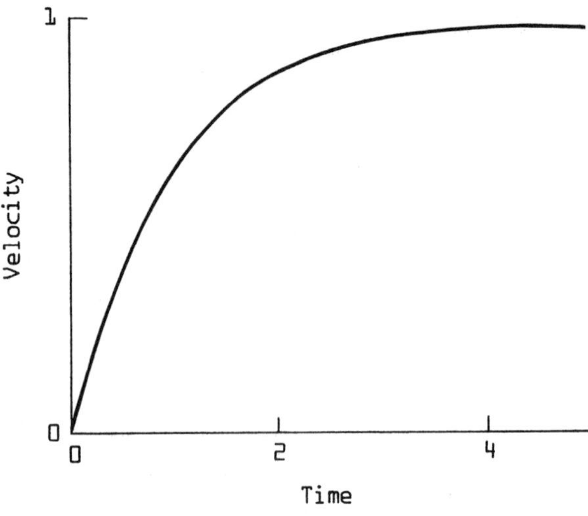

Figure 5.2 Step Response

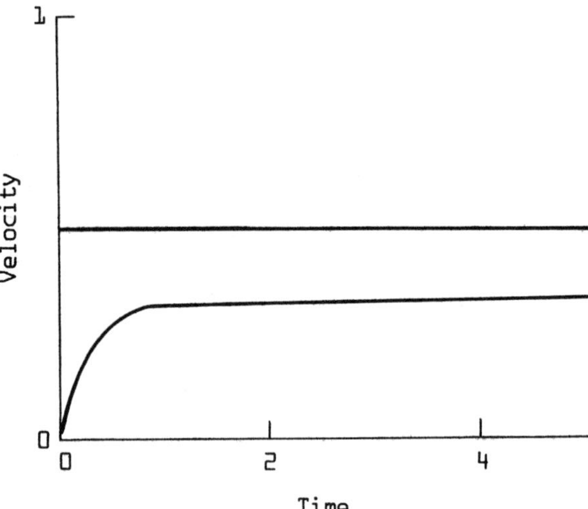

Figure 5.3 P-Control

form for improved computing speed, errors due to precision become the dominant consideration.

In this case, the errors that result from integer conversion affect the steady-state error, the very problem that the integral control action is designed to eliminate! In the incremental form of the PI algorithm, the integral action appears in a term $k_i\varepsilon$. For integer implementation, this must be expressed as $(k_{inum}\varepsilon)/k_{iden}$ so that gains can be represented with reasonable precision. (For large or small gains, either the denominator or numerator can be set to one to simplify the computation.) The problem arises when gains of less than one are used. In that case, whenever ε becomes smaller than k_{iden}/k_{inum}, integer truncation in the calculation will cause the result to be zero and *no further accumulation will take place.* This will

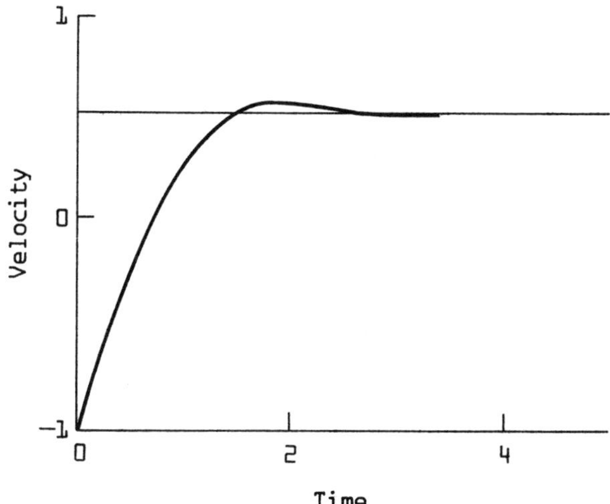

Figure 5.4 PI Control, Incremental

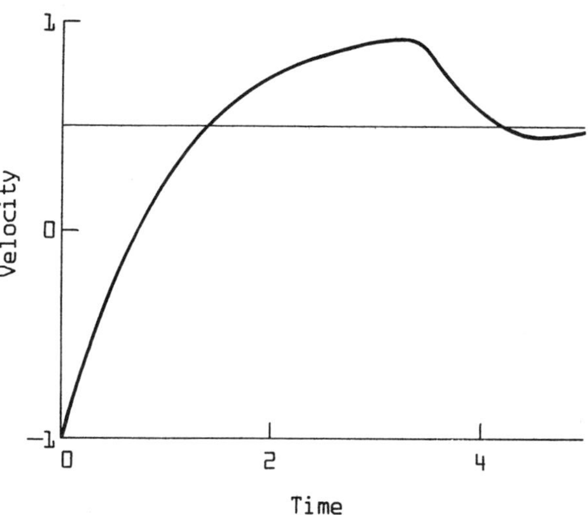

Figure 5.5 PI, Abs., Output Limit

then leave a steady-state error even though an integral term is included in the algorithm.

By contrast, in the absolute algorithm the multiplication by k_i can take place after the accumulation. As long as an error remains, the integral will continue to accumulate, thus eliminating the error. This will happen independent of the value of the integral gain. When limiting is added to the absolute form of the algorithm, the limit is applied to the accumulated (integrated) value. This limit is usually related to the physical saturation limits of the actuation system, but, since the accumulation is done before multiplication by the gain, the proper value of the limit will depend on the gain and will have to be changed every time the gain is changed. Furthermore, if the gain is changed while the process is under con-

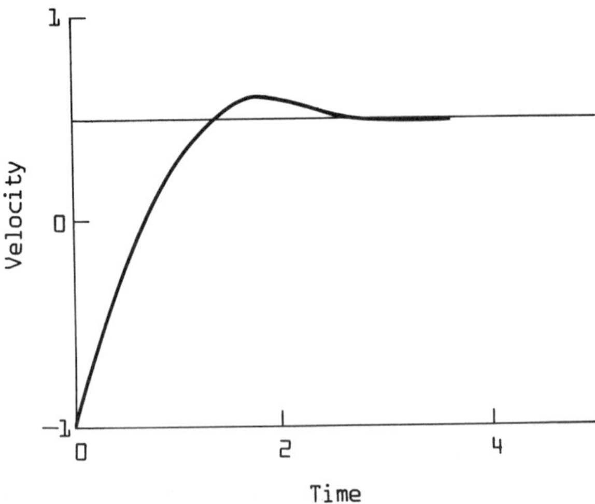

Figure 5.6 PI, Abs., Integ. Limit

trol, as it might be to accommodate some change in the nature of the process, there will be an output "bump" due to the multiplication of the same accumulated value by a new gain value. It might appear that these difficulties could be eliminated by reversing the order of the accumulation and the gain multiplication, but, even though the two forms are mathematically equivalent and cause no increase in computing time, the same precision problem exhibited by the incremental algorithm would be introduced.

This subject was examined in some detail here because of its importance in many control problems and because it is illustrative of problems that often occur when integer computation is used.

5.3 TASK SCHEDULING

With the nature of the control task now defined, we can proceed to the issue of running several of them at the "same time." The implication of running them at the same time is that there is some computational implementation available that will run the various control loops in such a way that, from the viewpoint of an external observer, they are running simultaneously. As with the discussion of the foreground tasks, this can range from true simultaneity achieved by running each task on its own processor to purely sequential operation with all tasks on the same processor. In the sequential mode, the processor must be fast enough to reduce task interference to a minimum.

A separate function will be used to schedule and run the various background tasks. Use of a scheduler makes the nature of the implementation as "invisible" as possible to the programmer responsible for the implementation of the control system. The control tasks themselves can be programmed in a way that need not consider whether sequential or parallel processing is being used, what kind of clocks are available, or what the processor is. As long as the processing capability is adequate, the job will be accomplished.

For a relatively simple problem such as our motor control, the scheduler must provide several basic services. These services are accessed by function calls to the scheduler to, create a task, enter a task onto the job queue, suspend a task, remove a task, and change the sample time. Creating a "task" causes the scheduler to allocate a block of memory to maintain the information needed to run that task. The task is not run, however, until the scheduler is asked to enter it into its job queue. Then, whenever that task's sample interval is done, the task will be run. Suspending a task from the job queue stops its execution, but does not remove from the list of possible tasks, whereas removing the task destroys any information the scheduler has about the task and recovers the space used for it. Most control tasks run continuously once they are initiated, however, tasks can also be scheduled to run only once and not be restarted automatically after each sample. To run such a task again, an explicit call to the scheduler to enter it into the job queue must be made each time it is to be run.

To be able to run each task, the scheduler must have information about what function is associated with the task, what the sample time is, whether the task is a run-once or run-continuous task, and, to enable several tasks to share the same executable function, a pointer to a data structure containing the parameters and state information about the task. The task creation function returns a "task identifier," which is used in all subsequent calls to let the scheduler know which task is being referred to. Fig. 5.7 is an example of a program that has two control tasks, each of which has a data structure to store its parameter information and a separate function to be executed to implement the control function. Once started, each task will run continuously until a "stop" signal is received.

```
(This code is executed after all of the parameters have been set for
each of the tasks.)

        task1_id = task_create(&function1, &data1, t_sample1, run_continuous)
        task2_id = task_create(&function2, &data2, t_sample2, run_continuous)

        enter_task_queue(task1_id)
        enter_task_queue(task2_id)

        Loop until both tasks are stopped
                if (stop1) suspend(task1_id)
                if (stop2) suspend(task2_id)
```

Figure 5.7

To control several motors, all using the same control algorithm, the function called will be the same for all of the tasks, but each will have its own data structure.

The "stop" signals could come from an external source or from a user intervention. The control action starts when the tasks are entered into the task queue.

5.4 BACKGROUND SCHEDULING

The program in Fig. 5.7 does not indicate how the scheduler itself runs. Task_create, enter_task_queue, etc., are functions that run when they are called by the background and service the data structures maintained by the scheduling section of the program. The scheduler is the function that must decide when each task is to run, set the timer so that the following task will be run at the correct time, then start the current task running. The scheduler can be made part of either the background or the foreground. Programming is simpler if the scheduler is part of the background, but the range of problems that can be addressed successfully with a background scheduler is much narrower than when a foreground scheduler is used.

When a function, or task, is running in the background, it can be interrupted by an external interrupt which will cause a foreground task to run. When the foreground task finishes its work, the background function will continue from where it left off. Once that background function begins, however, no other background function can run until it is done. If the scheduler is part of the background, then it cannot run until the current background task is done. Each background task is running as a function called by the scheduler, so, when it is done, it returns to the scheduler. At that time, the scheduler checks its task queue to see if any other tasks are ready to run. If any are, it will run the first one on the queue after setting the timer. If no tasks are ready, it can stay in a test loop, checking the time, until a task is ready to run. It could also call a "deep background" task, one that only runs when nothing else is scheduled. The deep background task could be used, for example, to check for the "stop" signal noted in Fig. 5.7, to interact with the operator, and so on. Using this method of scheduling, the program in Fig. 5.7 would have to be changed somewhat, as shown in Fig. 5.8. Since the scheduler is also a background task, entering the tasks into the task queue will not be enough to start control action. As soon as the tasks are entered, the scheduler must be called explicitly to start it running. Also, once the scheduler has been started, it will not return to the main program again until the whole system is stopped. Therefore, if a deep background function is desired, there must be a provision in the scheduler to know about such a function. This is most easily done by adding an additional mode to the "run-continuous" or "run-once" modes for "deep-background." Because the deep background task runs whenever there is time, the sample time is indicated as zero.

The data structure for the scheduler is shown in Fig. 5.9. Each time a new task is created, memory is allocated for a task descriptor block. When a task is removed, the space is freed. The task blocks are linked with a link pointer in each

(This code is executed after all of the parameters have been set for each of the tasks.)

```
task1_id = task_create(&function1, &data1, t_sample1, run_continuous)
task2_id = task_create(&function2, &data2, t_sample2, run_continuous)
task3_id = task_create(&stop_check, &data3, 0, deep_background)

enter_task_queue(task1_id)
enter_task_queue(task2_id)
enter_task_queue(task3_id)

Run the scheduler
```

Figure 5.8

block that points to the next block. An alternate structure to the linked list is to use an array of or table of descriptor blocks. This can be more efficient for small, fixed configuration problems. The task_state value in the descriptor block is used to keep track of the current status, which can be either active if the task has been entered into the task queue, or inactive. When the task is first created, its status is set to inactive.

```
Task Descriptor Block Structure:

    pointer_to_function     task_function
    pointer_to_structure    task_data
    integer                 task_type
    integer                 task_state
    float (or integer)      sample_time
    float (or integer)      time_left
    pointer_to_structure    next_task
```

Figure 5.9

The scheduler operates by maintaining a set of queues (or lists) that give it information on what tasks are to be run and when. The active task queue has as its first entry the currently running task. The next_task links connect the list in order of the current values of the time left until the task should run, time_left. Fig. 5.10(a) shows the sample time, time left, and next task pointers from the task descriptor blocks of three tasks, A, B, and C, at a time when A is running, B is the next to run, and finally C will run. The symbol "/" is used to indicate the end of the list.

	(a)			(b)			(c)			(d)		
	A	B	C	A	B	C	A	B	C	A	B	C
sample_time	5	7	4	5	7	4	5	7	4	5	7	4
time_left	0	2	3	5	1	2	4	0	1	1	4	0
next_task	B	C	/	/	C	A	/	C	A	B	/	A

Figure 5.10

When the current task finishes, the scheduler resets its time_left to its sample time and scans the active queue to find the correct position to insert it. The next_task pointer linkage is broken at that point and the task is inserted and thus "scheduled." Figure 5.10(b) shows the linkages after task A has finished, but before B is ready to run, (c) shows the linkages while B is running, and (d) shows the situation while C is running.

In addition, a list is maintained for inactive tasks, and if more than one deep background task is to be allowed, an additional queue is maintained for them. Because all of the task descriptor blocks, or task nodes, are linked with pointers, rearranging lists only requires that the pointers be changed. The data block itself is never moved. The program logic for the scheduler is shown in Fig. 5.11

5.5 BACKGROUND SCHEDULING CAVEATS

The primary advantage to background scheduling is that it is easy to program and requires minimal interaction with the computer hardware. There are, however, several limitations that must be observed if it is to be used successfully. These come mostly from the property that once a background task has been started, no other background task can be run until it finishes. The first consequence of this is that all of the background tasks must have the same priority. A task with high priority would imply that when its run time came up it would be able to interrupt the execution of any lower priority tasks that were currently running. With background scheduling, if a low-priority task were to start just before the time for a high-priority task, the high-priority task would have to wait for the low-priority task to finish before it could start.

A related restriction is that the execution time of the longest task should be relatively short with respect to the shortest sample interval. If it isn't, the actual intervals for the task with the short sample time would be extremely erratic. The same restriction applies to the "deep background" task (or tasks). The scheduling

```
Scheduler:
        current_task = head_of_queue
        set timer to current_task->time_left

        Loop forever
                Repeat until time out
                        Execute deep background

                Execute current_task->task_function(current_task->task_data)

                If (current_task->type = run_continuous)
                        current_task->time_left = current_task->sample_time
                        move current task to proper place in queue
                Else
                        move current task to inactive queue

                If (task_queue is not empty)
                        current_task = head_of_queue
                        set timer to current_task->time_left
                Else
                        turn timer off
```

Figure 5.11

algorithm for the deep background task used above actually implies the strictest restriction on its execution time. Because it will continue to start the deep background task as long as the clock hasn't run out, there is a guaranteed conflict between the deep background and the next background task to be run that will always cause it to run a little bit later than it was scheduled. If the deep background task is very fast, the error will be small and the best use will be made of the CPU resource. Other scheduling schemes can be used that will minimize the interaction. The simplest is to just run the deep background once for every time through the scheduler's major loop. For a program with widely spaced sampling, this would reduce the interference to almost nothing but would not use the CPU very well. A more complex method is to check the timer to see how much time is left and only run the deep background if there is enough time left. This requires a timer that is capable of returning the time left in the current cycle, and also means that either the user must send information to the scheduler on how long the deep background task takes to run, the scheduler must test it by running a timing test, or some preset time must be used.

Background scheduling is thus useful in situations where a number of tasks with similar operating time requirements and equal priority must be run. They will run most smoothly if the total load on the CPU is modest. If the tasks vary widely in execution time and/or priority, conflicts will result that cannot be arbitrated by the scheduler (to use a labor relations metaphor, a background scheduler is more like a mediator than an arbitrator). If these tasks use a large fraction of the CPU resource, timing conflicts will occur frequently, causing erratic timing. With equal priority tasks, this problem is not the fault of the background scheduling, however. It would occur with any scheduling method. When a smaller fraction of the CPU is used, there will still be occasional scheduling conflicts when the sample periods add up to a common multiple. These conflicts are also unavoidable, but can be minimized by proper phasing of the tasks.

5.6 SIMULATING REAL-TIME

Initial program verification and debugging using simulated real time is even more important for the multi-task case than it is for the single-task problem for which it was originally introduced. In the simulated mode, the numerical results can be checked for reasonableness and the timing can be verified in a reproducible and controllable way. Since "time" can be stopped, the state of the system can be examined at any moment and relations between variables can be checked.

For the background part of the program, the only change that has to be made is the addition of a call to the time simulation function in the scheduler. If a deep background task is included, it would probably be useful to break the time interval down to something smaller than the shortest sample interval so that the deep background program gets a chance to run several times for each time one of the regular background tasks runs. The time simulation function advances time on the simulated timer(s).

The motor simulation is a mirror image of the motor control. A data structure is maintained for all of the dynamic properties and states of each of the motors (see Fig. 5.12). For the simple motor model we have been using, the only motor parameter is its inertia, the velocity is the only state variable, and the only input is the torque command.

Simulated Motor Data Structure:

```
float   inertia
float   velocity
float   torque
```

Figure 5.12

The A/D and D/A functions must be changed so that, in the simulation mode, their inputs and outputs refer to the data stored in the appropriate block of this data structure. These blocks must thus be coordinated with the channel numbers selected in the controller data structure blocks. With the data structure shown, the blocks must be stored contiguously, with the block identification being its position in the array. For systems in which the tasks were not all operating on the same control object, a separate data structure would have to be defined for each type of external system. More complex linkages using interblock pointers and separate identification numbers could be used to maintain more generality.

The real motors are continuous-time devices. Therefore, *all* of the motor calculations must be done for every time step. The controllers are part of a computer control system and are thus discrete-time systems. They only run at their specified sample intervals so the input value, the motor torque, is only changed then and the motor's velocity is only sampled then.

The next chapter discusses mechanisms for implementing the interactions between the control software and the user. More general scheduling methods are treated in subsequent chapters.

MULTIPLE INDEPENDENT PROCESSES EXAMPLES

5.7 INTRODUCTION

This section contains two example programs that illustrate how multiple motor control tasks with fixed sampling periods can be scheduled. The number of tasks and their sampling intervals are specified at run-time. The task scheduler in the examples runs in the *background*; this means that once a task is executing, it cannot be pre-empted and must run to completion before the scheduler can dispatch the next task. Therefore, each task runs for a brief period and then gives up control to the scheduler until the next sampling instance. The sampling period must be much greater than the execution time, and the greater the difference between sampling period and execution time, the greater the number of concurrent tasks that the system can support. Foreground pre-emptive schedulers will be covered in later chapters.

In the first example, the scheduler is merged into the control program itself. The approach may be advantageous for systems with tight memory and performance constraints since it incurs the minimum memory and scheduling overheads. The disadvantages are that it is hard to maintain and does not scale up easily. The second example shows a more general approach where the background scheduler is independent of the tasks. This approach is much more flexible since the same scheduler can be applied to a variety of task types, the only common factor being that the tasks have to run at regular intervals. An added advantage is that the individual tasks need not know the specifics of the scheduling process.

The following files are common to both examples:

main3.c	The main program module containing the command processor.
rtsim3.c	The simulation module.
envir.h	Environment declaration file.
dash8.h	Declarations for Metrabyte DASH8 analog-to-digital data acquisition board driver module, simulated in rtsim3.c.
dac2.h	Declarations for Metrabyte DAC02 digital-to-analog board driver module, simulated in rtsim3.c.
time0.h	Declarations for simple timer functions, simulated in rtsim3.c.

The following files are specific to the first example in which the scheduler is embedded in the control program:

cntrl3.h Declarations for cntrl3.c

cntrl3.c The control module that implements PI control and task scheduling.

To generate the program, type:

```
cl /DSIMRT main3.c cntrl3.c rtsim3.c
```

The following files are specific to the second example in which the scheduler and task control system are derived from the *clotho* real-time multi-tasking kernel.

cntrl4.c A modified version of cntrl3.c using the general background scheduler.

bclotho.lib Library of routines that supports general background task scheduling.

bsched.c An abbreviated version of the general background scheduler.

To generate the program, type:

```
cl /AL /Gs /DSIMRT /DRTIME main3.c cntrl4.c rtsim3.c /link bclotho
```

The program must be compiled under the large memory model with stack checking disabled.

5.8 EXPLICIT BACKGROUND SCHEDULER

5.8.1 MAIN MODULE

The *main3.c* module implements a simple interface to allow users to specify the number of motors, set the sample intervals, control gains, and setpoints for each motor. The command is in the form of a command word (which may be abbreviated) followed by any arguments required by the command. For example:

```
setpoint 2 10.5 0.4 1.2
```

specifies for motor number 2, the proportional and integral gains plus the constant term in the control equation, respectively.

The command processor is essentially the same as that described in Chapter 4. One difference is that, instead of knowing the number of entries in the command table, the end of the table is marked with a NULL entry consisting of an ASCII NUL character for the command string and a NULL function pointer:

```
{ "\0", (void (*)())NULL }
```

When the command processor, *cmdint()*, sees the NUL command string, it knows that it has reached the end of the command table. Another difference is found in the *getcmd()* function, which extracts the command string from the input line. The previous version treats the input line and the command string as *char* arrays; this version uses pointers. We think that you will find the pointer version to be simpler.

5.8.2 CONTROL MODULE

This module implements both the Proportional Integral (PI) control algorithm and the task scheduling functions. Each motor is associated with a data structure describing its allocated i/o channel numbers, setpoints, and other control and scheduling parameters as shown below:

```
typedef struct motor {
     int ichan;          /* A/D channel number */
     int mchan;          /* D/A channel number */
     double v;           /* velocity */
     double vref;        /* velocity setpoint */
     double kp;          /* proportional gain */
     double ki;          /* integral gain */
     double ival;        /* integrator accumulated value */
     double vcon;        /* constant in control equation */
     double m;           /* controller output */
     double mmin;        /* lower limit for controller output */
     double mmax;        /* upper limit for controller output */
     double tsamp;       /* sample interval */
     double tleft;       /* time left to next sample */
} MOTOR;
```

The scheduler makes use of two fields: *tsamp*, the sampling interval, which normally does not change, and *tleft*, the time left to the next sampling instance. Motor control is performed by *pimotor()*, which uses information in its MOTOR descriptor argument to calculate the control output for a particular motor. For simplicity, we have elected to use a specialized descriptor data structure instead of a more general structure.

5.8.2.1 INITIALIZATION. The *setmot()* initialization function is the first statement executed by the program. It queries the user for the number of motors, allocates memory for the motor descriptors, initializes them with default values, and calls *sim_init()* to do the same for the simulation module. Note that the *setmot()* routine can only return if a valid entry is received for the number of motors since only then can the proper number of motor descriptors be allocated and initialized. The array of motor descriptors are referenced by the pointer variable

```
MOTOR *pm0;
```

This implies that the individual descriptors will be referenced using pointers of the form *(pm0+i)->tleft* instead of the equivalent array form *pm0[i].tleft*, although some compilers allow the latter form to be used with pointers.

The descriptor *motdef* contains the default field values that are used to initialize each newly allocated descriptor. The default field values are copied to the new descriptor with the *cpmotor()* routine. The ANSI C draft standard allows structures of the same type to be copied by a simple assignment statement. Hence, the descriptor can be initialized by a simple statement:

```
MOTOR *to, *from;
 ...
*to = *from;
```

If your compiler does not support structure assignment, you will have to either assign each field individually or perform a byte-by-byte copy operation. Individual field assignments are very portable, but can be quite tedious. The example shows a byte-by-byte copy operation in which the descriptor pointers are first copied to *char* pointers and the individual bytes making up the descriptor are copied:

```
register char *src, *dst;
unsigned count;

src = (char *)from;
dst = (char *)to;

for (count = 0; count < sizeof(MOTOR); count++)
     *dst++ = *src++;
```

This method implies that a *char* is the smallest unit of addressable memory with the least alignment restrictions, and all other types are integral multiples of a *char* type.

5.8.2.2 SCHEDULING. The scheduler is embedded in the function *control()*. The algorithm first determines, for all the tasks, the minimum positive time-left to the next execution (or sampling) instance. The minimum positive time-left, *tlmin*, determines when the next task (the one associated with this minimum) is to be dispatched. The timer is then set to this interval. The minimum time-left is contained in the *tleft* field of the motor descriptor. The *tleft* field can also be interpreted as the waiting time remaining until the task next gets to run. Thus, if *tleft* is zero or negative, the task will be dispatched in the current cycle, and the time when the task next gets to run is determined by its sampling interval contained in the *tsamp* field.

Next, the task descriptors are scanned for tasks that have to be dispatched in the current cycle. This is indicated if their *tleft* is less than or equal to zero. Tasks are dispatched by calling *pimotor()*, passing to it a pointer to the motor descriptor.

After returning from *pimotor()*, the *tleft* value is reset to *tsamp* since the next execution instance is the sampling period.

Then the *tleft* fields of all the motor descriptors are updated by subtracting from them the previously determined minimum positive time left, *tlmin*. Since the timer is set to *tlmin*, all tasks will have waited an interval of *tlmin* since the current round of tasks are dispatched and their *tleft* fields updated. This is not exactly accurate of course, since dispatching and executing tasks takes a certain amount of time, but the approximation is valid provided the execution time is short compared to the sample intervals for all the tasks.

Note that because floating point types are used for time, the statement

```
tleft -= tlmin;
```

may result in a small positive value that is very close to, but not quite exactly zero. This will cause the scheduler to malfunction. To prevent this from happening, an arbitrary time granularity of 0.001 seconds is imposed for values close to zero. This is not an elegant solution, and interested readers may want to modify the program to use a long integer type for time (perhaps in millisecond units) instead of floating point types.

There is a check to see if the timer has timed-out while the motor control tasks are executing. This can happen if the execution instances of several tasks happens to coincide and the total execution time exceeds *tlmin*. In this example, the program merely prints a message and dies. This may be acceptable for development and testing purposes, but once in production use, simply shutting down is not acceptable (especially for embedded control applications). The system must keep running, albeit with degraded performance. The designer must then precisely specify the time constraints and the permissible variation in sampling period for each task, and perhaps prioritize the tasks, to reduce sampling period variations for the more time-critical tasks. There must also be procedures in place to recover gracefully (as far as a graceful recovery is possible) from such events. However, bear in mind that there is only so much one can do when scheduler runs in the background.

As an exercise, how would you resynchronize the scheduler (i.e., adjust the time-left calculations) after a premature timeout? Does the scheduler have to be resynchronized?

5.8.3 Simulation Module

The simulation module, *rtsim3.c*, is adapted from the version in Chapter 4. The major difference is that it supports multiple motors—the inertia, torque, and speed parameters for each motor are now described by a data structure that is dynamically allocated in the *sim_init()* routine. It is assumed that the motor number is the same as the ADC and DAC channel numbers, i.e., channel 0 implies motor 0.

5.9 GENERAL BACKGROUND SCHEDULER

This example uses a special version of the *clotho* real-time multi-tasking kernel in which a background scheduler is substituted for the normal pre-emptive foreground scheduler. The kernel will be described in Chapter 8, but we shall describe an abbreviated version of the background scheduler contained in the file *bsched.c*.

This example differs from the previous one in that each task is associated with a task descriptor structure. Here is an abbreviated version of the structure:

```
struct _task {
    int t_id;               /* task id number */
    int t_pri;              /* effective priority */
    int t_flags;            /* flags */
    void (*t_func)();       /* routine executed by task shell */
    void *t_argp;           /* pointer to task argument structure */
    int t_tasktype;         /* task type (control, slice, etc) */
    int t_state;            /* task state code */
    long t_tleft;           /* time left before execution */
    long t_tsamp;           /* sampling time (for control tasks) */
    struct _task *t_next;   /* ptr to next task in a queue */
};
```

The *t_func* field points to the task function, and the *t_argp* field points to an argument block for that task. In the motor control example, *t_func* will point at *pimotor()*, and *t_argp* will point at the appropriate motor descriptor. The time left and the sampling interval are recorded in the *t_left* and *t_tsamp* fields, respectively, in millisecond units. The timer resolution is fixed by the kernel start-up code at 50 milliseconds. The other fields describing the task type and state need not concern us here.

Control tasks with fixed sampling intervals are grouped into a special task queue, *StlQueue,* in increasing *tleft* order. This queue is referenced by the background scheduler routines as the *stlq* parameter. There is a second queue for pre-empted task, referenced as the *urgentq* parameter; this is not used by the background version of the scheduler, but is kept to maintain compatibility with the foreground version.

Here is an example showing how to set up tasks for multiple motor control tasks using the kernel's *SetCntrlTask()* function:

```
for (i = 0; i < nmotors; i++)
    SetCntrlTask("MOTOR", pimotor, (void*)(pm0+i), 1000,
                 (long)((pm0+i)->tsamp * 1000));
```

The first argument is a name string; it is not currently used by the scheduler. The second argument is a pointer to the motor control function. The third argument is a void pointer to the i-th motor descriptor. The next argument,

PCONTROL, specifies a task priority, which in this example is set to 1000. The last argument is the sampling interval in milliseconds, taken from the *tsamp* field of the MOTOR descriptor. *SetCntrlTask()* automatically creates and initializes a task descriptor and sets the *t_tleft* field of the task descriptor equal to the *t_tsamp* field. This results in a staggered start—tasks with different sampling periods will start at different times and minimize crowding at the starting point. The pointer to the newly created task descriptor is automatically put into *StlQueue* in increasing *t_tleft* order; hence, the task at the head of the queue will be the one with the shortest *t_tleft*.

The scheduling logic is very similar to that described in the previous example.

5.9.0.1 START. The scheduler is started by a call to *start()*, which in turn calls *StlStart()*, passing to it pointers to the two task queues mentioned previously and a timer number reserved for the scheduler. The timer is set to the *t_tleft* value of the first task in the queue and execution chains to *StlDispatch()* to dispatch the first task. The *HeadTqueue()* function is used to obtain a pointer to the first task descriptor in the queue. Using the pointer dereferencing operator on the result of *HeadTqueue()*, we obtain the *t_tleft* value of the first task like so:

```
tnext = HeadTqueue(stlq)->t_tleft;
```

The timer[1] is set by a call to *SetDTimer()*. Since the tasks are ordered in increasing *t_tleft* order, this is the shortest time left to the next sampling instance among all the tasks in the queue.

5.9.0.2 SCHEDULING. The scheduler, *StlDispatch()*, is in the form of an infinite loop. It first waits for the timer to time-out. There are two versions here: one for real-time and one for simulated time. Let us look at the simulated time version first. While waiting for timeout, the program calls the multi-motor simulation routine, *do_simul()*, defined in *rtsim3.c*. It next calls the timer module's timer interrupt service routine, *chronos*, to simulate a timer interrupt. This version of *chronos()* is compiled for background mode; it only updates the software counters and does not dispatch any tasks (refer to *time.c* in the kernel files). One should use the *initialize* command to set a simulation time step of 0.05 seconds to properly match the resolution of the kernel's scheduling timer.

The other version of the wait procedure is designed for cases where the scheduling timer runs in real-time, perhaps synchronized with the hardware timer of the computer. If the time remaining is greater than 1 timer tick, a deep background task is executed. This background task may be used to collect process statistics, write acquired data to the disk, or get keyboard input from the user. In this example, it just soaks up CPU time.

---

[1]The timer module is *time.c* from Chapter 3.

When the timer times out, the scheduler calls *GetTqueue()*, which detaches the first task from the task queue, *stlq*, and returns a pointer to the detached task. The scheduler then calls *dec_tleft()* to decrement the previous timer setting from the *t_tleft* fields of all the remaining waiting tasks in *stlq*. The next timer setting is calculated by the function *set_tnext()*. This differs somewhat from the previous version since the next timer setting is calculated from the detached task's *t_tsamp* and the minimum *t_tleft* of the remaining tasks in the queue. Thus, if the next task in the queue has a zero or negative *t_tleft*, the timer is not set and *TimeUp()* will return true for the next task in the queue. Otherwise, the timer is set to *tnext*. The current task is dispatched with a pointer to an argument structure.

The task runs to completion and returns. Its *t_tleft* field is reset by the scheduler to the sample time, *t_tsamp*. The task is then inserted into the task queue, *stlq*, by a call to *EnterTqueue()*. The parameter STL_ENTER tells *EnterTqueue()* to insert the task in increasing "shortest-time-left" order.

As this code fragment demonstrates, the logic is the same as for the previous example; only the implementation details differ.

```
/**********************************************************************

FILE
    main3.c  -  d.c. motor velocity control, executive control file #3

ROUTINES
    main    -  main program
    cmdint  -  command interpreter
    fstr    -  extract command word
    help    -  print list of commands

REMARKS
    This version is intended for multi-motor control, to be
    used with modules cntrl3.c and rtsim3.c.

LAST UPDATE
    19 March 1985
        recast in module format
    01 April 1988
        copy over from main2.c and adapt for multiple motors

    Copyright (c) 1984-1988  D.M. Auslander and C.H. Tham

**********************************************************************/

/**********************************************************************
                              I M P O R T S
**********************************************************************/

#include <stdio.h>
#include <stdlib.h>     /* standard library function declarations */
#include <string.h>     /* standard string function declarations */

#include "envir.h"      /* environment definitions */
#include "dash8.h"      /* declarations for dash8.c */
#include "dac2.h"       /* declarations for dac2.c */
#include "time0.h"      /* declarations for time0.c */
#include "cntrl3.h"     /* declarations for cntrl3.c */

/**********************************************************************
                F O R W A R D   D E C L A R A T I O N S
**********************************************************************/

#ifdef ANSI

void    cmdint(char *);
char *  getcmd(char *, char *);
void    menu(void);

#else

void    cmdint();
char    getcmd();
void    menu();

#endif

/**********************************************************************
                      P R I V A T E   D A T A
**********************************************************************/

#define PROMPT  "READY "     /* defines the command processor prompt */
#define BUFSIZE 100          /* command input buffer size */

#define CMDLEN  12      /* max length of command name */

struct command {
    char cmd[CMDLEN+1];      /* command string (+1 for NUL terminator) */
    void (*cmdfunc)();       /* pointer to command function */
};

static struct command cmdtable[] = {

    { "gains",      gain },      /* specify position control gains */
    { "k",          gain },

    { "setpoint",   setv },      /* specify position setpoint */
    { "s",          setv },

    { "sampletime", setsmp },    /* specify sample time */
    { "t",          setsmp },

    { "go",         control },   /* start controller */
    { "g",          control },

    { "initialize", init },      /* initialize */
    { "i",          init },

    { "help",       menu },      /* print help menu */
    { "h",          menu },

    { "exit",       exit },      /* program exit */
    { "e",          exit },

    { "\0", (void (*)())NULL }   /* marks end of interpreter table */
};


/**********************************************************************
                      E N T R Y   R O U T I N E S
**********************************************************************/
```

```
/*-------------------------------------------------------------------------
PROCEDURE
    MAIN  -  this is the main program

LAST UPDATE
    1 April 1988
        copy and adapt from main2.c
-------------------------------------------------------------------------*/

main()
{
    char cbuf[BUFSIZE];      /* space for the user-typed command line */


    setmot();                /* set-up motor structures */

    menu();                  /* print command list to start. */

    for(;;)                  /* an endless loop. */
    {
        fputs(PROMPT, stdout);  /* print a prompt so that user will */
                                /*   know that the program expects  */
                                /*   an input.                      */

        fgets(cbuf, BUFSIZE, stdin);    /* read a NULL terminated string */
                                        /*   from the "standard input"   */
                                        /*   (normally the user console) */

        cmdint(cbuf);           /* call the routine that interprets  */
                                /*   the command line.               */
    }

}


/*************************************************************************
                    P R I V A T E    R O U T I N E S
*************************************************************************/

/*-------------------------------------------------------------------------
PROCEDURE
    CMDINT  -  command interpreter

SYNOPSIS
    static void cmdint(cline)
    char cline[];

PARAMETERS
    cline  -  command line

DESCRIPTION
    The command word is isolated and matched against the list of valid
    commands in the command table.  If a match is found, the routine
    associated with that command is executed.

LAST UPDATE
    1 April 1988
        adapt from main2.c
-------------------------------------------------------------------------*/

static void cmdint(cline)
char cline[];
{
    char cword[CMDLEN+1];     /* storage to hold the command word. */
    char *prest;              /* ptr to rest of line after command word */
    struct command *pcom;     /* ptr to the command structure list. */


    prest = getcmd(cline, cword);          /* isolate the command word */

    /*---------------------------------------------------------------------
        Search the command list for a match on the command word.
    ---------------------------------------------------------------------*/

    pcom = cmdtable;     /* initialize the pointer to the command list */

    while (pcom->cmd[0] != '\0')         /* while not at end of list */
    {
        /*  note: strcmp() returns zero if strings match  */

        if (strcmp(pcom->cmd, cword) == 0)
        {
            /*-------------------------------------------------------------
                Command word matches a name entry in the command
                interpreter table.  The associated function is
                executed  --  again, watch the parentheses!
            -------------------------------------------------------------*/

            (*pcom->cmdfunc)(prest);     /* execute associated func */

            break;                       /* break out of "while" loop */
        }

        pcom++;                          /* not found, next entry */
    }

    if (pcom->cmd[0] == '\0')
        printf("command not found : %s\n", cline);

}
```

```
/*-----------------------------------------------------------------------
FUNCTION
    GETCMD  -  isolate command word from input string

SYNOPSIS
    static char *getcmd(line, word)
    char *line, *word;

PARAMETERS
    line  -  command line
    word  -  where to put the command word

RETURNS
    pointer to rest of line (after the command word)

DESCRIPTION
    This is similar to the one in main2.c except that it uses pointers
    to address the 2 character arrays instead of array addressing.

    See how much simpler it is compared to the array version.

    Command words are assumed to be delimited by blanks.  Thus this
    routine finds the first blank-terminated word in the command line
    and copies it into the 'word' argument.

    The command line is a NUL terminated character array which is
    passed to this routine in the form of a NUL terminated character
    array.  Note that the command line CANNOT begin with a blank.

    getcmd() returns NULL if the input command line begins with a blank
    or carriage-return.

LAST UPDATE
    20 March 1988
        dump leading blanks
-----------------------------------------------------------------------*/

static char *getcmd(line, word)
char *line, *word;
{
    int i;          /* loop index */


    while ((*line == ' ') || (*line == '\t'))  /* skip leading blanks */
        ++line;

    for (i = 0; i < CMDLEN; i++)
    {
        if ((*line == ' ') || (*line == '\n') || (*line == '\0'))
            break;      /* end of word found, break out of for loop */
        *word++ = *line++;      /* append character to output word */
    }

    *word = '\0';    /* terminate command word with a NULL char */

    return(line);    /* return a pointer to the remainder of the line */

}



/*-----------------------------------------------------------------------
PROCEDURE
    MENU  -  print a list of commands

SYNOPSIS
    static void menu()

LAST UPDATE
    22 September 1984
-----------------------------------------------------------------------*/

static void menu()
{

    fputs("\n                COMMAND LIST\n\n", stdout);
    fputs("full command (or single-letter equivalent) arguments\n\n", stdout);

    fputs("initialize    (i)    delta_t\n", stdout);
    fputs("sampletime    (t)    motor_number tsamp\n", stdout);
    fputs("gains         (k)    motor_number kp ki c\n", stdout);
    fputs("setpoint      (s)    motor_number setpoint\n", stdout);
    fputs("go            (g)    number_of_iterations print?(0/1)\n", stdout);
    fputs("exit          (e) \n", stdout);
    fputs("help          (h) \n\n", stdout);

}

/************************************************************************

FILE
    rtsim3.c  -  simulation module for cntrl3.c

ENTRY ROUTINES
    tstep      -  advance one time step
    SetTimer   -  set count-down timer
    TimeUp     -  has count down completed?

    ad_init    -  simulates A/D initialization
    ad_start   -  simulates starting an A/D read
    ad_read    -  simulates reading A/D value
```

```
    ad_wread    -  simulates read from A/D

    da_init     -  simulates D/A initialization
    da_limits   -  returns simulation D/A output limits
    da_write    -  simulates write to D/A

    sim_reset   -  reset simulation parameters

PRIVATE ROUTINE
    simul       -  motor plant simulation

INITIALIZATION ROUTINE
    sim_init    -  initialize this module

REMARKS
    Implements multiple motor simulation for main3.c and cntrl3.c.

    We adopt the convention that the ADC and DAC channel number refers
    to the motor number, i.e., its index in the array of motor simulation
    descriptors.  For example, (pmsim0 + 0) points to the simulated
    motor "connected" to ADC and DAC channel 0; (pmsim0 + 2) points to
    the motor "connected" to ADC and DAC channel 2.  Of course, the
    ADC and DAC channels must be the same.

LAST UPDATE
    22 March 1985
        recast in module format.
    20 March 1988
        use ANSI features
    10 April 1988
        copy timer simulation from rtsim2.c

    Copyright (C) 1984-1988  D.M. Auslander and C.H. Tham

***********************************************************************/

/**********************************************************************
                              I M P O R T S
***********************************************************************/

#include <stdio.h>
#include <stdlib.h>

#include "envir.h"      /* environment specifications */
#include "dash8.h"      /* declarations for dash8.c */
#include "dac2.h"       /* declarations for dac2.c */
#include "time0.h"      /* declarations for time0.c */

/**********************************************************************
              F O R W A R D   D E C L A R A T I O N S
***********************************************************************/

#ifdef ANSI

extern void tstep(void);          /* these are referened outside of */
extern void sim_init(int);        /*   this simulation module.      */
extern void sim_reset(char *);

void simul(void);                 /* these are not referenced outside */
void runtimer(void);              /*   of this simulation module.     */

#else

extern void tstep();
extern void sim_init();
extern void sim_reset();

void simul();
void runtimer();

#endif

/**********************************************************************
                    P R I V A T E   D A T A
***********************************************************************/

#define VEL_SCALE       512.0   /* scale speed to A/D units */

#define ADMAX           2047    /* max A/D input value */
#define ADMIN          -2048    /* min A/D input value */

#define DASCALE         2047.0  /* scale D/A value to torque */
#define DAMIN          -2048    /* min. output value accepted */
#define DAMAX           2047    /* max. output value accepted */

static double t;                /* time */
static double dt;               /* simulation step size in seconds */

static long freq = 1000L;       /* timer frequency (ticks/sec) */
static long ticks;              /* how many ticks to timeout */
static int tflag;               /* set to 1 if timer runs out */

static int initflag = 0;        /* indicates if module initialized */

typedef struct motsim { /* motor simulation control structure */
    double inertia;             /* motor inertia */
    double speed;               /* motor speed */
    double torque;              /* applied torque */
} MOTSIM;

static MOTSIM *pmsim0;      /* pointer to first motor simulation block */

static int nmotor;              /* number of motors */
```

```
/************************************************************************
                    T I M E   S I M U L A T I O N
************************************************************************/

#ifndef RTIME

/*-----------------------------------------------------------------------
PROCEDURE
    TSTEP  -  advance time forward one step

SYNOPSIS
    void tstep(void)

LAST UPDATE
    10 March 1988
        check if simulation is initialized
-----------------------------------------------------------------------*/

void tstep()
{

    if (initflag)
    {
        simul();        /* compute one time step in the differential */
                        /*   equation for the motor system.      */

        t += dt;        /* increment time by dt */

        runtimer();     /* simulate timer run */
    }
    else
    {
        printf("simulation module not initialized\n");

        tflag = 1;
    }

}


/*-----------------------------------------------------------------------
PROCEDURE
    SETTIMER  -  set countdown timer

SYNOPSIS
    void SetTimer(ms)
    long ms;

PARAMETER
    period -  count down period in milliseconds

LAST UPDATE
    15 January 1988
-----------------------------------------------------------------------*/

void SetTimer(ms)
long ms;
{

    tflag = 0;                                /* timeout flag to false */

    ticks = ((ms * freq) + 500L) / 1000L;     /* 500 is for rounding */

    if (ticks <= 0L)
        printf("simulation time step too coarse\n");

}


/*-----------------------------------------------------------------------
FUNCTION
    TIMEUP  -  has timer timed out?

SYNOPSIS
    int TimeUp()

RETURNS
    1 if timer runs out, 0 otherwise

LAST UPDATE
    1 March 1985
-----------------------------------------------------------------------*/

int TimeUp()
{

    return(tflag);
}


/*-----------------------------------------------------------------------
PROCEDURE
    RUNTIMER  -  simulates timer run

SYNOPSIS
    static void runtimer()

LAST UPDATE
    20 March 1988
        one tick per simulation time step
```

```
------------------------------------------------------------------------*/

static void runtimer()
{

    if (!tflag)             /* if timeout, just return, otherwise... */
    {
        --ticks;

        if (ticks <= 0L)    /* time has run out */
            tflag = 1;
    }

}

#endif  /* ifndef RTIME */

/************************************************************************
                      A / D   S I M U L A T I O N

    These routines dummy the routines in dash8.c which drive the
    Metrabyte DASH8 A/D board.

************************************************************************/

void ad_init()
{
    int m;          /* motor number (also serves as loop index) */


    for (m = 0; m < nmotor; m++)
        (pmsim0 + m)->speed = 0.0;              /* motor is at rest */

}


void ad_start(channel)
int channel;
{
    /* nothing */
}


int ad_read(channel)
int channel;
{
    int rval;                   /* return value */


    if ((channel >= 0) && (channel < nmotor))
    {
        rval = (int)((pmsim0 + channel)->speed * VEL_SCALE);
    }
    else
    {
        rval = 0;
    }

    if (rval > ADMAX)                   /* apply converter limits */
        rval = ADMAX;
    else if (rval < ADMIN)
        rval = ADMIN;

    return(rval);
}



int ad_wread(channel)
int channel;
{

    return(ad_read(channel));
}


/************************************************************************
                      D / A   S I M U L A T I O N

    These routines dummy the routines in dac2.c which drive the
    Metrabyte DAC02 D/A board.  See rtsim2.c also.

************************************************************************/

void da_init()
{
    int m;


    for (m = 0; m < nmotor; m++)
        (pmsim0 + m)->torque = 0.0;

}


void da_limits(lo, hi)
int *lo, *hi;
{

    *lo = DAMIN;
    *hi = DAMAX;
```

```
}


int da_write(channel, value)
int channel, value;
{

    if ((channel >= 0) && (channel < nmotor))
    {
        if (value < 0)          /* OR with a binary number having 0's for */
            value |= ~0xfff;    /*   the lower 12 bits and 1's elsewhere  */
        else
            value &= 0xfff;     /* for positive values, just save the     */
                                /*   lower 12 bits.                       */

        (pmsim0 + channel)->torque = value / DASCALE;
    }

    return(0);
}


/***********************************************************************
                   P L A N T    S I M U L A T I O N
***********************************************************************/


/*----------------------------------------------------------------------
PROCEDURE
    SIM_RESET  -  reset simulation module

SYNOPSIS
    void sim_reset(cline)
    char *cline;

PARAMETER
    cline  -  user's input command line

REMARKS

LAST UPDATE
    20 March 1988
        adapt timer resolution to simulation time step
----------------------------------------------------------------------*/

void sim_reset(cline)
char *cline;
{

    sscanf(cline, "%lf", &dt);          /* get the step size */

#ifdef DEBUG
    printf("<init> dt = %f\n", dt);
#endif

    t = 0.0;                                /* reset time */
    freq = (long)(1.0 / dt  +  0.5);        /* adapt timer frequency */

    ad_init();          /* reset ADC (speed) */
    da_init();          /* reset DAC (torque) */

}



/*----------------------------------------------------------------------
PROCEDURE
    DO_SIMUL  -  special hook into simul() for demo purposes

SYNOPSIS
    void do_simul(void);

LAST UPDATE
    10 April 1988
        creation
----------------------------------------------------------------------*/

void do_simul()
{
    simul();
}


/*----------------------------------------------------------------------
PROCEDURE
    simul  -  simulates motor plant

SYNOPSIS
    static void simul(void)

REMARKS
    Solve the motor system differential equation.  This version uses
    the Euler method for integration; it isn't very efficient, but its
    easy to program!

    Simulates a motor with pure inertial load only.

LAST UPDATE
    1 April 1988
        add friction
----------------------------------------------------------------------*/

static void simul()
```

```
{
    MOTSIM *pms;          /* pointer to motor simulation descriptor */
    int m;                /* loop index (motor number) */
    double friction;      /* friction proportional to speed */


    for (m = 0, pms = pmsim0; m < nmotor; m++, pms++)
    {
        friction = pms->speed * 0.1;    /* 0.1 factor is arbitrary */

        pms->speed += (pms->torque - friction) * dt / pms->inertia;
    }

}


/*********************************************************************
          I N I T I A L I Z A T I O N    R O U T I N E
*********************************************************************/

/*-------------------------------------------------------------------
PROCEDURE
    SIM_INIT  -  initialize simulation module

SYNOPSIS
    void sim_init(nm)
    int nm;

PARAMETER
    nm  -  number of motors

REMARKS
    In a "real" real-time program, this function would be used to set
    up interrupts, set clock modes, etc.  In this simulation version,
    it sets time to zero and sets the motor simulation initial conditions.

LAST UPDATE
    20 March 1988
        rearrange sequence
-------------------------------------------------------------------*/

void sim_init(nm)
int nm;
{
    int m;                /* motor number (loop index also) */
    MOTSIM *pms;          /* pointer to motor simulation block */


    /* allocate memory for the motor simulation data structures */

    if ((pmsim0 = (MOTSIM *)calloc(nm, sizeof(MOTSIM))) != (MOTSIM *)NULL)
    {
        pms = pmsim0;         /* starting with first structure... */

        for (m = 0; m < nm; m++)
        {
            pms->inertia = 1.0;       /* initialize with defaults */
            pms->speed = 0.0;
            pms->torque = 0.0;

            pms++;                    /* next motor */
        }

        nmotor = nm;                  /* record number of motors */

        initflag = 1;
    }
    else
    {
        printf("INSUFFICIENT MEMORY: ");
        printf("cannot allocate %d simulation structures\n", nm);

        exit(1);
    }

}

/*********************************************************************

FILE
    envir.h  -  defines program environment

LAST UPDATE
    16 August 1987
        remove unnecessary clutter

    Copyright(c) 1985,1986,1987  D.M. Auslander and C.H. Tham

*********************************************************************/

/**********************   Operating System   **********************/

#define UNIX    0       /* 4.2 BSD, implies UNIX C compiler */
#define PCDOS   1       /* includes generic MSDOS family */
#define CPM     0       /* the CP/M family, including MP/M */


/*****************   Hardware or Machine Type   *****************/

#define IBMPC       1       /* standard PC, PC/XT, PC/AT */
#define COMPUPRO    0       /* Compupro 8086 or Dual Processor */
#define INTEL310    0       /* Intel 310 development system */
```

```
/***************************   Compilers   *************************/

#define CIC86       0       /* Computer Innovations C86 ver. 2.20M */
#define DESMET      0       /* Desmet C */
#define LATTICE     0       /* Lattice C ver. 2.15 */
#define MICROSOFT   1       /* Microsft C ver. 4.00 */

#if MICROSOFT
#define ANSI                /* use proposed ANSI C features */
#endif

/*********************************************************************

FILE
    dash8.h  -  interface declarations for dash8.c

LAST UPDATE
    18 November 1987

*********************************************************************/

#ifdef ANSI

extern void ad_init(void);
extern void ad_start(int);
extern int  ad_read(int);
extern int  ad_wread(int);

#else

extern void ad_init();
extern void ad_start();
extern int  ad_read();
extern int ad_wread();

#endif

/*********************************************************************

FILE
    dac2.h  -  interface declarations for dac2.c

LAST UPDATE
    18 November 1987

*********************************************************************/

#ifdef ANSI

extern void da_init(void);
extern void da_limits(int *, int *);
extern int  da_write(int, int);

#else

extern void da_init();
extern void da_limits();
extern int  da_write();

#endif


/*********************************************************************

FILE
    time0.h  declarations for time0.c

LAST UPDATE
    15 January 1988

*********************************************************************/

#ifdef ANSI

extern void SetTimer(long);
extern int  TimeUp(void);

#else

extern void SetTimer();
extern int  TimeUp();

#endif
/*********************************************************************

FILE
    cntrl3.h  -  exported declarations for cntrl3.c

LAST UPDATE
    1 April 1988

*********************************************************************/

#ifdef ANSI

extern void control(char *);
extern void gain(char *);
extern void setv(char *);
extern void setsmp(char *);
extern void init(char *);
extern void setmot(void);
```

```
#else

extern void control();
extern void gain();
extern void setv();
extern void setsmp();
extern void init();
extern void setmot();

#endif

/*********************************************************************

FILE
    cntrl3.c  -  PI Control of Servo Motor Speed for Multiple Motors

ENTRY ROUTINES
    control  -  execute control algorithm
    init     -  interpret command line for initialization
    gain     -  interpret command line for PI gains
    setv     -  interpret command line for setpoint
    setsmp   -  interpret command line for sampling rate
    setmot   -  allocate and initialize motor structures

PRIVATE ROUTINES
    pimotor  -  apply motor control
    cpmotor  -  copy motor descriptors
    getv     -  get velocity reading
    mact     -  send controller output to actuator

REMARKS
    This version implements multiple motor control; each motor has
    completely independent sampling interval, control parameters, etc.

LAST UPDATE
    20 March 1988
        include ANSI features

    Copyright (c) 1984-1988  D.M.Auslander and C.H. Tham

*********************************************************************/

/*********************************************************************
                    I M P O R T S
*********************************************************************/

#include <stdio.h>
#include <stdlib.h>
#include <math.h>

#include "envir.h"      /* environment definitions */
#include "dash8.h"      /* declarations for dash8.c */
#include "dac2.h"       /* declarations for dac2.c */
#include "time0.h"      /* declarations for time0.c */
#include "cntrl3.h"     /* exported declarations for this module */

#ifdef SIMRT
#ifdef ANSI
extern void tstep(void);
extern void sim_init(int);
extern void sim_reset(char *);
#else
extern void tstep();
extern void sim_init();
extern void sim_reset();
#endif
#endif

/*********************************************************************
          MODULE  PRIVATE  DATA  STRUCTURES  AND  VARIABLES
*********************************************************************/

#define ADCTOV      1.0         /* ADC units to velocity units */
#define MTODAC      1.0         /* output units to DAC units */

#define TIME_GRAIN  0.001       /* left time granularity */

/*-------------------------------------------------------*/
/*  This structure describes the control and configurational */
/*  parameters for velocity control of a d.c. motor.         */
/*-------------------------------------------------------*/

typedef struct motor {
    int ichan;        /* A/D channel number */
    int mchan;        /* D/A channel number */
    double v;         /* velocity */
    double vref;      /* velocity setpoint */
    double kp;        /* proportional gain */
    double ki;        /* integral gain */
    double ival;      /* integrator accumulated value */
    double vcon;      /* constant in control equation */
    double m;         /* controller output */
    double mmin;      /* lower limit for controller output */
    double mmax;      /* upper limit for controller output */
    double tsamp;     /* sample interval */
    double tleft;     /* time left to next sample */
} MOTOR;

static MOTOR *pm0;        /* pointer to the structure for motor #0 */
static int nmotors;       /* number of motors */

/*-----------------------------------------------------------------*/
```

```
/*  motdef is a set of default values that is used to initialize  */
/*  newly allocated motor control structure.                      */
/*---------------------------------------------------------------*/

static MOTOR motdef = {
          0,      /* A/D channel defaults to 0 */
          0,      /* D/A channel defaults to 0 */
        0.0,      /* zero initial velocity */
     1000.0,      /* default velocity setpoint */
        1.0,      /* kp defaults to 1.0 */
        0.0,      /* no integrator by default, P control by default */
        0.0,      /* zero integration sum */
        0.0,      /* constant term in control equation */
        0.0,      /* no controller output initially */
    -2048.0,      /* lower output limit */
     2047.0,      /* upper output limit */
        0.5,      /* default sampling interval of 0.5 seconds */
       0.0        /* time left to next sample */
};

/*********************************************************************
              F O R W A R D    D E C L A R A T I O N S
*********************************************************************/

#ifdef ANSI

double  getv(int);
void    mact(int, double);
void    pimotor(MOTOR *, int);
void    cpmotor(MOTOR *, MOTOR *);

#else

double  getv();
void    mact();
void    pimotor();
void    cpmotor();

#endif

/*********************************************************************
                   E N T R Y    R O U T I N E S
*********************************************************************/

/*-------------------------------------------------------------------
PROCEDURE
    CONTROL  -  this function does the control

SYNOPSIS
    void control(cline)
    char cline[];

PARAMETER
    cline  -  user's input line that specifies the number of iterations
              and whether to trace the control action.

REMARKS
    The control output is calculated in two parts - first with only P
    action and then with I action added.  The output is limited to what
    the actuator can put out, with provisions against reset windup.

LAST UPDATE
    20 March 1988
        use ANSI features
-------------------------------------------------------------------*/

void control(cline)
char *cline;
{
    MOTOR *pm;            /* pointer to motor data structure */
    long nitr;            /* number of control iterations */
    long i;               /* iteration counter */
    int m;                /* motor number index */
    int prnt;             /* if set to 1, print output every iteration */
    double tlmin;         /* minimum time left to next sample */


    pm = pm0;             /* set pm to point at first motor structure */

    for (m = 0; m < nmotors; m++)
    {
        pm->ival = 0.0;       /* initialize the integrator */
        pm++;                 /* next motor */
    }

    /*  next get user specified iteration limit and print switch  */

    sscanf(cline, "%ld %d", &nitr, &prnt);

 #ifdef DEBUG
    printf("number of iterations = %ld\n", nitr);    /* verify/debug */
 #endif

    for (i = 0L; i < nitr; i++)   /* main iteration loop */
    {
        pm = pm0;         /* point to first motor structure */

        /*-------------------------------------------------------------
            Tlmin is initialized to a large number so we can use it
            to find the task with minimum time left by comparing its
            time left against tlmin and setting tlmin to the minimum
            time left until the motor request control.
        -------------------------------------------------------------*/
```

```
    tlmin = 1.e+37;      /* 10 to the power of 37 */

    /*-----------------------------------------------------------------
        Check each motor to see how much time is left until
        it will request control.  tlmin is set in this loop.
    -----------------------------------------------------------------*/

    for (m = 0; m < nmotors; m++)
    {
        double ttest;     /* time to next sample for this motor */

        /*-------------------------------------------------------------
            A time-left of zero implies that this is the current
            sampling instance for the motor.  Hence, the time
            to next sample from now is the sample interval.
        -------------------------------------------------------------*/

        if (pm->tleft <= 0.0)
            ttest = pm->tsamp;
        else
            ttest = pm->tleft;

        if (ttest < tlmin)       /* update new tlmin */
            tlmin = ttest;

        ++pm;                    /* next motor */
    }

    /*-----------------------------------------------------------------
        Set timer for next sample interval and adjust tleft's.
        Note that argument to settimer() is in milliseconds.
    -----------------------------------------------------------------*/

    SetTimer((long)(tlmin * 1000));

    /*-----------------------------------------------------------------
        Now apply control on any motor requesting it (tleft <= 0).
        The timer should be set before applying control because
        the control action can take a significant amount of time,
        especially if there are many motors to control.
    -----------------------------------------------------------------*/

    pm = pm0;         /* point at first motor structure */

    for (m = 0; m < nmotors; m++)
    {
        if (pm->tleft <= 0.0)
        {
            pimotor(pm, prnt);       /* perform PI control */

            /*-------------------------------------------------------
                Set time-left to the sampling interval to
                await the next execution instance for this
                particular motor.
            -------------------------------------------------------*/

            pm->tleft = pm->tsamp;
        }

        pm->tleft -= tlmin;      /* subtract timer setting from */
                                 /*   time left for all motors. */

        /*-------------------------------------------------------------
            tleft will be compared against 0.0 in the previous
            for(;;) loop; hence we have to impose a comparison
            granularity as tleft is a floating point number.
        -------------------------------------------------------------*/

        if (fabs(pm->tleft) < TIME_GRAIN)    /* adjust for time */
            pm->tleft = 0.0;                 /*  granularity    */

        pm++;                    /* next motor */
    }

    if (TimeUp())         /* timeout before calculations were done */
    {
        printf("sampling time constraints violated\n");
        exit(1);
    }

    while (!TimeUp())   /* wait for next sampling instance */
    {
#if SIMRT                     /* if this is a simulation, call tstep() */
        tstep();              /*   which advances time and simulates   */
#endif                        /*   the motor plant(s).                 */
    }
  }
}



/*------------------------------------------------------------------------
PROCEDURE
    INIT  -  process system initialization command

SYNOPSIS
    void init(cline)
    char *cline;

PARAMETER
    cline  -  data part of input command line, specifying step size
```

```
REMARKS
    This routine must be called before control() is called.

LAST UPDATE
    20 March 1988
        change sim_init()
-----------------------------------------------------------------------*/

void init(cline)
char *cline;
{

    ad_init();                /* initialize A/D */
    da_init();                /* initialize D/A */

#ifdef SIMRT
    sim_reset(cline);
#endif

}


/*----------------------------------------------------------------------
PROCEDURE
    GAIN  -  interpret input line for controller gains specification

SYNOPSIS
    void gain(cline)
    char *cline;

PARAMETER
    cline  -  pointer to null terminated input command line

REMARKS
    Note that in gain(), setv() and setsmp(), the input data is put
    into temporary storage first.  This is because the specified
    motor number may be out of range.

LAST UPDATE
    20 March 1988
        use ANSI features
-----------------------------------------------------------------------*/

void gain(cline)
char *cline;
{
    int mn;                   /* motor number */
    double kp, ki, vcon;      /* temporary gain and constant terms */

    if (sscanf(cline, "%d %lf %lf %lf", &mn, &kp, &ki, &vcon) == 4)
    {
        if ((mn >= 0) && (mn < nmotors))
        {
            /*
             *  Set the appropriate fields of the motor descriptor.
             *  Note that (pm0 + mn) is a pointer to the descriptor
             *  for the mn-th motor; hence the use of "->" to
             *  dereference the descriptor fields.
             */

            (pm0 + mn)->kp = kp;
            (pm0 + mn)->ki = ki;
            (pm0 + mn)->vcon = vcon;

#ifdef DEBUG
            printf("<gain> motor = %d, ", mn);
            printf("kp = %lf, ki = %lf, vcon = %lf\n", kp, ki, vcon);
#endif
        }
        else
            printf("gain: invalid motor number: %d\n", mn);
    }
    else
        printf("gain: invalid or insufficient parameters\n");

}


/*----------------------------------------------------------------------
PROCEDURE
    SETV  -  get velocity setpoint from command line

SYNOPSIS
    void setv(cline)
    char *cline;

PARAMETER
    cline  -  pointer to null terminated input command line

LAST UPDATE
    20 March 1988
        use ANSI features
-----------------------------------------------------------------------*/

void setv(cline)
char *cline;
{
    int mn;             /* motor number */
    double vref;        /* temporary holder for setpoint value */
```

```
    if (sscanf(cline, "%d %lf", &mn ,&vref) == 2)
    {
        if ((mn >= 0) && (mn < nmotors))
        {
            (pm0 + mn)->vref = vref;        /* record velocity reference */

#ifdef DEBUG
            printf("<setv> motor = %d, vref = %lf\n", mn, vref);
#endif
        }
        else
            printf("setv: bad motor number: %d\n", mn);
    }
    else
        printf("setv: invalid or insufficient parameters\n");

}



/*-------------------------------------------------------------------
PROCEDURE
    SETSMP  -  set sampling interval from command line specification

SYNOPSIS
    void setsmp(cline)
    char *cline;

PARAMETER
    cline  -  pointer to null terminated input command line

LAST UPDATE
    20 March 1988
        use ANSI features
-------------------------------------------------------------------*/

void setsmp(cline)
char *cline;
{
    int mn;                 /* motor number */
    double tsamp;           /* temporary holder for sample time */


    if (sscanf(cline,"%d %lf", &mn, &tsamp) == 2)
    {
        if ((mn >= 0) && (mn < nmotors))
        {
            (pm0 + mn)->tsamp = tsamp;      /* set sample interval */

#ifdef DEBUG
            printf("<setsmp> motor = %d, tsamp = %f\n", mn, tsamp);
#endif
        }
        else
            printf("setsmp: bad motor number: %d\n", mn);
    }
    else
        printf("setsmp: invalid or insufficient parameters\n");

}



/*-------------------------------------------------------------------
PROCEDURE
    SETMOT  -  allocate and initialize data structures for the number
               of motors requested by the user.
SYNOPSIS
    void setmot(void)

REMARKS
    This routine must be called as the first action of the main program.

    Motor descriptors initialized from defaults specified in "motdef"

LAST UPDATE
    20 March 1988
        use ANSI features
-------------------------------------------------------------------*/

void setmot()
{
    MOTOR *pm;              /* pointer to motor data structures */
    int nm;                 /* number of motors */
    char cbuf[20];          /* input line */
    int damin, damax;       /* D/A output limits */
    int done;               /* flag, if set, o.k. to return */
    int i;                  /* loop index */


    do
    {
        done = 1;

        /*
         *  Prompt user and get response line.  Because scanf() does not
         *  remove the newline character at the end of lines, fgets() is
         *  used instead since the newline character may cause trouble
         *  with other console functions.
         */

        fputs("How many motors? ", stdout);
```

```
        fgets(cbuf, 20, stdin);         /* get at most 19 characters */

        if (sscanf(cbuf, "%d", &nm) == 1)   /* decode input */
        {
            da_limits(&damin, &damax);      /* find DAC limits */

            motdef.mmin = (double)damin / MTODAC;   /* set output limits */
            motdef.mmax = (double)damax / MTODAC;

            /*
             *  Dynamically allocate memory for the required number of
             *  motor structures.  Note that calloc() is used instead of
             *  malloc() since calloc() is supposed to guarantee that the
             *  allocated block of memory has the correct alignment.
             *  Note also the use of "casts" in the allocation statement;
             *  though not strictly necessary, it is recommended as good
             *  programming style.
             */

            if ((pm0 = (MOTOR *)calloc(nm, sizeof(MOTOR))) == (MOTOR *)NULL)
            {
                printf("INSUFFICIENT MEMORY: ");
                printf("cannot allocate %d motor blocks\n", nm);
                exit(1);
            }

            for (i = 0, pm = pm0; i < nm; i++, pm++)
            {
                cpmotor(&motdef, pm);   /* init with defaults from motdef */

                pm->ichan = i;  /* set both A/D and D/A channels to i; the */
                pm->mchan = i;  /*    actual channels depends on your setup */
            }

            nmotors = nm;       /* record number of motor descriptors */

#ifdef SIMRT
            sim_init(nm);   /* if real-time simulation is to be used, */
#endif                      /*    initialize the simulation module.    */

            if (nm == 1)
                printf("\nmotor 0 has been initialized\n");
            else
                printf("\nmotors 0 to %d have been initialized\n", nm - 1);
        }
        else
        {
            printf("invalid entry\n");
            done = 0;
        }
    }
    while (!done);

}


/************************************************************************
                      P R I V A T E    R O U T I N E S
************************************************************************/

/*-----------------------------------------------------------------------
PROCEDURE
    PIMOTOR  -  apply PI control for motor

SYNOPSIS
    static void pimotor(pm, prnt)
    MOTOR *pm;
    int prnt;

PARAMETERS
    pm    -  pointer to motor structure requiring control
    prnt  -  if 1, print control output

LAST UPDATE
    20 March 1988
        use ANSI features
-----------------------------------------------------------------------*/

static void pimotor(pm, prnt)
MOTOR *pm;
int prnt;
{
    double m1;      /* intermediate result in control calculation. */
    double error;   /* error between reference and measured */


    pm->v = getv(pm->ichan);            /* obtain motor velocity */

    error = pm->vref - pm->v;           /* calculate error term */
    pm->ival += error;                  /* update integral of error */
    m1 = pm->kp * error + pm->vcon;     /* do P control first */

    /*
     *  Check for actuator limits and apply "reset windup" control.
     *  If the output would exceed actuator limits, set the integral
     *  term to zero to prevent the integral term from dominating
     *  the output and slow down corrective action.
     */

    if (m1 > pm->mmax)
    {
        pm->m = pm->mmax;
```

```
            pm->ival = 0.0;
        }
        else if (ml < pm->mmin)
        {
            pm->m = pm->mmin;
            pm->ival = 0.0;
        }
        else    /* output withing actuator limits */
        {
            pm->m = ml + (pm->ki * pm->ival);    /* now add integral term */
        }

        if (prnt)               /* print controller output */
        {
            int mn;             /* motor number */

            mn = (pm - pm0);    /* compute motor number for output */

            printf("motor = %d, v = %7.3lf, m = %7.3lf\n", mn, pm->v, pm->m);
        }

        mact(pm->mchan, pm->m); /* send controller output to actuator */

}


/*-----------------------------------------------------------------------
PROCEDURE
    CPMOTOR  -  copy one motor descriptor to another

SYNOPSIS
    static void cpmotor(from, to)
    MOTOR *from, *to;

PARAMETERS
    from  -  pointer to source
    to    -  pointer to destination

REMARKS
    Standard (K&R) C does not allow entire structures to be assigned
    (this will change with the proposed ANSI X3J11 standards).  This
    restriction is very inconvenient and this routine gets around this
    by doing a byte-by-byte copy of the descriptor contents.  This
    technique may not work on all computers, but it is reasonably
    robust and is much easier than doing field by field assignments.

    If you are using an ANSI conforming C compiler, just do a structure
    assignment.  The compiler will take care of the rest.

LAST UPDATE
    20 March 1988
        use ANSI features
-----------------------------------------------------------------------*/

static void cpmotor(from, to)
MOTOR *from, *to;
{

#ifdef ANSI     /* can do structure assignment */

    *to = *from;

#else           /* do explicit byte by byte copy */

    register char *src, *dst;   /* source and destination pointers */
    unsigned count;             /* byte count */


    src = (char *)from;     /* make fast copy of source pointer */
    dst = (char *)to;       /* make fast copy of destination pointer */

    for (count = 0; count < sizeof(MOTOR); count++)
        *dst++ = *src++;

#endif

}


/*-----------------------------------------------------------------------
FUNCTION
    GETV  -  get current motor velocity

SYNOPSIS
    static double getv(channel)
    int channel;

PARAMETER
    channel  -  A/D channel from which to read the velocity

RETURNS
    current motor velocity

REMARKS
    Note that the conversion of raw ADC units to velocity units
    uses the ADCTOV conversion factor.

LAST UPDATE
    20 March 1988
        use ANSI features
```

```
---------------------------------------------------------------------*/

static double getv(channel)
int channel;
{

    return((double)ad_wread(channel) * ADCTOV);
}



/*----------------------------------------------------------------------
PROCEDURE
    mact  -  send controller output to D/A converter

SYNOPSIS
    static void mact(channel, output)
    int channel;
    double output;

PARAMETERS
    channel -  D/A channel number
    output  -  controller output

REMARKS
    Multiply by conversion factor and add 0.5 for rounding.

LAST UPDATE
    20 March 1988
        use ANSI features
---------------------------------------------------------------------*/

static void mact(channel, output)
int channel;
double output;
{

    da_write(channel, (int)((output * MTODAC) + 0.5));
}
/**********************************************************************

FILE
    cntrl4.c  -  PI Control of Servo Motor Speed for Multiple Motors

ENTRY ROUTINES
    control  -  execute control algorithm
    init     -  interpret command line for initialization
    gain     -  interpret command line for PI gains
    setv     -  interpret command line for setpoint
    setsmp   -  interpret command line for sampling rate
    setmot   -  allocate and initialize motor structures

PRIVATE ROUTINES
    pimotor  -  apply motor control
    cpmotor  -  copy motor descriptors
    getv     -  get velocity reading
    mact     -  send controller output to actuator

REMARKS
    This version implements multiple motor control; each motor has
    completely independent sampling interval, control parameters, etc.

LAST UPDATE
    20 March 1988
        include ANSI features

    Copyright (c) 1984-1988  D.M.Auslander and C.H. Tham

**********************************************************************/

/**********************************************************************
                    I M P O R T S
**********************************************************************/

#include <stdio.h>
#include <stdlib.h>
#include <math.h>

#include "envir.h"      /* environment definitions */
#include "dash8.h"      /* declarations for dash8.c */
#include "dac2.h"       /* declarations for dac2.c */
#include "time0.h"      /* declarations for time0.c */
#include "cntrl3.h"     /* exported declarations for this module */

#include "user.h"

#ifdef SIMRT
#ifdef ANSI
extern void tstep(void);
extern void sim_init(int);
extern void sim_reset(char *);
#else
extern void tstep();
extern void sim_init();
extern void sim_reset();
#endif
#endif

/**********************************************************************
          MODULE  PRIVATE  DATA  STRUCTURES  AND  VARIABLES
**********************************************************************/

#define ADCTOV      1.0         /* ADC units to velocity units */
```

```
#define MTODAC      1.0         /* output units to DAC units */

#define TIME_GRAIN  0.001       /* left time granularity */

/*---------------------------------------------------------*/
/*  This structure describes the control and configurational */
/*  parameters for velocity control of a d.c. motor.        */
/*---------------------------------------------------------*/

typedef struct motor {
    int ichan;        /* A/D channel number */
    int mchan;        /* D/A channel number */
    double v;         /* velocity */
    double vref;      /* velocity setpoint */
    double kp;        /* proportional gain */
    double ki;        /* integral gain */
    double ival;      /* integrator accumulated value */
    double vcon;      /* constant in control equation */
    double m;         /* controller output */
    double mmin;      /* lower limit for controller output */
    double mmax;      /* upper limit for controller output */
    double tsamp;     /* sample interval */
    double tleft;     /* time left to next sample */
} MOTOR;

static MOTOR *pm0;        /* pointer to the structure for motor #0 */
static int nmotors;       /* number of motors */

/*-------------------------------------------------------------*/
/*  motdef is a set of default values that is used to initialize  */
/*  newly allocated motor control structure.                   */
/*-------------------------------------------------------------*/

static MOTOR motdef = {
          0,      /* A/D channel defaults to 0 */
          0,      /* D/A channel defaults to 0 */
        0.0,      /* zero initial velocity */
     1000.0,      /* default velocity setpoint */
        1.0,      /* kp defaults to 1.0 */
        0.0,      /* no integrator by default, P control by default */
        0.0,      /* zero integration sum */
        0.0,      /* constant term in control equation */
        0.0,      /* no controller output initially */
    -2048.0,      /* lower output limit */
     2047.0,      /* upper output limit */
        0.5,      /* default sampling interval of 0.5 seconds */
        0.0       /* time left to next sample */
};

/*********************************************************************
               F O R W A R D     D E C L A R A T I O N S
*********************************************************************/

#ifdef ANSI

double  getv(int);
void    mact(int, double);
void    pimotor(MOTOR *);
void    cpmotor(MOTOR *, MOTOR *);

#else

double  getv();
void    mact();
void    pimotor();
void    cpmotor();

#endif

/*********************************************************************
                    E N T R Y    R O U T I N E S
*********************************************************************/

/*-------------------------------------------------------------------
PROCEDURE
    CONTROL  -  this function does the control

SYNOPSIS
    void control(cline)
    char cline[];

PARAMETER
    cline  -  user's input line that specifies the number of iterations
              and whether to trace the control action.

REMARKS
    The control output is calculated in two parts - first with only P
    action and then with I action added.  The output is limited to what
    the actuator can put out, with provisions against reset windup.

LAST UPDATE
    20 March 1988
        use ANSI features
-------------------------------------------------------------------*/

void control(cline)
char *cline;
{
    MOTOR *pm;              /* pointer to motor data structure */
    long i;                 /* iteration counter */
    int m;                  /* motor number index */
```

```
    prologue();           /* prepare scheduling kernel */

    pm = pm0;             /* set pm to point at first motor structure */

    for (m = 0; m < nmotors; m++)
    {
        pm->ival = 0.0;     /* initialize the integrator */

        SetCntrlTask("motor", pimotor, (void *)pm, 1000,
                      (long)(pm->tsamp * 1000.0  +  0.5));

        pm++;               /* next motor */
    }

    start();              /* start the scheduler */

}


/*-----------------------------------------------------------------------
PROCEDURE
    INIT  -  process system initialization command

SYNOPSIS
    void init(cline)
    char *cline;

PARAMETER
    cline  -  data part of input command line, specifying step size

REMARKS
    This routine must be called before control() is called.

LAST UPDATE
    20 March 1988
        change sim_init()
-----------------------------------------------------------------------*/

void init(cline)
char *cline;
{

    ad_init();                /* initialize A/D */
    da_init();                /* initialize D/A */

#ifdef SIMRT
    sim_reset(cline);
#endif

}
```

```
/*-----------------------------------------------------------------------
PROCEDURE
    GAIN  -  interpret input line for controller gains specification

SYNOPSIS
    void gain(cline)
    char *cline;

PARAMETER
    cline  -  pointer to null terminated input command line

REMARKS
    Note that in gain(), setv() and setsmp(), the input data is put
    into temporary storage first.  This is because the specified
    motor number may be out of range.

LAST UPDATE
    20 March 1988
        use ANSI features
-----------------------------------------------------------------------*/

void gain(cline)
char *cline;
{
    int mn;                     /* motor number */
    double kp, ki, vcon;        /* temporary gain and constant terms */


    if (sscanf(cline, "%d %lf %lf %lf", &mn, &kp, &ki, &vcon) == 4)
    {
        if ((mn >= 0) && (mn < nmotors))
        {
            /*
             *  Set the appropriate fields of the motor descriptor.
             *  Note that (pm0 + mn) is a pointer to the descriptor
             *  for the mn-th motor; hence the use of "->" to
             *  dereference the descriptor fields.
             */

            (pm0 + mn)->kp = kp;
            (pm0 + mn)->ki = ki;
            (pm0 + mn)->vcon = vcon;

#ifdef DEBUG
            printf("<gain> motor = %d, ", mn);
            printf("kp = %lf, ki = %lf, vcon = %lf\n", kp, ki, vcon);
#endif
        }
        else
            printf("gain: invalid motor number: %d\n", mn);
    }
```

```
        else
            printf("gain: invalid or insufficient parameters\n");

}



/*-----------------------------------------------------------------------
PROCEDURE
    SETV  -  get velocity setpoint from command line

SYNOPSIS
    void setv(cline)
    char *cline;

PARAMETER
    cline  -  pointer to null terminated input command line

LAST UPDATE
    20 March 1988
        use ANSI features
-----------------------------------------------------------------------*/

void setv(cline)
char *cline;
{
    int mn;             /* motor number */
    double vref;        /* temporary holder for setpoint value */


    if (sscanf(cline, "%d %lf", &mn ,&vref) == 2)
    {
        if ((mn >= 0) && (mn < nmotors))
        {
            (pm0 + mn)->vref = vref;          /* record velocity reference */

#ifdef DEBUG
            printf("<setv> motor = %d, vref = %lf\n", mn, vref);
#endif
        }
        else
            printf("setv: bad motor number: %d\n", mn);
    }
    else
        printf("setv: invalid or insufficient parameters\n");

}



/*-----------------------------------------------------------------------
PROCEDURE
    SETSMP  -  set sampling interval from command line specification

SYNOPSIS
    void setsmp(cline)
    char *cline;

PARAMETER
    cline  -  pointer to null terminated input command line

LAST UPDATE
    20 March 1988
        use ANSI features
-----------------------------------------------------------------------*/

void setsmp(cline)
char *cline;
{
    int mn;                 /* motor number */
    double tsamp;           /* temporary holder for sample time */


    if (sscanf(cline,"%d %lf", &mn, &tsamp) == 2)
    {
        if ((mn >= 0) && (mn < nmotors))
        {
            (pm0 + mn)->tsamp = tsamp;        /* set sample interval */

#ifdef DEBUG
            printf("<setsmp> motor = %d, tsamp = %f\n", mn, tsamp);
#endif
        }
        else
            printf("setsmp: bad motor number: %d\n", mn);
    }
    else
        printf("setsmp: invalid or insufficient parameters\n");

}



/*-----------------------------------------------------------------------
PROCEDURE
    SETMOT  -  allocate and initialize data structures for the number
               of motors requested by the user.
SYNOPSIS
    void setmot(void)

REMARKS
    This routine must be called as the first action of the main program.
```

```
    Motor descriptors initialized from defaults specified in "motdef"

LAST UPDATE
    20 March 1988
        use ANSI features
-----------------------------------------------------------------------*/

void setmot()
{
    MOTOR *pm;              /* pointer to motor data structures */
    int nm;                 /* number of motors */
    char cbuf[20];          /* input line */
    int damin, damax;       /* D/A output limits */
    int done;               /* flag, if set, o.k. to return */
    int i;                  /* loop index */


    do
    {
        done = 1;

        /*
         *  Prompt user and get response line.  Because scanf() does not
         *  remove the newline character at the end of lines, fgets() is
         *  used instead since the newline character may cause trouble
         *  with other console functions.
         */

        fputs("How many motors? ", stdout);
        fgets(cbuf, 20, stdin);          /* get at most 19 characters */

        if (sscanf(cbuf, "%d", &nm) == 1)    /* decode input */
        {
            da_limits(&damin, &damax);       /* find DAC limits */

            motdef.mmin = (double)damin / MTODAC;    /* set output limits */
            motdef.mmax = (double)damax / MTODAC;

            /*
             *  Dynamically allocate memory for the required number of
             *  motor structures.  Note that calloc() is used instead of
             *  malloc() since calloc() is suppose to guarantee that the
             *  allocated block of memory has the correct alignment.
             *  Note also the use of "casts" in the allocation statement;
             *  though not strictly necessary, it is recommended as good
             *  programming style.
             */

            if ((pm0 = (MOTOR *)calloc(nm, sizeof(MOTOR))) == (MOTOR *)NULL)
            {
                printf("INSUFFICIENT MEMORY: ");
                printf("cannot allocate %d motor blocks\n", nm);
                exit(1);
            }

            for (i = 0, pm = pm0; i < nm; i++, pm++)
            {
                cpmotor(&motdef, pm);    /* init with defaults from motdef */

                pm->ichan = i;  /* set both A/D and D/A channels to i; the */
                pm->mchan = i;  /*   actual channels depends on your setup */
            }

            nmotors = nm;          /* record number of motor descriptors */

#ifdef SIMRT
            sim_init(nm);     /* if real-time simulation is to be used, */
                              /*   initialize the simulation module.    */
#endif

            if (nm == 1)
                printf("\nmotor 0 has been initialized\n");
            else
                printf("\nmotors 0 to %d have been initialized\n", nm - 1);
        }
        else
        {
            printf("invalid entry\n");
            done = 0;
        }
    }
    while (!done);

}


/*************************************************************************
                     P R I V A T E    R O U T I N E S
*************************************************************************/

/*-----------------------------------------------------------------------
PROCEDURE
    PIMOTOR  -  apply PI control for motor

SYNOPSIS
    static void pimotor(pm, prnt)
    MOTOR *pm;
    int prnt;

PARAMETERS
    pm    -  pointer to motor structure requiring control
    prnt  -  if 1, print control output
```

```
LAST UPDATE
    20 March 1988
        use ANSI features
    10 April 1988
        modify for clotho background scheduler
----------------------------------------------------------------------*/

static void pimotor(pm)
MOTOR *pm;
{
    double ml;       /* intermediate result in control calculation. */
    double error;    /* error between reference and measured */
    int mn;          /* motor number */


    pm->v = getv(pm->ichan);            /* obtain motor velocity */

    error = pm->vref - pm->v;           /* calculate error term */
    pm->ival += error;                  /* update integral of error */
    ml = pm->kp * error + pm->vcon;     /* do P control first */

    /*
     *  Check for actuator limits and apply "reset windup" control.
     *  If the output would exceed actuator limits, set the integral
     *  term to zero to prevent the integral term from dominating
     *  the output and slow down corrective action.
     */

    if (ml > pm->mmax)
    {
        pm->m = pm->mmax;
        pm->ival = 0.0;
    }
    else if (ml < pm->mmin)
    {
        pm->m = pm->mmin;
        pm->ival = 0.0;
    }
    else    /* output withing actuator limits */
    {
        pm->m = ml + (pm->ki * pm->ival);   /* now add integral term */
    }

    mn = (pm - pm0);    /* compute motor number for output */

    printf("motor = %d, v = %7.3lf, m = %7.3lf\n", mn, pm->v, pm->m);

    mact(pm->mchan, pm->m); /* send controller output to actuator */

}
```

```
/*-----------------------------------------------------------------------
PROCEDURE
    CPMOTOR  -  copy one motor descriptor to another

SYNOPSIS
    static void cpmotor(from, to)
    MOTOR *from, *to;

PARAMETERS
    from  -  pointer to source
    to    -  pointer to destination

REMARKS
    Standard (K&R) C does not allow entire structures to be assigned
    (this will change with the proposed ANSI X3J11 standards).  This
    restriction is very inconvenient and this routine gets around this
    by doing a byte-by-byte copy of the descriptor contents.  This
    technique may not work on all computers, but it is reasonably
    robust and is much easier than doing field by field assignments.

    If you are using an ANSI conforming C compiler, just do a structure
    assignment.  The compiler will take care of the rest.

LAST UPDATE
    20 March 1988
        use ANSI features
----------------------------------------------------------------------*/

static void cpmotor(from, to)
MOTOR *from, *to;
{

#ifdef ANSI     /* can do structure assignment */

    *to = *from;

#else           /* do explicit byte by byte copy */

    register char *src, *dst;   /* source and destination pointers */
    unsigned count;             /* byte count */


    src = (char *)from;     /* make fast copy of source pointer */
    dst = (char *)to;       /* make fast copy of destination pointer */

    for (count = 0; count < sizeof(MOTOR); count++)
        *dst++ = *src++;

#endif

}
```

```
/*-----------------------------------------------------------------------
FUNCTION
    GETV  -  get current motor velocity

SYNOPSIS
    static double getv(channel)
    int channel;

PARAMETER
    channel  -  A/D channel from which to read the velocity

RETURNS
    current motor velocity

REMARKS
    Note that the conversion of raw ADC units to velocity units
    uses the ADCTOV conversion factor.

LAST UPDATE
    20 March 1988
        use ANSI features
-----------------------------------------------------------------------*/

static double getv(channel)
int channel;
{

    return((double)ad_wread(channel) * ADCTOV);
}



/*-----------------------------------------------------------------------
PROCEDURE
    mact  -  send controller output to D/A converter

SYNOPSIS
    static void mact(channel, output)
    int channel;
    double output;

PARAMETERS
    channel -  D/A channel number
    output  -  controller output

REMARKS
    Multiply by conversion factor and add 0.5 for rounding.

LAST UPDATE
    20 March 1988
        use ANSI features
-----------------------------------------------------------------------*/

static void mact(channel, output)
int channel;
double output;
{

    da_write(channel, (int)((output * MTODAC) + 0.5));
}
/************************************************************************

FILE
    bsched.c  -  special abbreviated version of stlsched.c

ENTRY ROUTINES
    StlDispatch  -  schedule and dispatch tasks
    StlStart     -  initialize timer

PRIVATE ROUTINES
    dec_tleft  -  decrement t_tleft for all tasks in queue
    set_tnext  -  set time to next sampling instance tnext
    deep_background

REMARKS
    The routines reference the STL queue as a parameter rather than
    as a global variable.  This is to allow the STL queue to be
    implemented as a soft timer-driven event queue.
    Note that multiple STL queues driven by different timers can be
    easily added later, only requiring the timer-number parameter to
    be passed as well as the queue pointer.

LAST UPDATE
    11 February 1986
        add event tasktype recognition
    14 April 1988
        make this abbreviated non-interrupt driven version

    Copyright (c) 1985 - 1988  D.M. Auslander  and  C.H. Tham

************************************************************************/

/************************************************************************
                              I M P O R T S
************************************************************************/

#include <stdio.h>

#include "envir.h"          /* environment definitions */

#include "config.h"         /* system configuration header */
#include "types.h"          /* type definitions */
```

```
#include "task.h"           /* task descriptor definitions */
#include "tqueue.h"         /* task queue module definitions */
#include "dispatch.h"       /* dispatcher module declarations */
#include "time.h"           /* time module definitions */

extern TASK *curtask;       /* pointer to current task descriptor */

/************************************************************************
               F O R W A R D   D E C L A R A T I O N S
************************************************************************/

void dec_tleft(long, TQUEUE *);
void set_tnext(TQUEUE *, TQUEUE *);
void deep_background(void);

/************************************************************************
           MODULE  PRIVATE  DATA  STRUCTURES  AND  VARIABLES
************************************************************************/

static long tnext = 0L;         /* time to next sampling instance */

/************************************************************************
                   E N T R Y   R O U T I N E S
************************************************************************/

/*-----------------------------------------------------------------------
PROCEDURE
    STLDISPATCH  -  STL dispatcher/scheduler (background non preemptive)

SYNOPSIS
    void StlDispatch(stlq, urgentq, stltimer)
    TQUEUE *stlq, *urgentq;
    int stltimer;

PARAMETER
    stlq     -  STL task queue
    urgentq  -  queue of urgent waiting tasks
    stltimer -  timer to use for stl scheduling

REMARKS
    1. No other scheduler can be running while this is running.
    2. Since scheduler is background, obviously non pre-emptive.

LAST UPDATE
    10 April 1988
        specially modified to call plant simulation
-----------------------------------------------------------------------*/

void StlDispatch(stlq, urgentq, stltimer)
TQUEUE *stlq, *urgentq;
int stltimer;
{

    for (;;)            /* infinite loop */
    {
#ifdef SIMRT
        while (!TimeUp(stltimer))
        {
            do_simul();
            chronos();
        }
#else
        while (!TimeUp(stltimer))
            if (ReadDTimer(stltimer) > (1000L / TICKRATE))
                deep_background();
#endif

        if ((curtask = GetTqueue(stlq)) == TNULL)
            panic("background StlDispatch: no task to dispatch");

        dec_tleft(tnext, stlq);
        set_tnext(stlq, urgentq);

        if (tnext > 0)
            SetDTimer(stltimer, tnext);

        (*curtask->t_func)(curtask->t_argp);

        curtask->t_tleft = curtask->t_tsamp;

        EnterTqueue(curtask, stlq, STL_ENTER);
    }
}


/*-----------------------------------------------------------------------
PROCEDURE
    STLSTART  -  start STL dispatcher/scheduler module

SYNOPSIS
    StlStart(stlq, urgentq, stltimer)
    TQUEUE *stlq, *urgentq;
    int stltimer;

PARAMETER
    stlq     -  STL task queue
    urgentq  -  queue of urgent waiting tasks
    stltimer -  timer for stl scheduling

REMARKS
    This function is used to initialize this module and to start the
```

```
    STL timer.  If a task is ready to run immediately (tleft == 0),
    that task is dispatched.

    StlStart should to be called whenever a new task (or a new group
    of tasks) is put into the STL queue since the queue may initially
    be empty and the timer not set.

LAST UPDATE
    18 March 1985
-----------------------------------------------------------------------*/

void StlStart(stlq, urgentq, stltimer)
TQUEUE *stlq, *urgentq;
int stltimer;
{

    if (stlq == TQNULL)
        panic("StlStart: stlq is NULL");

    if (!EmptyTqueue(stlq))
    {
        tnext = HeadTqueue(stlq)->t_tleft;

        SetDTimer(stltimer, tnext);
    }

    StlDispatch(stlq, urgentq, stltimer);

}


/***********************************************************************
                   P R I V A T E    R O U T I N E S
***********************************************************************/

/*---------------------------------------------------------------------
PROCEDURE
    DEC_TLEFT  -  decrement t_tleft for all tasks in queue

SYNOPSIS
    static void dec_tleft(deltime, taskq)
    long deltime;
    TQUEUE *taskq;

PARAMETERS
    deltime  -  amount to decrement (ms)
    taskq    -  task queue in question

REMARKS
    Normally used to decrement by tnext.

LAST UPDATE
    15 February 1985
-----------------------------------------------------------------------*/

static void dec_tleft(deltime, taskq)
long deltime;
TQUEUE *taskq;
{
    register TASK *task;


    if ((task = HeadTqueue(taskq)) != TNULL)
    {
        do
        {
            task->t_tleft -= deltime;

            task = task->t_next;
        }
        while (task != TNULL);
    }

}


/*---------------------------------------------------------------------
PROCEDURE
    SET_TNEXT  -  set time to next sampling, tnext

SYNOPSIS
    static void set_tnext(stlq, urgentq)
    TQUEUE *stlq, *urgentq;

PARAMETERS
    stlq     -  stl task queue
    urgentq  -  queue of urgently waiting tasks

REMARKS
    Uses side-effects to change tnext.

    Tnext is the minimum of (curtask->tsamp, stlq->tleft)

LAST UPDATE
    10 April 1988
        special background version, ignore urgentq.
-----------------------------------------------------------------------*/

static void set_tnext(stlq, urgentq)
TQUEUE *stlq, *urgentq;
{
```

```
    register TASK *task;


    tnext = MAXLONG;            /* re-initialize for comparison */

    if (((task = HeadTqueue(stlq)) != TNULL) && (task->t_tleft < tnext))
        tnext = task->t_tleft;

    if ((curtask != TNULL) && (curtask->t_tsamp < tnext))
        tnext = curtask->t_tsamp;

}



/*-----------------------------------------------------------------------
PROCEDURE
    DEEP_BACKGROUND  -  runs when nothing else is running

SYNOPSIS
    static void deep_background()

REMARKS
    This is called by the non pre-emptive scheduler when waiting for
    time to sample.  Currently, this routine does nothing and is used
    as a place holder.  Any routine you put in here MUST BE SHORT!

LAST UPDATE
    12 March 1985
-----------------------------------------------------------------------*/

static void deep_background()
{
    int i;


    for (i = 0; i < 500; i++)    /* idle loop */
        ;

}
```

CHAPTER 6

THE OPERATOR'S CONSOLE

The primary interaction between the computer and the system user or operator, when such interaction is part of the system design, is a console device. The console device usually consists of some form of visual display and a keyboard. These devices can range from highly specialized, dedicated pushbuttons, and numeric displays, to general-purpose terminals with color and graphics. The design of the computer/operator interface is based on the same principles as other parts of the real-time system: the operator must be able to respond to situations within time constraints that are imposed by the external systems. In addition, all of the console activity must take place without disturbing the control and data acquisition functions that are the primary tasks.

The critical elements in the interaction are the communication of relevant information to the operator and the operator's ability to enter commands and information. These functions take a great deal of careful design to avoid having the operator hunting through manuals or menus to find out how to call up the needed information or how to formulate the appropriate command. This chapter will address some of the basic techniques for organizing and scheduling the console functions, and some methods for presenting the operator with easy-to-find information and providing a simple command entry that can operate in parallel with control.

6.1 CONSOLE DEVICES

The material in this chapter will be directed toward applications using general purpose console terminals rather than specially designed consoles. These consoles consist of a screen, a typewriter style keyboard, and, perhaps, an additional data entry device such as a mouse. We will consider only the keyboard as the data entry device.

The keyboard and the screen are logically independent devices, even though they may be housed as part of the same "terminal." The keyboard interface to the computer is usually via a stream of characters on a serial line. This is a single electrical connection so that the information must be sent in serial form, one bit after another. Keyboards commonly use the ASCII (American standard code for information interchange) to represent characters. This is a 7-bit code, which therefore has 2^7=128 unique codes. Of these, 96 represent the characters on the keyboard (upper case, lower case, numbers, punctuations, special symbols). The remaining codes are called "control" characters and are used for a variety of signalling and control purposes. Other codes are also used, notably the EBCDIC code of IBM, but ASCII is the most widely used. An eighth bit is often added to the code, doubling the number of possible combinations. This eighth bit is used for two distinct purposes. The first use is as a *parity* bit for error detection. An *even* or *odd* parity can be used. In even parity, for example, before a character is transmitted, the number of "one" bits out of the seven bits representing the character are counted (an "A" is 1000001 in the 7-bit ASCII code, which, as an example, has two "one" bits). In even parity, the transmission rule is that the 8-bit character sent will always have an even number of "one" bits. Since the "A" has 2, the parity bit is set to zero for an 8-bit code of 01000001. The 7-bit code for "C" is 1000011; to keep even parity, the eighth bit would have to be "one," giving an 8-bit code of 11000011. The receiving end must know in advance what kind of parity convention is being used. When a character is received, the number of "one" bits is again counted. If it is not even (in even parity), then a transmission error must have occurred. The receiver can then take action to ignore the character, signal to the transmitter to send it again, and so on. The parity method of error detection will find all possible one-bit errors; however, any multi-bit errors involving an even number of bits will be missed.

Parity is useful when signals are sent in a noisy environment. When the noise level is low, however, as it usually is when a keyboard is connected directly to a computer, the eighth bit can be used to signal an "alternate" character set. The alternate character set can be for graphics, for additional characters not in the usual 96-character ASCII set (Greek letters for example). It can also indicate special attributes as used, for example, in some word processing software for "soft" hyphens or end-of-line indicators inserted by the word processor rather than by the user.

The signal representing the character is transmitted over a single data path. Because there is no way of knowing when a character will be typed, the signal protocol is *asynchronous* with respect to characters, but *synchronous* within the character. The beginning of an arriving character is signalled by a *start* bit. It is followed by the 7 or 8 bits of the ASCII code, which are in turn followed by a *stop* bit, for a total of 10 bits. The start and stop bits are the overhead associated with the asynchronous protocol. At minimum, the start bit must be present so that the receiver will know when a character is starting. Otherwise, if the leading bit of the code is a zero, there will be no way to detect it. The stop bit serves for further error detection—if it isn't there, something has happened in transmission and a *framing error* is indicated.

Within the character frame, the bits appear at uniformly spaced time intervals. The transmitter and receiver must be synchronized in advance in order for the character to be successfully decoded. The bit rate within the frame is called the *Baud* rate and has units of bits per second. Figure 6.1 shows the signal sent for the letter "A" using even parity. The start and stop bits are marked and the bit values are noted for the 8 code bits. The ASCII code is received after the "start" bit, in backwards order. The parity bit is in position 9, and the code 1000001 is read from time positions 8 down to 2.

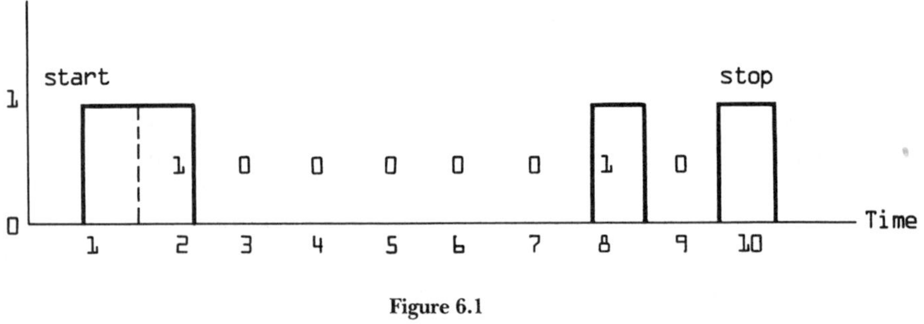

Figure 6.1

Two types of screen interfaces are commonly encountered. The first is the direct analog of the keyboard interface just described. ASCII characters are sent over a serial line from the computer to the console, where they are interpreted and displayed on the screen. The second type of interface is *memory mapped.* A section of the computer's memory is set aside as an "image" of the screen. Circuitry in the computer system takes the information from that section of memory and displays it on the screen. The information stored in the memory image can itself have two different forms. In one case, the ASCII code for the character is stored at the position at which it is to be displayed. The display circuitry translates the character code into a set of dots for actual display. In a *bit-mapped* display, the actual dots are stored in the memory image of the screen and all the display circuitry does is display them on a dot-for-dot basis. Software must then be used to put the dot pattern corresponding to a particular character into the correct memory locations. The bit-mapped screen allows for much more flexible displays, including graphics, but it takes more memory to map the screen and more software and computing time to translate the character codes into bit patterns.

Use of a bit-mapped screen is primarily a background task. A certain amount of computing time must be devoted to adding information to the screen memory, but there is no interaction outside the computer. Our interest centers on the interactions outside the computer, so for further discussion we will assume the use of a console connected to the computer through a serial link.

6.2 THE SERIAL INTERFACE

The circuitry that stands between the computer and the serial line, the serial interface, is responsible for conversion of the serial signal that is transmitted between the computer and the terminal into a parallel digital word and vice versa. The device that does the actual serial/parallel conversion is a *UART*, universal, asynchronous, receiver/transmitter. The receive and transmit sections of the interface operate completely independently. Because of this independence, there are two common mechanisms for getting the character *echo* that appears on the screen after the user presses a key. In *full duplex* mode, there are two independent transmission paths. The serial packet describing the character is sent from the keyboard to the computer. After it is received, the computer sends the character back to the terminal so that it will appear on the screen as an echo. Both the keyboard and computer can transmit at the same time. In *half duplex* mode, there is only a single transmission path, so instead of using that path to send the echo character, the echo is generated locally by the terminal, and the transmission path is reserved for characters sent from the terminal to the computer or from computer to terminal, but not both at the same time. Most real-time situations have dual transmission paths, so full duplex operation will be assumed here.

In addition to the UART, the serial interface has registers to store the characters being received and sent, and a status register to keep track of what is going on. When a character from the terminal is received at the interface, the character is converted from serial form to parallel form and stored in the received character *buffer*. At the same time, the bit in the status register that indicates "character ready" is turned on. (Note that "on" and "off" are used here in the logical sense; the actual voltage associated with "on," for example, can be either high or low depending on the hardware used.) The computer accesses the received character buffer register as an input port, and can read the character. When the character is read by the computer, the interface automatically turns the "character ready" bit in the status register off. To send a character to the terminal, the computer places the character into the transmit buffer register. This automatically initiates the parallel-to-serial conversion process to build the serial packet. At the same time, the interface turns off the bit in the interface that indicates "transmitter buffer empty." When the serial packet has been dispatched, the "transmitter buffer empty" bit will be turned back on.

In addition to these basic functions, the interface will also provide information in the status register for various error conditions, framing error (common when the baud rates of receiver and transmitter don't match), overrun (when a new character is placed into the received character buffer before the old one has been read), and parity errors. Other control lines are also made available to control modems, or issue signals that can be used if more than the minimum number of wires are used in the serial connection.

Interfaces as described buffer a single character in each direction. Any further buffering of characters must be done in software. More sophisticated interfaces are available that provide more buffering, but they are usually used for systems that must attach a large number of terminals, such as time-shared computers.

6.3 ASYNCHRONOUS (INTERRUPT) PROCESSING

There is no way to predict when characters will arrive from the terminal because characters are generated when users type them. To avoid tying the CPU down watching for characters, it is efficient to use an asynchronous interrupt process to receive the incoming characters and store them for use whenever the background task needs them. The console receiver interrupt handler runs whenever an interrupt is initiated by the "data ready" flag on the serial interface. The handler (see Fig. 6.2) saves registers, checks to see if the memory area for storing characters (the "buffer") has room, and, if it does, stores the character.

```
Character Ready Interrupt:

        Save machine state
        If (store_character_received is not successful)
                Set error flag

        Restore machine state
        return
```

Figure 6.2

In the case of a full buffer, there are two choices, both of which involve the loss of information. One is to ignore the character that just arrived, and the other is to throw away the oldest character in the buffer even though it has not yet been processed. It is not possible to wait for room to become available in the buffer because that can only happen if the background program that uses the characters can run. If this foreground handler waits, however, the background will never run.

The characters are buffered into a section of the computer's main memory. The best way to organize that memory is as a first-in, first-out (FIFO) buffer. When a FIFO buffer is established through software, it can be set up in "ring" form. A ring buffer can be set up with two control variables: (1) a pointer to the location behind the oldest character in the buffer; and (2) a pointer to the newest. Buffer empty or full is indicated by the oldest and newest pointers overlapping. The memory layout to create a ring buffer is given in Fig. 6.3. The memory positions with x's represent the received data. The pointer "top" points at the highest memory address in the buffer, and the pointer "bottom" points at the lowest memory address. The "top" and "bottom" are considered to be logically connected, as shown by the arrows, to give the ring buffer. The "front" and "rear" labels are the front and rear of the received data viewed as a variable length worm crawling around the ring!

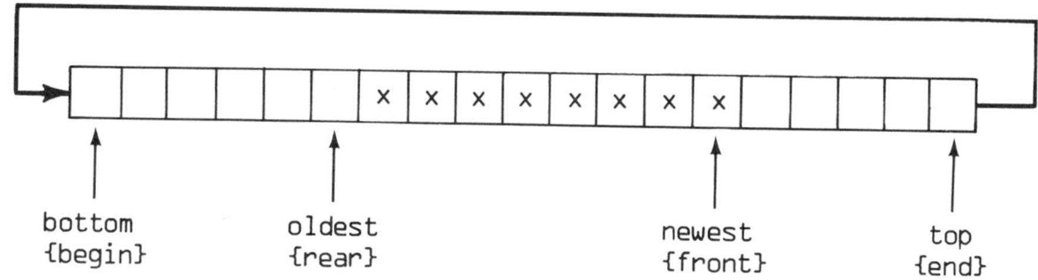

Figure 6.3

There are at least two functions used to service the buffer. The one to put characters into the buffer is called from the foreground interrupt service routine, while the function to take characters out of the buffer is called from the background task that interprets the information. Fig. 6.4 shows the store_character function, and Fig. 6.5 shows the get_character function.

```
Store_character(character):

    next = front + 1            (Location for new character)
    If(next > end)
            next = begin        (Wraparound)
    If(next == rear)
            return(buffer_full)
    *next = char                (Put new character in buffer)
    front = next                (Update pointer)
    Return
```

Figure 6.4

The key to the management of the ring buffer is the test for whether the "pointer_to_next" points past the end of the buffer. If it does, the pointer is reset to point to the beginning of the buffer, thus establishing the "ring-like" characteristic. An important property of this method of managing a buffer is that the amount of computing time is independent of the size of the buffer, so that there is no computing time penalty for using larger buffers.

Arrays and indices can be used to manage the buffer when using compilers that do not have sufficiently flexible pointer operations. The front and rear pointers are replaced by subscripts into the array, and the wraparound is achieved by using the subscripts corresponding to the beginning and end of the array.

Figure 6.5 shows the complementary process of removing a character from the buffer. Again, the wraparound to implement the ring buffer is the key to efficient implementation. The abnormal return in this case is when the buffer is already empty.

```
get_character:

        If(front == rear)
                Return(buffer_empty)
        Else
                rear = rear + 1
                If(rear == end)
                        rear = begin                (Wraparound)
                Return(*rear)
```

Figure 6.5

In the software implementation of a first-in, first-out (FIFO) buffer, a ring buffer, the most efficient solution is to move the pointers and leave the data stationary. It is interesting to contrast this with the hardware solution, a shift register, where the data is moved from register to register as it progresses from beginning to end. The hardware components carry out their processing in parallel, on all registers at the same time, so moving the data is efficient. Computers, by contrast, must do their computations sequentially, so the ring buffer becomes a more efficient solution.

6.4 ECHOES, SPECIAL CHARACTERS, AND HANDSHAKING

The functions described above will handle a simple, half-duplex serial channel, since they do not include any provisions for echoing the characters back to the terminal. On the other hand, it could also work for communication with another computer, where no echo was needed. For communication with a terminal, several special characters must be treated differently. The most important is the

RETURN. It signals the end of the line from the terminal, but, if echoed, will only return the cursor to the beginning of the current line. Thus, the "echo" must include a LINEFEED as well as the return so the cursor will advance to the next line.

Other special cases for echo processing are the key to erase the previous character (usually the RUBOUT, DELETE, or BACKSPACE keys), and the character used to instruct the computer to ignore the previous line (characters commonly used for this function include control-C, control-X, ESCAPE, DELETE, RUBOUT). For these characters to be effective, a convention must be established to define a "message." If the program processing the data takes it a character at a time, it is not possible to "ignore the previous character" because the character has already been processed. The usual method of accomplishing these "erase" tasks is to establish the input line as the message unit. Characters that are buffered by the foreground function will not be processed by the background program until a complete line has been received, as signaled by the receipt of a RETURN.

An additional control variable for the received character buffer can be used to control access of the background to the buffer, so characters will never be removed from an incomplete line. This variable counts the number of complete lines in the input buffer; for every RETURN received it is incremented, for every RETURN removed from the buffer, it is decremented.

The erase functions move the pointer_to_next backward to "erase" the indicated characters from the buffer. The single character erase causes the pointer_to_next to move backward one position. An echo of a BACKSPACE, a space (blank), and another backspace will cause the screen display to erase the offending character. A line erase causes the pointer_to_next to move back to the previous RETURN. In either case, the pointer is never backed up past the point at which the buffer becomes empty.

6.4.1 IMPLEMENTING THE ECHO

Current operating systems have three ways of dealing with the echo: (1) Send the echo character to the serial output without regard for current activity; (2) Buffer the echo characters and give them preference over any other characters being sent to the terminal; and (3) Buffer the echo characters but give the echo the lowest priority so that other processing will be completed before the echo buffer is serviced. All of these methods produce the same result when no other screen activity is taking place. However, because the incoming characters cause interrupts, the user can "type ahead," that is, enter characters in advance of when they are called for. If this is done while other characters are being sent to the terminal, the three methods will differ dramatically. The first will cause a jumble on the screen because characters will be sent to the interface while it is in the middle of other characters, so the terminal will typically see several illegal characters. The second method will give preference to the echo characters, and will therefore intermix the characters being echoed with the others, but all of the characters will be echoed correctly. The third method provides the neatest screen, but the user is typing blind during type-ahead and will not see the characters echoed until they are used. The second and third methods require the use of a separate buffer for echoes; the first does not.

6.4.2 Handshaking/Buffer Full

When the incoming character buffer fills up, information will be lost unless something is done to prevent new characters from arriving. When a person is the source of the characters, an audible signal works well. Thus, instead of echoing the character typed, an echo of the BELL character will ring a bell or sound a tone to indicate that the character has not been received. When the communication is with another machine, though, a more formal procedure is necessary. This interchange, or *handshake*, has three common forms for serial communication; the use of an additional signal wire is most common for closely connected devices, such as printers, while two common software protocols can be used without any additional wires. The software protocols are more general and can be used for local connections and for remote connections through telephone or other communication networks where it is not possible to have additional wires. The two protocols are similar and involve the transmission of special characters to signal buffer full/empty conditions. The characters used are from the nonprinting portion of the ASCII character set.

The Xon/Xoff protocol uses the control-S (DC3) and control-Q (DC1) characters. When the receiving buffer is nearly full, the receiving device sends a control-S to signal to the transmitting device to stop sending characters. A margin is usually allowed on the assumption that the transmitting device is also processing input and output asynchronously and therefore may send several more characters before the control-S is processed. When the buffer has enough room to start receiving characters again, the receiving device sends a control-Q. This protocol is normally used for communication from the user to the computer when the user wants to "freeze" the terminal screen.

The other software protocol uses the ETX and ACK characters for buffer control. The transmitting device appends the ETX character to the end of a string of characters when they are sent. When the ETX is removed from the buffer by the processing program, an ACK is sent back to the transmitter indicating that it is OK to send another message. The messages must each be short enough so that they will not overflow the buffer.

6.4.3 Implementation with Buffer Control

The receive and transmit functions become slightly more complex when these additional buffer control and special characters are considered. To make the functions more modular, it will be useful to define a data structure to use for buffer bookkeeping. This structure will keep track of the pointers to oldest and newest characters, number of characters in the buffer, etc. The definition for the structure is shown in Fig. 6.6.

Structure buffer:

pointer_to_character	buff	(the pointer to the actual data storage—the space must be allocated during initialization)
integer	number_of_characters	
pointer_to_character	p_oldest	
pointer_to_character	p_newest	
pointer_to_character	p_end	(the end of the buffer, for use in wraparound calculation)
integer	buffer_size	

Figure 6.6

The function to receive characters is a foreground function that answers the interrupt caused by a character being received by the serial interface. The version given in Fig. 6.7 is for communication with a terminal. If the buffer for input characters fills up, the character just received is ignored and a BELL character is put into the transmit buffer so the user is warned that input characters have been lost.

```
Receive_character:

    Get character from the serial interface
    If(character is CHARACTER_DELETE or LINE_DELETE)
        Buffer_erase(character,receive_buffer,echo_buffer)

    Else if(receive_buffer is full)
        Buffer_in(BELL,transmit_buffer)

    Else
        Buffer_in(character,echo_buffer)
        Buffer_in(character,receive_buffer)
        If(character is a RETURN)
            Increment full_line_counter
            Buffer_in(LINEFEED,echo_buffer)

    Transmit_wake_up          (Wake up the transmitter, if necessary)
    Return
```

Figure 6.7

The buffer_in function is very similar to the store_character function described above, except that it can operate on any buffer by having a pointer to the buffer passed to it. The buffer structure described above is used to perform the buffer update functions. Transmit_wake_up is needed to re-enable the interrupt for the transmitter in case the transmitter buffer had been empty. A flag is set in the transmit_character function when both the echo and transmit buffers are empty.

The end-of-line is indicated by the RETURN character in the figure; however, some systems could use other characters for that purpose.

This version of the character handling functions requires three buffers: the receive and transmit buffers and an additional buffer for the echo. Other buffers could be used if more elaborate buffer overflow control were being used.

The buffer_erase function takes care of resetting the buffer control variables and echoing the BACKSPACE-SPACE-BACKSPACE sequences that erase the characters on the screen. Figure 6.8 shows the buffer_erase function. It requires three arguments: the special character being processed, the buffer from which the erasure should be made, and the buffer that will echo to the screen.

```
Buffer_erase(character, r_buffer, e_buffer)

        If(r_buffer->number_of_char <= 0
                OR r_buffer->newest = End_of_Line)
                        return
                                                        (Nothing to erase!)
        If(character is CHARACTER_DELETE)
                buffer_backspace(r_buffer,e_buffer)
                Return
        Else If(character is LINE_DELETE)
                Repeat until an End_of_Line or the end of the buffer is reached
                        buffer_backspace(r_buffer,e_buffer)
        Return

Buffer_backspace(r_buffer,e_buffer)

        If(r_buffer->number_of_char > 0)
                Backup r_buffer->newest             (with wraparound)
                Buffer_in(BACKSPACE,e_buffer)
                Buffer_in(SPACE,e_buffer)
                Buffer_in(BACKSPACE,e_buffer)
                Decrement r_buffer->number_of_char
        Return
```

Figure 6.8

The transmit_character function must check both the transmit and the echo buffers. Other than that, it is nearly the same as the simpler version used earlier; the transmit_character function is shown in Fig. 6.9. The order in which the transmit and echo buffers are checked determines the priority that will be used—as written here, the transmit buffer will be emptied before the echo buffer is examined. "Type-ahead" characters will thus be echoed after the present output is completed. If both of the buffers are found to be empty, the interrupt is disabled so that there will not be continual interrupts because no new characters are being added to the buffer.

```
Transmit_character:    (Get here when the "transmitter buffer empty"
                       interrupt occurs)

        If(transmit_buffer and echo_buffer are empty)
                Disable interrupt
                Return

        If(transmit_buffer is not empty)  (This order of buffer check
                                          will give priority to the
                                          transmit buffer)
                buffer_out(character,transmit_buffer)
                Send character to serial interface
                Return

        Else                    (If transmit buffer is empty, echo buffer
                                must have a character)
                buffer_out(character,echo_buffer)
                Send character to serial interface
                Return
```

Figure 6.9

These foreground functions take care of the character-by-character interaction between the computer and the serial interface. On the receive side, putting the function into the foreground and driving it with interrupts guarantees that no incoming characters will be lost while other background activities are going on. On the transmit side, there is no danger of missing characters because the characters are being generated by the program. However, the speed of the serial device is relatively slow, so using a foreground function to actually send the characters out makes the most efficient use of the CPU resource.

The ultimate speed limitation for receipt of characters is determined by the speed of the interrupt processing. In order not to miss any characters, the foreground function must be completely finished before the next character arrives. Most serial interfaces include a flag that indicates if one or more new characters have been put into the data buffer before being read by the computer. As long as this flag is present, the fact that characters have been missed can at least be detected. There will also be a flag bit present on most UARTs for a "framing error," indicating that there was no stop bit in the expected place.

6.5 MESSAGE ENCODING/DECODING

While the foreground functions handle the character-by-character interaction with the serial interface, the actual generation and interpretation of messages is done by background tasks. Because there is only a single stream of characters to (or from) the console, but there can be many background tasks, it is necessary to design the background tasks in such a way that no more than one of them is accessing the console at a time. An easy way to do that is to assign all console interaction to a single background task. That single task can be responsible for all of the user interaction, which is practical in systems like the multi-motor control system, or it can be the "traffic-director" for any of the other background tasks that want to communicate with the operator.

Compilers provide extensive facilities for handling the interaction with the operator and formatting data, so any design we do should take maximum advantage of those features. Most of the formatting functions are based on a line-oriented interaction, that is, user input is processed a line at a time and output is produced a line at a time. However, the highest level of input and output functions are built on the scientific computing model in which the program waits for the user to complete a message before continuing its processing. This is unacceptable for a real-time system. However, most compilers also provide formatting facilities that operate with arrays of characters instead of the console. To use these, we must provide functions that interact with the foreground routines described above in such a way that lines are the message units that are interchanged. Figure 6.10 shows the functions to accomplish this. The input function makes use of the "full_line_counter" to know when one or more complete lines is in the input buffer. The character arrays used by these functions to represent lines of characters use whatever conventions the particular compiler defines to delimit character *strings.* Functions to operate on these strings, concatenate them, copy them, find the length of a string, etc., are also part of some compiler packages.

These functions, background and foreground, combine to make a complete package for dealing with formatted input and output in a real time system. The encoding and decoding functions of the operating system make the crucial link to do the actual formatting of the data. These functions are complete, all the way from the compiler level code to the interaction with the serial interface itself. In operating systems that are already interrupt driven, it may be possible to use operating system calls for some of the lower level functions and let the operating

```
get_line:

        If(full_line_counter <= 0)
                return(data_no_available)

        Initialize string array for line to be received
        Repeat until a RETURN is received
                buffer_out(character,receive_buffer)
                If(character is a RETURN)
                        Return(line)
                Else
                        Add character to line

send_line(line):

        If(buffer_room(transmit_buffer) < length(line))
                Return(no_room_in_buffer)

        For i = 1 to length(line):
                buffer_out(line(i),transmit_buffer)

buffer_room(buffer)

        Return(buffer->number_of_char - buffer->buffer_size)
```

Figure 6.10

system's foreground functions handle the console. In order to achieve real-time operation, the operating system must implement the equivalent buffering functions, including tests for whether any data is ready, so that it will not be necessary to wait for data.

6.6 OPERATOR FUNCTIONS FOR MULTI-MOTOR CONTROL

The command language introduced in Chapters 4 and 5 allowed the operator to set values for the controller parameters, setpoints, and sampling times. It operated as part of the initialization procedure; once the "go" command was given, the operator was cut off from the control system. The only thing that could be done if a change was to be made would be to stop the control, make the change, then restart the control. The console functions just developed can be used to provide real-time operator interaction as well as start-up control. Once the "go" command is typed and control starts, a low-priority background task ("deep background") takes care of communicating with the operator. This task needs a command language protocol to define the real-time operator interaction. Since a protocol has already been defined for the initialization part of the operator interaction, it can also be used for the real-time part; in fact, it would be useful to use the same command interpreter to handle the real-time command input as is used for initialization.

The sequence of events to use the same command interpreter in both places is shown in Fig. 6.11. The events that are highlighted in the figure are the places where the function to interpret commands is called. In effect, by following the sequence of function calls, the command interpreter calls itself, as shown in Fig. 6.12. The only restriction on the second invocation of the command interpreter is that it cannot call "control" again!

This structure is called a *recursion* and, in general terms, means that an action is expressed in terms of itself. The classic example of a recursion is the computation of the factorial, or the product of all of the integers from 1 to some specified number. A simple way to write a program to compute the factorial is shown in Fig. 6.13.

When are recursions legal? There are two major conditions. The first is that the recursion have an end. If all calls to the recursive function result in self calls, the process will continue indefinitely. In the factorial case, the end is when the argument reaches zero. Then, instead of doing a recursive call with (n-1), the function returns the value 1. Each subsequent version of factorial up the recursive chain can then execute its return until the original calling function is reached. The second condition is the same as the condition for re-entrance, that is, that the function does all of its intermediate storage in local variables.

The recursion in the control program has an end. It is normally only two levels deep and is terminated when a "quit" command is typed. There are, however, some restrictions on the re-entrance properties. Most commands are re-entrant. The exceptions are the "go" command, which can only be used from the initial version of the command interpreter, and the "quit" command, which only makes sense from the real-time version.

The other issue that must be faced in using the command interpreter recursively is its access to the serial interface. The choices that can be made depend on the environment that the program is to be run in. If the program will be run on a stand-alone computer with no operating system, the serial interface functions discussed above are the only links to the console and must be activated as soon as the program starts running. In that case, there is no conflict. If, however, the program is to be run in an operating system environment, it might be convenient to use the console I/O facilities for the initial part of the interaction and not activate the real-time functions until control mode is entered. This can be accomplished in at least two ways. Different code can be used for the I/O calls, with the command interpreter acting strictly on an array of characters that is passed to it, or a

```
Main Program for Motor Control:

        Initial Set-up
        Command_interpreter
        Exit

Command_interpreter:

        Read in command
        If(command is valid)do_it
        Else    Error

(If the command is "go," the control program is executed)

Control:

        Set up schedule for background
                (i.e., sample time for each loop)
        Schedule the Operator interaction             (The operator
                                                      interaction must
                                                      be scheduled as
                                                      a low priority
                                                      background task)
        Initialize interrupts for timers and console
        Call background scheduler

Operator_interaction:

        If(line ready)call command_interpreter
        Return
```

Figure 6.11

```
Motor Control
        Command Interpreter
                Control
                        Command Interpreter
```

Figure 6.12

```
Factorial(n):

        If(n = 0)
                return(1)
        Else
                return(n * factorial(n-1))
```

Figure 6.13

common set of calls can be used with an internal flag indicating whether to use the real-time functions or the operating system versions.

To improve the real time usefulness of the command interpreter, several additional commands should be added. Basic loop controls would allow individual loops to be turned on or off, or set into a manual state, and a set of commands allowing the operator to find out the current values of setpoints, process values, errors, instrument outputs, etc., should be added.

6.7 FORMATTED SCREEN OPERATOR INTERFACES

Command interpreters are a very flexible way to formulate an operator interface, and are very useful where a wide variety of relatively unpredictable actions could be taken by a skilled operator. When the options are more constrained, however, display screens with information in fixed locations are easier to use, more accurate to use, can display more information, and require less training.

A text-based terminal or console can be used to build formatted screens for operator input and/or display as long as the system has the ability to position the text cursor anyplace on the screen and perform a nonblocking read from the keyboard. Other features, such as color, and bold, blinking, or reverse video are useful but not necessary. The console interaction methods discussed above can form the basis for such a system.

6.7.1 LABELLED VALUES

The heart of a formatted screen is a labelled value. It is a data item associated with a label, displayed at a fixed position on the screen. When used for input, the operator moves to the desired item by using cursor (arrow) keys, control keys, or a pointing device such as a mouse, then types the new value for the item. When the operator finishes typing, the new value replaces the old value. When used for display, the value on the screen is updated by the computer when it changes, so the value shown is always current.

By moving around such a screen, an operator can monitor and control a whole set of variables, responding only to those requiring attention. Attention can be drawn to important information by color or blinking, for example, indicating the highest priority actions.

6.7.2 Action Inputs

When the operator wants an action to take place, the easiest thing to do is to press a special character on the keyboard causing that action. Most keyboards have a set of *function* keys that can serve well for this purpose. By putting the action key definitions on the screen, a variety of functions can be performed by the same set of keys, depending on the situation. If these keys are detected at a low level in the input chain, the action can be performed without disturbing any other operations.

6.7.3 Screen Management Program

A simple screen manager is described here that can be used to build applications of the sort described. By separating the general management functions from the machine/operating system-specific operations, a system that can be used on almost any computer can be constructed.

At its heart are two data structures—one for labelled values, and a second for action keys. A third data structure is added for static labels. These are technically a special case of a labelled value, but it is convenient to define them separately.

Fig. 6.14 shows the data structure for the labelled value. Each labelled value item on the screen is identified with an instance of this structure.

```
structure labelled_value:
   integer              id_number
   integer              x_data,y_data
   integer              data_field_width
   pointer              address_of_data
   pointer              address_of_character_to_data_function
   pointer              address_of_data_to_character_function
   integer              highlight,blink,intensify,color
   integer              x_label,y_label
   character_string     label
   pointer              up,down,left,right
```

Figure 6.14

Several fields in the data structure perform the necessary functions of specifying the location on the screen of the data and the label. The address of the data is specified so the screen manager functions can find or change the value when necessary.

Since the nature of the data is not fixed, it could be integer, float, text, etc., the screen manager makes no assumptions about that. Instead, it treats all interaction with the screen and keyboard strictly in terms of text characters. Each labelled value field has two functions specified—one to convert from data to text, so current data values can be displayed, and the other to convert from text to data, so operator inputs can be stored in usable form.

The "up, down, left, right" items in the data structure are pointers to other data instances of the same type. They control where the focus of attention will shift when the user presses the associated cursor keys.

The data structure for action keys is shown in Fig. 6.15. It is much simpler than the labelled value data structure, requiring only the key code generated by the keyboard when that key is pressed, the function to be executed when it is pressed, a function key ID number, and a label. The ID and label are used to put the action key definitions on the screen.

```
structure function_key:
    integer                 key_code
    pointer                 address_of_action_function
    integer                 key_number
    character_string        label
```

Figure 6.15

The overall program structure is simple. Most of the work goes on at the lowest level. Each time the low-level function (named get_input_string) is called, it checks to see if a character is available from the keyboard. If none is available, it returns. If a character is available, it is checked to see if it is one of the special characters. There are three types of special characters: those that end the input and/or move the user's focus to another item, those that edit the current data entry (erase character or erase line), and action keys.

The low-level function maintains a data buffer; any characters not trapped by the special character test are placed in the buffer. If the character is an arrow or ENTER (Return), when get_input_string returns, it indicates that the character buffer is complete and can be acted on. It also returns the character code, so the upper level functions can take whatever action is necessary.

If an editing key is detected, the character buffer is modified accordingly. If a function key is detected, the associated function is called. When either an editing or function key has been input, after completing its activity, get_input_string returns as if no character had been typed. Fig. 6.16 shows the main logic for this function. Get_input_string is also responsible for modifying the screen display as the user types.

```
get_input_string:
  if(no character available)return(no_character)
  if(character is action key)
        call associated function
        return(no_character)
  if(character is editing key)
        modify character buffer
        return(no_character)
  if(character is arrow or enter)
        return(character)
```

Figure 6.16

The next level function is only responsible for interpreting the data that was typed. It does this by passing the character string to the character_to_data function specified for the current item and then displays the new data item. It can then reset the character buffer to get it ready for the next input.

At the highest level, the main responsibility is to move the input focus from one item to another. This is done by following the up, down, etc., pointers in the data structure, depending on the key that was last typed.

6.7.4 SCREEN BACKGROUND

Because the low-level functions return after every character check, regardless of whether the user typed anything, it is possible to run a background function in parallel with the screen manager. This function, which is supplied by the programmer, can be used for general-purpose computing and for screen management functions. In screen management, it provides the mechanism for updating the displayed values. It is called for every keyboard scan, and calls the display function for the values to be updated.

The background function is useful for any general computing functions that do not take too much time, and can tolerate the uncertainty in how often they are called. Depending on the user input, the screen manager will do more or less work, so the frequency with which the background function is called will also vary.

6.7.5 NESTED SCREENS

One of the actions that can be taken as a result of pressing a function key is to switch to a new screen. This requires a recursion; the action key function is called from within the high-level function running the screen management. To bring up another screen, the screen management function must be called by the action key function, which is thus a recursive call. As long as the rules for recursion are followed, that is, all intermediate data stored on the stack, the recursive call should not cause any difficulty at all. Screens can then be nested to any practical level providing a simple means for controlling complex systems.

OPERATOR CONSOLE EXAMPLES

6.8 INTRODUCTION

The console interface module, *console.c*, provides application programs with a simple character-based terminal interface. The console is assumed to be a remote ASCII terminal which communicates with the computer over an asynchronous serial line. This type of terminal is quite common; it is often used in control systems to display process data and obtain operator input. The routines in *console.c* buffer input and output characters, echo keyboard input, and implements a simple XON/XOFF line control protocol. Hardware dependencies are isolated in separate modules; the examples will show one implementation using a serial terminal connected to the IBM-PC's COM1 port, and another implementation using the IBM-PC's memory-mapped video display and keyboard as the console. The *xignal* package is used to simplify set-up and use of interrupts. A simple test program, *contest.c*, is included to demonstrate some of the features of the console interface.

The basic console interface resides in the following files:

console.h Declarations for console.c.

console.c Code module for the basic console interface.

cbuf.h Declarations for cbuf.c.

cbuf.c Character buffer management routines.

kcon.h Declarations for routines that deal with hardware dependencies; these routines reside in *kcon1.c* (serial port version) and *kcon2.c* (video display and keyboard version).

The following files are specific to the serial port example:

kcon1.c The portion of the console interface that deals with the IBM-PC's COM1 serial port.

com.h Declarations for com.c.

com.c Routines to manipulate the COM1 hardware.

The following files are specific to the video display and keyboard example:

kcon2.c The portion of the console interface that deals with the IBM-PC's memory-mapped video display and keyboard.

8259.h Declarations about the 8259 interrupt controller used in the IBM-PC.

conkbisr.asm A front-end to the console keyboard interrupt service routine; it decodes the keyboard scan code and passes it to the keyboard handler in *console.c.*

model.h Memory model declarations for conkbisr.asm.

prologue.h Compiler specific declarations for conkbisr.asm.

epilogue.h Compiler specific declarations for conkbisr.asm.

The following are support files common to both examples:

envir.h Environment declarations.

inout.h Port input and output mapping macros.

xignal.h Declarations for the xignal package.

To generate the COM1 version of the test program:

```
cl /Gs contest.c console.c kcon1.c cbuf.c com.c /link xignal
```

The /Gs option disables run-time stack overflow checks; it is not strictly necessary for small memory model programs. To run the program, you need to connect a serial terminal to the COM1 port and set the terminal for DCE[1] operation at 9600 bits-per-second, 8-bit word, no parity, and 1-stop bit.

To generate the video display and keyboard version of the test program:

```
masm conkbisr /ml
cl /Gs contest.c console.c kcon2.c cbuf.c conkbisr /link xignal
```

6.9 APPLICATION INTERFACE LAYER

The console interface consists of two layers: a device-independent layer that is also the interface presented to application programs, and a device-dependent layer. The device-independent portion is implemented in *console.c*. This module provides input and output buffering and simple XON/XOFF line control.

There are two versions of the device dependent layer: *kcon1.c* for the IBM-PC's COM1 serial port, and *kcon2.c* for the IBM-PC's video display and keyboard. These two hardware-dependent modules provide the same set of interface routines, allowing them to be substituted for each other in a manner that is transparent to *console.c*.

---

[1]Data Communicating Equipment in Bell parlance. The COM1 port is a DTE (Data Terminating Equipment) and most serial terminals are set up as DTEs also. To get a DTE terminal to communicate with the COM1 port, you may need to connect pin2 of one to pin3 of the other and vice versa (often called a *null modem*).

The basic application interface routines are:

congetc Get a character from the console.

conputc Send a character to the console.

conread Get up to *n* characters from the console, or until a carriage return or linefeed character is encountered.

conwrite Send *n* characters to the console screen.

conioctl Interface for miscellaneous functions.

coninit Initialization routine, must be called before any of the other routines in the module.

In addition to these routines, there are 3 interrupt service routines that are called only by the hardware dependent layer:

conscsig Called whenever the console screen is ready to receive a . character

conkbsig Called whenever a character is available from the console keyboard.

conersig Called whenever a transmission line error is detected in the console connection.

Their declarations are not exported in the *console.h* header file, since only the hardware-dependent modules are supposed to know about them.

6.9.1 Buffers

The design of the console interface is based on buffered character streams. There are three buffers: (1) the input buffer for characters from the keyboard; (2) the echo buffer for echo feedback of keyboard input; and (3) the output buffer used by applications to send data to the console screen. The output buffer has priority over the echo buffer in that characters in the echo buffer are sent to the console screen only if the output buffer is empty.

The buffers are implemented as circular first-in first-out queues using services provided by the *cbuf.c* buffer management module. Each buffer is associated with a control structure that is dynamically allocated along with the actual buffer memory. This control structure contains pointers to the beginning and end of buffer memory plus pointers to the front and rear of the character queue. Here is the definition from *cbuf.h*:

```
typedef struct _cbuf {
    int cb_id;               /* buffer id number */
    char *cb_begin;          /* ptr to start of buffer */
    char *cb_end;            /* ptr to end of buffer */
    char *cb_front;          /* ptr to front of queue */
    char *cb_rear;           /* ptr to rear of queue */
} CBUF;
```

The actual buffer memory is marked by pointers *cb_begin* and *cb_end*. Characters are inserted at the rear of the queue and removed from the front. Two pointers, *cb_front* and *cb_rear*, point to the front and rear of the character queue, respectively. More precisely, *cb_front* points to the buffer location just before the first character, and *cb_rear* points to the last character in the queue. The queue is empty if they both point at the same location.

To put a character into the queue, *cb_rear* is first advanced to the next buffer location, wrapping around to the beginning of the buffer if necessary. If *cb_rear* ends up pointing at the same location as *cb_front*, the buffer is full and no characters can be inserted; otherwise, the new character is written to the location pointed to by *cb_rear*. This scheme results in one unusable buffer location in order to detect a buffer full condition, hence the buffer creation routine, *newcbuf()*, always allocates an extra buffer location to compensate. The routine to put a character into the queue is *putcbuf()*.

To get a character from the buffer, *getcbuf()* first checks if there are characters in the buffer. The buffer is empty if both *cb_front* and *cb_rear* point to the same location. If the buffer is not empty, *cb_front* is advanced to the next location, wrapping around to the beginning of the buffer if necessary. The character pointed to by *cb_front* is then returned, after being cast to an *int*.

Both *getcbuf()* and *putcbuf()* return an *int* value in order that a buffer empty or full condition can be indicated by a return value of -1. This allows the NUL character (ASCII value 0) to be treated like any other character. It is sometimes useful to be able to undo the effects of *putcbuf()* and *getcbuf()*, especially in terminal control functions. The *unputcbuf()* and *ungetcbuf()* are provided primarily for this reason. Readers are encouraged to peruse the code in *cbuf.c* to see how this is done.

6.9.2 TERMINAL CONTROL

The console normally operates in what is termed *cooked* (as opposed to *raw*) mode. In this mode, the two console input functions, *congetc()* and *conread()*, act much like the standard C *getchar()* and *read()* routines, returning only when a complete line[2] is collected in the input buffer. Certain characters, such as backspace, receive special handling. These niceties are bypassed in *raw* mode and no special meaning is accorded to characters. In *raw* mode, the console input function *congetc()* does not wait for a complete line, but instead, returns immediately with a character if one is available, and with -1 if the input buffer is empty. In both modes, control-C is interpreted as a signal to terminate execution. Readers using the *console.c* in their own programs may wish to substitute their own interpretation for control-C.

[2]Lines are character strings terminated by a carriage return, line feed, or NUL character.

Let us next examine how the *console.c* module interfaces to the hardware-dependent layer. It is assumed that the console device is capable of generating interrupts for 3 conditions: (1) Whenever a character is available from the keyboard; (2) Whenever the console screen is ready to accept a character; and (3) Whenever a transmission line error is detected. These signals must be simulated for devices that do not support them. The 3 routines, *conscsig()*, *conkbsig()*, and *conersig()*, are designed to be called by hardware-dependent interrupt service routines to handle these 3 events.

6.9.2.1 KEYBOARD INPUT. When a character is available from the console keyboard, an interrupt is generated. The keyboard interrupt service routine calls *conkbsig()*, passing to it a 16-bit integer argument with the ASCII value of the character in the least significant byte. This scheme allows information, such as keyboard scan codes, to be passed in the most significant byte. The scan code is present in the nonserial terminal version of the program, but is ignored to maintain compatibility with the serial terminal version. The incoming character is put into the keyboard input buffer. If the buffer is full, an ASCII BEL character is transmitted to alert the operator. The operator can remove characters from a full buffer with the backspace[3] key.

Characters such as backspace, carriage return, control-X, XON, and XOFF receive special handling. Since characters are always put into the input buffer first, these and other console control characters must first be removed from the input buffer [by *unputcbuf()*] before further processing.

A count of the number of complete lines is maintained in the *linecount* variable, which is updated whenever a carriage return or linefeed character is received. By waiting until at least one complete line is available before returning, the console input routines allow simple editing to be performed on the input line. A backspace causes the previous character to be removed from the input buffer. It is echoed to the screen as a sequence of 3 characters—backspace, space, and backspace again to erase the previous character and place the cursor over the erased (now blank) character position. This type of backspace response is also known as destructive backspace. There is an erase-line function, assigned to the control-X key. The input buffer is emptied by repeated calls to *unputcbuf()* until a carriage return or linefeed is removed or the buffer is empty. A backspace-space-backspace sequence is echoed to the console for each character removed.

The operator can halt screen output by typing control-S (XOFF), and resume by typing control-Q (XON). When a XOFF is received, the flag variable *xoffflag* is set and screen output is suppressed by a call to *ksleep()*, disabling character transmission to the console. The exact ksleep mechanism is hardware-dependent and is hidden in a device-dependent layer. Setting the *xoffflag*

---

[3]A quirk of the IBM-PC keyboard BIOS is that it does not return an ASCII value of 127 (DEL) for the DEL key.

prevents the buffer output routine, *putoutbuf()*, from calling *kwakeup()* to initiate screen output.

Before *conkbsig()* exits, it calls *kwakeup()* (if the console is not in the XOFF state) to activate asynchronous transmission of outgoing characters to the console. This is required since the edge-triggered transmit interrupt may be deactivated if a character was not transmitted for the previous transmit interrupt. Since *conkbsig()* is called by the keyboard interrupt service routine, will calling *kwakeup()* create a conflict between the keyboard and screen output interrupts? With COM1, there is no conflict since the screen output interrupt is not triggered until the transmitter holding register is empty again, by which time the keyboard interrupt will have long since returned. With the video display, screen output is not asynchronous.

6.9.2.2 SCREEN OUTPUT. The screen output routine, *conscsig()*, is designed to be called by an interrupt service routine that is triggered whenever the console is ready to receive a character. The characters are obtained from the output and echo buffers, with priority given to the output buffer. The hardware-specific details of sending a character to the screen are handled by the *kputc()* routine. If both the output and echo buffers are empty, the *tbmtflag* variable is set.[4] This flag is also returned by *conscsig()* to indicate the state of the output and echo buffers to the calling routine.

6.9.2.3 TRANSMISSION LINE ERROR. The *conersig()* function is intended for remote serial terminals; it is called whenever transmission line errors such as parity or framing errors are detected. Assuming that the console hardware can asynchronously signal such errors (COM1 has this capability), an interrupt service routine will read the appropriate status port and pass the result to *conersig()*. Determining the type of error from the status byte (or word) is obviously hardware dependent. This example just sends a "LINE ERROR" message to the console. There is no direct analogue for transmission line errors with the IBM-PC video display and keyboard interface.

6.9.2.4 OUTPUT BUFFER CONTROL. Characters are placed in the output buffer by the *putoutbuf()* routine. If the output buffer is full, the routine checks if the console is in a XOFF state. If not, it calls *kwakeup()* to activate the transmit interrupt to remove characters from the output buffer and make room for more characters. *Putoutbuf()* always calls *kwakeup()* before returning (unless the console is in a XOFF state) in case the edge-triggered transmit interrupt is disabled.

A problem arises if the console is in a XOFF state and the output buffer is full. The simplest solution is to wait until a XON is received from the console. This means that *conputc()*, and hence *conwrite()*, should not be called from a

---

[4]This tbmtflag flag is very useful in asynchronous serial drivers that do not support XON/XOFF to indicate whether to call kputc() in the putoutbuf() routine without the need for a kwakeup() routine.

foreground routine that runs with keyboard interrupts disabled, since doing so will create a *deadlock* situation where *putoutbuf()* is waiting for a XON, but will never receive one since keyboard interrupts are disabled.

There is a partial solution; the 8259 interrupt controller can be programmed in the Special Mask Mode.[5] In this mode, only the in-service interrupt requests are disabled; all other interrupt requests, even ones with lower priority, will cause an interrupt to be generated.

Another solution is for the foreground routines to pass characters to a background routine (using a circular buffer perhaps) for subsequent transmission to the console screen. This can easily be extended to multiple foreground routines (e.g., the multiple motor example in Chapter 5) by giving each foreground routine its own channel (buffer) to a background screen output management routine. However, should the XOFF state persist, even this foreground-background buffer will eventually be filled unless the foreground routines can be suspended until a XON is received from the console. Unfortunately, foreground routines that perform critical tasks such as process control cannot be suspended. This is a difficult design issue that often arises whenever access to resources required by real-time processes may be blocked.

6.10 SERIAL TERMINAL AS CONSOLE

The IBM-PC COM1 asynchronous serial port is based on the 8250 UART.[6] This UART has only one external interrupt line which, in the PC, is connected to the IRQ4 input (interrupt vector 9) of the 8259 programmable interrupt controller. An interrupt can be generated when (1) the transmitter holding register is empty; (2) data is available in the receive buffer; (3) a line error (such as parity or overrun) has occurred; or (4) there is a change in the modem line status. The interrupt service routine must read the Interrupt Identification Register to determine which condition has triggered the interrupt. There is a register on the 8250 to specify which combination of the above events will cause the interrupt request line to be asserted.

The *com.c* module provides a set of routines to manipulate the COM1 hardware. The *cominit()* routine sets up the asynchronous communications parameters such as baud rate and parity. The *comienb()* routine specifies which combination of the four events is allowed to trigger an interrupt, and the *comidis()* routine inhibits interrupt triggering. The control bytes to specify the interrupt triggering event is defined in the *com.h* header file; they are:

DAV_ENB	Data Available in the receive buffer.
THRE_ENB	Transmitter Holding Register is empty.

[5]Refer to the appropriate IBM Technical Reference Manuals and Intel data sheets for the 8259.

[6]Universal Asynchronous Receiver and Transmitter.

RLS_ENB	Error in the receiver line status.
MLS_ENB	Change in the Modem Line Status.

In the example program, COM1 is set to generate an interrupt for the first 3 conditions by the statement:

```
comienb(1, DAV_ENB | THRE_ENB | RLS_ENB);
```

The *kcon1.c* module provides the COM1 hardware interface layer for console.c. The *kinit()* initialization routine calls

```
xignal(XIGCOM1, com1isr);
```

to install *com1isr()* as an interrupt service routine to handle COM1 interrupts.

When a COM1 interrupt is generated, the CPU vectors to xignal's front-end interrupt service routine for COM1. This front-end routine saves the CPU state and calls *com1isr()*, which reads the Interrupt Identification Register of the 8250 to determine which of the 3 events (data available, transmitter ready, and line error) has caused the interrupt. It then calls the appropriate routine in *console.c* to handle the event, passing the keyboard input character to *conkbsig()* and the error status byte to *conersig()* if those routines are called.

The *ksleep()* routine puts the transmitter to sleep by calling

```
comidis(1, THRE_ENB);
```

to prevent the 8250 from generating an interrupt when the transmitter holding register is empty, while allowing the other two conditions, receive data available and receive line error, to continue to trigger interrupts. This facility is used to implement XON/XOFF line control.

If a character was not sent to the transmitter during the last transmitter holding register empty (THRE) interrupt, that particular trigger is deactivated since the interrupt is edge-triggered. Thus, the THRE trigger mechanism must be explicitly reactivated when a character is to be transmitted. The *kwakeup()* routine checks if the THRE status bit in the 8250 is set. If the THRE interrupt mechanism is active, *kwakeup()* should never see that bit set since an interrupt will be generated the moment THRE is set and the interrupt service routine will send a character to the transmitter, causing the THRE status bit to be immediately cleared. Thus, the only time that *kwakeup()* will see the THRE status bit set is if there was no output character to transmit during the last THRE triggered interrupt.[7] In this situation, the THRE interrupt mechanism is reactivated by calling *conscsig()* to

---

[7]There is one situation where this scheme breaks down, and that is where a higher priority event interrupts before a character can be sent to the transmit buffer register and the new interrupt service routine sends a character to the transmit buffer register. If this is a possibility, then checking the THRE bit and sending a character to the transmit register must be done inside a critical section.

send a character from the output or echo buffer to the transmitter (via the *kputc()* routine). The *txdis* flag indicates if the THRE trigger was disabled by a previous call to *ksleep()*; if so, a call is made to *comienb()* to re-enable the THRE trigger.

6.11 VIDEO DISPLAY AND KEYBOARD AS CONSOLE

Although the *console.c* module was designed for remote serial terminals, it is possible to adapt the module to use the IBM-PC keyboard and memory-mapped video display as a console by simply substituting *kcon2.c* and *conkbisr.asm* for *kcon1.c*.

6.11.1 VIDEO DISPLAY OUTPUT

The IBM-PC monitor is a memory-mapped display, making it rather difficult to implement asynchronous screen output since there is no equivalent to the COM1 serial port's THRE interrupt. Screen output is thus implemented synchronously using DOS calls in the *kputc()* routine. An important point to note is that DOS's screen output functions are non re-entrant; it must be invoked only within a critical section, i.e., no other routines can invoke the same set of DOS function calls until the current call returns. The simplest way to create a critical section on the IBM-PC is to disable interrupts via the *cli* instruction. Unfortunately, this does not work for DOS and BIOS calls since they always re-enable interrupts (with the *sti* instruction) when they execute. To get around this, interrupts are disabled by masking out the 8259 programmable interrupt controller's interrupt request inputs. The 8259's original interrupt mask is restored after the DOS call returns. Although this method is simple to implement, it has several disadvantages. First, it is not efficient. Readers who need greater screen update efficiency should consider writing directly to display memory since even a BIOS call to write a single character takes about 1 millisecond on a 4.77 MHz IBM-PC. Second, because all interrupts are disabled during the write operation, interrupt requests that occur during this period may be missed. Third, all interrupt-driven routines are put on hold during the write operation, which can cause all manner of performance-related problems.

Unfortunately, there is no simple solution to these problems. Writing directly to display memory usually requires code to accommodate several different video adapters and perform screen management functions such as cursor positioning and scrolling. Another solution is to synchronize screen output to a software timer using the *time.c* module discussed in Chapter 3. This will make screen output asynchronous, but even slower than DOS calls.

6.11.2 KEYBOARD INPUT

The keyboard interrupt service routine, *conkbisr()*, is implemented in assembly language because the functions it needs to perform are rather difficult to implement in C and very easy to do in assembly language. This routine assumes that *xignal* was used to set up interrupts. When *xignal()* is first called, it copies the contents of vectors 0 to 15 to vectors 200 to 215. When *xignal()* is called with the XIGKB argument, it installs its own keyboard interrupt service routine at vector 9, but since there is a copy of the original vector at 209, external keyboard interrupt handlers such as *conkbisr()* can call on the original BIOS keyboard interrupt service routine to perform hardware handshaking and buffering. This is precisely what *conkbisr()* does.

When *conkbisr()* is invoked, it first calls the original keyboard interrupt service routine to read the keyboard interface port and perform the messy housekeeping required by the hardware. It then calls a BIOS routine (via interrupt vector 22) to determine if an ASCII character has been entered. If an ASCII character is available, it calls the BIOS again to obtain the character and its scan code; the BIOS returns the information in the AX register, with the scan code in AH and the ASCII value in AL. The contents of the AX register is then pushed on the stack to be passed as an argument to *conkbsig()*.

Assembly language programs are very dependent on the compiler's assembly language interface. In this example, all names are preceded by an underscore character since that is how the Microsoft C compiler (version 4.00 and above) stores variable and function names. The file *model.h* defines the memory model used, *prologue.h* contains the messy declarations to set up a code segment, and *epilogue.h* contains declarations to end the code segment. Do not be concerned if you have not done any assembly language programming before. You do not need to know assembly language in order to follow the logic of the keyboard character capture process.

6.11.3 MISCELLANEOUS ROUTINES

In this version, the *kwakeup()* routine calls *conscsig()* repeatedly in a loop until the output and echo buffers are empty, as indicated by the value returned by *conscsig()*. There is no equivalent action to deactivate the transmitter, hence *ksleep()* is an empty routine in this version.

6.12 THE DEMONSTRATION PROGRAM

The demonstration program *contest.c* implements proportional speed control of a motor with asynchronous keyboard command input. The video display version of the program does not support asynchronous console output, but the serial version does. The control and plant equations are embedded in the *control()* routine.

6.12.1 INITIALIZATION

The console system is initialized in the main program by calling *coninit()*. The control and plant simulation routine, *control()*, is installed as a timer interrupt service routine, making it an asynchronous foreground routine that can run while *conread()* waits for a complete line to be typed in. The main program then goes into an infinite loop, reading console keyboard input and passing the input line to *cmdint()* for interpretation.

6.12.2 Keyboard Commands

The primitive command interpreter is similar to that encountered in the example programs for earlier chapters. For simplicity, only two commands are recognized: the *s* command to specify the speed setpoint, and the *k* command to specify the proportional gain. These two commands call *setv()* and *gain()* to parse the arguments and update the setpoint and gain variables. The variables are updated with interrupts disabled since they are referenced by the asynchronous foreground *control()* routine.

6.12.3 Plant Routine

The routine is installed through *xignal* as a timer interrupt service routine and is executed about 18 times a second; hence, the time-step variable, *dt*, for the speed equation is set to 0.0549 seconds. The speed and control output is printed to the console every half second using *conwrite()*. Yes, this violates the rule about writing to the screen in foreground routines, but it does serve to demonstrate the deadlock situation very nicely.

With a serial terminal for a console, the output character stream will occasionally overlap the incoming keyboard input and the outgoing echo characters, thus exercising the stream control functions of the console interface module. Readers may recall that if the console output buffer is full, the console output routine will wait indefinitely until buffer space becomes available. Since *conwrite()* is called in a timer interrupt service routine, COM1 interrupts are temporarily disabled since they have lower priority than the timer interrupt. If screen output is turned off via XOFF and the output buffer becomes full, a deadlock situation will occur since the program cannot respond to a XON keyboard input to clear the *xoffflag*. Clearing the *xoffflag* flag will allow the screen output routine to start transmitting characters from the output buffer, creating buffer space for more output characters and allowing *putoutbuf()* to return.

As an exercise, consider how you might solve this deadlock problem without using any of the methods discussed in the earlier sections.

6.13 CONCLUSIONS

This set of example program modules shows how hardware-specific functions can be isolated from the terminal control function. This allows the same terminal control module, *console.c*, to be used with an asynchronous serial terminal and a memory-mapped video display by using different hardware-specific modules.

Efficiency does suffer when the underlying hardware is very different from the design assumption of an interrupt-driven serial terminal. Greater efficiencies (or simpler code) can always be obtained by writing a hardware-specific console driver. For example, the IBM-PC keyboard-monitor console can be done very simply by substituting DOS and BIOS calls for *congetc()* and *conputc()*. The designer will have to decide what is best for the application.

As an exercise, integrate the console interface program to the multiple motor control example in the last chapter.

OPERATOR CONSOLE EXAMPLES: FORMATTED SCREEN

6.14 INTRODUCTION

The previous set of examples shows how to implement an operator interface using a terminal-style interaction. These interfaces are easy to implement and excellent for debugging use because they can be changed very easily. They make very few demands on the display or keyboard hardware, so are also relatively machine independent.

Operator interfaces that are intended for production use, however, should be more intuitive so that process information can be deduced quickly, and operator changes can be made with a minimum of effort. This example is a simple version of a text-based interface that displays process parameters and internal variables in fixed positions on the screen, and allows for changes in parameters to be made by "moving" to a place on the screen with cursor keys and then entering the new value.

6.15 FILES

The screen interface functions and the sample application are in the following files:

screen.h	Definitions of the screen management data structures.
screen.c	The screen management functions.
scr_def.h	Definitions of machine-specific values.
scr_msc.c	Machine-specific functions for screen and keyboard interaction. This version is for the IBM-PC family using the Microsoft C compiler.
scr_mtr.c	The sample application.

6.16 SAMPLE PROBLEM

A simulated motor with a velocity controller is used as a sample application. The operator screen contains four data fields, the velocity, the setpoint, and the proportional and integral controller gains. These are maintained in the indicated order, from top to bottom, on the screen. The value of velocity is updated as it changes, so the screen displays only the current velocity.

The other three variables are inputs. The values displayed can be changed by the operator, and the change will be reflected immediately in the system's performance.

The motor simulation is in the screen background function, as is the update of velocity value on the screen. This function (scr_bkg() in scr_mtr.c) is called after every check for input characters from the keyboard. How often it runs depends on the speed of the processor and the speed of the keyboard interaction software. It could be used for actual control if the uncertainties in how often it gets to run were within the time demands of the system being controlled. The control could also be moved to an asynchronous task without changing the basic structure of the user interaction.

6.17 SCREEN MANAGEMENT FUNCTIONS

The screen management system functions as the controlling routine once it is initiated. The functions in screen.c are machine-independent, so could be used with almost any computer. They could be used as the upper level functions with the terminal I/O functions in the previous section.

The machine-specific functions are all collected in the function scr_msc.c. A version of this function could be written for any hardware/operating system combination capable of operating with a formatted screen and nonblocking keyboard input.

The screen management functions operate on three data bases, for each of the major operations that it can do: display labels (text only), display labelled values that can be changed by the operator, and respond to function key inputs. Each of these has an associated data structure defined in screen.h.

The lowest level of the screen manager, get_str(), checks for incoming characters and does special character processing. The special characters are referred to by name, with the names defined in scr_def.h. Unless a character is a special character, it is placed in the input buffer. When an end-of-message character is detected, the return from get_str() indicates that a complete line has been input by the user and is ready for processing. Get_str() returns after every test for an incoming character, whether one was detected or not. Get_str() is also responsible for rewriting the screen information to reflect user input.

When an input line is complete, it is sent to a function specified by the programmer for conversion to data and storage. It then becomes available for use by the underlying programs.

6.18 MS/PCDOS INTERFACE

Whenever possible, C library functions are used for the screen and console interface. Most of these are defined as part of the Microsoft graphics library, and include functions to set the text position, check for keyboard input, control text attributes and color, and so on.

MS/PCDOS function call 7 is used to read in the characters and the extended codes. Once it has been determined that a key was struck, DOS function 7 will return the character ASCII value. If the key is not a standard ASCII key (such as a function or cursor key), function 7 returns a zero. A second call will then get a key code.

Rather than return two values, if an extended code is detected, the eighth bit of the character code is set, giving 256 possible characters.

The other function that doesn't use the library is scr_sinp(), which is used to get the character under the cursor on the screen. This uses an Interrupt-10 call, which is actually part of the ROM-BIOS (i.e., part of the computer's hardware, rather than the operating system).

```
/**********************************************************************

FILE
    console.h  -  public interface declarations for console module

LAST UPDATE
    16 May 1988
        add ANSI features

    Copyright(c) 1986,1987  D.M. Auslander and C.H. Tham

**********************************************************************/

#define CONECHO     1
#define CONRAW      2

#ifdef ANSI

extern int      congetc(void);
extern void     conputc(char);
extern int      conwrite(char *, int);
extern int      conread(char *, int);
extern int      conioctl(int, void *);
extern void     coninit(void);

#else

extern int      congetc();
extern void     conputc();
extern int      conwrite();
extern int      conread();
extern int      conioctl();
extern void     coninit();

#endif

/**********************************************************************

FILE
    console.c  -  operator console terminal control program

EVENT ROUTINES
    conscsig  -  handle console screen ready event
    conkbsig  -  handle console keyboard character ready event
    conersig  -  handle console line error event

APPLICATION INTERFACE ROUTINES
    congetc   -  get a char from the console keyboard
    conputc   -  send a char to the console screen
    conwrite  -  send an arary of char to the screen
    conread   -  read a line from the console keyboard
    conioctl  -  general i/o control
    coninit   -  initialize this module

PRIVATE ROUTINES
    raw_getc   - "raw" form of congetc()
    putoutbuf  -  put outgoing char into output buffer
    echo       -  echo keyboard input

REMARKS
    This module provides an interface between an operator console
    and an application program.  It is designed with an asynchronous
    remote console in mind, but does not perform any hardware
    specific manipulations directly.

    Hardware specific stuff are to be implemented in another module,
    with the following interface functions:

    kinit    -  initialize hardware
    kputc    -  send a character to the console screen port
    ksleep   -  deactivate console screen transmission
    kwakeup -  reactivate console screen transmission
    krest    -  restore computer and hardware for program exit

LAST UPDATE
    16 May 1988

    Copyright(c) 1986,1987  D.M. Auslander and C.H. Tham

**********************************************************************/

/**********************************************************************
                              I M P O R T S
**********************************************************************/

#include <stdio.h>
#include <stdlib.h>

#include "envir.h"           /* environment specifications */
#include "cbuf.h"            /* character buffer management declarations */
#include "kcon.h"            /* hardware dependent console services */

#include "console.h"

/**********************************************************************
                         P R I V A T E   D A T A
**********************************************************************/

#define MAXTRIES    3          /* # of retries in case of error */

static int rawflag = 0;        /* 0 => cooked, 1 => raw mode */
static int echoflag = 1;       /* 0 => do not echo, 1 => echo */
```

```
static int xoffflag = 0;        /* 1 => XOFF is active */
static int tbmtflag = 1;        /* indicates tx buffers are empty */
static int linecount = 0;       /* count of complete lines entered */

#define INBUFSIZE   128         /* input buffer size */
#define OUTBUFSIZE  256         /* output buffer size */
#define ECOBUFSIZE  128         /* echo buffer size */

static CBUF *inbuf;             /* ptr to input buffer structure */
static CBUF *outbuf;            /* ptr to output buffer structure */
static CBUF *ecobuf;            /* ptr to echo buffer structure */

#define CTRLC   3               /* control - C */
#define CTRLX   24              /* control - X */
#define BEL     '\07'           /* ASCII bell character */
#define XON     17
#define XOFF    19
#define DEL     127

/*************************************************************************
              F O R W A R D   D E C L A R A T I O N S
*************************************************************************/

#ifdef ANSI

extern int conscsig(void);
extern void conkbsig(int);
extern void conersig(int);

static int  raw_getc(void);
static int  putoutbuf(char);
static void echo(char);

#else

int  conscsig();
void conkbsig();
void conersig();

int  raw_getc();
int  putoutbuf();
void echo();

#endif

/*************************************************************************
        H A R D W A R E   S P E C I F I C   R O U T I N E S
*************************************************************************/

/*-----------------------------------------------------------------------
PROCEDURE
    CONSCSIG  -  called when console screen is ready to accept a char

SYNOPSIS
    int conscsig(void)

LAST UPDATE
    19 October 1987
-----------------------------------------------------------------------*/

int conscsig()
{
    int c;


    if ((c = getcbuf(outbuf)) < 0)      /* first try output buffer */
        c = getcbuf(ecobuf);            /* then try echo buffer */

    if (c >= 0)             /* buffer(s) not empty */
        kputc((char)c);
    else
        tbmtflag = 1;       /* output and echo buffers are empty */

    return(tbmtflag);
}



/*-----------------------------------------------------------------------
PROCEDURE
    CONKBSIG  -  called when char available from console keyboard

SYNOPSIS
    void conkbsig(c)
    int c;

PARAMETER
    c  -  lower 8 bits contain ascii char

REMARKS
    This is called by an interrupt service routine which passes the
    ASCII character in the lower 8 bits of the argument.  The upper
    8 bits is specific to the hardware and application.

    In the case of a serial terminal, the upper 8 bits is 0.  In the
    case of the IBM-PC keyboard, the upper 8 bits is the scan code.
    The scan code is currently ignored.

LAST UPDATE
    19 October 1987
-----------------------------------------------------------------------*/
```

```
void conkbsig(c)
int c;
{

    c &= 0xFF;                        /* mask off upper 8 bits */

    if (putcbuf((char)c, inbuf) < 0)     /* input buffer full */
    {
        if ((c == '\b') || (c == DEL))
        {
            unputcbuf(inbuf);
            echo((char)c);            /* echo backspace */
        }
        else
            putcbuf(BEL, ecobuf);    /* ring bell to indicate buffer full */
    }
    else
    {
        switch (c)
        {
            case CTRLC:      /* control-C terminate program */

                krest();     /* replace this with your ^C handler */
                exit(0);

                break;

            case CTRLX:      /* control-X, erase line */

                if (!rawflag)
                {
                    unputcbuf(inbuf);    /* remove ^X from input buffer */

                    while (1)            /* loop to dump line */
                    {
                        c = unputcbuf(inbuf);

                        if ((c == '\r') || (c == '\n') || (c < 0))
                            break;       /* end of line - break */
                        else
                            echo('\b'); /* backspace on screen to erase */
                    }
                }

                break;

            case '\b':       /* backspace */
            case DEL:        /* DEL */

                if (!rawflag)
                {
                    unputcbuf(inbuf);             /* remove bs or DEL char */

                    if (unputcbuf(inbuf) >= 0)   /* remove backspace'd char */
                        echo((char)c);            /* backspace on screen */
                }
                else
                    echo('\b');

                break;

            case XON:        /* resume transmission */

                if (!rawflag)
                {
                    unputcbuf(inbuf);        /* remove xon char */
                    xoffflag = 0;
                }

                break;

            case XOFF:       /* stop transmission */

                if (!rawflag)
                {
                    unputcbuf(inbuf);        /* remove xoff char */
                    xoffflag = 1;

                    ksleep();                /* put tx to sleep */
                }

                break;

            case '\r':       /* carriage return */
            case '\n':       /* line feed */

                ++linecount;     /* another line is received */

            default:         /* note: no break from previous case! */

                echo((char)c);

                break;
        }
    }

    if (!xoffflag)
        kwakeup();

}
```

```
/*----------------------------------------------------------------------
PROCEDURE
    CONERSIG  -  called if line error detected

SYNOPSIS
    void conersig(lstat)
    int lstat;

PARAMETER
    lstat  -  line status register value

REMARKS
    The line status value is ignored for now.  It can be used to
    provide a more precise error disgnosis than just "LINE ERROR".

LAST UPDATE
    19 October 1987
----------------------------------------------------------------------*/
/*ARGSUSED*/
void conersig(lstat)
int lstat;
{
    static char *msg = "LINE ERROR";


    while (*msg != ' ')
        putcbuf(*msg++, outbuf);

    kwakeup();
}


/***********************************************************************
    A P P L I C A T I O N    I N T E R F A C E    R O U T I N E S
***********************************************************************/

/*----------------------------------------------------------------------
FUNCTION
    CONGETC  -  get a character from the console keyboard

SYNOPSIS
    int congetc()

RETURNS
    input character

REMARKS
    This routine will wait until an entire line (terminated by a
    carriage-return) is available before returning the first char
    in the input stream.  It is assumed that the character input
    is interrupt driven.

LAST UPDATE
    19 October 1987
----------------------------------------------------------------------*/

int congetc()
{
    int c;


    if (rawflag == 0)
        while (linecount == 0)  /* wait until a complete line is avail */
            ;

    c = raw_getc();             /* get the input char from buffer */

    if (rawflag == 0)
        if (c == '\r')          /* translate CR to NL */
            c = '\n';

    return(c);
}



/*----------------------------------------------------------------------
PROCEDURE
    CONPUTC  -  send a character to console screen

SYNOPSIS
    void conputc(c)
    char c;

REMARKS
    Translate '\n' to carriage return - newline pair.

LAST UPDATE
    19 October 1987
----------------------------------------------------------------------*/

void conputc(c)
char c;
{

    putoutbuf(c);

    if (rawflag == 0)
        if (c == '\n')
            putoutbuf('\r');

}
```

```
/*---------------------------------------------------------------------------
FUNCTION
    CONWRITE  -  write n characters to the console screen

SYNOPSIS
    int conwrite(s, n)
    char *s;
    int n;

PARAMETERS
    s  -  ptr to array of characters
    n  -  number of char to write

RETURNS
    number of char transmitted

REMARKS
    If output buffer is full, will wait until buffer space is available.

LAST UPDATE
    16 May 1988
        replace conputs()
---------------------------------------------------------------------------*/

int conwrite(s, n)
char *s;
int n;
{
    int i;      /* iteration variable */


    for (i = 0; i < n; i++)
        conputc(*s++);

    return(i);
}


/*---------------------------------------------------------------------------
FUNCTION
    CONREAD  -  get a string from console keyboard

SYNOPSIS
    int conread(buf, size)
    char *buf;
    int size;

PARAMETER
    buf   -  char array supplied by caller
    size  -  buffer size

RETURNS
    number of char read, excluding NUL terminator if present.

REMARKS
    Wait until a complete line is available, then copy line into
    supplied buffer.

LAST UPDATE
    16 May 1988
        replace congets()
---------------------------------------------------------------------------*/

int conread(buf, size)
char *buf;
int size;
{
    int c;              /* input char */
    int i;              /* size counter */


    i = 0;

    do
    {
        c = congetc();

        if (c < 0)                      /* must be in raw mode */
            break;

        *buf++ = (char)c;               /* copy to caller supplied buffer */

        ++i;                            /* update bytes copied */
    }
    while (((c != '\r') && (c != '\n')) || (i >= size));

    if (i < size)
        *buf = '\0';                    /* NUL terminate line */

    return(i);
}


/*---------------------------------------------------------------------------
PROCEDURE
    CONIOCTL  -  i/o control for miscellaneous functions

SYNOPSIS
    int conioctl(cmd, data)
    int cmd;
    void *data;
```

```
PARAMETER
    cmd   -  command code, list is defined in console.h
    data  -  generic data ptr to possible arguments

RETURNS
    depends on command code

LAST UPDATE
    16 May 1988
        new
-------------------------------------------------------------------------*/

int conioctl(cmd, data)
int cmd;
void *data;
{
    int rval = 0;


    switch (cmd)
    {
        case CONECHO:

            echoflag = *(int *)data;
            break;

        case CONRAW:

            rawflag = *(int *)data;
            break;

        default:

            break;
    }

    return(rval);
}


/************************************************************************
                     P R I V A T E   R O U T I N E S
************************************************************************/

/*-----------------------------------------------------------------------
FUNCTION
    RAW_GETC  -  "raw" form of getc()

SYNOPSIS
    static int raw_getc(void)

RETURNS
    input char if one is available, -1 if not

REMARKS
    This function is the same as getc() except that it does not wait
    for a complete line to be available.  It also does not echo the
    input character.  If no char is available, -1 is returned.

LAST UPDATE
    19 October 1987
-------------------------------------------------------------------------*/

static int raw_getc()
{
    int c;


    c = getcbuf(inbuf);

    if ((c == '\r') || (c == '\n'))       /* c is end of line marker */
        --linecount;                      /* update line count */

    return(c);
}



/*-----------------------------------------------------------------------
FUNCTION
    PUTOUTBUF  -  put a char into output buffer

SYNOPSIS
    static int putoutbuf(c)
    char c;

RETURNS
    c   if successful
    -1  if buffer full

LAST UPDATE
    19 October 1987
-------------------------------------------------------------------------*/

static int putoutbuf(c)
char c;
{
    int rval;             /* return value */


    while ((rval = putcbuf(c, outbuf)) < 0)      /* buffer full?! */
    {
```

```
        if (!xoffflag)          /* wake up transmitter if not */
            kwakeup();          /*  in XOFF state */
    }

    if (!xoffflag)
        kwakeup();              /* wake-up transmitter to tx last char */

    tbmtflag = 0;               /* there is output char to transmit */

    return(rval);
}


/*----------------------------------------------------------------------
PROCEDURE
    ECHO  echo input character to monitor screen

SYNOPSIS
    static void echo(c)
    char c;

PARAMETER
    c  -  input character

LAST UPDATE
    19 October 1987
----------------------------------------------------------------------*/

static void echo(c)
char c;
{

    if (echoflag)
    {
        switch (c)
        {
            case '\r':      /* carriage return */
            case '\n':      /* linefeed */

                putcbuf('\r', ecobuf);      /* echo as carriage return */
                putcbuf('\n', ecobuf);      /*  - linefeed pair.       */

                break;

            case '\b':      /* backspace */
            case DEL:       /* delete */

                putcbuf('\b', ecobuf);
                putcbuf(' ', ecobuf);
                putcbuf('\b', ecobuf);
                break;

            default:

                putcbuf(c, ecobuf);
                break;
        }

        tbmtflag = 0;
    }
}


/**********************************************************************
          I N I T I A L I Z A T I O N     R O U T I N E S
**********************************************************************/

/*----------------------------------------------------------------------
PROCEDURE
    CONINIT  -  initialize console subsystem

SYNOPSIS
    void coninit(void)

REMARKS
    Allocate and initialize buffers, then call hardware specific
    initialization routine initcon().

LAST UPDATE
    19 October 1987
----------------------------------------------------------------------*/

void coninit()
{

    if ((inbuf = newcbuf(INBUFSIZE)) == NULL)
    {
        printf("cannot allocate console input buffer\n");
        exit(1);
    }

    if ((outbuf = newcbuf(OUTBUFSIZE)) == NULL)
    {
        printf("cannot allocate console output buffer\n");
        exit(1);
    }

    if ((ecobuf = newcbuf(ECOBUFSIZE)) == NULL)
    {
        printf("cannot allocate console echo buffer\n");
```

```
        exit(1);
    }

    kinit();         /* system specific initialization */

}

/**********************************************************************

FILE
    cbuf.h  -  declaration header for cbuf module

LAST UPDATE
    10 May 1988
        use function prototypes if ANSI compiler

**********************************************************************/

typedef struct _cbuf {
    int cb_id;              /* buffer id number */
    char *cb_begin;         /* ptr to beginning of buffer memory */
    char *cb_end;           /* ptr to end of buffer memory */
    char *cb_front;         /* ptr to front of buffer */
    char *cb_rear;          /* ptr to rear of buffer */
} CBUF;

#define CBNULL  (CBUF *)0

#ifdef ANSI

extern CBUF *   newcbuf(unsigned);
extern int      putcbuf(char, CBUF *);
extern int      getcbuf(CBUF *);
extern int      unputcbuf(CBUF *);
extern int      ungetcbuf(char, CBUF *);
extern unsigned countcbuf(CBUF *);
extern void     resetcbuf(CBUF *);

#else

extern CBUF *   newcbuf();
extern int      putcbuf();
extern int      getcbuf();
extern int      unputcbuf();
extern int      ungetcbuf();
extern unsigned countcbuf();
extern void     resetcbuf();

#endif

/**********************************************************************

FILE
    cbuf.c  -  circular character buffer

ENTRY ROUTINES
    newcbuf     -  create new buffer
    putcbuf     -  put a char into buffer
    getcbuf     -  get a char from buffer
    unputcbuf   -  undo a putcbuf
    ungetcbuf   -  undo a getcbuf
    countcbuf   -  how many in buffer?
    resetcbuf   -  reset buffer

REMARKS
    The buffer is organized as a circular queue or ring buffer.  Two
    pointers, one to the front and another to the rear of the queue
    are maintained.  The front pointer points to the location just
    before the first data item while the rear pointer points at the
    last data item in the queue.

    Thus a PUT operation is: *((rear + 1) % bufsize) = data
    and a GET operation is:  data = *((front + 1) % bufsize)

    -1 is returned if any operations fails.

    A very basic assumption is that address of end of buffer memory is
    greater than address of beginning of buffer memory.

LAST UPDATE
    15 March 1985  by  Haam

    Copyright (c) 1985  D.M. Auslander and C.H. Tham

**********************************************************************/

/**********************************************************************
                            I M P O R T S
**********************************************************************/

#include <stdio.h>
#include <stdlib.h>

#include "envir.h"
#include "cbuf.h"               /* declaration header file */

/**********************************************************************
        MODULE  PRIVATE  DATA  STRUCTURES  AND  VARIABLES
**********************************************************************/

static int cbufid = 0;          /* cbuf id number */

/**********************************************************************
```

```
                    E N T R Y    R O U T I N E S
*********************************************************************/

/*-----------------------------------------------------------------------
FUNCTION
    NEWCBUF  -  create a new buffer structure

SYNOPSIS
    CBUF *newcbuf(size)
    unsigned size;

PARAMETERS
    size  -  size of buffer

RETURNS
    pointer to allocated buffer structure, NULL if error

LAST UPDATE
    15 March 1985
-----------------------------------------------------------------------*/

CBUF *newcbuf(size)
unsigned size;
{
    CBUF *buf;


    if ((buf = (CBUF *)calloc((unsigned)1, sizeof(CBUF))) != CBNULL)
    {
        char *p;

        if ((p = (char *)malloc(size + 1)) != NULL)
        {
            buf->cb_id = cbufid++;
            buf->cb_begin = p;
            buf->cb_end = p + size;
            buf->cb_front = buf->cb_rear = p;
        }
        else    /* cannot allocate buffer */
        {
            free((char *)buf);      /* free allocated structure */
            buf = CBNULL;
        }
    }

    return(buf);
}


/*-----------------------------------------------------------------------
FUNCTION
    PUTCBUF  -  put a character into the buffer

SYNOPSIS
    int putcbuf(c, cbuf)
    char c;
    CBUF *cbuf;

PARAMETERS
    c     -  character data
    cbuf  -  pointer to buffer control structure

RETURNS
    non zero if successful, -1 otherwise

LAST UPDATE
    15 March 1985
-----------------------------------------------------------------------*/

int putcbuf(c, cbuf)
char c;
CBUF *cbuf;
{
    register char *p;              /* fast pointer into buffer */


    if ((p = cbuf->cb_rear + 1) > cbuf->cb_end)
        p = cbuf->cb_begin;        /* wrap pointer round to beginning */

    if (p != cbuf->cb_front)       /* buffer not full */
    {
        *p = c;                    /* enter character data */

        cbuf->cb_rear = p;         /* update rear pointer */

        return((int)c);
    }
    else    /* buffer full! */
    {
        return(-1);                /* indicate this fact */
    }
}


/*-----------------------------------------------------------------------
FUNCTION
    GETCBUF  -  get a character from buffer

SYNOPSIS
    int getcbuf(cbuf)
```

```
    CBUF *cbuf;

PARAMETERS
    cbuf  -  pointer to buffer control structure

RETURNS
    char if buffer not empty, -1 otherwise

LAST UPDATE
    15 March 1985
------------------------------------------------------------------------*/

int getcbuf(cbuf)
CBUF *cbuf;
{

    if (cbuf->cb_front != cbuf->cb_rear)        /* buffer not empty */
    {
        if (++(cbuf->cb_front) > cbuf->cb_end)      /* wrap around */
            cbuf->cb_front = cbuf->cb_begin;

        return(*(cbuf->cb_front));
    }
    else    /* buffer empty */
    {
        return(-1);
    }
}



/*-----------------------------------------------------------------------
FUNCTION
    UNPUTCBUF  -  undo a putcbuf

SYNOPSIS
    int unputcbuf(cbuf)
    CBUF *cbuf;

PARAMETERS
    cbuf  -  pointer to buffer control structure

RETURNS
    char last put in if successful, NULL if otherwise

REMARKS
    Character is retreived from rear of buffer queue.

LAST UPDATE
    15 March 1985
------------------------------------------------------------------------*/

int unputcbuf(cbuf)
CBUF *cbuf;
{
    register int c;


    if (cbuf->cb_front != cbuf->cb_rear)        /* buffer not empty */
    {
        c = *(cbuf->cb_rear);                   /* retreive character */

        if (cbuf->cb_rear == cbuf->cb_begin)    /* adjust pointers */
            cbuf->cb_rear = cbuf->cb_end;
        else
            --(cbuf->cb_rear);
    }
    else
        c = -1;         /* signify empty buffer */

    return(c);
}



/*-----------------------------------------------------------------------
FUNCTION
    UNGETCBUF  -  undo a getcbuf

SYNOPSIS
    int ungetcbuf(c, cbuf)
    char c;
    CBUF *cbuf;

PARAMETERS
    c     -  character data
    cbuf  -  pointer to buffer control structure

RETURNS
    non zero if successful, -1 otherwise

REMARKS
    Character is inserted into front of buffer queue.

LAST UPDATE
    15 March 1985
------------------------------------------------------------------------*/

int ungetcbuf(c, cbuf)
char c;
CBUF *cbuf;
{
    register char *p = cbuf->cb_rear;       /* fast buffer pointer */
```

```
    int error = 0;                          /* error flag */


    if (p == cbuf->cb_front)          /* rear == front, buffer empty */
    {
        *p = c;                           /* enter character */

        if (p == cbuf->cb_begin)          /* adjust front pointer */
            cbuf->cb_front = cbuf->cb_end;
        else
            --(cbuf->cb_front);
    }
    else    /* buffer not empty, could be full */
    {
        if (p == cbuf->cb_end)            /* set p just before rear */
            p = cbuf->cb_begin;
        else
            ++p;

        if (p != cbuf->cb_front)          /* buffer not full */
        {
            *(p = cbuf->cb_front) = c;

            if (p == cbuf->cb_begin)      /* adjust front pointer */
                cbuf->cb_front = cbuf->cb_end;
            else
                --(cbuf->cb_front);
        }
        else    /* buffer full! */
        {
            error = 1;      /* cannot insert into full buffer */
        }
    }

    return(error ? -1 : 1);
}


/*-----------------------------------------------------------------------
FUNCTION
    COUNTCBUF  -  how many in buffer?

SYNOPSIS
    unsigned countcbuf(cbuf)
    CBUF *cbuf;

PARAMETERS
    cbuf  -  pointer to buffer control structure

RETURNS
    number of characters currently in buffer

LAST UPDATE
    24 May 1987
        ptrtoabs() for big memory model
    10 May 1988
        delete ptrtoabs() - not necessary since buffer in same segment
-----------------------------------------------------------------------*/

unsigned countcbuf(cbuf)
CBUF *cbuf;
{
    unsigned count;          /* number of characters in buffer */


    if (cbuf->cb_rear > cbuf->cb_front)          /* no wrap around */
    {
        count = cbuf->cb_rear - cbuf->cb_front;
    }
    else if (cbuf->cb_rear < cbuf->cb_front)     /* warp around */
    {
        count = cbuf->cb_rear - cbuf->cb_begin + cbuf->cb_end - cbuf->cb_front + 1;
    }
    else    /* front == rear */
    {
        count = 0;
    }

    return(count);
}



/*-----------------------------------------------------------------------
PROCEDURE
    RESETCBUF  -  reset buffer

SYNOPSIS
    void resetcbuf(cbuf)
    CBUF *cbuf;

LAST UPDATE
    31 March 1985
-----------------------------------------------------------------------*/

void resetcbuf(cbuf)
CBUF *cbuf;
{

    if (cbuf != CBNULL)
        cbuf->cb_front = cbuf->cb_rear = cbuf->cb_begin;
```

```
}

/**********************************************************************

FILE
    kcon.h  -  common declarations for hardware dependent console services

LAST UPDATE
    16 May 1988
        add ANSI function prototypes

**********************************************************************/

#ifdef ANSI

extern void kputc(char);     /* send char to output hardware */
extern void kinit(void);     /* initialize console hardware */
extern void ksleep(void);    /* turn off transmitter */
extern void kwakeup(void);   /* wake up transmitter */
extern void krest(void);     /* reset console hardware */

#else

extern void kputc();
extern void kinit();
extern void ksleep();
extern void kwakeup();
extern void krest();

#endif

/**********************************************************************

FILE
    kcon1.c  -  interface between console.c and IBM-PC's COM1 port.

ROUTINES
    com1isr   -  COM1 interrupt service routine
    kputc     -  send a char to be transmitted
    kwakeup   -  wake up interrupt system
    kinit     -  initialize interrupts and hardware
    krest     -  restore interrupts and hardware

REMARKS
    This version interfaces the terminal control program, console.c
    to the IBM-PC's COM1 asynchronous serial port.

LAST UPDATE
    19 October 1987

**********************************************************************/

/**********************************************************************
                         I M P O R T S
**********************************************************************/

#include <stdio.h>

#include "envir.h"          /* program environment declarations */
#include "xignal.h"         /* xignal module declarations */
#include "inout.h"          /* in() and out() library mapping */
#include "com.h"            /* IBM-PC COM port decleartions */
#include "kcon.h"           /* exported hardware interface routines */

#ifdef ANSI
extern void conkbsig(int);       /* from console.c */
extern void conscsig(void);
extern void conersig(int);
#else
extern void conkbsig();
extern void conscsig();
extern void conersig();
#endif

/**********************************************************************
                    P R I V A T E   D A T A
**********************************************************************/

#define CONBUF      COM1BASE        /* port buffer register */
#define CONSTAT     COM1BASE+LSR    /* line status register */
#define CONIIR      COM1BASE+IIR    /* interrupt identification reg */

#define CONTHRE     THRE_MASK       /* THRE bit mask */

static int txdis = 0;               /* 1 => transmit disabled */

/**********************************************************************
    A P P L I C A T I O N   S P E C I F I C   R O U T I N E S
**********************************************************************/

/*--------------------------------------------------------------------
PROCEDURE
    COM1ISR  -  COM1 interrupt service routine

SYNOPSIS
    called by xignal's COM1 interrupt handler

REMARKS
    Read Interrupt Identification Register and depending on the type
    of interrupt, redirect to one of the console module's handler.
```

```
LAST UPDATE
    19 October 1987
--------------------------------------------------------------------------*/

void com1isr()
{

    switch (in(CONIIR))
    {
        case DAV_IID:       /* receiver Data Available */

            conkbsig(in(CONBUF));
            break;

        case THRE_IID:      /* Transmitter Holding Register Empty */

            conscsig();
            break;

        case RLS_IID:       /* Receiver Line Status fault */

            conersig(in(CONSTAT));
            break;

        default:

            break;
    }
}


/*-------------------------------------------------------------------------
PROCEDURE
    KPUTC  -  send char to monitor screen

SYNOPSIS
    void kputc(c)
    char c;

LAST UPDATE
    19 October 1987
--------------------------------------------------------------------------*/

void kputc(c)
char c;
{

    out(CONBUF, c);
}
```

```
/*-------------------------------------------------------------------------
PROCEDURE
    KWAKEUP  -  "wake-up" console hardware

SYNOPSIS
    void kwakeup(void)

REMARKS
    The IBM-PC interrupts are edge triggerred, so if a char was not
    transmitted in the last tx_ready interrupt, that interrupt will not
    trigger again.  This routine checks if the "Transmitter Holding
    Register Empty" bit in the status is set; if the tx was transmitting
    characters, this routine will never see that bit set since an
    interrupt will occur the moment THRE is set.  Thus if this routine
    sees that THRE is set, it means that there was no char to transmit
    during the last tx_ready interrupt.  Thus, we get a char from the
    output buffer and transmit that, reactivating the tx_ready interrupt
    response.

    The other purpose for this routine is to enable the UART interrupts
    if they were disabled in response to an XOFF character.

    Note that this routine should only be called when there is something
    to transmit, either from the main output buffer or the echo buffer.

LAST UPDATE
    19 October 1987
--------------------------------------------------------------------------*/

void kwakeup()
{

    if (txdis)
    {
        comienb(1, DAV_ENB | THRE_ENB | RLS_ENB);   /* enable interrupts */
        txdis = 0;
    }

    if (in(CONSTAT) & CONTHRE)                /* tx ready */
    {
        conscsig();
    }

}


/*-------------------------------------------------------------------------
PROCEDURE
    KSLEEP  -  put tx hardware to sleep
```

```
SYNOPSIS
    void ksleep()

REMARKS
    Disable COM1 THRE interrupts.  This is done by calling comidis()
    instead of masking the 8259 interrupt controller since we still
    wish to receive receive interrupts.

LAST UPDATE
    20 October 1987
---------------------------------------------------------------------*/

void ksleep()
{

    comidis(1, THRE_ENB);

    txdis = 1;
}


/*---------------------------------------------------------------------
PROCEDURE
    KINIT  -  co-ordinate system specific initializations

SYNOPSIS
    void kinit()

REMARKS
    Use services in the xignal module to set up comlisr() as the COM1
    interrupt handler.

    comienb() tells the serial port to generate interrupts.  This
    routine resides in the file com.c

LAST UPDATE
    19 October 1987
---------------------------------------------------------------------*/

void kinit()
{

    cominit(1, 9600, 0, 8, 1, 1, 1);

    xignal(XIGCOM1, comlisr);   /* install comlisr() */

    comienb(1, DAV_ENB | THRE_ENB | RLS_ENB);   /* enable COM1 interrupts */

    in(CONBUF);         /* clear serial input buffer */
    in(CONSTAT);        /* clear line status port */
}


/*---------------------------------------------------------------------
PROCEDURE
    KREST  -  restore system for program exit

SYNOPSIS
    void krest(void)

LAST UPDATE
    20 October 1987
---------------------------------------------------------------------*/

void krest()
{

    comidis(1, 0);      /* disable COM1 interrupt generation */

    xignal(XIGALL, XIG_DFL);        /* restore interrupt vectors */

}

/*********************************************************************

FILE
    kcon2.c  -  interface between terminal control layer and hardware

ROUTINES
    kputc     -  send a character to screen
    kwakeup   -  wakeup
    kinit     -  initialize this module
    krest     -  restore system for program exit.

REMARKS
    This version interfaces the terminal control program, console.c
    to the monitor and keyboard using DOS and BIOS calls.

LAST UPDATE
    16 May 1988
        use ANSI features

*********************************************************************/

/*********************************************************************
                           I M P O R T S
*********************************************************************/

#include <stdio.h>
#include <dos.h>        /* MSC dos function declarations */
```

```
#include "envir.h"
#include "inout.h"
#include "8259.h"
#include "xignal.h"
#include "kcon.h"       /* common exported interface declarations */

extern conkbisr(void);          /* from conkbisr.asm */

#ifdef ANSI
extern void conkbsig(int);      /* from console.c */
extern int  conscsig(void);
extern void conersig(int);
#else
extern void conkbsig();
extern int  conscsig();
extern void conersig();
#endif

/*********************************************************************
                    E N T R Y   R O U T I N E S
*********************************************************************/

/*-------------------------------------------------------------------
PROCEDURE
    KPUTC  -  send char to monitor screen

SYNOPSIS
    void kputc(c)
    char c;

REMARKS
    DOS is non re-entrant.  The bdos() call must take place within
    a critical region.  Since DOS functions enables interrupts by
    executing sti, we have to prevent interrupts from reaching the
    CPU by masking out the 8259 interrupt controller.

LAST UPDATE
    19 October 1987
-------------------------------------------------------------------*/

void kputc(c)
char c;
{
    int mask;           /* interrupt mask */


    mask = in(MASKPORT);         /* save current mask state */

    out(MASKPORT, 0xFF);         /* mask out all interrupts */

    bdos(2, c, 0);               /* call DOS to print char */

    out(MASKPORT, mask);         /* restore previous interrupt mask */

}



/*-------------------------------------------------------------------
PROCEDURE
    KWAKEUP  -  "wake-up" console hardware

SYNOPSIS
    void kwakeup(void)

REMARKS
    The IBM-PC's monitor screen is memory mapped and there is no
    interrupt for when it is ready to accept a character.  So this
    routine merely calls conscsig() to print the characters until
    the output and echo buffers are empty.  While not ideal in terms
    of throughput, it is the simplest way of maintaining compatibility
    with the asynchronous serial terminal version of the operator
    console code.

    Note that this routine should only be called when there is something
    to transmit, either from the main output buffer or the echo buffer.

LAST UPDATE
    19 October 1987
-------------------------------------------------------------------*/

void kwakeup()
{

    while (!conscsig())
        ;

}



/*-------------------------------------------------------------------
PROCEDURE
    KSLEEP  -  put tx to sleep

SYNOPSIS
    void ksleep(void)

REMARKS
    Suppose to put the transmitter to sleep in the asynchronous serial
    terminal version.  This version does nothing but is included for
    compatibility with the serial port version.
```

```
LAST UPDATE
    20 October 1987
----------------------------------------------------------------------*/

void ksleep()
{
    /* for compatibility with serial terminal version only */
}



/*----------------------------------------------------------------------
PROCEDURE
    KINIT  -  co-ordinate system specific initializations

SYNOPSIS
    void kinit(void)

REMARKS
    Set up conkbisr() (defined in conkbisr.asm) as the keyboard
    interrupt service routine.

LAST UPDATE
    19 October 1987
----------------------------------------------------------------------*/

void kinit()
{

    xignal(XIGKB, conkbisr);

}



/*----------------------------------------------------------------------
PROCEDURE
    KREST  -  restore system for program exit

SYNOPSIS
    void krest(void)

LAST UPDATE
    20 October 1987
----------------------------------------------------------------------*/

void krest()
{

    xignal(XIGALL, XIG_DFL);

}

/************************************************************************

FILE
    com.h  -  com.c module exported declarations

LAST UPDATE
    19 June 1985  by  Haam

************************************************************************/

/************  base addresses of 8250 i/o address block  ************/

#define COM1BASE    0x3F8
#define COM2BASE    0x2F8

/*******  offsets of various registers from the base address  *******/

#define RXBUF       0         /* Receiver Buffer */
#define TXBUF       0         /* Transmitter Buffer */
#define IER         1         /* Interrupt Enable Register */
#define IIR         2         /* Interrupt Identification Register */
#define LCR         3         /* Line Control Register */
#define MCR         4         /* Modem Control Register */
#define LSR         5         /* Line Status Register */
#define MSR         6         /* Modem Status Register */

/**********************  line status bit masks  *********************/

#define DAV     0x01      /* Rx ready (Data Available) */
#define THRE    0x20      /* Tx ready (Transmitter Buffer eMpTy) */

/*****  interrupt enable and identification bits for IER and IIR  *****/

#define DAV_ENB     1     /* enable Rx ready interrupt */
#define THRE_ENB    2     /* enable Tx ready interrupt */
#define RLS_ENB     4     /* enable Rx line error interrupt */
#define MLS_ENB     8     /* enable modem line interrupt */

#define MLS_IID     0     /* modem line interrupt id bit */
#define NONE_IID    1     /* no interrupts pending */
#define THRE_IID    2     /* Tx ready interrupt id bit */
#define RLS_IID     6     /* Rx line error interrupt id bit */
#define DAV_IID     4     /* Rx ready interrupt id bit */

/******************  Line Status Register Mask  ******************/

#define THRE_MASK   0x20    /* Transmitter Holding Register Empty */
#define DAV_MASK    0x01    /* Data Available */
```

```
/****************  Interrupt Vectors, Masks and EOI ****************/

#if 0
#define BASEVEC      8               /* Base vector */

#define COM1VEC      (BASEVEC+4)     /* COM1 interrupt vector */
#define COM2VEC      (BASEVEC+3)     /* COM2 interrupt vector */

#define COM1MASK     0x10            /* COM1 interrupt mask */
#define COM2MASK     0x08            /* COM2 interrupt mask */

#define COM1EOI      0x64            /* EOI byte for COM1 */
#define COM2EOI      0x63            /* EOI byte for COM2 */
#endif

/************************  exported routines  ************************/

#ifdef ANSI

extern int  cominit(int, int, int, int, int, int, int);
extern int  comienb(int, int);
extern int  comidis(int, int);

#else

extern int  cominit();
extern int  comienb();
extern int  comidis();

#endif
/***********************************************************************

FILE
    com.c  -  IBM PC non bios COM programming

ENTRY ROUTINES
    cominit  -  initialize com
    comienb  -  enable com interrupts
    comidis  -  disable com interrupts
    comin    -  com input
    comout   -  com output

PRIVATE ROUTINES
    combase  -  get base address of COM device

REMARKS
    This module supplies COM programming routines that are independent
    of the BIOS.  The BIOS limit of only 2 COM devices are overcomed.
    It is assumed that all COM devices use the INS8250 chip.

LAST UPDATE
    24 June 1985

***********************************************************************/

/***********************************************************************
                          I M P O R T S
***********************************************************************/

#include "envir.h"                  /* environment declarations */
#include "inout.h"                  /* i/o function mapping */
#include "com.h"                    /* exported module declarations */

/***********************************************************************
                     P R I V A T E    D A T A
***********************************************************************/

/************  table of baud rates and associated divisor  ************/

#define BAUDTABSIZ      16      /* number of entries in baud table */

static int baudtab[BAUDTABSIZ][2] = {
    {    50, 0x900 },
    {    75, 0x600 },
    {   110, 0x417 },
    {   135, 0x359 },               /* actually 134.5 baud */
    {   150, 0x300 },
    {   300, 0x180 },
    {   600, 0x0C0 },
    {  1200, 0x060 },
    {  1800, 0x040 },
    {  2000, 0x03A },
    {  2400, 0x030 },
    {  3600, 0x020 },
    {  4800, 0x018 },
    {  7200, 0x010 },
    {  9600, 0x00C },
    { 19200, 0x006 }                /* baud rate not recommended by IBM */
};

/***********************************************************************
               F O R W A R D    D E C L A R A T I O N S
***********************************************************************/

#ifdef ANSI
int combase(int);
#else
int combase();
#endif

/***********************************************************************
                   E N T R Y    R O U T I N E S
```

```
*************************************************************************/

/*-----------------------------------------------------------------------
FUNCTION
    COMINIT  -  initialize com device

SYNOPSIS
    int cominit(com, baud, parity, wordsize, stopbits, rts, dtr)
    int com, baud, parity, wordsize, stopbits, rts, dtr;

PARAMETERS
    com       -  com device (1 for COM1, 2 for COM2 etc...)
    baud      -  baud rate (135.5 is specified as 135)
    parity    -  0  -  none, 1  -  odd, 2  -  even
    wordsize  -  5, 6, 7, 8
    rts       -  initial RTS state (0 or 1)
    dtr       -  initial DTR state (0 or 1)

RETURNS
    0  if all is well,  -1  otherwise

REMARKS
    Wider range of baud rates than possible with DOS's MODE command.

LAST UPDATE
    4 May 1985
-----------------------------------------------------------------------*/

cominit(com, baud, parity, wordsize, stopbits, rts, dtr)
int com, baud, parity, wordsize, stopbits, rts, dtr;
{
    int base;                /* base address */
    char lcr;                /* LCR control byte */
    char mcr;                /* MCR control byte */
    int i;                   /* iteration variable */


    if ((base = combase(com)) < 0)       /* invalid com specifier */
        return(-1);

    for (i = 0; i < BAUDTABSIZ; i++)
        if (baudtab[i][0] == baud)       /* baud rate is supported */
            break;

    if (i < BAUDTABSIZ)
    {
        out(base+LCR, 0x80);             /* access divisor latch */

        out(base, baudtab[i][1] & 0xFF);
        out(base+1, baudtab[i][1] >> 8);
        out(base+LCR, 0x00);             /* reset DLAB */
    }
    else
        return(-1);


    lcr = 0;                             /* initialize LCR byte */

    switch (wordsize)
    {
        case 5:     lcr &= ~0x01;        break;
        case 6:     lcr |= 0x01;         break;
        case 7:     lcr |= 0x02;         break;
        case 8:     lcr |= 0x03;         break;
        default:    return(-1);          /* invalid word size */
    }

    switch (parity)
    {
        case 0:     lcr &= ~0x08;        break;      /* no parity */
        case 1:     lcr &= ~0x10;        break;      /* odd parity */
        case 2:     lcr |= 0x10;         break;      /* even parity */
        default:    return(-1);                      /* invalid parity */
    }

    switch (stopbits)
    {
        case 1:     lcr &= ~0x04;        break;      /* 1 stop bit */
        case 2:     lcr |= 0x04;         break;      /* 1.5 if wordsize=5 */
        default:    return(-1);                      /* error */
    }

    out(base+LCR, lcr);                  /* set line control */


    mcr = (char)in(base+MCR);

    if (rts && dtr)
        out(base+MCR, mcr | 0x03);
    else if (dtr)
        out(base+MCR, mcr | 0x01);
    else if (rts)
        out(base+MCR, mcr | 0x02);

    return(0);
}


/*-----------------------------------------------------------------------
FUNCTION
```

```
    COMIENB  -  enable com interrupts

SYNOPSIS
    int comienb(com, intrps)
    int com, intrps;

PARAMETERS
    com     -  com id
    intrps  -  which interrupts to enable (defined in com.h)

RETURNS
    0  if all is well,  -1 otherwise

LAST UPDATE
    4 May 1985
-----------------------------------------------------------------------*/

int comienb(com, intrps)
int com, intrps;
{
    int base;                   /* base address */


    if ((base = combase(com)) >= 0)
    {
        out(base+MCR, in(base+MCR) | 0x08);     /* enable them */
        out(base+IER, intrps & 0x0F);           /* select interrupts */

        return(0);
    }
    else                        /* com id error */
        return(-1);

}



/*----------------------------------------------------------------------
FUNCTION
    COMIDIS  -  disable com interrupts

SYNOPSIS
    int comidis(com, intrps)
    int com, intrps;

PARAMTERS
    com    -  com id
    intrps -  what interrupts to disable

RETURNS
    0  if all is well,  -1 otherwise

LAST UPDATE
    4 May 1985
-----------------------------------------------------------------------*/

int comidis(com, intrps)
int com, intrps;
{
    int base;                   /* base address */


    if ((base = combase(com)) >= 0)
    {
        intrps &= 0x0F;                 /* mask off extraneous bits */

        if (intrps == 0)                /* disable all interrupts */
        {
            out(base+IER, 0);
            out(base+MCR, in(base+MCR) & ~0x08);
        }
        else
        {
            out(base+IER, (~intrps) & 0x0F);
        }

        return(0);
    }
    else
        return(-1);

}


#if 0       /* taken out to save code space */

/*----------------------------------------------------------------------
FUNCTION
    COMOUT  -  non interrupt driven com character output

SYNOPSIS
    int comout(com, c)
    int com;
    char c;

PARAMETERS
    com  -  com id
    c    -  output character

RETURNS
    0  if all is well,  -1 otherwise

LAST UPDATE
```

```
    4 May 1985
-----------------------------------------------------------------------*/

int comout(com, c)
int com;
char c;
{
    int base;           /* com base address */
    int mcr;            /* MCR address */
    int lsr;            /* LSR address */


    if ((base = combase(com)) >= 0)
    {
        mcr = base+MCR;
        lsr = base+LSR;

        while (!(in(lsr) & THRE))   /* wait for THRE */
            ;

        out(base, c);

        return(0);
    }
    else
        return(-1);

}


/*-----------------------------------------------------------------------
FUNCTION
    COMIN  -  non interrupt com input

SYNOPSIS
    int comin(com)
    int com;

PARAMETERS
    com  -  com id

RETURNS
    input char cast to int if all is well,  -1 otherwise

LAST UPDATE
    4 May 1985
-----------------------------------------------------------------------*/

int comin(com)
int com;
{
    int base;                   /* com base address */
    int lsr;                    /* LSR address */
    int c;                      /* input value */


    if ((base = combase(com)) >= 0)
    {
        lsr = base+LSR;

        while (!(in(lsr) & DAV))        /* wait for DAV */
            ;

        c = in(base);
    }
    else
        c = -1;

    return(c);
}

#endif


/***********************************************************************
                P R I V A T E    R O U T I N E S
***********************************************************************/

/*-----------------------------------------------------------------------
FUNCTION
    COMBASE  -  get com base address from com id

SYNOPSIS
    static combase(com)
    int com;

PARAMETERS
    com  -  com id  (1 for COM1, 2 for COM2 etc...)

RETURNS
    base address if all is well,  -1 otherwise

LAST UPDATE
    24 June 1985
-----------------------------------------------------------------------*/

static int combase(com)
int com;
{
    int base;                   /* base address */
```

```
    switch (com)
    {
        case 1:         /* COM1 */

            base = COM1BASE;
            break;

        case 2:         /* COM2 */

            base = COM2BASE;
            break;

        default:

            base = -1;
    }

    return(base);
}

/**********************************************************************

FILE
    kcon2.c  -  interface between terminal control layer and hardware

ROUTINES
    kputc    -  send a character to screen
    kwakeup  -  wakeup
    kinit    -  initialize this module
    krest    -  restore system for program exit.

REMARKS
    This version interfaces the terminal control program, console.c
    to the monitor and keyboard using DOS and BIOS calls.

LAST UPDATE
    16 May 1988
        use ANSI features

**********************************************************************/

/**********************************************************************
                            I M P O R T S
**********************************************************************/

#include <stdio.h>
#include <dos.h>         /* MSC dos function declarations */

#include "envir.h"
#include "inout.h"
#include "8259.h"
#include "xignal.h"
#include "kcon.h"       /* common exported interface declarations */

extern conkbisr(void);          /* from conkbisr.asm */

#ifdef ANSI
extern void conkbsig(int);      /* from console.c */
extern int  conscsig(void);
extern void conersig(int);
#else
extern void conkbsig();
extern int  conscsig();
extern void conersig();
#endif

/**********************************************************************
                    E N T R Y   R O U T I N E S
**********************************************************************/

/*--------------------------------------------------------------------
PROCEDURE
    KPUTC  -  send char to monitor screen

SYNOPSIS
    void kputc(c)
    char c;

REMARKS
    DOS is non re-entrant.  The bdos() call must take place within
    a critical region.  Since DOS functions enables interrupts by
    executing sti, we have to prevent interrupts from reaching the
    CPU by masking out the 8259 interrupt controller.

LAST UPDATE
    19 October 1987
--------------------------------------------------------------------*/

void kputc(c)
char c;
{
    int mask;           /* interrupt mask */


    mask = in(MASKPORT);        /* save current mask state */

    out(MASKPORT, 0xFF);        /* mask out all interrupts */

    bdos(2, c, 0);              /* call DOS to print char */

    out(MASKPORT, mask);        /* restore previous interrupt mask */
```

```
}


/*------------------------------------------------------------------------
PROCEDURE
    KWAKEUP  -  "wake-up" console hardware

SYNOPSIS
    void kwakeup(void)

REMARKS
    The IBM-PC's monitor screen is memory mapped and there is no
    interrupt for when it is ready to accept a character.  So this
    routine merely calls conscsig() to print the characters until
    the output and echo buffers are empty.  While not ideal in terms
    of throughput, it is the simplest way of maintaining compatibility
    with the asynchronous serial terminal version of the operator
    console code.

    Note that this routine should only be called when there is something
    to transmit, either from the main output buffer or the echo buffer.

LAST UPDATE
    19 October 1987
------------------------------------------------------------------------*/

void kwakeup()
{

    while (!conscsig())
        ;

}


/*------------------------------------------------------------------------
PROCEDURE
    KSLEEP  -  put tx to sleep

SYNOPSIS
    void ksleep(void)

REMARKS
    Suppose to put the transmitter to sleep in the asynchronous serial
    terminal version.  This version does nothing but is included for
    compatibility with the serial port version.

LAST UPDATE
    20 October 1987
------------------------------------------------------------------------*/

void ksleep()
{
    /* for compatibility with serial terminal version only */
}


/*------------------------------------------------------------------------
PROCEDURE
    KINIT  -  co-ordinate system specific initializations

SYNOPSIS
    void kinit(void)

REMARKS
    Set up conkbisr() (defined in conkbisr.asm) as the keyboard
    interrupt service routine.

LAST UPDATE
    19 October 1987
------------------------------------------------------------------------*/

void kinit()
{

    xignal(XIGKB, conkbisr);

}


/*------------------------------------------------------------------------
PROCEDURE
    KREST  -  restore system for program exit

SYNOPSIS
    void krest(void)

LAST UPDATE
    20 October 1987
------------------------------------------------------------------------*/

void krest()
{

    xignal(XIGALL, XIG_DFL);

}
```

```
/***********************************************************************

FILE
    8259.h  -  8259A definitions, IBM-PC version

SYNOPSIS
    #include "8259.h"

DESCRIPTION
    This file contains useful definitions for default operation of the
    Intel 8259A Programmable Interrupt Controller in the IBM-PC.

LAST UPDATE
    30 April 1985

AUTHOR
    Haam Tham   18 February 1985

    Copyright(c) 1985,1986  D.M. Auslander and C.H. Tham

***********************************************************************/


#define BASE8259    0x20              /* base address */

#define EOIPORT     (BASE8259+0)      /* where to send EOI */
#define MASKPORT    (BASE8259+1)      /* 8259 mask port */

#define BASEVEC     8                 /* base vector */

#define TMRVEC      BASEVEC           /* timer vector */
#define KBVEC       (BASEVEC+1)       /* keyboard vector */
#define COM2VEC     (BASEVEC+3)       /* COM2 device vector */
#define COM1VEC     (BASEVEC+4)       /* COM1 or (AUX) vector */
#define PRNVEC      (BASEVEC+7)       /* parallel printer vector */

#define AUXVEC      COM1VEC           /* an alternative definition */

#define TMRMASK     0x01              /* disable timer mask */
#define KBMASK      0x02              /* disable keyboard mask */
#define COM2MASK    0x08              /* disable COM2 mask */
#define COM1MASK    0x10              /* disable COM1 mask */
#define PRNMASK     0x80              /* disable printer port mask */

#define AUXMASK     COM1MASK

#define TMREOI      0x60              /* timer specific EOI */
#define KBEOI       0x61              /* keyboard specific EOI */
#define COM2EOI     0x63              /* COM2 specific EOI */
#define COM1EOI     0x64              /* COM1 specific EOI */
#define PRNEOI      0x67              /* printer specific EOI */
#define NSEOI       0x20              /* non specific EOI */
```

```
;***********************************************************************
;
; FILE
;   conkbisr.asm  -  keyboard interrupt decode (Microsoft C version 4)
;
; SYNOPSIS
;   masm conkbisr /ml;
;
; LAST UPDATE
;   27 May 1985
;       modify to support big memory model
;   12 September 1987
;       compiler and name change
;   19 October 1987
;       special version for operator console example
;
;   Copyright(c) 1986,1987  D.M. Auslander and C.H. Tham
;
;***********************************************************************

BIOS_KBINT  EQU     209     ; relocated BIOS keyboard interrupt routine
BIOS_KBREAD EQU     22      ; BIOS keyboard query routine

    INCLUDE model.h

IF LARGEMODEL
    EXTRN   _conkbsig:FAR
ENDIF

    INCLUDE prologue.h

    PUBLIC  _conkbisr

IFE LARGEMODEL
    EXTRN   _conkbsig:NEAR
ENDIF

;-----------------------------------------------------------------------
; PROCEDURE
;   CONKBISR  -  special keyboard interrupt decoding routine
;
; REMARKS
;   This routine is set in ISrvFunc[1] and is called by KbIntSR
;
;   It calls the normal BIOS service routine to decode the keyboard
;   entry.  If an ascii character is available, it calls the BIOS
;   again to remove it from the BIOS buffer and passes it to conkbsig().
;   The ascii character will be in the lower byte and the scan code
;   will be in the upper byte.
```

```
;
;   The user MUST supply a routine called conkbsig() for this to work.
;
; LAST UPDATE
;   20 October 1987
;       change names by prepending "_con"
;-----------------------------------------------------------------------

IF LARGEMODEL
_conkbisr       PROC    FAR
ELSE
_conkbisr       PROC    NEAR
ENDIF

    int     BIOS_KBINT          ; call BIOS interrupt service routine

    mov     ah, 1               ; code for "is ascii char available?"
    int     BIOS_KBREAD         ; call BIOS again

    jz      kbexit              ; ZF=1 means no luck

    mov     ah, 0               ; char avail, remove it from BIOS buffer
    int     BIOS_KBREAD         ; AL <- ascii, AH <- scan code

    push    ax                  ; argument to in_kbbuf

    call    _conkbsig           ; call user's kb routine

    add     sp, 2               ; remove argument from stack

kbexit:

    ret

_conkbisr       ENDP


    INCLUDE epilogue.h

    END

;**********************************************************************
;
; FILE
;   model.h  -  define memory model
;
; REMARKS
;   The definitions LARGEMODEL, SMALLMODEL, MEDIUMMODEL and COMPACTMODEL
;   are mutually exclusive.  The symbols LCODE and LDATA means large
;   (>64k) code and large data segments.
;
; LAST UPDATE
;   12 February 1988
;
;**********************************************************************

SMALLMODEL      EQU     1       ; 1 code segment, 1 data segment
MEDIUMMODEL     EQU     0       ; multiple code segments, 1 data segment
COMPACTMODEL    EQU     0       ; 1 code segment, multiple data segments
LARGEMODEL      EQU     0       ; multiple code and data segments

IF SMALLMODEL
LCODE   EQU     0
LDATA   EQU     0
%out    SMALL MODEL
ENDIF

IF MEDIUMMODEL
LCODE   EQU     1
LDATA   EQU     0
%out    MEDIUM MODEL
ENDIF

IF COMPACTMODEL
LCODE   EQU     0
LDATA   EQU     1
%out    COMPACT MODEL
ENDIF

IF LARGEMODEL
LCODE   EQU     1
LDATA   EQU     1
%out    LARGE MODEL
ENDIF
;**********************************************************************
;
; FILE
;   prologue.h  -  C86 style assembly prologue for Microsoft C
;
;**********************************************************************

IF  LCODE
    AP  EQU 6       ; argument ptr to stack arguments
ELSE
    AP  EQU 4
ENDIF


    _DATA   SEGMENT WORD PUBLIC 'DATA'
    _DATA   ENDS
    CONST   SEGMENT WORD PUBLIC 'CONST'
```

```
    CONST   ENDS
    _BSS    SEGMENT WORD PUBLIC 'BSS'
    _BSS    ENDS


    DGROUP  GROUP _DATA, CONST, _BSS

    _TEXT   SEGMENT BYTE PUBLIC 'CODE'
            ASSUME cs:_TEXT, ds:DGROUP


;***********************************************************************
;
; FILE
;   epilogue.h  -  C86 style assembly module epilogue for Microsoft C
;
;***********************************************************************

    _TEXT   ENDS

/***********************************************************************

FILE
    envir.h  -  defines program environment

LAST UPDATE
    16 August 1987
        remove unnecessary clutter

    Copyright(c) 1985,1986,1987  D.M. Auslander and C.H. Tham

***********************************************************************/

/**********************   Operating System   ***********************/

#define UNIX    0       /* 4.2 BSD, implies UNIX C compiler */
#define PCDOS   1       /* includes generic MSDOS family */
#define CPM     0       /* the CP/M family, including MP/M */


/******************   Hardware or Machine Type   ******************/

#define IBMPC       1       /* standard PC, PC/XT, PC/AT */
#define COMPUPRO    0       /* Compupro 8086 or Dual Processor */
#define INTEL310    0       /* Intel 310 development system */


/*************************   Compilers   ************************/

#define CIC86       0       /* Computer Innovations C86 ver. 2.20M */
#define DESMET      0       /* Desmet C */
#define LATTICE     0       /* Lattice C ver. 2.15 */
#define MICROSOFT   1       /* Microsft C ver. 4.00 */

#if MICROSOFT
#define ANSI                /* use proposed ANSI C features */
#endif

/***********************************************************************

FILE
    inout.h  -  maps compiler's 8-bit i/o function names

REMARKS
    Different compilers call their 8-bit port i/o routines by different
    names.  This file contains macros to map these names to the generic
    in() and out().  This makes programs much more portable across
    different compilers

    Note: compiler #define's must be placed before this file.

***********************************************************************/


#if CIC86           /* Computer Innovations C86 */

#define in(port)            inportb((unsigned)(port))
#define out(port, value)    outportb((unsigned)(port), value)

#endif

#if DESMET          /* Desmet C  */

#define in(port)            _inb(port)
#define out(port, value)    _outb(port, value)

#endif

#if LATTICE         /* Lattice C (Version 2.15) */

#define in(port)            inp(port)
#define out(port, value)    outp(port, value)

#endif

#if MICROSOFT       /* Microsoft C Version 4.00 and above */

extern int inp(unsigned);
extern int outp(unsigned, int);

#define in(port)            inp(port)
#define out(port, value)    outp((port), value)
```

```
#endif

/*********************************************************************

FILE
    xignal.h    (IBM-PC version)

SYNOPSIS
    #include "xignal.h"

LAST UPDATE
    22 May 1985  by  Haam
        downgrade requirement for envir.h
    02 October 1985  by  Haam
        add stuff for Compupro
    10 September 1987  by  Haam
        name change to xignal

AUTHOR
    Haam  Tham  18 February 1985

*********************************************************************/

/*********************  locals - for IBM-PC  *********************/

#if IBMPC

#define XIGALL      0               /* vectors 0 to 15 */

#define XIGTMR      1
#define XIGKB       2
#define XIGCGA      3
#define XIGCOM2     4
#define XIGCOM1     5
#define XIGLPT2     6
#define XIGFDSK     7
#define XIGPRN      8
#define XIGFPE      9

#define XIGAUX      XIGCOM1
#define XIGLPT1     XIGPRN

#define NXIG        10

#define XIGTMR0     XIGTMR      /* compatibility with Compupro version */
#define XIGKEYB     XIGKB

#endif  /* if IBMPC */


/*********************  locals - for Compupro  *********************/

#if COMPUPRO

#define XIGALL      0

#define XIGPIO4     1
#define XIGSRX4     3
#define XIGSTX4     4
#define XIGSRX2     5
#define XIGSTX2     6

#define XIGTMR0     12
#define XIGTMR1     13
#define XIGTMR2     14
#define XIGSCRN     17
#define XIGKEYB     18

#define XIGFPE      20

#define NXIG        21

#define XIGTMR      XIGTMR0     /* compatibility with IBM version */
#define XIGKB       XIGKEYB

#endif  /* if COMPUPRO */


/**************  Some Standard Xignal Definitions  **************/

extern XIG_IGN();           /* actual functions are used instead of */
extern XIG_DFL();           /*  casting (*int())() since some       */
extern BADXIG();            /*  compilers cannot perform the cast.  */

extern  int (*xignal(int, int (*)()))();


/******  Floating Point Stuff, modelled on UNIX definitions  ******/

#define     FPE_INTOVF  0x1         /* integer overflow */
#define     FPE_INTDIV  0x2         /* integer divide by zero */
#define     FPE_FLTOVF  0x3         /* floating overflow */
#define     FPE_FLTDIV  0x4         /* floating divide by zero */
#define     FPE_FLTUND  0x5         /* floating underflow */


#define XIGALRM     XIGTMR  /* Unix to Local xignal number mapping */

/***********************************************************
Formatted Screen Test Program

copyright (c) 1988, D. M. Auslander
```

```
This program simulates a simple motor control system and maintains an
operator console using a formatted screen display.  The operator sees
the current motor speed and setpoint constantly displayed, and can make
changes to the setpoint or the controller gains without disturbing the
control.

The motor and controller are simulated in a "screen-background" function
that is run every time the keyboard is checked for a character.  The
program is thus completely synchronous in its present form.

The synchronous structure would suffice for control of a slow process,
but an asynchronous structure would be needed if the characteristic time
of the actual process was too fast.

The program can be run with Microsoft C or Microsoft Quick C.  It uses
the following files:

scr_mtr.c   (this file)
screen.c
screen.h
scr_def.h
scr_msc.c

There is no assembly language required -- all console/keyboard interaction
is done with DOS function calls.  All of the machine-specific parts of the
program are concentrated in scr_msc.c and scr_def.h

***********************************************************/

#include <stdio.h>
#include "screen.h"
#include "scr_def.h"

static float vel = 0.0, cntrli = 0.0;      /* Motor velocity and controller
       integrator values */
static float setpoint = 1.0, kp = 0.2, ki = 0.0002;     /* Controller parameters */
static int rtv=0;             /* Screen manager return value */

struct scr_item *alc_item(); /* Declaration for screen related items */
static struct scr_item *si;
struct scr_msg *alc_msg();   /* Declaration for message allocation */
static struct scr_msg *psm;
struct act_key *alc_akey();
static struct act_key *pact,*pact2;
int scr_bkgr(),quit();          /* Forward declarations */
int fcd(),fdc(),idc(),icd();
                /* Functions to process screen input and output */

main()
{
beginning();      /* Perform any machine specific initialization that
        is necessary */
si = alc_item(6);   /* Allocate space for screen items */


/* The items are set-up by calls to the function set_item().  It takes
all of the specifications needed for an item and stores them into the
data structure.  The first argument gives the address of the beginning
of the array of items to be set.  The second argument is the index for
the particular item.  These are must be contiguous entries from
the allocated set.

The up, down, right, left, and next entries are the associated item
indices, not their addresses.

The general form for the set_item function is:

set_item(pfi,itno,ix,iy,ifw,pdat,f_cd,f_dc,d_on,xl,yl,slab,
              iup,idown,iright,ileft,inext)

This Screen has four data items:
Velocity
Setpoint
Kp
Ki

The velocity is an output, so the cursor is never directed to it.
The other three are inputs.

Note that the screen coordinates are done in engineering graph style,
specifying x and y rather than row and column.    The origin for (x,y)
is at the upper left of the screen.
*/

set_item(si,0,40,7,10,&setpoint,fcd,fdc,1,20,7,"Setpoint",2,1,0,0,1);
set_item(si,1,40,8,10,&kp,fcd,fdc,1,20,8,"Kp",0,2,1,1,2);
set_item(si,2,40,9,10,&ki,fcd,fdc,1,20,9,"Ki",1,0,2,2,3);
set_item(si,3,40,6,10,&vel,fcd,fdc,1,20,6,"Velocity",0,0,0,0,-1);
                                               /* -1 is list terminator */

/* The action keys call functions that cause immediate actions.  They are
checked every time a character is entered */

pact = alc_akey(1);          /* Create an action key list */
/* The only action in this case is to leave the program!  The call to
set up the action keys includes a key label which is placed on the lower
part of the screen */

set_akey(pact,0,F1,quit,1,"Exit", "");/* Enter the F1 function in the list */

/* Define message only items -- These are labels without values */
```

```
psm = alc_msg(1);     /* Allocate space for screen messages */
set_msg(psm,0,20,3,"Velocity Control System",-1);
                      /* -1 indicates the end of the list */

/* This now starts the screen program running.    The initialization
puts the display on the screen, then scr_run services the display.
Scr_run() returns the code set by the function that caused the exit.
That code can be used to determine an action, but isn't used here.
*/

scr_init(si,psm,pact,scr_bkgr);            /* Initialize the first screen */
rtv = scr_run();

ending();      /* Any clean-up needed by the machine-specific functions */
}

quit()
{
scr_rv(1);     /* Set the return value so scr_run() will exit */
}

/* These are the character-to-data and data-to-character functions that
handle all of the data going to or from the screen.  Not all of these
are used in this example */

fcd(ps,s,id,pf)             /* Convert input characters to data and store in
---------              data structure */

struct scr_item *ps;
char *s;
int id;
float *pf;
{
sscanf(s,"%f",ps->p_data);
}

fdc(ps,s,id,pf)        /* Convert data to characters and store in data structure
----------             */
struct scr_item *ps;
char *s;
int id;
float *pf;
{
sprintf(s,"%7.3g",*pf);
}

icd(ps,s,id,pi)             /* Convert input characters to data and store in
---------              data structure */

struct scr_item *ps;
char *s;
int id;
int *pi;
{
sscanf(s,"%d",ps->p_data);
}

idc(ps,s,id,pi)             /* Convert data to characters and store in data structure
----------             */
struct scr_item *ps;
char *s;
int id;
int *pi;
{
sprintf(s,"%d",*pi);
}

/* The screen background function is run after every character check.  It
is used here to simulate both the motor and the controller and to display
the velocity value on the screen */

scr_bkgr()     /* Screen background function */
{
struct scr_item *ps;
float error,torque;
float inertia = 1.0, damping = 0.1;
float delta_t = 0.003;

/* This is a very simple model of the motor and controller, with
no limits or other nonlinearities. */

error = setpoint - vel;
cntrli += error;
torque = kp * error + ki * cntrli;

vel += (torque / inertia - damping * vel) * delta_t;


ps = &si[3];
/* Display the velocity */
disp_dat(ps);
}
/* Screen management functions -- generic, for any computer or terminal
Maintains a formatted screen that allows the user to move around from item
to item and enter new data.

While the screen is being maintained (by scr_run()), calls are made to a
background function so additional processing can be done.
This can include output screen display, etc.

The background function is passed as a pointer when the screen is
initialized, scr_init().  If a NULL pointer is passed, no function is
```

```
run.

Last revision: 9-Sept-85
               28-Dec-85, DMA, change call to cd and dc functions
               1-Jan-86, DMA, added background call
               18-May-86, DMA, added switch for background call
               18-July-86, DMA, changed "includes" ; added function key
                      immediate execution
               22-July-86, DMA, added screen message capability
               26-Aug-86, DMA, bugs
               5-Jan-88, DMA, re-organize for multi-screen use
               8-Jan-88, continuing
               17-Jan-88, DMA, added new entry function, scr_show()

copyright (c) 1985,1986,87,88  D. M. Auslander
*/

#include <stdio.h>
#include "screen.h"          /* Structures and other definitions */
#include "scr_def.h" /* Machine/compiler dependent definitions */

struct scr_item *first, *last;      /* Pointers to the beginning and end of the
                            list of items */


static struct act_key *key_cur = NULL;     /* Pointer to current end of list */
static struct scr_msg *msg_cur = NULL;
static struct scr_item *pcur = NULL;       /* Current item */
static int (*pbkgr_cur) () = NULL;
               /* Pointer to current background function */
static int retval;           /* Can be set to cause scr_run to return
               Is set to a value by calls to scr_rv(v).  Scr_run() returns that
               value, or 0 if the return is by striking the CHAR_EXIT key */

/* Variables for the display of the current item. */
static int display_flag = DATA_AND_LABEL;
static int dsp_hi = 1;              /* Default to reverse video. */
static int dsp_bl = 0;
static int dsp_in = 0;
static int dsp_color = 0;

               /* Flag that allows the user to change highlighting with cursor
                      movement. */

scr_show(ps)   /* Initialize then run a screen
------------   Returns the screen return value (see above) */
struct scr_all *ps;
{
scr_init(ps->pf,ps->pmessg,ps->pkey,ps->pbkgr);
return(scr_run());
}

scr_init(pf,pmessg,pkey,pbkgr)      /* Initialize the screen
------------  */
struct scr_item *pf;  /* Pointer to the first item in this screen */
struct scr_msg *pmessg;      /* Pointer to list of screen messages */
struct act_key *pkey; /* Action key list */
int (*pbkgr) ();              /* Screen background program */
{
struct scr_item *pi;
struct scr_msg *pm;
struct act_key *pk;
int i = 0;

retval = 0;            /* Return value */
pcur = pf;                      /* Set references for current screen */
msg_cur = pmessg;
key_cur = pkey;
pbkgr_cur = pbkgr;

pk = pkey;
pi = pf;
clr_scr();

while(pi != (struct scr_item *)NP)
       {
       disp_lab(pi);
       disp_dat(pi);
       pi = pi->next;
       }

pm = pmessg;
while(pm != (struct scr_msg *)NP)
       {
       pos_cur(pm->x_msg,pm->y_msg);        /* Position the cursor */
       /* Print the message */
       putst(pm->pmsg, pm->hilite, pm->blink, pm->intensify, pm->color);
       pm = pm->pnxt_msg;           /* Next message */
       }

while(pk[i].key_code != 0)
       {
       if(pk[i].key_num)
              {
              set_key_label(pk[i].key_num, pk[i].label_1, pk[i].label_2);
              }
              i++;
       }
}

set_item(pfi,itno,ix,iy,ifw,pdat,f_cd,f_dc,d_on,xl,yl,slab,
              iup,idown,iright,ileft,inext)
/*--------- Set the data for an item block */
```

```
int ix,iy,ifw,d_on,xl,yl;
int iup,idown,iright,ileft,inext,itno;
struct scr_item *pfi;
char *pdat,*slab;
int (*f_cd)(),(*f_dc)();
{
struct scr_item *psi;

psi = pfi + itno;

psi->current = 0;
psi->id = itno;
psi->x = ix;
psi->y = iy;
psi->fw = ifw;
psi->p_data = pdat;
psi->fun_cd = f_cd;
psi->fun_dc = f_dc;
psi->dspl_on = d_on;
psi->x_lab = xl;
psi->y_lab = yl;
strcpy(psi->lab,slab);
psi->up = pfi +iup;
psi->down = pfi + idown;
psi->right = pfi + iright;
psi->left = pfi + ileft;

/* Use set_atr after set_item to get these guys set. */
psi->hilite = 0;
psi->blink = 0;
psi->intensify = 0;
psi->color = 0;

if(inext >= 0)
        psi->next = pfi + inext;
else
        psi->next = (struct scr_item *)NP;
}

set_atr(ps,hi,bl,in,color,on)               /* Set field attributes
-----------------------                     */
struct scr_item *ps;
short hi,bl,in,color,on;     /* highlite, blink, intensify, display_on */
{
if(ps)
        {
        ps->hilite = hi;
        ps->blink = bl;
        ps->intensify = in;
        ps->color = color;
        ps->dspl_on = on;
        }
}


set_msg_atr(pm,hi,bl,in,color,on)           /* Set message attributes
-----------------------                     */
struct scr_msg *pm;
short hi,bl,in,color,on;     /* highlite, blink, intensify, display_on */
{
if(pm)
        {
        pm->hilite = hi;
        pm->blink = bl;
        pm->intensify = in;
        pm->dspl_on = on;
        pm->color = color;
        }
}
/* Set the display attributes for the current item. */

set_dsp(hi, bl, in, color)
{
dsp_hi = hi;
dsp_bl = bl;
dsp_in = in;
dsp_color = color;
}

struct scr_item *alc_item(n) /* Allocate space for n screen items
---------------------------- */
int n;
{
char *malloc();
struct scr_item *pi;

if((pi = (struct scr_item *)malloc(sizeof(struct scr_item) * n)) == (struct scr_item *)
        {
        printf("Not enough memory for screen memory\n");
        exit();
        }
return(pi);
}

struct scr_msg *alc_msg(n)   /* Allocate space for n screen message units
-------------------------    */
int n;
{
char *malloc();
struct scr_msg *pi;
if((pi = (struct scr_msg *)malloc(sizeof(struct scr_msg) * n)) == (struct scr_msg *)NP)
        {
```

```
        printf("Not enough memory for screen message memory\n");
        exit();
        }
return(pi);
}

set_msg(marray,i,xm,ym,pm,inxt)      /* Set the i-th element in the
------------------------------              message array */
struct scr_msg marray[];
int i,xm,ym,inxt;
char *pm;
{
marray[i].x_msg = xm;
marray[i].y_msg = ym;
marray[i].pmsg = pm;
marray[i].hilite = 0;
marray[i].blink = 0;
marray[i].intensify = 0;
marray[i].dspl_on = 1;
marray[i].color = 0;

if(inxt >= 0)marray[i].pnxt_msg = marray + inxt;
else   marray[i].pnxt_msg = (struct scr_msg *)NP;
}


/* Set up a list of action keys
The initial call, crt_akey(), sets up a list of specified maximum
size and initializes it to no entries.  Calls to
set_akey are made to add new items to the list.  The action key items
*must* be numerically contiguous to reduce search time.
*/

struct act_key *alc_akey(n)  /* Set up an action key list with room for
---------------------------- n entries.  The list is initialized empty */
int n;
{
struct act_key *key_list,*kl;
                                    /* Pointer to function key list */
int i;

if((key_list = (struct act_key *)malloc((n + 2) * sizeof(struct act_key)))
        == (struct act_key *)NP)
        {
        printf("No memory left (allocating action key list)\n");
        exit();
        }

for(i = 0,kl = key_list; i < n; i++,kl++)kl->key_code = 0;
                      /* List terminators */
(key_list + n + 1)->key_code = -1;  /* End of array */

return(key_list);
}

set_akey(pkl,ik,code,pfun,key,str_1,str_2)/* Set up an action key for ik-th entry
-----------------------                      */
struct act_key *pkl;
int ik;
int code;
int (*pfun)();          /* Pointer to action function */
int key;
char *str_1;
char *str_2;
{
pkl[ik].key_code = code;
pkl[ik].key_fun = pfun;
pkl[ik].key_num = key;
if(key != 0)
        {
        strcpy(pkl[ik].label_1,str_1);
        strcpy(pkl[ik].label_2,str_2);
        }
}

scr_rv(v)       /* Set the return value
----------      */
int v;
{
retval = v;
}

static struct scr_item *psicur;
static char chcur[3] = {0,8,0};      /* String to restore characters */
static new_cur[2] = {0xdb,0};        /* Temporary cursor */

scr_curitem(ppi)
/*----------------*/
struct scr_item **ppi;
{
*ppi = psicur;
return(psicur->id);
}

scr_run()               /* Run the screen operations
---------      */
{
struct scr_item *pf;  /* Pointer to the first item in this screen */
char cch_scr();
struct scr_item *psi;
int xcur,ycur;        /* Saved cursor positions */
```

```
pf = pcur;
if(pf == NULL)
        {
        printf("Attempt to run a screen that hasn't been initialized\n");
        exit();
        }

pos_cur(pf->x,pf->y);           /* Position the cursor for the first item */
psi = pf;                       /* Initialize item pointer */

psicur = psi;
do_current(psi);

for(;;)
        {
        int c;

        c = read_dat(psi);
        if((c == CHAR_EXIT) || retval)      /* User has typed the exit character
                        or the return value was set */
                {
                clr_scr();     /* Clear the screen */
                pos_cur(0,0); /* Cursor to home */
                return(retval);
                }

        if(c != 0)
                {
                switch(c)
                        {
                        case UP_ARROW:
                                if(psi->up)
                                        {

                                        undo_current(psi);
                                        psi = psi->up;
                                        do_current(psi);

                                        }
                                break;

                        case DOWN_ARROW:
                                if(psi->down)
                                        {

                                        undo_current(psi);
                                        psi = psi->down;
                                        do_current(psi);

                                        }
                                break;
                        case RIGHT_ARROW:
                                if(psi->right)
                                        {

                                        undo_current(psi);
                                        psi = psi->right;
                                        do_current(psi);

                                        }
                                break;
                        case LEFT_ARROW:
                                if(psi->left)
                                        {

                                        undo_current(psi);
                                        psi = psi->left;
                                        do_current(psi);

                                        }
                        }

                pos_cur(psi->x,psi->y);             /* Reposition the cursor */
                }
        if(pbkgr_cur != NULL) /* Do background if it is turned on */
                {
                chcur[0] = cch_scr(&xcur,&ycur);
                                /* Get the current cursor position
                                and the character at that position */
                /*  putst(new_cur, 0,0,0,0);  no new cursor */

                (*pbkgr_cur)();       /* Call the background function */

                /* pos_cur(xcur,ycur); */    /* Restore cursor */
                /* putst(chcur, 0,0,0,0); */  /* Restore the character */
                }
        }
}

disp_dat(ps)   /* Display the data item pointed at by ps
------------   */
struct scr_item *ps;
{
char ds[100];

pos_cur(ps->x,ps->y);         /* Make sure cursor is properly postitioned */

if(ps->dspl_on && (ps->p_data != (char *)NP))
        {
        (*(ps->fun_dc))(ps,ds,ps->id,ps->p_data);
                                /* Convert data to character form */
        }
```

```
else
        {
        ds[0] = ' ';            /* Blank string */
        ds[1] = 0;
        }

ssize(ds,ps->fw);               /* Make the string the correct length */

if(ps->current &&
        ((display_flag == DATA_ONLY) || (display_flag == DATA_AND_LABEL)))
        {
        putst(ds, dsp_hi, dsp_bl, dsp_in, dsp_color);
        }
else
        {
        /* Write the string */
        putst(ds, ps->hilite, ps->blink, ps->intensify, ps->color);
        }
}


ssize(s,w)      /* Make string s width w
----------      */
char *s;
int w;
{
int l;

if((l = strlen(s)) == w)return;                 /* Nothing to do! */
if(l > w)
        {
        int l_old;

        l_old = l;

        while((l = strlen(s)) > w)
                {
                if(s[l-1] == ' ')s[l-1] = 0;
                else if(s[0] = ' ')
                        {
                        register i;

                        for(i = 0; i < l; i++)s[i] = s[i+1];
                        }
                if(l_old == l)break; /* No change -- get out */
                else    l_old = l;
                }
        if(strlen(s) != w)    /* Still too big?? */
                {
                strcpy(s,"*");
                padl(s,' ',w);/* Print just a * for string too long */
                }
        }
else padl(s,' ',w);             /* Make it bigger by left padding */
}

padl(s,c,w)             /* Left-fill string s with character c
-----------             */
char c,*s;
int w;
{
int ls,i,n;

ls = strlen(s);
if(ls >= w)return;

n = w - ls;             /* Amount of padding */

for(i = ls; i >= 0; i--)     /* Copy original to leave space */
                s[i + n] = s[i];

for(i = 0; i < n; i++)s[i] = c;     /* Fill */
}


disp_lab(ps)    /* Display label for item pointed to by ps
------------    */
struct scr_item *ps;
{
if(ps->lab[0] == 0)return;          /* No label */

pos_cur(ps->x_lab,ps->y_lab);               /* Position cursor at start of label */

if(ps->current &&
        ((display_flag == LABEL_ONLY) || (display_flag == DATA_AND_LABEL)))
        {
                putst(ps->lab, dsp_hi, dsp_bl, dsp_in, dsp_color);
        }
else
        {
        /* Print it */
        putst(ps->lab, ps->hilite, ps->blink, ps->intensify, ps->color);
        }
}

static char s[100],*pps;            /* Storage for incoming message */
static int newstr = 1;              /* Flag to start new message */

read_dat(ps)        /* Read new data for item ps -- return the terminating
------------        character */
struct scr_item *ps;
{
```

```
int c,get_str();

if(newstr)
        {
        pps = s;        /* Initialize for new string */
        *pps = 0;
        newstr = 0;
        }

c = get_str(s,ps->fw,ps->x,ps->y,&pps);    /* Read in the string of characters */

if(c == 0)return(0);               /* No character */

if(strlen(s) > 0)
        {
        if(ps->p_data != (char *)NP)
                (*(ps->fun_cd))(ps,s,ps->id,ps->p_data);
                          /* Convert characters to data */
        newstr = 1;       /* Next character will start a new string */
        }

disp_dat(ps);/* Display the new data */
return(c);
}

get_str(s,w,x,y,ps)          /* Read a string
--------------------          */
char *s,**ps;
int w,x,y;
{
int rtrn = 0;  /* Return flag */
int dum;

for(;;)
        {
        int c;

        c = char_in();          /* Get a character from keyboard in raw mode
                                (no processing, no waiting) */
        if(c == 0)return(c);

        if(key_cur != (struct act_key *)NP) /* Check for an action key */
                {
                struct act_key *pk;

                pk = key_cur;

                while(pk->key_code != 0)     /* Scan the list */
                        {
                        if(c == pk->key_code)
                                {
                                int xcur,ycur;

                                chcur[0] = cch_scr(&xcur,&ycur);
                                /* Get the current cursor position
                                and the character at that position */
                                /*  putst(new_cur, 0,0,0,0); no new cursor */

                                (*(pk->key_fun))();
                                        /* Execute the function */

                                /*  pos_cur(xcur,ycur);    Restore cursor */
                                /* putst(chcur, 0,0,0,0); */
                                                /* Restore the character */
                                return((char)0);
                                /* Return as if no character had been typed */
                                }
                        pk++;
                        }
                }

        switch(c)
                {
                case RETURN:  rtrn = 1;     /* Done */
                              break;

                case DELETE:  /* Back up the buffer by one character */
                        if(*ps > s)
                                {
                                (*ps)--;
                                **ps = ' ';     /* Blank character */
                                pos_cur(x,y);  /* Erase char on screen */
                                putst(s, 0, 0, 0, 0);

                                **ps = 0;       /* Erase character */
                                }
                        break;

                case LINE_DELETE:

                        {
                        int j,n;

                        n = strlen(s);
                        for(j = 0;j < n; j++)s[j] = ' ';
                        pos_cur(x,y);  /* Erase line on screen */
                        putst(s, 0, 0, 0, 0);


                        break;
                        }
```

```
			case UP_ARROW:		/* Treat arrows like returns */
			case DOWN_ARROW:
			case RIGHT_ARROW:
			case LEFT_ARROW:
			case CHAR_EXIT:
				rtrn = 1;
				break;


			default:	/* Put any other character into the buffer */
				*(*ps)++ = c;
				**ps = 0;
			}
		pos_cur(x,y);		/* Print the message so far */
		putst(s, 0,0,0,0);
		if(rtrn)return(c);
		}
}

e_msg(x,y,msg)		/* Print an error message at the indicated point
-------------		*/
int x,y;
char *msg;
{
pos_cur(x,y);
putst(msg, 0,0,0,0);
}


/* Make the scr_item pointed to by psi the current item and then refresh it
	on the screen.  This will cause the item to be refreshed with the
	characteristics related to the current item, as opposed to its
	database characteristics. */
do_current(psi)

struct scr_item		*psi;

{
if(psi)
	{
	psicur = psi;
	psi->current = 1;

	/* Refresh the data after the label so that the cursor gets left
		in a reasonable position. */
	disp_lab(psi);
	disp_dat(psi);
	}
}

/* Set a screen items database to reflect that it is no longer the current
	item, hence it should be refreshed as it is defined in the database,
	not as if it were the current item. */

undo_current(psi)

struct scr_item		*psi;

{
if(psi)
	{
	psi->current = 0;
	disp_lab(psi);
	disp_dat(psi);
	}
}

/* Set the display mode to:
	DATA_ONLY, LABEL_ONLY, or DATA_AND_LABEL

*/

set_display_mode(value)

int	value;

{
display_flag = value;
}
/* Header filer with defintions for the screen management package
Contains structures and other definitions that are generic
(i.e., do not change with compiler/computer)

Last Update:	9-Sept-85
		28-Dec-85, DMA, add id to structure
		18-July-86, DMA, separate machine/compiler dependent
			parts; add function key input for immediate
			action
		23-July-86, DMA, added screen message capability
		17-Jan-88, DMA, added scr_all structure
		18-Jul-88, SMK, changed status vars to shorts, added color

copyright (c) 1985,86,87,88 D. M. Auslander
*/

#define NP (char *)0 /* Null pointer */
#defineLABEL_ONLY		1
#defineDATA_ONLY		0
#defineDATA_AND_LABEL		2
#defineLABEL_SIZE		9

/* Structure for a screen item */
```

```
struct scr_item
        {
        int id;                 /* Identification number */
        int x;                  /* Location of item */
        int y;
        int fw;                 /* Field width for data */
        char *p_data;           /* Pointer to actual data */
        int (*fun_cd)();        /* Pointers to functions that will process the
                                data -- cd is character-to-data (i.e., user
                                input), dc is data-to-character */

        int (*fun_dc)();
        short hilite;           /* Attributes of displayed field */
        short blink;
        short intensify;
        short dspl_on;          /* Display on/off switch */
        short color;
        short current;          /* Is this the current field ? */
        int x_lab;              /* Location of label */
        int y_lab;
        char lab[80];           /* The label itself */
        struct scr_item *up;    /* Pointers to items that are connected via
                                arrow commands */
        struct scr_item *down;
        struct scr_item *right;
        struct scr_item *left;
        struct scr_item *next;       /* Link to next item in full list */
        };

struct scr_msg          /* Structure for screen messages, i.e., information
                        that doesn't change and has no associated data */

        {
        int x_msg;      /* Message starting coordinates */
        int y_msg;
        short hilite;           /* Attributes of displayed field */
        short blink;
        short intensify;
        short dspl_on;          /* Display on/off switch */
        short color;
        char *pmsg;     /* Pointer to the text of the message */
        struct scr_msg *pnxt_msg;    /* Pointer to the next message
                                     in the list (NULL for the last) */

        };

/* Immediate action keys:
When the specified key is struck, the associated function is
executed.  The return is as if no key had been struck.

Structure definition:
*/

struct act_key          /* Terminate list with key_code = 0 */
        {
        int key_code;           /* ASCII code */
        int (*key_fun)();       /* Pointer to the function */
        int key_num;
        char label_1[LABEL_SIZE];
        char label_2[LABEL_SIZE];
        };

/* Screen structure -- all of the elements needed to define a screen */

struct scr_all
        {
        struct scr_item *pf;  /* Pointer to the first item in this screen */
        struct scr_msg *pmessg;       /* Pointer to list of screen messages */
        struct act_key *pkey; /* Action key list */
        int (*pbkgr)();               /* Screen background program */
        };
/* Functions used by the screen management package

scr_ibm.c

This file is for the IBM-PC, using the Microsoft v5 compiler

Last Update: 4-Jan-88
        13-Jan-88, DMA, add extended codes
        18-July-88, DMA, move putst() here and add attributes to it

copyright (c) 1985,86,87,88 D. M. Auslander
*/

#include <graph.h>
#include <dos.h>
#include "scr_def.h"

/* Register structures as defined in dos.h -- (comment here, not code)

struct WORDREGS {
    unsigned int ax;
    unsigned int bx;
    unsigned int cx;
    unsigned int dx;
    unsigned int si;
    unsigned int di;
    unsigned int cflag;
    };

struct BYTEREGS {
    unsigned char al, ah;
    unsigned char bl, bh;
    unsigned char cl, ch;
    unsigned char dl, dh;
```

```
    };

union REGS {
    struct WORDREGS x;
    struct BYTEREGS h;
    };

*/
static struct WORDREGS wregs;       /* Word registers */
static struct BYTEREGS bregs;       /* Byte registers */
static union REGS r;

clr_scr()       /* Clear the screen
---------       */
{
_clearscreen(0);
}

pos_cur(x,y)    /* Position the cursor
------------    */
int x,y;
{
_settextposition(y,x);
}

char_in()       /* Check for a character from the keyboard
---------          Return 0 if no character or the ASCII code if a character
                   is detected */

{
if(kbhit())
        {
        r.h.ah = 7;    /* Get a character */
        intdos(&r,&r);/* Call DOS */
        if(r.h.al != 0)return(r.h.al & 0x7f);        /* Return character value */
        else
                {       /* Get extended code */
                r.h.ah = 7;
                intdos(&r,&r);/* Call again */
                return(r.h.al | 0x80 & 0xff);
                                  /* Set high bit for extended codes */
                }
        }
return(0);      /* No character ready */
}

char cch_scr(px,py)   /* Read the cursor location and the character
-------------------      at that location */
int *px,*py;
{
char scr_sinp();
unsigned int cp;
struct rccoord rc;

rc = _gettextposition();     /* Get the cursor location */
*px = rc.col;
*py = rc.row;
return(scr_sinp());
}

char scr_sinp()              /* Get the character at the current cursor position */
{

r.x.ax = 0x0800;      /* Interrupt 10H function number */
r.x.bx = 0;                  /* Active page */

int86(0x10,&r,&r);

return((char)(r.x.ax & 0xff));       /* Return the character */
}
/* The following not used in screen.c, so not implemented --
rdc_scr(px,py)  Read the cursor position
--------------Returns the cursor mode
int *px,*py;   */

char ch_scr()           /* Read the character at the current cursor position
-------------              */
{
char scr_sinp();

return(scr_sinp());
}


putst(st,hilite,blink,intense,color)   /* Send a NULL terminated string
------------------------------------      to the console. Do not append a newline */
char *st;
int hilite,blink,intense,color;
{
int oldcolor,oldbkg;

if((color > 7) || (color < 1))color = 7;     /* Default to white */

if(hilite)
        {
        if(color == 7)color = 0;
        oldbkg = _getbkcolor();
        _setbkcolor(7L);            /* White background */
        }

if(intense)color += 8;            /* Intensify */
```

```
if(blink)color += 16;
oldcolor = _settextcolor((long)color);
_outtext(st);

if(hilite)_setbkcolor((long)oldbkg);
_settextcolor((long)oldcolor);
}

beginning() /* Initialization
----------- Dummy for IBMPC */
{}

ending()    /* Reset
--------    Dummy for PC */
{}

set_key_label(ik,s1,s2)     /* Display function key labels
-----------------------     */
int ik;
char *s1,*s2;
{
int x;
char buf[10];

x = 10 * (ik - 1);  /* Horizontal location */

pos_cur(x,23);
sprintf(buf,"F%d",ik);
putst(buf,0,0,0,WHITE);

pos_cur(x,24);
putst(s1,0,0,0,WHITE);

pos_cur(x,25);
putst(s2,0,0,0,WHITE);
}

scr_cur_on()    /* Turn the screen cursor on
------------    */
{
_displaycursor(_GCURSORON);
}

scr_cur_off()   /* Turn cursor off
-------------   */
{
_displaycursor(_GCURSOROFF);
}

/* Header filer with definitions for the screen management package
scr_ibme.h

This file is for the IBM-PC

Last Update:  9-Sept-85
              28-Dec-85, DMA, add id to structure
              18-July-86, DMA, Separated machine/compiler dependent
                      definitions from structures
              19-Jan-88, DMA, Changed definitions for extended codes,
                      renamed file to scr_ibme.h

copyright (c) 1985,86,87,88 D. M. Auslander
*/


#define UP_ARROW      0xc8
#define DOWN_ARROW    0xd0
#define RIGHT_ARROW   0xcd
#define LEFT_ARROW    0xcb
#define ESC           0x1b
#define RETURN        0xd
#define DELETE        0x8     /* Backspace */
#define LINE_DELETE   0x1b    /* Escape */
#define BACKSPACE     0x08
#define DEL           0xd3
#define INS           0xd2
#define TAB           0x09
#define HOME          0xc7
#define PGUP          0xc9
#define PGDN          0xd1
#define END           0xcf

        /* Function keys */
#define F1            0xbb
#define F2            0xbc
#define F3            0xbd
#define F4            0xbe
#define F5            0xbf
#define F6            0xc0
#define F7            0xc1
#define F8            0xc2
#define F9            0xc3
#define F10           0xc4

#define CTRL_A        0x01
#define CTRL_B        0x02
#define CTRL_C        0x03
#define CTRL_D        0x04
#define CTRL_E        0x05
#define CTRL_F        0x06
#define CTRL_R        0x12
```

```
#define CHAR_EXIT     0x5    /* Exit character -- cntrl-E */

/* Color Definitions for PC - text */

#define BLACK 0
#define BLUE 1
#define GREEN 2
#define CYAN 3
#define RED 4
#define MAGENTA 5
#define BROWN 6
#define WHITE 7
```

CHAPTER 7

PRIORITY SCHEDULING

The success of the scheduling method used to achieve multi-motor control depends on all of the background control tasks having the same priority and similar sample intervals. Any conflicts between control tasks are resolved implicitly in favor of whatever task happens to be first in the list, or whichever started running slightly earlier. Once one of the control tasks is started, no other control task can be run until the current task is finished. Although restrictive, these conditions permit the use of a scheduler that is quite simple in its structure and can run in the background along with the control tasks. When these conditions cannot be met, a scheduler that can take task priorities into account must be used. A priority-based scheduler can no longer be run in the background, but, because it must be able to suspend the operation of a task when a task of higher priority is scheduled to run, the scheduler must become part of the foreground.

7.1 FOREGROUND/BACKGROUND

Foreground tasks are executed in direct response to hardware interrupts. They are typically very short so that they will not interfere with other foreground tasks. Most foreground tasks are time critical, that is, they must be executed within a short time of the occurrence of the interrupt to avoid loss of data or other malfunctions. In the most critical cases, a foreground task can be run with all other interrupts disabled to assure that it will be completed in time. Foreground tasks are responsible for managing the input and output data streams, doing whatever buffering and processing is necessary. As such, they represent a set of parallel processes. They could each be implemented in a separate processor, or can coexist in the same processor and use the interrupt hardware for scheduling their operation. When the job of one of these tasks becomes too demanding of computational resources, it is common practice to redesign the hardware so that the bulk of the processing takes place on a separate processor.

Terminal character processing is a good example of such a situation. The foreground tasks described in the previous chapter have to be run for every incoming or outgoing character, an acceptable load when one terminal is involved. When a system must communicate with many terminals, however, the load on the CPU to process every character can become a sizeable portion of its capability. At this point, there is the danger of missing some incoming characters (there is no danger of loss of information on the outgoing side; however, the rate at which characters are sent will be reduced). Interface devices are available which alleviate the CPU load by buffering characters from many terminals and only transferring the characters to the computer when it is ready for them.

Background tasks run when no interrupts are being processed. When an interrupt occurs, whatever background task is in progress is suspended while the interrupt is processed, and is resumed when the foreground task finishes. Other than the loss of time, the background task is not affected by the operation of the foreground. Communication between the foreground and background takes place through data buffers and flag variables to signal conditions that initiate or terminate activities. Semaphores, a special case of flag variables, are widely used to coordinate real-time activities.

The scheduler is the bridge between the foreground and background worlds. Its purpose is to control the operation of the background, but it can run as part of either the background or the foreground. It runs in response to any event that requires that a decision be made about which background task should be running. Some interrupts require rescheduling, for example, when a clock timer runs out, and rescheduling is always required when a background task completes its work.

7.2 BACKGROUND PRIORITIES

A simple example of priority scheduling of background tasks occurs when multiple control tasks are being run, as in the discussion of background scheduling in Chapter 5, but when there is substantial variation in the sampling time of the different tasks. This occurs, for example, if the objects being controlled are not all motors, or if motors of different sizes were being controlled. If all of these control tasks are treated with equal priority, then a long sample-time task can be started just before it is time for a short sample-time task to run. The short sample-time task would be delayed until the long sample-time task had completed execution and would then run. If both tasks have the same execution time, as they do in the multi-motor example, the amount of time associated with the delay is independent of which task happens to start first. However, the delay as a fraction of the sample time would be much worse for the short sample-time task. This would adversely affect the dynamic performance of the short sample-time task much more than it would affect the performance of the long sample-time task.

Other instances in which priorities must be assigned to background tasks could occur when the function of the system is expanded. Still within the context of control, several other functions could be added that run on a sample-time basis, as the control modules themselves do. They could include data logging, system identification, control optimization, management information system functions, and so on. Data logging, for instance, would run as a task scheduled for regular sample intervals. Each time it ran it would collect information from a variety of instruments and write that information to a disk file, tape, printer, or other logging device. This information provides historical information on plant operation that can be used to diagnose the causes of malfunctions, improve plant operation, design new controller algorithms, and so on. It would be scheduled along with the control tasks, but definitely has lower priority whenever a timing conflict arises. If background scheduling were to be used, once the logger started running it would lock out a waiting control task until it finished.

An additional issue that makes foreground scheduling desirable is the way in which the low-priority background ("deep background" task) is handled. With background scheduling, there is a trade-off between having the deep background interfere with the control tasks, or leaving idle CPU time as a buffer between the control and low-priority background. The only way to satisfy both alternatives is to have a priori knowledge of the computing time required by the deep background so that it will not be started if any interference would result. Not all tasks have a predictable computing time, so that solution is not general. It also involves an undesirable level of complexity.

Dealing with the low-priority background is greatly simplified when foreground scheduling is used, because a low-priority task can be pre-empted whenever a control task is ready to run. This scheduling method also improves the CPU usage because low-priority background tasks can be started at any time without concern for interference.

7.3 FOREGROUND SCHEDULING

The role of the scheduler can be deduced from a typical timing diagram of the events and tasks that constitute a control system. In this example, assume that there are two control tasks, C1 and C2, with C1 having higher priority than C2, no deep background tasks, one hardware timer that is producing "ticks" that are being used to time the control sampling interval, a timer interrupt service task, T1, and the scheduler itself. Figure 7.1 shows a typical sequence; the column labelled

"CPU" indicates the task that gains control of the CPU as a result of the indicated event. Time runs from top to bottom.

EVENT	CPU
–	C2
Timer interrupt	T1
T1 finished (tick counted)	C2
Timer interrupt	T1
Time count at zero	SCH
C1 scheduled to run, C2 suspended	C1
Timer interrupt	T1
T1 finished	C1
C1 finished	SCH
C2 resumed	C2
Timer interrupt	T1
T1 finished	C2
C2 finished	SCH
Neither C1 nor C2 scheduled	idle
...	

Figure 7.1

Most of the timer interrupts are treated entirely in the foreground. The timer interrupt function runs and decrements the counter that it is using to keep track of the time to the next scheduling event. When it is done, as long as that counter has not run out, there is no need to reschedule the control tasks. Rescheduling can be initiated from the foreground or from the background. When the timing counter does run out, the scheduler is initiated from the foreground. When a control task finishes, the scheduler is invoked from the background.

When a low-priority background is involved, it will be scheduled to run when no other foreground or background tasks are running. In the timing chart of Figure 7.1, the low-priority background would be run when the CPU becomes "idle."

7.4 TASK STRUCTURE FOR CONTROL

The task structure discussed so far has evolved from the needs of the multi-motor control problem. By extending the control problem to the control of a variety of control objects, all with different characteristic time scales, the need for foreground scheduling is established. The control tasks run at regular time intervals so the scheduler is designed for tasks that can be rescheduled immediately after the clock runs out. The actual rescheduling is done by the scheduler, so this structure minimizes latency error while also reducing the programming tasks required of the user.

The deep background is used for lower priority tasks. In work thus far, it has served as the means of controlling the user's console. There are, however, other tasks of similar priority that should also be handled in the background. These might include reading and writing to the system storage volumes (disk or tape), performing statistical analysis of historical data, generating graphic displays, and the like. All of these tasks have the common property that they should run as often as possible, but that as long as they are not delayed for too long, there is no need to run on a fixed schedule. These tasks can be accommodated by generalizing the deep background scheduling to include more than one task, all with equal priority. Their peculiar needs can be satisfied with a scheduling algorithm that gives each one a "time slice," that is, access to the CPU for a fixed amount of time. When that time is up, the task is suspended and the next task gets its turn.

Two variants of time-slice scheduling can be used. One, which is particularly applicable to the control environment, is that each task has a fixed time slice, and always gets the same time slice. In control problems, many of these low-priority background tasks run as long as the control system is operational. The task that manages the console interface is a good example. In other cases, however, the task has a fixed mission and will suspend itself when that mission is accomplished. In these cases, it is a good idea to give some form of priority to tasks that are short, with lower priority to those that will require large amounts of computing time. This information is not always known in advance (and it is also possible that advance information, if given, might not be accurate), so a simple priority scheme can be set up in which all tasks start with equal priority. After each time slice, if the task is not completed, its priority is lowered and its time slice is lengthened. Longer tasks will thus get the efficiency of longer time slices at the expense of lower priority.

Many low-priority tasks will depend on information from other background tasks or from foreground tasks. Each task is responsible for making its own connections with whatever information sources it needs. If the information is not available, the task will have to suspend itself.

Figure 7.2 shows an expanded timing sequence for a system that includes time-sliced, low-priority background tasks. As in Figure 7.2, the control tasks are C1 and C2 (C1 has higher priority), timer T1 is used for the control scheduling, and SCH denotes the control scheduler. In addition, there is another timer, T2, two low-priority background tasks, D1 and D2, and a deep background scheduler, DSCH.

The presence of the low-priority background tasks in this timing sequence appears when the control tasks are idle. Each of the tasks is run for its time slice, as long as no control tasks want to run. In order to make the time kept by timer 2 correspond to the actual CPU time used by the low-priority task rather than to elapsed time, the count maintained by the timer 2 interrupt service routine is only decremented when low-priority tasks are actually running. Otherwise, it would be possible for a deep background task to start running and be interrupted almost immediately by a control task that might use up all of its time slice!

EVENT	CPU
—	C2
Timer 1 interrupt	T1
Counter out of time	SCH
C1 ready to run	C1
Timer 1 interrupt	T1
Interrupt service routine done	C1
Timer 2 interrupt	T2
Interrupt service routine done (no count because Control is running)	C1
C1 finished	SCH
Resume C2	C2
Timer 1 interrupt	T1
Interrupt service routine done	C2
C2 done	SCH
No control tasks pending	DSCH
Run D1 for time slice	D1
Timer 1 interrupt	T1
Interrupt service routine done	D1
Timer 2 Interrupt	T2
Interrupt service routine done (with count on)	D1
Timer 1 Interrupt	T1
Interrupt service routine done	D1
Timer 2 Interrupt	T2
Time slice finished	DSCH
Suspend D1, start D2	D2
...	

Figure 7.2

If other interrupts were active, such as the console, encoder inputs, other timers, etc., they would also appear in the time sequence table. Since all of the tasks are responsible for their own communication and information retrieval, none of these other interrupt service routines can cause the scheduler to run. Because of this, the low-priority background tasks cannot interrupt each other to service asynchronous events, so they must all have the same priority when running, except for the priority that is associated with the assignment of time slices.

Another consequence of the presence of additional asynchronous tasks is that the main scheduler would have to be run with interrupts enabled so that very high priority interrupts such as encoders would not be missed. In such circumstances, the scheduler must be protected against one of its timers running out before it has had a chance to complete the scheduling. This can be done by disabling the scheduling timer(s) while the scheduler itself is running.

7.5 TIME-BASED, FIXED-PRIORITY SCHEDULING

Before proceeding with the more general scheduling algorithm, we can use material that has already been discussed to develop a scheduling algorithm that is relatively simple and will work well for many control problems. The basis for the algorithm is the software implementation of multiple timers. In its simplest form, the multiple timer software will call a specified function whenever its software timer runs out. The function called is part of the foreground because it is executed in response to an interrupt. As such, it is not normally suitable for running a control algorithm, which will not be short enough to avoid interfering with other foreground functions.

This can, however, be remedied by noting that for a task to be part of the background it must be completely interruptable and re-entrant. That is, the state of the interrupt controller must be such that any interrupts that arrive will be honored. This can be accomplished with most interrupt control hardware by sending an end-of-interrupt signal to the interrupt control hardware *before* calling the function that implements the control algorithm.

With this modification, interrupts can be serviced while the control algorithm (or any other task that can be time-scheduled) is running. Care must be taken, though, to make sure that both the interrupt service functions (the low-level functions that save registers, etc.) and the time-based scheduler are completely re-entrant. Although the control task has been "redefined" to be part of the background, until it finishes there has been no "return" from the original interrupt from the clock event that initiated it. Thus, from the point of view of re-entrance properties, the control task remains part of the foreground!

Finally, the issues of priorities and task pre-emption must be considered. Priorities can be handled by adding a priority indication to the data structure describing each of the control tasks. For every clock tick, all of the software counters are decremented. Of those that have reached zero, including the task currently running (if there is one), the task having the highest priority is executed. If, while a task is running, another task with higher priority reaches the "ready-to-run" state, the current task is pre-empted and the higher priority task is run. The task that was running remains in the suspended state caused by the clock interrupt. Thus, no special consideration has to be given to the "pre-emption" case.

The normal interrupt actions that save process states are sufficient to preserve the pre-empted task's state until it gets a chance to complete.

The scheduling algorithm is shown in Fig. 7.3, and Fig. 7.4 gives the data structure used by the scheduler to maintain status information about each of the tasks.

```
->Timer Interrupt:

    Update running time

    For all timers
        If timer is active and
        if it is not locked
            decrement timer count

    Find highest priority among pending tasks
    and among tasks currently in service

    Send End-of-Interrupt signal to hardware
    interrupt controller

    If the highest priority task is pending (i.e.,
    a task that hasn't been started yet)
        Call that task

    Return
```

Figure 7.3

This scheduling method can be extended to cover interrupts from sources other than the clock, but it remains restricted to problems for which the priorities do not change dynamically. The reason for this is that the intermediate storage for state information of in-service but suspended tasks is done in the same manner as any other interrupt tasks, using the stack. As long as tasks are reactivated in the reverse of the order in which they were suspended, the state information will be restored properly. Otherwise, it will not be restored properly and the system will crash.

7.6 TASK SUSPENSION

In general, task suspension and reactivation is not as orderly as it is when background or fixed-priority scheduling is used. The effective priority of a task can change several times during its execution, making it impossible to guarantee the last-suspended/first-activated order necessary for use of a single stack. An example of this occurs when several tasks make use of some system resource that can only be used by one task at a time. If the resource is busy, and another task needs it, that task must be suspended until the resource is available. In effect, the priority of the task is lowered while it waits for the needed resource. Doing this requires that the system memory area, used to keep track of variables that are local to functions, function and interrupt return information, function arguments, and other system housekeeping (the task execution *context*), must be explicitly manipulated and saved by the scheduler by using a separate stack area for each task. Running the scheduler in the background is less complex in this regard because tasks are always complete before the scheduler gets to run again, so there is no intermediate information to be saved.

Task Data Structure:

Long Integer	Countdown-timer
Logic	Active-Flag
Logic	Lock-Flag
Integer	Priority
Logic	In-Service-Flag
Pointer-to-Function	Service Function
Pointer-to-Structure	Data to be serviced

Figure 7.4

7.7 STACKS

Stacks were introduced in Chapter 4 as a means of assigning local memory to functions as they are called, and then relinquishing the memory for re-use on returning. Stacks serve the same purpose for interrupts, preserving the state information of the function being interrupted and providing local storage for the interrupt service function(s) to run.

They are implemented by a combination of special-purpose registers and general-purpose memory. A register is used as a *stack pointer* to establish the access to the stack. The content of that register is the address in memory of the top of the stack (or, depending on the implementation details, the address of the memory location one past the top of the stack). It is thus a pointer to either the last item put on the stack or a pointer to the place where the next item placed on the stack will be put. In actual implementations, the stack can grow either "up," that is, from lower numbered memory locations to higher numbered locations, or "down." The principle is unchanged and the term "top" is used in either case for the item most recently added to the stack. The terms pop and push are often used to refer to putting items on the stack or taking them off.

The use of stacks in computer systems is almost universal for function calls. To illustrate, we can first use a function call in which no arguments (parameters) are passed and no local variables are used. The main problem to take care of in a function call is preserving the information about where the call came from so that the function can return to the calling program. The computer's hardware implementation of the function call is usually designed to make use of the stack pointer register for this purpose. The sequence of events is illustrated in Fig. 7.5, which shows the state of the stack (and stack pointer) before, during, and after the call.

Before the call, the stack pointer is directed to the last-used location in the stack (i.e., the top of the stack); information already in the stack is designated by x's and is not of relevance to the function call except to note that it is not disturbed. At the time of the execution of the call instruction, the CPU saves the return address by putting it on the stack. This happens within the hardware implementation of the call instruction. The return address is the address of the instruction that would have been executed next had the call not been executed. This is the place that processing should resume when the called function completes its work. That address is maintained in another CPU register, the *program counter* (PC). The stack pointer is first incremented, and then the return address is copied into memory at the place the stack pointer is referencing ("pointing" to).

```
              SP->  Return Address
SP-> xxx            xxx                SP-> xxx


  Before          During                 After
```

Figure 7.5

When the function executes a return instruction, the process is reversed. The return address is copied from the stack to the program counter and the stack pointer is decremented.

It is critical to the success of this procedure that the state of the stack at the time the return instruction is executed be the same as it was just after the call was executed. If it isn't, the return trail will be lost and the return will be to the wrong place!

Interrupts are implemented in exactly the same fashion. At the time of the interrupt, the CPU performs the equivalent of a call instruction in order to start the interrupt service routine running. Other information, such as CPU flags, might be saved on the stack at the same time. The return from an interrupt causes the instruction that would have been executed if the interrupt had not occurred to be executed, which is the same as the return from a function. In addition, there might be some additional elements to an interrupt return that reset the interrupt hardware.

This structure can handle nested calls with no difficulty. Each time a call is used, the stack looks exactly as it does in the BEFORE section of the figure. The top of stack information (xxx) is the most recently generated return address. Each new call will add a new return address to the stack. The depth of nesting is limited only by the amount of memory space that is allocated to the stack. Each return instruction drops the stack down one level. Fig. 7.6 shows the stack through the calling sequence F1->F2->F3 and associated returns. The return addresses are written as R1, R2, and R3. The function identified as "calling" is the function that first called F1. As calls and returns are intermixed, the stack grows and shrinks.

				SP-> R3
			SP-> R2	R2
		SP-> R1	R1	R1
	SP-> xxx	xxx	xxx	xxx
Function executing	calling	F1	F2	F3

(a) Calling

	SP-> R3			
	R2	SP-> R2		
	R1	R1	SP-> R1	
	xxx	xxx	xxx	SP-> xxx
Function executing	F3	F2	F1	calling

(b) Returning

Figure 7.6

7.8 ARGUMENTS AND LOCAL VARIABLES

The next step in the protocol for function calling is taking care of the arguments that are passed from the calling program to the called program. The actual mechanisms for doing this are dependent on the specific compiler being used, but the method described here which uses the stack is very common. Before making the function call, all of the arguments are put onto the stack. The call is then made, which puts the return address on the stack also. Parameters are accessed relative to where the stack pointer was at the entry point. This is done by saving the stack pointer in a CPU register that is used specifically for that purpose. Since all functions will be using that register in the same way, it must be saved by having its contents put on the stack before copying the stack pointer. Depending on the CPU design, different registers can be used for this purpose. To maintain generality, we will refer to it as the *stackframe* register. Any other registers to be saved can then be copied to the stack also, and the function can then be executed. Fig. 7.7 shows this sequence of events as a function is called and begins execution.

Local variables are handled in a similar manner. Before beginning execution, the stack pointer is moved ahead to leave space for any local variables that will be used by the function. The local variables can then be stored or retrieved by accesses relative to the stack frame register's contents.

(a) The calling function:

Put the arguments onto the stack
Call the function
Remove the arguments from the stack

(b) The called function:

Save the stack frame register by putting it onto the stack
Copy current stack pointer to stack frame register
Make room for local variables by incrementing the stack pointer

Execute the body of the function

Restore the stack pointer to its original state by copying the stack frame pointer to the stack pointer
Restore the stack frame register
Return

Figure 7.7

When the function is ready to return, the procedure is reversed. Copying the stack frame register back to the stack pointer has the effect of making the space used by the local variables available for use again and of "cleaning up" the stack by restoring the stack pointer to its original state. Because the state of the stack must be exactly the same at the time of the return as it was at the time of entry, using the stack frame pointer assures the integrity of the stack regardless of what the function has done (unless the function erased the return information). The function can also use the stack to save and restore any registers that it will use if the conventions of the particular compiler require that the registers be saved.

Putting the storage space for the local variables on the stack also satisfies the requirements of recursion and reentrance. Each time the function is re-entered, either via a recursion or as a result of being called from more than one interrupt level, a new stack frame is created, thereby providing new storage space for the local variables. Each version of the function has its own private storage space so that the intermediate information from previously called copies of the function is not disturbed.

7.9 PRIVATE STACKS

All of these procedures are normally taken care of by the compiler and are completely invisible to the programmer using a high-level language. When each function returns, the stack is cleaned up and made ready for the next function call. When foreground scheduling is used, however, tasks can be suspended because a task of higher priority is ready to run. Furthermore, suspended tasks can be restarted in any order since priorities can change dynamically. Thus, a suspended task could have its preserved information in the middle of the stack at the time it is restarted, rather than on the top of the stack. This would make restarting it impossible because there would be no room for additional information on the stack without destroying information left there by other suspended tasks. For that reason, each task is given its own private stack space, usually by allocating space from the free memory pool.

7.10 THE TASK CONTROL BLOCK

All of the primary information about each task, and the information that is saved whenever the task is suspended, is maintained in the task's control block. Figure 7.8 displays the data structure of the task control block. The task identification number and task name are used to display system status to the operator and to allow operator intervention. Two entries in the task control block are dependent on the actual CPU used: the array used to save the registers, task_reg[], and the item used for the flags, task_flags. The size and nature of these entries will be different if a different CPU is used.

Two separate areas are reserved for stack operations. The first, the user stack area, is the active stack area that is used by the task while it is executing. The other is the system stack area. It is used to save the system stack that existed at the time the task was activated. This assures that when the task finishes or is suspended, the system stack can be restored to its previous state. The final entry in the task control block is a pointer to the next block in the queue.

Structure Task_Control_Block

integer	task_id	(ID number)
character	task_name[]	
integer	task_priority	
integer	task_registers[]	
integer	task_flags	
pointer-to-function	task_func()	(function to be executed when this task is activated)
pointer-to-data	task_data	(data structure that is passed to task_func() when it is activated)
integer	task_type	(Type of task, i.e., control, time-slice, etc.)
integer	task_state	(Current state of this task's activity)
long integer	time_left	(Amount of time left until this task is to be activated)
long integer	sample_time	
pointer-to-integer	user_stack	[Pointer to the space reserved for the stack used by task_func()]
integer	user_stack_size	
pointer-to-integer	system_stack	(Space to preserve the system stack as it was found on activation of this task)
integer	system_stack_size	
pointer-to-structure	next_task	(Pointer to the next task in the queue)

Figure 7.8

CONTROL OF A THERMAL SYSTEM

7.11 INTRODUCTION

The simplified scheduling method, using fixed priority scheduling, is used in this sample program to control a simulated thermal system. The program is constructed in such a way that it can be converted into a controller for a real thermal system by substituting appropriate I/O functions for the simulation functions.

A second goal is the development of a graphic user interface. It shows process information on the screen in a graphic format, and allows user interaction through the use of arrow keys to increase or decrease certain values in the program or change program operating mode. The design of this screen display interface relies on a data structure definition to represent the information needed for each component of the display.

7.12 PROGRAM FILES

The program has three main sections: the main program that implements the control, the section that implements the graphic screen display, and the real-time scheduler.

The file associated with the control system is:

therm.c	The main program.

The files associated with the graphic display are:

pdsp.c	The graphic display functions.
display.h	Data structures for the graphic display.
dparam.h	Parameter definitions.
con_msc.c	The machine-specific graphic functions.

The functions that take care of the real time scheduling are:

time.c	The scheduler and associated support functions.
time.h	Scheduler definitions.
config.h	Configuration information.
8259.h	Hardware-dependent definitions for the IBM-PC family interrupt controller.
xignal.h	Definitions for the interrupt software.

The file

envir.h establishes environmental definitions for all program components.

The "make" file shown in Fig. 7.9 an be used to compile the program.

```
#
# Program: Therm
#

.c.obj: cl -c  -Gs $*.c

therm.obj : therm.c display.h dparam.h xignal.h envir.h

pdsp.obj : pdsp.c

con_msc.obj : con_msc.c

time.obj : time.c envir.h config.h time.h 8259.h

alarm.obj : alarm.c alarm.h inout.h

therm.exe : therm.obj pdsp.obj con_msc.obj time.obj alarm.obj xignal.lib
        link therm pdsp con_msc time alarm,therm,,xignal /NOI;
```

Figure 7.9

7.13 CONTROL OBJECT

The system to be controlled consists of an electrical heater and an object to be heated, which can be envisioned as a hotplate and a pot. A power amplifier produces a voltage across the heater in response to a command voltage from the computer's digital-to-analog converter. Two temperatures are read, one from the pot and one from the heater, which are read into the computer through its analog-to-digital converter (see Fig.7.10)

In order to introduce more generality into the program, so it can be used almost anywhere, the control is done for a simulated object rather than using the actual thermal system. The simulation uses the following differential equations to describe the system:

$$\frac{d\theta_1}{dt} = -\frac{q_{12} + q_{10}}{C_1} \tag{7.1}$$

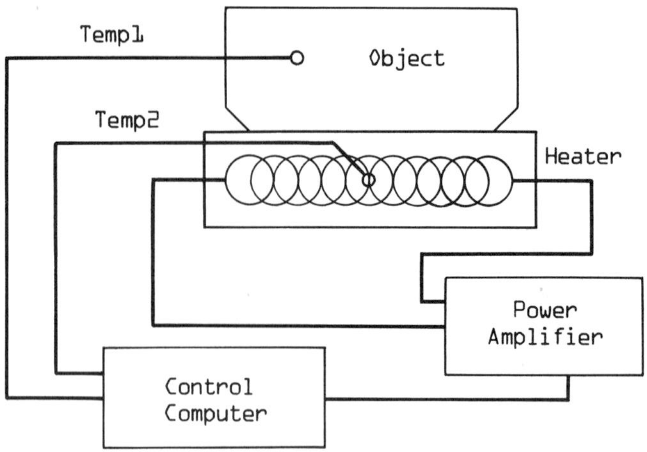

Figure 7.10 Thermal System.

and

$$\frac{d\theta_2}{dt} = \frac{q_{12} - q_{20} + q_v}{C_2} \tag{7.2}$$

where

$$\theta_1 \text{ and } \theta_2$$

are the temperatures of the object and heater, and the q's are heat transfer rates, which are linearly proportional to temperature differences, except for the heater coil input, which depends on voltage

$$q_v = \frac{V^2}{R_h} \tag{7.3}$$

Numerical solution of these equations is accomplished in the simulation by use of the Euler integration algorithm, and is implemented in the function sim_h(). Each time sim_h() is called, the simulation is carried forward by one time step.

7.14 THE CONTROLLER

A cascade control structure is used, with proportional plus integral control algorithms (PI) in each loop. The inner loop is used to control the heater temperature, which changes more quickly than the pot temperature. This is the same control structure that was used for motor position control in Chapter 3; the PI control algorithm was discussed in Chapter 2.

The PI control algorithm itself is implemented in the function pi_cntrl(), which accepts as arguments the information needed for the control. Both the integrator value and the final output are changed, so they both appear in the argument list as pointers (i.e., their addresses are passed).

The functions loop1() and loop2() compute the respective error values for each loop and then call pi_cntrl(). Note that loop2() uses the output of loop1() as its setpoint. This means that if the two are run at the same time, loop1() should be run first. This restriction must be taken into account when assigning priorities for real-time operation.

7.15 "PURE" SIMULATION

These functions are all that is required to simulate the system behavior. A main routine must be added to set values for the parameters, run the simulation and control functions in appropriate sequence, and print results.

Running the functions in correct sequence is dependent on the nature of each. The simulation function represents the solution to an ordinary differential equation. The numerical solution is discretized in time. The accuracy of the resulting solution depends on the step size, which is represented by the variable *dt* in the program. As long as *dt* is small enough, the solution will not depend on the actual value of *dt*. Thus, when the program is run in a loop, sim_h() is run every time, with each time around the loop advancing time by *dt*.

The control algorithms, however, are designed for digital controller implementation and thus are inherently discrete in time. They should only be run when the sample interval is over. The sample intervals for the two loops are tsmp1 and tsmp2.

Figure 7.11 shows a fragment of a program to do the simulation. There are three timing variables. $t1$ and $t2$ count time for each of the control loops and are checked to cause the controller to run. Running time, t, is incremented within sim_h().

7.16 REAL-TIME OPERATION

In the actual system, three different operating modes are provided. The first is the simulation mode shown above. The variable "rltm" controls the real-time mode; mode 0 is the pure simulation mode. Mode 2 is the full real-time mode, and mode 1 is an intermediate which uses the same scheduler as the real-time mode but does not actually invoke any interrupts.

The scheduler used is the chronos system described in this chapter. It provides for fixed priority scheduling and is ideal for control tasks. Setting up for scheduling requires a call to the function NewDTimer() to allocate a soft-timer for each task and a call to SetDTimer() to establish the time to the next run for each task. The scheduling is shown in Fig. 7.12. InitTime() is the function that chronos uses to initialize all its internal variables. The argument tells chronos how much time, in milliseconds, there is between ticks of the real time clock.

```
for(;;)
        {
        if(t1 >= tsmp1)
                {
                loop1();            /* Control */
                t1 = 0.0;
                }
        if(t2 >= tsmp2)
                {
                loop2();
                t2 = 0.0;
                }
        t1 += dt;
        t2 += dt;
        sim_h();           /* Run the simulation */
        if(t > t_end)break;        /* Check for end of simulation */
        }
```

Figure 7.11

If the true real-time mode is in effect, after the tasks have been scheduled the internal clock is set (setalarm()) and the interrupts are armed by signal(). If the intermediate mode (rltm = 1) is used, this last step is skipped, and chronos is called from the background loop.

Each time a task is called, it must schedule its next interrupt with another call to SetDTimer(). This is shown for the loop1 controller in Fig.7.13

7.17 MUTUAL EXCLUSION

Whenever information is interchanged between different priority levels, care must be taken that critical transfers are not interrupted midway, leading to possibilities of inconsistent and corrupted information. This is done by calling functions to do all such transfers, rather than just reading or writing the relevant variables. These functions, such as get_ref1(), set_m1(), etc., disable interrupts for the data transfer and then re-enable them when the data has been transferred to a local variable.

7.18 AUTOMATIC/MANUAL OPERATION

Most control systems provide two operating modes: an automatic mode in which the controller is active, and a manual mode in which the operator controls the actuation output directly, in this case the voltage to the power amplifier. In this system, the mode is controlled by the variable "cmode," cmode=0 for manual and

```
InitTime(mstick);          /* Initialize chronos */

if((tn0 = NewDTimer(sim_h,&dum,100)) < 0)
        {
        printf("Can't allocate timer\n");
        exit();
        }
SetDtimer(tn0,(long)(1000.0 * dt));                /* Set sample interval */

if((tn1 = NewDTimer(loop1,&dum,90)) < 0)
        {
        printf("Can't allocate timer\n");
        exit();
        }
SetDtimer(tn1,(long)(1000.0 * tsmp1));             /* Set sample interval */


if((tn2 = NewDTimer(loop2,&dum,80)) < 0)
        {
        printf("Can't allocate timer\n");
        exit();
        }
SetDtimer(tn2,(long)(1000.0 * tsmp2));             /* Set sample interval */
...

if(rltm == 2)
        {
        setalarm(mstick);              /* set the system clock */
        xignal(XIGTMR,chronos);        /* Turn on the interrupt */
        }
```

Figure 7.12

cmode=1 for automatic. In manual mode, the operation of the control tasks is blocked. (This is done in the pure simulation, by just not calling them, and in the scheduled cases by stopping the timers associated with the control tasks by calling StopDTimer().)

7.19 OPERATOR INTERFACE

For normal operation of a system such as this, the operator needs to be able to get a quick visual check of the system status, to be able to change the setpoint if in automatic mode or the actuation output in manual mode, and to change the mode. These all operate as the background part of the control

```
loop1(pdum)              /* Outer loop
——                  */
int *pdum;               /* Dummy argument from scheduler */
{
float mm;

if(rltm >= 1)SetDtimer(tn1,(long)(1000.0 * tsmp1));
                         /* Set sample interval */
errt1 = get_ref1() - get_th1();
pi_cntrl(errt1,&i1,i1min,i1max,kp1,ki1,m1min,m1max,&mm);
set_m1(mm);
}
```

Figure 7.13

program, using whatever CPU time is left over from operation of the simulation and control tasks.

The output portion of the operator interface is handled by a general-purpose graphical display program. It establishes and maintains displays consisting of a vertical bar whose length changes as the value of an associated variable changes, and a short horizontal bar whose vertical position changes with the value of an associated variable. On displays that support it, the color of these moving elements can be selected. Printed values of the variables can also be enabled; they move with the display.

Figure 7.14 shows a screen image (from an IBM CGA in 640x200 monochrome mode) of the operator display. Three complexes are on the screen, along with several operator messages. The leftmost complex is the pot temperature, the main object of the control. The vertical line gives the temperature and the associated moving bar gives the setpoint. At the moment shown, the process temperature was slightly below the setpoint. The middle complex gives the output voltage, that is, the actuation output. It has no second variable so the short horizontal bar is not displayed. The righthand complex gives the temperature and setpoint for heater.

The display as shown also has printed values for all the variables displayed. This tends to clutter the display, but is very useful for debugging work. The printed values can be turned off easily.

The two text fields in the screen give the time (in seconds, since the system was turned on) and the control mode (automatic or manual).

7.20 DISPLAY FUNCTIONS

The display package is broken into two parts. One part is used to make specific calls to graphics hardware to draw lines, position the cursor, and print text. It is system dependent and has to be rewritten for each new system for which it is used.

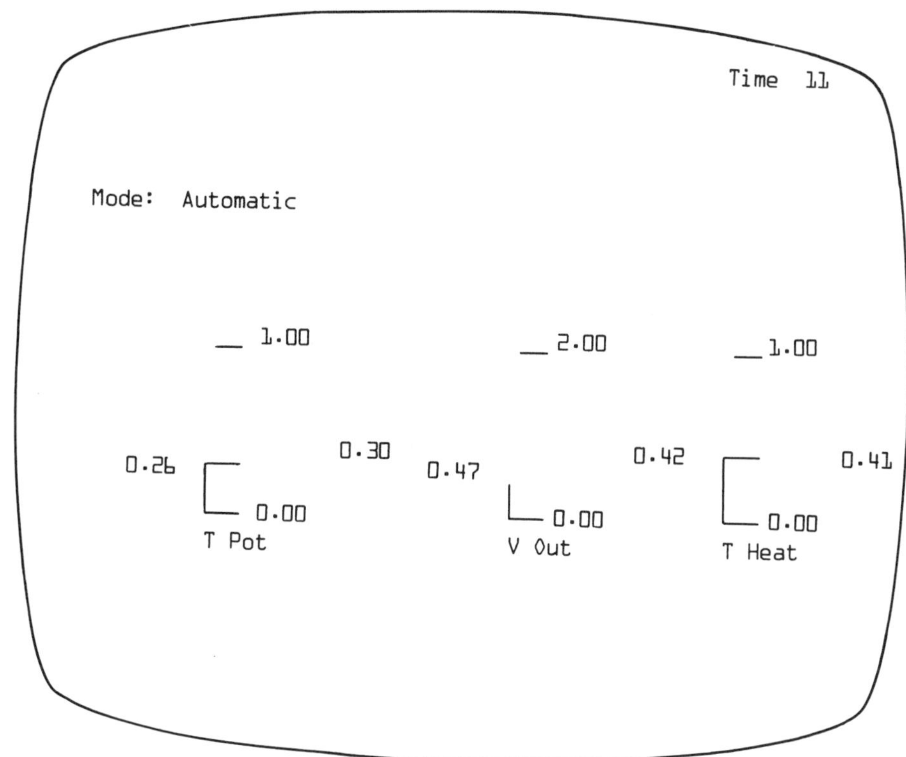

Figure 7.14 Screen Display

The other part is independent of the particular graphics display used. It controls the display generation and maintenance. Each display complex is described by a data structure, shown in Figure 7.15.

All of the information associated with one display complex is contained in one structure of this type. The first item tells the display manager what function to call to get the current value of each of the variables associated with this complex, followed by the coordinates specifying where the complex is to be located on the screen. Vbot and vtop specify the top and bottom scales. Note that it is assumed that the two associated variables have the same scale and units, as with a temperature and its setpoint. Other information gives the text for the labels, and the color of the graphic part of the display plus some variables that are used internally by the display manager function.

The user program can either manipulate the elements of this structure directly, or use a function to set them. The function is used by the thermal system control program. Each display requires that memory be allocated for its data structure, then the definition of the elements of the display. This is shown in Figure 7.16.

```
struct display
{
        float (*fv1)(),(*fv2)();  /* Functions called to get data */
        float x,y;                /* Position of the bottom of
                                     the vertical bar */
        float vbot,vtop;          /* Variable values at the top and bottom of the
                                     line */
        float val1,val2;          /* Stored data values */
        float lngth;              /* Line length (in cm) */
        int lcolor;               /* Data display color */
        char *label;              /* Label for this display */
        char *fmt;                /* String with format to convert data */
        char *dblnk;              /* String of blanks to erase old data */
        float l1old,l2old;        /* Saved values of the graphic locations */
        int v1line,v1data,v2bar,v2data;
                                  /* Flags indicating whether associated
                                     information should be displayed */
};

typedef struct display DISPLAY;
```

Figure 7.15

```
struct display d1,d2,d3;

/* Definition of dsp_set, for reference: */
/* dsp_set(pd,x,y,label,lngth,lcolor,vbot,vtop,fv1,fv2,fmt,dblnk)*/

/* First display, pot temperature */
dsp_set(&d1,3.0,2.,"T_Pot",6.,1,0.0,1.0,get_th1,get_ref1,"%4.2f","     ");

/* Second display, voltage to heater */
dsp_set(&d2,10.0,2.,"V_Out",6.,2,0.0,2.0,get_act,fv2b,"%4.2f","     ");
dsp_flag(&d2,1,1,0,0);    /* No second variable */

/* Third display, heater temperature */
dsp_set(&d3,15.0,2.,"T_Heat",6.,3,0.0,1.0,get_th2,get_ref2,"%4.2f","     ");
```

Figure 7.16

The dsp_set() function sets up the elements of the data structure according to the argument list shown in the commented definition. Get_th1, get_ref1, etc., are the names of the functions that return values for process variables. For each call, the first argument is the address of the data structure for that display. This allows the display manager software to be as general as possible; it can simultaneously maintain any number of displays.

The call to dsp_flag() changes the default settings for the flags, which is to display text and graphics for both variables. For the output voltage display, only the first variable is to be displayed (the second is a dummy and isn't used).

Generation of the actual display is done in two stages. In the first stage, the screen is initialized with a call to init_scr() and then the static part of the display is drawn with a call to dsp_init(). Its only argument is the address of the data structure. In the second stage, dsp_data() is used to show the changing part of the display. It also takes the address of the data structure as its argument. Finally, when the display is to be shut off, the screen is restored to its previous mode with a call to rst_scr().

The detailed operation of the display management functions is in the file pdsp.c.

7.21 OPERATOR INPUT

The operator input to run the process is very simple. In most cases, only a single variable is to be manipulated—the setpoint or the output voltage. This is done with the arrow keys; up-arrow increases the value, down-arrow decreases it. If large changes are needed, a shift-arrow is used. When in automatic mode, the arrow keys control the setpoint, while in manual mode, they control the output voltage.

The only other input is to change mode. The "m" key changes to manual and the "a" key changes to automatic (lower or upper case). These keys are read in using a nonblocking input function called char_in(). It returns a zero if no character is available, so the program never waits for the user to type.

The character input function is system dependent and is included with the system dependent screen functions. In many cases, the keyboard interrupt is already buffered by the operating system, so all that is necessary is an appropriate call to the operating system. For the example here, using PCDOS, this is the case. If the operating system will not buffer characters, or if there isn't any operating system, the keyboard interrupt must be set up explicitly.

```
/*****************************************************************
Real time simulation of a thermal control system

File: therm.c

This program schedules a simulation of a thermal control system to
run at highest priority, with its controller running at lower priority.

The background uses the screen graphic display package to maintain a
display of the system's state and to get operator input for changing setpoint
or control mode.


copyright (c) 1987, D.M. Auslander

Created: 30-June-87

Updates:
       12-July-87, DMA, initial debugging
       14-July-87, DMA, add scheduling
       18-Aug-88, DMA, modified for Microsoft C and xignal
*/

#include <stdio.h>
#include "display.h"
#include "dparam.h"
#include "envir.h"
#include "xignal.h"

#define UP 0xc8         /* Key definitions */
#define RIGHT 0xcd
#define LEFT 0xcb
#define DOWN 0xd0
#define SH_UP 0x38    /* Note that these (shifted arrows) are not unique */
#define SH_DOWN 0x32

extern float get_th1(),get_ref1(),get_act(),get_th2(),get_ref2(),get_m1();
extern float fv2b();
extern int loop1(),loop2(),sim_h(); /* Functions that are scheduled */
extern int chronos();         /* Scheduler */

static float v2a,v2b; /* Dummy variables */
static int rltm = 2;  /* Flag to indicate real time operation
                      0 - Pure simulation
                      1 - Use scheduler, but no clock interrupt
                      2 - Full real time, with clock
                      */
static int cmode = 1; /* Control mode; 0 - manual, 1 - automatic */
static float t;              /* Running time */
static float t1,t2;  /* Computation of sampling interval for non-real-time */
static float dv = 0.02,dvl = 0.1,dm = 0.02,dml = 0.1;     /* Increment
                                        associated with arrow keys */

/* Simulation system variables: */

static float th1;     /* object (pot) temperature */
static float th2;     /* heater temperature */
static float th0;     /* ambient temperature */
static float k12;     /* heat transfer coefficient, object-to-heater */
static float k10;     /* heat transfer coefficient, object-to-ambient */
static float k20;     /* heat transfer coefficient, heater-to-ambient */
static float q12;     /* heat transfer rate. object-to-heater */
static float q10;     /* heat transfer rate, object-to-ambient */
static float q20;     /* heat transfer rate, heater-to-ambient */
static float qv;      /* electrical energy input to heater */
static float c1;      /* heat capacity * mass, object */
static float c2;      /* heat capacity * mass, heater */
static float rh;      /* heater electrical resistance */
static float vmax;    /* maximum voltage from power amplifier */
static float v;       /* voltage input to power amplifier */
static float vp;      /* voltage output from power amplifier
                            (unity voltage gain) */
static float dt;      /* simulation step size */

/* Controller variables: */

static float errt1;         /* temperature error for object (pot) */
static float errt2;         /* temperature error for heater */
static float kp1, kp2;      /* controller proportional gains */
static float ki1, ki2;      /* controller integral gains */
static float ref1;          /* reference (desired) temperature
                            of object */
static float ref2;          /* reference temperature for heater */
static float m1min,m1max;   /* output limits, outer control loop */
static float m2min,m2max;   /* output limits, inner control loop */
static float i1min,i1max;   /* integrator limits, outer loop */
static float i2min,i2max;   /* integrator limits, inner loop */
static float tsmp1;         /* sample time, outer loop */
static float tsmp2;         /* sample time, inner loop */
static long mstick;         /* millisec per clock tick */
static float i1,i2;         /* integrator values, outer, inner loop */
static float m1,m2;         /* controller outputs */

static int tn0,tn1,tn2;     /* Timer ID numbers for scheduler */

main()
{
struct display d1,d2,d3;
int i,dum;
char cbuf[50];
long ReadClock();
float tm,tmold = -10.0;
```

```
/* Initialize simulation and controller variables */

th1 = 0.0;     /* Temperatures */
th2 = 0.0;

i1 = 0.0;      /* Controller integrators */
i2 = 0.0;

m1 = 0.0;      /* Controller output */
m2 = 0.0;

/* Parameter values */

c1 = 4.0;      /* Heat capacities */
c2 = 4.0;

k12 = 1.0;     /* Heat transfer coefficients */
k10 = 0.3;
k20 = 0.1;

vmax = 4.0;    /* Maximum voltage */
rh = 1.0;      /* Electrical resistance */
th0 = 0.0;     /* Ambient temperature */

t = 0.0;       /* Initialize running time */
dt = 0.25;     /* Simulation time step */

tsmp1 = 2.0;   /* Sample times for control */
tsmp2 = 1.0;
mstick = 50;   /* Tick period in millisec */

m1min = m2min = i1min = i2min = 0.0;      /* Limits */
m1max = 2.0;
m2max = 1.0;
i1max = 1.0;
i2max = 2.0;

ref1 = 0.2;    /* Setpoint */

kp1 = 0.7;     /* Controller gains */
kp2 = 1.7;
ki1 = 0.4;
ki2 = 0.4;

/* Definition of dsp_set, for reference:
dsp_set(pd,x,y,label,lngth,lcolor,vbot,vtop,fv1,fv2,fmt,dblnk)  */

/* First display, pot temperature */
dsp_set(&d1,3.0,2.,"T_Pot",6.,1,0.0,1.0,get_th1,get_ref1,"%4.2f","     ");

/* Second display, voltage to heater */
dsp_set(&d2,10.0,2.,"V_Out",6.,2,0.0,2.0,get_act,fv2b,"%4.2f","     ");
dsp_flag(&d2,1,1,0,0);        /* No second variable */

/* Third display, heater temperature */
dsp_set(&d3,15.0,2.,"T_Heat",6.,3,0.0,1.0,get_th2,get_ref2,"%4.2f","     ");


init_scr();    /* Initialize the screen */
dsp_init(&d1);/* Display the screen static part */
dsp_init(&d2);
dsp_init(&d3);

mv_cur(15.0,18.0);    /* Print the label for time */
printf("Time:");

/* Schedule the control tasks
Highest priority is for the simulation, then loop1, then loop2.
Loop1 is given higher priority because, if they happen to request service
simultaneously, loop1 produces data that loop2 uses.  This is the reverse of
the normal convention that would give higher priority to the faster loop.
*/

if(rltm >= 1)
    {
    InitTime(mstick);     /* Initialize chronos */

    if((tn0 = NewDTimer(sim_h,&dum,100)) < 0)
        {
        printf("Can't allocate timer\n");
        exit();
        }
    SetDTimer(tn0,(long)(1000.0 * dt));        /* Set sample interval */

    if((tn1 = NewDTimer(loop1,&dum,90)) < 0)
        {
        printf("Can't allocate timer\n");
        exit();
        }
    SetDTimer(tn1,(long)(1000.0 * tsmp1));            /* Set sample interval */


    if((tn2 = NewDTimer(loop2,&dum,80)) < 0)
        {
        printf("Can't allocate timer\n");
        exit();
        }
    SetDTimer(tn2,(long)(1000.0 * tsmp2));            /* Set sample interval */

    if(cmode == 0)
        {
        StopDTimer(tn1);      /* Don't allow controllers to run if in
```

```
                                manual mode */
                StopDTimer(tn2);
                }
        if(rltm == 2)
                {
                setalarm(mstick);           /* set the system clock */
                xignal(XIGTMR,chronos);     /* Turn on the interrupt */
                }
        }
/* Set dummy variables */
v2a =  v2b = 0.0;

t1 = tsmpl;    /* Initialize sample interval so controller runs immediately,
                        only used for pure simulation (rltm = 0) */
t2 = tsmp2;
mode_msg();             /* Put mode indicator on screen */

for(i = 0; ;i++)
        {
        int chr;

        if(rltm == 0)
                {               /* Use this to run a "pure" simulation --
                                i.e., no real time at all */

                if(cmode)               /* Check to see if mode is automatic */
                        {
                        if(t1 >= tsmpl)
                                {
                                loop1();        /* Control */
                                t1 = 0.0;
                                }
                        if(t2 >= tsmp2)
                                {
                                loop2();
                                t2 = 0.0;
                                }
                        t1 += dt;
                        t2 += dt;
                        }
                sim_h();        /* Run the simulation here if not real time */
                }

        if(rltm == 1)chronos();             /* Run the scheduler from the background */
        if(rltm >= 1)tm = ReadClock() / 1000.0;
        else    tm = t;

        if((tm - tmold) >= 1.0)
            {
            mv_cur(16.0,18.0);          /* Print the current time */
            printf("%5.0f",tm);
            tmold = tm;
            }

        dsp_data(&d1);
        dsp_data(&d2);
        dsp_data(&d3);

        chr = char_in();        /* Read the keyboard */

        if(chr)         /* If character has been entered */
                {
                switch(chr)
                        {
                        case UP:
                                if(cmode)set_ref1(get_ref1() + dv);
                                else    set_act(get_act() + dm);
                                break;

                        case DOWN:
                                if(cmode)set_ref1(get_ref1() - dv);
                                else    set_act(get_act() - dm);
                                break;

                        case SH_UP:
                                if(cmode)set_ref1(get_ref1() + dv1);
                                else    set_act(get_act() + dm1);
                                break;

                        case SH_DOWN:
                                if(cmode)set_ref1(get_ref1() - dv1);
                                else    set_act(get_act() - dm1);
                                break;

                        case 'm':
                        case 'M':       /* Set to manual mode */
                                if(cmode)
                                        {
                                        cmode = 0;      /* Set mode */
                                        mode_msg();    /* Set mode indicator on screen */

                                        if(rltm >= 1)
                                            {
                                            StopDTimer(tn1);  /* Turn off controllers */
                                            StopDTimer(tn2);
                                            }
                                        }
                                break;

                        case 'a':
                        case 'A':       /* Set to automatic mode */
                            if(!cmode)
```

```
                        {
                        /* Set integrators for bumpless transfer;
                        "atomic" change is not necessary because the control
                        can't run until the mode is changed. */

                        m1 = get_th2();       /* Set outer loop so inner
                                                 loop is in balance */

                        if(ki1 != 0.0) /* Don't change the integrator
                                          value if the integral gain is zero. */
                                {
                                i1 = (m1 - kp1 * (ref1 - get_th1()));
                                }
                            if(ki2 != 0.0)
                                {
                                i2 = v;
                                }
                            cmode = 1;
                            if(rltm >= 1)
                                {
                                StartDTimer(tn1);
                                StartDTimer(tn2);  /* Turn Controllers on */
                                }
                            mode_msg(); /* Set mode indicator on screen */
                            }
                        break;

                    }

            if(chr == '\r')break;
            }
        }
if(rltm == 2)
        {
        setalarm(0L);         /* Set timer back to DOS */
        xignal(XIGTMR,XIG_DFL); /* Turn off interrupt */
        }
rst_scr();            /* Reset the screen */
}

/* Functions that return process variables -- these are all "atomic"
processes and must disable interrupts while fetching data.

When doing a non-real-time simulation, dummies must be supplied for
enable() and disable().
*/

float get_th1()
{
float vv;

disable();
vv = th1;
enable();
return(vv);
}

float get_th2()
{
float vv;

disable();
vv = th2;
enable();
return(vv);
}

float get_m1()
{
float vv;

disable();
vv = m1;
enable();
return(vv);
}

float get_act()
{
float vv;

disable();
vv = v;
enable();
return(vv);
}

float get_ref1()
{
float vv;

disable();
vv = ref1;
enable();
return(vv);
}

float get_ref2()
{
float vv;

disable();
```

```
vv = ref2;
enable();
return(vv);
}

/* Set process values -- also atomic */

set_ref1(val)
float val;
{
disable();
ref1 = val;
enable();
}

set_ref2(val)
float val;
{
disable();
ref2 = val;
enable();
}

set_m1(val)
float val;
{
disable();
m1 = val;
enable();
}

set_act(val)
float val;
{
disable();
v = val;
enable();
}


float fv2b()   /* Return a value for the process variable
------------   */
{
return(v2b);
}

/* Controller functions */

pi_cntrl(erp,pt_intg,intmin,intmax,kp,ki,mmin,mmax,pt_m) /* Compute a
--------------------------------------------------------- PI control */
float erp,*pt_intg,intmin,intmax,kp,ki,mmin,mmax,*pt_m;
{
float flim();

/* New integrator value */
*pt_intg = flim(*pt_intg + ki * erp, intmin,intmax);

/* Controller output */
*pt_m = flim(kp *erp + *pt_intg, mmin, mmax);     /* Controller output */
}

loop1(pdum)           /* Outer loop
-------          */
int *pdum;            /* Dummy argument from scheduler */
{
float mm;

if(rltm >= 1)SetDTimer(tn1,(long)(1000.0 * tsmp1));    /* Set sample interval */

errt1 = get_ref1() - get_th1();
pi_cntrl(errt1,&i1,i1min,i1max,kp1,ki1,m1min,m1max,&mm);

set_m1(mm);
}

loop2(pdum)           /* Inner loop
-------          */
int *pdum;            /* Dummy argument */
{
float mm;

if(rltm >= 1)SetDTimer(tn2,(long)(1000.0 * tsmp2));    /* Set sample interval */

set_ref2(get_m1());          /* Use output of outer loop for setpoint */
errt2 = get_ref2() - get_th2();
pi_cntrl(errt2,&i2,i2min,i2max,kp2,ki2,m2min,m2max,&mm);
set_act(mm);
}

/* Simulation task -- This can be replaced by data in and out for
a real control problem */

sim_h(pdum)           /* Simulation; use the Euler method to integrate one step
-------          each time called. */
int *pdum;            /* Dummy argument from chronos */
{
float flim();

if(rltm >= 1)SetDTimer(tn0,(long)(1000.0 * dt));       /* Set sample interval */

q12 = k12 * (th1 - th2);     /* Heat transfer rates */
q10 = k10 * (th1 - th0);
```

```
q20 = k20 * (th2 - th0);

vp = flim(get_act(),0.0,vmax);      /* Power amplifier output */
qv = vp * vp / rh;          /* Electric power into the heater */

th1 -= dt * (q12 + q10)/c1;         /* Pot temperature */
th2 += dt * (q12 - q20 + qv)/c2;    /* Heater temperature */

t += dt;              /* Increment time */
}

float flim(x,xmin,xmax)
float x,xmin,xmax;
{
if(x < xmin)return(xmin);
if(x > xmax)return(xmax);
return(x);
}

mode_msg()      /* Print a mode indicator on screen
----------      */
{
mv_cur(0.0,13.0);

if(cmode)
        {
        printf("Mode: Automatic");
        }
else
        {
        printf("Mode: Manual    ");
        }
}

/* These dummies must be supplied if rltm != 2 -- they can be supplied
here or in a separate file. */

/*
enable(){}
disable(){}
*/

/* They are commented out at this point since the default parameter setting
is to run real time. */

/* Panic routine shuts off interrupts and exits (called from chronos) */

panic(msg)      /* Shut off real time and exit
----------      */
char *msg;
{
if(rltm == 2)xignal(XIGTMR,XIG_DFL);
printf("<Panic> %s\n",msg);
exit();
}
/* Control display functions -- maintain graphic displays of
system variables.

Each  display has two variables,  one displayed by a vertical line
whose length changes in proportion to the variable value, and the
other variable represented by a short horizontal bar whose position
moves in proportion to its value.

Typical uses are for displaying a process output variable and the
associated setpoint, or, when only the vertical bar is used, to display
other process variables, output values, etc.

Each display is described by a data structure containing all of the
relevant information.  Functions are provided to fill the structure and
operate on it, so the user programmer need only declare the structure
and assign storage for it.

When defining display units in a user program, all that is needed is
to define the storage space for each and call the set-up program.
The storage is allocated with one of the following declarations:

DISPLAY temp_dsp;

or to define a group of displays with,

DISPLAY dsp[10];

or to use the memory allocator,

DISPLAY *pr_dsp;
char *malloc();
...
pr_dsp = (DISPLAY *)malloc(NDSP * sizeof(DISPLAY));

Then, the function dsp_set() is called to put data into the structure.

copyright (c) 1987, D. M. Auslander

Created: 25 June 87

Updates:
            10-July-87, DMA, bugs
*/

#include "display.h"  /* Contains the description of the data structure */
#include "dparam.h"         /* Contains system-specific parameters */
```

```
/* Set up a structure for a display --
pd is a pointer to a (blank) structure -- space for the structure must
be assigned in the **calling** function */

dsp_set(pd,x,y,label,lngth,lcolor,vbot,vtop,fv1,fv2,fmt,dblnk)   /*
--------------------------------------------------------------   */
struct display *pd;
float (*fv1)(),(*fv2)();      /* Functions called to get
                                 data */
float x,y;              /* Position of the bottom of the vertical bar */
float vbot,vtop;        /* Variable values at the top and bottom of the
                        line */
float lngth;            /* Line length (in cm) */
int lcolor;             /* Data display color */
char *label;            /* Label for this display */
char *fmt;              /* String with format to convert data */
char *dblnk;            /* String ob blanks to erase old data */
{
pd->x = x;
pd->y = y;
pd->label = label;
pd->lngth = lngth;
pd->lcolor = lcolor;
pd->vbot = vbot;
pd->vtop = vtop;
pd->fv1 = fv1;
pd->fv2 = fv2;
pd->fmt = fmt;
pd->dblnk = dblnk;
dsp_flag(pd,1,1,1,1);         /* Default is for all displays to be on */
}

dsp_flag(pd,v1l,v1d,v2b,v2d) /* Set the enabling flags for each of the
----------------------------    itemss */
int v1l,v1d,v2b,v2d;
struct display *pd;
{
pd->v1line = v1l;
pd->v1data = v1d;
pd->v2bar = v2b;
pd->v2data = v2d;
}


dsp_init(pd)  /* Initialize a display -- put on the labels, blank the spot
------------     where the line goes, etc. */
struct display *pd;
{
char cc[50];            /* Space for a character buffer */
float x,y,lngth;
int lcolor;

x = pd->x;      /* Copy to local variables */
y = pd->y;
lngth = pd->lngth;
lcolor = pd->lcolor;

mv_cur(x,y - laboff);           /* Move cursor to label position */
pstr(pd->label);                /* Write the label to the screen */

drawl(x,y,x,y + lngth,backc);         /* Erase the old line */

/* Draw the top and bottom tick bars */

drawl(x + bx,y,x + bx + bw,y,lcolor);       /* Bottom */

sprintf(cc,pd->fmt,pd->vbot);               /* Value */
mv_cur(x +  bx + bw + blx,y);               /* Print it */
pstr(cc);

drawl(x + bx,y + lngth,x + bx + bw,y +lngth,lcolor);     /* Top */

sprintf(cc,pd->fmt,pd->vtop);               /* Value */
mv_cur(x +  bx + bw + blx,y + lngth);             /* Print it */
pstr(cc);

pd->val1 = pd->vbot;         /* Initialize values to point to the bottom */
pd->val2 = pd->vbot;

pd->l1old = 0.0;                  /* Old length values */
pd->l2old = 0.0;
}

dsp_data(pd)            /* Display the data
------------               */
struct display *pd;
{
float x,y,lngth,vbot,vtop;
float val,lnew,l1old,l2old,lim();
char cc[50];
char cbuf[20];

int lcolor,color;

x = pd->x;      /* Copy to local variables */
y = pd->y;
lngth = pd->lngth;
lcolor = pd->lcolor;
vbot = pd->vbot;
vtop = pd->vtop;
l1old = pd->l1old;
l2old = pd->l2old;
```

```
if(pd->v1line || pd->v1data)
	{
	val = (*(pd->fv1))(); /* Get the value of the first variable */

	if((pd->v1line) && (val != pd->val1))
		{
		/* Only proceed if the value has changed and the line
		is to be drawn */

		lnew = (val - vbot) * lngth / (vtop - vbot);
		lnew = lim(lnew,0.0,lngth);

		/* Check to see if line goes up or down */
		if(lnew > l1old)color = lcolor;
		else         color = backc;
		drawl(x,y + l1old,x,y + lnew,color);      /* Draw */
		pd->l1old = lnew;    /* Save the new line length */
		}

	if(pd->v1data && (val != pd->val1))
		{
		/* Write the data value */

		if(pd->v1line)
			mv_cur(x - v1x,y + l1old);
		else
			mv_cur(x - v1x,y + v1y);

		pstr(pd->dblnk);     /* Erase old value */
		if(pd->v1line)
			mv_cur(x - v1x,y + lnew);
		else
			mv_cur(x - v1x,y + v1y);

		sprintf(cc,pd->fmt,val);
		pstr(cc);     /* Print value */
		}
	}
pd->val1 = val;        /* Save value */

/* Now do second value */

if(pd->v2bar || pd->v2data)
	{
	val = (*(pd->fv2))(); /* Get the value of the first variable */

	if(pd->v2bar && (pd->val2 != val))
		{
		/* Only draw if bar is enabled and data has changed */

		lnew = (val - vbot) * lngth / (vtop - vbot);
		lnew = lim(lnew,0.0,lngth);

		/* Erase the old value; Check first for overlap with top
		and bottom fiducial marks */

		if((l2old > ltol) && (l2old < (lngth - ltol)))
			{
			drawl(x + bx,y +  l2old,x + bx + bw,y + l2old,backc);
			}

		/* Draw the new value's bar */
		if((lnew > ltol) && (lnew < (lngth - ltol)))
			{
			drawl(x + bx,y +  lnew,x + bx + bw,y + lnew,lcolor);
			}
		pd->l2old = lnew;     /* Save the new line length */
		}

	if(pd->v2data && (pd->val2 != val))
		{
		/* Write the data value */

		if(pd->v2bar)
			mv_cur(x + v2x,y + l2old);
		else
			mv_cur(x + v2x,y + v2y);

		pstr(pd->dblnk);     /* Erase old value */
		if(pd->v2bar)
			mv_cur(x + v2x,y + lnew);
		else
			mv_cur(x + v2x,y + v2y);

		sprintf(cc,pd->fmt,val);
		pstr(cc);     /* Print value */
		}
	}
pd->val2 = val;              /* Save the value */
}

float lim(x,xmin,xmax)              /* Return x or its limits
-----------------------          */
float x,xmin,xmax;
{
if(x < xmin)return(xmin);
else if (x > xmax)return(xmax);
return(x);
}
/* Data structure definition for the control display functions

copyright (c) 1897, D.M. Auslander
```

```
Created 26-June-87

Updates:

FIle: display.h

This file contains the definition of the data structure defining
a process control type of screen display.

When defining display units in a user program, all that is needed is
to define the storage space for each and call the set-up program.
The storage is allocated with one of the following declarations:

DISPLAY temp_dsp;

or to define a group of displays with,

DISPLAY dsp[10];

or to use the memory allocator,

#define NDSP 10
DISPLAY *pr_dsp;
char *malloc();
...
pr_dsp = (DISPLAY *)malloc(NDSP * sizeof(DISPLAY));

Then, the function dsp_set() is called to put data into the structure.
*/

struct display
        {
        float (*fv1)(),(*fv2)();     /* Functions called to get
                              data */
        float x,y;            /* Position of the bottom of
                              the vertical bar */
        float vbot,vtop;      /* Variable values at the top and bottom of the
                              line */
        float val1,val2;      /* Stored data values */
        float lngth;          /* Line length (in cm) */
        int lcolor;           /* Data display color */
        char *label;          /* Label for this display */
        char *fmt;            /* String with format to convert data */
        char *dblnk;          /* String of blanks to erase old data */
        float l1old,l2old;    /* Saved values of the graphic locations */
        int v1line,v1data,v2bar,v2data;
                              /* Flags indicating whether associated
                              information should be displayed */
        };

typedef struct display DISPLAY;
```

```
/* Display-specific parameters for the control value display package.

copyright (c) 1987, D. M. Auslander

These values are expressed in nominal units of centimeters, so most
will be fairly independent of the display being used.

The screen mode, and any others that might be unique, will have to be
changed for each display type.

All of the dimensional information is relative to the point (x,y), which
defines the coordinate location of the bottom of the val1 line.

Created 26-June-87

Updates:

*/

static float laboff = 1.0;   /* Distance to the bottom of the label
                             from y */
static float bx = 0.2, bw = 0.6;    /* Distance from x to bars,
                                    bar width */
static float v1x = 2.0, v1y = 4.0;
                             /* Location relative to (x,y) of the
                             start of the printed val1 */
static float v2x = 3.0, v2y = 4.0;
static float blx = 0.2;             /* Distance from the right end of a fixed
                             bar to its label */
static float ltol = 0.05;    /* Distance between moving bar and fixed bar
                             that defines "overlap"  */
static int backc = 0;        /* Background color */
/* Console control for a character-oriented screen --
This version is set up for the Microsoft C compiler.

The coordinates used for input to all functions are in the
graphics coordinate space, with the origin as (0,0) at the
lower left.

copyright (c) 1987-88 D.M.Auslander

Created:      10-July-87
Updates:
              15-July-87, DMA, fix CGA1 color table
              18-Aug-88, adapt for Microsoft C Compiler

This version is set up for various graphic modes on the IBM.
The control "defines" are:
CGA1    color graphics adapter, 640x200, monochrome
CGA2    color graphics adapter, 320x200, color
EGA             enhanced graphics adapter, 640x320, color
```

```
VGA     video graphics array, 640x480, color
*/

#include <stdio.h>
#include <graph.h>
#include <dos.h>


#define EGA

#ifdef EGA
static int srow = 350, scol = 640,smode = _ERESCOLOR,rmode = 3;
static int crow = 25, ccol = 80;    /* Size of character screen */
/* Output color map */
static int c_out[] =
    {0,1,2,3,4,5,6,7,8,9,10,11,12,13,14,15,16};
#endif

#ifdef CGA1
static int srow = 200, scol = 640,smode = _HRESBW,rmode = 3;
static int crow = 25, ccol = 80;    /* Size of character screen */
/* Output color map */
static int c_out[] = {0,1,1,1,1,1,1,1,1,1,1,1,1,1,1,1};
#endif

#ifdef CGA2
static int srow = 200, scol = 320,smode = _MRES4COLOR,rmode = 3;
static int crow = 25, ccol = 80;    /* Size of character screen */
/* Output color map */
static int c_out[] = {0,1,2,3,4,5,6,7,8,9,10,11,12,13,14,15};
#endif

static float sht = 20.0, swdth = 20.0;     /* Screen height and width (cm) */

init_scr()              /* Initialize the screen
----------              */
{
_setvideomode(smode);
}

rst_scr()       /* Restore the screen to its original state
----------      */
{
_setvideomode(_DEFAULTMODE);
}

mv_cur(x,y)     /* Move the cursor to a location specified in the **graphic**
-----------     coordinate space.  Origin is lower left. */
float x,y;
{
int r,c;
r = (sht - y) * (crow -1) / sht + 1.5;     /* Compute row/col coordinates */
c = x * (ccol - 1) / swdth + 1.5;
_settextposition(r,c);              /* Move the cursor */
}

pstr(s)         /* Write the string to the screen at the
-------         current cursor location */
char *s;
{
fputs(s,stdout);
}

drawl(x1,y1,x2,y2,color)     /* Draw a line from (x1,y1) to (x2,y2)
------------------------     */
float x1,y1,x2,y2;
int color;
{
int xi1,xi2,yi1,yi2,dx,dy,incx = 1, incy = 1, reg,i,n,ix,iy;
int clr;

yi1 = (sht - y1) * (srow -1) / sht + 1.5;  /* Compute row/col coordinates */
xi1 = x1 * (scol - 1) / swdth + 1.5;
yi2 = (sht - y2) * (srow -1) / sht + 1.5;  /* Compute row/col coordinates */
xi2 = x2 * (scol - 1) / swdth + 1.5;

sclim(&xi1,&yi1,&xi2,&yi2);         /* Limit values to inside the screen */

clr = _setcolor(c_out[color]);
_moveto(xi1,yi1);
_lineto(xi2,yi2);
_setcolor(clr);     /* Set color back to default */
}

sclim(x1,y1,x2,y2)           /* Limit values to inside the screen
----------------------              */
int *x1,*x2,*y1,*y2;
{
*x1 = ilim(*x1,1,scol);
*x2 = ilim(*x2,1,scol);
*y1 = ilim(*y1,1,srow);
*y2 = ilim(*y2,1,srow);
}

ilim(x,xmin,xmax)     /* Limit value of x to <xmin,xmax>
-----------------     */
int x,xmin,xmax;
{
if(x < xmin)return(xmin);
if(x > xmax)return(xmax);
return(x);
}
```

```
/* Register definitions for DOS calls -- structure definitions are
in dos.h
*/

static struct WORDREGS wregs;       /* Word registers */
static struct BYTEREGS bregs;       /* Byte registers */
static union REGS r;

char_in()       /* Check for a character from the keyboard
---------       Return 0 if no character or the ASCII code if a character
                is detected */

{
if(kbhit())
        {
        r.h.ah = 7;     /* Get a character */
        intdos(&r,&r);/* Call DOS */
        if(r.h.al != 0)return(r.h.al & 0x7f);       /* Return character value */
        else
                {       /* Get extended code */
                r.h.ah = 7;
                intdos(&r,&r);/* Call again */
                return(r.h.al | 0x80 & 0xff);
                                /* Set high bit for extended codes */
                }
        }
return(0);      /* No character ready */
}
/*********************************************************************

FILE
        time.c  -  timing routines

ENTRY ROUTINES
        chronos     -  timer interrupt service routine

        NewDTimer   -  allocate new countdown timer
        FreeDTimer  -  deallocate countdown timer
        SetDTimer   -  set countdown timer
        ReadDTimer  -  read countdown timer
        StopDTimer  -  freeze timer
        StartDTimer -  unfreeze timer

        CisDTimer   -  set tm_isf field to 0

        NewITimer   -  allocate new interval timer
        FreeITimer  -  deallocate interval timer
        SetITimer   -  set interval timer
        ReadITimer  -  read interval timer

        ReadClock   -  time telling

PRIVATE ROUTINES
        reset_dtimer  -  reset countdown timer
        reset_itimer  -  reset interval timer

INITIALIZATION ROUTINES
        InitTime     -  initialize timer module
        InitSysTime  -  system initialization for task scheduling

DESCRIPTION
        These routines implement multiple timers in software, using a
        single hardware clock as the real-time base.  Actual and
        simulation routines are included.

        Note the implementation of multiple prioritized timer interrupts
        in chronos().  Only countdown timers are associated with interrupt
        service routines.

        The first two timers are reserved by the kernel for time telling
        and task scheduling.

LAST UPDATE
        03 May 1985
                restructure allocation routines
        04 February 1986
                put enable() & disable() in #if BACKGROUND
        1 December 1987
                implement tm_flag[]
        26 January 1988
                use the new void types and add ANSI features

        Copyright (c) 1985-1988  D.M. Auslander  and  C.H. Tham

*********************************************************************/

#define KERNEL

/*********************************************************************
                                                    I M P O R T S
*********************************************************************/

#include <stdio.h>
#include <limits.h>                 /* ANSI data size limits */

#ifndef INT_MAX
#define INT_MAX             0x7FFF
#endif

#ifndef LONG_MAX
#define LONG_MAX            0x7FFFFFFL
#endif
```

```c
#include "envir.h"                /* environment definitions */

#include "config.h"               /* system configuration header */
#include "8259.h"                 /* hardware dependent declarations */
#include "time.h"                 /* time module declarations */

#ifdef ANSI

extern int  enable(void);    /* enable CPU interrupt response */
extern int  disable(void);   /* disable CPU interrupt response */
extern void seoi(int);       /* send specific EOI to 8259 */
extern void panic(char *);   /* abort execution */

#else

extern int  enable();        /* enable CPU interrupt response */
extern int  disable();       /* disable CPU interrupt response */
extern void seoi();          /* send specific EOI to 8259 */
extern void panic();         /* abort execution */

#endif

/***********************************************************************
              F O R W A R D   D E C L A R A T I O N S
***********************************************************************/

#ifdef ANSI

static void   reset_dtimer(int);
static void   reset_itimer(int);

#else

void   reset_dtimer();
void   reset_itimer();

#endif

/***********************************************************************
                      P R I V A T E   D A T A
***********************************************************************/

static long tm_dtime[MAXDTIMERS];          /* count down timers */

static int tm_used[MAXDTIMERS];            /* timer in use flag */
static int tm_lock[MAXDTIMERS];            /* used for virtual time */
static int tm_flag[MAXDTIMERS];            /* timeout flags */
static int tm_pri[MAXDTIMERS];             /* priority (countdown only) */

static int tm_isf[MAXDTIMERS];             /* interrupt in service flag */
static void (*tm_tsr[MAXDTIMERS])();       /* timeout service routines */

static void *tm_argp[MAXDTIMERS];   /* ptr to arguments */

static long tm_itime[MAXITIMERS];   /* interval timers */
static int tm_iused[MAXITIMERS];    /* interval timer in use flag */

static long clock;                         /* countdown since system started */
static long mstick;                        /* milliseconds per tick */

#ifdef CLOTHO

#define ISF             0                  /* whether to use tm_isf field */
#define AUTO_EOI        0                  /* enable and send EOI to 8259 */

#else

#define ISF             1                  /* whether to use tm_isf field */
#define AUTO_EOI        0                  /* enable and send EOI to 8259 */

#endif

#define UNUSED          0                  /* timer unused */
#define USED            1                  /* timer in use */
#define UNLOCK          0                  /* timer unlocked */
#define LOCK            1                  /* timer locked */
#define FOREGROUND

/***********************************************************************
                              E N T R Y   R O U T I N E S
***********************************************************************/

/*---------------------------------------------------------------------
PROCEDURE
       CHRONOS  -  Timer Interrupt Service Routine

SYNOPSIS
       void chronos(void)

DESCRIPTION
       First decrements count down timers.  Count down timers are only
       decremented if they are in use (ie. allocated to a task) and
       if the timer is not locked.  Interval timers are the exception
       and are all incremented regardless since it's probably faster to
       do so than check if they are in use.

       Next, the countdown timer array, tm_dtime[], is scanned for zero
       or negative times.  If time is zero or negative, see if user has
       specified an interrupt service routine (tm_tsr not NULL).  If so,
       set the In Service Flag (tm_isf) and execute the routine, clearing
       tm_isf on completion.

       If two or more service routines are due for service, the one with
```

```
        the highest priority will be executed first.  Only service routines
        with equal or higher priority can interrupt a currently in service
        routine.  Priority is set by the user when the timer is allocated.
        The larger the number, the higher the priority.

        Service routines are passed a pointer which may point to a scalar
        argument or an aggregate argument block (eg. structures).  This
        pointer is cast to a char type pointer.

        Chronos() may be used in programs where the "interrupt" routine
        never returns;  the "interrupt" service routine may be a task
        dispatcher or scheduler.  In such cases, two courses of action are
        possible depending on whether the dispatcher/scheduler is
        foreground or background.  In the case of a background scheduler,
        we normally want to disable the in service flag and also reset
        the hardware interrupt controller.  This is to allow another timer
        interrupt to be generated and passed to chronos() without the
        intervention of the dispatcher/scheduler.  For a foreground
        dispatcher/scheduler that uses the timer, it will want to control
        exactly when it gives up control, so we do not want to send
        EOI's or enable interrupts here, but allow the foreground
        dispatcher/scheduler to do so with CisDTimer().

        The in-service-flag may be ignored by means of the ISF conditional
        compilation switch.  The service routine has the task of reseting
        the hardware interrupt controller.  CisDTimer() performs both actions.

        Chronos() functions like a level triggered interrupt controller.
        As long as other conditions are satisfied, a zero or negative
        count will result in execution of the associated service routine.

        Note the use of register pointers for speed.

        New:   A timeout service routine is only invoked once when the
               count-down timer times out.  The timer must be reset by
               SetDTimer() before the timeout handler can be invoked again.

LAST UPDATE
        28 February 1985
                add ISF test
        04 February 1986
                use enable() and disable() only if BACKGROUND
        1 December 1987
                lock timer when isr active, release on reset
        26 January 1988
                use the new void pointer types
------------------------------------------------------------------------*/

void chronos()
{
        int maxpri;                     /* max. pri. of in-service routine */
        int index;                      /* index into timer array */
        int istat;                      /* interrupt status on entry */
        int i;                          /* iteration counter */
        register long *p;               /* fast pointer to timer times */


        istat = disable();              /* critical section, disable interrupts */


        ++clock;                        /* update clock */

        /*-----------------------------------------------------------------
           Upon system clock interrupt, increment all interval timers.
           May be faster than checking if they are used b4 incrementing.
        -----------------------------------------------------------------*/

        for (p = tm_itime, i = 0; i < MAXITIMERS; i++, p++)
                ++(*p);

        /*-----------------------------------------------------------------
           If a countdown timer is active and it is not locked, its
           time value is decremented.  Does not check if timer has
           timed out since this is taken care of by tm_flag[] and to
           do so here will increase the overheads.  The tm_lock[]
           check is needed because we may need to stop certain timers.
           Have to check if timer is in use because a timeout service
           routine may be attached to a timer.
        -----------------------------------------------------------------*/

        for (p = tm_dtime, i = 0; i < MAXDTIMERS; i++, p++)
                if ((tm_used[i] == USED) && (tm_lock[i] == UNLOCK))
                        --(*p);

#ifdef FOREGROUND               /* use timeout service routines */

        /*-----------------------------------------------------------------
           Find the highest priority of all timer interrupt routines
           currently in service and set maxpri to that priority.
        -----------------------------------------------------------------*/

        maxpri = -INT_MAX;

        for (i = 0; i < MAXDTIMERS; i++)
                if ((tm_isf[i] > 0) && (tm_pri[i] > maxpri))
                        maxpri = tm_pri[i];

        /*-----------------------------------------------------------------
           Find any pending service routine with greater or equal
           priority.  If index >= 0, such a routine exists and index
           is its offset in tm_tsr[].
        -----------------------------------------------------------------*/
```

```
        index = -1;

        for (i = 0; i < MAXDTIMERS; i++)
        {
                if ((tm_dtime[i] <= 0L) && (tm_pri[i] >= maxpri)
                        && (tm_isf[i] == 0) && (tm_tsr[i] != (void(*)())NULL)
                        && (tm_lock[i] == UNLOCK) && (tm_flag[i] == 0))
                {
                        index = i;
                        maxpri = tm_pri[i];
                }
        }

        if (index >= 0)
        {
#if ISF
                tm_isf[index] += 1;   /* indicate routine in service */
#endif
#if AUTO_EOI
                enable();

                seoi(TMRVEC);         /* specific EOI to intrp. controller */
#endif
                tm_flag[index] = 1;   /* prevent further use until reset */

                (*(tm_tsr[index]))(tm_argp[index]);

#if AUTO_EOI
                disable();
#endif
#if ISF
                tm_isf[index] -= 1;   /* indicate routine done */
#endif
        }

#endif /* ifdef FOREGROUND */

        if (istat)
                enable();                       /* release mutual exclusion */

}


/*-----------------------------------------------------------------------
FUNCTION
        NewDTimer  -  allocate countdown timer

SYNOPSIS
        int NewDTimer(func, argp, pri)
        void (*func)(), *argp;
        int pri;

PARAMETERS
        func  -  pointer to service routine
        argp  -  pointer to argument(s)
        pri   -  priority

RETURNS
        timer index if successful, -1 if not.

LAST UPDATE
        26 January 1988
                change func type to void
-----------------------------------------------------------------------*/

int NewDTimer(func, argp, pri)
void (*func)(), *argp;
int pri;
{
        int i;                                          /* iteration variable */
        int istat;                                      /* interrupt status */


        istat = disable();    /* disable interrupts, critical section */

        for (i = 0; i < MAXDTIMERS; i++)
                if (tm_used[i] != USED)
                        break;

        if (i < MAXDTIMERS)
        {
                tm_pri[i] = pri;
                tm_tsr[i] = func;
                tm_argp[i] = argp;
                tm_lock[i] = UNLOCK;
                tm_flag[i] = 0;
                tm_used[i] = USED;
        }
        else
                i = -1;

        if (istat)                      /* exit critical section, re-enable intrp */
                enable();

        return(i);
}


/*-----------------------------------------------------------------------
PROCEDURE
```

```
        FreeDTimer  -  free allocated timer

SYNOPSIS
        void FreeITimer(timer)
        int timer;

PARAMTERS
        timer  -  timer index number

DESCRIPTION
        Set associated used field to 0, indicating timer is free.  Note that
        you MUST ensure that the timer you are returning is obtained with
        NewDTimer.  Otherwise, you will screw-up the system for sure.

LAST UPDATE
        3 May 1985
-------------------------------------------------------------------*/

void FreeDTimer(timer)
int timer;
{

        if ((timer < 0) || (timer >= MAXDTIMERS))
        {
                panic("FreeDTimer: nonexistant countdown timer");
        }
        else if (tm_used[timer] == USED)
        {
                reset_dtimer(timer);
        }
        else
                panic("FreeDTimer: countdown timer not allocated");

}



/*------------------------------------------------------------------
PROCEDURE
        SETDTIMER  -  set countdown timer

SYNOPSIS
        void SetDTimer(n, ms)
        int n;
        long ms;

PARAMETERS
        n   -  timer id
        ms  -  time in milliseconds

DESCRIPTION
        Set countdown timer 'n' for ms milliseconds.  If ms is less than
        the resolution of the time-base, tm_dtime is set to zero.
        A negative value of ms deallocates the timer.

LAST UPDATE
        1 December 1987
                reset tm_flag
-------------------------------------------------------------------*/

void SetDTimer(n, ms)
int n;
long ms;
{
        int istat;              /* interrupt status */
        long tmp;               /* temporary to hold tick calculations */


        if ((n < 0) || (n >= MAXDTIMERS))
                panic("SetDTimer: nonexistent timer");
        else if (tm_used[n] == UNUSED)
                panic("SetDTimer: timer not allocated");

        tmp = ms / mstick;

        istat = disable();              /* begin mutual exclusion */

        tm_flag[n] = 0;                         /* reset tm_flag */

        if (ms >= 0L)
        {
                tm_dtime[n] = tmp;
        }
        else            /* release timer */
        {
                tm_used[n] = UNUSED;
                tm_tsr[n] = (void(*)())NULL;
        }

        if (istat)
                enable();                       /* release mutual exclusion */

}



/*------------------------------------------------------------------
FUNCTION
        ReadDTimer  -  read countdown timer

SYNOPSIS
        long ReadDTimer(n)
```

```
	int n;

PARAMETER
	n  -  timer number

RETURNS
	time in milliseconds

REMARKS
	The time left is only accurate to the precision allowed by the
	system clock rate.  If quantization is 10 ms, then ReadDTimer()
	will report 10 ms even if actual time left is 1 ms.

LAST UPDATE
	12 February 1985  by  author
----------------------------------------------------------------------*/

long ReadDTimer(n)
int n;
{

	if ((n < 0) || (n >= MAXDTIMERS))
		panic("ReadDTimer: nonexistant timer");

	return(tm_dtime[n] * mstick);
}



/*---------------------------------------------------------------------
PROCEDURE
	STOPDTIMER  -  stop timer from counting down

SYNOPSIS
	void StopDTimer(n)
	int n;

PARAMETER
	n  -  timer number

DESCRIPTION
	This routine should only be used by the system to freeze timers
	used by background process for virtual timing, ie. time proceeds
	only when that process is running.  An important use is for
	background scheduling.

	As this is an internal system routine, error checking is lax.

SEE ALSO
	StartDTimer() to restart stopped timers

LAST UPDATE
	12 February 1985
----------------------------------------------------------------------*/

void StopDTimer(n)
int n;
{
	int istat;				/* interrupt status */


	if ((n < 0) || (n >= MAXDTIMERS))
		panic("StopDTimer: nonexistent timer");

	istat = disable();

	tm_lock[n] = LOCK;

	if (istat)
		enable();
}



/*---------------------------------------------------------------------
PROCEDURE
	STARTDTIMER  -  stop timer from counting down

SYNOPSIS
	void StartDTimer(n)
	int n;

PARAMETER
	n  -  timer number

REMARKS
	This routine should only be used by the system to restart timers
	frozen by a StopDTimer call.

SEE ALSO
	StopDTimer() to stop timers

LAST UPDATE
	12 February 1985  by  author
----------------------------------------------------------------------*/

void StartDTimer(n)
int n;
{
	int istat;			/* interrupt status */
```

```
	if ((n < 0) || (n >= MAXDTIMERS))
		panic("StartDTimer: nonexistent timer");

	istat = disable();

	tm_lock[n] = UNLOCK;

	if (istat)
		enable();

}


/*----------------------------------------------------------------------
PROCEDURE
	CISDTIMER  -  clear in service flags (software and hardware)

SYNOPSIS
	void CisDTimer(n)
	int n;

PARAMETER
	n  -  countdown timer number

REMARKS
	The purpose is to allow another invocation of the timeout service
	routine at the next timer interrupt.

LAST UPDATE
	1 December 1987
		clear tm_flag
----------------------------------------------------------------------*/

void CisDTimer(n)
int n;
{
	int istat;			/* interrupt status */


	if ((n < 0) || (n >= MAXDTIMERS))
		panic("CisDTimer: nonexistant timer");

	istat = disable();

	tm_isf[n] = 0;
	tm_flag[n] = 0;

	seoi(TMRVEC); /* send specific EOI to interrupt controller */

	if (istat)
		enable();
}


/*----------------------------------------------------------------------
PROCEDURE
	SETTSR  -  install timeout service routine

SYNOPSIS
	void SetTsr(n, func, argp, pri)
	void (*func)(), *argp;
	int n, pri;

PARAMETERS
	n     -  timer id
	func  -  pointer to service routine
	argp  -  pointer to argument structure
	pri   -  priority

REMARKS
	There had better be no mistakes when specifying timer.

LAST UPDATE
	26 January 1988
		use the new void types
----------------------------------------------------------------------*/

void SetTsr(n, func, argp, pri)
void (*func)(), *argp;
int n, pri;
{
	int istat;				/* interrupt status */


	if ((n < 0) || (n >= MAXDTIMERS))
		panic("SetTsr:  nonexistant timer");

	istat = disable();

	tm_pri[n] = pri;
	tm_tsr[n] = func;
	tm_argp[n] = argp;
	tm_lock[n] = UNLOCK;
	tm_flag[n] = 0;
	tm_used[n] = USED;

	if (istat)
		enable();
```

```
}


/*-----------------------------------------------------------------------------
FUNCTION
	TIMEUP  -  has timer run out?

SYNOPSIS
	int TimeUp(n)
	int n;

PARAMETER
	n  -  timer number

RETURNS
	0  if timer has not timed out
	1  if it has timed out

LAST UPDATE
	29 January 1988
		created as this makes more sense than reading the timer
-----------------------------------------------------------------------------*/

int TimeUp(n)
int n;
{


	if ((n < 0) || (n >= MAXDTIMERS))
		panic("TimeUp:  nonexistant timer");

	return(tm_dtime[n] <= 0L ? 1 : 0);
}



/*-----------------------------------------------------------------------------
FUNCTION
	NewITimer  -  allocate interval timer

SYNOPSIS
	int NewITimer()

RETURNS
	timer index if successful, -1 if not.

LAST UPDATE
	3 May 1985
-----------------------------------------------------------------------------*/

int NewITimer()
{
	int istat;						/* interrupt status */
	int i;							/* iteration variable */


	istat = disable();	/* disable interrupts, critical section */

	for (i = 0; i < MAXITIMERS; i++)
		if (tm_iused[i] != USED)
			break;

	if (i < MAXITIMERS)
	{
		reset_itimer(i);

		tm_iused[i] = USED;
	}
	else
		i = -1;

	if (istat)				/* exit critical section, re-enable intrp */
		enable();

	return(i);
}



/*-----------------------------------------------------------------------------
PROCEDURE
	FreeITimer  -  free allocated interval timer

SYNOPSIS
	void FreeITimer(timer)
	int timer;

PARAMETERS
	timer  -  timer index number

DESCRIPTION
	Set associated used field to 0, indicating timer is free.  Note that
	you MUST ensure that the timer you are returning is obtained with
	NewITimer.  Otherwise, you will screw-up the system for sure.

LAST UPDATE
	3 May 1985  by  author
-----------------------------------------------------------------------------*/

void FreeITimer(timer)
int timer;
{
```

```
	if ((timer < 0) || (timer >= MAXITIMERS))
	{
		panic("FreeITimer: nonexistant interval timer");
	}
	else if (tm_iused[timer] == USED)
	{
		reset_itimer(timer);
	}
	else
		panic("FreeITimer: interval timer not allocated");

}


/*-----------------------------------------------------------------------
PROCEDURE
	SetITimer  -  set interval timer

SYNOPSIS
	void SetITimer(n);
	int n;

PARAMETERS
	n   -  timer id

REMARKS
	Set interval time value to 0.

LAST UPDATE
	13 October 1984
-----------------------------------------------------------------------*/

void SetITimer(n)
int n;
{

	if ((n < 0) || (n >= MAXITIMERS))
		panic("SetITimer: nonexistant timer");

	tm_itime[n] = 0;

}


/*-----------------------------------------------------------------------
FUNCTION
	ReadITimer  -  read interval timer

SYNOPSIS
	long ReadITimer(n);
	int n;

PARAMETERS
	n   -  timer id

RETURNS
	interval value in milliseconds

LAST UPDATE
	13 October 1984
-----------------------------------------------------------------------*/

long ReadITimer(n)
int n;
{

	if ((n < 0) || (n >= MAXITIMERS))
		panic("ReadITimer: nonexistant timer");

	return(tm_itime[n] * mstick);
}


/*-----------------------------------------------------------------------
FUNCTION
	ReadClock  -  read system time

SYNOPSIS
	long ReadClock()

RETURNS
	time elasped in milliseconds since system is born

LAST UPDATE
	12 February 1985
-----------------------------------------------------------------------*/

long ReadClock()
{

	return(clock * mstick);
}


/***********************************************************************
			P R I V A T E   R O U T I N E S
***********************************************************************/
```

```
/*------------------------------------------------------------------------
PROCEDURE
        reset_dtimer  -  reset countdown timer

SYNOPSIS
        static reset_dtimer(n)
        int n;

PARAMETER
        n  -  timer id

LAST UPDATE
        1 December 1987
                clear tm_flag
-------------------------------------------------------------------------*/

static void reset_dtimer(n)
int n;
{

        tm_dtime[n] = LONG_MAX;
        tm_used[n] = UNUSED;
        tm_lock[n] = UNLOCK;
        tm_flag[n] = 0;
        tm_pri[n] = PZERO - 1;
        tm_isf[n] = 0;
        tm_tsr[n] = (void(*)())NULL;
        tm_argp[n] = (void *)NULL;

}


/*------------------------------------------------------------------------
PROCEDURE
        reset_itimer  -  reset interval timer

SYNOPSIS
        static void reset_itimer(n)
        int n;

PARAMETER
        n  -  timer id

LAST UPDATE
        12 February 1985
-------------------------------------------------------------------------*/

static void reset_itimer(n)
int n;
{
        tm_itime[n] = 0L;
        tm_iused[n] = UNUSED;

}


/*************************************************************************
                        I N I T I A L I Z A T I O N   R O U T I N E S
*************************************************************************/

/*------------------------------------------------------------------------
PROCEDURE
        INITTIME  -  initialize this module

SYNOPSIS
        void InitTime(ms)
        long ms;

PARAMETER
        ms  -  milliseconds per tick

LAST UPDATE
        12 February 1985
                separate countdown and interval timers.
-------------------------------------------------------------------------*/

void InitTime(ms)
long ms;
{
        int i;                                  /* iteration variable */


        mstick = ms;
        clock = 0L;


        for (i = 0; i < MAXDTIMERS; i++)
        {
                reset_dtimer(i);
        }

        for (i = 0; i < MAXITIMERS; i++)
        {
                reset_itimer(i);
        }

}


#ifdef CLOTHO           /* used by clotho kernel only */
```

```
extern void InitSysTime(void (*)());

/*-----------------------------------------------------------------------
PROCEDURE
        INITSYSTIME  -  allocate and initialize timers for system

SYNOPSIS
        void InitSysTime(dispatcher)
        void (*dispatcher)();

PARAMETER
        dispatcher  -  pointer to clotho's scheduler/dispatcher

REMARKS
        timer 0  -  reserved for normal dispatcher
        timer 1  -  reserved for control-task dispatcher/scheduler

LAST UPDATE
        12 February 1985
-----------------------------------------------------------------------*/

void InitSysTime(dispatcher)
void (*dispatcher)();
{

        if ((SLC_TIMER >= MAXDTIMERS) || (STL_TIMER >= MAXDTIMERS))
                panic("InitSysTime: check SLC_TIMER & STL_TIMER < MAXDTIMERS");

        tm_used[SLC_TIMER] = USED;
        tm_lock[SLC_TIMER] = UNLOCK;
        tm_flag[SLC_TIMER] = 0;

        tm_used[STL_TIMER] = USED;
        tm_lock[STL_TIMER] = UNLOCK;
        tm_flag[STL_TIMER] = 0;

#ifdef FOREGROUND

        /*****  set up timer for time-slice priority dispatcher  *****/

        tm_tsr[SLC_TIMER] = dispatcher;
        tm_argp[SLC_TIMER] = (void *)SLC_TIMER;
        tm_pri[SLC_TIMER] = PZERO + 1;       /* has low priority */
        tm_dtime[SLC_TIMER] = 0;             /* start background next */


        /*****  set up timer for control-task STL dispatcher  *****/

        tm_tsr[STL_TIMER] = dispatcher;
        tm_argp[STL_TIMER] = (void *)STL_TIMER;
        tm_pri[STL_TIMER] = INT_MAX;         /* has very high priority */
        tm_dtime[STL_TIMER] = LONG_MAX;

#endif /* ifdef FOREGROUND */

}

#endif /* ifdef CLOTHO */

/************************************************************************

FILE
        time.h  -  timer module definitions

LAST UPDATE
        26 January 1988
                add ANSI function prototypes

************************************************************************/

/************************   Timer Type Codes   ************************/

#define DTIMER        0x01          /* count-down timer type */
#define ITIMER        0x02          /* interval timer type */

/*****************************  Exports  ******************************/

#ifdef ANSI

extern void chronos(void);
extern int  NewDTimer(void(*)(), void *, int);
extern void FreeDTimer(int);
extern void SetDTimer(int, long);
extern long ReadDTimer(int);
extern void StopDTimer(int);
extern void StartDTimer(int);
extern void CisDTimer(int);
extern int  TimeUp(int);
extern void SetTsr(int, void(*)(), void *, int);
extern int  NewITimer(void);
extern void FreeITimer(int);
extern void SetITimer(int);
extern long ReadITimer(int);
extern long ReadClock(void);
extern void InitTime(long);

#else

extern void chronos();
extern int  NewDTimer();
extern void FreeDTimer();
extern void SetDTimer();
```

```
extern long ReadDTimer();
extern void StopDTimer();
extern void StartDTimer();
extern void CisDTimer();
extern int  TimeUp();
extern void SetTsr();
extern int  NewITimer();
extern void FreeITimer();
extern void SetITimer();
extern long ReadITimer();
extern long ReadClock();
extern void InitTime();

#endif

/**********************************************************************

FILE
        config.h  -  system configuration header file

LAST UPDATE
        21 January 1986
                fine tune for IBM-PC hardware

        Copyright(c) 1985, 1986  D.M. Auslander and C.H. Tham

**********************************************************************/

#define TICKRATE         20          /* clock ticks per second (>18) */

#define MAXHARDTIMERS     1          /* number of hardware timer available */

#define MAXDTIMERS        4          /* number of soft countdown timers */
#define MAXITIMERS        2          /* number of soft interval timers */

#define MAXUSRSTACK    2048          /* max size of each user stack */
#define MINUSRSTACK      32          /* min size of each user stack */

#define SYSBUFSIZ        64          /* size of each system buffer in bytes */
#define MAXSYSBUF         8          /* total number of system buffers */

#define MAXTASKS         16          /* maximum number of resident tasks */
#define MAXEVENTS         8          /* maximum number of events/semaphores */
#define MAXSEMS           8          /* maximum number of semaphores */

#define MAXQUANTUM     1000          /* maximum quantum in milliseconds */
#define MINQUANTUM       50          /* minimum quantum in milliseconds */

#define PCONTROL       1000          /* minimum priority of control tasks */
#define PSERVER         100          /* mininum priority of server tasks */
#define PSLICE           10          /* default priority of slice tasks */
```

```
#define PZERO            0          /* floor on task priority */
#define PIDLER          -1          /* Idler priority, must be < PZERO */

#define SLC_TIMER        0          /* timer reserved for slice scheduling */
#define STL_TIMER        1          /* timer reserved for STL scheduling */


/**********************************************************************

FILE
        8259.h  -  8259A definitions, IBM-PC version

SYNOPSIS
        #include "8259.h"

DESCRIPTION
        This file contains useful definitions for default operation of the
        Intel 8259A Programmable Interrupt Controller in the IBM-PC.

LAST UPDATE
        30 April 1985

AUTHOR
        Haam Tham      18 February 1985

        Copyright(c) 1985,1986  D.M. Auslander and C.H. Tham

**********************************************************************/


#define BASE8259     0x20              /* base address */

#define EOIPORT      (BASE8259+0)      /* where to send EOI */
#define MASKPORT     (BASE8259+1)      /* 8259 mask port */

#define BASEVEC      8                 /* base vector */

#define TMRVEC       BASEVEC           /* timer vector */
#define KBVEC        (BASEVEC+1)       /* keyboard vector */
#define COM2VEC      (BASEVEC+3)       /* COM2 device vector */
#define COM1VEC      (BASEVEC+4)       /* COM1 or (AUX) vector */
#define PRNVEC       (BASEVEC+7)       /* parallel printer vector */

#define AUXVEC       COM1VEC           /* an alternative definition */

#define TMRMASK      0x01              /* disable timer mask */
#define KBMASK       0x02              /* disable keyboard mask */
#define COM2MASK     0x08              /* disable COM2 mask */
#define COM1MASK     0x10              /* disable COM1 mask */
#define PRNMASK      0x80              /* disable printer port mask */
```

```
#define AUXMASK         COM1MASK

#define TMREOI          0x60                /* timer specific EOI */
#define KBEOI           0x61                /* keyboard specific EOI */
#define COM2EOI         0x63                /* COM2 specific EOI */
#define COM1EOI         0x64                /* COM1 specific EOI */
#define PRNEOI          0x67                /* printer specific EOI */

#define NSEOI           0x20                /* non specific EOI */


/**********************************************************************

FILE
    xignal.h    (IBM-PC version)

SYNOPSIS
    #include "xignal.h"

LAST UPDATE
    22 May 1985  by  Haam
        downgrade requirement for envir.h
    02 October 1985  by  Haam
        add stuff for Compupro
    10 September 1987  by  Haam
        name change to xignal

AUTHOR
    Haam  Tham  18 February 1985

**********************************************************************/

/**********************  locals - for IBM-PC  *********************/

#if IBMPC

#define XIGALL          0               /* vectors 0 to 15 */

#define XIGTMR          1
#define XIGKB           2
#define XIGCGA          3
#define XIGCOM2         4
#define XIGCOM1         5
#define XIGLPT2         6
#define XIGFDSK         7
#define XIGPRN          8
#define XIGFPE          9

#define XIGAUX          XIGCOM1
#define XIGLPT1         XIGPRN

#define NXIG            10

#define XIGTMR0         XIGTMR          /* compatibility with Compupro version */
#define XIGKEYB         XIGKB

#endif  /* if IBMPC */


/**********************  locals - for Compupro  ********************/

#if COMPUPRO

#define XIGALL          0

#define XIGPIO4         1
#define XIGSRX4         3
#define XIGSTX4         4
#define XIGSRX2         5
#define XIGSTX2         6

#define XIGTMR0         12
#define XIGTMR1         13
#define XIGTMR2         14
#define XIGSCRN         17
#define XIGKEYB         18

#define XIGFPE          20

#define NXIG            21

#define XIGTMR          XIGTMR0         /* compatibility with IBM version */
#define XIGKB           XIGKEYB

#endif  /* if COMPUPRO */


/***************  Some Standard Xignal Definitions  ***************/

extern XIG_IGN();               /* actual functions are used instead of */
extern XIG_DFL();               /*  casting (*int()) () since some      */
extern BADXIG();                /*  compilers cannot perform the cast.  */

extern  int  (*xignal(int, int (*)()))();


/******  Floating Point Stuff, modelled on UNIX definitions  ******/

#define     FPE_INTOVF  0x1         /* integer overflow */
#define     FPE_INTDIV  0x2         /* integer divide by zero */
#define     FPE_FLTOVF  0x3         /* floating overflow */
#define     FPE_FLTDIV  0x4         /* floating divide by zero */
```

```
#define     FPE_FLTUND  0x5          /* floating underflow */


#define XIGALRM     XIGTMR  /* Unix to Local xignal number mapping */

/**********************************************************************

FILE
    envir.h  -  defines program environment

LAST UPDATE
    16 August 1987
        remove unnecessary clutter

    Copyright(c) 1985,1986,1987  D.M. Auslander and C.H. Tham

**********************************************************************/

/**********************   Operating System   ***********************/

#define UNIX    0       /* 4.2 BSD, implies UNIX C compiler */
#define PCDOS   1       /* includes generic MSDOS family */
#define CPM     0       /* the CP/M family, including MP/M */


/*****************   Hardware or Machine Type   *****************/

#define IBMPC       1       /* standard PC, PC/XT, PC/AT */
#define COMPUPRO    0       /* Compupro 8086 or Dual Processor */
#define INTEL310    0       /* Intel 310 development system */


/*************************   Compilers   *************************/

#define CIC86       0       /* Computer Innovations C86 ver. 2.20M */
#define DESMET      0       /* Desmet C */
#define LATTICE     0       /* Lattice C ver. 2.15 */
#define MICROSOFT   1       /* Microsft C ver. 4.00 */

#if MICROSOFT
#define ANSI                /* use proposed ANSI C features */
#endif
```

CHAPTER 8

EVENT DRIVEN SCHEDULING

Up until now, we have conveniently divided tasks into control tasks with fixed sampling times and background time-sliced tasks. Although such tasks are asynchronous in the sense that their execution is not synchronized with respect to each other, they are still synchronized to an internal periodic clock. In general, a real-time system will have to respond to external asynchronous events which may be nonperiodic.

Previously, external asynchronous events, such as the occurrence of an encoder transition, were handled by short interrupt service routines, bypassing the scheduler. In general, there may be events that require more processing time than can be allowed for in an interrupt service routine. For example, if the temperature in a chemical reactor rises above a safe level, a complicated and lengthy procedure may be required to immediately raise the alarm and effect an orderly shutdown. Complications also arise if there is more than one task synchronizing with the same event. For example, in an automated assembly line, a robot and a vision system may be waiting for the arrival of a part, with the assembly sequence determined by what the part is and when it arrives. As the examples suggest, the complicated and relatively lengthy processing required by such events makes it impractical to implement the event handler(s) as an interrupt service routine.

One solution is to have the event trigger a simple interrupt service routine that just sets a flag; tasks synchronizing with the event can wait in a loop, constantly checking the flag. However, it is wasteful, especially in a single-processor environment, to have CPU resources needlessly consumed by high-priority tasks in idle waiting. Another problem is that tasks cannot be pre-empted. This is clearly unacceptable, especially if the events are time critical and it is essential that the system repsond to them in a timely fashion.

It is obvious that the occurrence of a high-priority event that requires significant processing time to service must force a change in the normal task schedule. Tasks waiting for an event are suspended. When the event is signalled, the current executing task is pre-empted and the pending tasks added to the active task list. A priority scheduler is then called to select the highest priority task for execution. This form of scheduling is known as Event Driven Scheduling. The use of priority to represent the "urgency" of an event allows one to handle time critical events that require a guaranteed response time, and also to synchronize less time critical tasks. Because it is a more general scheduling paradigm, event driven scheduling can perform time based scheduling; the timer "time-out" is treated as just another event.

The earlier chapters dealt mainly with time based scheduling because of their immediate application to control tasks that operate at fixed sample intervals. We have delayed the introduction of event driven scheduling even though it is a more general and powerful scheduling mechanism because asynchronous events are more difficult to deal with. The asynchronous nature of event driven scheduling serves also as an introduction to concepts that are central to multi-tasking systems, whether time sliced or event driven.

8.1 TASK CONTROL

The event driven scheduling system requires that:

1. events must be defined;
2. tasks waiting for events should be suspended so as not to waste CPU resource in idle waiting;
3. the occurrence of an event must be made known to the event scheduler;
4. the scheduler must then release tasks that are pending on that event and schedule them for immediate execution, subjected to modification by priority.

8.1.1 DEFINING EVENTS

Events may be externally or internally generated. External events are those that depend on the state of the world outside the computer, such as the arrival of a part in an assembly cell. Such events are usually detected by hardware which signals the computer by means of an interrupt or perhaps by setting bits in an i/o port that is periodically polled by the computer. External events are thus asynchronous in nature. Internally generated events are those arising from the execution state of the computer. For example, many computers have hardware that traps conditions such as attempting to divide by zero or trying to access nonexistent or protected memory. Such events are normally detected by the computer's hardware. Finally, there is the software-triggered event. For example, a vision system may signal that it has finished identifying a part so that other tasks waiting for that part can proceed. Internally generated events are mostly synchronous. The exceptions are events such as the "tick" of the system clock used for time-based scheduling, though such events may be viewed as being externally generated.

Events that are signalled by means of an interrupt often require an interrupt service routine to save the machine state and perform any housekeeping required by the signalling hardware. Hence, such hardware-triggered events must be predefined and an interrupt service routine installed for each trigger source. One could of course perform the machine-dependent housekeeping in the pending task, but that would make the event triggering nontransparent to the tasks.

Software-generated events are not hardware dependent, and a general signalling mechanism can be written to accommodate them. Thus, cooperating tasks can allocate an event identifier (id) which they can then use to synchronize with each other. Except for the response-time requirement, this is not unlike a mailbox or a message passing scheme.

8.1.2 Task Suspension

Tasks waiting for an event can be suspended through a "pend" system call which "blocks" (i.e., causes the task to be suspended) until the occurrence of the event. As far as the task is concerned, nothing further happens until the event takes place, at which time it returns from the "pend" system call. Thus, event synchronization is completely transparent to the task, making it very simple to set up an event driven control system once the scheduler is in place.

When the event scheduler receives a "pend" request, it first checks that the task is pending on a valid or predefined event. The pending task is removed from the active task list and is added to the list of tasks that are waiting for that particular event. The scheduler then dispatches a task from the "ready-to-run" list.

In this limited context, one can view task suspension as dynamically lowering the priority of a task to such low levels that it will never get to run, unless the waited-for event occurs that causes the task's priority to be increased to levels sufficient to pre-empt other tasks. This distinguishes the current scheduling methodology from the "fixed-priority" scheduling described in Chapter 7.

8.1.3 SIGNALLING

When an event occurs, the foreground portion of the event handler gains control, either through an interrupt in the case of hardware-triggered events, or through a system call for software-triggered interrupts. The handler then has to decide which of the pending tasks (if any) to activate. The foreground handler can release one waiting task or it can release all waiting tasks to compete for CPU resources. The released task (or tasks) is placed into the "ready-to-run" list and the priority scheduler is called to dispatch a task from among the "ready-to-run" tasks. The event handling tasks must therefore have a high priority to ensure that they get to run as soon as possible after the event occurs.

The use of priority allows one to tailor the response to the importance of the event. Tasks that handle events such as a serious fault can be accorded such high priority that they will pre-empt all other tasks. Tasks pending on less important events such as the completion of vision processing can have lower priority, which in some cases may be lower than that of some sample-time control tasks. The system integrator can thus adjust the priority of the event tasks to reflect the importance of the event to the overall functioning of the system.

Software-triggered events can be used as a general mechanism to synchronize two or more tasks. However, the philosophy behind event driven scheduling is not quite the same as other synchronization methods such as semaphores, which are usually used for resource allocation in multi-tasking systems. In an event driven control system, all tasks waiting for an event should be executed when the event occurs. The waiting tasks could be sample-time control tasks, which require a more or less constant sampling interval for proper operation. Having more than one task pending on an event is generally not a good idea in a real time system because then we can no longer guarantee a response time for each task; only the response time of the highest priority task can be guaranteed.

8.2 TASK STRUCTURE

An event driven task usually spends most of its time waiting for the event. The structure shown in Fig. 8.1 is typical.

```
Task
   Initialization

   Loop Forever
      Wait for Event A
      .
      .
      .
   End Loop

End Task
```

Figure 8.1

The task consists of an infinite loop, and execution depends on the occurrence of some event, labelled A. This waiting is transparent to the task; it merely has to make a "pend" system call. A sample time control task can be implemented by having the event be the timer timeout. In this case, either the timer automatically resets or there must be some provision for setting the timer.

Figure 8.2 shows the structure applied to the multi-motor control problem. Each motor control loop is implemented by a separate task which shares the same piece of pure (i.e., re-entrant) code, but operates on different data.

```
i-th motor control task:
        Turn off power amplifier                 (Initialization Section)
        Do validity and safety checks
        Set timer for sampling time using auto-reset mode

        Loop Forever                    (Control Section)
                Suspend for timer       (This can be done at the
                                        beginning or end)
                Get motor velocity      (Or process variable measurement
                                        for other control problems)
                Call the motor computation function
                Send control output to power amplifier
        End-of-loop
```

Figure 8.2

8.3 THE MULTI-MOTOR CONTROL EXAMPLE

Each task is assumed to have its own timer which may be simulated in software if there are insufficient hardware timers. The timer is initially set with the sample interval and put into auto-reset mode, if that mode exists. Auto-reset will restart the timer using the same sample time as soon as the previous interval runs out; this minimizes latency errors. If auto-reset is not available, the timer must be reset immediately on return from the suspended "wait" system call.

The wait call can be placed at the beginning or the end of the control loop. Placing the wait call at the beginning of the loop will cause the task to wait for one sample period before executing for the first time. Thus, as long as the tasks do not all have the same sample time, they will not all try to execute at the same time when the system is first turned on. If some tasks have the same sample time, the initial timer setting can be varied for each task, staggering the sampling instances. The sample time can be reset to the correct value when the control part of each task first executes.

8.4 MULTI-TASKING

A multi-tasking computer system is one in which several tasks are active at the same time. In a system with only one processor (a uniprocessor system), a control program decides when each task gets to run and how much CPU resource it gets. This control program is the scheduler-dispatcher; the scheduler decides when to run the task and the dispatcher executes the task. For convenience, we have used the term scheduler to refer to the combination scheduler-dispatcher. We have discussed various forms of scheduling in the previous chapters, ranging from time-slice scheduling used in traditional operating systems to the fixed sample time and event driven systems, which are better suited to real-time control applications. The previous discussions have so far neglected several important aspects of multi-tasking systems; we shall address these issues here.

8.5 MUTUAL EXCLUSION

In a multi-tasking uniprocessor system with a pre-emptive scheduler, a task may be interrupted and pre-empted at any time. With a time-slice scheduler, that may happen when the current time slice is up. In fixed sample time systems, a higher priority task may need to run before the current task has completed its loop. An event driven system is by nature asynchronous, and tasks may be pre-empted and rescheduled at unpredictable times. These situations should not concern us but for the fact that in most systems of any size, certain resources such as memory and input/output devices may be shared between several tasks. Tasks may communicate with each other by using common memory locations; input/output devices such as disk drives and Analog-to-Digital (A/D) converters may have to be shared.

To illustrate the problems that can result unless access to shared resources is carefully controlled, let us consider an example where two tasks communicate with each other by reading and writing to a shared memory location. The first task, the writer, starts writing to the memory location but before it can finish, it is pre-empted by another task which attempts to read the same memory location. Since the first task has not completed its write operation, the contents of the memory location will not be valid; the second task will be reading garbage. This can easily happen with a user interface task that allows the user to dynamically change parameters, such as control gain, which are used by the control tasks. The problem is worse if the second task writes to the same memory location; when the first task resumes later on, it will continue its interrupted write and the memory location will contain garbage.

Let us look at another example. A high-speed Analog-to-Digital converter is multiplexed into several channels, each used by a different task. Obviously, if one task has selected a channel and is about to initiate an A/D conversion, we cannot allow another task to change the channel until the first task has finished its A/D operation.

As the examples show, only a single task may access a shared resource at any time. Once a task has access, all other tasks are excluded until the task that has access relinquishes it. This is known as *mutual exclusion*. The region of code where a task has exclusive access is known as the *critical region*. A task executing in a critical region may be pre-empted, but no other task can be in the same critical region until the first task relinquishes control. There exist many algorithms to ensure mutual exclusion; in fact, whole books have been devoted to the subject. In this chapter, we shall look at some of the simpler ones that can be easily implemented on a small computer.

Since the only way one task can pre-empt another on a single processor system is via an interrupt, the simplest way to ensure exclusive access is to disable interrupts in the critical region, as shown in Fig. 8.3.

```
non critical region code
.
.

Disable Interrupts

    .
    .
        critical region code
    .
    .

Enable Interrupts
```

Figure 8.3

The functions to enable and disable interrupts may have to be written in assembly language. The interface between assembly language routines and a "high" level language such as **C** is dependent on the compiler implementation, and the reader is advised to consult his/her compiler documentation. Figure 8.4 is an example that can be used with most C compilers that run on the IBM-PC. Any code that has to run with interrupts disabled should be kept as short as possible.

With cooperating tasks, a way of controlling access to a critical section without disabling interrupts in the critical section is through the use of a flag variable, which indicates when access is allowed. Reading and writing this flag variable must of course be *atomic*, meaning that the read or write is uninterruptible. Some processors support an atomic "test-and-set" instruction, which reads a memory location and then sets it to a non-zero value. Thus, a task wishing to go into a

```
enable PROC

  sti
  ret

enable ENDP
```

Figure 8.4

critical region performs an atomic test-and-set operation on a flag. If the flag is zero, no other task is in the critical section. The flag must be cleared when the task exits the critical region. If the test-and-set returns with the flag set, that indicates that another task is in the critical region; waiting tasks can wait, performing test-and-sets until the flag returns clear. If two or more tasks attempt a test-and-set at the same time, then by the atomic nature of the operation, only one call will return with the flag clear; the other calls will return with the flag set (see Fig. 8.5).

```
again:

        if Test-and-Set (flag) returns clear

                enter critical region
                clear flag on exit

        else

                goto again
```

Figure 8.5

If the processor does not support an atomic test-and-set operation, we can write a simple function to implement it by disabling interrupts before accessing the flag variable (see Fig. 8.6).

A test-and-set function is best implemented at a very low level in assembly language. An atomic test-and-set is easy to implement, but it suffers from the disadvantage that there may be times when tasks are idly waiting for others to relinquish control. More sophisticated systems may provide a pre-emptive *semaphore* mechanism, whereby tasks that cannot access a resource are automatically suspended and another task scheduled in its place. When the resource becomes available, a waiting task is reactivated. This process is not unlike the event driven

```
Function Test-and-Set (flag)

        allocate temporary variable

        disable interrupts

        save flag in temporary variable
        set flag

        enable interrupts

        return value of temporary variable

End Function
```

Figure 8.6

scheduling mechanism discussed earlier. A task wishing to access a shared resource performs a "pend" operation on a semaphore variable. If the resource is not available, the task is automatically suspended. When the resource becomes available, the pending task resumes execution where it left off; thus, when the task returns from the pend call, the resource is available. All this is transparent to the calling task. When the task has finished, it signals the system so that other waiting tasks can get their turn. Figure 8.7 is an example of how such a mechanism might operate.

```
... semaphore variable may be initialized elsewhere ...


Pend on semaphore S

    .
    .
    critical section code
    .
    .

Signal done to semaphore S
```

Figure 8.7

As the example illustrates, a pre-emptive semaphore mechanism makes it very easy to implement critical regions. If there is more than one task waiting for access, the semaphore mechanism must queue the tasks and decide which task to release when the resource becomes available. The above example is a very simple one; other types of semaphores can be used to keep track of the number of waiting tasks and control how many tasks can have access at any one time. The reader is advised to refer to the bibliography for more details.

The discussion so far assumes a uniprocessor system. In multiprocessor systems where tasks are distributed among several processors, there will usually be some form of hardware support for atomic operations.

While the discussion has focused on controlling access to shared resources, one should keep in mind that in real-time control applications, no task should be kept waiting if at all possible. There should be sufficient resources available to minimize sharing. Under this assumption, we have not addressed other multitasking issues such as deadlocks. Resource sharing may be unavoidable if tasks are to communicate with each other whether through explicit reads and writes into shared memory or through some system furnished mechanism such as mailboxes or message passing. The system designer should always keep in mind that a real-time system needs to respond to external events in a timely manner and any form of waiting may be detrimental to that goal.

EVENT DRIVEN SCHEDULING EXAMPLE

8.6 INTRODUCTION

This example program illustrates both synchronous and asynchronous event driven scheduling and also fixed sample time scheduling. The program uses the *Clotho* real-time kernel to implement a fixed sample time "control" task together with several tasks that are activated when certain keys on the keyboard are hit. The program can also serve as a preliminary introduction to the facilities of the *Clotho* real-time kernel, which is described in more detail in the next section.

A variable named *count* is accessed by three tasks: a sample time scheduled task, *print_count()*, which runs every second and prints out the current value of *count*, plus two asynchronous event driven tasks—*inc_count()*, which increments *count*, and *dec_count*, which decrements *count*. *Inc_count* is activated whenever the 'i' key is hit, whereafter it runs every 0.5 seconds, incrementing count every time it runs, for a total of 5 seconds before suspending itself to wait for the next time the 'i' key is hit. *Dec_Count*, which decrements the count variable, is activated whenever the 'd' key is hit, and it runs every 0.75 seconds for a total of 7.5 seconds before suspending itself to await the next 'd' key event. We can actually see this happening by observing the value of *count*, which is printed every second by *print_count()*. If we hit both the 'i' and the 'd' key, we can see the value of count oscillating around some value as *inc_count()* and *dec_count()* compete with each other to raise and lower the count value. The program is set up to run indefinitely, but there is a provision to terminate the program by hitting the *ESC* key, which triggers a high-priority task to effect an orderly exit back to DOS.

Although one tends to associate an event driven scheduling system as being associated with asynchronous external events, the triggering event may also be software generated. In the example program, there is a task called *reset()*, which is activated by *print_count()* whenever the value of *count* exceeds 20; *reset()* sets the value of *count* to zero.

8.7 INITIALIZATION

There is a special function called *InitUser()* which is called by the kernel to setup and initialize user tasks. A task is implemented in the form of a **C** function. Task setup is accomplished by a call to *NewTask()*, which allocates and initializes a task descriptor. Please refer to the section describing the kernel for a more detailed explanation of the arguments to *NewTask()*. The task descriptor pointer returned by *NewTask()* is then put into an appropriate task queue.

An event handle, in the form of a small integer, must be allocated for each event that can cause scheduling changes. This is accomplished by a call to *NewEvent()*. A *Pend()* call is then made with 2 arguments: the value of the event handle, and a task descriptor pointer for that event. This associates the task with the event handle and immediately suspends the task to await the event.

8.8 PRIORITIES

Note that the task priorities of *inc_count()* and *dec_count()* are the same as *print_count()*, forcing all 3 tasks to compete equally for CPU resources should they all want to run at the same time. This illustrates the fact that event synchronized tasks need not always be high-priority items requiring immediate service. Task priority can be used to tailor the response to the importance of the event, at the cost of introducing some uncertainty in the response time. The priority of the *reset()* task is higher than *print_count*, *inc_count*, and *dec_count*, to ensure that action is taken as soon as the triggering condition is discovered. In a real control system, software-detected fault or limit conditions such as tank overflow may be handled by a software-triggered task which must have sufficiently high priority to pre-empt other less important tasks. The task with the highest priority is triggered by the user hitting the *ESC* key, effecting an orderly exit to DOS.

8.9 EVENT HARDWARE INTERFACE

The system must be able to detect an external asynchronous event. In this example, whenever a key is pressed, it generates an interrupt. A keyboard interrupt service routine, *kbisr()*, defined in the file kbisr.asm, is associated with the keyboard interrupt by a call to system utility *setivec(vector number, function pointer)*. This routine calls on the IBM-PC BIOS to decipher the scan code and determine if an ASCII character is available. If so, it performs a context switch and calls on the function *kbsig()*, which determines if the key is an "event" key, i.e., if the key is one of 'i', 'd', or 'ESC'. If not, *kbsig()* returns and the program resumes where it left off; otherwise, it notifies the event manager, identifying the event using the designated event handle. Tasks pending on that event are released, and all ready-to-run tasks are rescheduled according to priority.

Note that *kbsig()* is considered "system" routine and executes in system space instead of user space. It needs to be loaded into the system entry table, defined in main.c.

8.10 GENERATING THE EXAMPLE PROGRAM

The example program consists of two source files: the **C** source file kbsched.c, and the assembly language source file kbisr.asm. The **C** program is compiled with the Microsoft **C** compiler (vers 5+) using the command line:

```
cl/Alfw /Gs /DLARGEMODEL kbsched.c /link clotho
```

and the assembly program is assembled with MASM (Microsoft Assembler) using

```
masm kbisr /ml;
```

THE CLOTHO REAL-TIME KERNEL

8.11 INTRODUCTION

Clotho is a real-time multi-tasking kernel designed for writing process control, scheduling, and data logging applications for the IBM-PC family of microcomputers. The kernel supports several pre-emptive scheduling schemes: time-slice scheduling for non-time critical tasks, fixed sample time scheduling for classical process control tasks and event driven scheduling to handle asynchronous events. All three schedulers can be simultaneously active.

Clotho is intended to be used primarily as a learning tool to explore the issues involved in designing a real-time system for process control, data acquisition, process scheduling, and exception handling. Readers are encouraged to study the innards of the kernel, understand it, make improvements, and otherwise modify the kernel to better serve their applications.

Clotho can also be used in actual control applications where the dynamics of the controlled systems have time constants of several hundred milliseconds or longer. On an IBM-PC (4.77-MHz 8088), it takes about 10 to 15 milliseconds to switch between fixed sample time scheduled tasks; on a 16-MHz 80386 machine, the context switching time can be less than 1 millisecond. Clotho will probe for the presence of an 8087, 80287, or 80387 math coprocessor when it starts up, and save the coprocessor state when switching between tasks. The kernel is written almost entirely in Microsoft **C** (version 5.1) with a few modules written in assembly language.

8.12 GETTING STARTED

The kernel is supplied as a large memory model library[1] *clotho.lib*, and a set of C header files. All the header files required by user applications are "included" in a single header file, *clotho.h*. Tasks are written as C routines which are compiled and linked with clotho.lib to generate an executable program. The task routines are called by the scheduler at the appropriate moment. The following example program sets up a single task that prints the elapsed time every second for 10 seconds.

```
#include <stdio.h>
#include "clotho.h"
```

[1]A medium memory model library and a special version for the QuickC environment are also included in the library set.

```
static void ticktock()
{
    long ms;  /* elapsed time in milliseconds */

    while (1)
    {
        ms = ReadClock();     /* get elapsed time */

        if (ms > 10000L)      /* 10 seconds have elapsed */
        {
            panic("time is up");
        }
        else
        {
            printf("%ld\n", ms / 1000L);
        }

        WaitNextSamp();       /* wait for next sampling instance */
    }
}

main()
{
    prologue();    /* initialize kernel */

    SetCntrlTask("TICKTOCK", ticktock, (void *)NULL, PCONTROL, 1000L);

    start();  /* begin application */
}
```

The main function, *main()*, must be supplied by the application. The routine, *prologue()*, initializes the kernel and must be called prior to any of the Clotho library functions. The next call is to *SetCntrlTask()* to set up *ticktock()* as a fixed sample time scheduled task (PCONTROL) to be executed every 1000 milliseconds (1000L). The first argument, TICKTOCK, is a name (which must be less than 16 characters) to be associated with the task. In the current implementation, this name is not used except as a task identifier for error messages. The third argument to *SetCntrlTask()* is a pointer to the area of memory containing arguments for the task routine, but since *ticktock()* does not require arguments, the pointer is set to NULL. Once the task is set up, *start()* is called to start Clotho. The program then runs until it is aborted or the computer is rebooted.

The task routine, *ticktock()*, is implemented as an infinite loop. It calls *ReadClock()* to get the elapsed time in milliseconds. If the elapsed time is less than 10 seconds, it prints the time; otherwise, it calls *panic()* to print a message and abort the program. The call to *WaitNextSamp()* at the bottom of the loop causes *ticktock()* to be suspended until the next sampling instance, which in this case comes after an interval of 1 second.

This example program can be found in the file *ticktock.c*. To compile and generate an executable program using Microsoft C version 5.0 and above, do:

```
cl /Alfw /DLARGEMODEL=1 /Gs ticktock.c /link clotho
```

As this simple example illustrates, it is quite easy to develop a real-time control application using Clotho to schedule the control task. There is a set of routines defined in *user.c* to simplify task setup. We have already encountered *SetCntrlTask()*, which sets up a fixed sample time scheduled task and *WaitNextSamp()*, which causes the task to wait until the next sampling instance. Following is a list of the task setup routines and their arguments:

```
TASK *  SetCntrlTask(name, func, argp, priority, tsamp);
TASK *  SetBkgndTask(name, func, argp, priority);
int     SetEventTask(name, func, argp, priority);
void    WaitNextSamp(void);

void (*func)(), *argp;
char *name;
int priority;
long tsamp;
```

SetBkgndTask() sets up a time-sliced task, also known as a background task since such tasks only run when no fixed sample time and event driven tasks wants to run. Both *SetCntrlTask()* and *SetBkgndTask()* return a pointer to a TASK data structure (which is ignored in the previous example). This TASK data structure is the task descriptor and contains information that is used by the task schedulers and dispatcher. Interested readers are encouraged to peruse the file *task.h* where TASK is defined. *SetEventTask()* sets up *func()* as an event driven task. It puts the task on an event queue and returns an event identifier. This event identifier can be used by other tasks to wait for the event or to notify the event manager that the event has occurred. The third parameter, *argp*, is a pointer to an area of memory containing the arguments (if any) to the task routine. This way, multiple copies of the same routine, if written in a re-entrant manner, can be used to simultaneously control several processes, each with different control parameters. We have already seen this in Chapter 5. The *priority* parameter sets the task priority; the larger the priority value, the higher the priority. PCONTROL is the starting priority level for control tasks, and PSLICE is the corresponding level for time-sliced tasks. The lowest priority level for user tasks is PZERO. These symbols are defined in the file *config.h*, which is included in *clotho.h*, and their intentions should be followed in all applications using Clotho.

Let us next examine Clotho's various scheduling schemes in more detail.

8.13 SCHEDULING

Clotho's scheduling system is divided into two parts: the scheduler and the dispatcher. The scheduler decides the execution order of a given type of task, and the dispatcher executes the task. There are 3 schedulers in Clotho; they are:

1. Fixed Sample Time scheduler implemented in *stlsched.c*
2. Time-Slice scheduler implemented in *slice.c* and *rrbsched.c*
3. Event Driven scheduler implemented in *event.c*

The dispatcher is implemented in *dispatch.c*. Let us look at the main *Dispatch()* routine:

```
if (curtask == TNULL)
    if ((curtask = GetTqueue(CwaitQueue)) == TNULL)
        if ((curtask = GetTqueue(ReadyQueue)) == TNULL)
            if ((curtask = GetTqueue(SliceQueue)) == TNULL)
                panic("Dispatch: slice queue empty");
```

If there are no currently executing tasks, *curtask* will be NULL and the dispatcher will look through the series of task queues, *CwaitQueue*, *ReadyQueue*, and *Slice-Queue* in this order for the next task to dispatch. These queues are used by the schedulers and will be described in the relevant scheduler sections. Note that there must be at least one task to dispatch; otherwise the system will abort. Clotho ensures this by setting up a time-sliced *idler* task whose sole purpose is to soak up unused CPU cycles.

8.13.1 Fixed-Sample-Time Scheduling

This is also known as control task scheduling, since traditional digital control algorithms always assume a fixed sample interval. Control tasks tend to be time critical since the dynamic systems they control may become unstable if the control tasks are not promptly dispatched at the proper sampling intervals. To ensure that they are dispatched at the requested intervals, fixed sample time tasks are assigned quite high priorities—the base priority for control tasks has been arbitrarily set at 1000 (defined as PCONTROL in *config.h*).

Scheduling information is stored in the *t_tsamp* and *t_tleft* fields of the task descriptor data structure, TASK. The *t_tsamp* field records the sampling interval in milliseconds, and the *t_tleft* field records the number of milliseconds to the next sampling instance. *SetCntrlTask()* creates a new task descriptor and sets the *t_tleft* field equal to the *t_tsamp* field, which in turn is obtained from the *tsamp* parameter. The pointer to the newly created task descriptor is automatically put into the "Shortest-Time-Left" queue, *StlQueue*, in increasing *t_tleft* order. Hence, the task at the head of the queue will be the one with the shortest *t_tleft*. This results in a staggered start—tasks with different sampling periods will start at different times and minimize crowding at the starting point.

When a control task is dispatched, the scheduler updates the *t_tleft* fields of all waiting control tasks by subtracting the *t_tleft* value of the about-to-be-dispatched task from the *t_tleft* of the waiting control tasks. This reflects the fact that the about-to-be-dispatched task (and all the other fixed sample time tasks) have been waiting for *t_tleft* milliseconds since the scheduler was last called to dispatch a task. Just before it is dispatched, the *t_tleft* field of the control task is reset to *t_tsamp*. The control task scheduling timer is set to the shortest time remaining to next sampling instance; the timer control module will trigger the scheduler at the preset elapsed time. The use of the shortest time left is the reason the scheduler-dispatcher, *StlDispatch()*, implemented in the file *stlsched.c*, is also called the Shortest-Time-Left Scheduler.

If two or more fixed sample time tasks need to run at the same sampling instance, only the task with the highest priority is dispatched. The rest of the tasks that want to run at the current sampling instance are put into a special queue named *CwaitQueue*. Tasks in this queue are arranged in priority order, with the highest priority task at the head of the queue. All the tasks in this queue have *t_tleft* equal to or less than 0.

When the control task is done and calls *WaitNextSamp()*, it invokes *StlWait()*, which inserts the task into *StlQueue* in ascending *t_tleft* order. Remember that the *t_tleft* field was reset to *t_tsamp* just before the task was dispatched.

The scheduler then checks *CwaitQueue*; if there are tasks present, the highest priority task at the head of the queue is dispatched. If *CwaitQueue* is empty, the main scheduler is invoked to dispatch a time-sliced background task.

If a control task needs to run but the currently running control or event task is not finished yet, which task to pre-empt is decided on the basis of priority. The pre-empted control or event driven task is placed in *CwaitQueue*.

If CPU contention does not occur too frequently, control tasks will be able to execute at more or less the correct sampling intervals. However, if one or more control tasks cannot finish their loop well before the next sampling instance, it implies that CPU resources have been over-committed and the computer does not have sufficient performance for the application. The scheduler will abort with a suitable error message.

Recall that when a control task is first set up, the system sets *t_tleft* to *t_tsamp* by default. Therefore, when the kernel is started by a call to *start()*, the time to when a fixed sample time task first executes is equal to the sampling interval. The time to first execution can be changed by modifying the *t_tleft* field of the task descriptor. However, if you want to do this, you cannot use *SetCntrlTask()* but must instead use the lower level *NewTask()* function (see *task.c*), which returns a pointer to the task descriptor but does not put the task into *StlQueue*.

8.13.2 TIME-SLICE SCHEDULING

In time-slice scheduling, CPU time is allocated in units known as *quanta*. At the end of its quantum, the task is suspended and another task dispatched in its place. By rapidly switching between tasks and giving each a small slice of CPU resources at a time, the computer can give the impression of running multiple concurrent tasks. This form of multi-task scheduling is very common in multi-user operating systems. In Clotho, time-slice scheduling is intended for non-time critical tasks which run whenever fixed sample time and event scheduled tasks are not running. Examples of non-time critical tasks that can be time-sliced are terminal interaction and calculating process statistics.

There are many variations on time-slice scheduling. The simplest scheme is to allocate an equal amount of CPU time to each task in strict rotation. This is known as Round-Robin Scheduling. Clotho uses round-robin scheduling. This is implemented in two files: *rrbsched.c* which implements the round-robin scheduler, and *slice.c*, which integrates the time-slice scheduler into the kernel.

There is a slightly more sophisticated form of time-slice scheduling known as exponential scheduling. Each task is initially allocated a certain amount of CPU time, and execution frequency is determined by priority. At the end of each time slice, the quantum is doubled (up to a predefined maximum) but the execution priority is halved. Tasks that have been running for a long time will end up with large quanta, but newer and higher priority tasks will be scheduled more often.

In a "static" system where tasks are not dynamically created and destroyed, an exponential scheduler is of limited value; a round-robin scheduler is simpler and serves equally well. In a multi-user operating system, an exponential scheduler increases the quantum and decreases the priority until the task performs an i/o operation such as reading from a disk, after which the quantum and priority are reset to their original values. This allows lengthy CPU intensive tasks to minimize context switching overhead and gives higher priority and better response time to tasks that need to perform frequent i/o operations.

Since individual tasks can perform i/o outside of Clotho, there is no easy way for Clotho to monitor a task's i/o operations, making an exponential time-slice scheduler quite impractical. Of course, one can always trap calls to DOS i/o routines and reset the task's quantum and priority after such a call. How would you go about doing this and would you get better "performance" from your system?

Clotho has both time-slice and fixed sample time scheduling. Both schedulers are clocked off different software-based timers. The timers are implemented in *time.c* where the two scheduler tasks are installed as time-out routines on two preallocated software timers. The software timers are managed by the *chronos()* routine, which is triggered by interrupts from the PC's hardware timer.

By convention, the priority of a time-slice task is always lower than that of a fixed sample time control task. Therefore, a control task can always pre-empt a time-slice task. Whenever a time-slice task is pre-empted by a control task, it is put at the head of the time-slice task queue, *SliceQueue*, and the software time-slice scheduling timer is stopped. When the control task finishes, the pre-empted time-slice task is resumed and the time-slice scheduling timer restarted. This ensures that each time-slice task gets its full quantum, subject to the granularity of the software timer.

On Clotho, background tasks are normally written as routines running in an infinite loop. Unlike fixed sample time scheduled tasks, there is no need to wait for a sampling instance; the system will transparently interrupt and suspend the task at the end of a quantum and resume it later in due course. A demonstration of both fixed sample time and time-slice scheduling can be found in *demo1.c*.

8.13.2.1 DEMO1.C. This program sets up 3 fixed sample time "foreground" tasks and 8 time-slice "background" tasks. One of the foreground tasks, *clock()*, implements a clock, running every second to print the elapsed time in hour:minute:second format on the upper left side of the screen. The other two foreground tasks are implemented by one routine, *fgtask()*, which prints an integer that is incremented at every sample instance. The two tasks differ only in their display parameters, which are contained in the parameter blocks defined by:

```
static struct _display d_fg1, d_fg2;
```

Similarly, the 8 background tasks are implemented by just one routine, *bgtask()*, which runs in an infinite loop, displaying the loop count at every iteration.

The data from the tasks are displayed using *video_WriteString()*, which writes a NUL terminated string directly to video memory. This routine is re-entrant (unlike the DOS and BIOS routines), and is a member of a family of video routines in the assembly language file *video.asm*. One of the problems we have encountered is that the Microsoft *sprintf()* function is not re-entrant—it must be used within a critical section. Until Microsoft (or your compiler vendor) can guarantee that their library routines are re-entrant, one should assume that the compiler's library routines are not re-entrant. In this example, the critical sections are implemented by disabling interrupts within the critical section. What effect does this have on context switching and scheduling in a real-time system?

The tasks are set up in the *main()* routine. After *prologue()* is called to initialize the kernel, the tasks are set up by calls to *SetCntrlTask()* and *SetBkgndTask()*. Note that the foreground task FG2 runs every 2 seconds at a slightly higher priority than FG1. To compile and generate an executable program, do:

```
cl /Alfw /DLARGEMODEL=1 /Gs demo1.c /link clotho
```

8.13.3 EVENT DRIVEN SCHEDULING

There may be situations where the system is required to handle events that occur rarely and/or whose occurrences cannot be predicted. Examples of events are the arrival of a part on an assembly line, exceeding the safe operating temperature in a chemical reactor, or when an operator presses the START button. There may be more than one task waiting for an event; for example, pressing the START button can send several tasks into action.

In Clotho, event driven tasks are also known as event scheduled tasks. The event can be synchronous and internally generated, such as the detection of an out-of-range value during a calculation, in which case the event is sometimes termed an "exception." Events can be asynchronous and externally generated, such as the operator pressing a key on the keyboard, in which case the event is normally termed an "interrupt." Event scheduling is quite a general concept which can encompass time-based scheduling such as fixed sample time and time-slice scheduling, where scheduling is triggered by time-out events.

Clotho's event manager is implemented in the file *event.c*. Each type of event is identified by a small unique integer known as the event handle. To ensure that event handles are unique, they are allocated with a call to *NewEvent()*, which allocates and initializes a per-event data structure defined thus:

```
typedef struct {
    int e_id;                   /* event handle */
    TQUEUE *e_queue;            /* tasks pending */
} EVENT;
```

A task queue is associated with each event, allowing more than one task to wait on an event. There are two basic operations: to Pend on an event, and to Notify the event manager that an event has occurred.

```
void Pend(event_handle, task_pointer)
int event_handle;
TASK * task_pointer;
```

A call to *Pend()* puts the task referenced by the task pointer into the task queue for that event. Waiting tasks are sorted in order of priority with the highest priority task at the head of the queue. If the task pointer is NULL, it is interpreted to mean the calling task, in which case the task is suspended until the event manager is notified of an occurrence of the event. *Pend()* is called with a non-NULL task pointer only during task setup to place the task in the proper event queue. Tasks set up this way [i.e., those set up by *SetEventTask()*] should not call *Pend()* as their first statement since they will be suspended immediately after being triggered by the event. The task should only call *Pend()* after it has finished processing the event and is ready to await the next occurrence. The structure of an event driven task is very similar to that of a fixed sample time task—an infinite loop with a call to *Pend()* at the bottom of the loop.

The occurrence of an event may trigger an interrupt service routine or be detected by software. In either case, the event manager must be informed by calling *Notify()*, with the event identifier. If the task that is pending on the event has a higher priority than the notifying task, it is dispatched, while the notifier is suspended and placed in the *ReadyQueue*. If the notifying task has the higher priority, the pending task is put into the *ReadyQueue* instead. If there is more than one task pending on the same event, the highest priority task among the pending tasks and the notifier is dispatched while the rest is put into the *ReadyQueue*. The advantage of this scheme is that the event response time can be tailored to the importance or urgency of the event. The disadvantage is that the worst-case event response time cannot be predicted without knowing the priorities of the other tasks in the system. In a purely event driven real-time system, a guaranteed response time is very important. However, in an environment that also supports fixed sample time control tasks, one must balance event response time against the need to run control tasks at sampling intervals that are determined by dynamic stability constraints. The solution adopted in Clotho is to use priority to tailor the response latency to the importance of the task. Thus, dangerous fault conditions or events requiring immediate attention can be assigned very high priorities to ensure timely service; less important conditions or synchronization schemes can be accorded lower priority. The more time critical the response, the more deterministic the response time.

There is an example of event driven scheduling in the file *kbsched.c*. This example program also shows the use of the *Suspend()* and *Resume()* calls to explicitly suspend and resume tasks.

8.14 SYNCHRONIZATION

The kernel provides 3 services to aid in task synchronization and resource management. The simplest way to implement mutual exclusion is to disable interrupts in the critical section. Clotho provides two functions, *disable()* and *enable()*, to disable and enable interrupts. The next simplest method is to use a lock variable and the atomic test-and-set function *tas()* to control entry into a critical section. Last, Clotho supports blocking semaphores, which are implemented in the file *sem.c*.

8.14.1 DISABLING INTERRUPTS

The first method is used in many of the example programs and also in *demo1.c*, and we shall not discuss it any further. Suffice it to note that its greatest advantage is its simplicity, while the disadvantage is that interrupts are disabled for *all* tasks. It also disables the scheduling timers and interrupt-based event detection.

8.14.2 TEST AND SET

An atomic test-and-set operation sets a specified bit (or bits) to 1 and returns the previous value of the bit. The term *atomic* means that the test-and-set operates like a single uninterruptible instruction. To ensure that only one task is executing in a critical section, a lock bit or variable is allocated for the critical section. A task wishing to enter the critical section performs a test-and-set operation on the lock variable. If the test-and-set returns 0, then the critical section is available and the task is the only one with access, because if another task were to perform a test-and-set on the same lock variable, a non-zero value will be returned. Since the test-and-set is atomic, out of several tasks "simultaneously" performing a test-and-set on an available lock, a zero value will be returned to only one task. The other tasks may choose to keep doing test-and-sets until a zero value is returned. When a task exits a critical section, it must set the lock value to zero (this assumes that assignment is atomic) in order that other tasks may acquire the lock.

Clotho provides a test-and-set function, *tas()*, which acts on a pointer to an integer lock variable, setting the lock variable to 1 and returning the previous lock value. The following code fragment shows how a critical section can be implemented using the *tas()* function:

```
int lock = 0;

while (tas(&lock) == 1)
    ;

 ... critical section code ...

lock = 0;
```

The advantages of test-and-set are that it is easy to use and interrupts need not be disabled inside critical sections. What are the disadvantages? Tasks can wait a long time before they acquire the lock. The only time the waiting tasks can acquire the lock is when the first task is outside of the critical section. This is quite pronounced in Clotho if the execution time within the critical section is a substantial portion of the task's overall loop execution time. This characteristic is demonstrated in the example program *demo2.c*. To compile and generate an executable program, do:

```
cl /Alfw /DLARGEMODEL=1 /Gs demo2.c /link clotho
```

Run the program for several minutes. Background tasks 1 to 8 use the *tas()* function to control access to the same critical section. We can also deduce from *demo2.c* that the background tasks spend a considerable portion of their execution time inside the *sprintf()* function.

8.14.3 BLOCKING SEMAPHORES

A semaphore is a type of signalling mechanism (in the computer sense) used for task synchronization and resource allocation. The lock variable used in a test-and-set operation can be considered a binary semaphore since it is used to signal the availability of a critical section and it has only two possible states: set or clear.

A counting semaphore differs from the binary semaphore in that it is not restricted to only two states. In the test-and-set example, if the lock is not available, it is up to the task to keep trying to acquire the lock. With a blocking or pre-emptive semaphore, the system can automatically suspend a task if the lock is not available. Thus, a call to the wait semaphore routine only returns when the lock is acquired. This not only simplifies the task's housekeeping chores, but also affects task scheduling by eliminating "busy-waits."

Clotho implements a kind of pre-emptive counting semaphore. The implementation code can be found in the file *sem.c*. Before a semaphore can be used, it must first be allocated by a call to *NewSem()*, specifying an initial semaphore count (more about this later). *NewSem()* returns a semaphore id value. Here is the semaphore descriptor structure:

```
typedef struct {
    int sem_count; /* semaphore count */
    TQUEUE *sem_queue;  /* tasks pending */
} SEM;
```

Note that each semaphore structure has a task queue for suspended tasks. Tasks in the semaphore queue are sorted in priority order with the highest priority task at the head of the queue.

There are two basic semaphore functions: Pend, to wait on a semaphore, and Release, to free up a semaphore. These are implemented in Clotho by the routines *Psem()* and *Vsem()* (after Dijkstra's P and V semaphore operations) passing to them the semaphore id returned by *NewSem()*. Here is a simple example of mutual exclusion using a binary blocking semaphore:

```
int lock;

lock = NewSem(1);

Psem(lock);

  ... critical section code ...

Vsem(lock);
```

When a *Psem()* is executed, if the semaphore count is less than or equal to zero, the calling task is suspended; otherwise, the call returns and the calling task continues to run. In both cases, the semaphore count is decremented after the less-or-equal-to-zero test. If the calling task is suspended, it is placed into the task queue associated with that particular semaphore. When a *Vsem()* is executed, if the semaphore count is less than zero, there are tasks waiting on the semaphore; otherwise the call returns and the calling task continues to run. In both cases, the semaphore count is incremented after the less-than-zero test. If there are suspended tasks, the first task in the queue is released and its priority compared against that of the calling task. The lower priority task is put into the *ReadyQueue*. If the priorities are the same, the released task is put into the *ReadyQueue*. By suspending a task only when the semaphore count is zero or negative, one can set up quite sophisticated resource allocation and execution synchronization schemes by using multiple semaphores with different initial semaphore counts.

The example program, *demo3.c*, demonstrates the use of a binary blocking semaphore to ensure mutually exclusive access to the non-re-entrant *sprintf()* function. To compile and generate an executable program, do:

```
cl /Alfw /DLARGEMODEL=1 /Gs demo3.c /link clotho
```

Run the program for a minute or so. Compare the behavior of the 8 background tasks with that shown by *demo1.c* and *demo2.c*. Can you explain why the background tasks seem to be switching between themselves very rapidly in no particular order?

Interested readers may wish to look at *demo4.c* for another example of semaphore usage.

8.15 INTER-TASK COMMUNICATION

If two tasks wish to communicate, the simplest way is to pass data through previously agreed-on global variables. However, access to these variables must take place in a critical section to prevent data corruption. The critical section can be implemented with any of the synchronization mechanisms discussed in this chapter, but remember that time critical, fixed sample time control tasks and event driven tasks should not be made to wait for resources (such as access to a critical section). Above all, the synchronization mechanism must not suspend these two types of tasks. The simple disable-enable scheme seems to work quite well for fixed sample time and event-driven tasks provided interrupts are disabled only to access the common variables and the number of these variables is kept small. For time-slice tasks, there are more options since they can afford to be suspended if a resource is not immediately available.

Another means of communication is to pass messages through a circular character buffer. Clotho provides a set of routines to set up and manipulate circular character buffers (see *cbuf.c*). Let us look at an example where circular buffers may be used. Suppose there is a data acquisition task that samples process variables. The acquired data must be written to disk, but the acquisition task cannot do so because it would take too much time or another task may have control of the disk resource at that time. One solution is to create a background time-slice task to write the acquired data to disk. These two tasks can set up a circular buffer; the acquisition task puts the formatted data into the buffer, and the "logging" task gets data from the buffer and writes it out to disk.

Using circular character buffers involves quite a bit of housekeeping for the tasks involved. Clotho provides a mailbox mechanism for passing messages between tasks. This is implemented in the file *message.c*, and there is an example program demonstrating its use in *demo5.c*.

8.16 SYSTEM ORGANIZATION

This section requires some knowledge of the 8086 memory models and assembly language programming. Readers who just want to use Clotho to build applications can skip this section. The kernel is written in Microsoft C version 5.1 using the large memory model (code and data can both be greater than 64 Kbytes in size). Because Clotho is written in a high level language and runs on top of DOS, certain compiler and DOS peculiarities cannot be avoided.

8.16.1 TASK STRUCTURE

A task descriptor structure is created for every task. This descriptor (defined in the file *task.h*) contains all the information that Clotho keeps about a task.

```
struct _task {
    int t_id;                  /* task id number */
    char t_name[TNAMELEN];     /* task name */
    int t_pri;                 /* effective priority */
    int t_reg[NOREG];          /* execution task state (registers) */
    int t_flags;               /* flags */
    void (*t_func)();          /* routine executed by task shell */
    void *t_argp;              /* pointer to task argument structure */
    int t_tasktype;            /* task type (control, slice, etc) */
    int t_state;               /* task state code */
    long t_tleft;              /* time left before execution */
    long t_tsamp;              /* sampling time (for control tasks) */
    int *t_usrstack;           /* ptr to allocated stack memory */
    unsigned t_ustacksize;     /* allocated user stacksize */
    struct _task *t_next;      /* ptr to next task in a queue */
};

typedef struct _task TASK;
```

We have already encountered the scheduling parameters such as *t_pri*, *t_tleft*, and *t_tsamp*. Since each task is written as a C routine, the descriptor has a pointer *t_func* which points at the routine, and a pointer *t_argp*, which points at the argument block for that routine. These two pointers correspond to the *func* and *argp* parameters of

```
TASK *  SetCntrlTask(name, func, argp, priority, tsamp);
```

and related task setup routines. The *t_tasktype* field identifies the type of task, and hence the associated scheduler. The three task types defined in *task.h* are: STL_TASK for fixed sample time or shortest-time-left scheduled tasks, SLC_TASK for time-slice tasks, and EVT_TASK for event driven tasks.

Each task has its own stack space that is distinct from the stack space of all the other tasks. This task stack is allocated from the heap during task setup, which means that the stack size must be specified in advance. The default stack size used by the simplified setup routines such as *SetCntrlTask()* is 2 Kbytes. The stack information is maintained in the fields *t_usrstack*, which points to the stack memory, and *t_ustacksize* which records the size of the stack in units of 2-byte words. Therefore, the default stack size is 1 Kword. If the default is too much or insufficient, readers can use the lower level *NewTask()* defined in *task.c*, which allows greater control of stack size and other parameters. A point to note is that Clotho actually allocates 16 bytes more than the specified stack size. This is because the task stack is aligned on a 16-byte paragraph boundary and the extra 16 bytes ensure that the task gets all of its requested stack space after allowing for segment alignment. However, the *t_ustacksize* field only records the requested stack size, not the actual allocated stack size.

An array, *t_reg[]*, is allocated to hold 8088 machine register values. Offsets into this array are defined in two files: *task.h* and *task86.h*, which is an assembly language include file used by the context switcher. It is **very important** that the offset definitions in these 2 files match. During setup, the task function's CS and IP values and the task stack's SS and SP values are placed into the register array. The CPU's registers are initialized from the *t_reg[]* array, and an interrupted task's CS:IP and SS:SP values will be copied into *t_reg[]*. Why is it that an interrupted task's CS:IP and SS:SP values cannot be left on the task stack?

Clotho maintains a global task descriptor pointer, *curtask*, which always points at the currently executing task. This task pointer is used by the schedulers and the dispatcher and user programs must not modify its value.

8.16.2 TASK QUEUES

Clotho's schedulers uses singly-linked task queues, hence the *t_next* field in the task descriptor structure. The queue descriptor structure is really quite simple:

```
typedef struct _tqueue {
    int tq_id;          /* queue id number */
    TASK *tq_head;      /* pointer to head of queue */
    TASK *tq_tail;      /* pointer to tail of queue */
} TQUEUE;
```

There are 5 system-defined queues (see *initsys.c*). They are:

CwaitQueue This is a queue of interrupted or pre-empted fixed sample time control tasks. This queue has the highest priority since we want to resume a control task as soon as possible; otherwise, there may be grave consequences for the controlled system. Tasks in this queue are sorted by priority.

ReadyQueue This is a queue of ready-to-run tasks. This queue is designed for event driven tasks that are released by the event manager, but have not had their chance to run yet because a higher priority task is currently executing.

Readers may notice that the existence of both *CwaitQueue* and *ReadyQueue* is unnecessary—one queue will suffice. There are two queues because the fixed sample time and event driven schedulers are designed and implemented at different times. Consolidating the functions of both queues into a single *ReadyQueue* seems a good exercise in understanding the function of these two queues and how they are used by the schedulers.

CntrlQueue This is a queue of all the fixed sample time scheduled control tasks. The tasks in this queue are ordered in descending *t_tleft* order; the task at the head of the queue is the one with the shortest time left to the next scheduled execution period.

SliceQueue This is a queue of all the time-slice scheduled tasks. Tasks in this queue are maintained in round-robin fashion by the scheduler.

SuspdQueue This is a queue of the suspended tasks in the system (excluding tasks pending on events). Clotho provides a mechanism whereby a task can explicitly suspend another task given the task descriptor pointer. This is intended to be used by exception or fault handlers to shut down control tasks, but we are sure readers will find other ways of using this feature.

8.16.3 CONTEXT SWITCHING

A context switch is a change in the execution thread. This may happen when (a) a task requests a system service such as *Pend()*, (b) a timer interrupt occurs; or (c) an external interrupt signals an event. These three situations change the execution context from a task to the Clotho kernel. However, such changes will not all result in a scheduling change; for example, a timer interrupt will not result in a scheduling change unless one of the fixed sample time or time-slice software timers have timed out. The term context switch is also used loosely to describe switching execution from one task to another. This actually involves a switch from task space to kernel space and out again to task space.

What happens in a context switch? The state of the currently executing task must be saved so that the task can be resumed exactly where it left off. This also involves switching from the task stack to the system stack, and is further complicated by the need to pass arguments from task to system space if the context switch results from a system call.

The context switching code is written in assembly language and resides in the file *kernel.asm*. Clotho recognizes only two types of entry into system space: a system call and an interrupt. System calls are handled by the assembly language function *syscall*, that is the principle means for a task to request system services such as pending on a semaphore (more about semaphores later). Interrupts are handled by interrupt service routines that call *gateway* to pass control to the system through a software interrupt (*gateway* is implemented as a software interrupt). Note that *syscall* also serves as a front-end for *gateway* to process system call arguments. *Gateway* saves the current state of the task, including the task stack in the *t_reg[]* array of the task descriptor pointed to by *curtask*. If an 8087 or 80x87 math coprocessor is present, the coprocessor state will be saved in the task stack. Next, *gateway* copies the arguments (if any) from the task stack to the system stack and switches execution context to system space by an indirect call to the system entry point (more about this later). When the call returns, the task pointed to by *curtask* is dispatched by *_runuser*, which switches to the task stack, restores the math coprocessor state (if a math coprocessor is present), and resumes where that task left off.

Gateway requires a system entry code argument that is really an offset into a table of entry points, *EntryTab[]*, defined in *initsys.c*. In addition to the entry code, *gateway* also requires the number of 16-bit argument words and the argument words themselves. *Gateway* only copies arguments between task and system stack if there are arguments.

An important point to note is that interrupts are disabled while executing in system space, i.e., the kernel is not interruptible. This places a constraint on the minimum interrupt latency and response time to external events, but it does simplify the kernel since it does not have to be fully re-entrant. Most of the kernel functions are re-entrant. Readers looking for a significant real-time project may consider making the kernel fully re-entrant. Readers wishing to tackle this project are advised to equip themselves with hardware-assisted debugging aids.

8.16.4 TIME—CHRONOS

The fixed sample time and the time-slice schedulers are clocked by two separate software timers, which in turn are clocked by interrupts generated by IBM-PC family's only available hardware timer.[2] The use of software timers is forced by the lack of multiple hardware timers. The structures of these software timers have been described elsewhere in the book. They are implemented in the file *time.c*, and the routine that manages the timers is *chronos()*. The fixed sample time and time-slice schedulers are installed as time-out routines on two specially reserved software timers. The timers are prioritized and are set to the schedulers' base priority values (PCONTROL and PSLICE).

---

[2]The IBM-PC family actually has 3 count-down timers, but only one is generally available for program use. The other two are dedicated for dynamic memory refresh and sound generation.

The front-end timer interrupt service routine, *cron*, is implemented in assembly language in *kernel.asm*. When a timer interrupt occurs, *cron* pushes two words on the stack: the number of arguments (zero in this case), and the entry code for *chronos()*. Execution branches to *gateway* by means of a software interrupt. In the interest of speed, memory is allocated in *cron's* code segment for the two values pushed on the stack so that *cron* can execute a segment override to directly push the values on the stack.

Due to the abysmal performance of the 4.77-MHz IBM-PC, the timer interrupt interval (i.e., the tick interval) is set to 50 milliseconds. DOS defaults to approximately 55 milliseconds; we chose 50 milliseconds because it is easier to count time in units of 50 than 55. Thus, tasks cannot be scheduled with a resolution better than 50 milliseconds. Readers who are using 80286 and 80386 machines may want to change the timer interrupt interval. This can be done by changing the TICKRATE definition in *config.h* and recompiling the kernel, or by seeing how the tickrate is set in *initsys.c* and following the same procedure in your *main()* just before calling *start()*.

8.16.5 Memory Organization

Code space is allocated by the compiler and loader. A program file is compiled into a module and each module has its own code and data segments, the names of which are *modulename*_TEXT and *modulename*_DATA (see compiler documentation). Segment names need not concern us unless we wish to access code or data from assembly language routines. In Clotho, data space is divided between system space and user space. System space is that used by the kernel, while user space is that used by the task routines. The system data space uses the default data (_DATA) and stack (STACK) segments which are set up when the program is loaded into memory by DOS. All initialized global variables reside in the default data segment _DATA.

8.17 FUNCTION SUMMARIES

All of the user-accessible functions in Clotho are described in this section. The functions are listed in alphabetical order so they can be used for reference in studying the sample programs.

```
PROCEDURE
        CisDTimer - clear in service flags (software and hardware)

FILE
        time.c

SYNOPSIS
        void CisDTimer(n)
```

```
int n;
```

PARAMETER

n — countdown timer id

REMARKS

The purpose is to allow another invocation of the timeout service routine at the next timer interrupt.

FUNCTION

countcbuf — how many in buffer?

FILE

cbuf.c

SYNOPSIS

```
unsigned countcbuf(cbuf)
CBUF *cbuf;
```

PARAMETER

cbuf — pointer to buffer control structure

RETURNS

number of characters currently in the buffer

FUNCTION

disable — disable 8086 external interrupt response

FILE

libc.asm

This module is shared with the stand-alone xignal module.

SYNOPSIS

```
int disable(void)
```

RETURNS

1 if interrupt was previously enabled, 0 otherwise

FUNCTION

ega_info — return information about EGA (if it exists)

SYNOPSIS

```
int ega_info(mode, memsize, features, switches)
```

```
        int *mode, *memsize, *feature, *switch;

PARAMETERS
        mode      - 0 = color, 1 = monochrome
        memsize   - 0 = 64K, 1 = 128K, 2 = 192K, 3 = 256K
        feature   - feature bit settings
        switch    - EGA switch settings

RETURNS
        0 if no EGA present
        1 if EGA present

REMARKS
        Reference: Augie Hansen, "Detecting Display Systems,"
             PC Tech Journal, Vol. 5 No. 7, July 1987.
```

```
PROCEDURE
        EnterTqueue - enter task descriptor in queue, sorted on key

FILE
        tqueue.c

SYNOPSIS
        void EnterTqueue(task, taskq, key)
        TASK *task;
        TQUEUE *taskq;
        int key;

PARAMETERS
        task   - pointer to task node
        taskq  - pointer to recipient task queue
        key    - insertion key

REMARKS
        Currently has 2 insertion keys: (defined in tqueue.h)
             PRI_ENTER - insert on highest priority
             STL_ENTER - insert on shortest time left
```

```
FUNCTION
        enable - enable 8086 external interrupt response

FILE
        libc.asm

        This module is shared with the stand-alone xignal module.
```

```
SYNOPSIS
        int enable(void)

RETURNS
        1  if interrupt was previously enabled, 0 otherwise
```

```
PROCEDURE
        error - print error message

FILE
        error.c

SYNOPSIS
        void error(mesg)
        char *mesg;

PARAMETER
        mesg - pointer to message string

REMARKS
        Message is displayed by using writing to video memory.
```

```
PROCEDURE
        FreeDTimer - free allocated count-down timer

FILE
        time.c

SYNOPSIS
        void FreeITimer(timer)
        int timer;

PARAMETER
        timer - timer id

REMARKS
        You MUST ensure that the timer you are returning is
        obtained with NewDTimer; otherwise, you will screw
        up the system for sure.
```

```
PROCEDURE
        FreeITimer - free allocated interval timer

FILE
        time.c
```

SYNOPSIS
```
void FreeITimer(timer)
int timer;
```

PARAMETER
timer – timer id

DESCRIPTION
You MUST ensure that the timer you are returning is obtained with NewITimer; otherwise, you will screw up the system for sure.

FUNCTION
getcbuf – get a character from buffer

FILE
cbuf.c

SYNOPSIS
```
int getcbuf(cbuf)
CBUF *cbuf;
```

PARAMETER
cbuf – pointer to buffer control structure

RETURNS
character if buffer not empty, -1 otherwise

FUNCTION
getivec – return 32-bit pointer to interrupt service routine

FILE
libc.asm

This module is shared with the stand-alone xignal module.

SYNOPSIS
```
long getivec(vecno)
int vecno;

void far *getivec(vecno)
int vecno;
```

PARAMETER
vecno – vector number (0..255)

RETURNS
segment in DX and offset in AX

REMARKS

Two alternative declarations for the return value are possible: one can declare it as a 32-bit long or a far pointer, depending on whether your compiler supports Microsoft's far pointer type. Personally, I prefer a 32-bit long return type since the "far" keyword is definitely nonstandard.

It is assumed that the vector entry will not be asynchronously changed while we are reading it, hence we do not disable interrupts.

FUNCTION

GetTqueue – get task descriptor at head of queue

FILE

tqueue.c

SYNOPSIS

```
TASK *GetTqueue(taskq)
TQUEUE *taskq;
```

PARAMETER

taskq – pointer to task queue

RETURNS

pointer to task descriptor at head of queue

REMARKS

The head node is disconnected from the rest of the queue.

PROCEDURE

intset – install interrupt service routine

FILE

intset.c

SYNOPSIS

```
void intset(intcode, func)
int intcode;
void (*func)();
```

PARAMETERS

intcode – interrupt id (defined in intset.h)
func – pointer to interrupt handler

REMARKS

This works somewhat like xignal().

PROCEDURE

movblock – move a block of memory from one location to another

FILE

libb.asm

SYNOPSIS

```
void movblock(src_offset, src_segment, dest_offset,
              dest_segment, nbytes)
unsigned src_offset, src_segment, dest_offset,
              dest_segment, nbytes;
```

PARAMETERS

```
src_segment  – segment component of source address
src_offset   – offset component of source address
dest_segment – segment component of destination address
dest_offset  – offset component of destination address
nbytes       – number of bytes to move
```

REMARKS

Uses the movsb instruction.

FUNCTION

newcbuf – create a new buffer structure

FILE

cbuf.c

SYNOPSIS

```
CBUF *newcbuf(size)
unsigned size;
```

PARAMETER

size – size of buffer

RETURNS

pointer to allocated buffer structure, NULL if error

FUNCTION

NewDTimer – allocate countdown timer

FILE

time.c

SYNOPSIS

```
int NewDTimer(func, argp, pri)
void (*func)(), *argp;
int pri;
```

PARAMETERS

```
func - pointer to service routine
argp - pointer to argument(s)
pri  - priority
```

RETURNS

timer id if successful, -1 if not

FUNCTION

NewEvent – allocate new event descriptor

FILE

event.c

SYNOPSIS

```
int NewEvent(void)
```

RETURNS

positive event number if all is well, -1 if otherwise

FUNCTION

NewITimer – allocate interval timer

FILE

time.c

SYNOPSIS

```
int NewITimer()
```

RETURNS

timer id if successful, -1 if not

FUNCTION

NewMessage – allocate a new message handle

FILE

message.c

SYNOPSIS

```
int NewMessage(void)
```

RETURNS

message handle (small integer ≥ 0)

```
FUNCTION
        NewSem -nallocate new semaphore

SYNOPSIS
        int NewSem(n)
        int n;

PARAMETER
        n - initial semaphore count

RETURNS
        positive semaphore handle  if all is well, -1 if otherwise
```

```
FUNCTION
        NewTask - create and initialize a task descriptor.

FILE
        task.c

SYNOPSIS
        TASK *NewTask(name, func, argp, tasktype, priority,
             stacksize, quantum)
        char *name;
        void (*func)(), *argp;
        int tasktype, priority;
        long quantum;
        unsigned stacksize;

PARAMETERS
        name      - task name string
        func      - task function
        argp      - pointer to argument structure
        tasktype  - control, time-slice ...etc.
        priority  - initial execution priority
        stacksize - required size of task stack in words
        quantum   - quantum (time-slice) or sampling time (control)

RETURNS
        pointer to task descriptor
REMARKS
        This is the routine called by SetCntrlTask() and its
        brethren.
```

```
PROCEDURE
        Notify - signal occurrence of an event

FILE
        event.c
```

SYNOPSIS

```
void Notify(en)
int en;
```

PARAMETER

en – event id number

FUNCTION

offset – returns offset portion of pointer

FILE

liba.asm

SYNOPSIS

```
unsigned offset(ptr)
void *ptr;
```

RETURNS

offset portion of pointer

REMARKS

Works the same in all memory models and on code and data pointers.

PROCEDURE

panic – very bad error, print message and die

FILE

error.c

SYNOPSIS

```
void panic(mesg)
char *mesg;
```

PARAMETER

mesg – pointer to message string

REMARKS

Message is displayed by using writing to video memory.

FUNCTION

peekw – peek at a 16-bit word in memory

FILE

libb.asm

SYNOPSIS
```
unsigned peekw(offset, segment)
unsigned offset, segment;
```

PARAMETERS
```
segment   – segment component of memory address
offset    – offset component of memory address
```

RETURNS
```
16-bit word at segment:offset
```

PROCEDURE
```
Pend – pend on an event
```

FILE
```
event.c
```

SYNOPSIS
```
void Pend(en, task)
int en;
TASK *task;
```

PARAMETERS
```
en – event id number (i.e., the "handle")
task – task pointer
```

REMARKS
```
Calling task will be suspended until event occurs.
```

PROCEDURE
```
pokew – poke a 16-bit word into memory
```

FILE
```
libb.asm
```

SYNOPSIS
```
void pokew(offset, segment, word)
unsigned offset, segment, word;
```

PARAMETERS
```
segment   – segment component of destination address
offset    – offset component of destination address
word      – 16-bit word to "poke" into memory
```

FUNCTION
```
probe87 – probe for presence of 8087, 80287 and 80387
```

FILE

probe87.asm

SYNOPSIS

```
int probe87(void)
```

RETURNS

0 if no NDP present
1 if 8087
2 if 80287
3 if 80387

REMARKS

This is used by Clotho to see if a math coprocessor is present.

PROCEDURE

prologue – kernel initialization

FILE

initsys.c

SYNOPSIS

```
void prologue(void)
```

REMARKS

This must be called before any other Clotho routines.

PROCEDURE

Psem – wait on semaphore

FILE

sem.c

SYNOPSIS

```
void Psem(n)
int n;
```

PARAMETER

n – semaphore number

REMARKS

If the semaphore count is less than or equal to 0, suspend task; otherwise task execution continues. In both cases, the semaphore count is decremented.

```
FUNCTION
        putcbuf - put a character into the buffer

FILE
        cbuf.c

SYNOPSIS
        int putcbuf(c, cbuf)
        char c;
        CBUF *cbuf;

PARAMETERS
        c    - character data
        cbuf - pointer to buffer control structure

RETURNS
        non-zero if successful, -1 otherwise
```

```
PROCEDURE
        PutTqueue - enter task descriptor at tail of queue

FILE
        tqueue.c

SYNOPSIS
        void PutTqueue(task, taskq)
        TASK *task;
        TQUEUE *taskq;

PARAMETERS
        task  - pointer to task descriptor
        taskq - pointer to recipient task queue
```

```
FUNCTION
        ReadClock - read system time

FILE
        time.c

SYNOPSIS
        long ReadClock()

RETURNS
        time elasped in milliseconds since system is born via start()
```

FUNCTION

ReadDTimer – read count-down timer

FILE

time.c

SYNOPSIS

```
long ReadDTimer(n)
int n;
```

PARAMETER

n – timer id

RETURNS

time in milliseconds

REMARKS

The time left is only accurate to the precision allowed by the system clock rate. If quantization is 10 ms, then ReadDTimer() will report 10 ms even if actual time left is 1 ms.

FUNCTION

ReadITimer – read interval timer

FILE

time.c

SYNOPSIS

```
long ReadITimer(n);
int n;
```

PARAMETERS

n – timer id

RETURNS

interval value in milliseconds

PROCEDURE

readseg – read segment registers

FILE

libb.asm

SYNOPSIS

```
void readseg(segment)
struct { int code, stack, data, extra; } *segment;
```

PARAMETER
    pointer to a structure to hold the segment register values

---

PROCEDURE
    Receive – receive a message (called by user task)

FILE
    message.c

SYNOPSIS
```
void Receive(mh, size, mptr)
int mh, size;
void *mptr;
```

PARAMETERS
    mh – message handle
    size – size of message block in bytes
    mptr – message datum pointer

REMARKS
    Calling task may be suspended until the entire message is placed in the buffer pointed to by parameter mptr.

PROCEDURE
    resetcbuf – reset buffer

FILE
    cbuf.c

SYNOPSIS
```
void resetcbuf(cbuf)
CBUF *cbuf;
```

PARAMETER
    cbuf – pointer to buffer control structure

PROCEDURE
    Resume – resume a suspended task, called by user tasks

FILE
    suspend.c

SYNOPSIS
```
void Resume(t)
TASK *t;
```

PARAMETERS

t – task to be resumed, cannot be NULL

REMARKS

See Suspend().

FUNCTION

segment – returns segment portion of pointer (segment:offset)

FILE

liba.asm

SYNOPSIS

```
unsigned segment(ptr)
void *ptr;
```

PARAMETER

ptr – pointer in segment:offset format, with segment in hi word

RETURNS

segment portion of 32-bit pointer

REMARKS

Works only with large (i.e., 32-bit) pointers in segment:offset format. It does not distinguish between code and data.

PROCEDURE

Send – send a message (called by user tasks)

FILE

message.c

SYNOPSIS

```
void Send(mh, size, mptr)
int mh, size;
void *mptr;
```

PARAMETERS

mh – message handle
size – size of message block in bytes
mptr – message datum pointer

REMARKS

Calling task may be suspended if message buffers are not immediately available.

```
PROCEDURE
        seoi – send specific EOI to interrupt controller

FILE
        machine.c

SYNOPSIS
        void seoi(dev)
        int dev;

PARAMETER
        dev – device code
```

```
FUNCTION
        SetCntrlTask – create and set up a fixed sample time task

FILE
        user.c

SYNOPSIS
        TASK *SetCntrlTask(name, func, argp, priority, tsamp)
        void (*func)(), *argp;
        char *name;
        int priority;
        long tsamp;

PARAMETERS
        name      – string with a symbolic task name
        func      – ptr to function comprising task
        argp      – ptr to data block comprising arguments
                        (NULL if none)
        priority  – initial task priority
        tsamp     – sample period in milliseconds
```

```
PROCEDURE
        SetBkgndTask – create and set up a time-sliced background
                            task

FILE
        user.c

SYNOPSIS
        TASK *SetBkgndTask(name, func, argp, priority)
        void (*func)(), *argp;
        char *name;
        int priority;

PARAMETERS
```

```
        name      - string with a symbolic task name
        func      - ptr to function comprising task
        argp      - ptr to data block comprising arguments
                       (NULL if none)
        priority  - initial task priority
```

```
PROCEDURE
        SetDTimer - set count-down timer

FILE
        time.c

SYNOPSIS
        void SetDTimer(n, ms)
        int n;
        long ms;

PARAMETERS
        n  - timer id
        ms - time in milliseconds

REMARKS
        Set countdown timer 'n' for 'ms' milliseconds.  If ms is
        less than the resolution of the time-base, tm_dtime
        is set to zero.

        A negative value of ms is a fatal error.
```

```
FUNCTION
        SetEventTask - create and set up an event driven task

FILE
        user.c
SYNOPSIS
        int SetEventTask(name, func, argp, priority)
        int (*func)();
        char *name, *argp;
        int priority;

PARAMETERS
        name      - string with a symbolic task name
        func      - ptr to function comprising task
        argp      - ptr to data block comprising arguments
                       (NULL if none)
        priority  - initial task priority

RETURNS
        event id
```

```
PROCEDURE
        SetITimer - set interval timer

FILE
        time.c

SYNOPSIS
        void SetITimer(n);
        int n;

PARAMETERS
        n - timer id

REMARKS
        Set interval time value to 0.
```

```
PROCEDURE
        setivec - install a function as interrupt service routine

FILE
        libc.asm

        This module is shared with the stand-alone xignal module.

SYNOPSIS
        void setivec(vecno, sizeof(isr), isr)
        int vecno;
        void (*isr)();

PARAMETERS
        vecno         - vector number (0..255)
        sizeof(isr)   - size of the function pointer
        isr           - routine to be vectored to

REMARKS
        Installs isr as an interrupt service routine.  If isr is a
        32-bit pointer in segment:offset form, then the specified
        segment is used.  If isr contains just the 16-bit offset as
        indicated by the sizeof(isr) argument, the current code
        segment will be assumed for the segment portion.
```

```
PROCEDURE
        SetTsr - install timeout service routine

FILE
        time.c
```

SYNOPSIS

```
void SetTsr(n, func, argp, pri)
void (*func)(), *argp;
int n, pri;
```

PARAMETERS

```
n    - timer id
func - pointer to service routine
argp - pointer to argument structure
pri  - priority
```

REMARKS

Install func() as a timeout service routine.

PROCEDURE

StackTqueue - enter task descriptor at head of queue

FILE

tqueue.c

SYNOPSIS

```
StackTqueue(task, taskq)
TASK *task;
TQUEUE *taskq;
```

PARAMETERS

```
task  - pointer to task descriptor
taskq - pointer to task queue
```

REMARKS

Included for efficiency considerations.

PROCEDURE

start - start system running

FILE

initsys.c

SYNOPSIS

```
void start(void)
```

REMARKS

This must be the last routine called in main().

PROCEDURE

StartDTimer - stop timer from counting down

```
FILE
        time.c

SYNOPSIS
        void StartDTimer(n)
        int n;

PARAMETER
        n - timer number

REMARKS
        This routine should only be used by the system to
        restart timers frozen by a StopDTimer call.
```

```
PROCEDURE
        StopDTimer - stop timer from counting down

FILE
        time.c

SYNOPSIS
        void StopDTimer(n)
        int n;

PARAMETER
        n - timer id
REMARKS
        This routine should only be used by the kernel to freeze
        timers used by background process for virtual timing,
        i.e., time proceeds only when that process is running.

        As this is an internal system routine, error checking is lax.

        See also StartDTimer() to restart stopped timers.
```

```
PROCEDURE
        Suspend - suspend a task, called by user tasks

FILE
        suspend.c

SYNOPSIS
        void Suspend(t)
        TASK *t;

PARAMETERS
        t - pointer to task to be suspended, if NULL, suspend
              calling task
```

REMARKS

Argument t is NULL denotes curtask. If so, update task state and put it into the SuspdQueue. Clear curtask and let Dispatch() dispatch the next task.

If t is not NULL, we merely mark it for suspension by Dispatch(). The reason is that there is no way to locate the queue that the task is in (other than a time consuming exhaustive search). This is complicated by the existence of dynamically created event and semaphore queues.

I blush to admit that this is a design flaw due to using singly linked task queues instead of doubly linked queues. One future project will be to restructure the system such that we can find the queue for a task given a ptr to the task descriptor.

So for now, we mark the task and let Dispatch() and Execute() take care of it when the task comes up next.

FUNCTION

tas – atomic test and set function

FILE

liba.asm

SYNOPSIS

```
int tas(lock)
int *lock;
```

PARAMETER

lock – pointer to a lock variable

RETURNS

status of lock – 0 if available, 1 if otherwise

REMARKS

Tas() is a tool for mutual exclusion. It is guaranteed to be atomic by doing a xchg 1 with the lock variable. Since a 16-bit word sized transfer on machines with an 8-bit bus may not be atomic, we make doubly sure that it will be atomic by disabling external interrupts. This is implemented in assembly since we wish to restore the original interrupt status and doing it in C is just too messy.

FUNCTION

TimeUp – has timer run out?

FILE

time.c

```
SYNOPSIS
        int TimeUp(n)
        int n;

PARAMETER
        n - timer id

RETURNS
        0  if timer has not timed out
        1  if it has timed out
```

```
FUNCTION
        ungetcbuf - undo a getcbuf

FILE
        cbuf.c

SYNOPSIS
        int ungetcbuf(c, cbuf)
        char c;
        CBUF *cbuf;

PARAMETERS
        c    - character data
        cbuf - pointer to buffer control structure

RETURNS
        non-zero if successful, -1 otherwise

REMARKS
        Character is inserted into front of buffer queue.
```

```
FUNCTION
        unputcbuf - undo a putcbuf

FILE
        cbuf.c

SYNOPSIS
        int unputcbuf(cbuf)
        CBUF *cbuf;

PARAMETER
        cbuf - pointer to buffer control structure
```

RETURNS

character last put in if successful, NULL if otherwise

REMARKS

Character is retrieved from rear of buffer queue.

PROCEDURE

video_GetCursor – get current cursor position

FILE

video.asm

SYNOPSIS

```
void video_GetCursor(row, col)
int *row, *col;
```

PARAMETERS

row – pointer to row value
col – pointer to column value

REMARKS

This routine calls the BIOS and hence is not re-entrant.

FUNCTION

video_GetMode – get current video mode

FILE

video.asm

SYNOPSIS

```
int video_GetMode(void)
```

RETURNS

```
 0 – bw40              CGA
 1 – co40              CGA
 2 – bw80              CGA, EGA, VGA
 3 – co80              CGA, EGA, VGA
 4 – 320X200           CGA
 5 – 320X200 grey      CGA
 6 – 640X200           CGA
 7 – mono              MDA, CGA, EGA
 8 – 160x200           PCjr
 9 – 320x200           PCjr
10 – 640x200           PCjr
11 – internal          EGA
12 – internal          EGA
13 – 320x200           EGA
```

```
        14 - 640x200          EGA
        15 - 640x350 b/w      EGA
        16 - 640x350          EGA
        17 - 640x480 b/w      MCGA, VGA
        18 - 640x480          VGA
        19 - 320x200          MCGA, VGA
```

REMARKS

This routine calls the BIOS and hence is not re-entrant.

PROCEDURE

video_PutCursor - set cursor position

FILE

video.asm

SYNOPSIS

```
void video_PutCursor(row, col)
int row, col;
```

PARAMETERS

row - row position of cursor
col - column position of cursor

REMARKS

This routine is re-entrant; it does not call the BIOS.

Position of upper left corner is (row = 0, col = 0).

PROCEDURE

video_ReadChar - read the character and attribute at the specified position

FILE

video.asm

SYNOPSIS

```
unsigned int video_ReadChar(row, col)
int row, col;
```

RETURNS

attribute (or color) in the high byte and the ASCII value in the low byte

REMARKS

This routine calls the BIOS and hence is not re-entrant.

PROCEDURE
```
video_SetMode - set video mode
```

FILE
```
video.asm
```

SYNOPSIS
```
int video_SetMode(mode)
int mode;
```

PARAMETER
```
mode - video mode (see video_GetMode)
```

REMARKS
```
This routine calls the BIOS and hence is not re-entrant.
```

PROCEDURE
```
video_Scroll - access BIOS video scrolling services
```

FILE
```
video.asm
```

SYNOPSIS
```
void video_Scroll(dir, nlines, lrow, lcol, rrow, rcol,
                  attr)
int dir, nlines, lrow, lcol, rrow, rcol, attr;
```

PARAMETERS
```
dir     - direction: 0 -> UP, 1 -> DOWN
nlines  - how many lines to scroll
lrow    - left corner row of scroll area
lcol    - left corner column of scroll area
rrow    - right corner row of scroll area
rcol    - right corner column of scroll area
attr    - video attribute (07)
```

REMARKS
```
nlines = 0 will clear the display.

This routine calls the BIOS and hence is not re-entrant.
```

PROCEDURE
```
video_WriteChar - display a character with given
                  attributes
```

FILE
```
video.asm
```

```
SYNOPSIS
        void video_WriteChar(row, col, c, color)
        int row, col;
        char c, colour;

PARAMETERS
        row     - row position of character
        col     - column position of character
        c       - the character
        colour  - the colour with which to display the character

REMARKS
        The color is an 8-bit quantity divided into the foreground
        component (bits 0 to 3) and the background component
        (bits 4 to 7).  Black is 0 and white is 7.  Thus,
        white-on-black is specified as 0x07 and reverse video
        (black-on-white) is 0x70.
        This routine is re-entrant - does not call the BIOS.
```

```
PROCEDURE
        video_WritePixel - write a pixel dot

FILE
        video.asm

SYNOPSIS
        void video_WritePixel(row, col, pixel)
        int row, col;
        int pixel;

PARAMETERS
        row    - row position of pixel
        col    - column position of pixel
        pixel  - the pixel colour value

REMARKS
        The video adapter MUST be placed in graphics mode before
        this routine is called (see video_SetMode() for information
        on video modes).

        The pixel parameter is actually the colour attribute byte
        for pixels that take up more than 1 bit.

        This routine calls the BIOS and hence is not re-entrant.
```

```
PROCEDURE
        video_WriteString - print a string with given attributes
```

FILE

```
video.asm
```

SYNOPSIS

```
void video_WriteString(row, col, s, colour)
int row, col, colour;
char *s;
```

PARAMETERS

```
row    - row position of cursor
col    - column position of cursor
color  - the color with which to display the string
s      - pointer to NUL terminated character string
```

REMARKS

This routine is re-entrant; it does not call the BIOS.

PROCEDURE

Vsem - release semaphore

FILE

```
sem.c
```

SYNOPSIS

```
void Vsem(n)
int n;
```

PARAMETER

n - semaphore number

REMARKS

If semaphore count is less than 0, there are tasks pending. Release the first task and execute either the released task or the calling task depending on which has the higher priority.

PROCEDURE

WaitNextSamp - wait for next sampling instance

FILE

```
user.c
```

SYNOPSIS

```
void WaitNextSamp(void)
```

REMARKS

Suspend the calling task until the next sampling instance. This routine should only be called by fixed-sample-time tasks.

```
/*********************************************************************

FILE
        demo1.c  -  simple multi-tasking test program

REMARKS
        This program sets up 3 foreground tasks and 8 background tasks.
        The foreground tasks are scheduled as sample-time control tasks
        which have to run at fixed intervals.  The background tasks just
        run forever.

        Mutual exclusion is achieved by disabling interrupts.

        Microsoft's sprintf() is not re-entrant! Aaugh!

LAST UPDATE
        23 May 1988

        Copyright(c) 1988  D.M. Auslander and C.H. Tham

*********************************************************************/

/*********************************************************************
                        I M P O R T S
*********************************************************************/

#include <stdio.h>

#include "clotho.h"

/*********************************************************************
                P R I V A T E   D A T A
*********************************************************************/

struct _display {
        char *label;            /* label to display */
        int lrow, lcol;         /* where to display label */
        int crow, ccol;         /* where to display count */
};

static struct _display d_fg1 = { "foreground 1: ",  8,  0,  8, 14 };
static struct _display d_fg2 = { "foreground 2: ", 10,  0, 10, 14 };

static struct _display d_bg1 = { "background 1: ",  4, 40,  4, 54 };
static struct _display d_bg2 = { "background 2: ",  6, 40,  6, 54 };
static struct _display d_bg3 = { "background 3: ",  8, 40,  8, 54 };
static struct _display d_bg4 = { "background 4: ", 10, 40, 10, 54 };
static struct _display d_bg5 = { "background 5: ", 12, 40, 12, 54 };
static struct _display d_bg6 = { "background 6: ", 14, 40, 14, 54 };
static struct _display d_bg7 = { "background 7: ", 16, 40, 16, 54 };
static struct _display d_bg8 = { "background 8: ", 18, 40, 18, 54 };

static long timelimit = 0L;             /* execution time limit of demo */

#define COLOR 0x07                      /* display text color = white on black */

/*********************************************************************
            F O R W A R D   D E C L A R A T I O N S
*********************************************************************/

#ifdef ANSI

static void clock(void);
static void fgtask(struct _display *);
static void bgtask(struct _display *);

#else

void clock();
void fgtask();
void bgtask();

#endif

/*********************************************************************
                                E N T R Y   R O U T I N E S
*********************************************************************/

/*-------------------------------------------------------------------
TASK
        CLOCK  -  pretends to be a clock

SYNOPSIS
        static void clock(void)

REMARKS
        Prints the time obtained from ReadClock().

LAST UPDATE
        23 May 1988
                creation
-------------------------------------------------------------------*/

static void clock()
{
        long elapsed;                   /* total elasped time in seconds */
        long hr, min, sec;              /* hour, minutes, seconds */
        char timestr[10];               /* time display string */


        while (1)
        {
                elasped = ReadClock() / 1000L;
```

```
                panic("Time's Up");

            WaitNextSamp();
        }

}



/*----------------------------------------------------------------------
TASK
        FGTASK  -  foreground task

SYNOPSIS
        static void fgtask(dp)
        struct _display *dp;

REMARKS
        They print the current invocation number and then wait for next
        sampling instance.

LAST UPDATE
        23 May 1988
                creation
----------------------------------------------------------------------*/

static void fgtask(dp)
struct _display *dp;
{
        int i = 0;
        char stat[12];


        video_WriteString(dp->lrow, dp->lcol, dp->label, COLOR);

        while (1)
        {
                disable();

                sprintf(stat, "%d", i);

                enable();

                video_WriteString(dp->crow, dp->ccol, stat, COLOR);

                if (++i < 0)
                        i = 0;

                WaitNextSamp();
        }
}



/*----------------------------------------------------------------------
TASK
        BGTASK  -  background task

SYNOPSIS
        static void bgtask(void)

REMARKS
        Runs in an infinite loop and print the current iteration number.

LAST UPDATE
        23 May 1988
                creation
----------------------------------------------------------------------*/

static void bgtask(dp)
struct _display *dp;
{
        int i = 0;
        char stat[12];


        video_WriteString(dp->lrow, dp->lcol, dp->label, COLOR);

        while (1)
        {
                disable();

                sprintf(stat, "%d", i);

                enable();

                video_WriteString(dp->crow, dp->ccol, stat, COLOR);

                if (++i < 0)
                        i = 0;
        }

}


/*----------------------------------------------------------------------
PROCEDURE
        MAIN  -  main program

SYNOPSIS
```

```
        main(void)

REMARKS
        First, call prologue() to setup system.

        Next, install ticktock() as a sample-time control task with a
        sample interval of 1 second (1000 milliseconds) using SetCntrlTask().

        Lastly, start the system.

LAST UPDATE
        23 May 1988
                creation
--------------------------------------------------------------------------*/

main()
{

        fputs("enter total running time in seconds > ", stdout);
        scanf("%ld", &timelimit);

        prologue();

        SetCntrlTask("CLOCK", clock, (void *)NULL, PCONTROL, 1000L);
        SetCntrlTask("FG1", fgtask, (void *)&d_fg1, PCONTROL+1, 1000L);
        SetCntrlTask("FG2", fgtask, (void *)&d_fg2, PCONTROL+2, 2000L);
        SetBkgndTask("BG1", bgtask, (void *)&d_bg1, PSLICE);
        SetBkgndTask("BG2", bgtask, (void *)&d_bg2, PSLICE);
        SetBkgndTask("BG3", bgtask, (void *)&d_bg3, PSLICE);
        SetBkgndTask("BG4", bgtask, (void *)&d_bg4, PSLICE);
        SetBkgndTask("BG5", bgtask, (void *)&d_bg5, PSLICE);
        SetBkgndTask("BG6", bgtask, (void *)&d_bg6, PSLICE);
        SetBkgndTask("BG7", bgtask, (void *)&d_bg7, PSLICE);
        SetBkgndTask("BG8", bgtask, (void *)&d_bg8, PSLICE);

        start();

        return(-1);    /* stop compiler from grumbling at /W2 warning level */
}


/*************************************************************************

FILE
        demo2.c  -  derived from demo1.c, use tas() for mutual exclusion

REMARKS
        This program sets up 3 foreground tasks and 8 background tasks.
        The foreground tasks are scheduled as sample-time control tasks
        which have to run at fixed intervals.  The background tasks just
        run forever.

        The background tasks uses atomic test-and-set for mutual exclusion.

        Microsoft's sprintf() is not re-entrant! Aaugh!

LAST UPDATE
        23 May 1988

        Copyright(c) 1988  D.M. Auslander and C.H. Tham

*************************************************************************/

/*************************************************************************
                              I M P O R T S
*************************************************************************/

#include <stdio.h>
#include <stdlib.h>
#include <string.h>

#include "clotho.h"

/*************************************************************************
                         P R I V A T E    D A T A
*************************************************************************/

struct _display {
        char *label;            /* label to display */
        int lrow, lcol;         /* where to display label */
        int crow, ccol;         /* where to display count */
};

static struct _display d_fg1 = { "foreground 1: ",  8,  0,  8, 14 };
static struct _display d_fg2 = { "foreground 2: ", 10,  0, 10, 14 };

static struct _display d_bg1 = { "background 1: ",  4, 40,  4, 54 };
static struct _display d_bg2 = { "background 2: ",  6, 40,  6, 54 };
static struct _display d_bg3 = { "background 3: ",  8, 40,  8, 54 };
static struct _display d_bg4 = { "background 4: ", 10, 40, 10, 54 };
static struct _display d_bg5 = { "background 5: ", 12, 40, 12, 54 };
static struct _display d_bg6 = { "background 6: ", 14, 40, 14, 54 };
static struct _display d_bg7 = { "background 7: ", 16, 40, 16, 54 };
static struct _display d_bg8 = { "background 8: ", 18, 40, 18, 54 };

static long timelimit = 0L;             /* execution time limit of demo */
static int lock = 0;                    /* lock for test-and-set, init to 0 */

/*************************************************************************
                    F O R W A R D    D E C L A R A T I O N S
*************************************************************************/

#ifdef ANSI
```

```
static void clock(void);
static void fgtask1(struct _display *);
static void bgtask1(struct _display *);
static void bgtask2(struct _display *);

#else

void clock();
void fgtask1();
void bgtask1();
void bgtask2();

#endif

/***********************************************************************
                         E N T R Y   R O U T I N E S
***********************************************************************/

/*-----------------------------------------------------------------------
TASK
        CLOCK  -  pretends to be a clock

SYNOPSIS
        static void clock(void)

REMARKS
        Prints the time obtained from ReadClock().

LAST UPDATE
        23 May 1988
                creation
-----------------------------------------------------------------------*/

static void clock()
{
        long elapsed;               /* total elapsed time in seconds */
        long hr, min, sec;          /* hour, minutes, seconds */
        char timestr[10];           /* time display string */
        char buf[4];                /* tmp buffer */


        while (1)
        {
                elasped = ReadClock() / 1000L;

                sec = elasped % 60L;
                min = elasped / 60L;
                hr  = elasped / 3600L;

                video_WriteString(0, 0, "        ", 0x07);
                ltoa(hr, timestr, 10);
                strcat(timestr, ":");
                strcat(timestr, ltoa(min, buf, 10));
                strcat(timestr, ":");
                strcat(timestr, ltoa(sec, buf, 10));

                video_WriteString(0, 0, timestr, 0x70);

                if (elasped >= timelimit)
                        panic("Time's Up");

                WaitNextSamp();
        }

}


/*-----------------------------------------------------------------------
TASK
        FGTASK1  -  foreground task

SYNOPSIS
        static void fgtask1(dp)
        struct _display *dp;

REMARKS
        They print the current invocation number and then wait for next
        sampling instance.

LAST UPDATE
        23 May 1988
                creation
-----------------------------------------------------------------------*/

static void fgtask1(dp)
struct _display *dp;
{
        int i = 0;
        char stat[12];


        video_WriteString(dp->lrow, dp->lcol, dp->label, 0x07);

        while (1)
        {
                disable();

                itoa(i, stat, 10);

                enable();
```

```
		video_WriteString(dp->crow, dp->ccol, stat, 0x07);

		if (++i < 0)
			i = 0;

		WaitNextSamp();
	}

}


/*-----------------------------------------------------------------------
TASK
	BGTASK1  -  background task

SYNOPSIS
	static void bgtask1(void)

REMARKS
	Mutual exclusion via test-and-set

LAST UPDATE
	23 May 1988
		creation
-----------------------------------------------------------------------*/

static void bgtask1(dp)
struct _display *dp;
{
	int i = 0;
	char stat[12];


	video_WriteString(dp->lrow, dp->lcol, dp->label, 0x07);

	while (1)
	{
		while (tas(&lock) == 1)
			;

		sprintf(stat, "%d", i);

		lock = 0;

		video_WriteString(dp->crow, dp->ccol, stat, 0x07);

		if (++i < 0)
			i = 0;
	}
}


/*-----------------------------------------------------------------------
PROCEDURE
	MAIN  -  main program

SYNOPSIS
	main(void)

REMARKS
	First, call prologue() to setup system.

	Next, install ticktock() as a sample-time control task with a
	sample interval of 1 second (1000 milliseconds) using SetCntrlTask().

	Lastly, start the system.

LAST UPDATE
	23 May 1988
		creation
-----------------------------------------------------------------------*/

main()
{

	fputs("enter total running time in seconds > ", stdout);
	scanf("%ld", &timelimit);

	prologue();

	SetCntrlTask("CLOCK", clock,  (void *)NULL, PCONTROL, 1000L);
	SetCntrlTask("FG1", fgtask1,  (void *)&d_fg1, PCONTROL+1, 1000L);
	SetCntrlTask("FG2", fgtask1,  (void *)&d_fg2, PCONTROL+2, 2000L);
	SetBkgndTask("BG1", bgtask1,  (void *)&d_bg1, PSLICE);
	SetBkgndTask("BG2", bgtask1,  (void *)&d_bg2, PSLICE);
	SetBkgndTask("BG3", bgtask1,  (void *)&d_bg3, PSLICE);
	SetBkgndTask("BG4", bgtask1,  (void *)&d_bg4, PSLICE);
	SetBkgndTask("BG5", bgtask1,  (void *)&d_bg5, PSLICE);
	SetBkgndTask("BG6", bgtask1,  (void *)&d_bg6, PSLICE);
	SetBkgndTask("BG7", bgtask1,  (void *)&d_bg7, PSLICE);
	SetBkgndTask("BG8", bgtask1,  (void *)&d_bg8, PSLICE);

	start();

	return(-1);   /* stop compiler from grumbling at /W2 warning level */
}

/*********************************************************************
```

```
FILE
        demo3.c  -  derived from m1.c, use blocking semaphores for exclusion

REMARKS
        This program sets up 3 foreground tasks and 8 background tasks.
        The foreground tasks are scheduled as sample-time control tasks
        which have to run at fixed intervals.  The background tasks just
        run forever.

        The background tasks uses blocking semaphores for mutual exclusion;

        Microsoft's sprintf() is not re-entrant! Aaugh!

LAST UPDATE
        23 May 1988

        Copyright(c) 1988  D.M. Auslander and C.H. Tham

**********************************************************************/

/*********************************************************************
                          I M P O R T S
**********************************************************************/

#include <stdio.h>
#include <stdlib.h>
#include <string.h>

#include "clotho.h"

/*********************************************************************
                   P R I V A T E   D A T A
**********************************************************************/

struct _display {
        char *label;            /* label to display */
        int lrow, lcol;         /* where to display label */
        int crow, ccol;         /* where to display count */
};

static struct _display d_fg1 = { "foreground 1: ",  8,  0,  8, 14 };
static struct _display d_fg2 = { "foreground 2: ", 10,  0, 10, 14 };

static struct _display d_bg1 = { "background 1: ",  4, 40,  4, 54 };
static struct _display d_bg2 = { "background 2: ",  6, 40,  6, 54 };
static struct _display d_bg3 = { "background 3: ",  8, 40,  8, 54 };
static struct _display d_bg4 = { "background 4: ", 10, 40, 10, 54 };
static struct _display d_bg5 = { "background 5: ", 12, 40, 12, 54 };
static struct _display d_bg6 = { "background 6: ", 14, 40, 14, 54 };
static struct _display d_bg7 = { "background 7: ", 16, 40, 16, 54 };
static struct _display d_bg8 = { "background 8: ", 18, 40, 18, 54 };
static struct _display d_bg9 = { "background 9: ", 20, 40, 20, 54 };

static long timelimit = 0L;         /* execution time limit of demo */

static int lock = 0;                /* lock variable - must init to 0 */

/*********************************************************************
           F O R W A R D   D E C L A R A T I O N S
**********************************************************************/

#ifdef ANSI

static void clock(void);
static void fgtask1(struct _display *);
static void bgtask1(struct _display *);
static void bgtask2(struct _display *);

#else

void clock();
void fgtask1();
void bgtask1();
void bgtask2();

#endif

/*********************************************************************
                   E N T R Y   R O U T I N E S
**********************************************************************/

/*--------------------------------------------------------------------
TASK
        CLOCK  -  pretends to be a clock

SYNOPSIS
        static void clock(void)

REMARKS
        Prints the time obtained from ReadClock().

        Since this is the only routine in which strcpy() and strcat() are
        used, there is no need to set up a critical section for them -
        assuming of course that sprintf() does not call on them.

LAST UPDATE
        23 May 1988
                creation
--------------------------------------------------------------------*/

static void clock()
{
```

```
	long elasped;			/* total elasped time in seconds */
	long hr, min, sec;		/* hour, minutes, seconds */
	char timestr[10];		/* time display string */
	char buf[4];			/* tmp buffer */


	while (1)
	{
		elasped = ReadClock() / 1000L;

		sec = elasped % 60L;
		min = elasped / 60L;
		hr  = elasped / 3600L;

		video_WriteString(0, 0, "         ", 0x07);

		ltoa(hr, timestr, 10);
		strcat(timestr, ":");
		strcat(timestr, ltoa(min, buf, 10));
		strcat(timestr, ":");
		strcat(timestr, ltoa(sec, buf, 10));

		video_WriteString(0, 0, timestr, 0x70);

		if (elasped >= timelimit)
			panic("Time's Up");

		WaitNextSamp();
	}

}


/*------------------------------------------------------------------------
TASK
	FGTASK1  -  foreground task

SYNOPSIS
	static void fgtask1(dp)
	struct _display *dp;

REMARKS
	They print the current invocation number and then wait for next
	sampling instance.

LAST UPDATE
	25 May 1988
		adapt from demo1.c  -  change sprintf() to itoa()
------------------------------------------------------------------------*/

static void fgtask1(dp)
struct _display *dp;
{
	int i = 0;
	char stat[12];


	video_WriteString(dp->lrow, dp->lcol, dp->label, 0x07);

	while (1)
	{
		disable();

		itoa(i, stat, 10);

		enable();

		video_WriteString(dp->crow, dp->ccol, stat, 0x07);

		if (++i < 0)
			i = 0;

		WaitNextSamp();
	}

}


/*------------------------------------------------------------------------
TASK
	BGTASK1  -  background task, type 1

SYNOPSIS
	static void bgtask1(dp)
	struct _display *dp;

REMARKS
	Mutual exclusion via blocking semaphores.

LAST UPDATE
	23 May 1988
		creation
------------------------------------------------------------------------*/

static void bgtask1(dp)
struct _display *dp;
{
	int i = 0;
	char stat[12];
```

```
        video_WriteString(dp->lrow, dp->lcol, dp->label, 0x07);

        while (1)
        {
                Psem(lock);

                sprintf(stat, "%d", i);

                Vsem(lock);

                video_WriteString(dp->crow, dp->ccol, stat, 0x07);

                if (++i < 0)
                        i = 0;
        }

}


/*-----------------------------------------------------------------------
PROCEDURE
        MAIN  -  main program

SYNOPSIS
        main(void)

REMARKS
        First, call prologue() to setup system.

        Next, install ticktock() as a sample-time control task with a
        sample interval of 1 second (1000 milliseconds) using SetCntrlTask().

        Lastly, start the system.

LAST UPDATE
        23 May 1988
                creation
-----------------------------------------------------------------------*/

main()
{

        fputs("enter total running time in seconds > ", stdout);
        scanf("%ld", &timelimit);

        prologue();

        SetCntrlTask("CLOCK", clock,  (void *)NULL, PCONTROL, 1000L);
        SetCntrlTask("FG1", fgtask1,  (void *)&d_fg1, PCONTROL+1, 1000L);
        SetCntrlTask("FG2", fgtask1,  (void *)&d_fg2, PCONTROL+2, 2000L);
        SetBkgndTask("BG1", bgtask1,  (void *)&d_bg1, PSLICE);
        SetBkgndTask("BG2", bgtask1,  (void *)&d_bg2, PSLICE);
        SetBkgndTask("BG3", bgtask1,  (void *)&d_bg3, PSLICE);
        SetBkgndTask("BG4", bgtask1,  (void *)&d_bg4, PSLICE);
        SetBkgndTask("BG5", bgtask1,  (void *)&d_bg5, PSLICE);
        SetBkgndTask("BG6", bgtask1,  (void *)&d_bg6, PSLICE);
        SetBkgndTask("BG7", bgtask1,  (void *)&d_bg7, PSLICE);
        SetBkgndTask("BG8", bgtask1,  (void *)&d_bg8, PSLICE);

        if ((lock = NewSem(1)) < 0)
                panic("cannot allocate sprintf lock semaphore");

        start();

        return(-1);    /* stop compiler from grumbling at /W2 warning level */
}

/**********************************************************************

FILE
        demo4.c  -  simple demo of Psem() and Vsem()

REMARKS
        This program sets up 3 foreground tasks and 3 background tasks.
        The foreground tasks are scheduled as sample-time control tasks
        which have to run at fixed intervals.  The background tasks just
        run forever.

        Mutual exclusion is achieved by disabling interrupts.

        Microsoft's sprintf() is not re-entrant! Aaugh!

LAST UPDATE
        23 May 1988

        Copyright(c) 1988  D.M. Auslander and C.H. Tham

**********************************************************************/

/**********************************************************************
                              I M P O R T S
**********************************************************************/

#include <stdio.h>

#include "clotho.h"

/**********************************************************************
                        P R I V A T E    D A T A
**********************************************************************/
```

```
struct _display {
        char *label;            /* label to display */
        int lrow, lcol;         /* where to display label */
        int crow, ccol;         /* where to display count */
};

static struct _display d_bg1 = { "background 1: ",  8, 40,  8, 54 };
static struct _display d_bg2 = { "background 2: ", 10, 40, 10, 54 };
static struct _display d_bg3 = { "background 3: ", 12, 40, 12, 54 };

static long timelimit = 50L; /* execution time limit of demo */
static int block = -1;                    /* block semaphore */

/*************************************************************************
          F O R W A R D   D E C L A R A T I O N S
*************************************************************************/

#ifdef ANSI

static void clock(void);
static void bgtask1(struct _display *);
static void bgtask2(struct _display *);
static void bgtask3(struct _display *);

#else

void clock();
static void bgtask1();
static void bgtask2();
static void bgtask3();

#endif

/*************************************************************************
                               E N T R Y   R O U T I N E S
*************************************************************************/

/*-----------------------------------------------------------------------
TASK
        CLOCK  -  pretends to be a clock

SYNOPSIS
        static void clock(void)

REMARKS
        Prints the time obtained from ReadClock().

LAST UPDATE
        23 May 1988
                creation
-----------------------------------------------------------------------*/

static void clock()
{
        long elasped;                   /* total elasped time in seconds */
        long hr, min, sec;              /* hour, minutes, seconds */
        char timestr[10];               /* time display string */


        while (1)
        {
                elasped = ReadClock() / 1000L;

                sec = elasped % 60L;
                min = elasped / 60L;
                hr  = elasped / 3600L;

                disable();

                sprintf(timestr, "%2ld:%2ld:%2ld", hr, min, sec);

                enable();

                video_WriteString(0, 0, timestr, 0x70);


                if (sec == 20L)
                        Vsem(block);
                else if (sec == 30L)
                        Vsem(block);
                else if (sec == 40L)
                        Vsem(block);


                if (elasped >= timelimit)
                        panic("Time's Up");

                WaitNextSamp();
        }

}


/*-----------------------------------------------------------------------
TASK
        BGTASK1  -  background task 1

SYNOPSIS
        static void bgtask1(dp)
        struct _display *dp;

REMARKS
```

```
        Runs in an infinite loop and print the current iteration number.
        Psem() at iteration == 1000.

LAST UPDATE
        23 May 1988
                creation
-----------------------------------------------------------------------*/

static void bgtask1(dp)
struct _display *dp;
{
        int i = 0;
        char stat[12];


        video_WriteString(dp->lrow, dp->lcol, dp->label, 0x07);

        while (1)
        {
                disable();

                sprintf(stat, "%d", i);

                enable();

                video_WriteString(dp->crow, dp->ccol, stat, 0x07);

                if (i++ == 1000)
                        Psem(block);

                if (i < 0)
                        i = 0;
        }

}


/*-----------------------------------------------------------------------
TASK
        BGTASK2  -  background task 2

SYNOPSIS
        static void bgtask2(dp)
        struct _display *dp;

REMARKS
        Runs in an infinite loop and print the current iteration number.
        Psem() at iteration == 2000.

LAST UPDATE
        23 May 1988
                creation
-----------------------------------------------------------------------*/

static void bgtask2(dp)
struct _display *dp;
{
        int i = 0;
        char stat[12];


        video_WriteString(dp->lrow, dp->lcol, dp->label, 0x07);

        while (1)
        {
                disable();

                sprintf(stat, "%d", i);

                enable();

                video_WriteString(dp->crow, dp->ccol, stat, 0x07);

                if (i++ == 2000)
                        Psem(block);

                if (i < 0)
                        i = 0;
        }

}


/*-----------------------------------------------------------------------
TASK
        BGTASK3  -  background task 3

SYNOPSIS
        static void bgtask3(dp)
        struct _display *dp;

REMARKS
        Runs in an infinite loop and print the current iteration number.
        Psem() at iteration == 3000.

LAST UPDATE
        23 May 1988
                creation
-----------------------------------------------------------------------*/
```

```
static void bgtask3(dp)
struct _display *dp;
{
        int i = 0;
        char stat[12];


        video_WriteString(dp->lrow, dp->lcol, dp->label, 0x07);

        while (1)
        {
                disable();

                sprintf(stat, "%d", i);

                enable();

                video_WriteString(dp->crow, dp->ccol, stat, 0x07);

                if (i++ == 3000)
                        Psem(block);

                if (i < 0)
                        i = 0;
        }

}


/*--------------------------------------------------------------------
PROCEDURE
        MAIN  -  main program

SYNOPSIS
        main(void)

REMARKS
        First, call prologue() to setup system.

        Next, install ticktock() as a sample-time control task with a
        sample interval of 1 second (1000 milliseconds) using SetCntrlTask().

        Lastly, start the system.

LAST UPDATE
        20 October 1986
--------------------------------------------------------------------*/

main()
{
        prologue();

        SetCntrlTask("CLOCK", clock, (void *)NULL, PCONTROL, 1000L);

        SetBkgndTask("BG1", bgtask1, (void *)&d_bg1, PSLICE);
        SetBkgndTask("BG2", bgtask2, (void *)&d_bg2, PSLICE);
        SetBkgndTask("BG3", bgtask3, (void *)&d_bg3, PSLICE);

        if ((block = NewSem(0)) < 0)
                panic("cannot alloc lock semaphore");

        start();

        return(-1);   /* stop compiler from grumbling at /W2 warning level */
}


/**********************************************************************

FILE
        demo5.c  -  test of message passing system

REMARKS
        This program sets up 1 foreground tasks and 5 background tasks.

        The foreground task pretends to be a clock.  3 of the background
        tasks share the same code; they merely increment and display a
        local integer variable.  The other 2 background tasks are divided
        into a message sender and a message receiver.  The sender sends
        the value of a local variable and then increments it.  The receiver
        receives the message in the form of an integer and prints it.

        Notice how the sender and receiver are synchronized?

        Microsoft's sprintf() is not re-entrant! Aaugh!

LAST UPDATE
        31 May 1988

        Copyright(c) 1988  D.M. Auslander and C.H. Tham

**********************************************************************/

/**********************************************************************
                              I M P O R T S
**********************************************************************/

#include <stdio.h>
#include <stdlib.h>
#include <string.h>
```

```
#include "clotho.h"

/***********************************************************************
                    P R I V A T E   D A T A
***********************************************************************/

struct _display {
        char *label;            /* label to display */
        int lrow, lcol;         /* where to display label */
        int crow, ccol;         /* where to display count */
};

static struct _display d_bg1 = { "background 1: ",  8, 40,  8, 54 };
static struct _display d_bg2 = { "background 2: ", 10, 40, 10, 54 };
static struct _display d_bg3 = { "background 3: ", 12, 40, 12, 54 };

static long timelimit = 0L;         /* execution time limit of demo */
static int mailbox = -1;            /* mailbox between sender & receiver */

/***********************************************************************
             F O R W A R D   D E C L A R A T I O N S
***********************************************************************/

#ifdef ANSI

static void clock(void);
static void fgtask1(struct _display *);
static void bgtask1(struct _display *);
static void sender(void);
static void receiver(void);

#else

void clock();
void fgtask1();
void bgtask1();
void sender();
void receiver();

#endif

/***********************************************************************
                    E N T R Y   R O U T I N E S
***********************************************************************/

/*-----------------------------------------------------------------------
TASK
        CLOCK  -  pretends to be a clock

SYNOPSIS
        static void clock(void)

REMARKS
        Prints the time obtained from ReadClock().

LAST UPDATE
        23 May 1988
                creation
-----------------------------------------------------------------------*/

static void clock()
{
        long elapsed;                   /* total elasped time in seconds */
        long hr, min, sec;              /* hour, minutes, seconds */
        char timestr[10];               /* time display string */


        while (1)
        {
                elasped = ReadClock() / 1000L;

                sec = elasped % 60L;
                min = elasped / 60L;
                hr  = elasped / 3600L;

                disable();

                sprintf(timestr, "%21d:%21d:%21d", hr, min, sec);

                enable();

                video_WriteString(0, 0, timestr, 0x70);

                if (elasped >= timelimit)
                        panic("Time's Up");

                WaitNextSamp();
        }

}


/*-----------------------------------------------------------------------
TASK
        BGTASK1  -  background task

SYNOPSIS
        static void bgtask1(void)

REMARKS
        Runs in an infinite loop and print the current iteration number.
```

```
LAST UPDATE
        23 May 1988
                creation
-----------------------------------------------------------------------*/

static void bgtask1(dp)
struct _display *dp;
{
        int i = 0;
        char stat[12];


        video_WriteString(dp->lrow, dp->lcol, dp->label, 0x07);

        while (1)
        {
                disable();

                sprintf(stat, "%d", i);

                enable();

                video_WriteString(dp->crow, dp->ccol, stat, 0x07);

                if (++i < 0)
                        i = 0;
        }

}


/*----------------------------------------------------------------------
TASK
        SENDER  -  produce and send messages

SYNOPSIS
        static void sender(void)

REMARKS
        The message is the value of a local integer variable.  This variable
        is incremented after every send.

LAST UPDATE
        31 May 1988
                creation
-----------------------------------------------------------------------*/

static void sender()
{
        int i;
        char stat[12];


        video_WriteString(6, 0, "sender: ", 0x07);

        i = 0;

        while (1)
        {
                disable();

                sprintf(stat, "%d", i);

                enable();

                Send(mailbox, sizeof(int), &i);

                video_WriteString(6, 9, stat, 0x07);

                if (++i < 0)
                        i = 0;
        }

}


/*----------------------------------------------------------------------
TASK
        RECEIVER  -  receives messages

SYNOPSIS
        static void receiver(void)

REMARKS
        The message is that sent by the sender() task.  Decode and print
        the value of the datum.

LAST UPDATE
        31 May 1988
                creation
-----------------------------------------------------------------------*/

static void receiver()
{
        int i;
        char stat[12];


        video_WriteString(8, 0, "receiver: ", 0x07);

        i = -1;
```

```
	while (1)
	{
		Receive(mailbox, sizeof(int), &i);

		disable();

		sprintf(stat, "%d", i);

		enable();

		video_WriteString(8, 10, stat, 0x07);
	}

}


/*----------------------------------------------------------------------
PROCEDURE
	MAIN  -  main program

SYNOPSIS
	main(void)

REMARKS
	First, call prologue() to setup system.

	Next, install ticktock() as a sample-time control task with a
	sample interval of 1 second (1000 milliseconds) using SetCntrlTask().

	Lastly, start the system.

LAST UPDATE
	20 October 1986
----------------------------------------------------------------------*/

main()
{

	fputs("enter total running time in seconds > ", stdout);
	scanf("%ld", &timelimit);

	prologue();

	SetCntrlTask("CLOCK", clock, (void *)NULL, PCONTROL, 1000L);

	SetBkgndTask("BG1", bgtask1, (void *)&d_bg1, PSLICE);
	SetBkgndTask("BG2", bgtask1, (void *)&d_bg2, PSLICE);
	SetBkgndTask("BG3", bgtask1, (void *)&d_bg3, PSLICE);

	SetBkgndTask("SEND", sender, (void *)NULL, PSLICE+1);

	SetBkgndTask("RECV", receiver, (void *)NULL, PSLICE+1);

	mailbox = NewMessage();

	start();

	return(-1);	/* stop compiler from grumbling at /W2 warning level */
}

/***********************************************************************

FILE
	kbsched.c  -  illustrates event driven scheduling via keyboard

REMARKS
	This program illustrates event driven task scheduling through
	asynchronous keyboard generated events.

	A count variable is accessed by 3 tasks:

		1)	a task runs every second, printing out the current value
			of count
		2)	another task runs every 0.5 seconds, incrementing count
			every time it runs
		3)	a third task runs every 0.75 seconds, decrementing count
			every time it runs.

	Upper and lower limits are set for the count.  Reaching the limits
	are events.  The overflow event handler suspends the incrementor
	and the underflow event handler suspends the decrementor.

	When a key is hit, an interrupt is generated.  The keyboard
	interrupt service routine (in the file kbisr.asm) calls the BIOS
	to decode the key and then calls kbsig() which decides what to
	do in response.

	If the 'i' key has been hit, the event manager notifies a task
	to "resume" the count incrementing task if it has been suspended.
	If the incrementor is not suspended, then hitting 'i' has no
	effect.

	If the 'd' key has been hit, the event manager notifies a task
	to "resume" the count decrementing task if it has been suspended.
	If the decrementor is not suspended, then hitting 'd' has no
	effect.

	Hitting the ESC key will abort the program.

	The scheduling of the increment and decrement tasks are
	driven by certain keyboard events.  We can see this in action
	by observing the count value which is printed out every second.
```

```
    Note that count is incremented or decremented with interrupts
    disabled; otherwise it is possible that the count decrement task
    can interrupt the count increment task in the middle of incrementing
    count, with disasterous results.

    To generate the executable program:

        cl /Alfw /Gs /DLARGEMODEL kbsched.c /link clotho

LAST UPDATE
    26 May 1988
        use suspend and resume instead

    Copyright(c) 1986-1988  D.M. Auslander and C.H. Tham

*************************************************************************/

/************************************************************************
                        I M P O R T S
*************************************************************************/

#include <stdio.h>
#include <bios.h>                       /* Microsoft specific */

#include "clotho.h"

/************************************************************************
                  P R I V A T E     D A T A
*************************************************************************/

#define MAXCOUNT     5       /* maximum allowable value of count */
#define MINCOUNT    -5       /* minimum allowable value of count */

static int count;            /* the infamous count variable */

static int escape;           /* "escape key has been hit" event id */
static int increment;        /* increment "count" event handle */
static int decrement;        /* decrement "count" event handle */
static int overflow;         /* count exceeds MAXCOUNT event handle */
static int underflow;        /* count less than MINCOUNT event handle */

static TASK *inc_task;
static TASK *dec_task;

/************************************************************************
              F O R W A R D    D E C L A R A T I O N S
*************************************************************************/

#ifdef ANSI

static void         kbsig(void);
static void         print_count(void);
static void         inc_count(void);
static void         dec_count(void);
static void         suspend_inc(void);
static void         resume_inc(void);
static void         suspend_dec(void);
static void         resume_dec(void);
static void         escape_handler(void);

#else

static void         kbsig();
static void         print_count();
static void         inc_count();
static void         dec_count();
static void         suspend_inc();
static void         resume_inc();
static void         suspend_dec();
static void         resume_dec();
static void         escape_handler();

#endif

/************************************************************************
               E N T R Y     R O U T I N E S
*************************************************************************/

/************************************************************************
             P R I V A T E     R O U T I N E S
*************************************************************************/

/*-----------------------------------------------------------------------
PROCEDURE
    KBSIG  -  keyboard signal routine

SYNOPSIS
    static void kbsig(void)

REMARKS
    This routine is called whenever an key is pressed

    If the key is one of ESC, 'i' or 'd', it notifies the event
    managerrelease tasks pending on these events, causing possible
    task rescheduling.

    The _bios_keybrd() routine calls the bios which enables interrupts.
    We cannot allow this to happen since kbsig() is installed as a
    keyboard interrupt service routine and executes in system space.
    Interrupts are disabled by masking out the 8259.

LAST UPDATE
```

```
        27 May 1988
                convert to be installed via intset()
----------------------------------------------------------------------*/

static void kbsig()
{
        int cc;                 /* scancode in hi-byte, ascii in lo-byte */
        int imask;              /* 8259 interrupt mask */


        imask = in(MASKPORT);           /* read current mask status */
        out(MASKPORT, 0xFF);            /* mask out all external interrupts */

        if (_bios_keybrd(_KEYBRD_READY))                /* ASCII key available ? */
        {
                cc = _bios_keybrd(_KEYBRD_READ);        /* get SCANCODE:ASCII */

                disable();              /* disable since bios enables interrupts */
                out(MASKPORT, imask); /* restore 8259 interrupt mask */

                switch (cc & 0xFF)
                {
                        case 27:        Notify(escape);                 break;
                        case 'i':       Notify(increment);              break;
                        case 'd':       Notify(decrement);              break;
                        default:                                        break;
                }
        }

        out(MASKPORT, imask);           /* restore 8259 mask */

}


/*----------------------------------------------------------------------
TASK
        PRINT_COUNT  -  priint count variable

SYNOPSIS
        static void print_count(void)

REMARKS
        Print the "count" value every second (or whatever period is set
        in the initialization routine).

        There is no need to put printf() in a critical section since this
        is the only task that calls printf() (and its internal routines).

LAST UPDATE
        16 May 1987
----------------------------------------------------------------------*/

static void print_count()
{

        while (1)
        {
                printf("%d\n", count);

                if (count >= MAXCOUNT)
                        Notify(overflow);

                if (count <= MINCOUNT)
                        Notify(underflow);

                WaitNextSamp();
        }

}



/*----------------------------------------------------------------------
TASK
        INC_COUNT  -  task that increments the count variable

SYNOPSIS
        static void inc_count(void)

REMARKS
        Note that count is incremented with interrupts disabled.

LAST UPDATE
        15 May 1987
----------------------------------------------------------------------*/

static void inc_count()
{

        while (1)
        {
                disable();

                ++count;

                enable();

                WaitNextSamp();
        }

}
```

```
/*-------------------------------------------------------------------------
EVENT
        RESUME_INC  -  resume incrementing

SYNOPSIS
        static void resume_inc(void)

REMARKS
        This is the handler in response to an 'i' keyboard input.

LAST UPDATE
        26 May 1988
                creation
-------------------------------------------------------------------------*/

static void resume_inc()
{

        while (1)
        {
                Resume(inc_task);

                Pend(increment, TNULL);         /* await next incarnation */
        }
}


/*-------------------------------------------------------------------------
EVENT
        SUSPEND_INC  -  suspend count incrementor

SYNOPSIS
        static void suspend_inc(void)

REMARKS
        This is the count overflow handler.

LAST UPDATE
        26 May 1988
                creation
-------------------------------------------------------------------------*/

static void suspend_inc()
{

        while (1)
        {
                Suspend(inc_task);

                Pend(overflow, TNULL);
        }
}


/*-------------------------------------------------------------------------
TASK
        DEC_COUNT  -  task that increments the count variable

SYNOPSIS
        static void dec_count(void)

LAST UPDATE
        15 May 1987
-------------------------------------------------------------------------*/

static void dec_count()
{

        while (1)
        {
                disable();

                --count;

                enable();

                WaitNextSamp();
        }

}


/*-------------------------------------------------------------------------
EVENT
        RESUME_DEC  -  resume decrementing

SYNOPSIS
        static void resume_dec(void)

REMARKS
        This is the handler in response to an 'd' keyboard input.

LAST UPDATE
        26 May 1988
                creation
-------------------------------------------------------------------------*/

static void resume_dec()
```

```
{

        while (1)
        {
                Resume(dec_task);

                Pend(decrement, TNULL);             /* await next incarnation */
        }
}


/*----------------------------------------------------------------------
EVENT
        SUSPEND_DEC  -  suspend count decrementor

SYNOPSIS
        static void suspend_dec(void)

REMARKS
        This is the count underflow handler.

LAST UPDATE
        26 May 1988
                creation
----------------------------------------------------------------------*/

static void suspend_dec()
{

        while (1)
        {
                Suspend(dec_task);

                Pend(underflow, TNULL);
        }
}


/*----------------------------------------------------------------------
EVENT
        ESCAPE_HANDLER  - called when escape key has been hit

SYNOPSIS
        Called by event manager.

LAST UPDATE
        11 May 1987
----------------------------------------------------------------------*/

static void escape_handler()
{

        panic("Terminated By User Request");

}


/************************************************************************
            I N I T I A L I Z A T I O N     R O U T I N E
************************************************************************/

/*----------------------------------------------------------------------
PROCEDURE
        MAIN  -  main program

REMARKS
        Set up print_count() as a sample time control task, executing
        once every second.  print_count() prints the count variable.

        Next, allocate event handles and set-up the tasks that increments
        and decrements the count variable.

        Finally, set up the ESC event handler and establish kbisr() as
        the keyboard interrupt service routine (see kbisr.asm).

        Note that calling Pend(event_id, task) in InitUser() will associate
        the task with the event id and install the task as an event handler.

LAST UPDATE
        26 May 1988
                new
----------------------------------------------------------------------*/

void main()
{

        prologue();

        SetCntrlTask("PRINT_COUNT", print_count, (void *)NULL, PCONTROL, 1000L);

        inc_task = SetCntrlTask("INC_COUNT", inc_count, (void *)NULL,
                                                PCONTROL, 500L);

        dec_task = SetCntrlTask("DEC_COUNT", dec_count, (void *)NULL,
                                                PCONTROL, 750L);


        increment = SetEventTask("INC_COUNT", resume_inc, (void *)NULL,
                                                PCONTROL+1);
```

```
        decrement = SetEventTask("DEC_COUNT", resume_dec, (void *)NULL,
                                                     PCONTROL+1);

        overflow = SetEventTask("NO_INC", suspend_inc, (void *)NULL,
                                                     PCONTROL+1);

        underflow = SetEventTask("NO_DEC", suspend_dec, (void *)NULL,
                                                     PCONTROL+1);

        escape = SetEventTask("ESCAPE", escape_handler, (void *)NULL,
                                                     PCONTROL+10);


        intset(INT_KB, kbsig);

        start();

}

;*********************************************************************
;
; FILE
;       kbisr.asm  -  keyboard interrupt decode (Microsoft C version 4)
;
; SYNOPSIS
;       masm kbisr /ml;
;
; LAST UPDATE
;       27 May 1985  by  Haam
;               modify to support big memory model
;       12 September 1987  by  Haam
;               compiler and name change
;       15 February 1988  by  Haam
;               support more memory models through LCODE and LDATA
;
; AUTHOR
;       Haam  Tham    18 February 1985
;
;*********************************************************************

BIOS_KBINT      EQU             209     ; relocated BIOS keyboard interrupt routine
BIOS_KBREAD     EQU             22      ; BIOS keyboard query routine


        INCLUDE model.h

IF LCODE
        EXTRN   _kbsig:FAR
ENDIF

        INCLUDE prologue.h

        PUBLIC _kbisr

IFE LCODE
        EXTRN   _kbsig:NEAR
ENDIF

;-------------------------------------------------------------------
; PROCEDURE
;       KBISR  -  special keyboard interrupt decoding routine
;
; REMARKS
;       This routine is set in ISrvFunc[1] and is called by KbIntSR
;
;       It calls the normal BIOS service routine to decode the keyboard
;       entry and if an ascii character is available, it calls the BIOS
;       again to remove it from the BIOS buffer and pass it to kbsig().
;       The ascii character will be in the lower byte and the scan code
;       will be in the upper byte.
;
;       The user MUST supply a routine called kbsig() for this to work.
;
; LAST UPDATE
;       15 February 1988
;               use LCODE and LDATA
;-------------------------------------------------------------------

IF LCODE
_kbisr          PROC    FAR
ELSE
_kbisr          PROC    NEAR
ENDIF

        int             BIOS_KBINT      ; call BIOS interrupt service routine

        mov             ah, 1           ; code for "is ascii char available?"
        int             BIOS_KBREAD     ; call BIOS again

        jz              kbexit          ; ZF=1 means no luck

        mov             ah, 0           ; char avail, remove it from BIOS buffer
        int             BIOS_KBREAD     ; AL <- ascii, AH <- scan code

        push            ax              ; argument to in_kbbuf

        call            _kbsig          ; call user's kb routine

        add             sp, 2           ; remove argument from stack

kbexit:

        ret
```

```
_kbisr       ENDP

      INCLUDE epilogue.h

      END
```

CHAPTER 9

TASK ORGANIZATION AND SCHEDULING FOR A CONTROL SYSTEM

This chapter illustrates the use of real time scheduling by working out the task structure for a multi-loop control system. The task structure developed is relatively independent of the particular real-time system used for implementation, but issues such as synchronization and mutual exclusion are identified within the tasks. The actual implementation is done using two different real-time operating system kernels: the one developed in Chapter 8, and a commercially available real-time system (VRTX from Ready Systems, Inc., Palo Alto, CA).

Although the task structures are very similar, the details of implementation differ. Our kernel is designed with an emphasis on control systems, making it very easy to set up and run control tasks. The commercial system is much more general and has more extensive facilities for intertask communication.

In keeping with our theme of motor control, the heart of the system is a motor-driven valve. The valve can be opened or closed to allow liquid to flow into a tank; the liquid flows out of the bottom of the tank. There is also a heater to control the temperature in the tank.

In order to make the example usable on any computer, the actual process is simulated. The only "real-time" component used is the computer's clock. By making the process simulation the highest priority task, it behaves like the real system in that no matter what happens in the control part of the program, the process continues. The use of the clock interrupt for task scheduling also guarantees that the control tasks will have the normal amount of asynchronous interaction so that problems such as mutual exclusion are tested even though the process is simulated. The example could be turned into a real control system by the substitution of data acquisition and actuation software for the simulation task.

9.1 THE PROCESS AND ITS MODEL

The system under control is shown in Fig. 9.1 In order to keep the simulation from getting too complex, several simplifying assumptions are made about the operation of the system:

1. The motor actuation signal is assumed to control the velocity directly.
2. The flow out of the tank is assumed to be linearly proportional to the height of liquid in the tank.
3. The liquid is assumed to be well mixed so that there are no temperature gradients in the tank.
4. It is assumed that there is no heat loss through the tank walls.

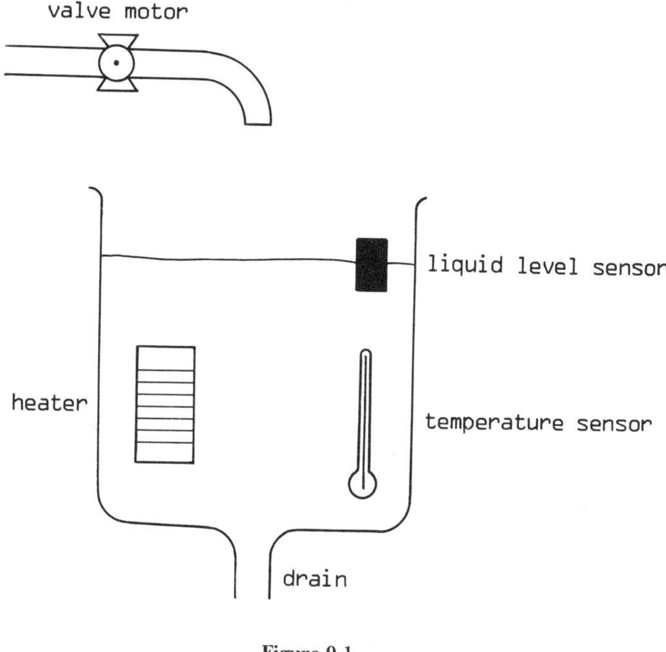

Figure 9.1

With these assumptions, the differential equations describing the response of this system can be developed. The valve position's rate of change is controlled by the control system output command

$$\frac{dx}{dt} = K_m \, m_{con} \tag{9.1}$$

where K_m is the scaling constant. The actual position is limited by the mechanical construction of the valve

$$x_{\min} \le x \le x_{\max} \tag{9.2}$$

The liquid flowrate into the tank is assumed to be proportional to valve position

$$Q_{in} = Q_{\max} \, x \tag{9.3}$$

while the flowrate out of the tank is taken to be proportional to the height of liquid in the tank

$$Q_{out} = K_q \, h \qquad (9.4))$$

The rate of change of the liquid height is related to the difference between inflow and outflow. For a straight-sided tank, the relationship is linear.

$$\frac{dh}{dt} = \frac{1}{A}(Q_{in} - Q_{out}) \tag{9.5}$$

where A is the cross-sectional area of the tank.

On the thermal side, the change in temperature depends on both the energy transport (convection) from the liquid flowing in and out of the tank and the energy added to the tank from the heater

$$\frac{d\theta}{dt} = \frac{1}{V}(Q_{in}\,\theta_{in} - Q_{out}\,\theta + H_{in}) \tag{9.6}$$

where V is the volume of liquid

$$V = A \, h \tag{9.7}$$

The simulation of these equations involves a numerical integration to get an approximate solution on a step-by-step basis. For simplicity, the numerical integration is done using the Euler method, which was also used in the motor simulations done earlier. This is not very efficient, but is simple to program and understand and a relatively small integration step size is required anyway in order to have data available on a timely basis for the controllers.

9.2 CONTROLLER CONFIGURATION

The liquid level control is set up as a cascade control. This is used in cases such as this where there are two measurements but only a single actuator. The inside loop is used to control the valve position. It is a normal single-input, single-output control loop (see Fig. 9.2). The setpoint for the valve position, however, comes from the output of the outer loop control, which controls the liquid level Fig. 9.2.

The block marked "valve" in Fig. 9.3 is the entire system represented by the diagram given in Fig. 9.2 The "command" output from the level control in Fig. 9.3

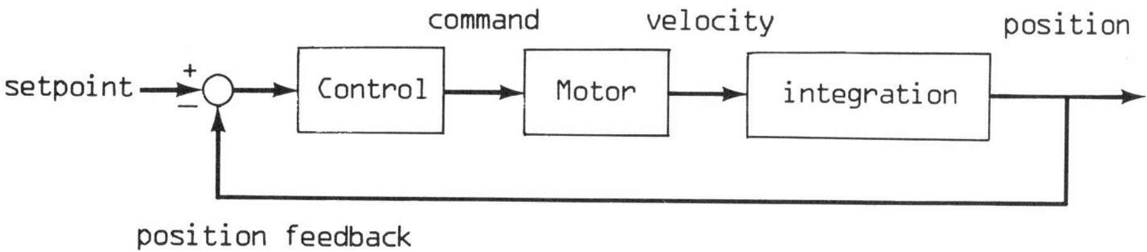

Figure 9.2

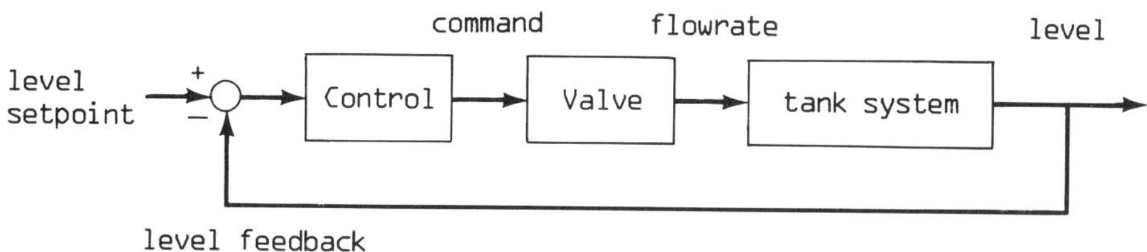

Figure 9.3

is the "setpoint" input in Fig. 9.2. The output of the valve control is valve position, which is directly proportional to flowrate into the tank (see Eq. 9.3).

9.3 TASK STRUCTURE: NORMAL OPERATION

The highest priority task is the process simulation. If the simulated process were to be replaced by a real process, the actuation control and data acquisition would remain as the high-priority task (or tasks). One or the other of these might also be implemented as part of the foreground if its computing time requirement were short enough.

During normal operation, the next highest priority level is occupied by the control tasks, the tasks responsible for the control loop calculations. Because of the cascade loop structure for the level control, this section of the system could be set up as either 2 or 3 tasks, with the cascade loop done as 1 or 2 tasks. Using 2 tasks for the cascade control allows a longer sample time for the liquid level loop than for the valve position control, and thus more efficient CPU usage. On the other hand, using 1 task, as will be done here, leads to a simpler program. Within the priority level of the control tasks, the task requiring faster sample time (valve control) is assigned the highest priority.

One level lower in priority than the control is the supervisory task. Its function is to generate the setpoints used by the control tasks. This could involve, for example, solving an optimization problem to get the combination of setpoints that would yield lowest price, changing product grade, etc. The process goal is often transmitted to the control computer from a plant management computer. In this example, the supervisory task will set the initial setpoints; then, at a prespecified time, it changes to new setpoint values.

The data logging task is at the next lowest priority level. Its function is to gather data about the process operation. The information gathered could be used for parameter adjustment, controller tuning, for example, management information on production rate, efficiency, etc., or diagnostic purposes to find out why a particular failure occurred.

Finally, the background task runs at the lowest priority. In the system being built here, the background task has two jobs: the first is to provide the operating system interface, and the second is to interact with the operator.

The nature of the operating system interaction depends on the needs of the particular real time software as well as the details of the operating system being used. The assumptions made here are that the real time software will use a single output stream for logging all information, and that the operating system can handle that stream without interfering with the real time operation. It is further assumed that the operating system contains parts that might not be re-entrant, so that all operating system interaction must be concentrated in one place.

The operator interaction is kept very simple for this example. The only function the operator has control over is stopping the system by pressing the ESCAPE key. This is an important function, however, because before the system is turned off and control returned to the normal operating system, all of the interrupts used specifically by the control program must be restored to their original state. More extensive operator interaction could be included by using any of the command processors discussed in earlier chapters.

When a background has several distinct functions, for example, in this case, if a more extensive operator interaction were to be used, it can be broken into several separate tasks. These tasks can then be scheduled as equal priority, time-sliced tasks. Both of the real time kernels we are using support time-sliced scheduling.

9.4 ALARMS

When something abnormal occurs, the task interaction must be modified to meet the needs of possibly dangerous conditions. As an illustration of such an alarm condition, this system checks for the level in the tank exceeding some preset limit. This is considered abnormal and potentially dangerous, so something must be done about it immediately. An alarm task is established to handle this condition. Its priority is just below that of the process simulation, and above the priority for the control tasks. That assures that the alarm task will run as soon as possible after an alarm condition has been detected.

The purpose of the alarm task is primarily to do whatever can be done to bring the system to a safe configuration. Because the condition is considered dangerous, the alarm task does not make any attempt to maintain production.

For this system, the alarm task can do this by shutting off the liquid inflow, and by turning off the heater. To accomplish that, the alarm task can take direct control of the actuation outputs, setting the valve position motor so that the valve starts closing, and turning off the heater. Since this would put the alarm task in conflict with the control and supervisory tasks, the alarm task first suspends those tasks so that they will not run at all. It can then send actuation commands directly to the actuation task (or, in this case, the simulation task).

Another function of the alarm task is to log the information associated with the alarm to the output stream and to inform the plant operators of the alarm condition by actuation of lights or whistles.

This completes the definition of all of the tasks, so the complete task structure can be shown in priority order (see Fig. 9.4).

TASK LIST, Highest Priority First:

Simulation
Alarm
Valve/Level Control
Temperature Control
Supervisor
Data Logger
Background (Output Stream and Operator Interaction)

Figure 9.4

9.5 INTER-TASK COMMUNICATION

In order for the whole control system to function properly, the exchange of information among the tasks must be both orderly, to maintain the integrity of the data, and timely, to make sure that command signals can be delivered at the proper moment.

Each task has its own private data area. All of its working data is stored in that area and is accessible using the standard types and classes of variables of whatever programming language is being used. When data are needed from another task, they are first copied into the local data area and then used. Because tasks can be interrupted, the intertask data copying process must be protected through implementation of some form of mutual exclusion. In single processor systems, mutual exclusion can be accomplished by disabling interrupts during the transfer. This assures that the data being transferred will not be corrupted during the transfer. Corruption of such data is possible if there is an interrupt before the data transfer is complete, and the result of the interrupt is to run the task that produces the data. If that task changes the data, when the copy program starts running again it will be copying modified data. However, the first part of the data transfer copied the premodification data. This could lead to inconsistent data, since part of the data set is from an earlier time than the rest of the data, or, it can even lead to completely incorrect data if the transfer was interrupted in the middle of a multi-byte transfer.

Disabling interrupts to achieve mutual exclusion works well for small systems, since it doesn't happen too often. For large systems, or if large amounts of data have to be transferred, it could be ineffective because it would keep more important tasks from running when they should. In those circumstances, it is possible to implement mutual exclusion methods that are completely software based. These methods are usually less efficient, in the sense that the transaction takes more time, but they improve system integrity by assuring that system priorities are properly observed.

The act of copying data from place to place also has a degree of inefficiency associated with it because of the CPU time used for moving data around. Although it is more efficient of CPU time to use shared global (external) memory for data that must be accessed by more than one task, it is very difficult to assure effective mutual exclusion without interfering with the priority structure.

Mutual exclusion must be used whenever the data transfer occurs between tasks at different priority levels, regardless of the direction of the transfer. Tasks at the same priority level cannot interrupt each other and so could share global data.

Figure 9.5 shows the data interchange structure for this system. The left-hand column lists the data-producing tasks, the middle column indicates the nature of the data, and the right-hand column shows the tasks that use the data. Most tasks are both consumers and producers of data.

Source Task	Data Description	User Tasks
Simulation	Process State	Valve Control Temp. Control
Data Logger		
Alarm	Alarm Type	Background
Valve/Level Control	Motor Command	Simulation
Temperature Control	Heater Command	Simulation
Supervisor	Level Setpoint Temperature Setpoint	Valve Control Temp. Control
Data Logger	Formatted Log Data	Background

Figure 9.5

9.6 SIMULATED REAL-TIME FOR DEBUGGING

Real-time operation means that tasks will run asynchronously, even in this case for which the controlled system is being simulated. Also, if the operating system being used is not re-entrant, debugging statements or interactive debuggers will not work except in the background task. To avoid those problems for initial debugging, it is desirable to have the ability to simulate the interrupts from the background task by calling a function that serves the role of an interrupt service routine. When this is done, the system will operate completely synchronously, with all tasks executing to completion before relinquishing control of the CPU. This mode is very effective for debugging the basic program logic since "print" statements can be put anywhere and breakpoints can be placed anywhere if a debugger is available. The program logic given below includes a flag variable to indicate whether simulated real-time operation is to be used. When it is, the timer interrupt service routine is called in a loop in the background task.

9.7 TASK SPECIFICATIONS

The operation of the program starts with the execution of a main routine. "Main" runs before real-time operation begins. It initializes the real-time functions, creates all of the tasks and arrays for communication, gets initial parameters from the user, and opens any files that will be used. Then it calls the real-time scheduler to begin control operation. The program logic for "main" is given in Fig. 9.6.

```
Main:
        Read value for simulated time flag
        Initialize real-time system
        Create all of the tasks and set priorities
        Create communication arrays
        If simulated time flag = FALSE
                Turn on timer interrupt
        Start real time operation
```

Figure 9.6

The program logic for all of the real time tasks is similar. A section at the beginning of the task may be present for initialization statements. These are executed only once when the task is first entered. The main body of the task is embedded in an infinite loop. The last statement of the loop suspends the task until it is time to run again. The only two variants in this case are in the supervisory task and the background. The supervisory task only has to set the initial setpoints; then, after a specified time, changes to new setpoints. It can then cease to be an active task since it has nothing further to do. The background task never suspends itself. It occupies all available CPU time not used by higher priority tasks. The program logic for the real-time tasks starts with Fig. 9.7 and continues with successive figures (Figs. 9.8 through 9.13).

```
Simulation:

        Loop forever
                If new actuation values are available
                        Copy values for motor and heater actuation
                Simulate one time step of system operation

                While requests for data are present
                        Send data to requesting task
                Suspend until next scheduled time
```

Figure 9.7

```
Alarm:

        Suspend until first alarm
        Record the time and type of alarm
        Suspend the control tasks and the supervisory task
        Send new actuation values: Send motor to valve-closed position
                and turn heater off

        Loop forever
                Format data indicating type and time of alarm
                Send formatted information to background for output

                Suspend until next alarm
                Record time and type of alarm
```

Figure 9.8

Valve/Level Control:

```
Loop forever
    If new setpoint is available
        Get new liquid level setpoint
    Request system state data
    Perform control algorithm calculation for liquid height
    Use output as setpoint for valve position control
    Perform control algorithm calculation for valve position
    Send new actuation value to simulation task
    Suspend until next scheduled time
```

Figure 9.9

Temperature control:

```
Loop forever
    If new setpoint is available
        Get new temperature setpoint
    Request system state data
    Perform control algorithm calculation for temperature
    Send new actuation value to simulation task
    Suspend until next scheduled time
```

Figure 9.10

Supervisor:

```
Send out initial setpoints for level and temperature
Suspend until time for setpoint change
Send out new setpoints
```

Figure 9.11

Data logger:

```
Loop forever
          Request system state data
          Get current time
          Format data
          Send formatted data to background for output
          Suspend until next scheduled time
```

Figure 9.12

Background:

```
Loop forever
          If simulated-time-flag = TRUE
                    Call timer service routine
          If any data has been received for output
                    Send data out
          If user has typed an ESCAPE
                    If simulated-time-flag = FALSE
                              Reset timer interrupt
                    Exit back to operating system
```

Figure 9.13

9.8 RESULTS

Figures 9.14, 9.15, and 9.16 show the temperature, liquid height, and valve position as a function of time during normal operation. The initial setpoints are 0.5 for both level and temperature, changing to 0.7 for temperature and 0.25 for level at time = 3000.

In a second case, the second level setpoint was set to 0.78. The height of liquid in the tank that causes an alarm is set to 0.8, so the overshoot on approach to the setpoint causes the liquid level to exceed the alarm value. Figure 9.17 shows the section of the output file around the time of the alarm. The alarm output is intermixed with the output from the data logger. The data logger's output has 6 columns: time, valve position, liquid level, temperature, valve motor command, and heater command. At the time of the alarm, the last two columns show the actuation commands, -1 for the motor and 0 for the heater. The alarm function in the simulation task does not have any reset mode, so it sends an alarm every time

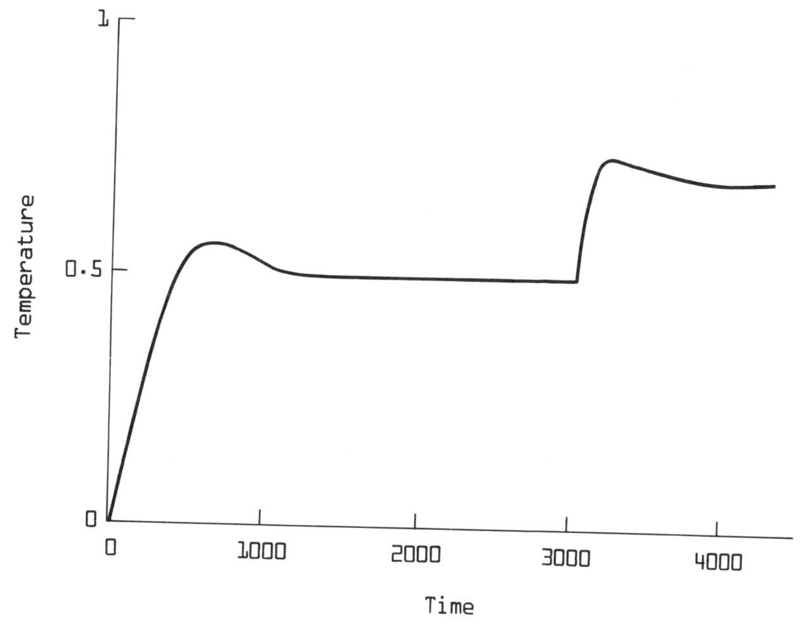

Figure 9.14

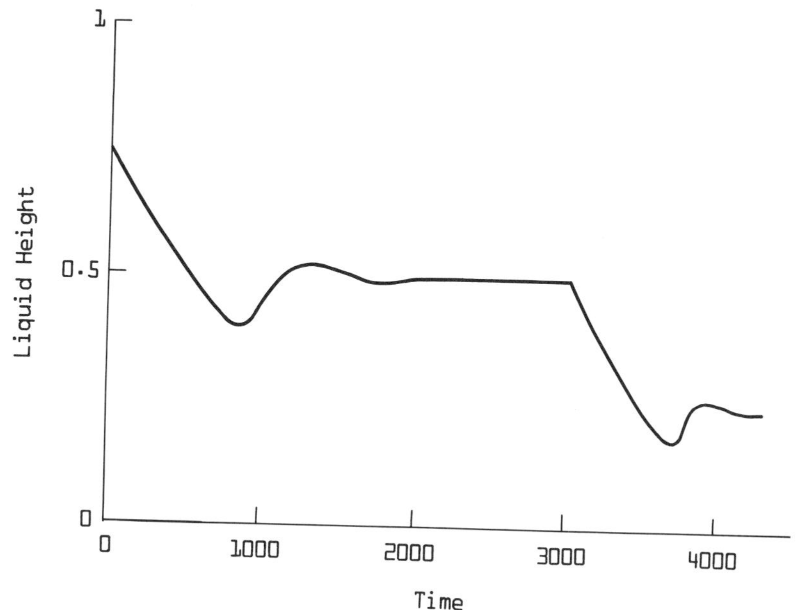

Figure 9.15

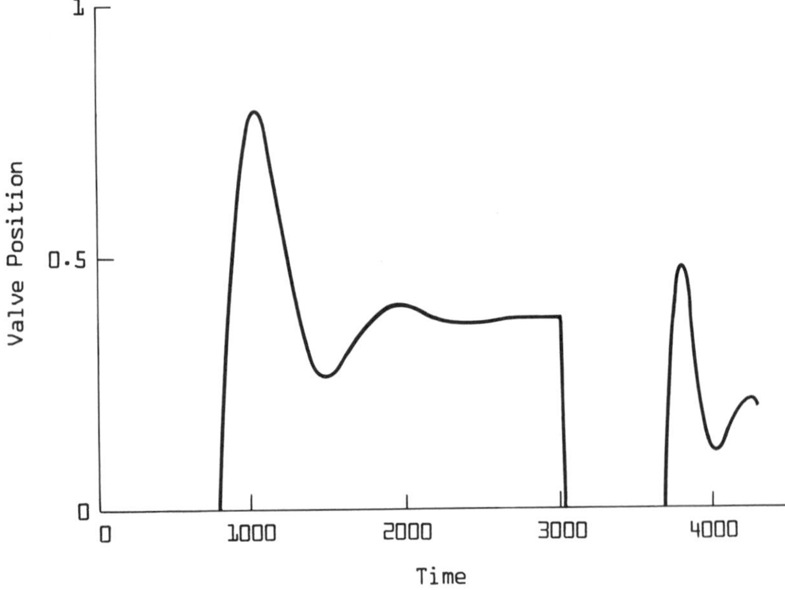

Figure 9.16

the simulation task runs until the height drops below the alarm level. This happens at time 3390, and the alarm signals disappear.

```
3270   1.000000   0.753805   0.708269    0.000000   0.404169
3290   1.000000   0.770996   0.708178    0.000000   0.395951
3310   0.991471   0.787592   0.707323   -0.085291   0.395951
ALARM #1 at time 3330
3330   0.912404   0.801740   0.706103   -0.260722   0.397146
ALARM #1 at time 3340
ALARM #1 at time 3350
3350   0.712404   0.804947   0.695573   -1.000000   0.000000
ALARM #1 at time 3360
ALARM #1 at time 3370
3370   0.512404   0.804120   0.685173   -1.000000   0.000000
ALARM #1 at time 3380
3390   0.312404   0.799320   0.674903   -1.000000   0.000000
3410   0.112404   0.790608   0.664762   -1.000000   0.000000
3430   0.000000   0.778916   0.654754   -1.000000   0.000000
3450   0.000000   0.767276   0.644896   -1.000000   0.000000
```

Figure 9.17

9.9 PARALLEL PROCESSING

Many real time systems are often limited by the processing speed available from the CPU. For well-partitioned jobs, it can often be more effective to use a set of processors operating in parallel rather than one much faster processor. Real time problems of the sort described in this chapter are already partitioned because of the task structure that is used for scheduling. In this example, each of the tasks could be run in a separate processor as long as facilities were available for intertask data communication. The trade-off in switching from single processor to multiple processor implementation is in the overhead associated with scheduling versus the overhead associated with communication. The scheduling overhead is very small in multi-processor systems, but the communication cost can be high.

CPUs in a multi-processor system can be bus connected or network connected. Bus connections allow direct access to shared peripherals and memory for communication and I/O, whereas network-connected systems cannot share facilities directly. The advantage to the network interconnection, on the other hand, is that such a connection can usually handle more processors. In either case, mutual exclusion must be observed in data interchanges. Because the processors are running in parallel, disabling of interrupts will not work because the other processors cannot be stopped. Some systems allow for locking of the bus so only one processor can have access for an extended period. This will work to provide mutual exclusion in bus connected systems that use shared memory for communication. Bus locking is effective in systems with a small number of processors, but in systems with more processors, or systems that require large amounts of data transfer, locking the bus will also lock out unrelated data transfers, thereby reducing the overall performance of the system.

Systems not using shared resources must use message passing over some form of communication channel for intertask data exchange. Mutual exclusion is inherently less of a problem when message passing is used, but the overhead can be high.

The design of the control system used in this example can be converted from single processor to multi-processor implementation without much change. The key design features that assure this convertibility are the use of separate program modules to isolate intertask data exchange, and the insistence that all data be copied into each task's local workspace before being used. If each task has its own processor, then priorities become irrelevant since all tasks run all the time. In addition, no scheduler is required. Several tasks could share a processor, in which case each such board would require, at minimum, a simple scheduler.

CLOTHO IMPLEMENTATION OF SCHEDULING FOR A CONTROL SYSTEM

The software used for scheduling in this example was written for educational use. As much as possible of the scheduler is written in C so that it is accessible for study and modification by users. It implements the functions needed for industrial implementation of multi-tasking systems, although it is not as fast in context switching as commercially available real time kernels. It is written for the IBM-PC family of computers running MS/PCDOS. Modification for other 8086 and derivative processors (80186, 80286, etc.) should be straightforward as long as they use the 8259 interrupt controller. The code is organized with machine dependent code as isolated as possible, so modification to other families of processors should be possible, although much more work. The software is available in source and/or executable form from the publisher or the authors.

In our examples, we are only using CLOTHO for scheduling; PCDOS is providing the input and output facilities albeit with the restriction of non-re-entrance so that all PCDOS references must be concentrated in the background task.

CLOTHO provides all of the scheduling services needed for real time and also has the interrupt service routines built into the package. If interrupts are needed from other devices, they can be added by mimicking the form used for the existing interrupt routines.

Time can be simulated for debugging purposes so that the program actually runs as a synchronous program even though it is structured as a multi-task program. This is accomplished by setting the external variable SimTime to a value of 1 while in *main()*, the initialization function. Calls must then be made to the function tick() every time a simulated tick of the clock is desired. This is usually done in a background function.

Two example programs are presented. The first is used to build a familiarity with the most basic features of CLOTHO. Its purpose is to tell time. The second example problem extends this experience into the full implementation of the tank level/temperature control.

9.10 TIME-TELLING PROGRAM

This program, c_time.c, keeps track of time and prints the current time and a count of the number of times a time-based task is executed. It has two tasks: the background task responsible for the printing and checking the console to see if the user has typed the job termination character (an ESCAPE), and a task that is called at fixed time intervals.

The user program can select whether real or simulated time is to be used. If simulated time is used, the timer interrupt will be turned off and there must be a call to the timer-tick simulation function [*tick()*]. This is usually done in a background function that will run whenever there is nothing else to do.

Tasks are entered into the scheduler's queue by calls to NewTask(). The call to NewTask includes as arguments:

- the task's name
- the address of the function that implements the task
- the address of an argument block
- a code identifying the type of task
- the task's initial priority
- the amount of stack space for the task
- the sample time interval (for control tasks)

The inclusion of an argument block allows the scheduler to pass that address to the task every time it starts executing. With this facility, tasks can be specified in a general way, but operate on different data every time they run, or, status information can be passed to the task on invocation.

There are three types of tasks, identified by the task-type code. They are:

- control tasks with known sampling time
- server tasks
- non-time critical time-slice tasks

Task priorities are specified by integers, with higher numbers implying higher priorities. The three task types each have baseline priorities, 1000 for the control tasks, 100 for the server tasks, and 10 for the time-slice tasks.

Each task has its own stack space. This is necessary because this scheduler allows for dynamically changing priorities, for example, when a task is suspended waiting for an asynchronous event. Stack sizes of 1K to 2K are usually adequate.

After the task has been specified, NewTask will return a "task descriptor," a value of type "pointer-to-task." The data type "task" is defined in the #include files. The task must then be entered into its appropriate queue with a call to *EnterTQueue()*. The arguments to EnterTQueue are:

- the task descriptor returned from NewTask
- the queue name
- a sort parameter

The queue name should match the type definition used for the task. It can be CntrlQueue, ServrQueue, or SliceQueue.

The sort parameter controls the order in which the task is entered onto the queue. It can be STL_ENTER to sort by time left until the next sampling instant, or PRI_ENTER to sort on the basis of task priority. If no sorting on entry into the queue is desired, the function *PutTQueue()* can be used as an alternative to *EnterTQueue()*. It has the same first two arguments as *EnterTQueue()*, but no third argument.

9.11 THE TASKS

Ticktock() is the task that runs at fixed time intervals. It increments a static variable named ic, then calls *wait()*. *Wait()* suspends the calling task until its next sample time.

Clock() is the background task. It consists of a forever loop that will be active anytime the CPU has nothing else to do, i.e., anytime there is neither a foreground routine running, nor a higher priority background task. If the sim_time flag is TRUE, the *tick()* function is called. This function simulates the clock by making the same call to the scheduler that would be made by the clock interrupt service routine. The current time is obtained with a call to *ReadClock()*. *Printf()* prints the value of the current time and also the value of ic, the variable incremented in *ticktock()*. Printing ic allows a check on whether the scheduling has been done properly.

The variable ic is created in *ticktock()* and accessed in *clock()* so it should be copied under mutual exclusion rather than the shared memory approach used here. It is an integer, however, and most instructions that operate on integers move both bytes within a single instruction, and so are noninterruptable. In any case, since the purpose of the program is to illustrate the basic scheduling functions of CLOTHO, there is no danger in not observing mutual exclusion. In the next example, all such data exchanges will be done under mutual exclusion.

Finally, *clock()* checks the console using PCDOS function 6. This function does a nonblocking input. That is, it returns whether or not a character has been input. All input characters except an ESCAPE are ignored. If an ESCAPE has been typed, the timer interrupt is reset (if real time is being used) and the program exits. The *panic()* function provides a means for exiting from C-Sched cleanly. It will print the message that is its argument, then reset all of the interrupts back to their DOS default before exiting.

9.12 THE CONTROL PROGRAM

The control program task structure and inter-task communication follow the outline established in this chapter exactly. The tasks are created in the *main()* routine with a series of *NewTask()*, *EnterTQueue()* calls.

9.12.1 DATA TRANSFER

Data are generated and used at different priority levels. The data can consist of any number of elementary memory units (a "float," for example, is 4 bytes). Reading or writing such data items is not an "atomic" process, so could be interrupted in the middle. If that were to happen, the process using the data would use part old data and part new data, which, in general, will produce "garbage!" In this program, data integrity is assured by identifying such critical sections of the program, and protecting them by disabling interrupts during the transfer time. To get data, a task makes a call to the function that can supply the needed data, the data are copied with interrupts disabled, interrupts are re-enabled, then the function returns. In this way, the data to be used is copied into the program space of the task needing the data, so, during further computation, its private copy of the data is used. The process of sending data is essentially the same. This is a simple method to implement, and is very efficient for small- to medium-sized, single-processor systems.

9.12.2 CONTROL TASK STRUCTURE

Control tasks use the same structure used by the major task in the time-telling program described above. They can have an initialization section, followed by an infinite loop. The loop includes a call to *wait()*, which causes the task to be suspended until its next sampling moment. Data is transferred to and from other tasks by calls to the input/output functions described above.

9.12.3 RESOURCE ALLOCATION: DATA LOGGING

The function of getting data to the outside world for later analysis is handled by the tasks data_log and filer. Data_log is implemented as a low priority control-type task, so that it runs at regular intervals. Each time it runs, it gets current data about the state of the system and formats the data into a character string. It then uses the character buffer, dataq, to send the characters to the filer, which is responsible for printing, transmitting, or storing the data. The character buffer is allocated during initialization by a call to *newcbuf()*; calls to *putcbuf()* and *getcbuf()* are used to communicate between data_log and filer. These functions implement a circular buffer.

"Filer" must use the operating system to get the data out. In this case, the operating system, PCDOS, is not reentrant, so only one task at a time is allowed to access it. The "filer" task illustrates two different methods of gaining access to DOS. One uses the "test and set" facility to get permission to gain access to DOS. The call to *tas()* returns when the test variable, doslock, is true. Access to DOS by other functions is prevented until it sets to zero (false) when filer has finished its call to DOS. The test-and-set facility provides a way to test a variable and then set its value in a protected environment so that the process cannot be interrupted. This is important for resource allocation because of the possibility that after the variable is tested, but before it is set, an interrupt will cause another task to become active. If that task were to use the same resource, there would be the possibility of a conflict because both tasks thought they had control of that resource. The test-and-set facility does not, however, provide for suspension of the calling task. It will "hang" in the while() loop until a higher priority task frees the desired resource. Its use must be carefully designed, therefore, so that deadlocks are avoided.

The other method uses a semaphore, which also provides for the test of the resource "lock" variable, but, in addition, will cause the task to be suspended until the resource becomes available. The semaphore is initialized in *main()* by calling *NewSem()*. A subsequent call to *Psem()* will return whenever DOS becomes free. DOS is released by a call to *Vsem()*. Either the test-and-set or the semaphore method can be used to allocate resources; the semaphore is more complex and uses more overhead, but requires less care with respect to possible deadlocks. Test-and-set is very useful when a nonblocking test is desired, so that if the resource is not available, the task will do something else.

9.12.4 ALARM

The alarm task is activated through the event detection mechanism. An event is defined in *main()* by a call to *NewEvent()*. The alarm task is high priority, so runs immediately after the system is initialized. Its first activity, however, is to call *Pend()*. It will then be suspended until the indicated event takes place. The actual detection of alarm conditions is done in the simulation section of the program. When an alarm condition is detected, the *Notify()* function is called. Since *alarm()* is "pending" on notification, it will again be secheduled to run. The *Notify()* function has two arguments: the first is the descriptor for the event that has occurred, the second is an indicator to the scheduler as to whether only one task should be released for rescheduling as a result of this event (NOTIFYONE), or whether all pending tasks should be released (NOTIFYALL).

9.12.5 TASK SUSPENSION

When the alarm task starts running, it immediately suspends the supervisory task and takes control of setting the setpoints itself. The suspension is accomplished by a call to *SuspendTask()*. It could also be structured to control the valve and heater directly if desired.

VRTX IMPLEMENTATION OF SCHEDULING FOR A CONTROL SYSTEM

VRTX, Versatile Real-Time Executive, is a scheduler for coordinating the operation of a set of semi-independent tasks that are coresident in the computer's memory. It is a product of Ready Systems, Inc., Palo Alto, CA, and is sold in several versions. It is available as a preprogrammed ROM for use in embedded applications, and, in the version we will be using, as a binary file for inclusion with programs running on the IBM-PC, XT, or AT (or compatibles) with the PCDOS operating system.

The software we are using for this example was made available to the University of California on extended loan. We would like to express our appreciation to Ready Systems for use of the software and also for their associated technical support.

In our examples, we are only using VRTX for scheduling; PCDOS is providing the input and output facilities albeit with the restriction of non-re-entrance so that all PCDOS references must be concentrated in the background task. Hunter & Ready also have modules for handling disk and other I/O interaction, but they are not used here.

VRTX provides all of the scheduling services needed for real time; the user provides whatever interrupt service routines are required. These routines are extremely simple, since all of the context switching, stack assignment, etc., is handled by VRTX. In the examples done here, the only interrupt is the clock, so the timer interrupt routine is the only one that need be supplied. The interrupt service routines must be in assembly language so that the appropriate registers can be saved. Figure 9.18 shows the assembly language timer interrupt routine used for both of the following examples.

The function saves the AX register, which will be restored by VRTX. All other registers are saved within VRTX. There are 3 VRTX function calls within the interrupt service routine. Ui_enter informs VRTX that an interrupt is being processed and that no scheduling should be done until a corresponding ui_exit call is made. The call to the DOS clock handler is done to retain the time-of-day function of PCDOS. This will work if the clock tick rate is not changed. It should be removed if the clock tick rate is modified. The ui_timer call activates the clock function within VRTX. It takes care of all clock-related scheduling activities, and assumes that there is a device external to VRTX that provides the stream of interrupts to operate the clock. Ui_timer tells VRTX that a clock pulse has arrived. Ui_exit restores the scheduling activity. VRTX will reschedule all the tasks based on whatever status changes have been caused by the interrupt. It also restores the

```
            PUBLIC CLK

CLK         PROC   FAR

        PUSH  AX            ; save ax on stack (restored by VRTX)
        MOV   AX, 16H       ; VRTX ui_enter function code
        INT   44H           ; enter interrupt level code
        INT   46H           ; call DOS clock handler through new vector
        MOV   AX, 12H       ; VRTX ui_timer function code
        INT   44H           ; announce another clock tick
        MOV   AX, 11H       ; VRTX ui_exit function code
        INT   44H           ; exit interrupt level code

CLK         ENDP
```

Figure 9.18

machine state and returns from the interrupt. Note that there is no RETURN or RETURN FROM INTERRUPT instruction in CLK.

The function ui_timer is the hook that we can use to establish the simulated time debugging environment. By putting a call to ui_timer in the background task, all of the task scheduling will be done as if a timer interrupt were present.

Two example programs are presented. The first is used to build a familiarity with the most basic features of VRTX. Its purpose is to tell time. The second example problem extends this experience into the full implementation of the tank level/temperature control.

9.13 TIME-TELLING PROGRAM

This program, v_time.c, keeps track of time and prints the current time and a count of the number of times a time-based task is executed. It has two tasks: the background task responsible for the printing and checking the console to see if the user has typed the job termination character (an ESCAPE), and a task that is called at fixed time intervals.

The main routine of v_time queries the user as to whether to use simulated real-time, then call *vrtxinit()*. Vrtxinit is responsible for assuring that all of the internal tables, pointers, and so on, are set up properly. It does not start any real-time scheduling activity, however, so the *main()* routine is still in control of the CPU.

If real-time is to be used, the *timeron()* function is called to set up the timer interrupt. The tasks are then "created," i.e., entered into VRTX's task table. The call to *sc_tcreate()* specifies the name of the task, its ID number, and its priority (low numbers imply high priority). An error variable is included in case the scheduling could not be accomplished. The ID number must be unique for each task and is the number that can be used to refer to that task.

These setup activities are followed by a call to *vrtxgo()*. This begins the real time scheduling activity. *Vrtxgo()* never returns. Exiting back to the operating system must be done from another task.

9.14 THE TASKS

Ttime() is the task that runs at fixed time intervals. It increments a static variable named ic, then calls *sc_tdelay()*. *Sc_tdelay()* suspends the calling task until the amount of time specified in its argument has elapsed.

Back() is the background task. It consists of a forever loop that will be active anytime the CPU has nothing else to do, i.e, anytime there is neither a foreground routine running, nor a higher priority background task. If the sim_time flag is TRUE, the *clk_sim()* function is called. This function simulates the clock by making a call to *ui_timer()*. The call to *ui_timer()* could be done by calling the interface function, but in clk_sim the compiler's *sysint()* function (system interrupt) is used to make a direct call to VRTX, bypassing the interface library. The current time is obtained from VRTX with a call to *sc_gtime()*. This is also done with a direct call using *sysint()*. *Printf()* prints the value of the current time and also the value of ic, the variable incremented in *ttime()*. Printing ic allows a check on whether the scheduling has been done properly.

The variable ic is created in *ttime()* and accessed in *back()* so it should be copied under mutual exclusion rather than the shared memory approach used here. It is an integer, however, and most instructions that operate on integers move both bytes within a single instruction, and so are noninterruptable. In any case, since the purpose of the program is to illustrate the basic scheduling functions of VRTX, there is no danger in not observing mutual exclusion. In the next example, all such data exchanges will be done under mutual exclusion.

Finally, *back()* checks the console using PCDOS function 6. This function does a nonblocking input. That is, it returns whether or not a character has been input. All input characters except an ESCAPE are ignored. If an ESCAPE has been typed, the timer interrupt is reset (if real time is being used) and the program exits.

9.15 THE CONTROL PROGRAM

The control program task structure and inter-task communication follow the outline established in this chapter exactly. The tasks are created in the main() routine with a series of *sc_tcreate()*'s.

9.15.1 MAILBOXES

All of the data interchange between tasks is done with VRTX's message passing facilities. There are two mechanisms for sending messages: mailboxes and message queues. Mailboxes are defined as memory locations that contain 32-bit variables (any 32-bit data type can be used). A mailbox is defined as empty when its value is zero. Mailboxes are used for both passing information and for controlling task synchronization and scheduling. A message is sent to a mailbox with a call to sc_post. Because the mailboxes are involved in scheduling, information cannot be written directly to the mailbox location, with the exception of initializing it. It can be initialized to either a zero or non-zero value, indicating it is either empty or contains a message.

A task can receive messages in two ways. When the *sc_pend()* call is used, the task will be suspended if the mailbox is empty. The task will remain suspended until something is posted to that mailbox. The task suspension will then be ended, and the task will be run whenever its priority is highest of all tasks that are ready. Tasks can also get messages with the *sc_accept()* call. If the mailbox is empty in that case, the empty state is indicated by the error variable and the task can continue.

Mailboxes are used to send actuation data from the control tasks to the simulation task, and are also used to send setpoints from the supervisory task to the control tasks. The message sent in each case is a pointer to the location of the new setpoint information. The receiving task uses the pointer to copy the information into its own workspace. Mutual exclusion is assured using this simple data transfer method as long as the receiver is the higher priority of the tasks involved. In that way, the copy process must be completed before the lower priority process can possibly run again to change the data. Data sent in the other direction, however, is not guaranteed to be protected since the receiving task (lower priority, in this case) can be interrupted in the middle of copying the data.

In general, to assure mutual exclusion, a handshake must be used. The data structure data_pointer (defined near the beginning of the program) can be used for that purpose. The handshake utilized two mailboxes. The message sent is a pointer to a data item of type data_pointer, shown in Fig. 9.19. The first item in the structure is the pointer to the data location, which is used as before. The second item is the mailbox used for the return part of the handshake. The sending task checks the return mailbox for a message before writing to the data area again. Depending on the nature of the information, either a blocking check [*sc_pend()*] or a nonblocking check [*sc_accept()*] can be used.

9.15.2 MESSAGE QUEUES

Message queues work very similarly to mailboxes, except that several messages can be posted to a queue before any messages have been processed. The messages are processed in the order that they were posted. Messages, as with mailboxes, are

```
struct data_pointer
        {
        float *pdat;
        long m_box;
        };
```

Figure 9.19

32-bit data items. Receipt of messages can also be blocking [*sc_qpend()*] or non-blocking [*sc_qaccept()*]. The actual queue maintenance is done by VRTX, so queues must be created with *sc_qcreate()* calls before they are used.

Queues are necessary when messages to a task can originate from several different sources. Since the sources are normally asynchronous, and could all have higher priority than the receiving task, several messages could be posted before the receiving task had any chance to run. An example of this is the mechanism used to send state information to the control tasks, and the data logging task. State information is sent only when requested. To request state information, a message is sent to the STATE_Q with a pointer to an item of type data_pointer. The desired information is copied to the location specified by the data pointer, and, when the copy operation is complete, a message is sent to the handshake mailbox. The requesting task does an *sc_pend()* on the handshake mailbox, thereby suspending itself until the information is available.

This same mechanism is used to send information to the background for relaying to PCDOS. Since the data being sent is in the form of strings, the data structure string_pointer is used instead of data_pointer. The handshake is used so that the sending task can be sure that the data has already been sent to PCDOS before it writes new messages to that data block.

The *alarm()* task uses a queue as its major scheduling mechanism. The queue is necessary rather than a mailbox because several alarms could be posted before *alarm()* had a chance to run if, for example, the alarms were sent from interrupt service routines. After initialization, the alarm task does an *sc_qpend()*. It will remain suspended until a message is posted to the ALARM_Q.

9.15.3 TASK SUSPENSION

The final VRTX facility that is used is the ability to explicitly suspend a task. This is done with the *sc_tsuspend()* call. The task whose ID is specified is suspended, and can only be restarted with a call to *sc_tresume()*. This form of suspension is used by the alarm task to suspend the control and supervisory tasks. It must do that so that it can take direct control of the actuation outputs.

```
/**************************************************************************

FILE
        simclock.c  -  test of simulated clock

REMARKS
        This simple program illustrates the use of a sample-time task
        to count 10 seconds.  We merely set up a task which runs every
        second and prints the time.

LAST UPDATE
        20 October 1986

        Copyright(c) 1986  D.M. Auslander and C.H. Tham

**************************************************************************/

/**************************************************************************
                              I M P O R T S
**************************************************************************/

/*
 *      These "include" files contain declarations that may be needed
 *      to create new tasks and set them up in the proper task queues.
 */

#include <stdio.h>

#include "envir.h"                  /* environment definitions */

#include "config.h"                 /* system configuration file */
#include "types.h"                  /* data type definitions */
#include "task.h"                   /* task module declarations */
#include "tqueue.h"                 /* task queue module declarations */
#include "systm.h"                  /* system interface declarations */
#include "kernel.h"                 /* miscellaneous kernel declarations */
#include "time.h"                   /* timer module declarations */

extern int SimTime;

extern TQUEUE *CntrlQueue;   /* queue of sample time control task */
extern TQUEUE *SliceQueue;   /* queue of time slice background tasks */


/*-------------------------------------------------------------------------
TASK
        TICKTOCK  -  pretends to be a clock

SYNOPSIS
        static ticktock()

REMARKS
        Prints the time obtained from ReadClock().  Since this is the
        only task that access DOS (via printf()), we do not need any
        special procedures to ensure exclusive access to DOS.

        Note the use of the panic() routine to abort and exit back to
        DOS.  This is the easiest way to do a clean abort.

LAST UPDATE
        20 October 1986
-------------------------------------------------------------------------*/

static ticktock()
{
        long ms;                        /* elasped time in milliseconds */


        while (1)
        {
                ms = ReadClock();

                if (ms > 10000L)                /* 10 seconds have elasped */
                {
                        panic("time is up");
                }
                else    /* print the time in seconds */
                {
                        printf("%ld\n", ms / 1000L);
                }

                wait(TWAIT, CntrlQueue);    /* wait for next sampling instance */
        }

}


/*-------------------------------------------------------------------------
PROCEDURE
        CLOCK  -  simulate a clock

SYNOPSIS
        static void clock()

REMARKS
        Each call to tick() simulates a tick of the system clock, which
        has a period of 50 milliseconds on the IBM-PC.

        Note that clock() is declared static to make it private to this
        file; a name such as clock() is too common to make it visible
        outside and chance a name conflict.
```

```
LAST UPDATE
	20 October 1986
------------------------------------------------------------------*/

static clock()
{
	int i;		/* loop counter */


	while (1)
	{
v_puts2(0, 60, "clock", 0x7);	/* DEBUG */

		for (i = 0; i < 1000; i++)		/* generate a little delay */
			;

		tick();

v_puts2(0, 60, "     ", 0x7);	/* DEBUG */

		for (i = 0; i < 1000; i++)		/* generate a little delay */
			;
	}

}

/*******************************************************************
	I N I T I A L I Z A T I O N    R O U T I N E
*******************************************************************/

/*-----------------------------------------------------------------
PROCEDURE
	MAIN  -  set up all user tasks

SYNOPSIS
	main()

REMARKS
	Only one task, scheduled every second.

LAST UPDATE
	20 October 1986
------------------------------------------------------------------*/

main()
{
	TASK *t;		/* task pointer */

	prologue();
	t = NewTask("TICKTOCK", ticktock, (char *)0, STL_TASK,
			PCONTROL, 256, 1000L);
	if (t == TNULL)
		panic("cannot create TICKTOCK");
	else
		EnterTqueue(t, CntrlQueue, STL_ENTER);


	t = NewTask("SIMCLOCK", clock, (char *)0, SLC_TASK,
			PSLICE, 256, 100L);

	if (t == TNULL)
		panic("cannot create SIMCLOCK");
	else
		EnterTqueue(t, SliceQueue, PRI_ENTER);

	SimTime = 1;

}
	start();

/*******************************************************************


FILE
	x_cntrl.c  - demo illustrating real-time multi-tasking control

SIMULATION ROUTINES
	simula		-  simulates a tank system

CONTROL ROUTINES
	valve_control	-  control flow valve
	temp_control	-  control temperature in tank
	supervisor	-  sets the setpoints
	alarm		-  "alarm" event handler - tank overflows
	control		-  do PI control calculations
	flimit		-  limit a variable

DATA LOGGING ROUTINES
	data_log	-  collect data
	filer		-  file the data away

CONTROL INTERFACE ROUTINES
	valve_actuate	-  send control output to valve actuator
	heat_actuate	-  send control output to heater

	get_vact	-  read valve actuation state
	get_hact	-  read heater state
	get_hset	-  read height setting
	get_tset	-  read temperature setting
	get_valve	-  read valve position
	get_height	-  read liquid height
```

```
        get_temp        -   read liquid temperature

        inchar          -   character input from terminal

INITIALIZATION ROUTINES
        InitUser

LAST UPDATE
        18 May 1987
                change to simplified Notify() interface

        Copyright(c) 1986,1987  D.M. Auslander and C.H. Tham

**********************************************************************/

#define VTRACE 1                /* 1 => trace executing by direct video write */
#define TAS             0       /* 1 => use test-and-set instead of semaphores */

/*********************************************************************
                        I M P O R T S
**********************************************************************/

/*
 *      These "include" files contain declarations that may be needed
 *      to create new tasks and set them up in the proper task queues.
 */

#include <stdio.h>

#include "envir.h"              /* environment definitions */

#include "config.h"             /* system configuration file */
#include "types.h"              /* data type definitions */
#include "task.h"               /* task module declarations */
#include "tqueue.h"             /* task queue module declarations */
#include "systm.h"              /* system interface declarations */
#include "kernel.h"             /* miscellaneous kernel declarations */
#include "event.h"              /* event scheduling module declarations */
#include "sem.h"                /* semaphore module declarations */
#include "time.h"               /* timer module declarations */
#include "cbuf.h"               /* character buffer module declarations */
#include "8259.h"

extern TASK *curtask;           /* pointer to currently executing task */

extern TQUEUE *CntrlQueue;      /* queue of sample time control task */
extern TQUEUE *ServrQueue;      /* queue of "server" tasks */
extern TQUEUE *SliceQueue;      /* queue of time slice tasks */

extern kbisr();

/*********************************************************************
                P R I V A T E    D A T A
**********************************************************************/

static TASK *valve_task;        /* pointer to valve control task */
static TASK *temp_task;         /* pointer to temperature control task */
static TASK *super_task;        /* pointer to supervisor task */

static float state[6];          /* plant state */

static int overflow;            /* tank overflow event handle */
static int escape;              /* "ESC key has been hit" event handle */

static CBUF *dataq;             /* buffer/queue to filer task */

/*******************  miscellaneous declarations  *******************/

#define ESCAPE 0x1B             /* ASCII value of the "escape" character */

#define VALVE_TSAMP      1000L  /* sampling period for valve control */
#define TEMP_TSAMP       4000L  /* sampling period for temp control */
#define DLOG_TSAMP       2000L  /* data logging sampling period */
#define SIMUL_TSAMP       500L  /* simulation period */
#define SUPER_TSAMP     60000L  /* supervisor period */
#define FILER_TSAMP     10000L  /* filer quantum */

/*********************************************************************
        F O R W A R D    D E C L A R A T I O N S
**********************************************************************/

float flimit();                 /* limits value to specified minima and maxima */

/*************  input/output logical interface routines  *************/

float get_hset();
float get_tset();
float get_valve();
float get_height();
float get_temp();
float get_vact();
float get_hact();

/*********************************************************************
**********************************************************************
        T A N K    S Y S T E M    S I M U L A T I O N
**********************************************************************
**********************************************************************/
```

```
/**  Timing variables to time execution of simulation loop  **/

static long start_time;      /* when simulation loop started (ms) */
static long end_time;        /* when 1 simulation loop ended (ms) */
static long xeq_time;        /* execution time for 1 simulation loop (ms) */


/***********************************************************************
              S I M U L A T I O N     R O U T I N E S
***********************************************************************/

/*-----------------------------------------------------------------------
TASK
       SIMULA  -  plant simulation

SYNOPSIS
       static simula()

REMARKS
       Simulates the tank system with inflow = Qin and outflow = Qout.

       Inflow is controlled by means of a valve which can be commanded
       to open or close.  As the valve slowly opens, the inflow naturally
       increases; thus the controller has to keep constant track of the
       valve position.

       The tank has a heating coil providing heat input Hin.

       Note that the plant parameters are all local to this function.
       This way, the only way the control and data acquisition programs
       can obtain state information is via well defined interfaces, just
       like in a real system.

LAST UPDATE
       14 February 1986
-----------------------------------------------------------------------*/

static simula()
{
       float delta_t = 0.1;        /* time constant */
       float area = 10.0;          /* tank cross sectional area */
       float volume;               /* liquid volume */
       float temp = 0.0;           /* liquid temperature in tank */
       float height = 0.75;        /* height liquid in tank */

       float safe_height = 0.8;  /* raise alarm if height exceeds this */

       float intemp = 0.0;         /* temperature of inflow */
       float Qin, Qout;            /* flow into and out of the tank */
       float Qmax = 1.0;           /* max flow with valve open all the way */
       float vc = 0.0;             /* valve control, 0 to 1.0 */
       float Kvc = 1.0;            /* scaling factor for vc_con */

       float Kq = 0.75;            /* Qout = Kq * height */

       float heat = 0.0;           /* heat input */

       char eflag = 0;             /* exception flag */


       for (;;)                    /* simula is an infinite loop */
       {
              float vact;                          /* valve actuation command */

#if VTRACE
              vtrace("simula");                    /* trace execution on screen */
#endif
              vact = get_vact();                   /* get valve actuation command */
              heat = get_hact();                   /* get heat actuation command */

#if 0
              start_time = ReadClock();            /* time the execution */
#endif


              vc += Kvc * vact  +  delta_t;        /* valve position */
              vc = flimit(0.0, vc, 1.0);           /* limit valve position */

              Qin = Qmax * vc;                     /* inflow depends on valve */
              Qout = Kq * height;                  /* outflow proportional to height */

              height += (Qin - Qout) * delta_t / area;
              volume = area * height;
              temp += (Qin * intemp  -  Qout * temp  +  heat) * delta_t / volume;


                /*-----------------------------------------------------
                     Determine the execution time for a simulation loop.
                     This is useful for setting the scale factor for time
                     and controller sample times.  It will only give relevant
                     information in real time operation since in simulated
                     time mode, xeq_time will always be zero since the clock
                     can only tick when the low priority background runs.
                -----------------------------------------------------*/
#if 0
              end_time = ReadClock();
              xeq_time = end_time - start_time;
#endif


              /*****************************************************
              Record plant state for input/output simulation tasks.
              *****************************************************/
```

```
		state[0] = vc;
		state[1] = height;
		state[2] = temp;
		state[3] = vact;
		state[4] = heat;

		/*********************************************************
		If the liquid level rises above a predefined "safe height",
		notify the alarm task.  In a real system, this condition
		will trigger an external interrupt which will cause the
		appropriate alarm event handler to run.  Here, we simulate
		the external interrupt with an exception.  An error flag
		(eflag) is used to prevent the exception condition from
		generating repeated calls to the alarm handler.
		In effect, the exception condition is edge triggered.
		*********************************************************/

		if (eflag == 0)
		{
			if (height > safe_height)
			{
				eflag = 1;
				Notify(overflow);
			}
		}


		wait(TWAIT, CntrlQueue);     /* wait for next simula run */
	}

}



/*********************************************************************
**********************************************************************
			C O N T R O L   T A S K S
**********************************************************************
*********************************************************************/

/*********************************************************************
	C O N T R O L   T A S K S   L O C A L   D A T A
*********************************************************************/

/**  Parameter structure for a Proportional-Integral controller  **/

typedef struct {
	float c_y;				/* measured variable */
	float c_set;				/* setpoint */
	float c_kp;				/* proportional gain */
	float c_ki;				/* integral gain */
	float c_int;				/* integrator value (cumulative) */
	float c_intmin;				/* lowr limit of integrator value */
	float c_intmax;				/* upper limit of integrator value */
	float c_m;				/* controller output */
	float c_mmin;				/* lower limit of actuation output */
	float c_mmax;				/* upper limit of actuation output */
} CONTROL_PARAMETERS;


static CONTROL_PARAMETERS valve_data = {
	0.0, 0.5, 0.0, 0.5, 0.0, -1.0, 1.0, 0.0, -1.0, 1.0 };

static CONTROL_PARAMETERS height_data = {
	0.0, 0.5, 0.0, 1.0, 1.0, -1.0, 1.0, 0.0, -1.0, 1.0 };


/*  Note that lower limits are zero since no cooling is available  */

static CONTROL_PARAMETERS temp_data = {
	0.0, 0.5, 0.0, 3.0, 0.7, 0.0, 0.5, 0.0, 0.0, 1.0, };


static float level_setpoint; /* heat input set point */
static float temp_setpoint;         /* temp input set point */


/*********************************************************************
	C O N T R O L   T A S K S   D E F I N I T I O N
*********************************************************************/

/*-------------------------------------------------------------------
TASK
	VALVE_CONTROL  -  controls liquid level using the valve

SYNOPSIS
	static valve_control()

REMARKS
	This is set up as a cascade scheme whereby the output of the
	height controller serves as the setpoint for the valve controller.

LAST UPDATE
	14 February 1986
-------------------------------------------------------------------*/

static valve_control()
{

	for (;;)
	{
#if VTRACE
```

```
            vtrace("valve ");
#endif
            height_data.c_set = get_hset();          /* get height setpoint */}
            height_data.c_y = get_height();          /* get liquid level */
            valve_data.c_y = get_valve();            /* get valve position */

            control(&height_data);              /* control calc for level */

            /*  The output of height control is the valve setpoint  */

            valve_data.c_set = height_data.c_m;

            control(&valve_data);               /* control calc for valve */

            valve_actuate(valve_data.c_m);      /* valve actuator output */

            wait(TWAIT, CntrlQueue);     /* wait for next sampling time */
        }

}


/*----------------------------------------------------------------------
TASK
        TEMP_CONTROL  -  temperature controller

SYNOPSIS
        static temp_control()

LAST UPDATE
        14 February 1986
----------------------------------------------------------------------*/

static temp_control()
{

        for (;;)
        {

#if VTRACE
            vtrace("temp  ");
#endif
            temp_data.c_set = get_tset();       /* get temp setpoint */
            temp_data.c_y = get_temp();         /* get temperature feedback */

            control(&temp_data);                /* do control calculations */

            heat_actuate(temp_data.c_m); /* send out actuation value */

            wait(TWAIT, CntrlQueue);     /* wait for next sampling time */
        }
}


/*----------------------------------------------------------------------
TASK
        SUPERVISOR  -  supervisory task, determines setpoints

SYNOPSIS
        supervisor()

REMARKS
        The heat input and liquid height set points (level_setpoint and
        temp_setpoint) are global variables local to this file.

        This supervisor routine generates a square-wave set points.

LAST UPDATE
        17 April 1986
----------------------------------------------------------------------*/

static supervisor()
{

        for (;;)
        {

#if VTRACE
            vtrace(" super");
#endif

            level_setpoint = 0.5;
            temp_setpoint = 0.5;

            wait(TWAIT, CntrlQueue);

            level_setpoint = 0.25;
            temp_setpoint = 0.7;

            wait(TWAIT, CntrlQueue);
        }
}


/*----------------------------------------------------------------------
TASK
        ALARM  -  task overflow alarm or exception handler
```

```
SYNOPSIS
        static alarm()

REMARKS
        The tank system is shut down and the control tasks suspended.

LAST UPDATE
        1 May 1986
---------------------------------------------------------------------*/

static alarm()
{
        long time;                      /* time alarm occurred */
        int istat;                      /* interrupt status */


        while (1)
        {
                char msg[32], *p;       /* message and pointer index */


#if VTRACE
                vtrace("ALARM ");
#endif

                time = ReadClock();

                SuspendTask(super_task);                /* supervisor */

                level_setpoint = 0.0;                   /* drain the tank */
                temp_setpoint = 0.0;                    /*   and cool it. */

                istat = disable();

                sprintf(msg, "ALARM at %ld\n", time);

                for (p = msg; *p != '\0'; )
                        if (putcbuf(*p, dataq) >= 0)
                                ++p;

                if (istat)
                        enable();

                Pend(overflow, TNULL);
        }

}


/*---------------------------------------------------------------------
PROCEDURE
        CONTROL  -  perform control calculations (PI control)

SYNOPSIS
        static control(param)
        CONTROL_PARAMETERS *param;

PARAMETERS
        param  -  pointer to control parameter data block

REMARKS
        Performs simple PI control calculation using data in parameter block.

LAST UPDATE
        14 February 1986
---------------------------------------------------------------------*/

static control(param)
CONTROL_PARAMETERS *param;
{
        float error;   /* error between measured variable and setpoint */


        error = param->c_set - param->c_y;

        param->c_int += param->c_ki * error;
        param->c_int = flimit(param->c_intmin, param->c_int, param->c_intmax);

        param->c_m = param->c_kp * error  +  param->c_int;
        param->c_m = flimit(param->c_mmin, param->c_m, param->c_mmax);

}


/*---------------------------------------------------------------------
FUNCTION

        FLIMIT  -  limit value to specified range

SYNOPSIS
        static float limit(lo, x, hi)
        float lo, x, hi;

PARAMETERS
        lo  -  lower limit
        x   -  value to be limited
        hi  -  higher limit

LAST UPDATE
        29 April 1986
```

```
----------------------------------------------------------------------*/

static float flimit(lo, x, hi)
float lo, x, hi;
{

        if (x < lo)
                x = lo;
        else if (x > hi)
                x = hi;

        return(x);
}



/**********************************************************************
***********************************************************************
                    D A T A   L O G G I N G
***********************************************************************
**********************************************************************/

static int doslock = 0;                   /* DOS access lock semaphore */


/**********************************************************************
            D A T A   L O G G I N G   R O U T I N E S
**********************************************************************/

/*-----------------------------------------------------------------------
TASK
        DATA_LOG  -  data logger

SYNOPSIS
        static data_log()

REMARKS
        The data logger obtains information from the process, formats
        the data and passes it into a character queue which connects to
        a background task (filer) which actually copies the data to a file.

LAST UPDATE
        14 February 1986
----------------------------------------------------------------------*/

static data_log()
{
        long time;              /* milliseconds since birth of system */
        float valve;            /* valve position */
        float height;           /* liquid level */
        float temp;             /* temperature */
        float vact;                         /* valve actuation command */
        float heat;                         /* heat input */

        char data[100];                     /* data buffer */
        char *dp;                           /* data pointer */


        for (;;)
        {

#if VTRACE
                vtrace("logger");
#endif


                valve = get_valve();
                height = get_height();
                temp = get_temp();
                vact = get_vact();
                heat = get_hact();

                time = ReadClock();

                sprintf(data, "%8ld %.3f %.3f %.3f %.3f %.3f\n",
                        time, valve, height, temp, vact, heat);

                 /*-------------------------------------------------------
                  The data string is put into a buffer queue to be
                  sent to the routine which saves the data onto
                  more permanent medium such as a disk file.
                 -------------------------------------------------------*/

                for (dp = data; *dp != '\0'; )
                        if (putcbuf(*dp, dataq) >= 0)
                                ++dp;

                wait(TWAIT, CntrlQueue);     /* wait for next sampling instance */
        }

}


/*----------------------------------------------------------------------
TASK
        FILER  -  saves data onto file

SYNOPSIS
        static filer(fp)
        FILE *fp;

PARAMETERS
```

```
        fp  -  file pointer

REMARKS
        This routine calls DOS to write-out data.  Since DOS is non re-entrant,
        we need to ensure exclusive access to DOS.  This can be done by using
        the test-and-set library function tas().  tas() is designed to perform
        an atomic read of the integer sized location specified by its argument
        and set that memory location to 1.

LAST UPDATE
        14 February 1986
-----------------------------------------------------------------------*/

static filer(fp)
FILE *fp;
{

        for (;;)
        {
                int c;

#if VTRACE
                vtrace("filer ");
#endif

                while ((c = getcbuf(dataq)) > 0)
                {
#if TAS
                        while (tas(&doslock) r== 1)  /* wait for dos to be avail */
                                ;
#else
                        Psem(doslock);
#endif

                        fputc((char)c, fp);

#if TAS
                        doslock = 0;                /* free dos */
#else
                        Vsem(doslock);
#endif
                }
        }

}


/************************************************************************
*************************************************************************
          I N P U T  / O U T P U T     S E C T I O N

        The routines in this section serves as logical interfaces to
        input/output device drivers, hiding the details of i/o from the
        control program.

        In a real system, these routines will activate valves, heaters
        and read sensors.  In a simulated system, these routines manipulate
        variables which are used by the i/o simulation system.

        Note that the i/o variables must be manipulated in a critical
        section - we cannot have a routine writing to a variable while
        another is reading it at the same time.

        Although critical sections can be implemented with semaphores,
        it is much simpler in this example to do so by disabling
        interrupts.

*************************************************************************
************************************************************************/

/************************************************************************
        I / O     T A S K S     L O C A L     D A T A
************************************************************************/

static float heat_input;            /* heat input to system */
static float valve_vel;             /* valve velocity */


/************************************************************************
                    I / O     R O U T I N E S
************************************************************************/

/*-----------------------------------------------------------------------
PROCEDURE
        VALVE_ACTUATE  -  set valve actuation velocity

SYNOPSIS
        static valve_actuate(vact)
        float vact;

PARAMETER
        vact  -  valve actuation velocity

REMARKS
        In a real system, this procedure will move a real valve.  If the
        system is simulated, this procedure sets a valve actuation variable.

LAST UPDATE
        29 April 1986
-----------------------------------------------------------------------*/

static valve_actuate(vact)
```

```
float vact;
{
	int istat;			/* interrupt status */


	istat = disable();

	valve_vel = vact;

	if (istat)
		enable();

}



/*-----------------------------------------------------------------------
PROCEDURE
	HEAT_ACTUATE  -  set heat actuation

SYNOPSIS
	static heat_actuate(hact)
	float hact;

PARAMETER
	hact  -  heat actuation input

REMARKS
	In a real system, this procedure will adjust power to a heating
	coil.  In a simulated system, this procedure sets a heat input
	variable.

LAST UPDATE
	29 April 1986
-----------------------------------------------------------------------*/

static heat_actuate(hact)
float hact;
{
	int istat;			/* interrupt status */


	istat = disable();

	heat_input = hact;

	if (istat)
		enable();

}
```

```
/*-----------------------------------------------------------------------
FUNCTION
	GET_VACT  -  get valve actuation value

SYNOPSIS
	static float get_vact()

RETURNS
	valve velocity actuation value

LAST UPDATE
	9 April 1986
-----------------------------------------------------------------------*/

static float get_vact()
{
	int istat;			/* interrupt status */
	float vact;			/* local copy of valve velocity */


	istat = disable();

	vact = valve_vel;

	if (istat)
		enable();

	return(vact);
}



/*-----------------------------------------------------------------------
FUNCTION
	GET_HACT  -  get heat actuation input

SYNOPSIS
	static float get_hact()

RETURNS
	heat input actuation value

LAST UPDATE
	9 April 1986
-----------------------------------------------------------------------*/

static float get_hact()
{
	int istat;			/* interrupt status */
	float heat;			/* local copy of heat input */
```

```
	istat = disable();

	heat = heat_input;

	if (istat)
		enable();

	return(heat);
}


/*--------------------------------------------------------------------
FUNCTION
	GET_HSET  -  get liquid level setpoint

SYNOPSIS
	static float get_hset()

RETURNS
	level setpoint

LAST UPDATE
	9 April 1986
--------------------------------------------------------------------*/

static float get_hset()
{
	int istat;			/* interrupt status */
	float hset;			/* local copy of level setpoint */


	istat = disable();

	hset = level_setpoint;

	if (istat)
		enable();

	return(hset);
}


/*--------------------------------------------------------------------
FUNCTION
	GET_TSET  -  get temperature setpoint

SYNOPSIS
	static float get_tset()

RETURNS
	temperature setpoint

LAST UPDATE
	9 April 1986
--------------------------------------------------------------------*/

static float get_tset()
{
	int istat;			/* interrupt status */
	float tset;			/* local copy of temperature setpoint */


	istat = disable();

	tset = temp_setpoint;

	if (istat)
		enable();

	return(tset);
}


/*--------------------------------------------------------------------
FUNCTION
	GET_VALVE  -  get valve position

SYNOPSIS
	static float get_valve()

RETURNS
	valve position

LAST UPDATE
	9 April 1986
--------------------------------------------------------------------*/

static float get_valve()
{
	int istat;		/* interrupt status */
	float valve;		/* local copy of valve position */


	istat = disable();

	valve = state[0];

	if (istat)
		enable();
```

```
        return(valve);
}


/*------------------------------------------------------------------------
FUNCTION
        GET_HEIGHT  -  get liquid level

SYNOPSIS
        static float get_height()

RETURNS
        liquid level

LAST UPDATE
        9 April 1986
------------------------------------------------------------------------*/

static float get_height()
{
        int istat;              /* interrupt status */
        float height;           /* local copy of liquid level */


        istat = disable();

        height = state[1];

        if (istat)
                enable();

        return(height);
}


/*------------------------------------------------------------------------
FUNCTION
        GET_TEMP  -  get tempearture

SYNOPSIS
        static float get_temp()

RETURNS
        temperature

LAST UPDATE
        9 April 1986
------------------------------------------------------------------------*/

static float get_temp()
{
        int istat;                      /* interrupt status */
        float temp;                     /* local copy of temperature */


        istat = disable();

        temp = state[2];

        if (istat)
                enable();

        return(temp);
}


/*------------------------------------------------------------------------
PROCEDURE
        KBSIG  -  keyboard signal

SYNOPSIS
        kbsig(cc)               called by keyboard interrupt service routine
        int cc;

PARAMETER
        cc  -  high byte is scan code, low byte is ascii

REMARKS
        This routine is called whenever an ascii key is available.

        For now, it just looks for the ESC key and ignores all others.
        This will serve nicely as the core for an event driven keyboard
        handling routine.

LAST UPDATE
        11 May 1987
------------------------------------------------------------------------*/

kbsig(cc)
int cc;
{
        int ascii;


        ascii = cc & 0xFF;

        if (ascii r== 27)
                Notify(escape);
```

```
}


/*--------------------------------------------------------------------
EVENT
        ESCAPE_HANDLER  - called when escape key has been hit

SYNOPSIS
        Called by event manager

LAST UPDATE
        11 May 1987
--------------------------------------------------------------------*/

static escape_handler()
{

        panic("Terminated By User Request");

}


/*********************************************************************
**********************************************************************
          I N I T I A L I Z A T I O N     R O U T I N E
**********************************************************************
*********************************************************************/

/*--------------------------------------------------------------------
PROCEDURE
        MAIN  -  set up all user tasks

SYNOPSIS
        main()

REMARKS

LAST UPDATE
        17 April 1986
--------------------------------------------------------------------*/

main()
{
        TASK *t;                /* task pointer */


        prologue();
         /*------------------------------------------------------------
                Set up simulation task "simula" to run every second.
                This task should have a very high priority since it
                the plant is supposed to react to control actions.
        -------------------------------------------------------------*/

        t = NewTask("SIMULA", simula, (char *)0, STL_TASK,
                        PCONTROL+100, 4096, SIMUL_TSAMP);

        if (t r== TNULL)
                panic("cannot create SIMULA");
        else
                EnterTqueue(t, CntrlQueue, STL_ENTER);


         /*------------------------------------------------------------
                Set up the liquid overflow alarm task.  Since this
                task is activated only when a liquid overflow is detected,
                we set it up as an event task.
         ------------------------------------------------------------*/

        if ((overflow = NewEvent()) < 0)
                panic("cannot allocate overflow event handle");

        t = NewTask("ALARM", alarm, (char *)0, SRV_TASK,
                        PSERVER+150, 512, 1000L);

        if (t r== TNULL)
                panic("cannot create ALARM");
        else
                Pend(overflow, t);


         /*------------------------------------------------------------
                Control tasks (valve and temperature) have priority between
                simulation and data logging.  Temperature control has lower
                priority than valve control partly because the time constant
                for the temperature response is longer than the valve response.
         ------------------------------------------------------------*/

        valve_task = NewTask("V_CONTROL", valve_control, (char *)0, STL_TASK,
                        PCONTROL+50, 1024, VALVE_TSAMP);

        if (valve_task r== TNULL)
                panic("cannot create V_CONTROL");
        else
                EnterTqueue(valve_task, CntrlQueue, STL_ENTER);


        temp_task = NewTask("T_CONTROL", temp_control, (char *)0, STL_TASK,
                        PCONTROL+40, 1024, TEMP_TSAMP);

        if (temp_task r== TNULL)
                panic("cannot create T_CONTROL");
```

```
    else
        EnterTqueue(temp_task, CntrlQueue, STL_ENTER);

    /*-----------------------------------------------------------
        Supervisor task has higher priority than data logger, but
        lower than the control task.  Its only duty at this time
        is to set the setpoints.  However, the superviser must run
        first to set the setpoints, hence we artificially set the
        time left field (t_tleft) to 0.
    -----------------------------------------------------------*/

    super_task = NewTask("SUPERVISOR", supervisor, (char *)0, STL_TASK,
                PCONTROL+30, 1024, SUPER_TSAMP);

    super_task->t_tleft = 0L;

    if (super_task r== TNULL)
        panic("cannot create SUPERVISOR");
    else
        EnterTqueue(super_task, CntrlQueue, STL_ENTER);

    /*-----------------------------------------------------------
        Initialize data logging routines and associated data.
    -----------------------------------------------------------*/

    if ((dataq = newcbuf(1000)) r== CBNULL)
        panic("cannot allocate dataq buffer");

    if ((doslock = NewSem(1)) < 0)
        panic("cannot allocate doslock semaphore");

    t = NewTask("DATALOGGER", data_log, (char *)0, STL_TASK,
                PCONTROL+10, 2048, DLOG_TSAMP);

    if (t r== TNULL)
        panic("cannot create DATALOGGER");
    else
        EnterTqueue(t, CntrlQueue, STL_ENTER);

    t = NewTask("FILER", filer, stdout, SLC_TASK,
                PSLICE+10, 2048, FILER_TSAMP);

    if (t r== TNULL)
        panic("cannot create FILER");
    else
        EnterTqueue(t, SliceQueue, PRI_ENTER);

    /*-----------------------------------------------------------
        Set up an event driven task to handle the case when
        an ESC key is hit, which is the user signalling an
        abort from the keyboard.  This requires a keyboard
        interrupt service routine, kbisr(), which is defined
        in the file kbisr.asm
    -----------------------------------------------------------*/

    if ((escape = NewEvent()) < 0)
        panic("cannot allocate escape event handler");

    t = NewTask("ESCAPE", escape_handler, (char *)0, SRV_TASK,
                PCONTROL+1000, 128, 1000L);

    if (t r== TNULL)
        panic("cannot create ESCAPE");
    else
        Pend(escape, t);


    setivec(KBVEC, kbisr);

}
    start();

/***********************************************************
This is a series of programs that illustrate the use of the
VRTX real-time kernel (from Ready Systems, Inc., Palo Alto, CA).

The sequence of programs starts with very simple programs to
use the time keeping facility and show how to create and
execute tasks.

The first program in the sequence simulates time by calling the
clock input function from the lowest priority task.  This method
will be used in all cases to do the initial program debugging.
It allows easy debugging of the programming logic and mathematics
because there are no actual asynchronous events.  Operating system
calls (e.g., printf, scanf) can be used anywhere in the program
because there are no re-entrance problems.

When the basic program logic is initialized, then the actual timer
interrupt is enabled and the program operates in real-time.  Problems
such as mutual exclusion can appear at this point that will not appear
in the simulated version, but calls to the operating system must be
carefully controlled since PCDOS is not re-entrant.

After the time-keeping function, a simple process control system will
be implemented.  The same sequence, using simulate time first and then
using real-time will be used.  In all cases, however, a simulation of the
actual plant will be used so that this test program can be run anywhere.
```

```
File: v_time.c

Compiler: Computer Innovations, C86 v2.3

Compile with the -i switch so that long names are recognized.

Linking instructions:

link v_time task sync clock memory chario vrtx bsp,,,s2s

Note: The functions task, sync, clock, etc., are the property of
       Hunter & Ready, Inc.  They provide the interface between the
       Computer Innovations C86 compiler and VRTX proper.
       Check with them to get copies.

Author:        D. M. Auslander
Creation Date: 29-Jan-86
Last Update:

copyright (c) 1986 D. M. Auslander

*****************************************************************/

/* This structure is used by the CIC86 compiler for communicating
with the operating system or implementing software interrupts. */

struct regval {unsigned int ax,bx,cx,dx,si,di,ds,es;};

static int sim_time = 1;
                    /* Flag to indicate whether time should be
                    real or simulated.  For faster execution of
                    the real-time version, this flag could be
                    set with "define," and conditional compilations
                    used, however, using sim_time as a variable
                    means that the program does not have to be
                    recompiled to switch from simulated time to
                    real-time.  */

#define ESCAPE 0x1b   /* The escape character */

/* The task defined below, ttime, does nothing but keep time.
Each time it is activated, it increments the time variable, ic,
then goes to sleep for the delay time, t_del.
*/

static int ic = 0;
static long t_del = 20;

ttime()
{
for(;;)
        {
        ic++;
        sc_tdelay(t_del);
        }
}

/* The task "back" always runs at the lowest priority.
For the simulated time case, the call to the time simulation
function is placed in this task.  It is also used to interact with
the user during operation.
*/

back()
{
for(;;)
        {
        struct regval rg;
        char char_in();             /* A function to return a character
                              from the console if one has been typed;
                              otherwise, it returns 0 */

        if(sim_time)clk_sim();             /* Simulate the clock */

        rg.ax = 0xa;   /* Code for sc_gtime */
        sysint(0x44,&rg,&rg); /* Call sc_gtime */

        printf("ic = %d time = %d\n",ic,rg.cx);

        /* When operating in real-time it is necessary to restore
        the interrupt status before exiting -- the PCDOS ^C exit
        will not do that, so a check for a user input is used to
        indicate the end of the program.
        */
        if(char_in() r== ESCAPE)
                {
                if(!sim_time)
                        timeroff();    /* Restore timer interrupts */
                exit();
                }
        }
}

/* The main program is used to initialize the system and set up the
default task structure.  Once VRTX is started, through the call
to vrtxgo(), control is never returned to main().
*/

main ()
{
int    err;
```

```
        printf("Simulate time (0/1)?: ");
        scanf("%d",&sim_time);

        vrtxinit (&err);

        if(!sim_time)timeron();       /* Turn on timer interrupt */

        sc_tcreate(ttime,1,10,&err); /* Create the time-telling
                                        task -- its id is 1 and its
                                        priority is 10 (low numbers
                                        imply high priority) */

        sc_tcreate(back,2,255,&err); /*Create the low priority
                                        (background) task with the lowest
                                        possible priority (255). */

        vrtxgo ();     /* Start VRTX -- this function never returns! */

}

clk_sim()              /* Simulate the clock by calling vrtx */
{
struct regval srr;

srr.ax = 0x12;/* ui_timer to announce clock tick */
sysint(0x44,&srr,&srr);
}

/* This function uses DOS function 6 to check the keyboard and
read in a character if one has been typed.  If nothing has been
typed, a 0 is returned. */

char char_in()
{
return((char)(bdos(6,0xff) & 0xff));
}
/************************************************************
This is a series of programs that illustrate the use of the
VRTX real-time kernel (from Ready Systems, Inc., Palo Alto, CA).

The sequence of programs starts with very simple programs to
use the time keeping facility and show how to create and
execute tasks.

The first program in the sequence simulates time by calling the
clock input function from the lowest priority task.  This method
will be used in all cases to do the initial program debugging.
It allows easy debugging of the programming logic and mathematics
because there are no actual asynchronous events.  Operating system
calls (e.g., printf, scanf) can be used anywhere in the program
because there are no re-entrance problems.

When the basic program logic is initialized, then the actual timer
interrupt is enabled and the program operates in real time.  Problems
such as mutual exclusion can appear at this point that will not appear
in the simulated version, but calls to the operating system must be
carefully controlled since PCDOS is not re-entrant.

After the time-keeping function, a simple process control system will
be implemented.  The same sequence, using simulated time first and then
using real-time will be used.  In all cases, however, a simulation of the
actual plant will be used so that this test program can be run anywhere.

File:          v_cntrl.c

Compiler:      Computer Innovations, C86 v2.3

Compile with the -i switch so that long names are recognized.

Linking instructions:

link v_cntrl task sync clock memory chario vrtx bsp,,,c86s2s

This link indicates the use of the software floating point library.
To use a floating point co-processor (8087, 80287, etc.), the interrupt
service routines (in bsp.asm) must be modified to save the state of the
co-processor on an interrupt.  Otherwise, the floating point instructions
will be non-re-entrant.

Note: The functions task, sync, clock, etc., are the property of
       Ready Systems, Inc.  They provide the interface between the
       Computer Innovations C86 compiler and VRTX proper. The file
       vrtx is the vrtx kernel.  If you already have a license for
       vrtx, the interface functions are available from me or from
       Ready Systems.  You must contact Ready Systems to purchase
       a license for VRTX itself.

Author:        D. M. Auslander
Creation Date: 5-Feb-86
Last Update:

copyright (c) 1986 D. M. Auslander

*****************************************************************/

#include <stdio.h>

/* This structure is used by the CIC86 compiler for communicating
with the operating system or implementing software interrupts. */

struct regval {unsigned int ax,bx,cx,dx,si,di,ds,es;};

struct data_pointer   /* Structure to implement data passing
```

```
                    from a source to a destination.  The
                    task wanting data send a message to a
                    queue.  The task having the information
                    checks the queue for messages, then sends
                    the data out as requested.  The message passed
                    to the data source has two parts: a pointer to
                    a data area for storage of the desired information,
                    and a mailbox for the data sender to use to notify
                    the receiver that the data is ready. */
        {
        float *pdat;    /* Pointer to the data area */
        long m_box;     /* Mailbox for notification */
        };

struct string_pointer /* Structure to implement passing of
                    character information.  Its operation is
                    the same as data_pointer, above. */
        {
        char *cdat;     /* Pointer to the data area */
        long m_cbox;    /* Mailbox for notification */
        };

static int sim_time = 1;
                    /* Flag to indicate whether time should be
                    real or simulated.  For faster execution of
                    the real-time version, this flag could be
                    set with "define," and conditional compilations
                    used, however, using sim_time as a variable
                    means that the program does not have to be
                    recompiled to switch from simulated time to
                    real-time.  */

#define ESCAPE 0x1b   /* The escape character */

/* Task ID numbers: */
#define T_SIM  1
#define T_VC   2
#define T_TM   3
#define T_SUP  4
#define T_BACK 5
#define T_LOG  6
#define T_ALARM       7

/* Queue ID numbers: */
#define STATE_Q       1       /* Queue id for state variable data queue */
#define OUT_Q         2       /* Queue id for DOS output queue */
#define ALARM_Q       3       /* Alarms are sent to this queue for processing */

#define ER_QFL 0xd    /* Queue full error code */

/* p_sim is the task that simulates the process being controlled.  It
is run at the highest priority to make sure that the process continues
running regardless of what the control system is doing.  Since it occupies
a substantial part of the CPU time, the whole system will run much slower
than the control system alone could run.
*/

/* State variables and static variables */

static float x = 0.0,h = 0.75,th = 0.0;
static float Qin,Qout,Vw;

/* Parameters */

static float delta_t = 0.1,Km = 1.0,Qmax = 1.0,Kq = 0.75;
static float A = 10.0;

/* Controller output variables */

static float m_con = 0.0,Hin = 0.0, THin = 0.0;

static long sim_del = 10;
static long xeq_time,start_time;    /* Used to measure how long it takes
                                    to execute the simulation task */
static long end_time;
static long v_box = 0;      /* Mail box for sending valve actuation signal */
static long th_box = 0;     /* Mail box heater actuation */
static float h_alarm = 0.8; /* If height goes above this, call alarm */

p_sim()         /* The simulation uses a simple Euler integration to
--------        perform the numerical integration of the differential
                equations. */
{
char *sc_qaccept();
struct data_pointer *pdp;   /* Pointer to communications structure for
                            information transmission */
int errd;
long rv = 1;
long alarml = 1;

for(;;)         /* The task is an infinite loop with a delay at the end */
        {
        long sc_gtime();
        char *sc_accept();
        float *pm_con,*pHin;

        /* First, check for new values for actuation variables */

        pm_con = sc_accept(&v_box,&errd);
        if(errd r== 0)m_con = *pm_con;      /* errd 0 => message was
                                            present */
        pHin = sc_accept(&th_box,&errd);    /* Check for new values for
```

```
    if(errd r== 0)Hin = *pHin;          actuation variables */
                                        /* errd 0 => message was
                                        present */
    start_time = sc_gtime();            /* Time the execution */

    x = x + Km * m_con * delta_t;       /* Valve position */

    if(x < 0.0)x = 0.0;                 /* Limit valve position */
    else if(x > 1.0)x = 1.0;

    Qin = Qmax * x;                     /* Flow into tank */
    Qout = Kq * h;                      /* Flow out of tank */
    h = h + (Qin - Qout) * delta_t / A; /* Liquid height */
    Vw = A * h;                         /* Liquid volume */

    th = th + (Qin * THin - Qout * th + Hin) * delta_t / Vw;
                                        /* Temperature */
    end_time = sc_gtime();
    xeq_time = sc_gtime() - start_time;
            /* This calculation of execution time is useful
            for setting the scale factor for time  and
            controller sample times.  It will only give relevant
            information in real-time operation -- in simulated
            time operation xeq_time will always be zero since
            the clock can only tick when the low priority
            background runs. */

    if(h > h_alarm)             /* Check alarm conditions */
        sc_qpost(ALARM_Q,&alarm1,&errd);

    do  /* Fill all requests for data */
        {
        pdp = (struct data_pointer *)sc_qaccept(STATE_Q,&errd);
                    /* Check the queue */
        if(errd r== 0)
            {
            pdp->pdat[0] = x;     /* Copy the state data */
            pdp->pdat[1] = h;
            pdp->pdat[2] = th;
            pdp->pdat[3] = m_con;
            pdp->pdat[4] = Hin;

            sc_post(&(pdp->m_box),&rv,&errd);
                    /* Send the message saying data is ready */
            }
        }while(errd r== 0);

    sc_tdelay(sim_del);   /* Delay for next time step */
    }
}

/* Control tasks --
all of the control tasks use the function control_calc() to do the actual
calculation.  The data is stored in a standard format, specified by
the structure control_data.  New setpoints can be sent to the control
tasks from a supervisory task through the mailboxes h_set and th_set.
*/

struct control_data
        {
        float c_y;              /* Measured variable */
        float c_set;            /* Setpoint */
        float c_int;            /* Integrator value */
        float kp;               /* Proportional gain */
        float ki;               /* Integral gain */
        float int_min;          /* Limits for integrator */
        float int_max;
        float m_min;            /* Limits for controller output */
        float m_max;
        float c_m;              /* Controller output */
        };

control_calc(pc)        /* Function to do a PI controller calculation
----------------        */
struct control_data *pc;
{
float error;
float lim();

error = pc->c_set - pc->c_y;
pc->c_int += pc->ki * error;
pc->c_int = lim(pc->c_int,pc->int_min,pc->int_max);

pc->c_m = pc->kp * error + pc->c_int;
pc->c_m = lim(pc->c_m,pc->m_min,pc->m_max);
}

float lim(x,min,max)  /* Return a bounded value of x
---------------------- */
float x,min,max;
{
if(x > max)x = max;
else if(x < min)x = min;
return(x);
}

/* Height and Valve control */

static long h_set = 0;        /* Mailbox for height set point */
static long v_t = 10;         /* Controller sample interval */

/* Data storage area for valve control */
```

```
static struct control_data valve_data =
        {0.0, 0.5, 0.0, 4.0, 0.0, -1.0, 1.0, -1.0, 1.0, 0.0};

static struct control_data height_data =
        {0.0, 0.5, 0.0, 5.0, 1.0, -1.0, 1.0, -1.0, 1.0, 0.0};

v_control()     /* This task controls the valve position and the
-----------     liquid tank level.  The controls act in a cascade
                arrangement with the output of the level control
                acting as the setpoint for the valve control.
                The height control could be run as a separate task,
                since it does not have to be run as often.  This would
                make more efficient use of the CPU at the expense of
                a more complex task structure. */
{
float state[6];             /* Storage space for state variables */
struct data_pointer dp;     /* Communication link for getting data */
int err;                    /* Error variable for calls to VRTX */
float *new_set;

dp.m_box = 0;           /* Make sure the mailbox starts out empty */
dp.pdat = state;        /* Address of target for data */

for(;;)
        {
        new_set = sc_accept(&h_set,&err);   /* Check for new setpoint */
        if(err r== 0)                       /* err = 0 r==> message */
                {
                height_data.c_set = *new_set;
                }

        sc_qpost(STATE_Q,&dp,&err);         /* Post a message asking for data */
        sc_pend(&(dp.m_box),0L,&err);       /* Wait for the answer */

        valve_data.c_y = state[0];  /* Valve position */
        height_data.c_y = state[1];

        control_calc(&height_data); /* Control calculation for level */

        valve_data.c_set = height_data.c_m; /* The output of the height
                                    control is the valve setpoint */
        control_calc(&valve_data);          /* Calculate the PI control */

        sc_post(&v_box,&(valve_data.c_m),&err);
                                    /* Send out actuation value */
        sc_tdelay(v_t);             /* Wait for next sample time */
        }
}

/* Temperature control task -- it can sample much more slowly
than the valve control task because of the slow dynamics of
the temperature system */

static long th_set = 0;             /* Mail box for setpoint */
static long th_t = 40;              /* Controller sample interval */

/* Data storage area for valve control */

static struct control_data temp_data =
        {0.0, 0.5, 0.0, 3.0, 0.7, 0.0, 0.5, 0.0, 1.0, 0.0};
                /* Low limits are zero since no cooling is available */

th_control()    /* This task controls the temperature in the tank
------------    */
{
float state[6];             /* Storage space for state variables */
struct data_pointer dp;     /* Communication link for getting data */
int err;                    /* Error variable for calls to VRTX */
float *new_set;

dp.m_box = 0;           /* Make sure the mailbox starts out empty */
dp.pdat = state;        /* Address of target for data */

for(;;)
        {
        new_set = sc_accept(&th_set,&err);  /* Check for new setpoint */
        if(err r== 0)                       /* err = 0 r==> message */
                {
                temp_data.c_set = *new_set;
                }

        sc_qpost(STATE_Q,&dp,&err);     /* Post a message asking for data */
        sc_pend(&(dp.m_box),0L,&err);   /* Wait for the answer */

        temp_data.c_y = state[2];   /* Temperature */

        control_calc(&temp_data);   /* Calculate the PI control */

        sc_post(&th_box,&(temp_data.c_m),&err);
                                    /* Send out actuation value */
        sc_tdelay(th_t);            /* Wait for next sample time */
        }
}

/* Supervisory task -- this task sends the setpoints to the control
tasks.  The source of the setpoints could be from the user console,
from another, management computer, or internally generated.  In this
case, the setpoints are programmed to change at a fixed time.
*/

supervisor()    /*
------------    */
```

```
{
/* The following variables must be static so that their values will
remain defined after the function returns.
*/
static float hset, thset;
int err;

hset = 0.5;
thset = 0.5;
sc_post(&h_set,&hset,&err);
sc_post(&th_set,&thset,&err);

sc_tdelay(3000L);            /* Wait until it is time to change */
hset = 0.25;
thset = 0.7;
sc_post(&h_set,&hset,&err);
sc_post(&th_set,&thset,&err);

/* The end of the function at this point, i.e., a return, causes the
VRTX scheduler to remove this task from its active queue.  In this
case, that is fine since the supervisor has nothing else to do.
*/
}

/* Alarm -- This is the highest priority of the control tasks.
It is activated by sending messages to the ALARM_Q.  When it
is activated, it suspends the supervisor and all of the control
tasks, turns the heater off and sends the valve towards closed by
setting the valve motor actuation signal to -1 (it is assumed that
the valve will stop safely by hitting its mechanical stop). */

alarm()
{
long alarm_n,*pa;
char *sc_qaccept();
int err;
float valve = -1.0,heat = 0.0;
long al_time,sc_gtime();
struct string_pointer sp;    /* Structure for sending messages to "back" */
char data_line[200];         /* Buffer for message */

sp.m_cbox = 1;         /* Initialize string data structure.  Mailbox starts
                          as 1 so that the first message can be sent */
sp.cdat = data_line;

pa = (long *)sc_qpend(ALARM_Q,0L,&err);     /* Wait for the first
                                               alarm */
al_time = sc_gtime(); /* Time of alarm */
alarm_n = *pa;         /* Alarm number */

/* Suspend the control tasks and send out new actuation values */
sc_tsuspend(T_VC,0,&err);    /* Valve control */
sc_tsuspend(T_TM,0,&err);    /* Temperature control */
sc_tsuspend(T_SUP,0,&err);   /* Supervisor */

sc_accept(&v_box,&err);              /* Empty the mailbox in case the old
                             setpoint had not yet been accepted */
sc_accept(&th_box,&err);

sc_post(&v_box,&valve,&err); /* New actuation values */
sc_post(&th_box,&heat,&err);

for(;;)        /* Start loop looking for other alarms for logging */
       {
       sprintf(data_line,"ALARM #%ld at time %ld\n",alarm_n,al_time);

       sc_pend(&(sp.m_cbox),0L,&err);       /* Make sure last message has been
                                        processed */

       do             /* Send out message logging the alarm */
       {
              sc_qpost(OUT_Q,&(sp),&err);
       }while(err r== ER_QFL);
                                        /* Send the string to "back" */

       pa = (long *)sc_qpend(ALARM_Q,0L,&err);     /* Wait for the next
                                                 alarm */
       al_time = sc_gtime(); /* Time of alarm */
       alarm_n = *pa;        /* Alarm number */
                             /* No action is needed on further alarms
                             since all possible actions have already
                             been taken.  Alarm specific actions could
                             be put here. */
       }
}

/* Data logging task -- responsible for keeping a record of relevant
data.  In this case, the data received is sent to the background task
for actual transmission to the console or disk file. */

static long t_log = 10;             /* How often the log function should run */

data_log()     /* This task has the function of logging data.
----------     It uses message queues to request information, and
               can also be set up with its own queues to log unsolicited
               information coming from other tasks. */
{
float state[6];                     /* Storage space for state variables */
struct data_pointer dp;             /* Communication link for getting data */
struct string_pointer sp;
char data_line[200];
int err;                     /* Error variable for calls to VRTX */
```

```
long tm;                    /* Time, for the log record */
int nq;

dp.m_box = 0;         /* Make sure the mailbox starts out empty */
dp.pdat = state;      /* Address of target for data */

sp.m_cbox = 1;        /* Initialize string data structure.  Mailbox starts
                      as 1 so that the first message can be sent */
sp.cdat = data_line;

for(;;)
        {
        sc_qpost(STATE_Q,&dp,&err);          /* Post a message asking for data */
        sc_pend(&(dp.m_box),0L,&err);        /* Wait for the answer */

        tm = sc_gtime();             /* Get the current time */

        sprintf(data_line,"%ld %f %f %f %f %f\n",
                tm,state[0],state[1],state[2],state[3],state[4]);
                        /* Format the result to a string */

        sc_pend(&(sp.m_cbox),0L,&err);       /* Make sure last message has been
                                     processed */
        do
        {
                sc_qpost(OUT_Q,&sp,&err);
        }while(err r== ER_QFL);
                                     /* Send the string to "back" */

        sc_tdelay(t_log);            /* Wait until time for next log */
        }
}

/* The task "back" always runs at the lowest priority.
For the simulated time case, the call to the time simulation
function is placed in this task.  It is also used to interact with
the user during operation.

Since this is the only task that runs when no interrupts are active,
all DOS function calls must be in this task.
*/

static out_line[200]; /* Buffer for cutput to DOS */

back()          /*
-------         */
{
for(;;)
        {
        struct regval rg;
        struct string_pointer *sp;
        char char_in();               /* A function to return a character
                              from the console if one has been typed;
                              otherwise, it returns 0 */
        char *sc_accept(),*pstr;
        int err;
        int dr = 1;           /* Data received flag */

        if(sim_time)clk_sim();                /* Simulate the clock */

        sp = sc_qaccept(OUT_Q,&err); /* Check for a string
                                     to be sent to DOS */
        if(err r== 0)         /* Any return code other than zero
                              indicates no message was available */
                {
                strcpy(out_line,sp->cdat);
                sc_post(&(sp->m_cbox),&dr,&err);
                              /* Ok to send more data */
                fputs(out_line,stdout);               /* Send out data */
                }

        /* When operating in real-time it is necessary to restore
        the interrupt status before exiting -- the PCDOS ^C exit
        will not do that, so a check for a user input is used to
        indicate the end of the program.
        */
        if(char_in() r== ESCAPE)
                {
                if(!sim_time)
                        timeroff();   /* Restore timer interrupts */
                exit();
                }
        }
}

/* The main program is used to initialize the system and set up the
default task structure.  Once VRTX is started, through the call
to vrtxgo(), control is never returned to main().
*/

main ()
{
int     err;

        printf("Simulate time (0/1)?: ");
        scanf("%d",&sim_time);

        vrtxinit (&err);

        if(!sim_time)timeron();      /* Turn on timer interrupt */

        sc_tcreate(p_sim,T_SIM,10,&err);
```

```
                         /* Create the simulation
                            task -- its id is 1 and its
                            priority is 10 (low numbers
                            imply high priority) */

    if(err != 0)
        {
        printf("Can't create p_sim. Error code %d.\n",err);
        exit();
        }

    sc_tcreate(alarm,T_ALARM,15,&err);
                         /* Create the alarm task.
                            Its priority is the highest of
                            all of the control tasks, but
                            is lower than the simulation
                            because the simulation represents
                            the physical system which cannat
                            be stopped! */

    if(err != 0)
        {
        printf("Can't create alarm. Error code %d.\n",err);
        exit();
        }

    sc_tcreate(v_control,T_VC,100,&err);
                         /* Create the valve control
                            task. Its priority is in between
                            the priority of the data logger
                            and the simulation .*/

    if(err != 0)
        {
        printf("Can't create v_control. Error code %d.\n",err);
        exit();
        }

    sc_tcreate(th_control,T_TM,120,&err);
                         /* Create the temperature control
                            task. Its priority is lower than
                            the priority of the valve control
                            task. */
    if(err != 0)
        {
        printf("Can't create th_control. Error code %d.\n",err);
        exit();
        }

    sc_tcreate(supervisor,T_SUP,180,&err);     /* Create the supervisor task.
                                  It runs at a priority higher than
                                  the data logger, but lower than
                                  the control tasks. */
    if(err != 0)
        {
        printf("Can't create supervisor. Error code %d.\n",err);
        exit();
        }

    sc_tcreate(back,T_BACK,255,&err);   /*Create the low priority
                                  (background) task with the lowest
                                  possible priority (255). */

    if(err != 0)
        {
        printf("Can't create back. Error code %d.\n",err);
        exit();
        }

    sc_tcreate(data_log,T_LOG,200,&err);
                         /* Data logging task -- this is
                            low priority task that runs when no
                            control or data acquisition tasks
                            need to run */

    if(err != 0)
        {
        printf("Can't create data_log. Error code %d\n",err);
        exit();
        }

    sc_qcreate(STATE_Q,10,&err); /* Create a queue for communication
                            of state information.  Any task
                            wanting state information sends a
                            message to this queue giving a
                            mailbox for the handshake and a
                            pointer to the data area for writing
                            the state information. */
    if(err != 0)
        {
        printf("Can't create STATE_Q. Error code %d.\n",err);
        exit();
        }

    sc_qcreate(OUT_Q,10,&err);    /* Create a queue for messages to
                            be output to the operating system.
                            Each message is a string of characters
                            that will be sent to DOS in the
                            background task, "back." */
    if(err != 0)
        {
        printf("Can't create OUT_Q. Error code %d.\n",err);
```

```
                exit();
                }

        sc_qcreate(ALARM_Q,10,&err); /* Create a queue for alarm
                                        messages. */

        if(err != 0)
                {
                printf("Can't create ALARM_Q. Error code %d.\n",err);
                exit();
                }

        vrtxgo ();      /* Start VRTX -- this function never returns! */

}

clk_sim()               /* Simulate the clock by calling vrtx */
{
struct regval srr;

srr.ax = 0x12; /* ui_timer to announce clock tick */
sysint(0x44,&srr,&srr);
}

/* This function uses DOS function 6 to check the keyboard and
read in a character if one has been typed.  If nothing has been
typed, a 0 is returned. */

char char_in()
{
return((char)(bdos(6,0xff) & 0xff));
}
```

BIBLIOGRAPHY

AUSLANDER, DAVID M., AND PAUL SAGUES. *Microprocessor for Measurement and Control.* Berkeley, CA:Osborne/McGraw-Hill, 1981.

BERZIUS, LUGI, AND VALDIS. "Rapidly Prototyping Real-Time Systems." *IEEE Software,* vol. 5 no. 5, September 1988.

COMER, DOUGLAS. *Operating System Design: The XINU Approach.* Englewood Cliffs, NJ: Prentice Hall, 1984.

CRAINE, J. FFYNOL, AND GRAHAM R. MARTIN. *Microcomputers in Engineering and Science.* Reading, MA: Addison-Wesley Publishing Co. 1985.

DEITEL, HARVEY. *An Introduction to Operating Systems.* Reading, MA: Addison-Wesley Publishing Co., 1984.

ELECTRO-CRAFT CORPORATION. *DC Motors, Speed Controls, Servo Systems.* Hopkins, MN: Electro-Craft Corp., 1980.

GEHANI, NARAIN. *Ada: An Advanced Introduction.* Englewood Cliffs, NJ: Prentice Hall, 1983.

GLASS, ROBERT. *Real-Time Software.* Englewood Cliffs, NJ: Prentice Hall, 1983.

HARBISON, SAMUEL P., AND GUY L. STEELE, Jr. *A C Reference Manual.* Englewood Cliffs, NJ: Prentice Hall, 1984.

HOGAN, THOM. *The C Programmer's Handbook.* Bowie, MD: Brady Communications Company, Inc., 1984.

HOROWITZ, ELLIS AND SARTAJ SAHNI. *Fundamentals of Data Structures.* Computer Science Press, 1982.

JAMSA, KRIS. *The C Library.* Berkeley, CA: Osborne/McGraw-Hill, 1985.

JONES, DOUGLAS L., AND THOMAS W. PARKS. *A Digital Signal Processing Laboratory. Using the TMS32010.* Englewood Cliffs, NJ: Prentice Hall, 1988.

KERNIGHAN, BRIAN W. AND P.J. PLAUGER. *The Elements of Programming Style.* New York, NY: McGraw-Hill, 1978.

KERNIGHAN, BRIAN W., AND DENNIS, M. RITCHIE. *The C Programming Language.* Englewood Cliffs, NJ: Prentice Hall, 1978.

MILLER, LAWRENCE H., AND ALEXANDER E. QUILICI. *Programming in C.* New York, NY: John Wiley and Sons, Inc., 1986.

NORTON, PETER. *Inside the IBM PC.* Englewood Cliffs, NJ: Prentice Hall, 1983.

NORTON, PETER. *The Peter Norton Programmer's Guide to the IBM PC.* Microsoft Press, 1985.

PETERSON, J., AND S. SILBERSCHATZ. *Operating System Concepts.* Reading, MA: Addison-Wesley Publishing Co., 1983.

RAYNAL, M. *Algorithms for Mutual Exclusion.* Cambridge, MA: MIT Press, 1986.

RECTOR, RUSSEL, AND GEORGE ALEXY. *The 8086 Book.* Berkeley, CA: Osborne/McGraw-Hill, 1980.

ROBERTS, STEVEN K. *Industrial Design with Microcomputers.* Englewood Cliffs, NJ: Prentice Hall, 1982.

SAVITZKY, STEPHEN. *Real-Time Microprocessor Systems.* New York, NY: Van Nostrand Reinhold, 1985.

TANENBAUM, ANDREW. *Operating Systems: Design and Implementation.* Englewood Cliffs, NJ: Prentice Hall, 1987.

ZAKS, RODNAY, AND AUSTIN LESEA. *Microprocessor Interfacing Techniques.* Sybex, 1979.

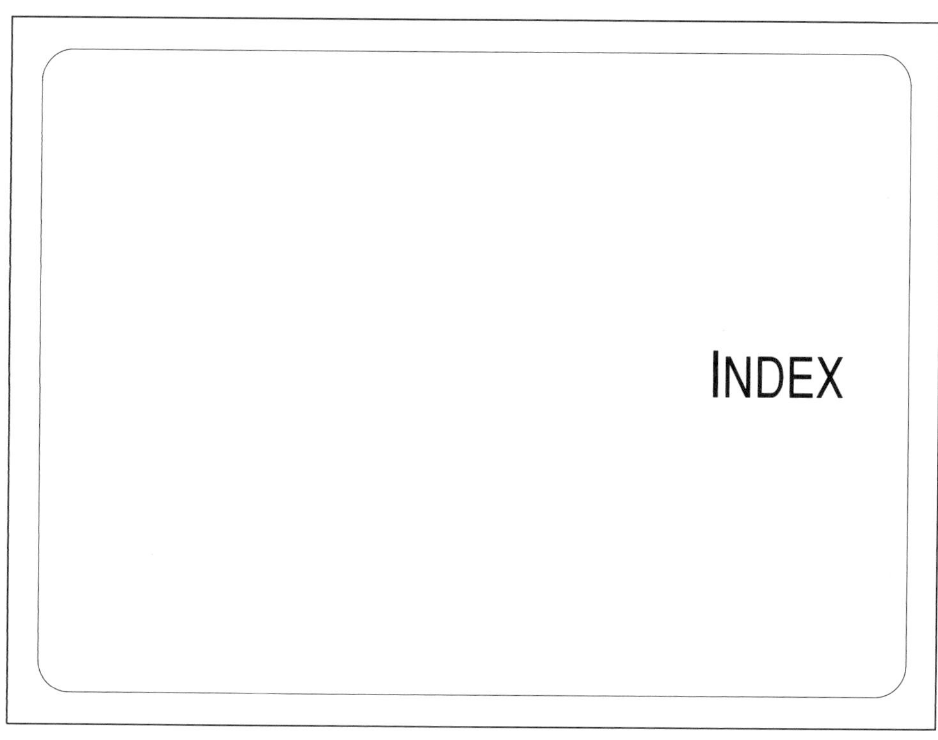

INDEX

C

D

K

L

M

N

O

P

Q

R

S

T

U

V

W

X